ENGINES OF THE IMAGINATION

How did men and women in earlier ages respond to their technologies? In his characteristically lucid and captivating style, Jonathan Sawday explores poetry, philosophy, art, and engineering to reveal the lost world of the machine in the pre-industrial culture of the European Renaissance.

In the Renaissance, machines and mechanisms appealed to familiar figures such as Shakespeare, Francis Bacon, Montaigne, and Leonardo da Vinci, as well as to a host of lesser-known writers and artists in the sixteenth and seventeenth centuries. This intellectual and aesthetic engagement with devices of all kinds would give rise to new attitudes towards gender as well as towards work and labour, and even fostered the beginnings of the new sciences of artificial life and reason which would be pursued by Descartes, Hobbes, and Leibniz in the later seventeenth century.

But writers, philosophers, and artists often had conflicting reactions to the technology that was beginning to surround them. For at the heart of the creation of a machine-driven world were stories of loss and catastrophe. Was technology a token of human progress or was it, rather, a sign of the fall of humanity from its original state of innocence? These contradictory attitudes are part of the legacy of the European Renaissance, and this historical legacy helps to explain many of our own attitudes towards the technology that surrounds us, sustains us, and sometimes troubles us today.

Jonathan Sawday is Professor of English Studies at the University of Strathclyde, Glasgow. He has taught at universities in Britain [...] United States. As well as writing many articles and essays [...] erature and culture, he is the author of *The Body Emblazoned* [...] and co-editor (with Tom Healy) of *Literature and the English* [...] (with Neil Rhodes) *The*

Praise for *Engines of the Imagination*:

'This is a magisterial work of myth-busting, and a marvellous demonstration of how art and literature may be used to reanimate the material imagination of an historical period. The old idea of the Renaissance as a pre-technological pause, or paradise, is gone for good.'

Steven Connor, *Birkbeck College, University of London, UK*

'Jonathan Sawday has written another big, beautiful, brilliant book that will change the way we all see (and hear) the Renaissance.'

Gary Taylor, *Florida State University, USA*

'This is a brilliant achievement . . . It has huge intellectual and imaginative range and is written with great vitality . . . This could be the book of the decade in Renaissance Studies.'

Neil Rhodes, *University of St Andrews, UK*

'Jonathan Sawday's pioneering and thoughtful work can change the course of the study of the Early Modern period . . . This illuminating book enlarges our sense of the Renaissance, redirects our focus, and shows us a world elsewhere we have not seen before.'

Arthur Kinney, *University of Massachusetts, Amherst, USA*

'*Engines of the Imagination* offers a fascinating picture of Renaissance encounters with technology. Engaging and entertaining, Sawday's book will become required reading for all students of the period.'

Mary Poovey, *New York University, USA*

ENGINES OF THE IMAGINATION

Renaissance culture and the rise of the machine

Jonathan Sawday

Routledge
Taylor & Francis Group

LONDON AND NEW YORK

First published 2007
by Routledge
2 Park Square, Milton Park, Abingdon, Oxon OX14 4RN

Simultaneously published in the USA and Canada
by Routledge
270 Madison Ave, New York, NY 10016

Routledge is an imprint of the Taylor & Francis Group, an informa business

© 2007 Jonathan Sawday

Typeset in Joanna and Scala Sans by
The Running Head Limited, Cambridge
Printed and bound in Great Britain by
MPG Books Ltd, Bodmin, Cornwall

British Library Cataloguing in Publication Data
A catalogue record for this book is available from the British Library

Library of Congress Cataloging in Publication Data
Sawday, Jonathan.
Engines of the imagination: Renaissance culture and the rise of the machine / Jonathan Sawday.
    p. cm.
  Includes bibliographical references and index.
  1. Machinery — History. I. Title.
  TJ17.S39 2007
  621.8094'0903—dc22

                              2007028583

ISBN10: 0–415–35061–1 (hbk)
ISBN10: 0–415–35062–x (pbk)
ISBN10: 0–203–69615–8 (ebk)

ISBN13: 978–0–415–35061–7 (hbk)
ISBN13: 978–0–415–35062–4 (pbk)
ISBN13: 978–0–203–69615–6 (ebk)

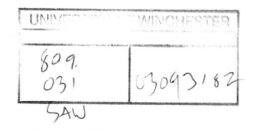

CONTENTS

List of illustrations   xi

Preface and acknowledgements   xv

1   The Renaissance machine and its discontents   1
     The world of Technē 1
     A world run upon wheels: the sound of the Renaissance 4
     Windmills and watermills 6
     Shame 18

2   Philosophy, power, and politics in Renaissance technology   31
     'The vital humour of the terrestrial machine' 31
     A water-driven world 34
     Watching machines with Montaigne 38
     Movement and the philosophy of machines 47
     Machines and social power 54
     The Renaissance megamachine: Rome 1585–6 58

3   The turn of the screw: machines, books, and bodies   70
     Of alienation and pins 72
     'What is't o'clock?': clock time and social status 76
     Print and mechanical culture 78
     The birth of the Renaissance machine 83

Georgius Agricola and the invention of mechanical labour 86
The syntax of the machine 96
The mechanical world of Agostino Ramelli 102
The body of the machine 108
Textual engines 111
Perpetual motions 116

4   Women and wheels: gender and the machine in the Renaissance   125
    Rosie the Riveter 125
    The Spinners 128
    Wheels 137
    Rotary punishment 139
    The wheel of Fortune 150
    'A thing made for Alexander' 160

5   'Nature wrought': artifice, illusion, and magical mechanics   166
    Metallic fantasies 166
    Fabricating nature 172
    Mechanical illusions 183
    'Bodies without souls' 185
    Mechanical women 199

6   Reasoning engines: the instrumental imagination in the
    seventeenth century   207
    Buying an instrument 207
    Francis Bacon and the reform of mechanism 210
    Seeing with machines 216
    Robert Hooke's artificial bodies 221
    The second Adam 228
    Clockwork reason 232
    The calculating machine 237
    Mechanical theology 242
    Political machines 245
    Sex machines 248

7   Milton and the engine   257
    Mechanical language 257
    Mechanical sight 259

The semi-omnipotent engine 265
The idea of the engine 270
Milton and industry 275
Milton and the machine 284

8 The machine stops   294
The interrupted idyll of Andrew Marvell 294
The happy return 299
Conclusion: The machine stops 310

Notes   319
Index   385

. . . *Order.* A letter of exhortation to a friend, to induce him to seek. He will reply: 'But what good will seeking do me? Nothing comes of it.' Answer: 'Do not despair.' Then he in turn would say that he would be happy to find some light, but according to religion itself it would do him no good even if he did thus believe, and so he would just as soon not look. The answer to that is 'the Machine'.

Blaise Pascal, *Pensées* (1662) trans. A. J. Krailsheimer
(Harmondsworth: Penguin Books, 1966), p. 33

Look round the world: Contemplate the whole and every part of it: You will find it to be nothing but one great machine, subdivided into an infinite number of lesser machines, which again admit of subdivisions to a degree beyond what human senses and faculties can trace and explain. All these various machines, and even their most minute parts, are adjusted to each other with an accuracy, which ravishes into admiration all men who have ever contemplated them.

David Hume, *Dialogues Concerning Natural Religion* (1779)
ed. Martin Bell (London: Penguin Books, 1990), p. 53

There once was a man who said, 'Damn!'
It is born upon me that I am
An engine that moves
In predestinate grooves
I'm not even a bus, I'm a tram.

Attributed to Maurice E. Hare (1886–1967)

ILLUSTRATIONS

1.1 Herri met de Bles (Civetta) (*c.* 1510–50), *The Copper Mine* (oil on   8
     panel), Galleria degli Uffizi, Florence, Italy, The Bridgeman Art
     Library.

1.2 Plaque depicting a winch mechanism for driving a transverse shaft   10
     by Ambrogio de Federico Barocci (fifteenth century) (stone), Palazzo
     Ducale, Urbino, Italy, The Bridgeman Art Library.

1.3 Hieronymus Bosch, *Triptych of the Haywain*: right wing of the triptych   12
     depicting Hell, *c.* 1500 (panel), Monasterio de El Escorial, Spain, The
     Bridgeman Art Library.

1.4 Zacharias Heyns, *Emblemata, Emblems Christienes, et Morales*   14
     (Rotterdam, 1625), plate 18. Glasgow University Library, Special
     Collections.

1.5 Pieter Brueghel the Elder (*c.* 1515–69), *Hunters in the Snow* (1565),   16
     Kunsthistorisches Museum, Vienna, Austria.

1.6 Carlo Saraceni, *Moses Defending the Daughters of Jethro* (1609–10)   17
     (oil on copper), 28.5 × 35.3 cm, National Gallery, London.

1.7 Mattheus Merian the Elder (1593–1650), Engraving of the   22
     construction of the Tower of Babel in *Icones Biblicae* (Strasbourg,
     1625), private collection.

1.8 Pieter Brueghel the Elder (*c.* 1515–69), *The Tower of Babel*, detail   23
     of the construction works, 1563 (oil on panel), Kunsthistorisches
     Museum, Vienna, Austria, The Bridgeman Art Library.

1.9   Pieter Brueghel the Elder (*c.* 1515–69), *Landscape with the Fall of*   27
       Icarus, *c.* 1555 (oil on canvas), Musées Royaux des Beaux-Arts de
       Belgique, Brussels, Belgium, Giraudon, The Bridgeman Art Library.

2.1   *Water Machine at Marly*, *c.* 1715 (engraving), French School   39
       (eighteenth century), private collection, The Stapleton Collection,
       The Bridgeman Art Library.

2.2   Vittorio Zonca, *Novo Teatro di Machine et Edificii* (Padua, 1607),   48
       p. 68.

2.3   Domenico Fontana, *Della trasportatione dell' obelisco Vaticano et delle*   60
       fabriche di Nostro Signore Papa Sisto V fatte dal Cavallier Domenico
       Fontana . . . Libro primo [secondo] . . . (Rome, 1590), plate 18. Glasgow
       University Library, Stirling Maxwell Collection.

2.4   Carlo Fontana, *Templum Vaticanum et ipsius origo cum ædificiis*   62
       maximè conspicuis antiquitùs, & recèns ibidem constitutis (Rome,
       1694), p. 131. Glasgow University Library, Special Collections.

2.5   Carlo Fontana, *Templum Vaticanum et ipsius origo cum ædificiis*   65
       maximè conspicuis antiquitùs, & recèns ibidem constitutis (Rome,
       1694), pp. 168–9. Glasgow University Library, Special Collections.

3.1   Georgius Agricola, *De Re Metallica libri xii: quibu officia, instrumenta,*   89
       machinae, ac omnnia denique ad metalicam spectantia, non modo
       lucluentissime describuntur (Basle, 1556), p. 220. Glasgow University
       Library, Special Collections.

3.2   Georgius Agricola, *De Re Metallica libri xii: quibu officia, instrumenta,*   91
       machinae, ac omnnia denique ad metalicam spectantia, non modo
       lucluentissime describuntur (Basle, 1556), p. 225. Glasgow University
       Library, Special Collections.

3.3   Georgius Agricola, *De Re Metallica libri xii: quibu officia, instrumenta,*   94
       machinae, ac omnnia denique ad metalicam spectantia, non modo
       lucluentissime describuntur (Basle, 1556), p. 152. Glasgow University
       Library, Special Collections.

3.4   Georg Andreas Boeckler, *Theatrum Machinarum Novum*   98
       (Nuremberg, 1662), title page. Glasgow University Library, Special
       Collections.

3.5   Agostino Ramelli, *Le diverse et artificiose machine del Capitano*   106
       Agostino Ramelli . . . (Paris, 1588), plate 27, Glasgow University
       Library, Special Collections.

3.6 Agostino Ramelli, *Le diverse et artificiose machine del Capitano*   107
     Agostino Ramelli... (Paris, 1588), plate 46, Glasgow University
     Library, Special Collections.

3.7 Agostino Ramelli, *Le diverse et artificiose machine del Capitano*   112
     Agostino Ramelli... (Paris, 1588), plate 188, Glasgow University
     Library, Special Collections.

3.8 Georg Andreas Boeckler, *Theatrum Machinarum Novum*   119
     (Nuremberg, 1662), p. 152. Glasgow University Library, Special
     Collections.

4.1 Norman Rockwell, 'Rosie the Riveter', Cover, *Saturday Evening Post*,   126
     29 May 1943.

4.2 Michelangelo Buonarroti (1475–1564), *Sistine Chapel Ceiling: The*   127
     Prophet Isaiah (fresco), Vatican Museums and Galleries, Vatican City,
     Italy, The Bridgeman Art Library.

4.3 Quirijn Gerritsz. van Brekelenkam (*c.* 1620–68), *The Spinner* (1653),   130
     Metropolitan Museum of Art, New York (oil on wood), 19 × 25¼ in.
     (48.3 × 64.1 cm), Purchase, 1871 (71.110).

4.4 Woman spinning and another carding wool, Luttrell Psalter, British   131
     Library, Add. MS 42130 f.193. Begun prior to 1340 for Sir Geoffrey
     Luttrell (1276–1345), British Library, London. © British Library Board.
     All Rights Reserved. The Bridgeman Art Library.

4.5 Diego Rodriguez de Silva y Velásquez (1599–1660), *The Fable of*   133
     Arachne, or The Spinners, c. 1657 (oil on canvas), Prado, Madrid,
     Spain, The Bridgeman Art Library.

4.6 Albrecht Dürer (1471–1528), *The Torture of St Catherine of Alexandria*   140
     (woodcut), Private Collection, Agra Art, Warsaw, Poland, The
     Bridgeman Art Library.

4.7 Giovanni Branca, *Le Machine. Volume nuouo et di molto artificio da*   145
     fare effetti marauigliosi... *arichito di bellissime figure* (Rome, 1629),
     plate 20, private collection.

4.8 Robert Recorde, *The Castle of Knowledge* (London, 1556), frontispiece. 156
     Glasgow University Library, Special Collections.

PREFACE AND ACKNOWLEDGEMENTS

This book sets out to explore the imaginative history of machines and mechanisms within European culture between 1450 and 1700. Drawing on the evidence of poetry, philosophical writing, and the visual arts as much as technical and technological treatises and images, *Engines of the Imagination* is a study of the world of the machine or device in what is usually known as 'pre-industrial' culture. In marshalling this evidence, the book sets out to map the features of a world whose outlines were shaped by familiar figures such as Leonardo da Vinci, Montaigne, Shakespeare, and (later) John Milton, as well as a host of lesser known poets, philosophers, *ingenarii* or engineers, and artists whose works appear in what follows. But these features are viewed from the perhaps unfamiliar perspective of the advent of mechanical culture in the European Renaissance.

Although it is always risky to commend a book to a prospective reader by telling them what it is *not* about, it is perhaps worth saying at the outset that this study is *not* a work of technological history, even if it has drawn on the insights and explorations of several generations of technological historians in its composition. Instead, its starting point is the idea of 'imaginative history' coined by the British filmmaker, poet, and artist, Humphrey Jennings. In his remarkable unfinished work *Pandaemonium*, sub-titled 'the coming of the machine as seen by contemporary observers', Jennings set out to record what he termed 'the imaginative history of the industrial revolution'.[1] Jennings's book is a collection of documents or records, culled from poetry, novels, diaries, biographies, memoirs, newspapers, and pamphlets (well over 300 items were represented in the truncated posthumously published version) which charts those 'moments in the history of the Industrial Revolution at which clashes and conflicts suddenly show themselves with extra clearness'.[2] His history is an inner mental record, as far as it can be reconstructed, of those who lived through the period of industrialization in Britain between 1660 and 1886.

For all its occasionally gnomic quality, *Pandaemonium* provides an immense stimulus for any cultural historian who seeks to fathom a subject as nebulous as the imaginative texture of the machine and mechanical labour in the past. As its title suggests, Jennings's work begins with those sections of John Milton's *Paradise Lost* (1667) that describe the creation of the fallen angels' new residence in Hell, Pandaemonium. For Jennings the building of Pandaemonium 'is equated with the industrial revolution and the coming of the machine . . . the building of Pandaemonium is the real history of Britain for the last three hundred years'.[3] For literary and cultural historians, however, 'The Renaissance', which we associate with the ideas, images, and writings of a European intellectual and cultural elite in the fifteenth, sixteenth, and seventeenth centuries, has all too frequently neglected technology as, in itself, a work of the imagination. In some sense, this neglect is a response to the ways in which early-modern people themselves wrote about and thought about machines, mechanisms, and their makers. After all, as Shakespeare reminds us, were not 'rude mechanicals' (a term that could be applied in the sixteenth century to any unskilled labourer) a collection of humble artisans, or worse, clownish buffoons?

In fact, of course, the inventors and fabricators of the beautiful and complex devices and instruments that came to permeate Renaissance culture were very far removed from this stereotype. Perhaps, indeed, this relative neglect of the imaginative history of technology, for all that it has begun to shift following recent scholarship, tells us rather more about our own response to technological culture, particularly among those of us who work in the arts and humanities, than it does about this earlier period?[4] At the same time, our sense of the symbolic significance of pre-industrial machines is inevitably coloured by the fact that they have been consigned to what has sometimes been termed the 'paleotechnic age', the age, that is, before the advent of steam power at the end of the seventeenth century, or the internal combustion engine and the electric dynamo at the end of the nineteenth century.[5] Surrounded as we are in the modern world by far more powerful, subtle, or transformative machines, the imaginative force of early-modern mechanisms easily escapes us. And yet, as I hope this book will demonstrate, many of our complex and contradictory attitudes towards our own technologies were, I believe, first shaped in the period of the European Renaissance.

One distinguished historian of Renaissance culture has understood technology as 'a distinctive product of western civilization [which] has proved to be more exportable than any other aspect of our cultural and social heritage'.[6] This view of the technological supremacy of Western culture is a pervasive and troubling one. In September 2001, for example, the Italian Prime Minister, Silvio Berlusconi, was reported as praising the 'superiority' of Western civilization and particularly its technology over the products of non-Western cultures. In particular, the 2001 atrocities in New York and Washington were to be understood as attacks 'on our civilization, of its discoveries and inventions, which have brought us democratic institutions, respect for the human, civil, religious and political rights of citizens, openness to diversity and tolerance of everything'.[7]

Historians of either culture or technology (let alone students of current affairs) would agree, I think, that both of these claims are nonsense. For centuries, European technological prowess ('our discoveries and inventions') lagged far behind the technological mastery of either the Islamic or the Chinese worlds, while many facets of European technology in the Renaissance were imported from beyond the boundaries of Christendom.[8] It is true, however, that at the end of the period covered by this book, technology began to play a dominant and self-defining role in Western societies of the kind expressed by the scholar of the Renaissance and the Italian politician. And certainly, this period sees the beginning of what economic historians have termed a 'new and unique phenomenon' in human culture: the 'affluence' of the West based on 'efficient economic organization'.[9] But this affluence was also based on a belief in the transformational power of technology that took root in the European Renaissance. No longer slaves to circumstance, at least in theory, early-modern people began to articulate the view that it was possible to 'conquer' the natural world with cunning machines, engines, and devices. It is in this sense, too, that it is proper to term the people who lived in Europe in this period as 'early modern' because, as John Gray has reminded us, 'modernity' in the sense of a belief that the future would be somehow different from the past, was also an invention of the technological culture of sixteenth-century Europe.[10]

The book's structure is, very broadly, chronological. In the opening chapter, we trace some of the founding myths of technology as they were understood in Renaissance art and literature, tracing the representation of those myths to their roots in some familiar and less familiar classical texts and biblical narratives. In chapter 2, we explore the impact of machines on the European imaginative and geographical landscape by following the ideas of three archetypal Renaissance figures: the artist-engineer Leonardo da Vinci, the philosopher Michel de Montaigne, and the engineer and architect Domenico Fontana. Together, Leonardo, Montaigne, and Fontana help us recreate something of the texture of pre-industrial Europe poised on the brink of the revolution in power generation, organization, and the inventive application of technology that we normally associate with the industrial revolution in the eighteenth century. As we shall see, early-modern Europe was very far from being a paleotechnic desert. Rather, machines of enormous power and complexity were an everyday reality for skilled and unskilled workers throughout the continent. Machines and mechanisms in the European Renaissance were far more than simply an efficient means of helping human beings to perform 'work' or 'labour'. Rather, the elaborate devices of the artist-engineers of the Renaissance reached deep into early-modern political, aesthetic, and philosophical structures of thought.

In chapter 3, we survey the greatest single source for our knowledge of the world of mechanical culture in the Renaissance: the printed machine books of the later sixteenth century. Concentrating on the work of two individuals, the German physician, historiographer, mining engineer, and metallurgist Georgius Agricola (1494–1555) and the Italian military engineer Agostino Ramelli (1531–1600), we learn how new images of mechanism and machinery began to shift the ways in which the idea of work or labour was conceived, almost two centuries prior to the more familiar analysis of the impact of the machine on human life to be found in the writings of Adam Smith and Karl Marx. In this chapter, we also explore the ways in which the new 'device' of printing helped to foster mechanical culture, and we encounter the great fantasy of Renaissance technology, the machine without end, or *perpetuum mobile*. Chapter 4 takes us into quite different territory, as we unravel some of the symbolic complexities surrounding the work of women with machines. Gender and technological history has become, in recent years, an area of intense study for cultural historians of the industrial revolution and its aftermath. And yet, some of our most pervasive attitudes towards gender, technology, and labour in the modern Western world had their roots in this earlier epoch.

The second half of the book traces the story of the machine and the related idea of the instrument in the later part of our period. Chapter 5 locates the

machine within the wider argument between 'art' and 'nature' that dominated late sixteenth- and early seventeenth-century artistic and literary
culture. Chapter 6 shows how this argument gave way to the pursuit of
mechanism in the work of the 'mechanical philosophers' of the later seventeenth century who, working in the years after Francis Bacon's manifesto
for a new study of 'nature wrought' or altered with the help of machines,
devices, and instruments, began to conceive of all of nature as a gigantic
engine. In this chapter, too, we shall follow the debate among both natural philosophers and poets as they conjured with the possibility of creating
artificial forms of life, aping the organic structures to be found in nature.
Chapter 7 is the most 'literary' section of the book, in that it is the only
chapter devoted to a single author: John Milton. There are very good reasons, I believe, for highlighting Milton and his writings in this way. Milton's
poetry, which still has the power to vex, move, thrill, and frustrate the
modern reader in almost equal measure, allows us an insight into the paradoxical engagement with machines or engines of probably Europe's foremost intellect in the seventeenth century. Milton's fascination with both the
idea and the reality of engines and machines is explored within the context of the arguments over language, instruments, and industry which had
emerged in seventeenth-century London at the time that he was labouring
on a poem which Humphrey Jennings saw as the starting point for mechanical culture: *Paradise Lost*. Finally, in chapter 8, some of the strands of thought
that this book has pursued are brought together as we pursue the fantasy of
a world recreated without machines or technology. The idea of technological erasure is, in the modern world, perhaps more beguiling or terrifying
than it has ever been. That early-modern Europeans, too, were equally fascinated with the prospect of starting anew by abandoning their devices and
instruments in pursuit of some purer communion with nature unalloyed by
human artifice, is the point at which we end.

At various points in this book, the reader will encounter definitions of
what, exactly, a machine might be, which range from the symbolic to the
severely technical. At the risk of prompting frustration, I have purposefully
withheld from offering a single conclusive definition of this most singular
of human artefacts, preferring to agree with one historian of technology
who has observed that the term 'machine' presents 'an almost hopeless
problem' of definition.[11] Similarly, cognate words such as 'engine' and
'mechanism' as well as a host of synonyms such as 'artifice', 'device', 'contrivance', 'apparatus', and 'invention' are used interchangeably in this study,
although the distinction (for example) between a 'mechanism' understood

as a means of modifying motion, and a 'machine' which modifies energy to carry out work was gradually emerging in the early-modern period. Usually, the technological definition of a machine rests on some form of distinction between a simple 'tool' and a more complex 'engine' or 'instrument' of some kind. This, certainly, was the distinction with which Karl Marx struggled in his many attempts at defining the effect of machines on the lives and fortunes of machine workers or operatives in the nineteenth century. But, equally, it has been suggested that the stone-age hand-axe might be thought of as 'forming a machine with the hand of its user . . . or with its user's whole body'.[12] Some technological historians, indeed, have suggested that all machines are essentially 'force-transmitting devices', a definition that might embrace a hand tool as well as an electronic computer, or even an idea.[13] Other definitions of machines are more imaginative, and in some ways, much more helpful, since they allow a wider range of cultural and metaphorical possibilities to come into play:

> a class of typhonic mindless organisms, exempt from the will of nature; . . . ever more intelligent, ever more versatile slaves; . . . pockets of decreasing entropy in a framework in which the larger entropy tends to increase; . . . a method of making power effective; . . . a piece of stone, the branch of a tree – the first tools in man's hands . . . an idea put into practice, an inspiration, an observation . . .[14]

I hope that, by the end of this book, the reader will also have begun to sense how mysterious is that complex of artefacts that we have come to know as 'machines'.

Acknowledgements

This book began its life as a short feature programme, written for BBC Radio 4. I am grateful to Mathew Dodd, the producer of *The Machine Mind*, for encouraging me in my earlier mechanical speculations, as well as to the contributors to that programme, in particular: Francis Spufford, Tom Standage, Kevin Jackson, Lucy Hartley, Clive Gamble, Doron Swade, and Steve Connor. My editors at Routledge, Polly Dodson and Liz Thompson, have demonstrated seemingly inexhaustible funds of patience and kind support. Similarly, I am grateful to Jonathan Jones, and Talia Rodgers at Routledge for her early encouragement of this project. Thanks, too, to Carole Drummond at The Running Head and to Roger Jordan, a meticulous copy-editor.

I should like to thank those friends, colleagues, and academic correspondents who have (always willingly, though sometimes unwittingly) contributed to the evolution of the ideas that are presented here. I am particularly grateful to Arthur F. Kinney, Neil Rhodes, Gary Taylor, and the anonymous 'US Reader 1' whose helpful notes, comments, and suggestions have made me rethink sections of this book. Others I should like to thank include: Derek Attridge, Dana Brand, Paul and Julia Brennan, Alexander Brodie, Clara Calvo, John Carey, I. F. ('Nobby') Clarke, Adam Max Cohen, Philip Cooke, Jonathan Crewe, John Cottingham, Tom Evans, Sheila Fisher, Peter Forshaw, Stephen Greenblatt, Tom Gretton, Paul Henry, Jane Hubert, Derek Hughes, Michael Hunter, James Knowles, Kate McLuskie, Gordon MacMullan, Marcos Martinón-Torres, David Matthews, Helen and Roger Millar, Lucy Mills, John Peacock, Murray Pittock, Ramie Targoff, Janet Todd, Suzanne Trill, Faye Tudor, Peter Ucko, Brian Vickers, Susan Wiseman, and Michael Witmore. I am particularly grateful to Edward Chaney and to Kevin Sharpe who provided much needed support at an early stage of this book's gestation. I am equally grateful to my colleagues in the Department of English Studies at the University of Strathclyde (particularly Nigel Fabb, Tom Furniss, Jonathan Hope, and Elspeth Jajdelska), all of whom have had to contend with my wearying obsessions with machines and mechanisms for far too long. Needless to say, the mistakes and errors that sharp-eyed readers will no doubt discover in these pages are all of my own creation.

I should like to thank the librarians and staff of The British Library, The Andersonian Library at the University of Strathclyde, Glasgow University Library, the Mitchell Library in Glasgow, and the National Library of Scotland in Edinburgh. I should also like to acknowledge the financial support I have received in working on this project from the UK Arts and Humanities Research Council, the British Academy, and the Principal of the University of Strathclyde.

My wife, Ruth Evans, is a medievalist who has managed to help me become a much better early modernist than I could ever have dreamed of becoming on my own. This book is dedicated to her with love and gratitude.

A note on texts and sources

In quoting from early-modern texts, I have tried to use modern editions wherever these are available. When quoting from sixteenth- and seventeenth-century material, or material available on EEBO (Early English Books Online), I have silently altered punctuation and spelling when it assists the modern reader. All quotations from Shakespeare, unless otherwise specified, are from Stanley Wells and Gary Taylor (eds.), *The Oxford Shakespeare* (Oxford: The Clarendon Press, 1994).

Jonathan Sawday
Glasgow

1

THE RENAISSANCE MACHINE AND ITS DISCONTENTS

The world of *Technē*

Just like our own machines, Renaissance machines were useful devices with which people worked and laboured. Acting upon the world, their avowed purpose was to make human existence more tolerable. But fabricated as they were out of a synthesis of poetry, architecture, philosophy, antiquarianism, and theology, as well as craft, skill, and design, Renaissance machines were also freighted with myth, legend, and symbolism. As products of human activity concerned, according to Aristotle, with 'bringing something into being', machines were manifestations of artifice rather than nature.[1] For, unlike natural objects, which Aristotle claimed 'have their origin in themselves', the Renaissance machine or engine belonged to that class of things lacking the power of replicability or reproduction.[2]

As an instrument or device wrought by human design or intellect, the machine was part of the world of *Technē* which Martin Heidegger, in the twentieth century, would come to describe as embracing 'the arts of the mind and the fine arts. *Technē* belongs to bringing-forth, to *poiēsis*; it is something poetic.'[3] In the modern world, the machine belongs, primarily, to the world of technology: a term used to describe the material practices by which people intervene in the natural world, but which did not exist in any recognizably modern sense until the eighteenth century.[4] Early-modern people were, of course, aware of the force of technology in their lives, though they were more likely to use words such as 'device', 'invention', 'engine', or 'instrument' to describe the objects crafted by *Technē*. And these terms had a wide applicability to a vast range of human practices, stretching from mental activity, via the arts of grammar, rhetoric, and logic, to simple tools, to more complex mechanical devices.

Sigmund Freud, however, has offered a quite different account of the technological impulse, which he related to a feeling of sadness. In *Civilization and Its Discontents* (1930), Freud wrote of how all the many tools, implements, instruments, machines, and engines that have come to inhabit the world may be understood as attempts to escape the limitations imposed upon the body and the mind by nature. At first, this supplementary effort appears remarkably successful: 'with every tool man is perfecting his own organs, whether motor or sensory, or is removing the limits to their functioning' Freud wrote.[5] He continued:

> Motor power places gigantic forces at his disposal ... thanks to ships and aircraft neither water nor air can hinder his movements; by means of spectacles he corrects defects in the lens of his own eye; by means of telescopes he sees into the far distance; and by means of the microscope he overcomes the limits of visibility set by the structure of his retina. In the photographic camera he has created an instrument which retains the fleeting visual impressions, just as the gramophone disc retains the equally fleeting auditory ones; both are at bottom materializations of the power he possesses of recollection, his memory. With the help of the telephone he can hear at distances which would be respected as unattainable even in a fairy tale. Writing was in its origin the voice of an absent person; and the dwelling house was a substitute for the mother's womb, the first lodging, for which in all likelihood man still longs, and in which he was safe and felt at ease.[6]

And yet, for all the triumphant cataloguing of humanity's accomplishments in which tools and devices may be considered as grafts extending our intellectual, sensory, and physical capacities, this story was also a tale of disappointment: 'We do not feel comfortable in our present-day civilization', Freud continued, as though the graft of technology had not fully taken on to its human stock.[7] 'Man has, as it were, become a kind of prosthetic God. When he puts on all his auxiliary organs he is truly magnificent; but those organs have not grown on to him and they still give him much trouble at times.'[8]

For Freud, machines were compensatory devices, but their presence in human life, paradoxically, worked to deepen a sense of human frailty. This paradox is a mirror of a more general argument revolving around the presence of the machine in Renaissance culture. As we shall see, in the course of the fifteenth, sixteenth, and seventeenth centuries, with the advent of ever-more complex and sophisticated machines, whether real or imagined, two conflicting attitudes towards the machine emerged to jostle, uneasily, against one another. This conflict arose from that original Aristotelian distinction between the natural world and the artificial world of Technē. Is Technē an expression of a utopian spirit, a drive to make the world in some measure better, or at least more comfortable or more secure? Or might it, instead, be thought of as gloomily dystopic: a vain attempt to shape the natural and human worlds whose end result is usually frustration and perhaps even disaster? In the European Renaissance, the clash of these two positions, one of which was characterized by optimism, the other by pessimism, was rooted in both classical myth and Christian theology.[9] And this clash, in turn, was to produce the idea of mechanical culture or the 'machine world' as it has also sometimes been known, of which we have become the inheritors.

The optimistic view of things held that Technē promised a partial theological restitution. Perhaps the original disaster of the Fall of humanity in the Garden of Eden could be alleviated by the invention and deployment of ingenious devices? Working in the service of humankind and understood as a product of human ingenuity, Technē was a manifestation of 'secondary creation'. Machines, tools, and devices represented a partial compensation, through God's grace, for that original punishment by which humanity was exiled from its place of origin.[10] With their help, so it was believed, a partial replica of the lost paradise might be confected. Machinery and mechanism, according to Francis Bacon, was one of the means by which humanity might mitigate the effects of 'the first general curse' in the development of the civilizing arts.[11] The world wrought with the help of machines could, of course, only ever be an imperfect version of what had been irretrievably lost in the primal disaster of the expulsion from Eden.

It was this fundamentally optimistic sense of the role of machines that, as we shall see, came to underpin the mechanical visions of Bacon's successors in England in the seventeenth century. Following Bacon, among the 'mechanic philosophers' who revelled in the new science of mechanics associated with Galileo, and who were equally enthralled at the prospects of nature revealed by their various devices and instruments, the belief arose that the world, human society, and perhaps even the individual were on the brink of being rendered calculable and hence predictable, perhaps even controllable. The world and all that it contained was understood as a series of 'engines', crafted or fabricated by the master-engineer who was God. The task of fallen humanity was to emulate and perhaps even to surpass the divine mechanisms to be found in nature. Might it even be possible to create better mechanical versions of those structures that God had organized in the first week of creation? Here, perhaps, is the origin of that Western belief in technological and social progress, a belief that was unknown (so it has been argued) either in antiquity or in the Middle Ages.[12]

At the very core of the pessimistic view of technology, however, was the conviction, often deep-rooted and unspoken, that the machine was fundamentally at variance with an ideal of 'nature', or even of God. Despite their usefulness, machines were products of fallible human reason, and as such they were always to be considered as tainted in some way by the primal act of transgression recounted in the opening verses of Genesis. So, in the pessimistic view of things, the machine was in no sense to be understood as a compensatory device by which the effects of the Fall of humanity were softened. Rather, it epitomized the moment of transgression, exile, and loss. The machine was a mark of shame. Indeed, it was only because we were fallen creatures that we felt the need to develop those prosthetic additions to the human form that the machine also came to represent.

A world run upon wheels: the sound of the Renaissance

In our own noisy post-industrial culture, we tend to think of the world inhabited by the contemporaries of Chaucer, and (later) Montaigne or Shakespeare as technologically silent when compared to the world we inhabit today. Of course, we know that early-modern people *used* machines of various kinds. How else could the cathedrals of medieval and early-modern Europe have been raised, or the books printed? But it is easy to assume that whatever sound might have been heard in the pre-industrial past was generated directly by humans, animals, or nature, and only rarely by machines or mechanical devices. Not until the late eighteenth and nineteenth centuries, so the argument goes, would the European cityscape ring to the sound of machine-driven industrial processes.[13]

Nevertheless, just occasionally, we are allowed to hear the rhythms of pre-industrial culture, as in this set of anonymous fourteenth-century verses, complaining about noise and smoke pollution, generated by the workshops of medieval blacksmiths. The poem begins:

Swarte smekyd smeþes smateryd with smoke
Dryue me to deth with den of here dyntes
Swech noys on nyghtes ne herd men neuer
What knavuene cry and clateryng of knockes![14]

[Swart smoky smiths, smattered with smoke
Driving me to death with the din of their blows.
Such a noise, at night, no man has ever heard:
What yelling of servants and clattering of knocks!]

And the verses end in a riot of onomatopoeia, evoking the clang and din of the blacksmith's forge, which needs no translation: 'Tik, tak! hic, hac! ticket, taket! tyk, tak! / Lus, bus! Lus, das! Swyth lyf thei ledyn . . .'[15] This is a poem whose subject is, simply, noise. Although those rhythmic hammer blows are not mechanically driven, the economic historian David Landes has observed that late-medieval Europe was 'as nowhere else, a power-based civilization'.[16] As we shall see, machines, particularly water-driven machines, generated much of the power that was also harnessed by those 'Swarte smekyd smeþes' at their forges and bellows. But elsewhere, mechanical noise is described as forming part of the texture of the soundscape of the early-modern city. An account of life in early seventeenth-century London, for example, to be found in Thomas Dekker's *The Seuen Deadly Sinnes of London* (1606), suggests something of the cacophony that assaulted the senses in the narrow streets of the city in Shakespeare's time. 'In every street' Dekker wrote:

> . . . carts and Coaches make such a thundring as if the world ranne vpon wheeles: at euerie corner, men, women, and children meete in such shoales, that postes are sette vp of purpose to strengthen the houses, least with iustling one another they should shoulder them downe. Besides, hammers are beating in one place, Tube hooping in another, Pots clincking in a third, water-tankards running at tilt in a fourth . . .[17]

For all that the ambient hum and roar of the modern city was absent from the early-modern world, it was, clearly, a noisy place in which to live and work.

It was in the nineteenth century that the idea of 'medieval' or 'Renaissance' culture came to express a quieter, less mechanized, more organic way of life. For a critic such as John Ruskin, the pre-industrial past functioned as a refuge from the noisy, cluttered, machine-driven age of the iron master, the industrialist, and the engineer. So Ruskin compared nineteenth-century Rochdale 'riveted together with iron' with its polluted stream and its city 'foaming forth perpetual plague of sulphurous darkness', with thirteenth-century Pisa, where, out of the 'scenery of perfect human life, rose dome and bell-tower burning with white alabaster and gold'.[18] Nineteenth-century commentators such as Ruskin, burdened by their sense of modern industry, tended to ignore the fact that there were large and powerful mech-anized devices, as well as sophisticated industrial processes, to be found in the heart of Renaissance cities. For example, a work such as Thomas Deloney's *The Pleasant Historie of Iohn Winchcomb* (first published in 1597), dedi-cated to the 'famous Cloth-Workers in England', announces a mechanized industrial presence in Elizabethan London:

> Within one roome being large and long,
> There stood two hundred Loomes full strong:
> Two hundred men the truth is so,
> Wrought in these Loomes all in a row.[19]

Spinning and weaving were activities that had been mechanized in parts of Europe for at least two hundred years before these verses were written. Deloney's two hundred machine operatives, tending their powerful looms, formed just a tiny proportion of the thousands of machine workers who populated sixteenth-century London. For this was indeed, in Dekker's evoc-ative phrase, a world that ran upon wheels.

Windmills and watermills

For all that Wordsworth may have hymned the technological sublimity of Westminster Bridge, the idea that technology was a fitting subject for art or for poetry is generally assumed to be the invention of the later nineteenth century.[20] Given this assumption, it has been all too easy to overlook the mass of evidence for a more general imaginative and artistic engagement with the machine as well as technology on the part of Renaissance writers and artists.

Yet, machines and devices of all kinds are to be found at every turn in Renaissance art. An image of a blast furnace, created about 1520, the work of Joachim Patenier (c. 1480–1524), hints at the ways in which technol-ogy was considered to be a fitting subject among artists of the sixteenth and seventeenth centuries. So, we find an altarpiece (1521) in St Anne's church at Annanberg, the work of Hans Hesse, in which miners labour with machines watched over by angels; miners (again) at work depicted by Hans Holbein theYounger (1497–1543) in a series of drawings now to be found in the British Museum; a landscape by Lucas van Gassel (c. 1500–70) in Brussels which includes one of the earliest known views of a railway; industrial landscapes by the brothers Lucas and Martin van Valckenborch (1530–97, 1535–1622 respectively). These images do not, in any way, constitute an emerging critique of mechanism. In fact, quite the reverse, they represent an optimistic celebration of machines and the human labour that works with machines. The art historian Francis Klingender has observed of such images that they 'foreshadow the concept that manual labour has a self-sufficient dignity and strength of its own' of a kind more commonly associated with Victorian images of human labour and machinery.[21] A painting such as The Copper Mine (c. 1540) of Herri met de Bles (c. 1510–50) (Figure 1.1, p. 8) shows the busy activity surrounding a mine's surface workings, including blazing forges, spoil heaps, and a great water wheel, powering various kinds of machinery. The artist was based in Antwerp, and his painting may be understood as responding to the trade in metals among South German banking families who had settled in that city.[22] An image such as this can also be understood as the aesthetic equivalent of a more obviously technological work such as Georgius Agricola's De Re Metallica (1556), an exhaustive study of all aspects of the German mining industry in the early part of the sixteenth century.

These scenes of Renaissance industry also remind us of how, within protestant culture, the term 'industry' would come to express the godly business of self-renewal and self-improvement, of the kind that R. H. Tawney, long ago, associated with the rise of industrial capitalism. Industry symbolized the 'daemonic energy' with which the 'Puritan flings himself into practical activities' purged of doubt, and 'conscious that he is a sealed and chosen vessel'.[23] Industry and industriousness denoted a zealous purposefulness, a single-minded pursuit of gain sanctioned by a pious awareness of God's continual presence within human affairs, of which worldly success could be understood as a sign of impending grace.

But an optimistic fascination with industry, labour, and mechanism surfaced in staunchly Roman Catholic Italy, too, long before any puritan pursuit of practical activity. In 1474, Duke Federico da Montefeltro ordered seventy-two machine drawings based on the work of the Sienese engineer Francesco di Giorgio Martini to be cut in stone relief and mounted on the

Figure 1.1 Herri met de Bles (Civetta) (c. 1510–50), *The Copper Mine* (oil on panel), Galleria degli Uffizi, Florence, Italy, The Bridgeman Art Library.

walls of his palace at Urbino (Figure 1.2, p. 10).[24] A century later, Giorgio
Vasari ordered a set of 'industrial murals' depicting the labour of alchemists,
jewellers, glass-workers, and dyers for the study of Francesco I de' Medici in
Florence, in a style 'partly heroic, partly realistic'.[25] These tokens of mechanical culture underline the extent to which the great patrons of Renaissance
art were also patrons of technology. Earlier in the sixteenth century, too, in
the paintings of the Florentine Piero di Cosimo (1462–1521), particularly
his *Vulcan and Aeolus* (c. 1495–1500), *The Discovery of Honey* (c. 1505–10), and
The Myth of Prometheus (1515), we can see a fascination with what might be
termed the 'mythic' origins of labour, human ingenuity, and mechanism.[26]
In di Cosimo's *The Building of a Double Palace* (c. 1521), something of the busy
activity of a Renaissance construction site can be glimpsed, with workmen
deploying different kinds of devices to raise the neoclassical building that
dominates the surrounding landscape. Labour and human ingenuity are celebrated, here, as foundational works of civilization by which monuments of
enduring beauty come to inhabit the world.

Informing all such images, too, was an idea of 'progress' that was to become such a vital component in the construction of mechanical culture. But
what of the pessimistic view of things? An image of a mine or a forge, for
example, may have celebrated human ingenuity, but no Renaissance artist
would have viewed such a scene without a certain degree of ambivalence.
For, underpinning these images was that great reservoir of classical myth
and narrative to be found in Ovid's *Metamorphoses*, in which human inventiveness is imagined as part of a history of decline. In the distant Golden
Age, Ovid writes, there was no need for the arts of civilization, the skills of
the miner, the blacksmith, or the ploughman:

> The peoples of the world, untroubled by any fears, enjoyed a leisurely and
> peaceful existence . . . The earth itself, without compulsion, untouched by
> any hoe, unfurrowed by any share, produced all things spontaneously.[27]

But with the coming of the 'age of hard iron', and with it the technological
arts of mining and husbandry, the innocent pastoral world was shattered for
ever. The earth no longer simply yielded its fruits. Instead it was rifled for
treasure – iron and gold – with which to fashion objects and instruments of
all kinds. 'War made its appearance' Ovid writes 'using both those metals in
its conflict.'[28]

This pessimistic view of technology is a mirror of the Christian idea of
technology as a by-product of the Fall. In Renaissance art, the idea of the

Figure 1.2 Plaque depicting a winch mechanism for driving a transverse shaft by Ambrogio de Federico Barocci (fifteenth century) (stone), Palazzo Ducale, Urbino, Italy, The Bridgeman Art Library.

Fall is encountered at its most extreme in the strange, hallucinatory images of Hieronymus Bosch (c. 1450–1516). In Bosch's art, machines and mechanisms of all kinds are ghostly presences, dimly realized as manifestations of human pain or torment. The right-hand panel of Bosch's famous triptych *The Garden of Earthly Delights* (c. 1510–15?) offers us an essentially industrial landscape, the Renaissance equivalent of Blake's dark satanic mills, featuring watermills and windmills, ceaselessly revolving, incandescent with the glare of fires, ovens, and furnaces.[29] Windmills can be discerned, again, in Bosch's *Adoration of the Magi* (c. 1510), while in the *Triptych of the Haywain* (c. 1500–5), hell is represented by a gigantic half-finished tower constructed with the aid of some obscure engine or windlass, driven by the energy of the devils who populate this infernal construction site (Figure 1.3, p. 12).

But among later Northern European artists, machines tended to appear in a quite different guise, reminding us of the optimistic view of technology as a restitution of some kind. Thus, in the paintings of the Dutch artist, Jacob van Ruisdael (1628/9–82), watermills and mill machinery are shown as monumental, heroic, presences in his landscape, calming and taming the elemental ferocity of water, which was one of the artist's favourite themes in his paintings.[30] Along with watermills, locks, bridges, and sluices, or his drawing of a *moddermolen* or mudmill (c. 1650s), now in the Metropolitan Museum of Art in New York, Ruisdael specialized in painting that seemingly ubiquitous device in the Dutch landscape, the windmill, which was portrayed with aerodynamic precision in his art.[31]

In Holland, the windmill represented one of the great power technologies of the period. Unsurprisingly, the device also featured prominently in the work of other landscape artists in the region: Jan Brueghel the Elder (1568–1625), Pieter Codde (1599–1673), Jan Brueghel the Younger (1601–78) are just a few of the many artists who were drawn to this unmistakable technological presence in the Flemish and Dutch landscape. Sometimes, as in *A Distant View of Dordrecht* (c. 1650) (*The Large Dort*) by Aelbert Cuyp (1620–91), now in the British Museum, the view of the town is dominated by the windmills that rival the *Grote Kerk*, the main church of the town, for the viewer's attention. In Jan van Goyen's (1596–1656) *A Windmill by a River*, by contrast, the bare, windswept landscape is the setting for an isolated windmill, registering a defiantly human presence amid the forces of nature.[32] It was not, however, in pursuit of the picturesque that Dutch painters set about depicting these complex mechanisms. The windmill, along with other signs of an artificially contrived human presence in the flat landscape, functioned, in art, as part of a mapping impulse. Mills and canals, along with distant church steeples, were marks on the land, helping to fix one's bearings in an otherwise featureless terrain of sky, water, and fenland.[33] The windmill was a guardian presence, demarcating the boundary between land and water. In an ink sketch by Constantijn Huygens III (1628–97) entitled *View of the Waal from the Town Gate at Zaltbommel* (1669), two windmills stand like sentinels on

Figure 1.3 Hieronymus Bosch, *Triptych of the Haywain*: right wing of the triptych depicting Hell, *c.* 1500 (panel), Monasterio de El Escorial, Spain, The Bridgeman Art Library.

the seashore, helping (both literally and aesthetically) to separate the sea from the land, which would otherwise threaten to merge into one another.

In purely functional terms, situated as they were so often by rivers and canals, windmills were powerful pumping engines. With their help, the surrounding fields and polders were preserved for agriculture. In Dutch art, they expressed the ingenuity by which the landscape was transformed and made serviceable to human needs, while they were also tokens of collective pride in Dutch technological mastery: 'God made the World' as the familiar motto had it 'but the Dutch made the Netherlands.'[34] The windmill thus symbolized what it was to dwell in this flat landscape that had to be wrested from the threat of inundation. 'Trial by water' Simon Schama writes, was one of the 'formative experiences in the creation of Dutch nationhood' as well as Dutch society, which he characterizes as having a 'diluvian personality'.[35] So, the windmill was made to perform work twice over: once, in actuality, draining the countryside, and a second time, in representation, signalling an emerging sense of geographic and even national identity.

But the windmill and watermill also fulfilled other functions, which alert us to a wider symbolic set of values which came to adhere to the idea of the machine. In an anonymous fifteenth-century English prose translation of Guillaugme de Deguileville's mid-fourteenth-century poem, Le Pèlerinage de la vie humaine, Christ is considered as the 'seed' who is first harvested, then winnowed and threshed and finally ground in a mill, 'broken, brused, tormented', in the passion and crucifixion.[36] By contrast, in his Emblemata of 1625, Zacharias Heyns (1566–1638) depicts a windmill standing on a rocky promontory, its sails turned towards the sun. Beneath the image is the Pauline dictum (adapted from 2 Corinthians 3. 6) 'the letter killeth, but the spirit giveth life'.[37] Heyns explains that the mill's dependence on wind power is similar to human dependence on the Holy Spirit for life (Figure 1.4, p. 14).

The machine is thus made to express some larger idea of the relationship between God and humanity. But a machine did not have to be the subject or theme of a painting or image in order to exert its symbolic influence in Renaissance art, whether emanating from north or south of the Alps. Earlier in the sixteenth century, the machine was put to symbolic work in Pieter Brueghel the Elder's Hunters in the Snow (1565), one of a cycle of pictures depicting the progress of the seasons. Brueghel's painting contains a small mechanical detail, easily overlooked. In the bottom right-hand corner of the image an icicle-festooned watermill, held fast in a frozen millpond, evokes the shivering immobility of the human and animal worlds held in

Figure 1.4 Zacharias Heyns, *Emblemata, Emblems Christienes, et Morales* (Rotterdam, 1625), plate 18. Glasgow University Library, Special Collections.

the grip of winter (Figure 1.5, p. 16). Once this detail in Brueghel's painting is noted, a network of ancillary meanings of the image begins to unfold, circulating around those related ideas of optimism and pessimism once more. Pessimistically, the machine is shown to be impotent in the face of the power of nature, which is able to reduce it to frost-bound stasis. But optimistically, the machine is emblematic of the social world that the frozen hunters are intent on rejoining. Something of the mythic archetypes of technological progress is at work, too, in the painting: the hunters, returning with their dogs and the single rabbit which is all they have been able to retrieve from the frozen forest, are representatives of an older, nomadic way of life. The machine, on the other hand, for all that it is held in the grip of winter, is a promise of a more secure existence. Remembering that this image is part of a cycle of paintings, the promise is that the land will, eventually, emerge from its wintry shroud, and with the spring thaw the mill's wheels will turn once more. The temporary retreat into a frozen Arcadia, which is shown to be a not entirely comfortable place, will, at last, come to an end.

Machines may be much more than extraneous details in the landscape. In Renaissance images, the machine, usually in the form of a mill of some kind, can often be glimpsed at the margin of the picture, through an opened window, or vaguely evoked in the middle or further distance. Such devices are particularly prevalent in religious painting. So, while the machine in the landscape may be understood as a sign of civility, it also reminds us of that promise of a theological restitution. It also might hint, emblematically, at the anguish suffered by Christ on the cross, imagined, as we have seen in the case of a fourteenth-century French poet, as a form of milling or grinding. In a depiction, for example, of the *Rest of the Holy Family on the Flight into Egypt* of c. 1525–50, attributed to the workshop of the 'master of the female half-lengths', the Virgin, St Joseph, and the infant Jesus are shown in the foreground. Behind them, in the middle distance, painted with an attentive eye to detail, can be discerned an overshot watermill and a sluice.[38] In the *Last Supper* (1531) by Pieter Coecke van Aelst (1502–56), through an opened window, behind Christ's right shoulder, we can see two windmills in the far distance. In Brueghel's *Carrying of the Cross* (1564), the route to Calvary is dominated by another windmill, perched precipitously on a craggy outcrop. The mill, in fact, is far easier to spot in the painting than the tiny figure of Christ struggling under the burden of his cross. Similarly, in the *Madonna and Child with the Young John the Baptist* (1497), the work of Fra Bartolommeo (1473–1517), the sacred figures are posed, conventionally, within an open *loggia*, while, behind them, the landscape unfolds to show, again, a watermill. In a picture now in the National Gallery in London known as *Moses Defending the Daughters of Jethro* (1609), by Carlo Saraceni (1579–1620, also known as Carlo Veneziano), an incident from the early life of Moses is depicted, in which Moses defends Jethro's daughters from a group of shepherds, intent on driving them away from a well (Exodus 2. 16) (Figure 1.6, p. 17). But dominating the left-hand side of the image, the artist shows us a complex water-lifting device, quite possibly derived from the machine designs of Agostino Ramelli, whose sumptuous *Le Diverse et Artificiose Machine* was published in a dual French and Italian edition at Paris in 1588. In his work, Ramelli traced the divine origins of the invention of mechanisms

Figure 1.5 Pieter Brueghel the Elder (c. 1515–69), *Hunters in the Snow* (1565), Kunsthistorisches Museum, Vienna, Austria.

Figure 1.6 Carlo Saraceni,
*Moses Defending the Daughters
of Jethro* (1609–10) (oil on
copper), 28.5 × 35.3 cm,
National Gallery, London.

and machines, recounting how this 'magnificent discipline' had flourished among the Chaldeans, and how it had become the object of study of Abraham. From Abraham, wrote Ramelli, knowledge of the discipline was passed to the Egyptians and thence to the Greeks.[39] Saraceni's pictorial device, then, may be understood as a sign of the ancient origins of mechanism, while it also recalled the memory of the patriarch, Abraham, and of the Egyptian transmission of mechanical knowledge to the Christian West. Alternatively, the mechanical device in Saraceni's image might also be a reminder of the labour of the Israelites in their Egyptian slavery, when they, like Samson, were put to work in the mills of their overlords.[40] Much later, in another biblical scene, Claude Lorraine's (1604–82) idyllic *Landscape with the Marriage of Isaac and Rebekah* (1648), almost as much effort as has been expended in rendering the detail of a watermill, churning away in the middle distance together with what appear to be a group of industrial buildings, as has been devoted to the human figures in the foreground, who are the painting's ostensible subject matter.

The windmill, present at Christ's passion or in the flight of the Holy Family, is a guardian presence, reminding the viewer, as in the case of the Dutch emblem of a windmill powered by the animating Holy Spirit, of theological restitution. But Renaissance artists were also accustomed to collapsing the past and the present, producing a timeless continuum. In Brueghel's *Carrying of the Cross*, the Passion is enacted within a contemporary context, as though the events told in the Gospels were happening on the outskirts of sixteenth-century Brussels.[41] In a similar fashion, the Holy Family, pausing on its journey by revivifying streams and rivers, is placed close to the familiar technological device of the mill, or the machine is glimpsed through an opened window, an incidental detail in the image.[42] In the fifteenth and sixteenth centuries, these same rivers and streams would have been the sites of numberless mills, sluices, dams, locks, and canals, powering the workshops of pre-industrial Europe. What better way, in other words, to remind the pious onlooker of the reality of the sacred, within the world of the here and now, than to situate the biblical narrative within the humdrum reality of everyday existence, which contained so many artful devices of this kind?

Shame

This rich artistic legacy was based, however, on a foundational myth of technology as transgression. Though the Bible may have celebrated King Uzziah, who 'loved husbandry' and who, with the help of 'cunning men', invested

Jerusalem with 'engines' against his enemies, his career ended in oblivion. Uzziah 'transgressed against the Lord' and died a leper (II Chronicles 26. 10–23). Uzziah thus joined a long line of cunning inventors who traced their lineage back to the fratricidal Cain, the inventor of cities, and which included Jabal ('the father of such as dwell in tents, and *such as have* cattle') who invented pastoralism, Jubal, the inventor of musical instruments, and Tubalcain 'the instructor of every artificer in brass and iron' (Genesis 4. 17–22).

For technology, the Bible story tells us, was the product of the Fall, though in exactly what way is not entirely clear. Genesis records that God 'took the man, and put him in the garden of Eden to dress and to keep it' (Genesis 2. 15), which suggests that the technological impulse is pre-lapsarian. But after the Fall, this technological impulse is tainted by shame. The first reaction of Eve and Adam, after their primal act of disobedience, is shame at their nakedness. Hence they fashion what the Authorized Version of the Bible (1611) quaintly terms 'aprons' by sewing fig leaves together as clothes (Genesis 3. 7). Shame is a mark both of civilization and of humanity's fallen state, while technology, here the sewing together of fig leaves, is understood as a prosthetic mask.[43] With God's discovery of this disobedience, betrayed by the suddenly clothed appearance of Eve and Adam, humanity is cursed to labour: 'out of the sweat of thy face shalt thou eat bread, till thou return unto the ground: for dust thou *art*, and unto dust shalt thou return' (Genesis 3. 19).

But then, in one of those curious reversals of which the creation story in Genesis seems so fond, the story is refashioned or reinscribed. An alternative myth of the appearance of technology is suddenly allowed to surface: 'Unto Adam also and to his wife did the LORD God make coats of skins, and clothed them' (Genesis 3. 21). God's care for his fallen creatures is touching, but puzzling. If we understand either the original fig-leaf 'aprons' fashioned by Adam and Eve or the ambiguous 'skins' fashioned by God of the revisionary story as metonyms for the earliest technological accomplishment of humanity, then is that same technology to be considered an unaided human response to the disaster that befell our primal parents? Or is it, rather, a divine gift, akin to the Promethean gift of fire, by which God bestowed upon humankind the means to help them to survive in the world that had suddenly become a place of exile and work?[44]

Pessimism, once more, is in competition with optimism. For Augustine, in the closing pages of the *City of God*, all the manifold inventions of human industry and ingenuity which are manifestations of *Technē*, and which included clothing, building, agriculture, navigation, pottery, sculpture, painting, theatre, arms, 'engines of war', eloquence, poetry, music, melody, geometry, and arithmetic formed what he termed a 'compressed pile of blessings'.[45] They were not, however, to be understood as 'rewards' of any kind. Rather, they were 'the consolations of mankind under condemnation'.[46] Augustine's view of Technē as a 'consolation' structured the wider interpretation of technology in the pre-industrial world. Thus, writes David Noble, 'technology came to be identified . . . with both lost perfection and the possibility of renewed perfection . . . not only as evidence of grace, but as a means of preparation for, and a sure sign of, imminent salvation'.[47]

This oscillation between two competing accounts of the technological impulse informed the two most familiar narratives of technology known to Renaissance artists, writers, and mythographers: the story of the construction and abandonment of the tower of Babel, and the story of the fall of Icarus. In the familiar story of Babel (Genesis 11. 1–9), we read how God was angered by the singleness of purpose with which the people of the 'plain in the land of Shinar' constructed a city and a tower in order to make themselves a 'name' (Genesis 11. 4). In retaliation, God confuses their speech, the city is abandoned, and the people doomed to wander. Babel thus emerges as a monument to the diversity of language in the world, as well as to the diffusion of peoples. Mythically, it helps to explain why, in the words of a modern prehistorian, there are humans everywhere.[48] But Babel is also a monument to technology. For the story may be read as an account of the transition, in human culture, from nomadic wandering (the era of the so-called 'hunter gatherers') to pastoralism, and hence to urban dwelling.[49]

In the Renaissance, the Babel story, with its familiar narrative of linguistic confusion, was understood as one of the three 'successive setbacks' (the others being the Fall and the Flood), which, to natural philosophers, signalled the loss of 'natural knowledge of the world and its operations'.[50] 'In the age after the Flood', wrote Francis Bacon in The Advancement of Learning, 'the first great judgment of God upon the ambition of man was the confusion of tongues, whereby the open trade and intercourse of learning and knowledge was chiefly imbarred.'[51] Dominion over nature was thus a matter of translation, as much as it was to do with experiment or practice.[52] This belief would prompt the Jesuit polymath Athanasius Kircher to publish his last book, Turris Babel (1679), in which he sought to explain how languages, peoples, and culture had become diversified since the catastrophe held to have taken place on the plain of Shinar.[53] Kircher's imaginative reconstruction of Babel, as Anthony Grafton puts it, 'stone by stone and arch by arch', would result in the devising of his fantastic (literally) translation machine, as though the appliance of technology could remedy this primal catastrophe.[54]

But if Babel represented the possibility of linguistic restitution, it also symbolized a degree of technological optimism.[55] In the late sixteenth and earlier seventeenth centuries, Northern European artists became fascinated with the idea of Babel as the foundation of the idea of craft or industry. Deploying all manner of imaginative machines in their images – cranes, hoists, wheels, gigantic pulley systems – artistic recreations of the construction of Nimrod's great tower expressed a dynamic story of human technical ingenuity. In artistic, if not theological terms, Babel was imagined as a technological utopia, forged with the help of elaborate and fantastical instruments and devices. Certainly, the artists who turned to this theme seemed to have rejected (or simply ignored) the traditional view of Babel, as described by Augustine in the *City of God* or Dante in the *Paradiso*, that 'the unaccomplishable task' ('*ovra inconsummabile*') of Babel was a work of 'arrogant impiety' or 'empty presumption' on the part of humanity.[56] They seemed blithely unaware, too, that Babel signalled the end of the pastoral idyll. Instead, Babel became a celebration of the world of *Technē*. Thus, in images produced by (among others) Holbein, Hendrick Van Cleve III (1525–89), Marten van Valckenborch (c. 1535–1612) and Lucas van Valckenborch (c. 1535–97), Pieter Balten (1525–98), Abel Grimmer (1570–1619), Pieter Brueghel the Younger (c. 1564–1638), Abraham Sauer (1543–93), Mathieu Merian (1593–1650), Tobias Verhaecht (1561–1631) and (above all) in the two well-known fantasy creations of Pieter Brueghel the Elder (1525–69) known, respectively, as the 'great' and the 'little' Tower of Babel of 1563, the Tower appears not as a terrible warning to humanity, but as an expression of a better, more organized, more accomplished, world (Figures 1.7 and 1.8).

In fact, to these Northern European artists, the construction of the great edifice was a far more compelling subject than its destruction. For all that protestant artists were perhaps acutely sensitive to the problem of linguistic confusion (the first polyglot Bible had been published in Antwerp in 1566), they chose to depict the moment *before* the tower was abandoned amid the confusion of tongues. Babel thus appears as a monument to innovation. In a miniature, for example, to be found in a breviary of the early sixteenth century, the work of the Flemish illuminator Gerard Horenbout (1465–1541), the incomplete tower of Babel is festooned with machines and devices of all kinds. In the foreground, artisans labour inside forges, while in the distance an enormous wheeled lifting machine, a purely imaginative device, is

Figure 1.7 Mattheus Merian the Elder (1593–1650), Engraving of the construction of the Tower of Babel in *Icones Biblicae* (Strasbourg, 1625), private collection.

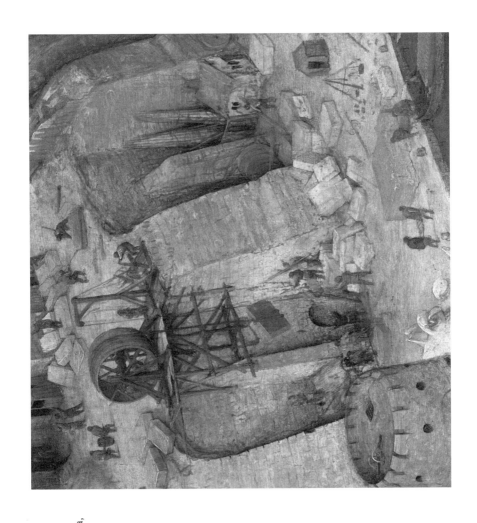

Figure 1.8 Pieter Brueghel the Elder
(c. 1515–69), *The Tower of Babel*, detail of
the construction works, 1563 (oil on panel),
Kunsthistorisches Museum, Vienna, Austria,
The Bridgeman Art Library.

deployed. Babel had become, for these artists, a biblical prototype of their own world of labour, industry, and manufacture.

The story of Icarus, the second great foundation myth of technology, lies behind Freud's image of humanity recasting itself as a 'prosthetic God' with the help of the 'graft' which technology came to represent. But, just as in the case of the Babel story, to Renaissance artists and mythographers, the tale of Icarus admitted of divergent, even contradictory interpretations. Daedalus, the father of Icarus, and fabricator of the Cretan labyrinth, was considered to be the archetype of cunning inventiveness. In Polydore Vergil's *De inventoribus rerum* (1499), a monumental investigation into what would become known as 'heurematography' (the study of discovery), Daedalus was the inventor of the saw, the hatchet, the plumb line, and significantly, given the tale that unfolds, of 'glue . . . for cementing wood together'.[57]

In Book VIII of the *Metamorphoses*, Ovid recounts how Daedalus, hoping to escape from the island of Crete, 'set his mind to sciences never explored before and altered the laws of nature' in fashioning wings for himself and his son.[58] Preparing for flight, Icarus is warned by his father to 'follow a course midway between the earth and heaven, in case the sun should scorch your feathers'.[59] But the advice is unheeded, and in any case proves untrustworthy. Exulting in the thrill of flight, Icarus soars upwards towards the sun which, rather than scorching his feathers (as his father had feared) instead melts the wax that holds together the feathery contraption: 'the unhappy father . . . saw the feathers on the water, and cursed his inventive skill'.[60] His fall echoes the larger Fall of humankind to be found in the opening chapters of Genesis or the decline of humankind from a mythical pre-technological golden age, or the disaster that encompassed the founders of Babel. For Daedalus had tampered with 'the laws of nature'. Ovid underlines his transgression at the conclusion to the tale, when he has a 'chattering lapwing' flapping its wings and crowing with joy from a muddy ditch, mocking the sorrowing Daedalus who has just buried his son's corpse.[61]

Tampering with the 'laws of nature' was exactly what machines, as they were understood in Renaissance culture, were designed to accomplish. Daedalus can thus be understood as the first in a long line of heroic but failed machine makers. In Renaissance art and literature, moreover, Icarus was to stand, or rather fall, alongside other examples of legendary overreachers who are punished for their presumptive interference with the designs of fate or providence.[62] Renaissance poets seized on the story of Daedalus and Icarus as an expression of human pride or, as Shakespeare has it in the first of his Henry VI plays (c. 1592), as an example of an 'over-mounting spirit'

(1 *Henry VI* IV. vii. 16). More brutally, and dismissively, in 3 *Henry VI* (1595), Shakespeare recalls the story of Icarus and Daedalus as an example of fathers betraying their all too credulous sons:

> What a peevish fool was that of Crete
> Who taught his son the office of a fowl!
> And yet for all his wings, the fool was drowned.
>
> *(3 Henry VI* V. v. 18–20)

For Christopher Marlowe, equally, the story of the fall of Icarus expressed 'selfe conceit'. Marlowe's *Tragicall History of Doctor Faustus* (1604, 1616) describes Faustus, at the opening of the play, as:

> . . . swolne with cunning, of a self conceit,
> His waxen wings did mount aboue his reach,
> And melting heauens conspirde his ouerthrow.[63]

As well as displaying intellectual *hubris*, the story of Icarus was also understood in the Renaissance as a social lesson: that one must learn to accept one's 'estate' or station in life. Thus, Arthur Golding, in his 1567 translation of the *Metamorphoses*, carefully glossed the advice of Daedalus to his son that he should follow 'a course midway between the earth and heaven, in case the sun should scorch your feathers', by means of an epistle dedicated to the politically ambitious Robert Dudley Earl of Leicester.[64] Golding's verses interpreted the Icarus story as a lesson in quietism. For, though the story of Daedalus is an example of how necessity 'Dooth make men wyse, and sharpes their wits to fynd their own redresse', yet:

> Wee also lerne by Icarus how good it is to bee
> In meane estate and not to clymb too hygh, but to agree
> Too wholsome counsell: for the hyre of disobedience is
> Repentance when it is too late for thinking things amisse[65]

More allusively, in an anonymous poem ('Love wing'd my hopes and taught me how to fly') to be found in Robert Jones's (fl. 1597–1615) collection of airs and songs, published in 1601, the story of Icarus was interpreted as an ambiguous warning which, once more, carried a social dimension:

LOVE wing'd my Hopes and taught me how to fly
Far from base earth, but not to mount too high:
> For true pleasure
> Lives in measure,
> Which if men forsake,
Blinded they into folly run and grief for pleasure take.

But my vain Hopes, proud of their new-taught flight,
Enamour'd sought to woo the sun's fair light,
> Whose rich brightness
> Moved their lightness
> To aspire so high
That all scorch'd and consumed with fire now drown'd in woe they lie.[66]

With that characteristic Renaissance delight in transposing elements from an older, mythic source onto a quite different theme, the poet has appropriated the story of Icarus to produce a lyric whose lesson is one of limiting human ambition. 'Love' (which might be read in either its sacred or profane sense) prompts the exhilarating release from 'base earth', but human pride and vanity ignores the moral, appropriate for a lyric designed to be set to music, that 'true pleasure . . . lives in measure' at its peril. All of these ideas may be associated with that fundamentally pessimistic view of the fate of fallen humanity, which labours to tame the elements with the help of devices and instruments, but whose end result is failure.

In the many pictorial renditions of the story of the fall of Icarus meaning seems to oscillate, once more, between pessimism and optimism.[67] We can see the oscillation in possibly the most famous Renaissance rendition of the legendary catastrophe: Brueghel's *Landscape with the Fall of Icarus* (c. 1558) (Figure 1.9). But Brueghel's painting presents another kind of puzzle, since Icarus himself is almost absent from the scene. Only a splash and a pair of legs mark the site of his catastrophe. Dwelling on that splash, in his poem 'Musée des Beaux Arts' (1938), W. H. Auden famously observed that the personal disaster of Icarus seems to have been oddly displaced from Brueghel's rendition of the scene. Instead, the overriding impression left on the viewer of the painting is one of indifference to the tragedy that has taken place. This indifference to the sight of 'something amazing, a boy falling out of the sky' was (for Auden) the whole point of the painting, which he understood to be a sardonic allegory on the nature of human suffering:

Figure 1.9 Pieter Brueghel the Elder (c. 1515–69), *Landscape with the Fall of Icarus, c.* 1555 (oil on canvas), Musées Royaux des Beaux-Arts de Belgique, Brussels, Belgium, Giraudon, The Bridgeman Art Library.

> . . . how everything turns away
> Quite leisurely from the disaster; the ploughman may
> Have heard the splash, the forsaken cry,
> But for him it was not an important failure.[68]

But it was not that 'the Old Masters' were 'never wrong' about human suffering, or that they were indifferent to the fate of others. Rather, it was that the
fall of Icarus expressed a larger truth about the relationship of human beings
to nature, to artifice, and to technology.[69] So, Icarus plunges, almost unno-
ticed, into the sea, while the everyday business of the world carries on: the
fisherman continues to fish, and the ploughman, the central and most arrest-
ing figure in the entire image, plods steadfastly behind the plough, his eyes
fixed on the furrows he is graving in the earth's surface. Only the shepherd,
leaning on his staff and gazing in slack-jawed amazement into the sky, tracing the invisible path of Daedalus, the survivor of the catastrophe, seems to
be aware that he is witness to something remarkable: the impossible sight of
humans, soaring into the demesne of the gods.

This indifference to the fate of Icarus on the part of two of the three human
figures in Brueghel's scene marks a significant departure from the Ovidian
text. In the Ovidian version of the story, as father and son soar aloft prior
to the disaster, Ovid speculates on the earth-bound inhabitants below who
might have seen these impossible prosthetic creatures in the sky above them.
As Golding's (1567) translation describes the scene:

> . . . The fishermen
> Then standing angling by the Sea, and shepeherdes leaning then
> On sheepehookes, and the Ploughmen on the handles of their Plough,
> Beholding them, amazed were: and thought that they that through
> The Aire could flie were Gods.[70]

All three figures – ploughman, shepherd, and fisherman, the traditional representatives of Renaissance pastoral and piscatorial modes – appear in Brueghel's
painting. But, as we also have noted, only Brueghel's shepherd marks their
flight, and even he seems unaware of the disaster that has encompassed one
of these voyagers. In some Renaissance pictorial depictions of the myth, such
as *Landscape with the Fall of Icarus* by Hans Bol (1534–93), the Ovidian version
of the narrative is followed closely, with the flight of Icarus and Daedalus
witnessed by awe-struck terrestrial observers, particularly the ploughman,
the fisherman, and the shepherd. Others, such as Pieter Van Der Borcht

(1540–1608), whose illustrations appeared in a 1591 edition of the *Meta-morphoses*, have the shepherd and the fisherman witnessing the fall, while the ploughman (following Brueghel's example) trudges behind his oxen, unaware of what has just taken place above him.[71]

Those versions of the story that concentrate on the Audenesque indifference to the fate of Icarus on the part of the ploughman and his companions mark a revisionary reading of Ovid's story that was familiar to Renaissance artists. Following this revisionary version, the true subject of Brueghel's image is the ploughman, rather than Icarus.[72] Attending to the useful though humble arts of civilization, working in harmony with nature, it is the ploughman, a simple tool user, whose example we should follow, rather than striving to emulate the more complex technology deployed by Daedalus and his son. It is not, in other words, by some heroic imaginative leap that humanity confirms its technological mastery over nature: Daedalian technology will prove to be a shaky foundation upon which to rear the arts of civilization, of which the city which glimmers in the middle distance of Brueghel's image is an emblem. Brueghel's painting, then, functions as a Flemish riposte to that earlier Renaissance commonplace which imagined that all of creation was placed at the service of humankind. So, in Marsilio Ficino's *Platonic Theology* (1482), a founding text of the Renaissance synthesis of Platonism and Christianity, the human creature is seen as the unproblematic lord of nature, the intellectual centre of the created universe, placed there by God to exercise sovereignty over the created world. That world has to be moulded to the human will through the resources of *Technē* which:

> . . . uses all the world's materials and uses them everywhere as though they were all subject to him: he uses the elements, stones, metals, plants, and animals, fashioning them into many forms and figures, which the beasts never do . . . he employs them all as though he were lord of all. He tramples on the earth, furrows the water, ascends into the air in the tallest of towers – and I am leaving aside the wings of Daedalus and Icarus.[73]

Brueghel rejects this triumphal narrative, preferring, rather, the Ovidian tale of decline, in which the earth no longer freely renders her riches to toiling humanity.[74] Following the pessimistic understanding of the myth, Daedalus and Icarus graft onto themselves devices that prove to be poor substitutes for the natural mastery of the air displayed by birds, or the simple skills of the ploughman, each of whom is following the pattern of behaviour dictated to them by a consciousness of their 'estate': their allotted position within the world, whether as a ploughman, a god, or a lapwing.

And yet, optimistically, *Landscape with the Fall of Icarus* is a painting replete with images of the positive attributes of the human ability to transform the landscape with the help of technology. The ships laden with goods, the ploughman cultivating the ground, even the fisherman harvesting the fruits of the sea, all may be taken as representatives of the human ability to improve and to civilize the world with the help of their inventions and devices; to produce, in short, the vision of the city which glimmers in the painting's middle distance with the enfolding arms of its port offering sanctuary. But as Freud reminds us in his later account of our complex responses to the world of *Technē*, the machine imagined as a kind of graft is often as much a burden as it is a source of solace. How the machine came to occupy this ambiguous position represents the thread of the narrative of this book.

2

PHILOSOPHY, POWER, AND POLITICS IN RENAISSANCE TECHNOLOGY

'The vital humour of the terrestrial machine'

To the modern viewer, Leonardo da Vinci's designs for mechanical devices of all kinds have become emblematic of the Renaissance engineer's art. Many of Leonardo's machine designs have been 'reconstructed' by modern engineers and designers in three dimensions. Ironically, these reconstructions may represent something of an imposture, since some modern technological historians now believe that the ingenious devices that Leonardo and his contemporaries and successors explored on paper were never actually realized as working mechanisms.[1] Modern reconstructions of these devices, in other words, may mark their very first appearance as three-dimensional forms. And, in any case, the reconstructed machine is inevitably decontextualized. Rather than a grimy, oily, battered mechanical reality, the reconstructed machine is presented behind a glass case within the confines of a modern art gallery, along with helpful exploratory diagrams and appropriate sections of Leonardo's manuscript drawings illustrating its archival 'source'. Fabricated out of lovingly varnished wood and polished metal, with its intricate working parts carefully scaled down, the reconstructed machine has become an art object, revealing the skill and craftsmanship of the twentieth-century model maker. It tells us very little of how devices of this kind were experienced by those who might have worked with them.

In order to attempt a true reconstruction of the devices which Leonardo and his contemporaries devised, we have to imaginatively re-place these remarkable objects into the landscape once more. That landscape was dominated by one element in particular: water. Water was, in more ways than one, the *raison d'être* of the early-modern machine. And nothing enthralled Leonardo quite as much as watery motion. Beginning in the early 1490s, Leonardo had embarked upon a series of studies of water in movement, a project that would culminate, towards the end of his life, in his apocalyptic visions of the world drowned in a universal deluge. Domination of such an unruly element was an alluring prospect, since it entailed mastery over Nature itself: 'Water is the driver of Nature', Leonardo wrote, claiming that 'Water, which is the vital humour of the terrestrial machine, moves by its own natural heat.'[2] In combining a mechanical term ('terrestrial machine') with a medico-corporeal image ('vital humour . . . natural heat'), Leonardo simultaneously seems to have imagined water as both a machine-like force and an organic entity. This combination of organism and machinery was characteristic of Leonardo's thinking. Just as his human anatomical studies grew out of his studies of mechanical systems, so the animating power of water in motion could be imagined as components of an engine – the 'recoil of a stroke' as he put it – to be investigated and represented with mechanical precision.[3]

For Leonardo, water was both an agent of change and a force of destruction. The destructive potential of water was captured most dramatically in Leonardo's 'deluge drawings' of his final years, in which humanity and the works of humanity are overwhelmed by cataclysmic surges of water.[4] Water, Leonardo wrote, would be the cause of some future catastrophe, since already it was refashioning the world:

> . . . in the end the mountains will be levelled by the waters, seeing that they wash away the earth which covers them and uncover their rocks, which begin to crumble . . . The waters wear away their bases and the mountains fall bit by bit in ruin into the rivers . . .[5]

Water, in this sense, was a *primum mobile* of the terrestrial world, tirelessly and endlessly shaping the earth. At other times, Leonardo imagined water as a wild creature, turning with an animated will against human beings and all their works of civility 'gnawing and tearing' at 'cities . . . lands, castles, villas, and houses . . .'[6]

Kenneth Clark has described the many studies of water in often-violent

motion as 'abstractions' of Leonardo's 'expressive feelings about the movement of water', which 'gradually came to demand a symbolic form'.[7] As
Clark has (elsewhere) observed, of all Leonardo's interests, 'the most continuous and obsessive was the movement of water'.[8] Claiming that water was
'both awe-inspiring and terrifying' for the artist, Michael White believes that
Leonardo wanted not merely to understand water, but more than that '. . . he
wanted to neuter it'.[9] Michel Jeanneret, too, describing how water 'runs like
an obsessional theme all through the writings and sketches in Leonardo's
notebooks' follows Ernst Gombrich in noting the sheer number of different
terms that Leonardo uses to describe the movement of water – risaltazione,
circolazione, revolutzione, ravvoltamento, raggiramento, sommergimento, and so on – some
seventy or more different words, figures of speech, or metaphors.[10]

But there is, perhaps, a simpler way of understanding Leonardo's obsession
with watery movement. Again and again, in his drawings, doodles, and notes,
we find Leonardo returning to the task of 'managing' water mechanically in a
host of different ways. These scattered jottings reflect Leonardo's professional
interests. 'Whilst still young', wrote Giorgio Vasari of Leonardo in his Lives of
the Artists (1550), 'he was the first to propose reducing the Arno to a navigable
canal between Pisa and Florence. He made designs for mills, fulling machines,
and engines that could be driven by water-power.'[11] In a memorandum of
1482, Leonardo noted 'certain water instruments' that he was engaged in
creating.[12] These 'instruments', which date from his first Florentine period
(1469–82), were predominantly pumps, Archimedean screws, a siphon,
and a double-action pump driven by a paddle wheel. Equally, canals and
lock systems were continually fascinating to him. In his first Milanese period
(1485–90), he devoted himself to vast projects involving basins, locks,
dredging mechanisms, and sluice gates.[13] In 1494, he was investigating the
canals around Vigevano, and trying to apply hydraulic and hydrodynamic
principles to the design of mill machinery. By 1502–3, working as chief
engineer to Cesare Borgia, he was undertaking canal works throughout central Italy, and later, assisting in the design of a defensive project to deviate
the River Arno for the Florentine Republic.[14] Towards the end of his life he
would undertake similar projects for the French king François I. Although
he had become, in Martin Kemp's words, a 'master of water', Leonardo's
projected 'Treatise on Water' (c. 1490), like so many of Leonardo's undertakings, was never completed.[15] Nevertheless, the manuscripts that he produced
throughout his career (amounting to over 5,000 pages) are dotted with
notes concerning water, drawings of water in motion, designs of water-
driven machinery, or machines that could raise water.[16]

A water-driven world

Leonardo's fascination with water is not difficult to explain. Water was the single most reliable source of power known to early-modern communities, providing the foundations upon which so much social, communal, and urban life depended. And just as in our own world, where the constant drone of distant electrical devices and unseen automobile traffic provides the acoustic backdrop to the life of the modern city-dweller, so the sound of running water can be understood as one of the 'keynote sounds' of the early-modern world, gushing through the innumerable pipes, conduits, and streams constructed to channel it to where it was needed not only for domestic and animal use, but, more importantly, to meet the community's demand for power.[17]

To Leonardo and his contemporaries, the demand for the reservoir of energy represented by water was inexhaustible.[18] In the years prior to the creation of Leonardo's water studies at the end of the fifteenth century, water-powered devices were undergoing a dramatic technological transformation, and Europeans were as restless in their pursuit of this seemingly endless energy source as we are, today, in our search for hydrocarbons in order to drive our own civilization. Water, of course, together with wind, gravity, and fire had been understood as an energy source for millennia.[19] Machines driven by these power sources were capable of astonishing outputs. The complex of watermills constructed by the Romans at Barbegal, near Arles in the south of France in the fourth century CE, for example, has been estimated at having been capable of generating 60kW of power (the power output of a modern automobile is in the range 40kW–100kW). This cluster of machines helped to sustain a population of over twelve thousand people.[20]

Such devices had generated power throughout Europe for over a thousand years. But in the later Middle Ages, Europe was facing an energy shortage as potentially devastating as that which now faces our own fossil-fuel-based culture.[21] It has been suggested that, in part, this crisis was a function of the effects of the plague, which had depleted the availability of human labour to such an extent that machines and mechanisms had to be developed as substitutes for vanished human muscle power. In Germany, for example, following the plague of 1348, almost one-third of the human population had disappeared, leading to industrial innovations such as the development of water-driven hammers and bellows in iron forges, where once humans would have been employed as the primary energy source.[22] But a more deep-seated problem was that wood, a primary fuel source, was becoming depleted.[23] An iron foundry, for example, might consume, annually, more than four hundred square miles of forest.[24] Thus, as early as the fourteenth century, we see the beginnings of the transition from firewood to coal as the primary energy source, and the start of the decline of the 'wood-and-water complex', which would give way, in turn, to the 'coal-and-iron complex' characteristic of continental Europe and North America in the nineteenth century.[25]

In the pre-industrial world, however, water represented a major threat to this transformational process. As the easily recovered (and low-grade) supplies of lignite – a soft form of coal to be found close to the surface – became exhausted, so attention was turned to the harder (and far more energy efficient) coals that could be retrieved only through sinking deeper mines. But mines, driven far beneath the earth's surface, were more prone to flooding, creating, in turn, a demand for more efficient and powerful pumping machines. Hence the emerging fascination with the 'management' of water in so many different forms in the period. Late-medieval and Renaissance water technology was thus an ancient technology redesigned in order to bridge the gap which had opened up between the demand for more fuel, and the difficulty of meeting that demand through the supply of coal in the period prior to the advent of more efficient, coal-fired, steam-driven, pumping engines which were developed in the final years of the seventeenth century.[26]

Leonardo's machine designs were thus part of a 'power revolution' in late-medieval and early-modern Europe. While both animal and wind power were much more efficiently harnessed in the medieval period, it was water power that underwent the greatest transformation.[27] From the fourteenth century onwards Europe was enjoying what we would now term a 'boom' in the design and production of ever-more complex water-driven machinery, together with the networks of dams, reservoirs, canals, and sluices required to store and transport the water used by the various machines that drew upon its power.[28] 'Water was the economic nerve centre of pre-industrial urbanization . . . without water, there could have been neither millers nor weavers, neither dyers nor tanners, nor would communities have existed.'[29]

The superstructure of much of late-medieval and Renaissance urban life rested on fluid foundations, which have been vividly described by the economic historian David Landes:

> Millwrights increased pressure and efficiency by building dams and ponds and by lining the wheels up to utilize the diminishing energy for a variety

of tasks, beginning with those that needed the most power, and descending. At the same time, the invention or improvement of accessory devices
– cranks, toothed gears – made it possible to use the power at a distance,
change its direction, convert it from rotary to reciprocating motion, and to
apply it to an increasing variety of tasks: hence not only grinding grain, but
fulling (pounding) cloth . . . hammering metal; rolling and drawing sheet
metal and wire; mashing hops for beer; pulping rags for paper.[30]

The water-based infrastructure that Leonardo was designing for his various
patrons in the early years of the sixteenth century was also the culmination of centuries of development. Jean Gimpel, the historian of medieval
technology, helps us understand the nature of that development and the
nature, too, of the continent's reliance on water, which in terms of scope
and complexity offered nothing comparable in antiquity.[31] For example (the
statistics are given by Gimpel), the river Robec, which joins the Seine at
Rouen, powered two watermills in the tenth century, four in the eleventh,
ten in the thirteenth, and twelve by the beginning of the fourteenth century.
What would eventually become known as the *départment de l'Aube*, in north-
eastern France, contained fourteen watermills in the eleventh century, sixty
in the twelfth, and over two hundred in the thirteenth century.

But the most staggering statistics are furnished by England. More than any
other European country, medieval and early-modern England, where the
forests had long since been felled, faced a particularly acute fuel shortage.
England was to become the first European country to shift from plant fuels
to meet its energy needs, to coal: a process that was already well under way
in the late sixteenth and seventeenth centuries.[32] It may, perhaps, be this
fact that helps to account for the astonishingly sophisticated development
of water technology in that country, well before the advent of steam power.
Norman England was a land accustomed to water-driven mechanisms of all
kinds. In 1086, the population of England (calculated from the Domesday
Book) may be estimated at roughly 1,400,000. This tiny population was
sustained by a complex water-powered infrastructure. The Domesday Book
records 5,624 watermills in England, each of which was supplying either
power, or the products of mechanical power, to, on average, fifty households. In post-conquest England, in other words, a mill of some kind existed
for every 250 people, a statistic which may suggest, in turn, how ubiquitous
the sight and sound of the grinding wheels of the turning mill must have
been in the period. Gimpel summarizes the proto-industrial landscape of
Norman England for us cartographically, commenting:

> A map of England's river system with its 5,624 Domesday water mills is an amazing site. It is literally covered with dots, especially the areas to the south of the Severn and the Trent. On rivers like the Wylye in Wiltshire the concentration of mills is remarkable: thirty mills along some ten miles of water; three mills a mile.[33]

Gimpel's analysis helps us to re-imagine the technologies of pre-industrial Europe. So, to the sound of running water which, as we have seen, Thomas Dekker described in early seventeenth-century London, we should add another ubiquitous sound which formed the acoustic backdrop to pre-industrial life: the shudder, creak, groan, and patter of great wood and iron water-powered mechanical devices, driving the workshops of pre-industrial Europe.[34]

Images of water wheels at work in medieval and early-modern cities (as opposed to technical illustrations of the device itself) show us how these devices operated as energy generating plants, clustered together, providing an unmistakable urban landmark. A fifteenth-century plan of the bridge mills at Corbeil in France, for example, shows a system of six devices churning the water, while the mills under the Grand Pont in Paris, depicted in an early fourteenth-century manuscript, suggest a procession of devices strung across the Seine which, by 1323, numbered some thirteen distinct mechanisms.[35] By the fifteenth century, the Seine, as it wound its way through Paris, was driving over seventy mills.[36] London, like other European cities, was also relying increasingly on mechanical water systems. In 1581, the Dutch engineer Peter Morris installed a great fixed wheel within an arch of London Bridge that worked pumps, supplying water drawn from the river directly to Londoners through a system of pipes.[37] The device proved to be an immense success and was soon supplemented by additional wheels and pumps under the arches of the bridge, while other types of mechanical pumping devices clustered along the banks of the Thames in the closing years of the sixteenth century.[38]

By the sixteenth century, water-powered devices had reached new levels of mechanical sophistication. The 'stangenkunst' (rod-engine) system, for example, allowed power to be transmitted, via networks of pivoted rods, from a particular water mill to the site where reciprocating motion was needed, often over a distance of several miles.[39] New industries, clustering around these radiating networks of mechanical linkage, had begun to emerge. One historian of energy has listed no fewer than seventeen 'industrial' processes that drew upon the power of watermills in pre-industrial society, claiming that 'to a significant degree the energy foundations of Western industrialization rest on these specialised uses of water wheels'.[40] The development of this proto-industrial landscape has even led some economic and technological historians to argue that our model of a dramatic transformation in industrial process in the mid to late eighteenth century is quite wrong. Instead of understanding the European industrial revolution as a sudden shift resulting from the advent of steam power, we should, rather, think of Europe, and particularly Britain, undergoing a proto-industrial water-powered revolution in the sixteenth and earlier seventeenth centuries.[41] These water-driven instruments and appliances were capable of Herculean labour. The Great Machine of Marly, built by the Walloon engineer Arnold de Ville between 1678 and 1685, was the greatest prime mover ever to have been constructed in the early-modern period. This machine, or rather series of machines, consisted of fourteen enormous water wheels driving over two hundred pumps. Built to power the hydraulic systems of Versailles for Louis XIV, and capable of generating seventy-five horsepower (56kW), and raising one million gallons of water each day to a height of over 500 feet, the machine was (to quote a modern commentator) a 'marvel of misapplied engineering skill' (Figure 2.1).[42]

Watching machines with Montaigne

In terming the skill betrayed in the construction of such a machine as 'misapplied', there is an implicit assumption that technology exists in a moral dimension. Did early-modern observers share this assumption? In order to answer this question, and to help us to understand the wider philosophical scope of early-modern technology, we can turn to an eyewitness to the machines of Europe in the age before the industrial revolution: Michel de Montaigne.

Montaigne is not a figure we would normally associate with machines. Alone in the tower of his chateau, on the banks of the River Dordogne, sitting beneath a ceiling inscribed with aphorisms culled from his voracious reading in his beloved classical authors, Montaigne spent his days, as he put it, 'leafing through now one book, now another, without order and without plan, by disconnected fragments' (Montaigne, 762).[43] The library, rather than the workshop or the mill, was Montaigne's natural arena. Indeed, Jean Starobinski's influential study of Montaigne specifically rejects any fascination on the part of the philosopher with 'technical activity'. Montaigne (Starobinski writes): '. . . has little to say about actions involving tools and

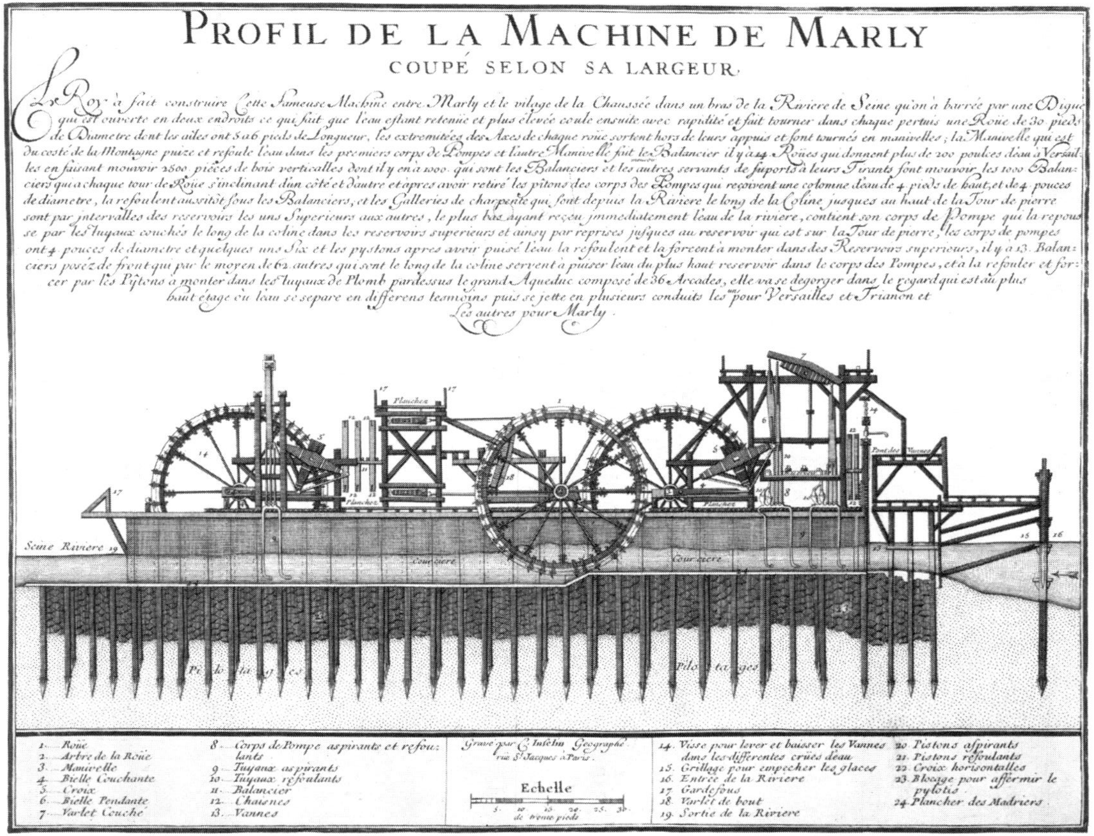

Figure 2.1 *Water Machine at Marly*, c. 1715 (engraving), French School (eighteenth century), private collection, The Stapleton Collection, The Bridgeman Art Library.

directed towards objects in the outside world . . . activity that requires an implement in order to "make" something, is a "mechanical" labor and as such is of little value'.[44] Claiming that, in this respect, Montaigne shared the prejudices of the minor nobility in disdaining the value of the 'mechanical arts' as opposed to the liberal arts, Starobinski's Montaigne is a philosopher of inwardness, concerned with the 'enrichment of personal experience' rather than the 'transformation of material objects'.[45] And yet, our dominant image of Montaigne as a pensive solitary ignores the fact that machinery of all kinds had an important bearing on his philosophical work.

Montaigne's fascination with machines is revealed in the record that he kept (with the help of an amanuensis) of his journey to Italy in 1580–1, following the publication of the first edition of his *Essays*.[46] The journey through France, Switzerland, Germany, Austria, and Italy would eventually cover over two and a half thousand miles and take him through thirteen European cities and over one hundred smaller towns and villages. Travelling towards his eventual destination, Rome, Montaigne's journey also traced the course of a number of European river systems. In premodern Europe, the river valleys represented the best (often the only) route available. Hence, for much of his seventeen-month odyssey, Montaigne was never far from the sound of running water: the diary is constantly recording rivers encountered, followed, forded or crossed.[47]

In following the course of these river valleys, Montaigne continually encountered water-powered mechanical devices. These machines fascinated him. Although he had claimed, at one point in his *Essays*, to be 'disgusted with innovation, in whatever guise' (Montaigne, 104) this crotchety observation stands in counterpoise with a delight in certain kinds of novelty: 'The novelty of things incites us more than their greatness to seek their causes', he also wrote (Montaigne, 162). To this end, novelties, particularly mechanical novelties were recorded in minute detail, filling page after page of the diary. Anything involving machinery, and, more particularly, the application of water power, or the mechanically assisted flow of water, was of interest. Basle and its environs, for example, were complimented on the 'infinite abundance of fountains in all this country; there is no village or crossroads where there are not very beautiful ones' – a comment that was echoed on seeing the fountains at Baden: 'flowing with streams of water, which have been erected sumptuously at the street corners' (Montaigne, 1070, 1075). At Neuchâteau, which Montaigne and his party visited on 13 September 1580, the library of the church of the Cordeliers was dismissed (by this most bookish philosopher), with the comment 'many books, but nothing rare'; of much greater interest, judging by the detailed description, was the community's water-raising engine (a treadmill), which consisted of:

> . . . a well from which water is drawn in very big buckets by working with the feet a wooden pedal, supported on a pivot, to which is connected a round piece of wood to which the rope of the well is attached . . . Next to the well is a big stone vessel raised five or six feet above the brim, up to which the bucket mounts; and without anyone touching it the water is poured into the same vessel, such a height that from it, by means of lead pipes, the well water is led to [the] refectory and kitchen and bakery, and spouts out of raised stone outlets in the form of natural springs.
>
> (Montaigne, 1061)

This description is characteristic of the diary's many accounts of machines at work. For Montaigne wanted to record not only the appearance of the machine, but also its underlying sequential motion. Understanding the machine depended on understanding the relationship between cause (the power generated by the human treadmill) and effect (the water pouring into the refectory, kitchen, and bakery). In similar fashion, Montaigne described the watermills at Schaffhausen in Switzerland; a water engine between Pfronten and Füssen in Germany; a fountain at Landsberg in Germany 'which spouts water out of a hundred pipes . . . and scatters it . . . the pipes being pointed in whatever direction is wanted'; at Augsburg, a water-driven clock and 'a machine consisting of two iron pistons which . . . beat and pressed the water at the bottom of [the] well and . . . forced it to gush through a leaden pipe'; a 'dripping apparatus' (a form of primitive shower) at La Villa and so on (Montaigne, 1081, 1093, 1100).

Montaigne was a keen observer of systems of hydraulic engineering, the generating stations and sub-stations of the sixteenth century, together with their associated canals, conduits, and pipelines: the transmission grid. At Constance, which he visited early in October 1580, he watched the construction of an enormous water-raising engine on the Rhine, which consisted of 'twelve or fifteen great wheels, by means of which they will continually raise a great quantity of water to a floor which will be one story higher' (Montaigne, 1082). A further system of wheels was being constructed in order to raise the water higher still, with the process being repeated a third time, until the mass of water, raised over fifty feet above its natural course, was released to flow 'through a big wide artificial canal and be led into their town to several mills grinding' (Montaigne, 1082).

But it was in the city of Augsburg, situated close to the confluence of the rivers Lech and Wertach (tributaries of the Danube) where he encountered the most impressive water works. Augsburg, which was also a centre of the metal industries, was a city dedicated to the flow of water. Montaigne stayed there for five days (15–19 October 1580), inspecting, first, the system of aqueducts and pumps constructed to provide abundant water to the city:

> We saw a big channel of water flowing . . . to the town gate by which we had entered; this water is conveyed from outside the town by a wooden aqueduct, which runs under the footbridge over which we had passed and above the river that flows through the town moat. This channel of water sets in motion certain very numerous wheels which work several pumps, and by two lead channels these raise the water of a spring . . . to the top of a tower at least fifty feet high. Here the water pours into a big stone vessel, and from this vessel it comes down through many conduits, and from there is distributed throughout the town, which by this means alone is all crowded with fountains. Individuals who want a rivulet to themselves are allowed it on payment to the town of ten florins of rent a year, or two hundred florins paid up for good. It is now forty years since the town has been adorned with this rich work.
>
> (Montaigne, 1095–6)

Water, harnessed to raise yet more water, flowing uninterrupted for forty years represented the most advanced technological accomplishment in this sphere since the time of the Romans.[48]

At Augsburg, these impressive works were complemented by an alternative use of water that the city had developed: a system of ponds and fountains. The ponds were a form of 'water joke' designed to amuse and edify the onlooker, as Montaigne went on to record:

> On all four sides of each pond there are many little pipes, some straight, the others bent upwards; through all these pipes the water pours very charmingly into these ponds, some sending the water in straight, the others spurting it upwards to the height of a pike. Between these two ponds there is a space ten paces wide floored with planks; through these planks go lots of little brass jets which cannot be seen. While the ladies are busy watching the fish play, you have only to release some spring: immediately all these jets spurt out thin, hard streams of water to the height of a man's head, and fill the petticoats and thighs of the ladies with this cool-

ness. In another place where there is an amusing fountain pipe, while you are looking at it anyone who wants to can open the passage to little imperceptible tubes, which from a hundred places cast water into your face in tiny spurts; and in that place is that Latin sentence: *you were looking for trifling amusements, here they are; enjoy them.*

(Montaigne, 1097–8)

In a city that had developed water-based technology to such a pitch, there is something ironic about the inscription that Montaigne recorded, as if the town fathers were aware that the creation of these *divertissements* was, in some way, a frivolous use of this technology. At Augsburg, too, Montaigne encountered another kind of water-raising device, a siphon:

Having once filled it with water, holding both holes up, you suddenly and dexterously turn it upside down, so that one end drinks out of a vessel full of water, and the other discharges it outside; when you have started this flow, the result is that, to avoid the vacuum, the water always keeps filling the tube and running out without stopping.

(Montaigne, 1098)

What seems to have appealed to Montaigne, in examining this device, is its capacity to initiate and sustain a seemingly endless flow. In the seventeenth century, the siphon would become known as 'the Philosopher's Engine' since it seemed to work, 'as if there were in them some *mysteries* in *Nature* more than in any other works' as a seventeenth-century commentator wrote.[49] But the siphon may have attracted Montaigne for rather more mundane reasons. Suffering as he was for so much of his journey from the painful effects of kidney stone, which made the passing of water a matter of acute suffering, one can understand how such a device, dedicated to initiating and sustaining uninterrupted flow, might have had more than simply an aesthetic appeal to this colic-stricken voyager.[50]

The flow and movement of water were always significant to Montaigne. We can see his engagement with water technology in the Italian sections of his journey. In the fifteenth and earlier sixteenth centuries, Italy had become the most technologically advanced society in Europe.[51] Today, we tend to think of Northern European visitors to Italy as concerned with the discovering of the works of the classical past, associated with the idea of 'The Grand Tour'. Hence, we easily forget that, at the time of Montaigne's visit, for all that the ruins of antiquity, as well as the palaces, churches, frescos, and works of art were to be admired and praised, Italy was essentially a modern culture. As Edward Chaney reminds us, here in the context of English visitors to Italy in the sixteenth and earlier seventeenth centuries: '. . . literature, music, mathematics, science, art, architecture, politics, banking, philosophy, historiography and much else were derived more or less directly from [the] experience of Italy'.[52] A visit to Italy, then, had about it something of the quality of those late nineteenth-century European visits to America, where industry, the production line, the scale of the new cities, were objects of wonder. So, although the past could be perceived in Italy in a way that was becoming famous throughout Europe, Italy also expressed the future.

Montaigne, keen to see the technological triumphs of Italian culture, devoted considerable time to the inspection of gardens. In the sixteenth century, gardens had become the forcing ground for exploring new, water-based, technological creations that would, in the course of time, result in contrivances of the kind to be found much later in the great water engine at Marly. Thus, in November 1581, he explored the still-unfinished gardens at Pratolino, begun in 1569, created by the architect-engineer Bernardo Buontalenti for the Grand Duke Francesco. From Pratolino, he moved on to the gardens of the Medici villa at Castello. After a lengthy stay in Rome, he visited (April 1581) the gardens of the Villa d'Este at Tivoli, the work of the humanist antiquarian Pirro Ligorio for the owner, the Cardinal of Ferrara.

Together, Pratolino, Castello, and Tivoli represented the apotheosis of the hydraulic engineer's art in the creation of what Roy Strong has termed the mannerist garden which was to become so influential throughout Europe in succeeding years.[53] Central to these extraordinary creations were the multitude of hydraulically powered fountains, automata, and statuary, all of which were closely observed by Montaigne. Everywhere he looked, in these gardens he was aware of the moving power of water, but dedicated to an aesthetic rather than utilitarian end. At Pratolino, as well as water-powered musical instruments, water was made to 'squirt . . . on your buttocks', while 'a thousand jets of water . . . give you a bath' (Montaigne, 1132). Fountains were everywhere, and the diary's comments reflect their ubiquity: 'Springing fountains . . . nothing but fountain jets . . . a beautiful fountain . . . dripping . . . water boiling . . . a fountain of fresh water in which each man may cool his glass' (Montaigne, 1132). At Castello, water flowed 'incessantly, drop by drop', where it also 'spurted up under [the] feet and between [the] legs, through an infinite number of tiny holes' so that the visitors were 'completely sprinkled'. A gardener operated the mechanism 'with such artifice that . . . he made these spurts of water rise and fall as he wanted' (Montaigne, 1135–6). At Tivoli, he saw 'the gushing of an infinity of jets of water checked and launched by a single spring that can be worked from afar off'. Tivoli was the home, too, of a mechanical organ 'effected by means of the water, which falls with great violence into a round arched cave and agitates the air that is in there and forces it, in order to get out, to go through the pipes of the organ and supply it with wind'. Water-powered mechanical birds, including an owl, a 'noise, as of harquebus shots . . . done by a sudden fall of water into channels' were admired, as were the 'ponds or reservoirs' surrounded by pillars from the top of which 'water comes out with great force, not upward but toward the pond' (Montaigne, 1175).

These extravagant creations, in which water power was transformed into movement and even sound, demonstrated the hydraulic engineer's virtuosity in harnessing the power and force of falling water to surprise and delight. But there was also a moral dimension to such works. Many years after Montaigne saw these hydraulic wonders, Francis Bacon, in his essay 'Of Gardens' (1625) would commend the provision of water in gardens 'in perpetual motion' as 'pretty things to look on'.[54] But were they anything more than that? Designed to impress, the marvellous Italian water-powered gardens that Montaigne observed in such detail somehow lacked the *moral* force of the water works he had witnessed north of the Alps.

For water, for Montaigne as much as it had been for Leonardo, was first and foremost a force for the public good. It was used to its best advantage when it was distributed throughout a city, or put to work to grind corn, or lift massive weights.[55] Impressive and amusing as they undoubtedly were, was there, perhaps, something luxuriously wasteful about the Italian water-powered gardens? We become aware of this possibility after Montaigne's third visit to Lucca on 21 October 1581. At Lucca, the disparity between water used as a frivolity and water used to promote the public good became apparent. On his first visit to the city, in August 1581, Montaigne had commented on how the villas of the local aristocracy 'have lots of water, but artificial – that is to say not running, not natural, or continuous' (Montaigne, 1240).

The distinction was important to Montaigne, outweighing the somewhat cloying aesthetic delight that Francis Bacon was later to identify. On the one hand, 'natural' water for Montaigne was water in motion. On the other hand, 'unnatural' water, such as he saw in the ponds and lakes of the local gentry at Lucca, was turbid, still and lifeless. On his third visit to the city, he passed a sad testimony to the neglect of public water works:

... I came across a machine that is half ruined owing to the negligence of the ... lords; and this lack does great harm to the surrounding country. This machine was made for the purpose of draining the soil in these marshes and making them fertile. A great ditch had been dug, at the end of which three wheels were kept continually in motion by means of a stream of running water which came falling down from the mountain onto them. These wheels, with certain vessels attached to them, drew the water from one side of this ditch, and on the other side poured it into another, higher ditch and channel; which ditch, made for this purpose and provided with walls on each side, carried this water into the sea. Thus the whole country around was drained.

(Montaigne, 1258–9)

From Montaigne's description, we may surmise that the machine he saw was related to one of the oldest water-raising devices known to civilization, and one that is still in use today in parts of the world: the *Noria*.[56] In failing to discharge their responsibility towards this machine, quite clearly, the local nobility had failed the community at large. The 'half ruined' machine, implicitly, stood as an ironic commentary on noble luxury, which, though it could fashion an exquisite water-animated statue, had neglected to understand that the primary purpose of water is to work.

For Montaigne, machines of all kinds were registers of human inventiveness by which life could be made more endurable, even, at times, comfortable and pleasurable. Donald Frame, in his biography of Montaigne, has noted the philosopher's fascination with 'all signs of human ingenuity' together with is appreciation of 'landscapes ... cultivated against [the] odds'.[57] But more puzzling, to the biographer, is Montaigne's evident (and otherwise rarely remarked) delight in machinery. This involvement with machines and 'gadgets' Frame finds 'surprising'.[58] But is it? Or rather, should we be surprised by this engagement with a world of mechanical devices?

Beyond their sheer ubiquity and utility, machines and mechanisms were tokens of civic order and harmony. These were values that Montaigne prized highly. Whether constructed by individuals out of philanthropic concern for their fellow citizens, or simply for profit, or else erected as part of a joint endeavour, machines helped to promote an aura of public *virtù* and civility. A well-regulated machine in operation pleased him, since it suggested a well-regulated civic life. In Switzerland, he noted approvingly the proliferation and quality of ironwork, concluding that 'there is no church so small as not to have a magnificent clock and sundial' (Montaigne, 1071).

He remarked, too, upon the skill which was displayed in the manufacture of turning spits in the kitchens of the inns in which he stayed, driven by springs, or else ingeniously drawing upon the power of rising hot air in the chimneys (smoke jacks) (Montaigne, 1073).[59] He recorded water-driven mills for sawing wood, pounding flax or shelling millet (Montaigne, 1080). Other kinds of devices included 'an iron machine, such as we had also seen elsewhere, by which they raise large stones to load the wagons without manpower' (Montaigne, 1081). Economy of effort always satisfied him. At Augsburg, for example, Montaigne encountered what can only be described as Europe's first mechanized entry system: the town gates consisted of a complex of remotely controlled iron chains, moving drawbridges, and sequential chambers, culminating in a room where the entrance fee to the town was extracted mechanically, 'the stranger . . . all the way along, sees no one to talk to'. The Augsburg entry system, he recorded, was 'one of the most ingenious things than can be seen. The queen of England sent an ambassador expressly to ask the city government to reveal the workings of these machines; it is said that they refused' (Montaigne, 1099–1100). For all that the Augsburg entry system has (to the modern reader) a slightly Heath Robinson/Rube Goldberg air about it, the point was that the device, or sequence of devices, required only two unseen operators. The entire security of the city, in other words, had been effectively mechanized.

Movement and the philosophy of machines

But as well as possessing a moral dimension, machines had a philosophical application. Having observed, with an uncharacteristically coy euphemism, prostitutes at work in Florence ('I went alone for fun to see the women who let themselves be seen'), Montaigne described a quite different kind of female industry adjacent to the red light district: 'I saw the shops of the silk spinners; they have certain machines by turning which one single woman can twist and turn five hundred spindles at once' (Montaigne, 1229). What Montaigne saw was quite possibly the contrivance to be found in Vittorio Zonca's *Novo Teatro di machine* (1607), the *filatoio da aqua* or multiple, water-powered spinning wheel, said to have originated in Lucca at some point before 1330 (Figure 2.2). The device was a supreme example of mechanical ingenuity that dazzled observers (Zonca wrote) while they contemplated 'how the mind of man could understand such variety of things, so many contrary motions moved by one single wheel'.[60] Understood in these terms, a machine such as the *filatoio da aqua* represented the complexities of the mind

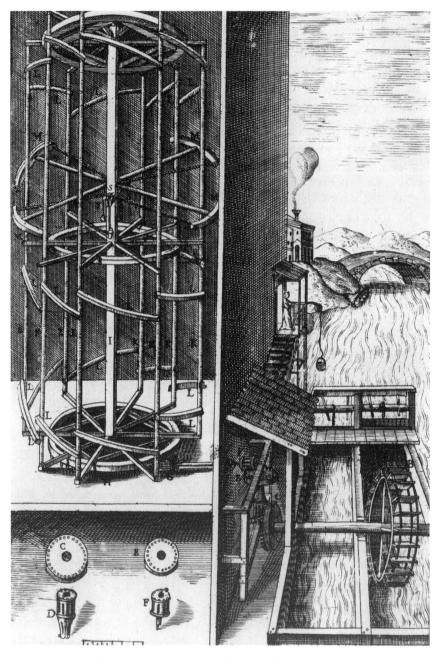

Figure 2.2 Vittorio Zonca, *Novo Teatro di Machine et Edificii* (Padua, 1607), p. 68.

itself. Here was the true 'philosopher's engine', which seemed to work as a model of human thought, driven by a single source of power, and yet capable of so many 'contrary motions' almost simultaneously: a sentiment that perfectly accords with Montaigne's fascination with his own contrary interior motions.

For mechanical motion may be philosophically satisfying, even pleasurable in its own right. Otto Mayr, the philosopher of the history of technology, has eloquently expressed what he terms the 'intellectual, almost spiritual appeal of machinery [which] becomes evident to everyone who experiences machines directly':

> It is this curious sense of fascination more than the wish to build something useful or the hope for material rewards that makes men devote their lives to machinery. Constructing, operating, even watching machines provides satisfactions and delights that can be intense enough to become ends in themselves. Such delights are purely aesthetic . . . the fascinations and delights of machinery are a historical force, insufficiently appreciated perhaps because of a cultural bias, but nevertheless real, a force that has affected not only our technology but also philosophy, science, literature, or in short, our culture at large.[61]

In articulating this sense of satisfaction, Mayr alerts us to something fundamental about Montaigne's engagement with mechanism and mechanical motion: the 'purely aesthetic' delights of the machine need have nothing whatsoever to do with the machine's purpose, let alone its output measured in terms of the useful 'work' that it might be designed to perform. This supposedly most purposeful of creations, in other words, can exist, in the mind and the eye of the spectator, as a purely mechanical expression of movement.[62] As far as we know, Montaigne was never interested in designing or building machines himself. He simply seems to have enjoyed watching machines in motion and at work, delighting in tracing the sequential movement of the machine's components, the interrelationship of its parts, and the transformation of the energy of falling water or rising heat into activity or sound. Interested in many different kinds of machines and devices, he would never dismiss them (even those encountered in the Italian gardens) as mere 'gadgets', though he was always quick to comment on whether or not a particular machine represented a genuine mechanical innovation, or was simply a version of a machine he had seen elsewhere. As such, he was something of a classifier of machines into their various kinds or types.

Although it was not until the later seventeenth century that machines began to be distinguished from 'mechanisms', Montaigne had already begun to appreciate machines as groups of similar parts forming components that could be transposed from one machine to the next, rather than as clusters of separate parts unique to that particular machine.[63]

In this respect, Montaigne begins to appear strikingly modern. In the nineteenth century, Franz Reuleaux, according to Lewis Mumford 'the first great morphologist of machines', argued that the attraction of the machine to the human observer does not lie in its ability to perform certain defined functions, such as overcoming resistance to perform useful 'work'.[64] Rather it is mechanical motion itself that acted as a spur to invent new devices. This delight in motion, which is (technically) no more than an 'accompanying phenomenon' of the machine, Reuleaux compared to a child's delight in machine movement:

> . . . certain minds are always irresistibly attracted by the motion itself, by the first impression gained solely from external appearances, from the overpowering influence of which even the most accomplished cannot boast themselves to be entirely free.[65]

Reuleaux helps us to understand why a machine whose purpose we may only dimly comprehend, nevertheless can be a source of amusement or even wonder. For the machine, in its constant movement, seems to echo or even imitate life itself. This, too, Montaigne seems to express in his response to different engines and devices. In this context, Mumford has suggested that, in the Renaissance, there took place 'a displacement of the living and the organic' that was concurrent with the development of new types or classes of machine. 'The machine' Mumford went on to argue 'was a counterfeit of nature, nature analysed, regulated, narrowed, controlled by the mind of man.'[66] If this claim is true, then we might think of the machine, together with the observation of machinery in operation, as a kind of thought experiment. It represented an opportunity to rethink, within the scope of a particular engine or device, the philosophical relationship between cause and effect, action and reaction.

Though Montaigne was no machine fabricator, he certainly *used* machines, though in a philosophical rather than a technical sense. In his philosophical writings, machines seemed to offer an entry point into a parallel universe of movement and motion. One of the striking aspects of Montaigne's habit of thought is his capacity to enter not just into the minds of others, particularly the minds of long-dead classical authors, but also into other possible states of being. In his essay 'An Apology of Raymond Sebond' (composed c. 1575–80), Montaigne had begun to speculate upon the nature of human intelligence, and whether it is to be found beyond the boundaries of the human world. Thus, famously we observe a philosopher playing with his cat: 'When I play with my cat, who knows if I am not a pastime to her more than she is to me?' Montaigne pondered (Montaigne, 401). The problem posed by Montaigne's cat is essentially one to do with cause and effect: who is the prime mover, to use a term common to both machines and theology? The human being who thinks they are acting as instigator? Or the cat, of whom we cannot even be sure that she is thinking, but with whom we find ourselves, nevertheless, playing, and to whom we appear to respond, as she does to us? We can understand this famous conundrum as a Renaissance version of the Turing test, proposed by the early computer scientist, logician, and cryptanalyst Alan Turing in 1950: 'when communicating with a computer, if the human cannot distinguish the computer from the human, then for all functional purposes the computer is human'.[67] But, as Montaigne put the matter: 'In natural things, the effects only half reflect their causes' (Montaigne, 481). The problem was to pierce beneath the surface reality of nature, and to try and understand the complete sequential relationship of cause and effect. Was the cat, in other words, playing with the philosopher or was it the other way round?

Viewing a machine in motion seems to have helped Montaigne to understand, philosophically, just this relationship of cause and effect. But if, for Montaigne, actual machines were tokens of harmony and order, machines in the abstract seemed to have functioned as an illustration of the limits of human autonomy. The ruins of ancient Rome, for example, he described as the remnants of an 'awesome . . . machine', as if the physical fabric of the fragmented ancient city expressed an abstract power and authority that was mechanical, or, at least inhuman, in some form (Montaigne, 1150). Another (animal-driven) machine prompted Montaigne to ponder on the abstract problem of whether or not reason is unique to human beings. Citing, from classical and scriptural sources, a water-raising machine said to have been used in ancient Persia, Montaigne wrote:

> The oxen that served in the Royal gardens of Susa to water them and turn certain great wheels for drawing water, to which there were buckets attached (like many that are to be seen in Languedoc), had been ordered to draw up to one hundred turns a day; they were so accustomed to this number that it

was impossible by any force to make them draw one turn more, and having done their task, they stopped short. We are in our adolescence before we know how to count up to a hundred, and we have just discovered nations which have no knowledge of numbers.

(Montaigne, 413)

Stoic regularity, as much as any knowledge of arithmetic, is the key here. Oxen cannot count and neither in Montaigne's day, any more than in our own, could machines.[68] The oxen, like the machine, for all that they move and fulfil their allotted tasks, can have no understanding of the limits of the design which has yoked them to the engine, and nor do they have any understanding of the will of the designer. Both the oxen and the machine would appear to lack purpose, even though what they are doing appears to be purposeful. Yet, in the case of the machine, it exists, as an animated testimony to the presence of its fabricator, who had endowed it with all the appearance of purpose.

And so, too, with the world: God, in this sense, was a mechanic, a skilled designer of a larger mechanism, who had left tokens of his presence engraved into the machinery of the universe: 'it is not credible that this whole machine should not have on it some marks imprinted by the hand of this great architect' Montaigne wrote, concluding that the 'stamp of . . . divinity' (a further mechanical analogy) was left on the world, if only we had the wit to perceive it (Montaigne, 395). Contemplating the universe, and quoting Cicero, Montaigne was drawn to contemplate its maker in terms of machinery: 'What preparations, what instruments, what levers, what machines, what workmen performed so great a work?' (Montaigne, 400).

The Montaigne who traversed Europe, in Sainte-Beuve's memorable phrase, 'sprinkling his stones and gravel over the roads' was a man who enjoyed ingenuity, innovation, and adaptability.[69] But Montaigne enjoyed technology, it seems, not just for its utilitarian functionality, nor even for the philosophical truth that it might reveal. Rather, he found something deeply satisfying in the rhythm and tireless repetition of the machine. More particularly, Montaigne enjoyed *watching* technology at work, since it seems to have helped him to rethink even the process of thought itself. In his essay 'Of the Education of Children', Montaigne wrote as if thought, or the effects of thought, could be understood as an essentially mechanical process resonating with images of release and flow, comparable to the hydraulic forces he had contemplated in his travels or discovered in the Italian gardens, and which operated so imperfectly in his own stone-wracked body. So, in describing the effect of poetry on the mind he wrote:

... just as sound, when pent up in the narrow channel of a trumpet, comes out sharper and stronger, so it seems to me that a thought, when compressed into the numbered feet of poetry, springs forth more violently and strikes me a much stiffer jolt.

(Montaigne, 130)

Poetry, here, has become a kind of hydraulic sound engine. To 'compress' a thought is a striking turn of speech, as though thinking could itself be subjected to hydraulic pressure that gushes out 'sharper and stronger' in poetry than if it merely leaked into the world through conversation or prose.

In similar fashion, the mind could be imagined, in another essay, as being comparable to material being worked upon by a machine: 'The more a mind is empty and without counterpoise, the more easily it gives beneath the weight of the first persuasive argument' (Montaigne, 160). Here, logic and rhetoric, the tools of reason, are transformed into a combination of balanced levers, one of the most fundamental of mechanical systems. In his essay 'That to Philosophise is to Learn How to Die', Montaigne interrupted his speculations on the inevitable dissolution of the individual in death to comfort himself with an observation culled from Lucretius: 'All things, their life being done, will follow you.' This aphorism he glossed with an equally aphoristic question: 'Does not everything move with your movement?' (Montaigne, 80). Movement and motion, the essence of that 'accompanying phenomenon' whereby we know ourselves to be in the presence of a machine, seems, at this point, to have entered into the core of Montaigne's thought. With the idea of motion or movement in mind, Erich Auerbach has commented on Montaigne's fascination with 'things':

Strictly speaking it is 'things' (les choses) after all which direct him – he moves among them, he lives in them; it is in things that he can always be found . . . From things he takes the animation which saves him from abstract psychologizing and from empty probing within himself. But he guards himself against becoming subject to the law of any given thing, so that the rhythm of his own inner movement may not be muffled and finally lost.[70]

In calling attention to rhythm and movement, it is as if Auerbach had encountered, in his reading of Montaigne, an enormously subtle watchmaker, softly listening to the almost imperceptible springs and flywheels that animate his thought and emotions.

Machines and social power

Watching machines through the eyes of Montaigne, we begin to sense how the machines that he had encountered in his travels through Europe had begun to enter deeply into his imaginative and philosophical world. Unknowingly, Montaigne stood on the cusp of what was to emerge as a new understanding of the role of technology in human life. What has been termed 'the classical dichotomy between thinkers and makers' had begun to collapse in Renaissance Europe, while the new distinction between the scientist and the engineer had not yet crystallized.[71] Like Leonardo, Montaigne appreciated the machine as a device, which, through its application of mechanical power, was able to transform not just nature, but also human life. In this respect, we can think of both Leonardo and Montaigne as sharing that optimistic sense of mechanism that we traced in the previous chapter.

Machines today are associated with power. The power associated with mechanisms in the early-modern period, however, existed in at least two distinct forms. First there was the 'power' of the machine seemingly to transform nature according to some pre-ordained plan or design. Nineteenth-century definitions of machines tended to see this transformation as a form of compulsion: 'a combination of resistant bodies so arranged that by their means the mechanical forces of nature can be compelled to do work accompanied by certain determinate motions'.[72] Early-modern people, similarly, tended to think of machines as devices for overcoming the resistance of animated nature. Machines were 'ingenious devices for cheating Nature, for getting something for nothing'.[73] Thus mechanics, in the words of Guido Ubaldo, whose *Mechanicorum liber* was published in 1577, were to be understood as a means of working '*against* nature or rather in *rivalry* with the laws of nature' (my emphasis).[74] Not until the earlier seventeenth century when Galileo, analysing the mathematical principles of the lever, and observing the operation of machines in the Venetian shipyards, began to think of machines in terms of 'force' or 'work', was it possible to estimate the relative 'power' of different types and classes of machines, and to realize that machines were not capable of 'cheating' nature, but that, rather, they worked in conformity with the laws of motion.[75]

But the second form of power associated with machinery is a much looser, sociological or even symbolic concept, whereby the 'power' of the machine is transformed, through metaphor, analogy, and symbol into a means of understanding larger social forces, or abstract entities at play in the world. One view of these relationships was expressed by Karl Marx, at his most technologically determinist, in his famous dictum that 'the hand-mill gives you society with the feudal lord; the steam-mill society with the indus-trial capitalist'.[76] In this formulation, society − a network of human social relations − is understood to be a product of technology. But if, for Marx, technology governed social relationships, it is equally possible to reverse the formula, so that technology is shown to be the product of those same social forces.

So, it has been suggested that one reason why Christian Europe embraced technological innovation was to do with social and religious change. By 1500, technological historians now agree, Europe had at last achieved technological parity with the Islamic world, superseding the inventions of classical antiquity, and leaving China, which had far exceeded Europe in technological innovation for centuries, as 'a magnificent dead end'.[77] In the slave-based economies of antiquity, so the argument goes, there was simply no need for new mechanical systems or devices since coerced human muscle was an almost infinite power resource. And this was the reason why, it has been suggested, there was no equivalent to the industrial revolution in the ancient world, or why the Roman Empire failed to mechanize.[78] Simi-larly, the relative absence of mechanical devices in, for example, the Indian subcontinent (gears, pulleys, cranks, and cams were unknown in India prior to the early thirteenth century) has been explained through a variety of socio-cultural factors: 'abundance of skilled labour, extreme specialization, and the marginal living of artisans with their minimum of simple tools'.[79]

By contrast, in other ancient cultures, particularly those that emerged in China and in Iraq, powerful, even despotic, systems of government and bureaucracy arose out of technological need and necessity, in order to plan, implement, and maintain the large-scale irrigational works undertaken by what Karl Wittfogel has termed 'hydraulic societies'.[80] More optimistically, some historians have gone so far as to claim that it was only in such socie-ties, also known as 'irrigation civilizations', that many aspects of the modern polis could evolve. The conception of 'man as a citizen', the codification of law, the development of a militia, the institution of social class, the organi-zation of knowledge, and even the creation of that great totem of intellectual and cultural historians, the emergence of the idea of the 'individual', could only have taken place within the 'technological polity' of the hydraulic or irrigation society.[81]

Medieval and Renaissance Europe was certainly a 'hydraulic society', though not of the kind to be encountered in the ancient Near East: European water-based engineering systems were not the products of gangs of slaves or coolies.

But pre-industrial Europe was also a society that was 'power-conscious to the point of fantasy'.[82] 'By the end of the fifteenth century', Michael Adas writes, 'the peoples of western Europe possessed an advantage of three or four to one over the Chinese in per capita capacity to tap animal and inanimate sources of power.'[83] No longer relying on forced labour, the pre-industrial European power revolution, in which animal, wind, and (above all) water power were harnessed much more effectively than in the past, was, it has been suggested, a reflection of profound religious and social change. So, it has been claimed that the history of pre-industrial technology is 'to some extent the history of religion':

> The Christian ideal of the infinite worth of man and the correlative aversion to submitting men to work which required no intelligence or judgment were among the principal factors which incited the evolution of mechanical power as a replacement for human muscles.[84]

The thesis that technological development is a reflection of a Christian ideal of the individual's value echoes an earlier claim made by the historian of Renaissance technology and designer of the IRT (which would become the New York City subway system), William Barclay Parsons. Writing in the 1930s, Parsons argued that the development of new mechanical devices in Europe, particularly in the fifteenth century, was a function of labour shortage arising out of a 'new social order . . . all men were now free'.[85] The machine is thus imagined as a liberating device, while it also is seen as part of a larger process of social change. It becomes a means of affirming the 'infinite worth' of each individual, as well as a method of grinding corn or lifting weights more efficiently, and more cheaply.

We might expect a distinguished engineer to see his craft as a historically liberating force. But is it true? Does the urge to create new machines in order to supplement or even replace human labour (pace Marx) arise out of a more comprehensive sense of human worth? Setting aside, for the moment, the uncomfortable fact of history that technologically advanced Western societies were still drawing upon the muscle power furnished by slaves until well into the second half of the nineteenth century, or that gangs of corvée (that is impressed) labour were deployed in the earlier stages of the construction of the Suez Canal (begun in 1859) until public outcry forced its designer, Ferdinand de Lesseps, to use more efficient mechanical excavators, this thesis may not be true even of the societies that White and Parsons are describing.[86] In the medieval period, technology may have helped liberate clerics on church estates from the drudgery of hand-grinding corn, thus allowing them to devote time to prayer and to contemplation.[87] But it is rather more difficult to sustain the argument that technology was a generally socially liberating force. Mills, for example, owned by the seigneurial lord, might even have represented a form of local tyranny. The mill owners and their agents jealously guarded their monopoly, so that the possession of individual hand mills among the peasants was outlawed.[88] Ownership of a machine, then, involved the protection of a significant capital investment, and sometimes that protection resulted in violence against the peasant or land worker who dared to install a rival, if much less sophisticated, mechanical device on their own account.

So, while we are accustomed to the early nineteenth-century idea of machine breaking, or 'Luddism', on the part of dispossessed cottage workers or agricultural labourers in England, we should be aware of earlier examples of the practice.[89] Machine breaking, in England, has a long history (there are records of riots against 'engine looms' among weavers dating from 1675), but in the pre-industrial age, the boot was, as it were, on the other foot.[90] The machine breakers might be the machine owners, and their ire was directed at those who challenged their monopoly over mechanism by constructing rival machines. Chaucer's fictional technologist, the miller in the *Canterbury Tales*, we might remember, is an overwhelmingly violent physical presence:

> The Miller was a stout carl for the nones,
> Full big he was of braun, and eek of bones;
> That proved wel, for over-al there he cam,
> At wrestling he wolde have alwey the ram.
> He was short-sholdered, brood, a thikke knarre,
> Ther nas no dore that he nolde heve of harre,
> Or brekke it, at a renning, with his heed.[91]

Like the mill machines with which he worked, Chaucer's miller is an irresistible force. He is also one of the very few pilgrims in the stories to be armed: 'A swerd and bokelar bar he by his syde.' His penchant for lifting doors off their hinges or breaking them 'at a renning, with his heed' may give some literary substance to Marc Bloch's account of domestic millstones being seized, throughout the medieval period, 'by the lord's officials in the very houses of the owners and broken in pieces'.[92]

The Renaissance megamachine: Rome 1585–6

If the mill expressed the power of the feudal lord, and the miller was understood as the jealous guardian of the mechanical status quo in medieval society, then, equally, the design or the installation of a particular piece of technology may be much less the product of cool, mechanistic, decision making than we sometimes care to think. Rather, certain kinds of machine or technological innovation may incorporate a political dimension into their design, so that a particular social outcome is engineered, consciously or unconsciously, into the artefact.[93] Such an interweaving of the technological and the social is closely allied to what Lewis Mumford has termed the 'megamachine'. Megamachines are structured organizations of human beings, brought together to achieve a defined end, which is usually largely symbolic or sacred. They embody, in their design and operation, hierarchies, schedules, timetables, and systems. The megamachine is an idea rather than a device, given physical expression in the agglomeration of parts, composed out of objects and human bodies, brought together, to achieve a purposeful outcome:

> These parts were brought together in a hierarchical organization under the rule of an absolute monarch whose commands, supported by a coalition of the priesthood, the armed nobility, and the bureaucracy, secured a corpse-like obedience from all the components of the machine.[94]

Writing in the 1930s, Mumford had plenty of examples of such megamachines to draw upon: the construction of the *Autobahn* system under Hitler, Mussolini's draining of the Pontine marshes, and the construction of the Moscow underground under Stalin being the most obvious examples. But megamachines were ancient. They had been used to construct the great pyramids of ancient Egypt, as well as in the fabrication of other sacred structures to be found scattered throughout the world, from Mesopotamia to Peru. The megamachine relied for its functioning on the organization of human beings into specialized groups, performing closely overseen, rigidly controlled, repetitive movements which, in a pathological form, might appear similar to an obsessive neurosis. The megamachine was ritualistic and restrictive, coercive, and yet productive. And paradoxically, what it achieved were structures of enduring beauty and complexity.[95]

We can see the Renaissance megamachine in operation in late-sixteenth-century Rome. The rebuilding of St Peter's and its environs was perhaps the greatest urban construction project of the later Renaissance.[96] By the time of

Montaigne's visit, this vast project was nearing completion. There remained, however, one pressing, but hitherto irresolvable problem. The obelisk, now standing in front of St Peter's, which had first been transported to Rome under the orders of the Emperor Caius Calligula from Heliopolis in 41 CE, and which had withstood the ravages of both time and barbarian invasion over the succeeding centuries, was to be moved some seven hundred metres to a new position in front of the remodelled cathedral. Objects of this size had never stirred since the slave societies of antiquity first fashioned and transported these behemoths in the Nile valley.[97] Spurred on by the example of pagan engineering skill, in August 1585, Pope Sixtus V appointed a council of churchmen, officials, and laymen to consider how the task of moving the four-hundred-tonne obelisk might be undertaken. Representations to the council were made from all over Italy and from further afield by some five hundred individuals. The eventual winner of this engineering competition was the forty-two-year-old architect Domenico Fontana (1543–1607). Fontana's plan was to surround the obelisk in a wooden framework (Figure 2.3), raise it vertically from its pedestal, then tilt it through ninety degrees so that it lay horizontally on a movable platform which would be drawn on rollers to the new site, where it would be restored to the vertical position and set on a new base.

Fontana was working without access to a science of mechanics of the kind that would emerge out of Galileo's work on the principles of the lever, or his later work on dynamics and materials first presented in his *Two New Sciences* of 1638. In shifting the obelisk, Fontana was operating with a combination of mathematical calculation, experience, and trial and error. The technology Fontana deployed on the project was not, in any sense, new: hoisting machines, pulleys, and capstans (a rotating drum fitted with levers) were all devices known to the ancient Greeks and Romans. The power source was equally traditional: human and animal muscle.

But what was most striking about Fontana's operation was its planned social effect on the city in which we can see the megamachine at work. During the year that it took to prepare the site, and move the obelisk to its new location, Rome was effectively placed under the equivalent of martial law. The papal edict of 5 October 1585, endowing Fontana with the necessary authority to undertake his task, indicates the nature of the subordination to the city to a technological imperative. The edict begins:

> We, Sixtus V, hereby confer on Domenico Fontana, architect to the Holy
> Apostolic Palace, in order that he may more easily and quickly achieve the

Figure 2.3 Domenico Fontana, *Della trasportatione dell' obelisco Vaticano et delle fabriche di Nostro Signore Papa Sisto V fatte dal Cavallier Domenico Fontana . . . Libro primo [secondo] . . .* (Rome, 1590), plate 18. Glasgow University Library, Stirling Maxwell Collection.

removal of the Vatican Obelisk to St Peter's Square, full power and authority to make use of any and every craftsman and labourer as well as their
tools, and if necessary to force them to lend or sell any of them to him, for
which he will duly satisfy them with a suitable reward.[98]

Then follow details of the 'planks, beams and timbers of any sort . . . to
whomsoever they belong' which Fontana was empowered to requisition
(though he was also obliged to pay compensation); the trees and forests
belonging to the various papal institutions which he was authorized to lop
down 'without any compensation'; the rights of way for animals used in
the project, and provision for their pasturage; the 'necessary objects' (these
are undefined) that he was authorized to demand from 'anybody' without
paying tax or duty; the food and equipment that he could also demand
both from within Rome and from the neighbouring districts; and finally,
the power he was granted to enter private property, and demolish buildings ('though the form of compensation to be paid must be firmly settled
beforehand'). The edict concludes:

> In short, we give to the here-named Domenico Fontana full authority to
> do, arrange and demand everything else that may be required . . . he, his
> agents, servants and household staff may everywhere and at every time
> bear every sort of arms . . . Subjects of the Apostolic See, whatever be their
> rank or station, we command, under pain of our displeasure and a fine
> of 500 ducats or more as we may determine, that they shall not dare to
> obstruct the work or in any wise to molest the aforesaid Domenico, his
> agents, or his workers, but without delay or any excuse, shall assist, obey,
> support and aid him.[99]

Armed with this wide-ranging commission, Fontana and his workers spent
the winter and spring of 1585–6 gathering materials, erecting the apparatus, levelling the ground, and rehearsing the operation. Shifting the obelisk
would involve the carefully coordinated efforts of hundreds of labourers and
horses, powering multiple winches and pulleys. As the many illustrations of
the undertaking, published after it had been completed, make clear, the area
in front of the church of St Peter's was to be transformed into a gigantically
complex system or network of machinery (Figure 2.4).

Religious ritual was evident at every stage of the undertaking. Preparations
were finally completed on 28 April 1586. The following evening, the workmen were confessed and given communion, and, on 30 April, following

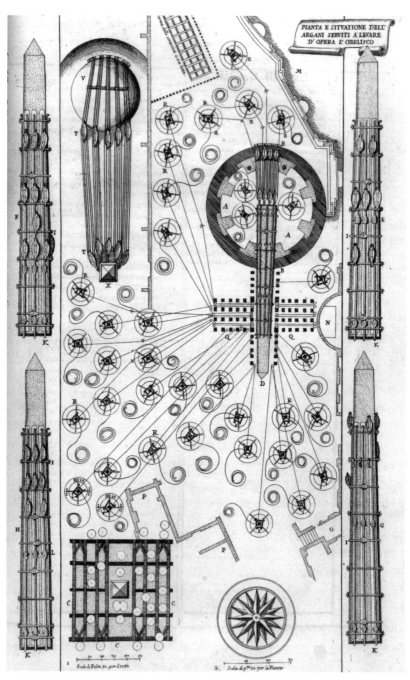

Figure 2.4 Carlo Fontana, *Templum Vaticanum et ipsius origo cum ædificiis maximè conspicuis antiquitùs, & recèns ibidem constitutis* (Rome, 1694), p. 131. Glasgow University Library, Special Collections.

two masses celebrated before dawn, men and animals were positioned. Under Fontana's direction, the workmen knelt once more and joined him in a *Pater Noster* and an *Ave Maria*. A technical undertaking had evolved into a pious spectacle, a theatre of machinery and mechanism, attracting thousands of spectators. Fontana's own account of the task, *Della Trasportione dell'obelisco vaticano* (published at Rome in 1590 and clearly devised as a form of self-advertisement for his engineering skill), describes the arrangements for preserving order and silence among the spectators, even the threat of execution that was levelled at any who might interfere with the operation in any way. The audience was immense:

> There were present the greater part of the College of Cardinals, the foreign ambassadors, the city officials, and many of the nobility not only of Rome, but from all parts of Italy. Every window facing the obelisk was occupied, as well as the whole edifice of St Peter's, the roofs of adjoining buildings and every point of vantage. So great was the multitude in the streets that the Swiss Guards and the Light Horse were ordered out to reinforce the police.[100]

Throughout the course of summer 1586, the obelisk was slowly raised, tilted, lowered onto its cradle, and then trundled to its new site, which it reached in early September. On 10 September, following further religious ceremony, and in front of another enormous crowd, the operation of hoisting the mass of stone into the vertical began, using forty windlasses, one hundred and forty horses, and eight hundred men. By sundown, after fifty-two distinct movements, the obelisk was hanging like a gigantic stone needle suspended within a network of ropes, beams, and pulleys, over its new resting place. The following day it was gently lowered into position and, on 28 September 1586, it was consecrated. It still stands, today, at the centre of the great colonnade fronting the church of St Peter, surmounted by a metal cross.[101] Buoyed up by this success, Fontana was to supervise the movement of three more obelisks in Rome.

Gazing on technology in operation is not a modern phenomenon, although accounts of the deployment of technology as a spectacle, in and of itself, are comparatively rare in the ancient economies of antiquity. However, an Egyptian tomb painting has survived which illustrates just this facet of ancient technology, and which also serves as a precursor to the efforts of Sixtus and his engineer. On the walls of a tomb at Deir el-Bersheh is an illustration of the transporting of an enormous six-metre-high alabaster statue (probably

weighing some sixty tonnes) of the *nomarch* (or provincial governor) Djehutihotpe, dating from the XII dynasty (around 2000 BCE). One hundred
and seventy-two men are depicted hauling the image, which was moved
some fifteen kilometres from quarries to the governor's city of Hermapolis,
on a sledge, while attendants beat out the time to accompany the rhythmi-
cal chanting of the toiling haulers, and poured lubricating oil or water in
front of the slowly shifting effigy. The project has been described as a form
of spectacular religious ceremony.[102] An accompanying text, found on an
adjacent inscription, recounts how 'the city assembled and let out cries of
joy. The spectacle was more beautiful than anything.'[103]

Fontana's activities in Rome, in the course of the summer of 1586, seem
to hearken back to this ancient idea of technology as both spectacle and
ceremony, which can thus be understood as the re-creation of an ancient
practice. There are, of course, illustrations and records that show us how,
in the medieval period, the great cathedrals were constructed. Yet, these
records and images tend to concentrate on the technical tasks of individual masons, glaziers, lead workers, and labourers, or else they show us the
operation of specific machines: cranes, treadmills, windlasses, and water-
powered saws. We are rarely shown an audience to the undertaking, other
than, perhaps, the prince or bishop who has commissioned or endowed the
work, and who is shown in order to commemorate his pious generosity.
Crowds of spectators, witnessing the construction of such buildings, are
virtually unknown, since it was God, rather than the master-designer, who
was to be praised, and that only in the completion of the entire edifice.[104]
A half-completed cathedral, or a cathedral under construction, could hardly
be thought of as a fitting paean of praise to the almighty, even if (in practice) such buildings were housing religious services long before they were
completed.

For Fontana and for his patron, however, just as for the ancient Egyptian
governor, the process of construction was part of the undertaking. The obelisk (or the statue) was not merely to be moved, but it had to be *seen* to be
moved. As such we can understand such projects as performances, as much
as they represented technological challenges. Hence, in the lavish illustrations that accompanied Fontana's account of moving the obelisk, we can see
groups of fashionably dressed spectators clustered around the site (Figure
2.5). Fontana and his helpers had transformed a technical task into an open-
air pageant, a celebration of the immense power and delicate accuracy of
men, animals, and machinery working in coordinated harmony. Fontana's
publication of his achievement is an example, too, of the ways in which

Figure 2.5 Carlo Fontana, *Templum Vaticanum et ipsius origo cum ædificiis maximè conspicuis antiquitùs, & recèns ibidem constitutis* (Rome, 1694), pp. 168–9. Glasgow University Library, Special Collections.

(in Elizabeth Eisenstein's words): 'Major public works, once published, became tourist attractions which vied with old pilgrimage sites and Roman ruins.'[105]

But the event also represented a fusion of religion, politics, and technology in a way that is comparable to what David Nye has described as the later creation of 'sublime technological objects' associated with American technological achievement beginning in the first half of the nineteenth century.[106] In Nye's analysis, the sight of vastly complex technological projects is cathartic. Thus, the construction of the Erie Canal in 1825 or the launch of Apollo XI in 1970 'purified and uplifted the mind and helped individuals see themselves as members of a larger community'.[107] Such projects were institutionalized, in America, as concrete manifestations of abstract ideals such as 'freedom' or 'democracy'. This, quite clearly, was not the case in sixteenth-century Rome any more than it was in Pharaonic Egypt. Rather, Sixtus' plan for the new Rome was to create a 'New Jerusalem' attracting pilgrims from all corners of the globe to its spiritual centres. In pursuing this ambition, he envisaged a network of broad, radial, streets, linking the various pilgrimage sites, and marked by the obelisks which, as Fontana had now demonstrated, could be shifted, though with great cost and labour, around the city.[108] This radial plan also conformed to a deeper, symbolic, sense of the relationship of the city to the world at large. As Ruth Eaton has observed, Renaissance architects and town planners:

> ... drew analogies between the city's layout and, on the one hand, the microcosm (the head signifying the centre of direction, the arteries the streets, and so forth) and on the other hand the macrocosm (the central *piazza* representing the sun, radial streets the rays, and so on). This desire to conform to the layout of the cosmos explains the repeated use of the rather impractical radial form, whose architectural parallel was the cupola-crowned church built to a central plan ... [109]

The symbolic analogy with the sun was underlined in the use of the obelisk: devised by the Egyptians in veneration of the sun, these had, in the course of time, been transported to Rome in antiquity as expressions of imperial rule and dominion. Now, repositioned and christianized, they expressed the church's universal dominion: 'these phallic beacons added a historical dimension to the urban landscape, broadcasting the message that even in ancient Egypt and Rome the victory of the church had been divinely preordained'.[110] The obelisk, a symbol of the vast economic as well as technological prowess of ancient society, had been re-inscribed (as well as rededicated) to the ideology of Christianity.

In embarking upon this immense and costly project, Sixtus had demonstrated the temporal power of the church over the lives of her devotees. It was also a vivid example of the ways in which Christian Europe had begun to fashion itself as a technological society, able to rival if not surpass the ancient world's mastery of mechanical force. Leonardo had envisaged the machine as a means of harnessing the forces of nature to the hand of human beings, while Montaigne had appreciated machines as tokens of philosophical rationality and social order. But Sixtus and his engineer had begun to glimpse the possibility that technology might express social and political power. Thus, the autocratic edict that acted as Fontana's warrant for the entire undertaking, Chant and Goodman observe, 'could not have been written by Popes of the early fifteenth century ... no other monarch in Europe had greater power over his subjects'.[111] Medieval municipal and ecclesiastical institutions were either defunct or they had become purely formal bodies, with no ability to check the virtually absolute power of papal authority.[112]

The obelisk project, together with the entire *renovatio Romae*, the Sixtine renovation of Rome, fused the glory of the ancient city with its revived Christian mission. The undertaking commanded the admiration of contemporary foreign commentators. The architect and masque designer, Inigo Jones, for example, studied Fontana's book on the transporting of the obelisk with great care.[113] John Wilkins, the English mathematician and savant, writing in the 1640s, noting that Fontana's undertaking had been described by no fewer than '56 several authors', wrote of the accomplishment as 'strange and glorious'.[114] Calculating the labour required to raise the monuments of antiquity, and relying largely on classical sources such as Herodotus, Wilkins estimated that the construction of Solomon's temple required 150,000 labourers, one of the Egyptian pyramids had involved the deployment of 360,000 individuals, while a second pyramid needed the labour of over a million.[115] Eventually, numbers were collapsed altogether into one vast agglomeration of nameless peoples: 'the *Ephesian* temple was built by all *Asia* joining together ... the whole work being not finished under the space of two hundred and fifteen years', Wilkins wrote.[116] Although Fontana's project was more limited in scope, Wilkins appreciated the far greater economy of the sixteenth-century engineer, who completed a work 'in some few days by five or six hundred men; and as the work was much lesse than many other recorded in Antiquity: so the means by which it was wrought, was yet far lesse ...'[117]

Wilkins was exaggerating. The labour involved required rather more than 'some few days'. And yet, the technical accomplishment of the moving of the Vatican obelisk, described by the English traveller and diarist John Evelyn in 1644 as the 'most stupendious invention by Domenico Fontana', easily blinds us to the social impact of the project.[118] Reading Fontana's self-aggrandizing account of the entire operation, one is struck by his organizational as much as his technical skill. The bodies of his labourers and animals had to be made to work with machine-like precision and harmony if they were to succeed. What had been devised in Rome was what Michel Foucault would later describe as the 'body–machine complex', where 'the regulation imposed by power is at the same time the law of construction of the operation'.[119]

What it also relied upon, of course, was that fundamental device associated with mechanical culture, the timetable, since, without the precise coordination of machinery, men, and animals, the obelisk could never have stirred in the first place. The timetable, understood as a device used to 'establish rhythms, impose particular operations, regulate the cycle of repetition', was as important to Fontana's project as the ingenious combinations of pulleys, capstans, and labour.[120] The timetable is not, strictly speaking, a machine of any kind, and yet, in its regulation of human activity to achieve a purposeful outcome, it has some of the attributes of a mechanism. In the distribution and regulation of individuals through space and time, ordering their movements, forming groups of people into precisely calibrated units who work in a regulated sequence, the timetable can be thought of as a mechanism by which individuals are welded together into more tractable or pliable or purposeful groups.[121]

The machine had thus come to occupy a symbolic domain, where it helped to illuminate the nature of social and political relationships. Broadly speaking, and remembering the juxtaposition of optimism and pessimism with which we began this enquiry, all three of those archetypical Renaissance figures – Leonardo the artist-engineer, Montaigne the philosopher, and Fontana the architect-engineer – understood machines to be operating within an optimistic framework. But in what other ways did the presence of machines, of the kind Leonardo was designing for his various patrons, or Montaigne was admiring on the rivers of Europe, or of the type that Fontana and his patron had set in motion in the piazza in front of St Peter's in Rome, redefine the nature of work itself? Human and animal bodies, working together to a pre-ordained plan, whose ultimate end was the glorification of God, powered Fontana's engines. The success of this sacred undertaking depended on the conjunction of mechanical force and the bodies of those consigned to the task. How the body, more specifically the human body, was to be linked ever more intimately to mechanism in the Renaissance is the theme of the next chapter.

3

THE TURN OF THE SCREW
Machines, books, and bodies

Machines and tools may exert a deep though unquantifiable influence on those who work with them. Indeed, the relationship between humans and their artificial devices may perhaps best be thought of as dynamic.[1] By the very fact of their existence, machines help to define the ways in which we approach different kinds of work that has to be undertaken. Confronted by a particular task, we, the heirs to the mechanical culture of the Renaissance, are furnished with a vast imaginary lexicon of movement that helps us to categorize the nature of the work which faces us, together with the skills which might be needed to accomplish the task.

So pervasive has this habit of mind and motion become that we may not even be aware of the extent to which a prosthetic supplement to our bodies is helping to determine our actions and movements, or even helping to shape our identity. Sometimes, indeed, only pain or injury reminds us that certain motions, particularly when repeated over and over again, are by no means 'natural' but are grafted onto the human frame. For example, the complex rotary twist of the muscles of the arm and shoulder (technically the supination and pronation of the forearm) is a fundamental mechanical motion in the modern world, enabling us to change a light bulb, manipulate a screwdriver, or open a bottle of wine. It is a deft physical movement that must once have helped our scavenging human ancestors to grub for roots, or twist berries and fruit from trees and bushes.[2] This physical motion was known to the ancient world as much as it was known in the European

Middle Ages or Renaissance. But with the advent of the screw as a fastening device in Europe in the fifteenth century, and hence the need to wield the tool which would evolve into the screwdriver with greater precision and dexterity, this motion began to form part of the specialized repertoire of human physical movements that identified the skilled mechanical craft worker.[3]

Of course, there are plenty of examples of technological devices determining human movement from earlier epochs: the ancient technology of the potter's wheel, for example, emerging around 3000 BCE, involved working with rotary motion to form and shape a lump of clay into an almost perfectly symmetrical form.[4] Learning to use a tool until it has become 'second nature' is one of the hallmarks of the modern craft worker. But the very term 'second nature', which mirrors the idea of the machine as part of 'secondary creation', indicates the extent to which these movements have to be learned at some stage. In this sense, human beings may themselves be thought of as products of *Technē*, where the tool or instrument may be said to exercise an unspoken authority over human movement. Tool users, like machine operatives, are human beings who have adapted themselves and their social identities to the demands of *Technē*.

The rise of mechanical culture involved a redefinition of human movement, as well as altering the pace and nature of human labour. But work, in early-modern communities, possessed a theological dimension, as much as it was a practical necessity. Work was part of the punishment of fallen humanity, though it was also a pathway to redemption expressed in the Benedictine expiation for humankind's original transgression *ora et labora* (pray and work).[5] At the same time, Renaissance 'work', it has been suggested, was much more akin to craft than to industry: work was a process 'which never repeats itself, never does anything twice in exactly the same way'.[6] This view of Renaissance work has helped to foster the idea of individuality as being one of the hallmarks of the Renaissance worker, author, or artist, engaged in producing objects all of which are uniquely crafted, whether it be a spoon or the ceiling of the Sistine chapel.

In part, we can explain the uniqueness of so many crafted objects in the early-modern world in terms of the absence, until the later eighteenth century, of any standardized system of measurement in European countries. Calibration and measurement are also basic 'tools' of mechanical culture. In Britain, for example, it was not until 1758 that a standard yard was produced and deposited in the House of Commons, while in France, which industrialized much later than Britain, it has been calculated that, under the pre-Revolutionary *ancien régime* there existed some 250,000 different units of weight and measurement, described with the help of no fewer than eight hundred different names.[7] Thus, early modern technology lacked that essential quality of 'I-see-what-you-see', and this absence, in turn, helps to explain the pedantically literal nature of so many descriptions of objects or procedures in the early-modern world.[8] Each thing, or process, had to be described in terms of some other thing, or process, based on assumed shared knowledge, or else described entirely anew, while measurement itself was constantly in flux, more often than not using the human body – hands, fingers, feet, stature – as an anthropomorphic calculating device to indicate length, breadth, and depth.[9] It is exactly this quality which Hamlet exploits to comic effect, when he has Polonius agree to his various descriptions of an insubstantial cloud as being, in turn, 'like a camel . . . like a weasel . . . like a whale' (III. ii. 365–70). Things were understood in terms of other things, and no two objects were ever exactly the same. We can only speculate as to the extent that early-modern discourse was bound up with the time-consuming business of rehearsing likenesses and unlikenesses, though this feature of early-modern life surfaces, I suspect, in the love of metaphors of affinity or disaffinity, similarity and dissimilarity, congruence and incongruence, which is so much a hallmark of Renaissance writing.

But this patchwork of endlessly repeated description does not mean that early-modern people, or, indeed, people from earlier epochs, had not begun to think of work and labour in sophisticated terms. In France, for example, Jean Bodin in his *Six Books on the Commonwealth* (1576) had attempted to analyse the phenomenon of the growth in wage labour in the period.[10] Nevertheless, the vocabulary with which early-modern people described work or labour was different from the terms that we now deploy in an industrial or post-industrial epoch. In order to understand this earlier vocabulary, we first have to turn, very briefly, to the ways in which the relationship between machines and labour was described by the two great philosophers of mechanical culture *after* the Renaissance: Karl Marx and Adam Smith.

Of alienation and pins

Marx has bequeathed to us the fundamental vocabulary with which we understand the relationship of humans and their machines. In the *Grundrisse* of 1857–8, Marx contrasted the skills of the craftsman, using simpler tools, to the 'alienation' of 'labour' deployed alongside complex machines. For Marx, the transition between simple tool use and the emergence of the machine worker signalled a shift in patterns of authority. Thus, Marx suggested that the craftsman 'animated' the tool 'with his own skill and dexterity'.[11] What was merely an object or thing was endowed with a measure of shape or definition by the animating force of human skill or purpose. With the coming of more complex machines, however, this relationship was fundamentally altered. So profound was this change, in Marx's view, that it was akin to a shift in syntax. Where once people had worked with machines, now machines worked with people. The fate of the machine 'operative' (a term which, the OED records, only began to be attached to those who worked with machines in the nineteenth century) was to be subordinated to his or her machine. It was the machine possessing 'skill and force in the worker's place' which became 'the virtuoso, with a spirit of its own in the mechanical laws that take effect in it'.[12] Marx continued:

> The worker's activity, limited to a mere abstraction, is determined and regulated on all sides by the movement of the machinery, not the other way round. The knowledge that obliges the inanimate parts of the machine, through their construction, to work appropriately as an automaton, does not exist in the consciousness of the worker, but acts upon him through the machine as an alien force, as the power of the machine itself.[13]

Marx had realized that machines, rather than being the passively obedient servants of human skill and ingenuity, had, rather, assumed the prerogative over their erstwhile masters. Roles had been reversed. Machine 'minders' (to use another term which came into vogue in the nineteenth century) were reduced to being no more than so many 'hands', whose primary task was the service of the machine. The machine thus controlled its 'minder' since the pace of work as well as the nature of the task was now understood as determined by the physical capacities of the device, even if the knowledge that had first animated the machine was human knowledge. So, Marx wrote, labour began to appear as 'a conscious organ, composed of individual living workers at a number of points in the mechanical system ... subjected to the general process of the machinery itself, it is itself only a limb of the system'.[14] In Marx's richly metaphoric language an exchange has taken place: human bodies have become machine like, while machines have begun to sprout their own 'limbs', composed from the bodies of the labour force.

Marx's analysis rested upon a clear distinction between the supposedly benign relationship that was held to exist between the worker and the tool, as opposed to the alienating force of the machine.[15] Labour, or rather, the labourers themselves, were spiritually and economically incapacitated by machinery. This incapacitation Marx related directly to the idea of the 'division of labour'. 'As the division of labour increases,' Marx wrote, so 'labour', by which he now meant the range of tasks to be undertaken, 'is simplified':

> The special skill of the worker becomes worthless. He becomes transformed into a simple, monotonous productive force that does not have to use intense bodily or intellectual faculties. His labour becomes a labour that anyone can perform.[16]

Devaluation of the labourer's skill was a process that was enhanced by the advent of machinery: 'Machinery brings about the same results on a much greater scale, by replacing skilled workers by unskilled, men by women, adults by children.'[17]

Marx's anatomy of industrial work was derived directly from Adam Smith's *Inquiry into the Nature and Causes of The Wealth of Nations* (1776). Comparing the agricultural labourer who, equipped with simple tools might in the same day pursue the several occupations of ploughman, harrower, sower of seed, and reaper of corn, to those engaged in 'manufactures', Smith observed that, in the latter case: 'the carpenter is commonly separated from . . . the smith. The spinner is almost always a distinct person from the weaver.'[18] From this observation stemmed Smith's larger claim that 'the invention of all those machines by which labour is so much facilitated and abridged seems to have been originally owing to the division of labour'.[19]

The reorganization of time, together with the idea of concurrent as opposed to consecutive activity, was fundamental to Smith's analysis. For the whole point of the 'division of labour' was that activity could be compressed. Instead of the worker first picking up a particular tool, completing the task, laying down the tool to pick up another, and beginning a new task ('sauntering' was Smith's evocative term for this process), all of these activities could take place simultaneously, using different workers, who were thus transformed into specialists. Smith's observation, that machinery was itself the outcome of some original division of tasks, was based on what Roy Porter has described as 'Smith's immortal pin manufacture example': the observation that just ten labourers were able to produce 48,000 pins in a single day, when compared to the solitary labourer who, attempting to undertake all the tasks required in the manufacture of these trivial objects, might be hard-pressed to produce even one pin in the same space of time.[20]

Smith's analysis, no matter how true it was in practice, was based on a misunderstanding of technological development in Europe. Work on *The Wealth of Nations* was begun in the early 1760s, when Smith held a professorship at the University of Glasgow.[21] Surrounded as he was by the burgeoning coal, iron, and textile industries of the region, he may be forgiven for believing that complex, power-driven machinery was a new phenomenon: 'Neither wind nor water mills of any kind were known in England so early as the sixteenth century, nor, as far as I know, in any other part of Europe north of the Alps', he wrote.[22] Despite this fundamental historical error, so influential would Smith's analysis become that it suggested a possible definition of what exactly constituted a machine as distinct from a tool. Thus Charles Babbage, for example, better known as the inventor of that distant forerunner of the modern computer, the Difference Engine, in his *On The Economy of Machinery and Manufactures* (1832), turned to Smith's analysis of the division of labour to explain the genesis of machinery. Machines, for Babbage, were simply collections of tools whose outcome was far more predictable than that produced by the individual tool user. Babbage argued that 'in cases where a blow from a single hammer is employed, experience teaches the proper force required'.[23] But mount the hammer on an axis so that it is 'lifted regularly to a certain height by some mechanical contrivance, . . . [then] it is not difficult to perceive that if the hammer always falls from the same height, its effect must always be the same'.[24] Repetition and regularity, in other words, were the hallmarks of the machine. Experience, skill, aptitude, or dexterity were all made redundant by the uniform blow of the mechanically driven hammer. By reducing all processes to the action of a simple tool, Babbage concluded that 'the union of all these tools, actuated by one moving power, constitutes a machine'.[25]

For Marx, this gain in productivity was purchased only at the cost of the labourer's task being made not only simpler (in contrast to the skills deployed by the craftsman) but also more enervating. But terms such as enervation, specialization, or alienation formed no part of the understanding of the relationship between machines and labour in pre-industrial culture. Rather, labour was understood in theological terms as a penance for the transgression said to have taken place in Eden. The 'dismal science' of political economy, as Thomas Carlyle is said to have responded to the works of Malthus and with it the analysis of work and productivity in terms of different mechanisms or systems that were to be developed in the course of the eighteenth and nineteenth centuries, lay in the distant future.[26]

'What is't o'clock?': clock time and social status

But that absence of reflective analysis did not mean that early-modern people were unaware of a deeper relationship between tools, machines, and labour. Historians of technology have documented one area in which mechanical culture impacted upon the lives of Europeans in the pre-industrial period. It has been claimed that the development in the course of the thirteenth century of the mechanical clock, and, later in the sixteenth century, of the portable timepiece or watch, marked a decisive shift in the everyday rhythms of life.[27] The miniaturized device of the watch seems to have appeared around 1550, in Nuremberg, and soon became known as the 'Nuremberg Egg'.[28] Though still a luxury item, watches (or 'dials' as they were more commonly known) were to become widely available in the sixteenth century, and with their wider distribution, so time itself became privatized or personalized. Time became the property, if not of everyman, then certainly of many. It was this factor, David Landes has claimed, which was to become: 'a major stimulus to the individualism that was an ever more salient aspect of Western civilization'.[29]

Carlo Cipolla, too, has traced the enormous impact of clocks and watches on Western culture in the course of the seventeenth century: 'People became very conscious of time . . . punctuality became at the very same time, a need, a virtue, and an obsession.'[30] But perhaps this device made its presence felt in other, less obvious, ways. Thus, a character in one of Shakespeare's plays asks another character the time: 'I pray you, what is't o'clock?' asks Rosalind of Orlando in Shakespeare's *As You Like It* (1600) (III. ii. 293). To us, this query is a commonplace. Posed in the course of a theatrical performance, of course, its meaning shifts so that it becomes a ploy by which interaction between two characters is initiated. Yet, replaced within its historical moment, this query alerts us to an emerging network of social and cultural meaning, precipitated by the presence of this novel time-measuring device, which competed with older social and cultural practices.

So, Orlando's reply to Rosalind reminds us that, in the early years of the seventeenth century, the memory of older ways of calculating time still existed: 'You should ask me what time o' day', he responds 'There's no clock in the forest' (III. ii. 294–5). In fact, Orlando is wrong. There are indeed clocks (or at least watches) in the forest. Earlier in the play, the melancholy Jaques had observed the Fool, Touchstone, draw just such a mechanical timepiece from his clothing:

And then he drew a dial from his poke,
And looking on it, with lack-lustre eye,
Says, very wisely, 'It is ten o' clock.'
'Thus we may see' quoth he 'how the world wags . . .'

(II. vii. 20–3)

To the modern audience, Jaques is mocking Touchstone's pretentious phi-
losophizing, based on his possession of a watch. But to Shakespeare's earlier
audiences, we might guess that the simple description of Touchstone's
pulling this device from his 'poke' (a word meaning either a small bag,
or wide full-bodied sleeve) would already have seemed incongruous, and
quite possibly comic. Fools or jesters were relatively humble members of
the household, and for them to have possessed the unlikely device of a clock
or watch might suggest that they had ideas above their station. To be in possession of the mechanical reckoning of time signalled social sophistication,
as Touchstone is reminding himself as he gazes (in Jaques's description), in
such an obviously self-satisfied way at his watch amid the alien environment
of wild nature.

The existence of the portable clock, or watch, even (as was now possible)
in the depths of the forest, had become a talismanic register of who, or even
what, one felt oneself to be, or wished to be. To 'own' time in this way was
to be urbane and precise. And to be in possession of such time was still a
relatively novel phenomenon. The ubiquity of Shakespeare's use of the device
by which one character asks another the time 'by the clock', or comments
on the passage of 'clock time' (as opposed to remarking upon the mere passage of time more generally) reminds us of the fact that, in the late sixteenth
and early seventeenth centuries, this possibility of mechanical punctuality
was still disarmingly new.[31] Moreover, to ask for clock time in the seventeenth century was to make implicit assumptions about the rank, status, or
wealth of the person to whom one was addressing this question: relatively
few people would have had the wherewithal, let alone the need, to be able
to afford to carry this luxurious item about them. Hence, a question such
as that posed by Rosalind in *As You Like It* might indicate a certain degree of
social deference, or even flattery. One did not ask the time from one's social
inferiors, only from those of equal or superior rank. Later, in the seventeenth century, a punctual ability to obey the dictates of clock time would be
linked, particularly by Puritans, to industriousness and even godliness: 'The
Puritan horror of waste of time helped not only to concentrate effort, to
focus attention on detail, but also to prepare for the rhythms of an industrial

society, our society of the alarm clock and the factory whistle', Christopher Hill has observed.[32] But the point, here, is that the machine or instrument was also beginning to function as a register of social standing, rather than simply as a utilitarian device for calculating the passage of time. The drive to accumulate machines or devices as indices of one's sense of wealth and worth in the world, a drive with which we are all too familiar, was already in play in the Forest of Arden.

Print and mechanical culture

The extent to which the diffusion of machines and devices in the Renaissance was intimately linked to the development and distribution of printed books and images cannot be overestimated. In more ways than one, the Renaissance machine was the invention of print culture. In the final years of the fifteenth century, following the adoption of the mechanical press, the development of redistributable type, and the use of high-quality paper and oil-based inks, it was now possible to produce and distribute in virtually identical copies, the all-important illustrations of the machines that a traveller such as Montaigne had seen appearing in France, Germany, and Italy in the sixteenth century. It was from exactly these regions that illustrations of new machines emerged.

Illustrations of machines in the pre-print age were, of course, legion. But in the pre-print age, as textual artefacts, machine illustrations were subject to misunderstandings of all kinds. By contrast, a fundamental product of the replicative capacities of the mechanical printing press was its capacity to produce 'uniform spatio-temporal images'.[33] Pre-print technical illustrations of course formed an important part of what has been termed 'technical communication', but such illustrations were also subject to distortion as they circulated in a hand-copied form.[34] Quite simply, printing made it much easier to refine an illustration of a mechanical device over and over again. Machines could thus become more complex since their intricate detail could be widely distributed and accurately copied, either as further refinements to the design, or as constructions in the real world. One no longer had to see a particular example of a machine in situ in order to duplicate it. Print, the child of mechanism, thus helped to spread the appreciation of mechanism: 'the difference between the hand-copied image that decays over the course of time and the repeatable engraving that can be *corrected and improved* is essential for understanding how visual aids were affected by print' writes Elizabeth Eisenstein (my emphasis).[35] Correction and improvement, a phrase that was to become associated with the issue and reissue of differ-ent 'editions' of the printed book, was also essential to the evolution and diffusion of more complex mechanisms.

In this respect, we can think of the printed book as a form of memory appliance. It represented a means of storing and recovering complex infor-mation and ideas. Of course, printed texts could become corrupted or be reproduced from inferior originals.[36] Moreover, even the worst 'bad quarto' of a Shakespeare play makes *some* kind of sense. Literary texts still 'work', even if they are 'wrong'. Machines, on the other hand, rarely do. In hand-copied drawings, mechanical details were often ignored or misunderstood: complex block and tackle systems were reduced to a single pulley; the threads on screw mechanisms were reversed. The machine had been, in effect, lost as a practical working device to future generations. Inevitably, mistakes were still made in printed images of machinery. But nevertheless, there was a tendency to trust a printed image far more than one might a hand-drawn illustration, even if, in reality, such trust was misplaced. Print had the effect of freezing a design at one stage of its evolution, which, in turn, made it easier to transmit technical information from one locality to another, or even, through time, from one generation to the next.[37] Improve-ment, the process by which a design or an idea could be reworked so that it became more efficient, or redesigned entirely and applied to an entirely different task, paradoxically, rested on that quality of fixity that seemed so unique to print.

The importance of print to the growth of scientific and intellectual culture in Europe in the sixteenth century has been comprehensively explored over the past few years.[38] Perhaps surprisingly, its importance to technological culture has been less widely appreciated. Printing was, after all, the applica-tion of mechanism to the task of generating texts, and hence disseminating ideas. But it was also an offshoot of advances in metallurgy and the devel-opment of metal industries, particularly in Southern Germany, in the early fifteenth century.[39] We can, though, only speculate as to the extent to which the enormous growth in the circulation of printed material in both Europe and the 'New World' of the Americas (a printing press had been established in Mexico City as early as 1533), even within populations that were largely illiterate, fostered an interest in the mechanical culture which was both generated by, and helped in turn to foster the spread of the mechanical presses.[40] Walter Ong, however, following Marshall McLuhan, has indicated some of the shifts in *mentalités* attributable to the advent of the printing press. For Ong, the printing press heralded the primacy of sight over hearing, the development of indexes and (later) dictionaries, the sense of a book being 'less like an utterance and more like a thing', the exploitation of 'typographic space' to generate meaning as in a poem such as George Herbert's 'Easter Wings', or space as a marker of silence or absence as in the instance of the famous blank page in Laurence Sterne's *Tristram Shandy* (1759–67). Even the development of the idea of the 'point of view', personal privacy, private ownership, and the sense of closure associated with literary texts, have been attributed to the advent of printing as a mechanical undertaking.[41]

The social effects of this new form of mechanical labour were incalculable. Certainly, writers and intellectuals now had to be aware, as they need never have been before, of the importance of mechanism in a practical sense, to the generation and distribution of their ideas. Just as modern authors, in the digital age, have had to acquaint themselves with at least some vestigial idea of digital technology if they are to distribute their words and thoughts either in the traditional form of the book, or by way of the newer technologies of e-mail, the web page, or the blog, so Renaissance writers became more aware of mechanism as it impinged on their professional lives. The simple fact that, as their works passed through the press authors were often expected to attend the print shop in order to make corrections to the proof copies of their texts as they were thrown off the machines, introduced authors to the inky, mechanical world of mechanisms and their ever more skilful human servants.[42] 'Professors', writes Eisenstein, 'came into closer contact with metal workers and mechanics' and this inevitable proximity of intellectual and mechanical labour helped to bring about the redefinition of certain kinds of 'work'.[43]

The print shop, too, represented a means of organizing work and labour that accorded in its outline with that idea of the 'division of labour' that can be associated with Adam Smith's later example of pin makers. In the world of manuscripts the many skills and tasks involved in producing a book, which included the raising, feeding, and then slaughtering of animals, the manufacture of vellum from their skins, the mixing of inks from organic and mineral sources which in turn had to be mined, collected, or harvested and then prepared, the process of copying, illuminating, binding and so on, were distributed widely through the community. Producing a manuscript book, in the pre-print era, mobilized a galaxy of seemingly unrelated skills and crafts. Printing, on the other hand, for all that it drew on an equally wide range of distributed tasks, tended to compress activity into a shop structure, which, in turn, involved workers pooling their skills under one roof.[44] Print brought people closer together, allowing them to learn from one another not only in communities of readers, but as producers of objects.

It was not, of course, that Europeans had never before had to work in conformity with a machine. The plough, after all, is a machine of sorts, though we more commonly refer to it, in its earlier forms, as a tool.[45] But the ploughman's work was solitary. Printing, on the other hand, in common with weaving and spinning, was gradually evolving into a 'shop' structure in Europe in the course of the fifteenth and sixteenth centuries.[46] The fifteenth- and sixteenth-century print shop was a place of bustling group activity, where the workers had to learn to adapt their bodies and their minds to labour together, with their activity governed by the rhythm of the operation of the press itself. The turn of the mechanical screw, quite literally, dictated the pace of labour and hence the rapidity (as well as the quality) with which bibles, almanacs, pamphlets, technical treatises, as well as the more familiar literary and philosophical works of the period could be generated and distributed. As Lucien Febvre and Henri-Jean Martin have commented, those who, in the late fifteenth and early sixteenth centuries, were learning to work with movable type had to develop an entirely new range of skills. Speed was a factor in this process: 'to work really fast a compositor has to handle the letters without pausing or looking: he has to become an automaton, just like a modern typist at the keyboard'.[47] What Michel Foucault has termed 'the automatism of habit', by which the body is recomposed in conformity with some exterior force (whether the exigencies of military drill, the factory, or even the school conceived of as 'a machine for learning') had its roots in a mechanism designed to press a blank sheet of paper against an ink-covered surface, over and over again.[48]

Authors were by no means aloof from this mechanical process. Indeed, they had to learn to accommodate themselves to the 'timetable' or 'schedule' that was a further manifestation of mechanical culture. A common complaint of authors, in the first decades of print, was that the printers and their servants were working too quickly or 'hedelynge [headlong] and in hast' as one author complained in 1509, suggesting that it was only with some difficulty that authors adapted themselves to the new pace set by the mechanisms of print, if, indeed, they have ever succeeded.[49] In the case of the print shop, the production of books was now working to a faster pace, since no printer would have wished the machines to stand idle, waiting for copy or emendations and corrections to the proofs.[50] That bane of authors and publishers alike, the deadline (and with it the familiar litany of excuses for missing deadlines, or producing poor copy), was an aspect

of mechanical culture that can be thought of as an offshoot of the development of print technology. The idea that a book should be finished on a
particular date, rather than when the author judged that the labour was at
an end, was an entirely new facet of intellectual work, as was the calculation
of the exact rate at which a given work could be printed.[51] Speed, together
with accuracy, would become new markers of 'efficiency', which would,
in the course of time, become a key term in the deployment of machinery.
Even one hundred years after the first appearance of the mechanical printing press, the efficiency of this device still had the capacity to astonish those
who observed it in operation: 'it would appear to be incredible if experience did not prove it to be true', wrote an anonymous French writer some
time before 1572, 'that four or five workers can produce in one day as much
excellent script as three or four thousand of the best scribes of the whole
world by this most excellent art of printing'.[52] Of course, this was an exag-
geration. As the bibliographer D. F. McKenzie has argued, the output of the
early-modern print shop was certainly much lower than was once imagined
by print historians.[53] Nevertheless, for all that it is easy to exaggerate the
volume of print production when compared to the production of texts by
non-mechanical methods, there arises a complaint on the part of authors
unknown in the world of the manuscript: that their works had been marred
or spoilt by the haste of the printers, anxious to keep their machines running at higher capacity. A Jacobean divine, Samuel Hieron, gives us a taste
of the quickened pace of intellectual labour. In the preface to his collected
sermons (published in 1614), Hieron explains that he lives 'farre from the
presse, and it requireth much time, to convey sheetes to and fro, betwixt
the compositors and me' and asks the reader to excuse the errors that have
crept into his work due to the 'hast of the printer, and my remoteness from
the citie'.[54]

But it was, in the end, the output of the print shops – the printed book
itself – which was the true signifier of the arrival of mechanical culture. As
Marshall McLuhan has famously argued, 'every aspect of Western mechanical culture was shaped by print technology' and he continued:

> Printing, remember, was the first mechanization of a complex handicraft;
> by creating an analytic sequence of step-by-step processes, it became the
> blue-print of all mechanization to follow. The most important quality of
> print is its repeatability; it is a visual statement that can be reproduced
> indefinitely, and repeatability is the root of the mechanical principle that
> has transformed the world since Gutenberg. Typography, by producing the

first uniformly repeatable commodity, also created Henry Ford, the first assembly line and the first mass production. Movable type was archetype and prototype for all subsequent industrial development. Without phonetic literacy and the printing press, modern industrialism would be impossible. It is necessary to recognize literacy as typographic technology, shaping not only production and marketing procedures but all other areas of life, from education to city planning.[55]

One might quibble with many elements of McLuhan's analysis here.[56] Yet, there is a truth to McLuhan's observations when we come to consider the idea of 'repeatability' which would, in time, give rise to the production lines of twentieth-century Detroit, Dagenham, and Tokyo. Print was indeed a 'mechanism of repeatability', as McLuhan has (elsewhere) written.[57] In introducing the idea of repetition, both as an activity, and as an output in the form of the printed book itself, work, as well as intellectual culture, was transformed by mechanical process. Quite simply, in virtually no other aspect of life, other than perhaps in the case of artefacts produced with the help of the highly skilled craft of working with the mechanical rotary motion of the potter's wheel, had it ever been possible to contemplate the production of any human artefact in considerable quantities of near uniform design, appearance, size, and quality prior to the advent of the printing press.

The birth of the Renaissance machine

Intimately associated with the rise of mechanical culture was the production and distribution of 'machine books'. The printed machine book, in which Renaissance engineers advertised their technical skills, would introduce new ways of seeing and hence understanding the very idea of mechanism, while it also promoted new ideas of motion, dexterity, and repetition. Yet, just as in the case of the production of medical texts, where the 'new' anatomists of the earlier sixteenth century still deferred to the classical authority of Galen, so the Renaissance engineers looked to the past, specifically the classical past, for their inspiration.[58]

The foundational work for Renaissance engineering was the De Architectura of Marcus Vitruvius Pollio (Vitruvius), first printed in an illustrated form in the edition of Fra Giocondo at Venice, in 1511. In the tenth and final book of De Architectura, Vitruvius discussed many different kinds of machines, defining them (somewhat unhelpfully) as: 'a combination of timbers fastened together, chiefly efficacious in moving great weights'. Of the different types of machine (rotary machines, 'climbing' machines (ladders), pneumatically driven machines, and so on), it was those designed to hoist great weights which were to be considered 'greater and full of grandeur' than any other, and these encompassed the various forms of siege weapon that had been devised by Roman military engineers.[59] For Vitruvius, machines existed in two forms, some of which could be considered mere 'machines', but others of which were dignified with the title 'engines'. As far as we can tell, the difference between the two was held to reside in the respective amount of effort required to make the machine work:

> The difference between 'machines' and 'engines' is obviously this, that machines need more workmen and greater power to make them take effect, as for instance *ballistae* and the beams of presses. Engines, on the other hand, accomplish their purpose at the intelligent touch of a single workman, as the *scorpio* or the *anisocycli* when they are turned.[60]

Machines that could work 'at the intelligent touch of a single workman' – devices, in other words, whose 'output' seemed to transcend their required 'input' – were the ideal form of mechanism, and these were the types of machine to which Renaissance designers and engineers aspired.

Intellectually, the genesis of the machine book was complex, combining many different kinds of ancient and contemporary source, some of which had been in circulation for many hundreds of years, while others were of relatively recent creation. Written and visual descriptions and depictions of Greek and Roman machines were to be found in both the Western and Eastern traditions.[61] Illustrations based on these sources together with an accompanying textual commentary had circulated in manuscript many years before the advent of the printed machine book. Indeed, the printed texts were often based on earlier, manuscript collections.[62] In the fourteenth century, for example, in the surviving manuscripts of the German military engineer Konrad Kyeser, we begin to see the emergence of a distinct technological *oeuvre*.[63]

But it was in Italy, in the hilltop town of Siena that the machine book, as a recognizable genre, was rooted. Siena was to the invention of machinery what, later, Bologna, Padua, and Leiden would become to the study of the human body. Siena was the birthplace of a 'school' of engineering and engineers, the most famous of whom were Taccola (Mariano di Iacopo) (1381–1458?) and Francesco di Giorgio Martini (1439–1501). These two early engineer-authors were to forge Europe-wide reputations for their ingenious and scholarly mechanical designs. Indeed, classical scholarship associated with the skills of the humanist, was as important as technical aptitude in the development of Renaissance machines. In much the same way that the humanists were gradually filling up the emergent private, princely and ecclesiastical libraries of Europe by retrieving the great, hitherto lost, classical *corpus* from Greek and Arabic manuscripts, so the engineer-authors of Siena set about the task of excavating the buried designs of the classical tradition of engineering from the past, particularly the Islamic past.[64] Works such as the thirteenth-century *Book of Knowledge of Ingenious Mechanical Devices* of al-Jazari, written in Diyarbakir in Asia Minor, and termed 'the most remarkable engineering document to have survived from pre-Renaissance times', gradually became known in the Christian West.[65] It was in Siena, too, that classical technology, to be discovered in the writings of Athenaeus, Philo of Byzantium, Heron of Alexandria, and Vitruvius, was married to new processes and designs in the works of these engineer-authors to produce the impressive manuscript collections in which Giorgio and Taccola displayed their mechanical contrivances.[66]

These manuscript volumes, rivals to the more familiar manuscripts of machines that Leonardo was to create (though rarely disseminate), were mostly compiled in the period c. 1420–85. They covered the whole range of civil and military engineering tasks which Renaissance architects and engineers might be called upon to perform: the installation of public water works, the design of complex devices for powering ships and boats, the creation of more accurate methods for measuring distance, for raising and transporting water, for fabricating construction devices and lifting machinery of all kinds. Most important of all, they showed how energy could be harnessed or transmitted using power from either living sources (humans and animals), or inanimate nature: gravity, wind, heat, and water.[67]

A particular favourite of these author-engineers, as it would be for the makers of the later printed machine books, was the investigation of ancient forms of artillery. Designs for trebuchets and catapults, together with siege engines of all kinds, were of continuing fascination in the period. Although, in the sixteenth century, such devices were to become redundant in the face of the innovation of gunpowder-powered artillery, ancient siege engines were regarded as the mechanical essence of the machine. They represented a kind of intellectual exercise by which it was possible to explore the action of wood, hemp, and metal under compression and sudden release. Thus, until well into the seventeenth century, machine books might contain anachronistic designs for devices that had not seen action on a European battlefield for

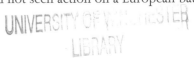

several hundred years.[68] It was as if a modern catalogue of different digital technologies – iPods, mobile phones, and laptops – also threw in a few examples of a typewriter for good measure. These ancient devices invested the world of mechanism with a kind of chivalric glamour, reminding the onlooker not only of the antiquity of mechanism itself, but also of its link to the noble practice of the arts of war. This residue of chivalry, as we shall see in due course, was to have a profound effect on the very different machines that came to be used by women, as opposed to men in early-modern societies.

Particularly striking, too, were the various mechanical devices that Taccola and Giorgio designed for work on construction sites, and which would reappear in the printed machine books. These, following the example of Vitruvius, were considered to be among the most noble of engines, equal in rank, almost, to the ancient siege engines which were so popular among Renaissance engineers. 'Ars sine scientia nihil est' ('Art without science is worthless') may have been the watchword of the architect, meaning that theory took precedence over mere skill or technique.[69] But, to the Sienese engineers, theory alone could not lever heavy stones forming a pediment into position a hundred metres above the ground. A fascination with lifting devices is not, perhaps, surprising given that the period during which Taccola and Giorgio were working was also the period of the most complex engineering project undertaken in fifteenth-century Europe: Filippo Brunelleschi's construction (in 1420–36) of the great dome for the (then) unfinished cathedral church of Santa Maria del Fiore, the Duomo of Florence. Brunelleschi has left us no illustrations of the machines that were used in raising the vast mass of material (computed at some 37,000 tonnes and involving four million bricks) over fifty metres above ground level.[70] However, Taccola, together with his contemporaries, Lorenzo Ghiberti, and Guiliano da Sangallo, as well as Leonardo, made copies of some of these devices, which were to reappear in the Sienese manuscripts. The most fabulous machine of all was the great ox hoist, constructed to Brunelleschi's design in the interior of the octagon supporting the dome in the cathedral in Florence and which, for over a dozen years, was to be the primary means of lifting bricks, tiles, stones, and timber high into the air.[71]

Georgius Agricola and the invention of mechanical labour

Circulating as manuscripts, the dissemination of such works could, however, have been only limited.[72] Print, of course, was to radically change this state of affairs. Addressing a much wider (though still specialist) public were the direct antecedents of the machine book: the printed technical works published in the earlier part of the sixteenth century that covered the 'technological arts' of mining and metallurgy. Beginning in the mid-1520s, and emanating from Germany, and particularly the mining centre of Augsburg, whose water-powered devices would so fascinate Montaigne in the 1580s, small treatises, known (by their titles) as *Probierbüchlein* (assaying booklets) had begun to appear.[73] From these collections of chemical 'recipes' for refining metals, constructing assay furnaces and crucibles, or separating (for example) silver from iron or lead, grew, in turn, the two most important works on technology in the mid-sixteenth century: the *Pirotechnia* of Vannoccio Biringuccio, first published at Venice in 1540, and the *De Re Metallica* of Georg Bauer, better known as Georgius Agricola, published at Basle in 1556. The *Pirotechnia* was to be reissued throughout the sixteenth century and well into the seventeenth, with a French translation appearing in 1556. Agricola's work, begun in 1533, was even more popular, appearing in Latin, German, and Italian editions, while Spanish and English translations may have been commissioned or even prepared but were never published.[74]

Both Biringuccio's and Agricola's works, though they were primarily technical treatises on every aspect of metallurgy and mining, showed illustrations of different kinds of machines and engines at work. The pages of Agricola's *De Re Metallica*, in particular, presented a cornucopia of illustrations of the often-complex devices associated with the mining industry. Agricola's many illustrations of machinery exploited the device of the 'keying mechanism' which had been so successfully deployed in the anatomy textbooks of the period.[75] Using this device, the different components in the machine were labelled, categorized, and anchored to the explanatory text. These illustrations were integral to the design of the work, as Agricola explained in the preface (dated from Chemnitz, Saxony, 1 December 1550) to *De Re Metallica*:

> . . . with regard to the . . . tools, vessels, machines, and furnaces, I have not only described them, but have also hired illustrators to delineate their forms, lest descriptions which are conveyed by words should either not be understood by men of our own times, or should cause difficulty to posterity, in the same way as to us difficulty is often caused by many names which the Ancients (because such words were familiar to all of them) have handed down to us without any explanation.[76]

Agricola had recognized the importance of text and illustration working together on the page to promote a new science of machines. For mechanical illustrations had to function in the future as well as in the present, when language might have shifted in unpredictable ways.

But more importantly, in combining human figures with his depictions of machinery, Agricola helped to produce new images of human labour. To show people at work, in the fields or in craft trades was, of course, nothing new; medieval illuminated manuscripts contained galleries of field and farm workers labouring with hoes, or trudging behind the ox-drawn plough. Equally, interior scenes of people at work, particularly women engaged in brewing or spinning, were a common feature of the medieval illustrators. Urban scenes of labour, in medieval art, appear, too, in the reliefs to be found in the upper arch of the main porch of San Marco in Venice, on the campanile of the Duomo in Florence, or in the stained-glass windows of Chartres cathedral, reflecting the church's view that the *artes mechanicae* were, optimistically, to be understood as 'a means of mitigating the curse of original sin'.[77]

But Agricola's illustrations radically shifted the ways in which human labour was now presented. Machines and humans are shown working together, in large, organized groups. Rather than labour being a solitary, repetitive, field-bound, task, or one demanding very limited human cooperation, Agricola's vistas of machine-induced labour are densely populated with human figures clambering into, or over, the machines that they are busily tending.[78] Often, indeed, Agricola seemed less interested in exploring the mechanical composition of his devices, than in showing us how the overall tasks associated with this industry were to be performed. In this respect his illustrations are very different from those of, say, Leonardo or the Sienese engineers, who tended to show the machine with its interior opened up to display, but in splendid isolation, often devoid of any human context. Instead, it was labour itself, broken down into its constituent parts, which claimed the attention of the reader of *De Re Metallica*, as the author unravelled the complex processes being developed in the mining and extraction of metallic ores. Through a combination of text and illustration, the reader was shown how the labourer's body was to move in conformity with the machinery that was to be deployed. What, in short, Agricola had invented was that most indispensable article of modern technological life: the technical instruction 'manual', or 'handbook'.[79]

Historians of print have puzzled over the implied readership of a work such as *De Re Metallica*: 'What was the point of publishing vernacular manuals outlining procedures that were already familiar to all skilled practitioners of certain crafts?'[80] The point was that labour or work was itself being redefined by machinery. As machines began to quicken the pace of labour,

Figure 3.1 Georgius Agricola, *De Re Metallica libri xii: quibu officia, instrumenta, machinae, ac omnnia denique ad metalicam spectantia, non modo lucluentissime describuntur* (Basle, 1556), p. 220. Glasgow University Library, Special Collections.

even the most unskilled task was broken down into a series of steps, so that operators could keep pace with their new devices. For example, illustrations from Book VIII of *De Re Metallica* show the operation of a water-powered ore-crushing machine (Figure 3.1).[81] First, Agricola describes the manufacture of the machine itself, going into considerable detail to provide alternative designs if suitable materials are not to hand ('. . . if an oak block is not available, two timbers are placed . . .'). Care is taken, as well, to ensure that the reader understands why the design incorporates certain details ('to prevent the stamp head from becoming broken . . . there is placed around it'. . .).

Alternative designs are evaluated and recommended ('Some divide the cam shaft with a compass into six sides, others nine; it is better for it to be divided into twelve . . .')[82] Finally the machine is put to work.

There follows the most important element in the discussion. Having constructed the machine, Agricola proceeds to deconstruct the tasks involved in working with it. Recognizing that the machine can only work within the context of organized labour, he analyses each of the peripheral tasks associated with tending the device, carefully indicating every act or movement of the labourers' bodies. Thus, one of the activities involved in working with the machine is to sieve the broken or crushed material that has been produced. In a modern instruction manual such as a cookery book, in which a similar operation was required, we might find the instruction 'separate the fine and coarse particles using a sieve', or more simply 'sieve the residue'. That would be enough, since it is assumed that most adults in our technological culture have been taught to use the simple but vital tool that is the sieve. Agricola, however, makes no such assumptions. Although the muscular action of sifting coarser particles from finer was a technique that must have been as old as agriculture itself, Agricola nevertheless shows how even this simple operation must be performed. He goes into immense detail concerning not only the movement of the worker's limbs, but also how the task may be performed using slightly different versions of the sieve. Each and every action is described over and over again:

> Some employ a sieve shaped like a wooden bucket . . . With an iron shovel the workman throws into this sieve broken rock, small stones, coarse and fine sand raked out of the dump; holding the handles of the sieve in his hands, he agitates it up and down in order that by this movement the dust, fine and coarse sand, small stones, and fine broken rock may fall through the bottom . . . Some use a sieve made of copper, having square copper handles on both sides, and through these handles runs a pole, of which one end projects three quarters of a foot beyond one handle; the workman then places that end in a rope which is suspended from a beam, and rapidly shakes the pole alternatively backwards and forwards. By this movement the small particles fall through the bottom of the sieve.[83]

The pedantically literal quality of the description is striking. No action is left to the imagination, but each is painstakingly described: 'throws into this sieve . . . holding the handles of the sieve in his hands, he agitates it up and down . . . places that end in a rope . . . rapidly shakes the pole alternatively

Figure 3.2 Georgius Agricola, *De Re Metallica libri xii: quibu officia, instrumenta, machinae, ac omnnia denique ad metalicam spectantia, non modo lucluentissime describuntur* (Basle, 1556), p. 225. Glasgow University Library, Special Collections.

backwards and forwards . . .' and so on. Here is what Foucault has described as the 'body–object articulation', whereby a new discipline is established that 'defines each of the relations that the body must have with the object that it manipulates'.[84] But added to the literal quality of Agricola's descriptions is the fact that the operation of the ore-crushing machine is accompanied by no fewer than six detailed (and hence costly) woodcut illustrations, three of which are devoted to the simple operation of using various forms of sieve (Figure 3.2). This level of detail helps to explain not only why, in its first Latin edition of 1556, *De Re Metallica* ran to some five hundred and forty folio pages, accompanied by a further eighty-six pages of preface, glossary, and index, but also why the work took over twenty years to produce.[85]

For Adam Smith and for Karl Marx, the division of labour preceded the idea of the machine. And this may indeed have been the case: the *Verlag* or 'co-ordination' system developed in medieval Nuremberg, and first mentioned in an ordinance of 1340, for example, was a means of subdividing production among groups of contractors, tasked with manufacturing small metal items such as knives and needles.[86] More akin to Smith's idea, however, is a medieval treatise on illumination that includes sixteen separate steps for painting a single acanthus leaf.[87] But, in the case of the work of the medieval illuminator, labour was understood as a series of consecutive tasks, rather than (as Adam Smith recognized) a series of tasks or movements that could be performed concurrently. *De Re Metallica*, predating Smith's analysis by over 200 years, recognizes this crucial difference. The sheer numbers of human figures in Agricola's illustrations suggest a variety of occupations. Specialists people Agricola's landscape: machine builders (using different simple tools), shovellers, sievers (five different methods of sieving are illustrated in the case of the ore crushing machine), wheelbarrow pushers, rakers, and so on. Each task is allotted its careful description, as though none were more or less important than the next. We also know that these are not representations of the same individual performing different tasks since Agricola's illustrators took considerable care to deploy artistic devices to suggest the individuality of the workers: their clothes are different, some are bearded, some clean shaven, some are old while others are young, and while men are in the majority, women also are shown in these scenes. The images, in other words, work synchronically as well as diachronically, showing some of the tasks that must be performed *at the same time* by different people, working to a pace which has become regulated by machinery.

More broadly, in artistic terms, we may think of this commitment to detailed observation of the quotidian as part of the emerging idea of 'naturalism' that would become a vital component in technical and scientific education. As Pamela H. Smith has argued:

> . . . in sixteenth-century German prints . . . images came to be understood as witnesses to facts. Images that increasingly invoked claims of factuality reinforced the techniques of observation and eyewitnesses as modes of acquiring knowledge.[88]

The desire to evoke 'factuality' is apparent, too, in the methods Agricola developed to depict both the naturalistic and symbolic qualities of the landscape in which his machines and labourers were situated. Agricola's world is also one in which human labour and mechanical devices have been yoked together within what is gradually emerging as an industrial landscape. Engine houses, sheds, discarded tools, piles of spoil, and general industrial clutter lying around are pictorial details to be found in the *De Re Metallica*, and these would later become stock elements in the depiction of the industrial landscapes of Northern Europe. The world depicted in *De Re Metallica* is fundamentally messy, which invests it, in turn, with an aura of modernity. At the same time, this landscape is still predominantly pastoral, or, more technically, sylvan. It is a pleasant, wooded, mountainous setting, in which the human world of towns and villages is glimpsed only in the distance, reflecting the actual geographic isolation of the mining districts of Bohemia, where Agricola lived and worked.[89]

But Agricola transforms this landscape by the intrusion of mysterious subterranean machines into the mountains' depths. At this point, his commitment to naturalism gives way to a more overtly symbolic register. Earth, or the mountainside, is cut away, or peeled back (again the similarity to the anatomical text books of the time might come to mind) to show startling images of a new, mechanical world, hidden from ordinary view. In one image, for example, a miner and his dog are shown strolling nonchalantly past a cut-away diagram of the surface gear of a pumping engine (Figure 3.3). But below them, buried beneath the earth, is a complex array of toothed wheels, drums, and chains, as though the earth itself had been transformed into the components of some vast pumping engine. This conceit, by which the machine is shown to inhabit both the surface and the depths of the world is, of course, an attempt at showing how the mining industry actually works. But the idea of buried or concealed machinery, suddenly exposed to human view through the device of treating the earth as a kind of organic skin covering that can be flayed back, is one which seems to have exercised a peculiar fascination for Agricola. In turn, it would be a technique that would become one of the most remarkable conventions of the machine books of the later sixteenth and seventeenth centuries. It is as if, in Agricola's imagination, machines are involved in a transaction between surface and depth. Mediating between the human world on the surface, and the metallic world beneath the ground, the earth is slowly transformed through the toil and skills of the miners into a series of gigantic hollow chambers or vaults, filled with machines and men. Many years later, in one of his sermons delivered in the early 1620s, the English poet and divine John Donne would imagine the human body as an impenetrable system of 'conduits and systems', where could be discovered 'furnaces of our spirits', as though the

Figure 3.3 Georgius Agricola, *De Re Metallica libri xii: quibu officia, instrumenta, machinae, ac omnnia denique ad metalicam spectantia, non modo lucluentissime describuntur* (Basle, 1556), p. 152. Glasgow University Library, Special Collections.

body was the setting for some arcane proto-industrial process.[90] In Agricola's images of the earth, hollowed and transformed by machines, that vision had already become a reality. But this, perhaps, is not surprising. Agricola had trained and worked as a physician, studying medicine at Venice, Bologna, and possibly Padua, the latter two places being centres of medical, and, more specifically, anatomical teaching in the first half of the sixteenth century.[91] He was also keenly interested in 'subterranean' things. From 1544 onwards, while he was busy gathering the materials for De Re Metallica, Agricola issued a series of works on geology, on subterranean waters, on mineralogy, and, most intriguingly, on animals which live underground – De Animantibus subterraneis (1548). In the remarkable production that was the De Re Metallica, the world of the organic body and the world of the inorganic machine collide with one another in the place which so clearly fascinated Agricola: the depths of the eviscerated earth.

In earlier-medieval and late-medieval depictions of human labour, particularly those to be found in richly illustrated devotional works, both the context in which the images of work appeared, and the subject matter of the books themselves emphasized the redemptive and punitive nature of human labour as well as the social order which underpinned every aspect of the labourer's life. Where a machine appears in such images, as Michael Camille has remarked in the case of a watermill in his analysis of the Luttrell Psalter (c. 1345), it is the absence of any human figures clustered around the machine that, to the modern eye, is remarkable. Instead the mill is 'an object of worth . . . the property of the lord who controlled this place for profit'.[92] Similarly, in the images of the most common machine to be found in the Psalter, the plough – 'the most important single piece of machinery in the feudal economy' – the message that is conveyed is socio-religious.[93] The ploughman, who could be a restlessly disturbing element in the social order, was also a reminder of the curse of labour, which was the punishment for Adam's and Eve's rebellion against God: 'In the sweat of thy face shalt thou eat bread' (Genesis 3. 19) as the biblical text had it. As Camille goes on to remark of another, later, depiction of human labour to be found in the fifteenth-century Les Très Riches Heures of the Duc de Berry, the labouring peasants in the fields 'are themselves reduced to schematic repetitive machines' working within a rigidly defined social and religious order.[94]

This socio-religious message, one which reminds the onlooker of social hierarchy while it also works to emphasize the divine order of that hierarchy, is entirely absent from the depictions of men and machines in the De Re Metallica. Rather, an infectious mechanical optimism inhabits the pages

of Agricola's text. There is nothing in the least machine-like in the depictions of the human figures labouring above and beneath the earth's surface.
Instead, miners and machines are shown to be working in intelligent, close-
knit, sociable, harmony with one another. Equally, there is no recognizable
sense of rank or hierarchy in these images. Agricola was a shareholder
in a mine known as the 'God's Gift' mine at Albertham, and he admired
the technological and practical skills required of the miner, as opposed
to the gold-hungry avariciousness of the mere 'digger'.[95] For the miner's
toil was, in Agricola's view, a foundational art of human civilization, the
means by which not only useful objects could be created out of metals, but
also objects of enduring beauty. Mining, which had long been associated
with the labour of slaves, was, rather, a calling of dignity. It was 'honour-
able employment for respectable people'.[96] In this respect, Renaissance
mechanical labour was entirely different from that transformation of labour
that Marx was to identify in the nineteenth-century factory system. Rather
than the despairing *ennui* and alienation which Marx saw as the hallmark of
mechanical labour in the factories and mills of the industrial revolution, the
Renaissance mechanical revolution as Agricola depicted it envisaged human
labour as communal, sociable, intelligent, and dignified.

The syntax of the machine

In the case of Leonardo, it has often been remarked that his designs were
'technological dreams . . . that led him to materialize in his imagination
and on paper, designs beyond the engineering possibilities of the time'.[97]
The possibility of fashioning wrought objects of great worth also endowed
Renaissance machines with a certain fantasy element. In his *Della tranquil-
litià dell' animo* ('On the Tranquillity of the Soul') composed around 1441,
Leon Alberti recounts the story of a statesman who, unable to sleep at night,
soothes his mind with mechanical fantasies:

> I am accustomed, most of all at night, when the agitation of my soul fills
> me with cares, and I seek relief from these bitter worries and sad thoughts,
> to think about and construct in my mind some unheard-of machine to
> move and carry weights, making it possible to create great and wonder-
> ful things.[98]

Such an imaginary machine was a form of solace, in much the same way
that Montaigne, a century later, understood machines as expressing control

and stability in a world that appeared to be unstable and disturbingly unpredictable. The machine might be imagined as a regularizing force, echoing the traditional Aristotelian view that machines are a means of rearranging nature to conform to human design.[99]

Such a response to machinery was a mirror of a much broader, and growing, Renaissance interest in the machine not just for what it does, but, rather, for what it might do. Renaissance machinery had come to inhabit fantasy as much as reality. The machine, with its tireless, obedient, repetitive concentration on a single task, was a glimpse, paradoxically, of a more idealized world. For Renaissance engineers were not responding to modern design criteria. Questions such as 'Will it work?' and 'Will it perform to its design specification?' and even 'Is it efficient?' were not the first, or even the last questions that they asked of their designs. Rather, as Kenneth Knoespel has explained, the Renaissance machine existed within the same intellectual framework as (say) an emblem book, with the onlooker being asked to 'puzzle out hidden mechanical relations' in the same way that a book such as Alciati's *Emblemata* (1531) 'requires the reader to puzzle out hidden morals'.[100] Complexity of design, rather than simplicity, was to be welcomed: 'encumbered by complex linkages and redundant – sometimes self-defeating – gear trains . . . it was not until the eighteenth century that the advantages of simplifying rather than complicating a machine began to be understood'.[101] Machines were *designed* to appear complex, since complexity was, in part, what helped to define a machine. Jessica Wolfe has shrewdly summarized the conceptual paradoxes that surrounded Renaissance machinery:

> Renaissance machines are only secondarily regarded as objects with specific functions and aims. Machines are means not ends . . . The most ineffectual or impractical machines are often more compelling to Renaissance culture than machines that 'work' in the modern sense of the term. Frequently regarded as unpredictable or mendacious, Renaissance machines do some of their finest work when they fail to work . . .[102]

Existing as a mental as a well as a physical construction, machines were to become the object of study not just of designers and engineers, but also of scholars and noblemen.[103] In the works of Jacques Besson, Jean Errard, Agostino Ramelli, Fausto Veranzio, Vittorio Zonca, Giovanni Branca, Georg Boeckler and their rivals and imitators, a new world of mechanical devices was displayed in printed form.[104] These 'theatres' of machines, as they were often entitled, should be understood as luxurious and collectable volumes

Figure 3.4 Georg Andreas Boeckler, *Theatrum Machinarum Novum* (Nuremberg, 1662), title page, Glasgow University Library, Special Collections.

(Figure 3.4).[105] Beautiful, costly, and sumptuous, in these works machines were disassembled, labelled, categorized, and explored. They were dedicated to noble patrons as advertisements for the mechanical ingenuity of their authors. Often plundering their designs from one another, within their pages the machine book authors laid out, in illustrative detail, the wonderful variety of mechanical creations which could be imagined (if not actually constructed) by the new generation of late sixteenth- and earlier seventeenth-century engineers.

Elizabeth Eisenstein has described the effect of the illustrations to be found in the machine books:

> In the hands of skilful artists, the somewhat prosaic functions of levers, pulleys, gears and screws were dramatized; engineering feats were illustrated in the same heroic vein as epic poems ... Presented by artful engravers as three-dimensional objects on two-dimensional planes, even the grimmest mining machinery acquired a certain dignity and aesthetic appeal.[106]

These works were, quite obviously, the products of skilful engineers. And yet, to speak of the authors of the machine books as though they were the equivalent to the work of modern engineers is misleading. The term 'engineer' existed in the sixteenth century in a different and rather richer sense than it does today. When, in Shakespeare's *Hamlet* (1603), the prince undertakes to eliminate the untrustworthy courtiers Rosencrantz and Guildenstern, he deploys a cunning and artful 'device' or plot, which is conceived of in terms of the devious skills of the military engineer. Unknowingly, the courtiers are carrying letters that will condemn them to death. Hamlet reflects on his own calculations:

> ... Let it work;
> For 'tis the sport to have the engineer
> Hoist with his own petard: and 't shall go hard
> But I will delve one yard below their mines,
> And blow them at the moon.

(III. iv. 189–93)

Hamlet's 'machinations' (again, a term which links machinery with deviousness or mental agility) suggest how the term 'engineer' is cognate with the word 'ingenious', and this, in the older sense, was indeed what the skills of the *ingenarius* or engineer represented. A fashioner of *ingenia*, his inventions were as much intellectual as practical schemes. The cogitating engineer was a creator of cunning devices, deploying wheels, springs, and balances.[107] As Otto Mayr points out, in trying to answer that vexing question, 'what is a machine', ingeniousness lay at the heart of the undertaking:

> The importance of ingenuity as an essential characteristic of the concept is highlighted by the ancient double meaning of the Greek and Latin words for machine, mechanism, engine, engineer, and their counterparts in modern languages: in addition to their customary technical meaning they often have the figurative connotation of ingenious artifice, clever trick, deception, a fact neatly illustrated by the word 'machination'.[108]

At their best, the devices of the engineer had a kind of terrible wit about them, as Hamlet, a true 'engineer' of the fate of his former schoolfellows, recognizes in confecting a plot which will 'delve one yard below their mines' to 'blow them at the moon' in a kind of mental counter-mine, indebted to the tactic used in sieges in the period. So, what has been termed the 'mechanical vocabulary' of Renaissance culture, embracing terms such as engine, device, motion, invention, and instrument, belonged to a 'semantic network' that might include 'any witty device from an emblem or epigram to a morsel of political advice'.[109] An 'instrument', for example, might take the form of a deed, a letter, an executive warrant, or a royal charter, as much as it might betoken an artificial mechanical device acting upon the natural world in some way. 'I kiss the instrument of their pleasures' says Othello, in courtly mode, when handed a letter from the Venetian senate (*Othello*, IV. i. 216), while in *Twelfth Night*, it is the 'instrument' of the disguised Viola which 'screws' Orsino from what he believes to be his 'true place' in Olivia's favour (*Twelfth Night*, V. i. 121).

For all that they might have been associated with wit, cunning, or mental ingenuity, the 'mechanical arts' in the sixteenth century out of which emerged real machines and devices were also understood as a sub-branch of the study of mathematics, and were thus held to comprise the socially inferior though 'useful' crafts, as opposed to the socially exclusive demesne of the 'liberal' arts.[110] Given this social hierarchy of knowledge, we can understand the machine books of the sixteenth and seventeenth centuries as part of a wider attempt in Europe to reorder the intellectual disciplines in a movement that would culminate, in the seventeenth century, with the triumph of the 'mechanical philosophy'. The machine book authors sought to promote their 'art' as an ancient and dignified discipline, underpinned by the classical tradition of engineering to be found in the writings of Vitruvius, rather than as the product of routine, unthinking, physical activity.

Engineering, moreover, did not, as yet, exist as a distinctive discipline, but was related to military science in the period; Shakespeare, for example, tends to use the terms 'pioneer' and 'engineer' interchangeably. In Henry V (1600), the professional soldiers Fluellen and Macmorris are presented as comically pedantic mining engineers who had studied their Latin texts of war and engineering – 'the Roman disciplines' (III. iii. 18) as Fluellen ponderously terms them – with care and attention. Military service, as we might expect, was often an important factor in the intellectual formation of the machine book authors. Nothing quite loosened the purse strings of the Renaissance prince or governor so much as the prospect of encouraging some new, and wonderful, technological invention which might be deployed, or might be threatened to be deployed, against one's enemies.[111] This reflection helps explain the ubiquitous presence of fantastic siege engines of various kinds in these texts, as though the engineer-authors were reminding their classically trained noble readership of the great military undertakings of antiquity.

Who were these engineer-authors? Ramelli, a Catholic soldier and military engineer, was certainly present at the siege of La Rochelle, one of the centres of French Protestantism, in 1572.[112] Besson's military credentials are less clear, though he was to be affected by the catastrophic French wars of religion of the late sixteenth century. He has been described as 'successor to Leonardo as engineer to the French court', which is most unlikely, given that he does not surface until he is heard of working in Paris in the 1550s, many years after Leonardo's death in 1519.[113] A citizen of Geneva and a protestant, Besson seems to have lived a cosmopolitan intellectual existence, designing water engines in Lausanne (1557) and then working in Rouen (1563), Paris (1565), and Orléans (1567) before eventually fleeing France and its religious wars and dying, 'unknown to the world', in London in 1573.[114] Jean Errard also pursued a military career, studying the art of fortification in Italy, and then working as engineer to the King of France in the 1580s. Under Henri IV he was made *premier ingenieux*, taking part in the sieges of Chartres (1591) and Dreux (1592).[115] More unlikely was the career of the cleric Veranzio (or Verantius, also known as Vrančić), Bishop of Csanàd in Hungary, who only became interested in machines, around 1608, in retirement.[116] Vittorio Zonca, on the other hand, whose posthumous work on machines has been described as 'the closest to the actual mechanical practice of the time', seems to have had a more conventional career; he is described as the 'architetto' (architect or designer) to the city of Padua in the early seventeenth century.[117]

The costly folios that these authors produced acted not only as advertisements for their skills, but also as a kind of certification by which, in the absence of any stable system of patents, they laid claim to the intellectual ownership of particular machines or devices. A system of patents, indeed the very concept of intellectual property rights, was still in its infancy in the sixteenth century. On the Continent, such a system was evolving: the first recorded design patent or 'privilege' had been awarded to Brunelleschi at Florence in 1421, while the first patent law had been promulgated in Venice in 1474.[118] But in England the patent system was no more than a means of raising money for favoured courtiers, which actively hampered any idea of invention or innovation in the modern sense.[119] Theft of one's ideas was an ever-present anxiety, and the machine book was a partial solution. Claiming the protection of a powerful dedicatee, investment in the machine book promised a twofold return: first in the price paid by the bookseller for the work itself, and second (and more importantly), in the hope that it might precipitate future commissions from other patrons who had read the book.

The mechanical world of Agostino Ramelli

The most luxurious machine book of the age was Ramelli's Le Diverse et Artificiose Machine ('Diverse and Artificial Machines'), which was published in Paris, in a dual French and Italian edition in 1588, and dedicated to Henri III of France. In his address 'To Kindly Readers', which prefaced Le Diverse et Artificiose Machine, Ramelli complained of how a rival had 'furtively robbed me of my special drawings . . .[and] after adding or subtracting some useless details devised by their foolish caprice, confusing them here and distorting them there to cover the theft, they printed them thus mutilated as their own'.[120] As well as underlining the problem of intellectual theft, Ramelli's comment on the adaptation of his designs through 'adding or subtracting some useless details' is significant in helping us to understand the ways in which mechanical culture was evolving. Ramelli's anger was directed at those who had abridged, or distorted, or supplemented his text of machinery, or who had treated it as if it were, indeed, a literary text, capable of embellishment or ornament in the hands of the imitator. Today, no engineer would aim to design a machine or mechanical system in which certain details of the design were acknowledged to be 'useless'. But Renaissance machine books had affinities with literary texts rather than modern engineering manuals. Just as the ability to invest a text with rhetorical devices inherited from the classical past was held to embellish a poem or a piece of prose, so a machine in its illustrated abstract form was rooted in the classical past, and ornamented with often very slight mechanical variation.

Equally, a certain degree of secrecy, of deliberate obscurantism, was at work in the production of the Renaissance machine book. Engineer inventors such as Ramelli were intent on displaying their mechanical prowess, while they may also, paradoxically, have been concerned to conceal vital elements of their different designs from rival engineer-inventors. Hopeful of being granted a royal 'privilege' or, perhaps better still, a commission, the machine-book author sought to parade his designs in front of an influential readership, while concealing what has been termed 'the rational core' of his mechanical designs with Mannerist embellishment.[121] The machine books thus functioned in a contradictory fashion, in ways that might remind us of Renaissance writers' more general love of concealment, hidden revelation, and secrecy. As an eighteenth-century commentator on the machine book authors of the sixteenth century wrote, it was as if Ramelli and his contemporaries had designed mechanisms 'in such a misshapen way as if they wished to show experts that they knew very well about such secrets but hid them so that others . . . should not be able to copy them'.[122]

In his dedicatory epistle to 'the most Christian King', Ramelli characterized his undertaking as 'mathematical or, as they are called, mechanical demonstrations'.[123] Ramelli's images are not so much engineering drawings, but, rather, 'technical illustrations'. That is, they cannot be compared to the typology of engineering illustration which has emerged in the modern age, and which might include designer's drawings (rough sketches), project drawings (small scale outline proposals), production drawings (which cover each detail of the particular product being manufactured) and presentation and maintenance drawings (produced at the end of the production process).[124] Instead, they combine sometimes all of these elements in a single illustration to produce what Joel Mokyr has described as 'idealized concepts' rather than 'real machines'.[125]

Despite Ramelli's claims that his work represented 'mathematical demonstrations', a 'science' of mechanics, by which the action of materials under stress could be analysed mathematically, did not (yet) exist. Hence, Renaissance machinery was often hugely 'over-engineered', as we would now say. But other elements were in play, too. Rather than 'form following function' as the dictum of modernist design has proclaimed, form was just as important as functionality. For it was in the form of the machine that the maker's individuality was expressed, or to use Montaigne's word 'stamped'. The designers of machines were responding to aesthetic and even literary conventions, similar to the conventions of Mannerism.[126] In keeping, too, with the prevailing aesthetic of the period, a machine that 'looked' antique (no matter how innovative it might have been) was held to lend a suitable aura of classical *gravitas* to the overall design. The 'best' machines tended to look as though they might have been deployed in some gigantic ancient engineering project or (better still) heroic military undertaking. Devices that might have been used in 'the pristine wars of the Romans', to recall the words of Shakespeare's Fluellen in *Henry V*, were the mark to be aimed at. Just as the epic poem, considered as an imitation of classical forms, or as a means of summoning up a heroic classical past into the present, was held to be the most dignified form of poetic utterance, so Renaissance engineers aspired to create machines that might have sprung from the pages of Vitruvius or the mind of Archimedes, rather than from the brain of the engineer himself. Imitation of antiquity was the goal in Renaissance engineering as much as it was in Renaissance poetry.[127] The ideal of creating an object that self-consciously looks 'new' and which is such a feature of our own technological culture, did not form part of the Renaissance engineer's catalogue of aspirations.

The second remarkable element in the appearance of these devices was the repetitive nature of the designs. Machine book authors understood their mechanisms as cumulative rather than as fixed to particular tasks. Today, we might consult an equivalent work, such as an engineering manual or a cookery book, to try and understand how a particular task, whether changing an oil filter or baking a particular kind of cake, might best be accomplished. We are not concerned, in other words, with all the other possible tasks contained within the pages of the manual or recipe book at the moment in which we turn to it. That is not, however, how the Renaissance machine book authors approached their subject. Rather, it was the machine as object, rather than the task for which it was designed, which claimed their attention. Equally, they were keen to instil in the reader a sense of machines as sequential devices, with each design building on the mechanical insights offered by its predecessor, often through exhibiting very small variations in the design which could have offered little or no mechanical advantage to what had gone before.

Today, the idea of a sequence — a succession of events — is fundamental to both narratives, particularly of the realist kind, and to mechanisms, both of which can be held to operate through 'sequential' motion. Yet, as any modern reader of Edmund Spenser's *The Faerie Queene* (1596), let alone Sir Philip Sidney's *The Countess of Pembrokes Arcadia* (1590), soon discovers, in order to engage with these vast works we have to abandon our conventional ideas of linear narrative sequence. Rather, as a modern editor of the *Arcadia* reminds us, 'the huge structure is kept under control by the establishment of narrative patterns, and echoes based on parallel or contrasting *sequences of action* which form a commentary on each other' (my emphasis).[128] The OED reminds us, too, that the term 'sequence' meant something rather different in the early-modern period from what it does today. 'Sequence' was a term which was never used either by sonnet writers or engineers to describe their works. Rather, the term was originally derived from the Latin word *sequentia*, denoting the long succession of notes sung on the final syllable of the *Alleluia* in ecclesiastical music. The *sequentia* thus signalled the *end* of a performance, rather than its continuation. Only in the late sixteenth century, around the time that machine books were appearing, did it come to possess its modern meaning of a succession of events or things, existing in a causative and temporal relationship to one another.

Sequence, in this new, modern sense, was, however, vital to the machine designs of Ramelli and his contemporaries. In fact, the very idea of 'sequentiality', the ordered arrangement of components through space and time, rests upon a fundamentally mechanical view of things. It is this, an essentially aesthetic quality, which helps us to understand the evident delight with which a designer such as Ramelli paraded his machines in front of the reader. Often, the explanatory text in Ramelli's work drew attention to the similarity of his designs, while stressing the overall sequentiality of the work. This habit of mind is, of courser, alien to the modern designer or 'inventor', anxious to demonstrate their mastery of mechanical difference, and their commitment to innovation and novelty. But for Ramelli and his contemporaries similarity was a praiseworthy quality: 'In the same way as with the preceding machine . . .' or 'Another kind of machine which similarly . . .' are phrases which pepper Ramelli's text, as are words such as 'likewise' and 'the same principle' and 'the same arrangement'.[129] 'The mechanism of the present machine is not very different from the preceding one', he says of a pumping engine (Figure 3.5) or, introducing a complex arrangement of Archimedean screws: 'the construction of this machine . . . is no different from the preceding one' (Figure 3.6).[130] Similarity was positive, even reassuring. Only very rarely does Ramelli stress the novelty of his designs, as in the case of a water-raising device.[131]

Figure 3.5 Agostino Ramelli, *Le diverse et artificiose machine del Capitano Agostino Ramelli*... (Paris, 1588), plate 27. Glasgow University Library, Special Collections.

Figure 3.6 Agostino Ramelli, *Le diverse et artificiose machine del Capitano Agostino Ramelli . . .* (Paris, 1588), plate 46, Glasgow University Library, Special Collections.

That Ramelli's machines were designed to be read, as much as used as design models was indicated in his dedicatory epistle to the King of France:

> I now present them [the machines] to you as a small offering . . . In addition to bringing you pleasure and not a little satisfaction, when somewhat removed from your kingly duties to take delight in reading and on occasion in putting them into operation . . .[132]

Clearly, though Ramelli hoped that some of his designs might actually be transformed into reality, and while we can read these self-deprecating phrases as a form of graceful self-commendation of the author's talents to the king, it is also clear that Ramelli saw his work, like a literary text, as designed to give 'pleasure' and 'satisfaction' to his reader. Moreover, Ramelli saw his task as providing both a universal 'grammar' of machinery, and a historical encyclopaedia of mechanism, in that it explored:

> . . . all the principles of the many machines and instruments which up to now have been constructed or are yet to be built in the future . . . by means of which stupendous operations and marvellous effects equal to the great miracles of nature have been produced in the world.[133]

Ramelli's designs thus stretched from the distant past into an imagined future, in which 'nature' would be equalled (if not surpassed) by the intricate devices that he had recorded on paper. In using the term 'grammar' I have in mind, too, the ways in which later, seventeenth-century, machine designers began to think of their designs in terms of a universal alphabet. Thus, the seventeenth-century Swedish engineer Christopher Polhem saw the five 'simple machines' identified by Heron of Alexandria (the lever, the wheel and axle, the pulley, the wedge, and the screw) as the 'vowels' of the machine, while other elements formed the 'consonants' out of which might be constructed entire mechanisms, just as one might construct text in the world of discourse.[134]

The body of the machine

If the machine book could be thought of as embodying principles analogous to grammar or literary forms in its design, then it was also a manifestation of an entirely different field of knowledge, that of anatomy. Like the anatomical textbooks that were appearing in the same period, and often emanating from the same intellectual centres – Padua, Paris, Rome – the machine books announced themselves as 'theatres' of machinery.[135] As we have already seen in the case of Domenico Fontana's gigantic machine set in motion in sixteenth-century Rome, theatrical spectacle, the sense of an audience watching the interplay of men and mechanisms, was to prove an important element in the 'staging' of Renaissance engineering. Equally, the theatres of anatomy, in the sixteenth and seventeenth centuries were the stage sets within which the human body was broken down, before an admiring audience, into its constituent components.[136] In a similar fashion, within the 'theatres' of machinery, mechanisms were disassembled, to show the reader how these devices were constructed. Inanimate engineering was embodied through the skilful use of perspective and shading, an illustrative device which (again) might remind us of the work of Vesalius and his imitators as they sought to invest the fragmented body with the depth of three-dimensional form.[137] Mechanical devices were shown, in situ, moving and working, just as the human 'machine' was displayed in the anatomical texts as a living (though dissected) entity. The new Vesalian, anatomical texts offered a vista of the human interior as a world of process, and so, in the case of machines, their mysterious mechanical interiors were dissected, enumerated, categorized, and opened to the public gaze. Elizabeth Eisenstein has speculated that 'the same visual devices to delineate machine parts and human organs – both hidden from readers before – may have encouraged new analogies between pump and heart or between mechanical piping and plumbing and human venous and arterial systems'.[138] Her speculations (which she acknowledges to be 'difficult to substantiate') are given added weight, I think, when we read of Ramelli describing his images as 'engraved on copper, like living figures'.[139] In that phrase, Ramelli was reminding his reader that his machines represented the abstract principles of mathematics transformed into embodied entities, 'palpable things', capable of producing 'astonishing effects'.[140] But Ramelli was also drawing upon a more ancient tradition (and one that seems to have informed Leonardo's thoughts on the matter) in which machines and the organic body were held to be analogous or even equivalent to one another. 'All engines may be looked upon to be a sort of Animals, with prodigious strong hands' observed Leon Alberti in his De re aedificatoria (1485), concluding that 'they move Weights just in the same Manner as we Men do with our Arms'.[141] The body, indeed, provided the archetype of the machine: 'the same Distention and Contraction of the Members and Nerves, which we use in pulling, thrusting or lifting, we are to imitate in our Engines', Alberti wrote.[142]

But this process was reversible. If the machine was held to be analogous to the body, as Alberti had suggested, then in working with a machine, the labourer's body now had to be brought into conformity with mechanism: a phenomenon which Michel Foucault attributes to eighteenth-century institutions and practices. If, too, in the printing shop, workers and writers had to learn to labour to a new rhythm, then the machine books of the sixteenth century set out to reinforce this lesson through the device of showing bodies (animal, but more often human) labouring at or even within the machines which were being constructed. This element in mechanical culture was represented in the machine books through the common device of showing the human body and the machine working together, a device that we have seen Agricola developing. This device can be traced back to an older artistic convention in which the exaggerated musculature and heroic poses of the machine workers were related to the depiction of the saints and heroes to be found in paintings, or on the ceilings of Renaissance churches and palaces.[143] It is also, of course, a device that was to be abandoned in representations of machinery in the late eighteenth and nineteenth centuries, as engineering drawing shifted from devoting attention to working with machines, to focus on the machine itself. For, as Marx came to recognize, it was the machine rather than the operative that would become the core of inventive attention.

In these earlier images there is, of course, no hint of that 'alienation' of labour that Marx, later, would identify in industrial mechanization. Although, in a work such as Ramelli's, machines are occasionally shown without any human presence, the more usual convention was to represent the machine in operation, with a human figure straining at a capstan bar, revolving a crank handle, or hauling on a block and pulley system. This was not merely a handy expedient by which the scale of the mechanism could be conveyed to the reader (and Renaissance machines, at least in their abstract form, tended towards a certain gigantism); it was also a lesson in how to work with machines. More than this, the juxtaposition of the human body with the machine served to emphasize the enormous theoretical power which the machine was capable of applying, visually reinforcing the oft-repeated claim in the text: 'by means of which one person alone will . . .' or 'with this next kind of machine one man alone can easily . . .'[144] These repeated comments are not, as we would now understand them, simply advertisements for the (usually non-existent) efficiency of the mechanism. Rather, the phrase indicated a very different attitude towards the relationship between the machine's operation and its power source. A phrase such as 'with the help of one man alone', which is a characteristic verbal formula in so many of Ramelli's textual comments on his drawings, suggests that the machine is not so much drawing upon human energy, as being assisted by it. The machine thus possesses a vestigial motive power of its own. In fact, so complex were the mechanical components that Ramelli and his fellow authors assembled, that many of them would have been all but impossible to operate, given the immense friction within the system, and the inertia that would need to be overcome by the operator.

The novelty of mechanical culture is underlined by the closing comments of Cyprian Lucar's book on estate management, *Lucarsolace* (1590), and one of the earliest 'How to' manuals to appear in print. By drawing on the many different kinds of mechanical examples contained in his text, Lucar argued, it would become possible to devise new machines, 'strange engines and instruments, not only for private pleasure, but also for sundrie purposes in the commonwealth . . .'[145] What those purposes might have been was, however, still obscure. But that machines might be designed for 'pleasure' as much as for 'sundrie purposes' is significant. Although Vitruvius had claimed that the noblest engines 'accomplish their purpose at the intelligent touch of a single workmen', and this was an ideal to which the machine authors constantly aspired, purposefulness was not the only end of Renaissance technology. Indeed, play and fantasy, as the machine books illustrate, have perhaps been far greater elements in the evolution of different forms of technology than is suggested by that popular (but wrong-headed) belief that 'necessity is the mother of invention'.[146]

Textual engines

Machine books have long been valued by historians of technology as sources of information as to when specific mechanisms or devices such as a particular gearing arrangement, for example, came into use. In some measure, too, they have been understood as heralds of the coming industrial revolution.[147] But for all that the pages of the works of Zonca, Ramelli, Strada, and Branca are crowded with workable devices, or devices that look as though they might work, many of their designs were purely fanciful. Ramelli's famous book wheel, for example, has, in recent years, attracted considerable amounts of comment, in part because it seems to foreshadow (at least conceptually) our own age of mass data storage and retrieval (Figure 3.7).[148] In part, too, it answers to the scholar's dream of the machine that will read, digest, and process vast amounts of text on his or her behalf, saving them the labour of actually reading what has been written. Equipped with such a

Figure 3.7 Agostino Ramelli, *Le diverse et artificiose machine del Capitano Agostino Ramelli . . .* (Paris, 1588), plate 188, Glasgow University Library, Special Collections.

device, wrote Ramelli, 'a man can see and turn through a large number of books without moving'.[149] Such devices, though of a rather simpler design, were certainly in use in Italy in the early sixteenth century when a wood-cut illustration, the frontispiece to an astrological work published in 1514, shows a vertical revolving bookcase in use.[150] In a creaking mechanical form, here were the distant ancestors of our own age of instantaneous data retrieval and storage. Ramelli's device promised the possibility of intellectual work without toil, circulating texts mechanically before the reader's eyes, albeit in a severely truncated form when compared with the millions of pages of text now made available by the networked computer.[151]

Circularity was a feature of the book wheel that mirrored the circulation of texts, documents, and ideas through communities of readers that had taken place many centuries before the advent of print. The book wheel thus represented, in abstract form, the art of writing itself, which was yet another manifestation of *Technē*. For writing was an 'invention' which fallen humanity had developed in the absence of the more insensible forms of communication available to God and the angels. As John Wilkins observed in his work on encryption and the art of 'secret writing' published in 1641: 'men ... that have *Organicall bodies*, cannot communicate their thoughts, so easy and immediate a way ... therefore have need of some corporeal instruments, both for the *receiving* and *conveying* of knowledge'. Language, just like a machine, was thus conceived as an 'instrument' devised as partial recompense for the disaster of Eden, even if its imperfect operation was made yet more imperfect by the secondary disaster of Babel.[152] Although Francis Bacon, in *The Advancement of Learning* (1605), would only grudgingly admit speech as an invention, for Ben Jonson speech was, unequivocally, 'the instrument of society'.[153] According to Thomas Hobbes in *Leviathan* (1651), writing, too, was to be considered as an 'invention' based on speech, which far outshone the later invention of printing.[154] And speech, too, could be considered an 'invention' without which, Hobbes wrote, civility was impossible: in the absence of speech 'there had been amongst men neither common-wealth, nor Society, nor Contract, nor peace, no more than amongst Lyons, Bears, and Wolves'.[155] Historians of technology and human evolution tend to agree with Wilkins and Hobbes, citing speech and writing as the first two stages of the technology of recording 'correlative' to the tool, which would lead, in the course of time to the Bronze, Iron, and Machine ages.[156] Writing is thus an 'extra-somatic information store', a prosthetic memory tool which works as an 'artificial substitute for a function that was previously performed in the body ... by the chromosomes of the germ cells'.[157]

But with the advent of print, this tool, for some, had begun to appear clumsy and even unwieldy. A more efficient mechanism was needed. For Erasmus, writing one hundred years before Hobbes, at the beginning of the print age, the work of the scholar, immersed in written documents and records, had become a mechanically circular task. It was a labour not of love, but bondage. Commenting on his self-imposed labour of collecting and publishing the thousands of proverbs from ancient texts that would become his *Adagorum Collectanea* (1500), a text which would itself expand with each edition (and there would be no fewer than twenty-seven editions in his lifetime), Erasmus began to see his undertaking as a mental mechanical punishment, a never-ending task of textual consumption and production. Leafing through the thousands of pages of the works of 'so many Poets, Grammarians, Orators, Dialecticians, Sophists, Historians, Mathematicians, Philosophers, Theologians', Erasmus wrote, 'you are fettered to the treadmill, you cannot budge an inch, as they say from your texts'.[158] Looking at the book wheel through the eyes of Erasmus, we can begin to see its seductive hold on the imagination. Just as nineteenth-century machine operatives would have to learn to accommodate their physical and intellectual capacities to the machines they now served, Erasmus had begun to sense that he was no longer the author of his own labours. Instead, he was being transformed into a component of a larger mechanical system, robbed of autonomy, Yet, if, as Ramelli claimed, with the force of great engines (treadmills being a particular favourite) it was possible 'for one man alone' to accomplish such Herculean tasks, then why should it not be possible to apply mechanical labour, in principle, to solitary mental activity?

Erasmus's complaint was aimed at the world of manuscripts, a world which ravaged the scholar labouring in the archive, even as the texts themselves seemed to crumble before his failing eyesight: 'you waste your eyesight on decaying volumes covered with mould, torn and mangled, eaten into everywhere by worms and beetles, and often mostly illegible'.[159] But how much more extreme would this multiplicity of textuality appear with the advent of print? Hence the book wheel, a device which seemed to consume (though not yet produce) texts mechanically. But perhaps even textual production, the act of writing itself, might be assisted in some mechanical fashion? In his essay 'A Consideration upon Cicero', Montaigne, having first commended the Italian mastery of print, went on to comment on how producing handwritten letters was a perpetual labour to him, since so much of the substance of the official letters he was constrained to write was simply formulaic: 'I would gladly give someone else the charge of adding those long harangues, offers, and prayers that we place at the end, and I wish that some new custom would relieve us of it', he wrote.[160]

What Montaigne was in need of, had he but known it, was a word-processing program, or at least that indispensable instrument of the modern office or academy, the Xerox machine. In 1647, in England, the first step towards such a device was announced by Sir William Petty who claimed to have invented:

> ... an Instrument of small Bulke and price, easily made, and very dura-ble, whereby any Man, even at the first sight and handling, may write two resembling Copies of the same thing at once, as serviceably and as fast (allowing two lines upon each page for setting the Instruments) as by the ordinary way.[161]

This device, whatever it may have been, was not merely an answer to Montaigne's worries over the endless production of circumlocutory documents, with their formulaic opening and closing phrases. Rather, it was a fore-taste of the later instruments and machines which would seek to mechanize nature, or at least the perception of nature, by sifting truth from falsehood, the authentic from the inauthentic. For with the help of his 'instrument', Petty suggested that not only lawyers, scriveners, merchants, 'intelligencers' (journalists), secretaries, and clerks would be able to duplicate their documents and records, but it would help scholars in their Erasmian labour of:

> ... transcribing of rare Manuscripts, and preserving Originals from falsifi-cation, and other injuries of time. It lesseneth the Labour of Examination, serveth to discover forgeries and surreptitious Copies, and to the trans-acting of all businesses of writing, as with ease and speed, so with much privacy also.[162]

However fanciful Petty's 'instrument' may have been, he had realized that one advantage of the machine over the human copyist was that it would tell no tales. The scribal transcription of private documents was an endless source of anxiety to those who, in the early-modern world, had reasons to keep their correspondence secret. Scriveners and personal 'secretaries' entrusted with copying or duplicating documents were individuals of immense power since they had access to the private thoughts of their employers, which they transcribed in written form.[163] Petty's 'instrument' was thus conceived of not merely as a 'useful' device in the execution of the law, trade, or commerce. Rather, it was imagined as a form of mechanical memory device, able to keep secrets in a way that no mere human toiler could be trusted.

At the very end of the seventeenth century, rumours of yet another miraculous writing device began to circulate, in the form of the 'writing engine' described in an anonymous pamphlet, published in Edinburgh in 1695. The 'writing engine', so it was promised, was capable of producing instantaneous copy. Using it, the operator could produce text 'ready and done before a man can set the Tipes, yea, its thought before some of them can correct what they have set, & the Engine is much cheaper: so the Engine is an excellent *Medium*, betwixt printing and the common way of writing'.[164] The typewriter would, in reality, have to wait until Remington's 'typing machines' began to appear in American offices in the early 1870s.[165] And yet print had made the problems faced by Erasmus and later Montaigne every bit as difficult as those that we face in the modern age. The creative energy released through print would involve, it seemed, a perpetual production, distribution, and consumption of texts and ideas by authors, printers, booksellers, and readers. Ramelli's iconic machine, the book wheel, irrespective of whether or not it actually worked, can thus be thought of as an attempt, no matter how crude, of regularizing or controlling the never-ending outpouring of texts from the mechanical presses. Just like a water wheel (to which in any case, the device was mechanically related), the book wheel was symbolically powered by the seemingly inexhaustible flow of printed matter, which it sought to regularize and channel. This world was, indeed, a *perpetuum mobile* of the mind, a never-ending conversion of intellectual energy into textual production. As such, the book wheel may also stand as a symbol for the one device that Renaissance engineers laboured, incessantly, to create: the machine that would represent the summit of mechanical culture, the *perpetuum mobile* itself, a machine that would never stop.

Perpetual motions

The perpetual motion machine has a long though not very distinguished history. Writing in 1931, Oswald Spengler saw in the idea of perpetual motion the 'secret ideal' of all mechanical culture, or *technics*. Spengler cited a thirteenth-century source (Petrus Peregrinus) as the archetype of the 'monk [who] busied himself in his cell with the idea of *Perpetual Motion*'.[166] Perpetual motion, wrote Spengler, represented an idea that:

. . . never thereafter let go its hold on us, for success would mean the final victory over 'God' or 'Nature' (*Deus sive Natura*), a small world of one's own creation moving like the great world, in virtue of its own forces and obeying the hand of man alone. To build a world oneself, to be oneself God – that is the Faustian Inventor's dream, and from it has sprung all our designing and re-designing of machines to approximate as nearly as possible to the unattainable limit of perpetual motion.[167]

That perpetual motion was, indeed, an 'unattainable limit' was recognized in the late fifteenth century by Leonardo: 'O speculators on perpetual motion, how many vain designs you have created in the like quest! Go and join up with the seekers after gold!'[168] In consigning the seekers after perpetual motion to the tribe of the alchemists and speculators, Leonardo had unwittingly anticipated, by four hundred years, the views of the US Patent Office, in the early years of the twentieth century. In 1911, the US Patent Officer, exasperated at the time spent on examining the claims of those who believed that they could override the first and second laws of thermodynamics, ruled that no patent for a perpetual motion machine could be admitted until an actual, working, model of such a machine had been filed with the office, and had been shown to run for one year.[169]

Renaissance engineers, speculators, and inventors were fascinated by the prospect of perpetual motion. In their quest for such devices, we can see a kind of theology of mechanics at work, which would, eventually, be subsumed (although never entirely replaced) by the science of mechanics associated with Galileo. Discovering the secret of perpetual motion obsessed long-forgotten inventors and fantasists, but also more familiar figures such as John Dee, Robert Fludd, and Vittorio Zonca.[170] Such devices were to become objects of scorn and ridicule in the nineteenth century: 'a manifest absurdity' is how one commentator described a hydraulic machine, while the work of Gaspar Schott, a skilled fabricator of automata in the sixteenth century, was dismissed with the comment 'the monstrosity of this scheme refutes itself'.[171] Today, the search for a *perpetuum mobile* has been transformed into the quest for infinite (free) energy.[172] In the sixteenth century, by contrast, the quest for perpetual motion can be thought of as both a response to the growing habit of thinking in terms of mechanisms, as well as a desire for economic gain. In 1559, for example, a committee of the Venetian Senate granted a 'privilege' for a perpetual motion device ('*motto perpetuo*') capable, so it was believed, of driving a mill or water lifting device.[173] But it was not always the utility or functionality, even, of such devices that attracted Renaissance engineers and their successors in the seventeenth century. Rather, they saw in the prospect of perpetual motion, mechanism perfected, moving only to its own self-directed end. The *Cochlergon* apparatus, for example, devised by Georg Boeckler in his *Theatrum Machinarum Novum* (1662), was not designed to fulfil any useful task (Figure 3.8). Rather, it existed simply as a demonstration of the possibility of endless movement, as well as the inventive genius of its creator. In the late 1630s, the inventor Edward Somerset, second Marquis of Worcester, devised a perpetual motion machine based on a revolving wheel and a system of descending and ascending weights and installed it in the Tower of London, demonstrating its operation to the king.[174] By the 1660s, John Evelyn understood devices of this kind as unremarkable, simply listing the operation of another machine in the course of a particularly sociable evening: 'I showed his majesty the perpetual motion sent to me by Dr Stokes, from Cologne; and then came in Monsieur Colbert, the French ambassador.'[175]

For others, however, the possibility of creating endless motion had clear theological implications, as Isaak de Caus suggested when he introduced an 'engine which shall move of itselfe' in his *New and Rare Inventions of Water-Works* (1659). Although the term 'perpetual motion' was used on the title page of the English translation of this work, de Caus himself was wary of introducing the term into the body of his text:

> . . . all that hath a beginning is subject to an Ende; and the word Perpetual or without End ought to be applied to God alone, who as he had no beginning cannot also have an end, so as it is folly & deceit in Men to make themselves beleeve that they can make perpetuall Works; seeing that themselves are mortal and subject to an end: so also are all their works: Therfore I will leave those wordes of perpetual or without end, and will shew the *Fabricke* of an *Engin* which shall move of itselfe . . .[176]

The perpetual motion device ran the risk of idolatrously aping the works of God. Designing an '*Engin* which shall move of itself', a self-activating and self-regulating device of some kind, was a more limited (and theologically sounder) ambition. For others, however, the perpetual motion machine was, indeed, a godlike apparatus that would replicate the divine skill with which God had fashioned the universe. But then, as an English contemporary of de Caus wrote, quoting Francis Bacon's *Novum Organum*, machines in general were nothing less than 'new creations, and imitations of Gods own works'.[177] 'Perpetuall motions' were likewise to be a feature of the imaginary

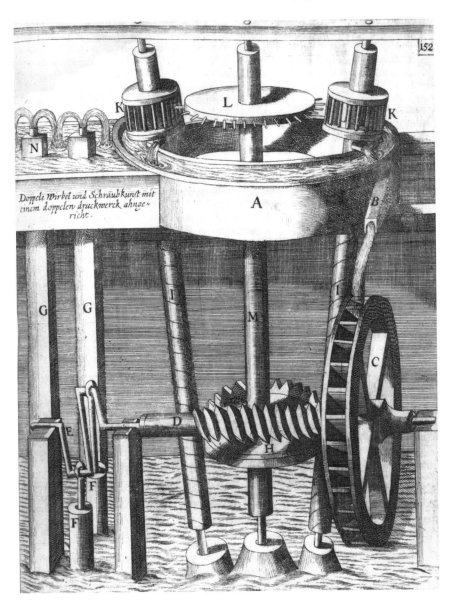

Figure 3.8 Georg Andreas Boeckler, *Theatrum Machinarum Novum* (Nuremberg, 1662), p. 152. Glasgow University Library, Special Collections.

gallery of mechanical devices which Bacon would describe in the engine houses of Salomons House, Bacon's vision of an ideal scientific community described in his *New Atlantis* (1624).[178] Similarly, for Thomas Powell, author of *Humane Industry or A History of Most Manual Arts* (1661), God was a designer of perpetual motions. 'The whole machine of the world', according to Powell, was nothing less than '. . . a kinde of Automaton or Engine that moves of it self, much like a great Clock with wheels and poyzes and counterpoyzes, that is alwaies in motion, though no body move it'.[179]

John Wilkins, the mathematician and (later) member of the Royal Society, was equally entranced by the idea of perpetual motion. In his *Mathematical Magick or The Wonders That may be Performed by Mechanicall Geometry* (1648), Wilkins set out to explore the ways in which mathematical rigour could be put to work in the service of humankind. For Wilkins, infected with mechanical optimism, the 'artificiall experiments' of machinery promised an escape from the theological disaster of the Fall. They offered the means 'whereby men do naturally attempt to restore themselves from the first generall curse inflected upon their labours'.[180] The emerging science of mechanics, moreover, was neither a slavish imitation of nature, nor was it to be understood as a means of assisting nature. Rather, machines and devices were designed to 'overcome, and *advance* nature': to remould nature, in other words, according to human ends.[181]

Wilkins was a determined rationalist. The title of his work on machines – *Mathematicall Magick* – was chosen ironically, Wilkins wrote, 'in allusion to vulgar opinion, which doth commonly attribute all such strange operations unto the power of magick'.[182] But for all his rationalism, Wilkins believed that the unattainable limit of perpetual motion might be achieved. Acknowledging 'the seeming facility [yet] real difficulty of any such contrivance', Wilkins understood that the problem was inherent to the nature of the mechanical systems with which he was dealing.[183] Various kinds of automaton were the closest he could envisage to such devices. Yet even these machines 'need a frequent repair of new strength, the causes whence their motion does proceed, being subject to faile and come to a period . . .'[184] Nevertheless, in the pages of *Mathematicall Magick*, Wilkins speculated on different kinds of device which might somehow provide the elusive wonder of perpetual motion. So, he set about exploring 'perpetual lamps' (chapter 12), 'Perpetual Motion by Magneticall Virtues' (chapter 13), 'continuall motion by solid weights in a hollow wheel or sphere' (chapter 14), and finally, using 'fluid weights' or water (chapter 15).

Today, common sense (as well as the laws of thermodynamics) tells us that the search for perpetual motion was a chimera, although that does not preclude our own contemporary fascination with the topic.[185] Seventeenth-century mechanists, too, could be as sceptical as any contemporary engineer: the search for a perpetual movement device, one seventeenth-century author cautioned, should be considered to be 'as a Rock and sand to be avoyded and shunned not as safe deeps to sayle in'.[186] Yet the machines devised by Renaissance mechanicians and engineers had revealed vistas of mechanical movement in which such a device seemed not only perfectly plausible, but perhaps inevitable. Moreover, in that analogical habit of mind which was so characteristic of the age, there were at least two examples of perpetual motion machines to be seen in the world which served as models for the engineer: the heavens themselves, and the human body, God's lesser creation. The world, the elements, and the body seemed to operate without any outward motive force, other than that divine fiat of creation described in Genesis by which the universe was created, or the breath or *pneuma* that had first animated the human body.[187]

Construction of a perpetual motion device was, then, a matter of imitating the creative workmanship of God. One such device was exhibited in London at the court of James VI and I in the early years of the seventeenth century, the invention (so it was claimed) of the Dutch inventor and engineer, 'part necromancer, part experimentalist', Cornelius van Drebbel (or Drebble).[188] Drebbel's device seems to have been a combination of a mechanical clock, and a species of mystical armillary sphere, which was offered as a model of the universe in miniature. It was described, in some detail, by the translator and author, Thomas Tymme, in the second part of his *Dialogue Philosophical* of 1612 ('wherein nature's secret closet is opened'). The machine or instrument was, according to Tymme: 'a memorable Modell and Patterne, representing the motion of the Heavens about the fixt earth, made by art in the imitation of nature . . . which instrument is perpetually in motion, without the means of steele, springs, and weights'.[189] In other words it was a machine for defending an older, pre-Copernican view of the universe. Composed of concentric rings of crystal glass, running (obscurely) on wheels of brass, the machine moved in such 'slow measure' that it was (Tymme believed) frictionless: the brass wheels (wrote Tymme) 'cannot weare . . . for that they are not forced by any poyse of waight'.[190] The machine is said to have entranced the king who 'could hardly believe that this motion should be perpetuall, except the mysterie were revealed unto him . . . in secret manner'.[191]

James was, of course, right to be sceptical. Drebbel's machine possessed a kind of poetic resonance. Its brass wheels which will never wear out might remind us of the ambiguous evocation of 'brass eternal slave to mortal rage' in Shakespeare's Sonnet 64, or, indeed, the wider argument with time which Shakespeare's sonnets as a whole represent. John Kerrigan, in his engaging discussion of Shakespeare's sonnets, has drawn our attention to the ways in which a preoccupation with the passage of time in the sequence of poems may be thought of as a response to the ever-more precise means of calibrating time, which (as we saw at the outset of this chapter) had penetrated even into the depths of the (imagined) forests of Arden. 'Clock time' Kerrigan writes, had, in the period of the composition of the sonnets, 'invaded men's lives' so that it had become 'the matrix of living', and he cites one poetic response to this phenomenon – a sonnet by the Marinist poet Ciro di Pers which begins: '*Mobile ordignio di dentate rote / Lacera il giorno e lo divide in ore ...*' ('The moving engine, with its toothed cogs, tears up the day and divides it into hours') and which concludes by meditating upon how the clock 'taps by the hour at the tomb to open' ('*ognor picchia a la tomba*').[192] The essence of the machine (as Ciro de Pers's poem demonstrates) is that, unlike human life, which gradually unwinds, the mechanical beat of the clock appeared, in theory at least, to be endless. The king's fascination (as Tymme reported the matter) with the prospect that any 'motion should be perpetuall' is, then, a mirror to that argument played out in the sonnets conceived of as memory devices: that devouring time could be held at bay by the equally artificial preservative of a printed book of poems.

Drebbel's machine, for all that it must have been pure fantasy, was to have a strange afterlife in poetry. It inspired Drebbel's countryman, the legal theorist Hugo Grotius (Huig de Groot), to compose a short Latin poem ('*In organum motus perpetui ...*') addressed to James, which imagines the sovereign, within the well-ordered commonwealth, as a kind of perpetual motion engine: 'The untired strength of never- ceasing motion, / A restless rest a toyl-less operation' the poem begins, and concludes by addressing the king directly as a 'motion' akin to the larger, heavenly motion, of the divinely ordered mechanism of the cosmos. The poem was translated into English by the Welsh poet Henry Vaughan and first published in Thomas Powell's *Humane Industry*:

> In You, whose minde (though still calm) never sleeps,
> But through your Realms one constant motion keeps:
> As your minde (then) was Heavens type first, so this
> But the taught *Anti-type* of your mind is.[193]

Did Vaughan's knowledge of Drebbel's perpetual motion engine, with its whirling rings, lie behind perhaps his most famous poetic image, that to be found in 'The World' which opens with his evocation of eternity 'like a great Ring of pure and endless light'?[194] Eternity, kingship, and the concept of endlessness are certainly bound together in the haunting image of the great 'ring' of luminosity. Equally, the king's sovereign power within his realm is imagined as an impossibly idealized mechanical force, or motion, which in contrast to the blind hits of chance or fortune, is governed by regularity and constancy. Fate, fortune, chance, and the random occurrences of daily life would seem to be abstractions that one might have thought banished by the advent of mechanical culture. After all, was not the essence of the machine, as Montaigne had understood the matter, its regularity and its predictability?

Of course, the opposite was the case. Although King James might have been imagined, poetically, as a kind of perpetual motion engine, governing the state with a 'constant motion' that would never swerve from the path of justice, this was not, however, how he saw his own position within the polity. In the advice written to his son, Prince Henry, and published as *Basilicon Doron* ('the kingly gift') in 1599, James set out his own vision of what it was to be a king. Underpinning his meditations on the art of governance, however, was his awareness that the state of all humankind, both kings and their subjects, was one of continual and restless change. '*Quia nihil nouum sub sole* ('there is no new thing under the sun') he wrote, quoting Ecclesiastes, before turning to another scriptural text, and another kind of device or instrument:

> ... such is the continuall volubility of thinges earthly according to the roundnesse of the world, and revolution of the heauenly circles: which is expressed by the wheeles in *Ezechiels* visions, and counterfeited by the Poets *in rota fortunae*.[195]

The obscure wheels in Ezekiel's visions ('a wheel in the middle of a wheel' Ezekiel 1. 16) were understood by James in terms of an equally fabulous device, the '*rota fortuna*' or wheel of fortune, turned by the fickle goddess who presides over human destiny: the goddess *Fortuna*.

The wheel of fortune is rarely thought of as a manifestation of technology. It is, rather, an emblematic expression of an abstract idea of the working of providence in human life. But the curious story of James and the perpetual motion machine, as well as the presence of this ubiquitous symbol of the obscure unravelling of fortune in Renaissance culture, alerts us to a further dimension of the engagement with machines on the part of people in the early-modern world. Fortune, visualized as a great wheel, was turned, almost exclusively in Renaissance culture, by a woman. And it is to the subject of women and wheels that we too shall now turn, as we begin to explore the symbolic realms of Renaissance mechanical culture.

4

WOMEN AND WHEELS

Gender and the machine in the Renaissance

Rosie the Riveter

On 29 May 1943, Norman Rockwell's iconic image of the relationship between women, labour, and technology in the modern world appeared on the cover of the *Saturday Evening Post* (Figure 4.1). Named after a popular song of the period, 'Rosie the Riveter' was a herald of the ways in which women, under the press of a war economy, were now held to be perfectly capable of assuming the heavy industrial tasks which had once been the preserve of those men who were now enlisted in the American armed forces. In Britain, America, and even more so in Japan and in Germany, occupations which formerly had been classified as being either 'male' or 'female' were being redistributed.[1]

Yet, for all her modernity, Rosie's origins were firmly rooted in a heroic ideal of masculinity associated with Renaissance images. Wittily playing off Michelangelo's sixteenth-century depiction of the prophet Isaiah on the Sistine Chapel ceiling (Figure 4.2), Rosie sits monumentally munching on a sandwich, imperiously crushing a copy of Hitler's *Mein Kampf* beneath her foot.[2] Throwing off the shackles of convention, Rosie seems to announce the forging of a new order of labour and work. The picture also echoes other familiar Renaissance images. Perched in front of the American flag, closer scrutiny reveals that behind her head, Rockwell has suggested a halo,

Figure 4.1 Norman Rockwell, 'Rosie the Riveter', Cover, *Saturday Evening Post*, 29 May 1943.

Figure 4.2 Michelangelo Buonarroti (1475–1564), *Sistine Chapel Ceiling: The Prophet Isaiah* (fresco), Vatican Museums and Galleries, Vatican City, Italy, The Bridgeman Art Library.

summoning up images of an alternative icon of femininity, the Madonna. Her goggles pushed up, legs apart, wearing bright red lipstick, this hybridization of the Old Testament prophet and the Madonna of the New Testament cradles in her lap a phallically emphatic pneumatic rivet gun.

Emerging from a scriptural and artistic past, sex, power and traditional gender roles seem to collide in this image of woman, seemingly at ease with technology. But, Rosie and her sisters were eventually to be pushed out of the factory and back into the home on the return of the men from Europe and the Pacific. So the appropriation of industrial clothing, heavy equipment, even the lunchbox usually prepared for the male worker by their (female) domestic helpmeet, reminds the viewer of how, with the benefit of hindsight, and for all the picture's good humour, Rosie is essentially a temporary man, a woman in drag. Her male counterpart was probably either stationed on some bleak Lincolnshire airfield or flying over Berlin in the daylight air raids that had begun just a fortnight before the picture's appearance.[3] Her appearance, in other words, is designed to remind us of his absence, an element that is reinforced by the nonchalant ease with which she cradles her homage to the air gunner's heavy calibre weaponry.[4]

In Rockwell's image, the rivet gun is symbolic of the entry of women into a world of industry and machines, opened to them because of the absence of men. As we shall see, with some significant exceptions, portraits of women working with machines are relatively uncommon until the early nineteenth century, when images illustrating the abuses of female and child labour in the textile mills of England and Scotland during the industrial revolution began to circulate. Historically, it may be the case that such images have conditioned us to see women as primarily victims of technology. Only in the twentieth century, when female factory labour becomes part of the propaganda of war art, are women represented approvingly in a technological milieu, as in the Canadian George Agnew Reid's *Women Operators*, 1919, which depicts female munitions workers, labouring with heavy industrial plant to produce artillery shells.

The Spinners

Rosie's artistic origins are rooted in the Mannerist art of the high Renaissance. As such, she is also caught up within a web of history and ideology enmeshing the idea of women, work, and industry in the early modern era, which has, in recent years, claimed the attention of historians.[5] But if Rockwell's image of a woman cradling a rivet gun hints at a historical as well as cultural dimension to the question of the interplay of women and machines, then where are we to discover the Renaissance equivalents of Rosie?

If Rosie's mid-twentieth-century rivet gun can also be considered as a symbolic substitute for the (absent) male, then, following Marina Warner, we might conclude that its Renaissance equivalent was the distaff. The distaff was a simple device used in spinning, whose phallic shape appears in contemporary prints as a signifier of female sexual desire and of female autonomy.[6] But the Renaissance counterpart of the rivet gun was not so much the ancient device of the distaff, but the more complex technology of the spinning wheel. A woman, seated at her spinning wheel, was one of the most popular of all forms of genre portraits involving female subjects in late Renaissance art. Such images were particularly common in the Netherlands. In The Spinner (1653) by Quirijn Gerritsz. van Brekelenkam (c. 1620–68) (Figure 4.3), an elderly couple sit in companionable harmony together. The man sits at his ease, gazing back at the viewer. Beside him, the woman is entirely engrossed in the operation of her complex machine, a spinning wheel of the old-fashioned 'great wheel' type. Significantly, she does not have the time to pause in her labours, to return our glance. We should, of course, be careful not to treat a Renaissance portrait as if it were the equivalent to a modern photograph, let alone a document of social commentary. In Dutch art, moreover, it may well have been the case that by the early seventeenth century the spinning wheel had become a conventional attribute of femininity associated with upper class women, rather than the representation of a habitually operated device.[7] Certainly, in the eighteenth century, following the introduction of more complex spinning machines in the cotton industry, the spinning wheel was to become a fashionable device, giving rise to the 'boudoir' spinning wheel, a highly decorative object of luxurious consumption, around which wealthy women might cluster in sociable groups.[8]

In the earlier period, artists whose chose to depict women seated at their spinning wheels were showing women at their labour according to idealized social codes, which announced their virtue, industry, and modesty. These images may be indebted to older, religious representations of women at work, such as a depiction of a woman labouring with her wheel to be found in the Luttrell Psalter (c. 1325–35) (Figure 4.4), or a fifteenth-century depiction by an unknown Hungarian master of the Virgin, seated at a spinning wheel, now to be seen in the National Museum in Budapest. Such images represented idealizations of the feminine virtues of industry, chastity, and modesty. A woman occupied with her spinning wheel was not

Figure 4.3 Quirijn Gerritsz. van Brekelenkam (c. 1620–68), *The Spinner* (1653), Metropolitan Museum of Art, New York (oil on wood), 19 × 25¼ in. (48.3 × 64.1 cm), Purchase, 1871 (71.110).

Figure 4.4 Woman spinning and another carding wool, Luttrell Psalter, British Library, Add. MS 42130 f.193. Begun prior to 1340 for Sir Geoffrey Luttrell (1276–1345), British Library, London. © British Library Board. All Rights Reserved, The Bridgeman Art Library.

only performing useful work, but she was also proclaiming her obedience to the economic needs of the household, while abstaining from frivolity or luxurious behaviour.

Today, the most famous image in seventeenth-century art of women engaged in mechanized labour is the painting known, variously, as *La Fabula de Aragne* (*The Fable of Arachne*) or *Las Hilanderas* (*The Spinners*), by Diego Velásquez, created about 1656–8. In Velásquez's image, there is no hint of domestic labour (Figure 4.5). By the time that Velásquez came to work on this image, the production of large-scale tapestries had evolved into a shop structure with highly organized and well-paid workers, particularly in late-medieval Flanders and Northern France.[9] And certainly, the painting was understood in terms of realism immediately prior to its being entered into the Spanish Royal Collections: in 1711 it was described as *'mugeres que travajavan en tapizería'* – 'women working in a tapestry workshop'.[10]

Weaving and spinning, in the sixteenth century, were symbolically related to the idea of the spinning out of words or text. In the dedicatory verses, for example, which prefaced her co-translation of the Psalms (1599), Mary Sidney, Countess of Pembroke, describes the entwined work of herself and her dead brother, Sir Philip Sidney, as akin to weaving a web of praise and prayer: 'hee [Sidney] did warpe, I weav'd this webb to end; / the stuffe not ours, our worke no curious thing'.[11] The ensuing textual tapestry is made of 'stuffe' provided by other workers, God and the Psalmist, and is then imagined as being presented to Queen Elizabeth as a rich 'cloth', commemorating the names of the sister and brother. But female subordination still seems to be the theme of this 'shop' of industry, praise, and prayer since, in providing the 'warp' or the longer, tougher, lengthwise thread attached to the loom before weaving begins, the dead male poet is imagined as creating the solid foundational structure around which his sister weaves her own thread of ornamentation.

Velásquez's image of women weaving, however, seems, at first, devoid of these complex textual and sacred undertones. And yet, the three alternative descriptive titles by which the image has been known – 'The Fable of Arachne', 'The Spinners', and 'Women Working in a Tapestry Workshop' – traverse a range of possibilities of meaning. Following the Ovidian title, 'The Fable of Arachne', the painting illustrates a purely fictional moment. It depicts a scene from Book VI of Ovid's *Metamorphoses* in which the mortal, Arachne, challenges the goddess, Minerva, to a competition in weaving.[12] In Ovid's tale, the goddess and her opponent set to work to weave their respective tapestries which, when they are completed, are indistinguishable from one

Figure 4.5 Diego Rodriguez de Silva y Velásquez (1599–1660), *The Fable of Arachne, or The Spinners*, c. 1657 (oil on canvas), Prado, Madrid, Spain, The Bridgeman Art Library.

another in terms of their craftsmanship. But Arachne, driven by the presumption that had caused her to challenge Minerva in the first instance, weaves into her tapestry scenes showing the crimes and deceptions of the gods, all of which involve abduction and rape: the rape of Europa by Jupiter, the story of Leda and the swan, the tricking of Danae by Jupiter, and so on. Enraged by her rival's success as well as the subject matter she had chosen, Minerva transforms her opponent into a spider, in one of the most horrific of all the many transformations recounted in the *Metamorphoses*:

> . . . the girl's hair dropped out, her nostrils and ears went too, and her head shrank almost to nothing. Her whole body, likewise became tiny. Her slender fingers were fastened to her sides, to serve as legs, and all the rest of her was belly; from that belly, she yet spins her thread, and as a spider is busy with her web as of old.[13]

In *Las Hilanderas*, however, Velásquez shows us the moment of revelation in which Minerva is confronted by the evidence of her rival's accomplishment. At the rear of the painting, in a brilliantly lit space, the classically draped Arachne stands before her tapestry, gesturing to the helmeted Minerva.[14] Three other women, richly costumed in seventeenth-century fashion, make up the group surrounding the tapestry, one of whom glances out of this stage setting at us, the viewers. Her glance, too, traverses the painting's foreground, which shows five women, who are busily manufacturing the thread used in the competition. These are the 'hilanderas' – the spinners – of one of the picture's alternative titles.

Like Velásquez's *Las Meninas*, *Las Hilanderas* seems to hint at some larger, programmatic, statement about the nature of art and illusion.[15] Thus, the tapestry in front of which Minerva and Arachne seem to stand has been identified as a rendition of Titian's painting, *The Rape of Europa* (c. 1559), suggesting that Velásquez was making a claim for the godlike status of the artist. Just as Arachne can equal Minerva in skill and accomplishment so Titian is Arachne's equal: his painting, translated into tapestry, is worthy enough to challenge the artistry of the gods.[16] In conformity with the dictates of Mannerism, by consigning the important mythological content of the painting to the rear of the image, Velásquez risked violating pictorial decorum in order to reconcile the myth with what Jonathan Brown terms 'visual reality'.[17] That reality centres on the spinning, whirling wheel that seems to intercede between the viewer of the painting and the various pictorial spaces receding behind it. To look into the painting, and particularly to peer into the brilliantly lit

background, we have to look past the revolving wheel whose motion is suggested by the flashes of light which trace its circumference.[18]

In Velásquez's image, rather than expressing modesty, silence, and industry, the seated, spinning woman seems to have been distracted by her
companion pulling back the red curtain to disclose the entire scene for
us, reminding us of a theatrical moment, or even the frozen motion of a
tableau vivant. Distracted from the task of operating her wheel, the spinner
seems more engrossed in exchanging confidences with the woman at the
extreme left of the image. On the opposite side of the painting, the woman
working with a skein of yarn also seems abstracted from her work, leaning towards her companion on the extreme right of the image, as if they,
too, are engaged in some intimate conversation. Only the brooding, solitary
figure in the very centre of the image, occupied with the menial task of
carding wool, seems to exhibit the customary degree of modesty associated
with such images of women at work with thread or yarn.[19] Her presence
reinforces that oscillation (described by Anne Rosalind Jones and Peter Stallybrass) between 'high' culture, associated with the courtly Ovidian myth
shown at the rear of the image, and the 'low' realm of quotidian, habitual
labour depicted in the painting's foreground.[20]

Mythologically, the spinning wheel reminds us of the fate of Arachne:
'from that belly, she yet spins her thread, as a spider is busy with her web
as of old'. Equally, the spinner and her wheel might represent the notion
of deceit or guile. For Arachne, the spider, weaves or spins her 'subtle web'
out of magic and deceit in Edmund Spenser's 'Bowre of Blisse' episode in
The Faerie Queene (1596) (II. xii. 77), while she fashions a 'curious network'
fabricated with 'divers cunning', which ensnares the unwary in Spenser's
earlier *Muiopotmos: or The Fate of the Butterfly* (1590).[21] Among the poets and
mythographers, the spider's web was emblematic of the spidery web of
words which, in *The Faerie Queene* once more, is woven by Detraction who
'faynes to weave false tales and leasings bad / To overthrow the good' (V. xii.
36). And in Velásquez's depiction of the woman spinning, we note that she
and her companion are indeed engaged in rapt conversation. Their trade is
in words as much as it is in thread.

Alternatively, the three central female figures in the image might also
remind the onlooker of the three most famous mythological female textile
workers: Clotho, Lachesis, and Atropos, the *Moirai* or fates of Greek myth,
known as the *Parcae* to the Romans, whose task it was to spin, measure, and
cut the thread of human life.[22] As an emblem either of craft, deceit, cunning, or fate, the presence of the spinning wheel has been identified as a

problem in one intriguing discussion of the painting, namely that 'it is difficult to imagine that many viewers would discover the story of Arachne and Athena [Minerva] in this painting . . . There is no competition between the spinner and the goddess; there are no looms; we do not see Arachne being transformed into a spider.'[23]

If, however, we follow Sigmund Freud, then it becomes clear that guilt, punishment, and shame are the motifs with which Velásquez's complex interweaving of myth and female labour is concerned. Writing (in 1931) of what he termed the 'riddle of femininity', Freud argued that 'it seems that women have made few contributions to the discoveries and inventions in the history of civilization', but for one exception: 'there is, however, one technique which they may have invented – that of plaiting and weaving'.[24] The 'unconscious motive for this achievement', Freud claimed, was an imitation of that process by which nature, at the onset of puberty, provides women with a protective, concealing, covering of the genitals with the arrival of the pubic hair. The woman sitting at her spinning wheel is thus manufacturing the means by which her 'genital deficiency' (her lack, that is, of a penis) will be concealed. Seated either at their loom or spinning wheel, women weave or spin thread out of which will be fashioned a more secure 'mat' than that which nature has provided to conceal this guilty secret of lack or absence.[25]

In such a Freudian reading of genre portraits of women spinning, the modestly downcast eyes of the virtuous and industrious female spinner express her shame or guilt: the guilt of the fallen Eve, doomed (like Arachne) to spin for her living, as the words of John Ball's famously revolutionary re-reading of the scriptural origins of labour, and the social origins of gentility, remind us: 'When Adam delved and Eve span, / Who was then the Gentleman?'[26] And, if we are to follow Freud a little further, then Eve's shame is also the shame of woman as a deformed male, aware that she has no 'instrument' of the kind furnished for Man. Even Freud, however, seems to have found his argument unconvincing. He concluded the discussion of the topic of women, weaving, and the absent phallus with an uncharacteristically submissive gesture of both apology and defiance: 'If you reject this idea as fantastic and regard my belief in the influence of lack of a penis on the configuration of femininity as an idée fixe, I am of course defenceless.'[27] Defenceless or not, more recent commentators have been rather less than convinced by Freud's account of the unconscious origins of weaving. So, Sadie Plant writes of how Freud 'pulls aside the veils, the webs of lies, the shrouds of mystery . . . and finds . . . Only "the horror of nothing to be seen." Good of her to cover it up for him.'[28]

And yet, Velásquez's painting seems to hint at (even if it refuses to reveal) so many of the themes around which Freud's analysis of the female task of weaving also circulates. Modesty and immodesty is certainly one of the themes of the image. Words, or conversation, are important to the image too. So, too, is punishment, and quite possibly deceit of craftiness, in the sense that came to be attributed to the ensnaring webs of the spider. The seated woman, posed at the very centre of the painting's foreground, might also be understood as rehearsing a gesture of shame, isolation, or even abjection. And finally, at the back of the entire image where the complex mythological narrative that informs the painting is actually to be discovered, looms a scene of rape, an expression of the violence done to mortal women by the immortal gods. This violence echoes the violence of Minerva who judges and punishes her opponent for her presumption.

Wheels

Svetlana Alpers has described the meaning as well as the effect of Las Hilan-deras as obscure, strange and unsettling.[29] She is surely right. But then the homely spinning wheel, which features so prominently in Velasquez's brilliantly ambiguous image, was itself an uncanny device. The spinning wheel was a technological innovation which incorporated a much older device into its composition: the turning potter's wheel, or, indeed, the very idea of the wheel itself. As such it may be considered to be an offshoot of one of the most basic technologies known to human beings, which has also come to symbolize civilization itself: the wheel. 'In the wheel we have one of the greatest as well as one of the oldest technological advances', write T. K. Derry and Trevor Williams.[30]

This may be true, yet the wheel is by no means a foundation stone of human technological culture: 'The more we learn about the wheel, the clearer it becomes that its history and influence have been distorted by the extraordinary attention paid to it in Europe and the United States', observes another historian of technology.[31] Our own reliance on all forms of rotary motion – particularly for transport, power, and representing the passage of time – tends to blinker us to the fact that many ancient and sophisticated world cultures, including the peoples of sub-Saharan Africa, southeast Asia, Australasia, Polynesia, and pre-colonial South and North America, have all functioned perfectly well for millennia without this supposedly ubiquitous marker of civilization.[32] Indeed, one of the greatest ironies of technological history is that the wheel was actually *abandoned* as a primary component in transport devices by those living in its place of origin – the Near East and North Africa – at some point between the third and seventh centuries CE.[33] More than this, the earliest examples of wheels integrated into carriages and carts, discovered in widely dispersed tombs in the Near East and in Europe, suggest that they may have originated not as utilitarian designs, but for ritualistic purposes or even as toys.[34]

For us, however, the wheel has come to express not just motion, but progress itself. It might be assumed that the Western idea of 'progress', bound up with the prospect of a turning wheel, may be indebted to the appearance, in the fourteenth century, of clock dials or 'faces' with their restlessly moving 'hands' marking the passage of time, although the OED tells us that these anthropomorphic terms for describing clocks and watches did not surface until long after these devices came to be widely distributed. In fact the turning wheel as a register of the passage of time is far more ancient than the mechanical clock, and its origin lay in the East rather than the West. Finely crafted geared wheels appeared as components in calendrical devices such as portable sundials in the first century CE, which in turn provide evidence for the transmission of mathematically driven technology from Islamic to Byzantine culture.[35] In other contexts and cultures, the wheel expresses not merely the idea of either circular motion or progress, but a restless state of change or movement from one geographic space to another, from one historical epoch to another, or, more profoundly, from one state of being to another. In some human cultures, moreover, the wheel has been, for centuries, primarily a fideistic rather than a utilitarian mechanism. The prayer wheel, for example, associated with the Tibetan Buddhist tradition, is a mechanical rotary device by means of which the devotee, who turns or attends the wheel, generates *mantras*. The wheel, in this tradition, also expresses larger, cosmic symbolism, the passage of the sun, of the 'wheel-turning king', or of any kind of cyclical motion in the world at large.[36] Containing sacred texts, the prayer wheel has also been related to the Chinese innovation of revolving libraries which might also contain sacred texts, and which would give rise to the 'fashion for mechanized piety' which (Lynn White Jr argues) swept China in the early twelfth century.[37]

Of course it is true that in their habitual reliance on the functional role of wheels early-modern people resembled us, their modern counterparts. Wheels were vital components in a host of prime movers. In art and in literature, fantastically ornate vehicles drawn through the streets are frequently depicted in the welcoming of princes and emperors, while pageant wagons involved in the performance of mystery plays trundled through the streets of medieval York. Indeed, the urban topography of the European city or town in the late medieval and Renaissance periods was already largely determined by the need to allow wheeled transport to pass through the streets, unlike the 'labyrinthine' streets of Islamic cities, with stairways, blind alleys, and enclosed courtyards, familiar from European descriptions of the souq.[38] Thomas Dekker's image of Shakespeare's London, in which 'carts and Coaches make such a thundring as if the world ranne vpon wheeles' reminds us of how the European city was already having to accommodate the free flow of wheeled traffic.

But wheels also performed a symbolic role within Western societies in the early-modern period. For the wheel was a mystery. Though it was an everyday and fundamental part of that mechanical superstructure by which nature and the environment were shifted or altered to human designs, it also had the capacity to express larger, more abstract forces at work in human life. Remembering the story of Arachne, and her transformation into a spinning spider as a punishment for daring to challenge the gods, memorialized in Velásquez's painting through the device of the spinning wheel, what other symbolic significance might have attached to the prospect of women and wheels in the pre-industrial world?

Rotary punishment

One answer to this question is suggested by one of the most popular religious cults of the Middle Ages and the Renaissance: the story of St Catherine of Alexandria. Among the one hundred and seventy or more individual lives of saints collected in the thirteenth-century compilation known as the Golden Legend of Jacobus de Voragine, the story of the martyrdom of Saint Catherine is, at once, one of the most detailed and one of the most bizarre. Versions of her story can be found scattered through numerous early- and late-medieval manuscript and printed collections, including one of the earliest books printed in English – Caxton's Golden Legend published in 1483.[39] She appears, too, in images made by an anonymous Netherlandish painter of the late fifteenth century, as well as in works by Dürer (Figure 4.6), Michelangelo (who portrayed the saint and her wheel on the ceiling of the Sistine Chapel), and the Spanish artist Fernando Gallego (c. 1440–1507).[40]

Saint Catherine, today, is associated with the spectacular firework that bears her name – the Catherine Wheel – a memorial to the key element in the story of her martyrdom. According to the story preserved in the Golden Legend, the highborn Catherine was persecuted for her Christian faith by the

Figure 4.6 Albrecht Dürer (1471–1528), *The Torture of St Catherine of Alexandria* (woodcut), Private Collection, Agra Art, Warsaw, Poland, The Bridgeman Art Library.

fourth-century Roman Emperor Maxentius. The emperor, of whom Gibbon records that 'pleasure' was his 'only business', enraged by her stubborn devotion, and having failed to persuade Catherine through various forms of privation to worship pagan gods, prepared an intricate form of torture for her.[41] She was to be placed inside a contraption consisting of:

> . . . four wheels studded with iron saws and sharp pointed nails . . . to have the virgin torn to pieces with these horrible instruments, thus terrorizing the rest of the Christians with the example of so horrible a death. It was further ordered that two of the wheels should revolve in one direction and the other two in the opposite direction, so that the maiden would be mangled and torn by the two wheels coming down on her, and chewed up by the other two coming against her from below. But the holy virgin prayed the Lord to destroy the machine for the glory of his name and the conversion of the people standing around; and instantly an Angel of the Lord struck that engine such a blow that it was shattered and four thousand pagans were killed.[42]

So terrible was the 'awful machine' devised by Maxentius that, in some versions of the Catherine story, the mechanism had the power to kill those who so much as gazed upon it.[43]

Catherine and her ghastly wheel, sometimes depicted as broken, thus entered the catalogue of Christian martyrology in the Middle Ages and in the Renaissance. But from Catherine's wheel, we can trace a whole sequence of later disciplinary devices and machines, many of which took the form of a wheel. In Pieter Brueghel the Elder's picture the *Triumph of Death* (c. 1565–6), for example, the horizon is punctuated by wheels, hoisted high into the air, onto which have been stretched human bodies.[44] These instruments exist within the same realm as the ambiguous and sinister 'apparatus' of malfunctioning turning wheels evoked by Franz Kafka in his harrowing 1919 story *In der Strafkolonie* ('In the Penal Settlement').[45] In this context, Michel Foucault observes, parenthetically, in his analysis of the 'mechanism' of judicial torture that 'The first degree of torture was the sight of the instruments', and for some, this was enough.[46] Exhibition, too, was the point of Catherine's legendary machine, which was not designed so that it should work more efficiently to inflict pain, or to accomplish tasks beyond the capacities of unassisted human labour. As an alternative (fifteenth-century) account of Catherine's wheels suggests, sight was the chief sense by which the machine was designed to act upon its victim. The emperor was advised that 'Katherine hasn't yet seen a torment frightening enough to make her do your will and sacrifice to our great gods . . . The horror of these turning wheels will scare her into honouring our gods.'[47] This was, in essence, a fantasy device: a mechanism of the mind rather than one that could actually have existed in the world.

There was, however, nothing fantastic about the spinning wheel, though its operation was predominantly reserved for women in early-modern Europe. But the spinning wheel, too, could function as a form of punishment. The female house of correction in seventeenth-century Amsterdam was the *Spinhuis* where (in the words of Simon Schama) 'from 1597 "fallen women" – vagrants, whores, and thieves – were sent for stiff doses of improvement at loom and wheel'.[48] The *Spinhuis* was also one of the sites of the city, catering for the tastes of the Renaissance sex-tourist who, on payment of a small sum, could watch the women at their work through a grill, or engage (as a contemporary records) in indecent banter, and even watch 'indecent actions' being performed for their benefit.[49] Elsewhere, in early-modern Europe, women might find themselves, quite literally, chained to their spinning wheels as punishment.[50] The spinning wheel was the female equivalent of the tread wheel, which was also a punishment device, transforming criminal energy into useful work. Was this, perhaps, the true context in which Montaigne saw women operating the *filatoio da aqua* in Florence, after he had wandered through the city's Red Light district? More fantastically, are we to imagine that Velásquez's image, with its group of chattering lower-class women, working with the spinning wheel and skeins of yarn, in front of a scene of rape, traces a shadowy reference to this other, punitive, aspect of women working with wheels? Svetlana Alpers has, I think, hinted at a very similar train of ideas when she writes of how Velásquez (echoing Titian and Rubens) was 'clearly attracted by the erotic interplay within a band of women' who have been taken 'inside to an imaginary workplace or studio' and set to work.[51]

Mechanical spinning was mind-numbingly repetitious, and hence its usefulness as a form of punishment. It was, moreover, a task that was undergoing a series of rapid technological shifts in the pre-industrial world. In the thirteenth century, in Europe, women had to develop the considerable manual skill required to operate the 'great wheel' as the earlier form of the spinning wheel was known. This device had begun to replace the more primitive technique of twisting together fibres to form a continuous thread using a spindle which was twirled, and a distaff, the stick used to hold the fibres ready for spinning, which we have already seen functioning as a symbol of female autonomy.[52] Later, in the fifteenth century, the 'great wheel' was to be replaced, in turn, by the more efficient 'Saxon wheel', familiar from illustrations to fairy stories, with the addition of a treadle in the earlier seventeenth century. This is the device that is shown at work in *Las Hilanderas*.[53]

The mechanization of this industry was already well established, at least in parts of Italy, by the sixteenth century, as we have seen in the case of Montaigne's visit to Florence. But, for all that Velásquez chose to depict his female workers in the foreground of Las Hilanderas as engaged in a busy, sociable activity, or that Montaigne watched groups of women working in what was, clearly, a space resembling our modern idea of a factory, the reality of spinning in early modern communities was usually that of isolated female labour. So, the more familiar image of women at work with machines is that of the spinster, labouring with her wheel in a reserved, domestic, environment. The solitude of the 'spinster', a term which once described the archetype of the solitary female, seems to have been enforced by legislation in some communities.[54] A sixteenth-century regulation, promulgated in the Ribble Valley, in Northern England, enforced solitude on women working at spinning, on payment of a fine:

> We are Agreyd, that no women, shall goe Abroade into theire neighbours howses with their distaves, neither daye nor night, nor spyne by the waye, for ev'ry tyme so doinge the spynner shall forfete and paye xiid.[55]

Although the regulation alluded to the older, more rudimentary, distaff and spindle technology employed by women prior to the advent of the spinning wheel in the thirteenth century, the wording of the edict indicates that this older technology was still being used three hundred years later.

It has been suggested that the fine was a 'precaution against embezzlement; thefts of yarn by women were a common offence'.[56] But the patriarchal tone of that 'we are agreed' might equally be understood as an attempt by men to regulate the working lives of women, tying them by legislative force to the domestic hearth, and preventing them associating together in unruly, 'gossiping' groups.[57] This English example of the fear of women gathering together armed with their spindles and distaffs is echoed in accounts of sixteenth-century German *Spinnstuben*, public spinning rooms, which were viewed suspiciously by the local authorities as potential sites of female disturbance and disorder in the community.[58] How appropriate, then, to turn the spinning wheel, which was one of the very few devices available to women to claim some measure of economic independence, and which, in other symbolic contexts, proclaimed their virtuous industry, into an instrument of punishment?

According to Adam Smith, mechanized spinning devices, which replaced the older device of the distaff and spindle, doubled the productivity of labour compared to earlier, non-mechanical, techniques.[59] But for all its repetitive nature, the task of spinning was by no means easy, and the advent of mechanization may even have made it rather more difficult. Operating the mechanized spinning wheel required a good deal of skill and dexterity.[60] Even for the skilled female operator, who might be assumed to have developed 'automatism of habit', work of this kind, if it were also subject to unforeseeable interruption, could hardly have been unthinking. But repetition made it an ideal task for mechanization. In the early seventeenth century, imaginative ideas of deploying hydraulic power in this process had begun to take hold. Giovanni Branca's *Le Machine* (1629) shows a woman seated at a hydraulically powered spinning device, operating a reversed Archimedean screw (Figure 4.7).

But for all that the work of Clotho, Lachesis, and Atropos had been imaginatively mechanized in Branca's image, solitary domestic spinning still predominated in early-modern communities.[61] Spinning was an economically vital task in early-modern society. A recent exploration of patterns of female labour in seventeenth-century England identifies spinning, along with dairying, brewing, and baking, as one of the 'key forms' of women's work in the period.[62] Although it was also notoriously badly paid, spinning was deemed to be as important as the labour required to till the fields. A 1613 pamphlet on the English cloth industry adopted the language of the Book of Proverbs to reinforce the economic importance of the task: 'men that would lay no hand to the plough, and women that would set no hand on the wheel' would equally deserve 'the censure of wise Solomon, Hee that would not labour should not eat'.[63] There is also some evidence to suggest that, for all its later association in Dutch art with the bourgeois virtues of industry and diligence, or its appearance in the eighteenth century as a fashionable social device, the chore of spinning tended to be concentrated in lower-class households.[64] Technological historians tend to agree, too, that women were assigned to this kind of textile work in pre-industrial societies in order to ensure that the productive labour of women would not be lost during their child-bearing years.[65] The spinning wheel was readily suited to the less structured, more diverse, and less easily categorized range of tasks facing working women, as opposed to gentlewomen, within sixteenth- and

Figure 4.7 Giovanni Branca, *Le Machine. Volume nuouo et di molto artificio da fare effetti marauigliosi . . . arichito di bellissime figure* (Rome, 1629), plate 20, private collection.

seventeenth-century communities. So, in her *Working Life of Women in the Seventeenth Century*, Alice Clark has suggested that spinning was peculiarly suited to the demands of female patterns of labour: 'the mechanical character of the movements, and the small demand they make on eye or thought, renders spinning wonderfully adapted to women whose serious attention is engrossed by the care or training of their children'.[66] Spinning, in this description, is not so much 'labour' as it is a useful diversion from the more 'serious' task of child rearing. It is important to note, here, that Clark is *not* suggesting that women are, somehow, mentally or physically more suited to this 'mechanical task'. Rather, her argument is that women were subjected to so many different kinds of demands on their time that a task which could be easily picked up, then set aside, was inevitably, one that fell within their demesne. As Mary Prior writes, here in the context of her study of working women in the urban economy of Oxford in the early-modern period: 'Asymmetry bred asymmetry. Because a man's work was clearly demarcated and limited, his day had a beginning and an end;' by contrast 'even when sitting down, women spun, knitted or sewed'.[67]

Spinning is a very clear example of a technological task being distributed according to perceived gender roles. The role of women in the development and deployment of technology in later periods, particularly in the nineteenth and early twentieth centuries, has been the subject of much academic research in recent years.[68] These enquiries into the relationship of women with machinery have tended to reflect a more generalized sense that working with machines has been, historically, a masculine preserve: 'women have been conditioned historically to feel that they cannot comprehend technology, that indeed technical matters constitute a male realm', writes Martha Moore Trescott.[69] Spinning and weaving, however, seem to have worked as exceptions to this rule. By the same token, women's labour in earlier periods has been understood, historically, as commonplace, unregulated, and by and large hidden. Until very recently, it was assumed that women's labour in the early-modern period did not figure in the historical record at all when compared to the labour of men where the records of craft guilds, for example, provide valuable information on the patterns of male labour.[70]

At its most extreme, the very concept of useful 'work' has been not infrequently defined, in Western industrial societies, by supposedly male ideals of labour. Thus, in the case of engineering, Cynthia Cockburn writes that:

> ... the norm for the industrial worker is male ... Engineering represents everything that is defined as manly – the propensity to control and manip-

ulate nature; the celebration of muscle and machine in action upon raw materials; the tolerance of, even pleasure in, dirt, *viz*, grease, swarf and metal shavings . . . Technical work involves the acceptance of physical risk – exposure to frequent accidents, cuts, contusions. It affords free movement round and about its object, in contrast to the physical confinement of much women's work. It implies control – designing solutions to physical problems, making energy work for you. The all-male workshop fosters and develops masculine patterns of relationships, it is the home of camaraderie based on the exchange of anecdote and slander concerning women.[71]

As well as indicating the historical bias at work in this field, Cockburn's account emphasizes the communal, sociable nature of male patterns of involvement in technology. For women's work in the early-modern period, by contrast, unless it took place within the ambiguously sexualized sphere of a place such as the Amsterdam *Spinhuis* or the dangerously subversive sociability of the German *Spinnstuben*, isolation, as we have seen, was more likely to have been the norm. Distaff and spindle technology was easily portable; a spinning wheel, on the other hand, was far too cumbersome an object to be readily moved from one location to another.[72] Cockburn draws our attention, too, to patterns of male behaviour which seem to be the direct result of labouring with machinery: the sense of control over nature and of the task in hand; the harmonious coming together of human muscle power and the machine; the idea of 'free movement' around the object of one's labours in comparison to the fixed position adopted by the seated spinning woman; and finally, and perhaps most important of all, that notion of 'camaraderie'. These characteristics of mechanical work are seen as offshoots of the historical appropriation of certain forms of technology by men.

The development of these attributes was a direct outcome of the mechanical culture of the early-modern period. As knowledge and experience of large-scale machines spread not only among machine workers, but also among the purchasers and readers of works such as the machine books in the later sixteenth and seventeenth centuries, working with such devices was invariably shown to be a male occupation. Here, of course, is a familiar story. So, Judy Wajcman has argued that 'it was only with the formation of engineering as a white, male, middle-class profession that "male machines and female fabrics" became the modern markers of technology'.[73] Wajcman sees this process as a nineteenth-century phenomenon, based around a developing 'idea of manliness':

> ... characterised by the cultivation of bodily prowess and individual achievement ... drawn around the engineering bastion. It was during and through this process that the term 'technology' took on its modern meaning. Whereas the earlier concept of the 'useful arts' had included needlework and metalwork as well as spinning and mining, by the 1930s this had been supplanted by the idea of technology as applied science.[74]

Wacjman's analysis assumes that the idea of 'technology' as masculine, together with an idea of 'manliness' associated with such technology, really only begins in this later period. Yet, an idea of 'manliness', cultivated through the encounter with machines, seems to have been at work long before the rise of the engineering professions in the nineteenth century. Thus, although Georgius Agricola's 1556 treatise on mining *De Re Metallica* showed women at work in the Bohemian mining industry, their labour tended to be unskilled: carrying, sorting, and sifting are the chief tasks in which the woodcut illustrations show them to be engaged. Unskilled female labour in the service of technology has a long history: a fifteenth-century image of a water mill shows two women, bent under their burdens of sacks of grain which are being carried to the mill, while a well-dressed man, perhaps the miller himself but more likely the landowner, watches their efforts approvingly. Gender divisions are even more pronounced in Ramelli's *Le Diverse et Artificiose Machine* (1588). Of the 195 illustrations in that volume, only seven (less than 4 per cent) depict female figures, and in these few instances, women are usually shown to be performing the ancillary tasks of carrying items. Only once is a woman shown to be operating a machine. A single illustration shows a woman turning a crank operating a pump to draw water from a well: a task that, given the division of domestic or household labour in the period, must have been a fairly common chore for women to have performed. Two other illustrations show women simply as onlookers, watching men at work with machines.

Machines, for Ramelli, are overwhelmingly masculine devices. With their help, men labour with other men to deploy mechanical force to compel nature to undertake work. Most remarkable of all, that device which revolutionized the European textile industry in the medieval period, and which was held to be, as we have seen, the technological preserve of women – the spinning wheel – simply does not appear in Ramelli's text.[75] As far as Ramelli was concerned, the spinning wheel, a female device, did not exist as a machine, just as, in his illustrations, the backbreaking labour of drawing water from a well (which many of his complex arrangements of gears, pumps, and pulleys were designed to facilitate), once it had been mechanized, was understood as implicitly male rather than female labour. 'Female machines' (i.e. machines designed to be operated by women), as well as female machine operators, are not to be found in the world of Renaissance mechanical culture, even if, paradoxically, the most technologically advanced instrument known to early-modern people was, in effect, reserved almost exclusively for the work of women.[76]

How did this paradoxical disjunction come about? Why did working with machinery come to be seen as the preserve of men, even as numberless women laboured with their spinning wheels? The answer lies not in any idea of the disproportion of physical strength, let alone supposedly differing male or female aptitudes, but rather in the classical antecedents of the machine. For Renaissance engineers, as we have seen, the most 'noble' instruments of all were those that could be operated 'at a single touch' by the operator, and of these kinds of machine, it was, in turn, those modelled on ancient military engines which represented the height of the engineer's aspirations. Machines had thus inherited some of the attributes of the art of warfare, which was, of course, an exclusively masculine preserve in the period. So, the machine was invested with 'dignity' or 'nobility', springing out of an older, chivalric, sense of masculinity. In this context, Cockburn's comments on the masculine appropriation of machinery in later periods become all the more relevant. She writes:

> Men's greater average physical stature and strength are often cited as a reason for men's preponderance in engineering occupations. Yet it is not self-evident that they should be male. Many machines, from the lever to the mill, have been developed precisely to substitute for human physical strength.[77]

Remarking on the fact that many women find that mechanical equipment is manufactured in such a way that makes it difficult for them to operate, Cockburn argues that 'this need not be conspiracy, it is merely the outcome of a pre-existing pattern of power', whereby women who operate machines are seen as substitutes for their male counterparts. The machine, in Cockburn's words, is 'lent' to women, in much the same way as machines more generally are only 'lent' to men by capital.[78] In the context of Renaissance machinery, the ideas of nobility and dignity deployed by the machine book authors invested their various inventions with a sense of military glamour, inherited from those older, chivalric, views of the arts of warfare. These

codes worked all the more effectively to promote the very idea of mechanism as an arena in which men laboured together with their machines and
devices to wage war not against one another, but against that archetypical
female symbol: nature.

Myth and symbolism may have as important a part to play in our understanding of the gendered nature of the technological past, in this respect,
as historical records or images: 'The Fates spun, and it was the assigned
fate of mortal women to spin.'[79] Was it (for example) an older, mythical
memory of the female Fates, whose task it was to spin out, measure, and
then cut the thread of human life, and who thus controlled human destiny,
which somehow made the local legislators of the Ribble Valley in sixteenth-
century England even more nervous at the prospect of women gathering
in groups to spin, measure, and cut thread? Or was there something more
politically fundamental about the male desire to carefully regulate women's
access to technology? Certainly, there are other examples of the regulation
of female time and activity in related contexts in the early-modern period.
Thus, Lena Cowen Orlin has explored the representation of needlework and
embroidery, another sanctioned female occupation in the early-modern
period, as 'an instrument of oppression'. Citing the care taken to ensure
that women who gathered in groups to pursue this activity were carefully
supervised with the lady of the house reading aloud from 'histories of virtuous women', Orlin concludes that work and communal reading 'presumably
prevented thoughts from wandering or tongues from wagging on inappro-
priate lines'.[80]

Nobody, of course, designed the spinning wheel in order to anchor women
more firmly to the household, let alone the prison or the workhouse. The
social effects, in other words, of working with a given machine may be largely
unforeseeable, even if the economic effects of depressing the price of labour
(which was the constant complaint of industrial workers in the nineteenth
century) were, indeed, predictable. But the question of the intersection of
women and technology in the early-modern period becomes even more
complex if we now turn to other kinds of evidence.

The wheel of Fortune

In the story of St Catherine and her wheel, the 'broken wheel' becomes
emblematic of the saint's divinely inspired power over the crude human
technology of terror deployed by her Roman persecutor. In similar fashion,
we find that, far from being constrained by their instruments or devices, in

other images and motifs from the medieval and Renaissance worlds, women who operate mechanical devices are invested with power, albeit of a symbolic character. But this power was not benign. Once more, the wheel was figured as an emblem of punishment, but this time it was a device driven by a female hand, and it was set to work to punish the great for the sin of pride or *hubris*. Thus the spinster would reappear in another guise altogether, as a sinister or even malevolent figure: an attribute which perhaps unravels even more of the rich texture of Velásquez's image of a woman seated at her turning wheel in seventeenth-century Spain.

In children's fairy stories, the figure of the elderly spinster, bent over her wheel, is often a sinister character. Deformed by her work, she is related to the mythic deformation suffered by Arachne, the spider and spinner of webs of deceit or guile, rather than to Penelope, at work on her loom, a figure of devotion and constancy. But the spinster is also related to the ambiguously powerful figure of Fortune. Fortune was, of course, a woman, turning her wheel incessantly. 'Let us mock the good housewife Fortune from her wheel' says Celia in Shakespeare's *As You Like It* 'that her gifts may henceforth be bestowed equally' (I. ii. 26–7). In Celia's homely image, Shakespeare conflates two aspects of fortune or fate, both of which are associated with women. In the image of Fortune and her wheel is the familiar image of *Fortuna* as Boethius or Chaucer might have depicted her. But in seating her in the familiar context of the spinning wheel, as a 'good housewife', Shakespeare is recalling the work of women labouring at their wheels, and hearkening back to the older allegory of destiny expressed in women who work with thread, that of the *Moirai* or Fates.

The wheel, fate, fortune, and the manufacture of thread or yarn are intertwined with one another in often-complex symbolic ways. Certainly, the wheel, in Renaissance Europe, also had a wider, mystical or cosmographical significance, and in this it can be compared to that fashion for 'mechanized piety' that is said to have emerged in twelfth-century China. Was not the pre-Copernican spherical universe, after all, depicted as a vast system of concentric rings, rotating around a common axle, whose still point was the earth itself, a structure which the imaginary perpetual motion machine of Cornelius Drebbel, admired by King James, was designed to imitate? The roundness of the universe, of which the wheel was emblematic, was confirmed not just by the observation of the wheeling heavens. Theologically and philosophically, in the words of the sixteenth-century English cosmographer, Thomas Blundeville, the circular universe imitated 'the chief idea or shape of Gods minde, which hath neither beginning nor ending, and therefore is compared to a circle'.[81]

But if the wheel was a symbolic expression of providence, it was also (para-doxically) an attribute of a far more fickle element in human life. The wheel, the epitome of circular motion and, indeed, of the very idea of circularity, was also expressive of the seemingly arbitrary or even whimsical turns of the individual's fate within either the political or personal realm. Thus, one of the omnipresent images in medieval and Renaissance culture is the emblem of the terrible goddess *Fortuna* which drew upon the everyday technological device of the fixed wheel to express humanity's necessary submission to fate or destiny: 'I torne the whirlinge wheel with the torninge cercle; I am glad to chaungen the lowest to the heyest, and the heyest to the lowest', says Fortune – a female figure – in Chaucer's fourteenth-century translation of the *De Con-solatione philosophiae* of Boethius.[82]

Boethius's text, composed in late antiquity, was hugely popular in the Renaissance.[83] Significantly, *Fortuna* is rarely evoked in those moments that see the lowly raised up. Rather, she is at her most potent when the great are cast down. We see Fortune and her wheel, for example, resurfacing in the pageant of the 'Mutabilitie Cantos', appended to the posthumous first folio edition of Spenser's *The Faerie Queene* in 1609. Fortune's wheel is an instru-ment of sportive cruelty, governing not just human life, but the lives of every mortal thing, the property of the rebellious goddess Mutabilitie in Spenser's fable. Just as in the labour of spinning, it is a woman who turns the wheel:

What man that sees the euer-whirling wheele
Of *Change*, the which all mortal things doth sway,
But that thereby doth find, and plainly feele,
How *MUTABILITY* in them doth play
Her cruel sports, to many men's decay?

(*FQ* VII. vi. 1)

Presenting her masque of change that, in its processional nature, seems to operate like the complex processions of mechanical figures to be found on the great public clocks of the period, Mutabilitie's claim is that:

. . . *Times* do change and moue continually.
So nothing here long standeth in one stay:
Wherefore, this lower world who can deny
But to be subiect still to *Mutablilitie*?

(*FQ* VII. vii. 47)

Change is here conceived of as a universal engine of perpetual motion, governing human existence in the sublunary world. In similar measure, in Shakespeare's *King Lear*, the image of the wheel expressed the larger turns of fate in human life. 'The wheel is come full circle! I am here' (V. iii. 174) exclaims Edmund, confronted by his brother Edgar towards the end of the play. Although the allusion, here, is possibly to the ancient technology of the potter's wheel to be found in a story recounted by Augustine, we can guess that Shakespeare's audience would have also recognized the more familiar image of the turning wheel of Fortune.[84]

Wheels and mechanical motion seem to haunt *King Lear*. In the play, wheels are associated primarily with the figure of the sovereign, Lear himself, as an emblem of his internal torment, 'bound / Upon a wheel of fire' (IV. vii. 46–7). The wheel of fire is a remembrance of the fate of Ixion, bound to whirl eternally on a wheel of fire, punished by Zeus for attempting to seduce Hera, and also, perhaps, of the fate of the criminal condemned to be broken on the wheel.[85] Earlier in the play, Lear is not so much fixed to the wheel, as he is a personification of the wheel. Just as in Grotius's poem to King James, where the sovereign's power in the political realm could be considered as a form of mechanical 'motion', so Lear's fall from power was imagined as a catastrophic mechanical failure, a technological collapse: 'Let go thy hand when a great wheel runs down a hill, lest it break thy neck with following it; but the great one that goes up the hill, let him draw thee after', so the Fool advises Kent (II. iv. 66–7). Here, the familiar image of Fortune turning her wheel has been reworked in terms of a larger industrial apparatus, of the kind that Montaigne had seen and admired on the rivers of Europe, or of the type that was to be found in the machine books of the period, or even beneath the arches of London Bridge at the time that the play was written. In the Fool's Machiavellian parable, Lear, the erstwhile ruler of Britain, has become a piece of malfunctioning technology, part of an ambiguously evoked system of pulleys for heaving weights.

Lear is crazily dismounted and incapable of driving the engine of state, but he still possesses the latent energy to crush those who insist on trying to harness the residue of force that remains. In *Hamlet*, too, Shakespeare has the courtier, Rosencrantz, develop the analogy of the sovereign with a malfunctioning machine at more length, comparing the concept of majesty (through a pun on weal/wheel) to:

> . . . a massy wheel
> Fixed on the summit of the highest mount,

> To whose huge spokes ten thousand lesser things
> Are mortised and adjoined, which when it falls
> Each small annexment, petty consequence,
> Attends the boist'rous ruin.
>
> (III. iii. 17–22)

This image is reminiscent of those depictions of Babel in the late sixteenth and seventeenth centuries, which showed the gigantic edifice festooned with stupendous machinery. Although the image of a 'massy wheel / Fixed on the summit of the highest mount' is suggestive of a wind-driven machine of some kind, or the complex machinery to be found in the machine books of the late sixteenth century, we do not have to anchor ourselves to a particular machine, or set of machines, to grasp the tenor of Shakespeare's metaphor. The image of the 'massy wheel' in *Hamlet* rests, in the end, on the turning wheel of fortune. The king's majesty, a vast imaginary engine, is a purposeful component in a larger mechanical system driven neither by wind nor water, but by providence or fate. The failure of this system precipitates the general ruin of the commonweal, in which the sovereign is envisaged as a component within the larger and more complex engine which is society, and from which no element of the mechanism can be considered detached. These Renaissance appropriations and transformations of the ancient image of *Fortuna* were associated with the failure of gigantic and cumbersome machines. Christian mythographers and poets understood this failure, in turn, as symbolic of the primal fall of humanity. The pagan goddess *Fortuna*, reinterpreted by the mythographers and poets, thus occupies an equivalent place to that occupied by Eve in the Old Testament story. Both were female figures held to be culpable for wider human transformation, usually for the worse.

The image of the turning wheel of fortune – 'the giddy round of fortune's wheel' as Shakespeare described fluctuations in human life in *The Rape of Lucrece* (1594) (ll. 952) – is omnipresent within Shakespeare's writing, particularly his history plays. This, of course, is not surprising in a sequence of plays whose plots are governed by a view of history that is, in the end, cyclical.[86] Rotary motion inhabits Shakespeare's idea of history, as it did those of his contemporaries. We encounter this idea of cyclical motion at the very end of *Henry V* (1600). In the epilogue to the play, Henry's brief and brilliant career is summed up by the Chorus: 'Fortune made his sword', before the audience is reminded of what they already know from the sequence of *Henry VI* plays, which, though they deal with a chronologically later period in English history, had already been performed on the London stage in 1600. This 'star of England', which is both Henry himself, and the nation's fortune, had attained its zenith. Its only trajectory, now, was downwards, tracing the circumference of the turning wheel of the heavens.

The verbose Fluellen, in Shakespeare's *Henry V*, explains for us something of the iconography of the restless mechanical symbol, with its female prime mover:

> Fortune is painted blind with a muffler afore her eyes, to signify to you that fortune is blind. And she is painted also with a wheel, to signify to you – which is the moral of it – that she is turning and inconstant and mutability and variation. And her foot, look you, is fixed upon a spherical stone, which rolls and rolls and rolls.
>
> *(Henry V III. vi. 29–34)*

It is not the blindness of Fortune (an attribute, after all, that she shares with those other Renaissance personifications, Justice, and Love) that is the essence of the 'moral'. Rather, it is her association with a turning wheel which best expressed her qualities of mutability and variation. Her precarious stance on a rolling stone also symbolizes her continual, restless, motion. That she was also a woman, the epitome of inconstancy so it was held, was also, of course, significant. What Fluellen is describing is an image such as that to be found on the title page of *The Castle of Knowledge* (1556) the work of the mathematician and astronomer, Robert Recorde (Figure 4.8). In Recorde's titlepage, blind Fortune, poised unsteadily on her rock, turns her wheel, with the help of a connecting rod and a crank. On the rim of the wheel is inscribed the Latin motto '*Qui modo scandit corruet statim*' – 'Whoever rises, will soon Fall.'[87]

These symbolic attributes of the ancient image of *Fortuna*, the goddess of human destiny who punishes the great for their pride, send us back, once more, to Velásquez's *Las Hilanderas*, with its three central female figures in the foreground echoing the ancient Greek trio of fateful female yarn workers – the *Moirai*. But if we study the image in terms of the more obvious attributes of the fixed wheel of fate, then a small detail in the picture's foreground becomes significant. The pose of the seated female figure at her wheel is curiously awkward. This awkwardness is a function of the fact that her bare left leg is extended, with her foot hovering above the floor, as if she has just kicked to one side, with her naked foot what might appear to be a ball of wool, of the kind which the woman working with the skein of thread holds in her right hand. Yet Velásquez seems to have invested this light, fibrous,

Figure 4.8 Robert Recorde, *The Castle of Knowledge* (London, 1556), frontispiece. Glasgow University Library, Special Collections.

stuff with a stony materiality, as if in remembrance of the rolling stone upon which the familiar figure of *Fortuna* was balanced. Arachne's fate or fortune is sealed; the wheel is about to plunge downwards, carrying her with it.

The wheel, driven by a female figure, is a restless symbol. And yet here is a further paradox. For one of the qualities of a fixed wheel is the strict regularity with which any point on its circumference traces a path through space and time. The wheel turns, in other words, but it always returns, and this is nature's point in *The Faerie Queene*, when she rejects Mutabilitie's claim to universal dominion. This attribute is the very opposite of the arbitrary qualities that we, today, might associate with the idea of mutability: a state of continual, restless, and above all, unpredictable or random change. The wheeled and wheel-turning goddess was thus not simply an expression of the blind and arbitrary hits of chance. Rather (as Michael Witmore points out) she could be invoked 'as the cause of any outcome that could not be predicted in advance'.[88] Only when seen retrospectively, are the effects of fortune, paradoxically, apparent. This paradox informs the climax of Christopher Marlowe's *Edward II* (1594), when Edward's nemesis, Mortimer, compares his state, moments before his execution, to the path traced by the circumference of the turning wheel of Fortune, and addresses the fickle goddess directly:

> Base Fortune, now I see, that in thy wheele
> There is a point, to which when men aspire,
> They tumble hedlong downe: that point I touchte,
> And, seeing there was no place to mount vp higher,
> Why should I greeue at my declining fall?[89]

Here the wheel has become a consolatory mechanism. Watching a wheel in motion should have led Mortimer to the conclusion that his fate was inevitable, even if the precise moment in time when the revolving wheel would precipitate his headlong plunge was rather harder to foresee. In similar fashion, in the third part of Shakespeare's *Henry VI*, it is the turning circumference of the wheel of Fortune that provides the focus of the image in which King Edward vainly struggles to assert his own sense of individuality and autonomy against the turning wheel: 'Though fortune's malice overthrow my state, / My mind exceeds the compass of her wheel' (*3 Henry VI* IV. iv. 19–20). Edward, of course, has misunderstood the nature of Fortune and her wheel. Malice is exactly what the fixed wheel did *not* express. Rather, its relentless and endless mechanical motion was suggestive of the more impersonal operation of fate or fortune in human affairs.

But within the political realm, the sovereign could also be imagined as the driving mechanical force within the commonwealth. We have seen King James described in these terms in a eulogistic poem of the early years of the seventeenth century. But earlier still, these were precisely the terms in which Sir Walter Raleigh expressed his own emotional attachment to Queen Elizabeth. In the puzzling poem of erotic complaint which Raleigh addressed to the queen, possibly written following his period of imprisonment in 1592, and known as 'The 21st and Last Book of the Ocean to Cynthia' (or sometimes, more simply, as 'The Ocean's Love to Cynthia') wheels, women, and water technology appear once more, though in a more obscure guise than was to be found in the designs of the Renaissance engineers:

> Or as a wheel forced by the falling stream
> Although the course be turned some other way,
> Doth for a time go round upon the beam
> Till, wanting strength to move, it stands at stay;
> So, my forsaken heart, my withered mind . . .[90]

Raleigh's image is clearly indebted to the idea of the turning wheel of Fortune, while it also incorporates the idea of the turning mill wheel. The turning water wheel, robbed of its motive power, yet possesses (as does Lear in Shakespeare's more forceful metaphor of the dismounted wheel) some latent energy. This last vestige of motive force allows the wheel to turn, fitfully, on its axis until it 'stands at stay'. In Raleigh's simile, the monarch is the stream, the energy source of the turning wheel, as well as the source of both the emotional and political power wielded by her courtiers on her behalf. Once the stream's 'course' is 'turn'd some other way', her eye alighting on some other favourite, then the courtly wheel, divested of its purpose, may turn briefly but its power both to move and to work on the queen's behalf has disappeared.[91] Raleigh's anthropomorphic simile, in which the ever-more slowly turning wheel reflects his own vanishing emotional and political attachment to the queen, is a curious inversion of the more familiar emblem of *Fortuna*. Rather than being subject to the turn of Fortune's wheel, Raleigh imagines himself to be the wheel, moved by the irresistible but fickle power of the sovereign's 'stream' of preferment.

The wheel of fortune is an ancient device, although the symbol was to be reinvigorated by the appearance of the many types of mechanical devices that were now appearing, whether on paper or beneath the arches of Old London Bridge. A wheel's motion was regular and predictable once it had started to turn, but herein lay the problem. Knowing when it would begin to revolve, feeling the first faint stirrings of this symbolic mechanism, was the Machiavellian trick that the Renaissance courtier had to learn if he was to preserve himself. 'Let go thy hand' was the advice of the Fool in *King Lear* as the wheel of power plunged out of control. And he was, of course, quite right. If to be attached to the turning mechanism as it began its descent was to court disaster, then even worse was to be linked to a mechanism that had spun out of control entirely. So, the turning wheel was an emblem of those terrible alterations of state which affected everyone, but none more so than the great in the courtly world of the earlier sixteenth century. Sir Thomas Wyatt's poetry, for example, abounds in circular revolving metaphors of collapse and change, which are associated, more often than not, with ambiguously powerful female presences. Wyatt, who suffered periods of imprisonment, also found himself punished by the turning wheel of Fortune, though it must have seemed, at times, to have been operated directly by a sovereign with whom conversation, in Stephen Greenblatt's memorable phrase, 'must have been like small talk with Stalin'.[92] Fortune, nevertheless, drove the mechanism by which Wyatt would find himself 'aghast' at the heart-stopping velocity with which his state could so suddenly shift: 'for dread to fall I stand not fast' he wrote, as though his day to day existence was bound up with the sickening apprehension that Fortune's mechanism might pause, but any cessation in its circular motion was, at best, momentary.[93] Wyatt experienced on more than occasion the giddy alteration of the turning wheel, when, poised at the summit of ambition, he found himself plunged into the abyss of imprisonment and fear of death as the turning wheel began to shift. This motion, for all that it might have been foreseeable, still prompted incredulity on the part of the victim:

> Is it possible
> For to turn so oft,
> To bring that lowest that was most aloft,
> And to fall highest yet to light soft:
> It is possible.[94]

Indeed it was. So, 'Good Fortune was my guyde', wrote Isabella Whitney in the commendatory verses prefacing her collection of poems *A Sweet Nosegay* (1573), 'though she ever hath denyde, to hoyce me on her Wheele'.[95] Fifty years later, in his 'Elegy' written following the death of John Donne in 1631, Thomas Carew would describe Donne's influence on English poetry in terms of the mechanism of the turning wheel, in a simile reminiscent of Raleigh's image of the gradual loss of momentum of a turning water wheel. With Donne's death, Carew wrote, it was as if the motive force of poetry had lost its prime mover. Though poetry is able to turn, falteringly, for a brief period following the withdrawal of the 'moving hand' that was the effect of Donne's poetic voice among his contemporaries, poetry has lost its impetus:

> So doth the swiftly turning wheel not stand
> In th'instant we withdraw the moving hand,
> But some small time maintain a faint weak course
> By virtue of the first impulsive force;[96]

And even in the twentieth century, the image has lingered on. The popular TV game show, 'Wheel of Fortune', originating in the 1980s in Los Angeles, and transmitted in the UK throughout most of the 1990s, featured a woman and a mechanical wheel. Although it might seem odd to compare the worlds of twentieth-century popular light entertainment to the very different worlds inhabited by Wyatt, Shakespeare, Isabella Whitney, Carew, or Velásquez in the Spanish court, yet this symbol of a woman and a mechanical device has remained a potent means of explaining the nature of flux or change in the sublunary world.

'A thing made for Alexander'

For all that they may have incessantly turned wheels in the early-modern world, either literally or symbolically, Freud reminds us of how rarely women have been celebrated as the designers of a particular technological device. We do not know who first designed the spinning wheel, or adapted it to work more efficiently. Given that, in early-modern Europe, women were so ubiquitously tied to this kind of machine, it is difficult to believe that female design ingenuity was not at work in the evolution of the device. But we have one, remarkable, instance of a woman as a designer of an engine, though one that operated in a purely imaginative literary realm.

Shakespeare's most forthright exploration of the nature of power and masculinity in the early-modern state, Coriolanus (composed c. 1608, but not published until 1623), takes us back to that much broader question of the relationship between technology and gender that we have been exploring throughout this chapter. And it also returns us, for the last time, to the three seated female figures occupying centre-stage in *Las Hilanderas*. The world of *Coriolanus* has been described as 'hard, tough, unaccommodating', and the play itself, one of Shakespeare's most 'masculine' plays.[97] Within this world, the central dilemma of the eponymous hero, Coriolanus, is expressed in the struggle between the pulls of kindred affiliation, and his decision to forswear his loyalty to the Republic and to join with his erstwhile foe though equal in military valour, Tullus Aufidius, who has besieged Rome. The ties binding Coriolanus to Rome are represented by the demands made upon him by the women in the play: his mother and his wife. At the play's outset, these women, Volumnia and Virgilia, are discovered by Valeria ('a chaste lady of Rome') sewing: the stage direction in the 1623 (folio) edition of the play (I. ii) reads: '*Enter Volumnia and Virgilia, mother and wife to Martius. They set them down on two low stools and sew.*' When Valeria joins with them on the stage, the tableau is complete. We watch three women working with thread and discussing the life of a man, a point emphasized by Valeria when she urges Virgilia to abandon her labour ('lay aside your stitchery'), and join her outdoors, in an allusion to the story of Penelope: 'You would be another Penelope. Yet they say all the yarn she spun in Ulysses' absence did but fill Ithaca full of moths' (I. iii. 84–6). Shakespeare's allusion to Penelope as a spinner, rather than a weaver, draws not on the Penelope story as related in *The Odyssey*, but on Ovid's account of her as a spinner found in the *Heroides*, a version of the story which was well known to Renaissance poets.[98] In associating her with spinning, rather than weaving, Shakespeare seems to have foresworn the myth of chastity and constancy, for the altogether darker idea of women as manufacturers of the filament of human life spun and cut by the *Moirai*. So, the play as a whole investigates this theme, exploring how the life of a man has been spun out for him by his mother, and how that thread is cut by the intercession of the women at the play's conclusion. Clotho, Lachesis, and Atropos, then, are the presiding geniuses of the story of Coriolanus.

In keeping with this trope, Coriolanus is not so much a man as he is a fabricated object: the technological creation of a woman, his mother Volumnia. It is the terrifying Volumnia who, as she recalls, had fashioned her son for one purpose, war. 'When yet he was but tender-bodied and the only son of my womb', she recounts to Coriolanus's wife, Virgilia:

> . . . I, considering how honour would become such a person – that it was no better than picture-like, to hang by th'wall if renown made it not stir – was pleased to let him seek danger where he was like to find fame. To a cruel war I sent him, from whence he returned his brows bound with oak. I

tell thee, daughter, I sprang not more in joy at first hearing he was a man-
child than now in first seeing he had proved himself a man.

(I. iii. 9–17)

Volumnia is intent on constructing a devastatingly destructive ideal of masculinity. In pursuit of her ideal, whereby a child can be moulded into a
hybridized 'man-child', she is prepared to renounce the bonds of maternal
affection. Masculinity is defined by war, for which Volumnia has shaped (or
as the play has it, 'framed') her son, and which she now seeks to visit on
her grandson, of whose infant 'mammocking' of a 'gilded butterfly' in his
teeth she so much approves. For Young Martius – Coriolanus's son – has, in
Volumnia's eyes, embarked upon that programme which she had so successfully designed for his father. In her fantasies, the child's casual tearing
apart of the living creature suggests that he, too, will eventually become
a mechanistic implement of war, a personification of death who with his
'mailed hand then wiping' ventures forth 'like to harvest-man that's tasked
to mow / Or all or lose his hire' (I. iii. 37–9).

'One does not need the help of a psychoanalytic approach', writes Janet
Adelman of this play, 'to notice that Volumnia is not a nourishing mother.'[99]
And Coriolanus, by the same token, is not a nourishing father or husband.
Rather, he is invested with vague evocations of vast, machine-like motion.
In his pursuit of implacable conquest, his 'thunder-like percussion' shakes
the world (I. v. 30). As Volumnia (once more) expresses the matter in per-
haps Shakespeare's most chilling evocation of machine-like purposefulness:
'These are the ushers of Martius. Before him he carried noise, and behind
him he leaves tears. Death, that dark spirit, in's nervy arm doth lie, which
being advanced, declines; and then men die' (II. i. 155–8).

Here is that conflation of the organic and the mechanical which we have
already encountered in Leonardo's thoughts on both machines and bodies,
or in the designs of the machine book authors of the late sixteenth century.
Sequential motion, or cause and effect, energize that irresistible 'nervy arm'
whose output is death. An anatomically precise mortality machine, Coriolanus bears 'death's stamp', as if Volumnia were the designer, but Death
the manufacturer: he is a 'thing of blood, whose every motion / Was timed
with dying cries' (II. ii. 107, 109–10). Regularity and motion, the attendant
features of this 'thing of blood', are marked by the shrieks of human misery,
caught up within the mechanism's resistless progress. And like a machine,
Coriolanus appears to have no interior self-knowledge, only the purposeful
motion invested in him by his designer: 'What his breast forges, that his

tongue must vent' (III. i. 257), says the patrician Menenius, bewailing his friend's inability to dissemble before the populace. Coriolanus, in this metaphor, is not so much forged by Vulcan or Volumnia, as he is the forge. But he is a forge that moves: 'When he walks', says Menenius:

> . . . he moves like an engine, and the ground shrinks before his treading. He is able to pierce a corslet with his eye, talks like a knell, and his 'hmh!' is a battery. He sits in state like a thing made for Alexander. What he bids be done is finished with his bidding. He wants nothing of a god but eternity and a heaven to throne in.
>
> (V. iii. 18–25)

'Thingness' rather than humanity defines Coriolanus. Like a 'thing made for Alexander', Coriolanus, who has been framed by his mother, can be compared to the fabulous war engines which were appearing, at almost the same moment as the play's composition, in the anachronistic designs of the machine books that we have already explored: torsion catapults, siege engines, mechanical artillery modelled on the devices which battered into submission the city of Tyre, in 332 BCE, whose walls had once resisted the artilleryless armies of Nebuchadnezzar, 250 years earlier, in a siege lasting thirteen years.[100]

But *Coriolanus* also raises a peculiarly modern (or even post modern) dilemma. What if our machines, crafted with such precision and care, were to turn against us, as though we had inadvertently invested them with the vestiges of will? *Coriolanus* thus foreshadows the fantasy, or nightmare, of the cyborg: a theme to which we shall turn in the next chapter of this book. Like the replicants in Ridley Scott's film, *Blade Runner* (1982), Coriolanus turns on those who have fashioned him and used him. It is the efforts of his mother, at the end of the play, to divert him from his machine-like purpose, to reinvest him with feelings of common humanity, which occasions his destruction. In this respect, the tragedy of Coriolanus is that he has been so skilfully framed by his maternal designer that the act of memory and of moulding himself, pliantly, to the demands of kinship and social existence is entirely beyond him. Framed for just one purpose, the memory of what it is to be human becomes a perversely unnatural act. Confronted, in the persons of his wife and son (and his mother) with the evidence of his humanity, Coriolanus, the machine, breaks down, in the effort to deny the ties of kinship and nature:

> . . . I'll never
> Be such a gosling to obey instinct, but stand
> As if a man were author of himself
> And knew no other kin.

(V. ii. 34–37)

That 'as if' suggests the impossibility of resolving the dilemma. If 'instinct' is indeed implanted in human beings by their maker, as the gosling obeys instinct in bonding with the first moving object that captures its attention after it has hatched, then in what sense are humans free? How can it be possible to stand 'as if a man were author of himself' if all our actions have already been scripted for us, as the machine's actions have been foreseen by its maternal fabricator associated with the ancient trinity of spinning women? In *Coriolanus* the final reduction of the hero to a reified state of 'thingness' is confirmed by his mortal enemy (though equal in remorseless commitment to the craft of war), Aufidius, who pronounces his true epitaph. In hearkening to 'instinct' and obeying, for the last time, the will of his maker-mother, Coriolanus has become no more than 'a twist of rotten silk' (V. vi. 98), a discarded, manufactured, piece of fabric, such as that which was being assembled by the trio of women, with their needles, at the play's outset.

Aufidius's epithet – 'a twist of rotten silk' – returns us to the main theme that we have been exploring in this chapter: labour, technology, and the gendered traffic of machines and machinery associated with the female figure of *Fortuna* and the older figures of the *Moirai* or fates, all of which are present, too, in Velásquez's image. We have also seen how Freud, noting that women were rarely seen as technological innovators, claimed that the one exception to this rule was to be found in the case of weaving, which he was driven to explain in terms of a genital absence. But there may be other ways of approaching this problem. For, if we understand the technological impulse as a means of bringing new artefacts into the world, artificial creatures which had never existed before in nature, then the masculine involvement in machines of all kinds can be understood as the equivalent of parturition. In this respect, the 'framing' of Coriolanus by his mother acts as a more general metaphor for the birth of artificial entities, devised (so it was once believed) for the control of unruly nature by humans. In the story of Arachne, as told by Ovid, or as visualized by Velásquez, the manufacture of perfect representations of the world would result only in punishment. But *Coriolanus* alerts us to a further element in the history of our relationship with machines. In *Coriolanus*, a woman is able to transform a human being into a mechanism of some kind. But what happens when men begin to perceive their artificial creations in terms of the labour of parturition?

In the sixteenth and seventeenth centuries, these ideas would culminate in the disturbing prospect of the manufacture of artificial women, a topic that we shall also encounter in the next chapter. For the moment, though, it is enough to reflect on the idea that machines, as manufactured artefacts, may well have come to symbolize better versions of ourselves. Certainly, the habit of mind whereby we think of living organisms in terms of the dominant technology of the day is centuries old: in the seventeenth century clockwork devices provided a model of human motion, in the nineteenth century the living organism became a heat engine, while today the computer provides the prevailing analogy with which we measure our own humanity.[101] Machines and mechanisms of all kinds, which we have seen glimpsed in the margins of a painted landscape, or transforming a Renaissance city, or appearing as ingenious designs with which nature can be shaped and altered, had begun to emerge not as inanimate expressions of human ingenuity, but as rivals to human existence, as though they possessed not merely motion and movement, but a degree of autonomy. Words that express our ideas of mechanism, words such as automatatism, automacity, and automaton, share the Greek prefix: αυτό-, auto-, which means, of course, 'self'. Attached to a machine, the prefix denotes that appearance of self-movement or self-activation, a quality that machines, in their operation, appear to possess. But the etymological conjunction of autonomy and automacity reveals a new prospect of the history of our relationship to mechanism. And it is to the curious history of the Renaissance automaton that we now turn.

5

'NATURE WROUGHT'
Artifice, illusion, and magical mechanics

Metallic fantasies

Norbert Weiner has claimed that 'the ability of the artificer to produce a working simulacrum of a living organism' is deeply rooted in technological history.[1] An early seventeenth-century religious poem might seem, at first, to be an unlikely place to test this hypothesis. Yet, written with staccato verve and energy, possibly in the same year (1609) that Shakespeare wrote *Coriolanus*, John Donne's Holy Sonnet 'Batter my heart, three person'd God' seems to substantiate Weiner's speculation. Donne's poem also introduces the next stage of our enquiry: the exploration of the contest between art and nature that underpinned the mechanical culture of Renaissance Europe.

Donne's 'Batter my heart' celebrates the paradoxes that lie at the centre of the Christian doctrine of redemption and salvation. The poem is, by turns, hectoring, threatening, argumentative, wheedling, flirtatious and, finally, submissive:

> Batter my heart, three person'd God; for, you
> As yet but knocke, breathe, shine, and seeke to mend;
> That I may rise, and stand, o'ethrow mee,'and bend
> Your force, to breake, blowe, burn and make me new.
> I, like an usurpt towne, to'another due,
> Labour to admit you, but Oh, to no end,

Reason your viceroy in mee, mee should defend,
But is captiv'd, and proves weake or untrue.
Yet dearely 'I love you,'and would be loved faine,
But am bethroth'd unto your enemie:
Divorce mee,'untie, or breake that knot againe,
Take mee to you, imprison mee, for I
Except you'enthrall mee, never shall be free,
Nor ever chaste, except you ravish mee.[2]

That famous ending, in which a feminized Donne (or, at least, a feminized poetic voice) implores a hyper-masculine God to exert His 'force' first to 'divorce' the narrator from Satan ('your enemie'), and then 'imprison . . . enthrall . . . ravish' them into salvation is one of Donne's most deliberately shocking investigations into the mysteries of the Christian faith.

The opening images of the poem evoke a craft that is rough and rudimentary: a village blacksmith's shop or the bustling activity of an iron works of the kind in which we might imagine Coriolanus to have been metaphorically forged. Conversely, Donne's own poetic persona is imagined as a tarnished vessel in need of divine restoration. In developing these images, Donne was drawing on Augustine's view of God as 'the great artificer', whose task it was to refashion and bring to perfection fallen humanity.[3] The problem, though, as Donne expresses it, is that the Divinity has been too subtle or gentle in the exercise of His mechanical craft: 'for, you / As yet but knocke, breathe, shine, and seek to mend' he observes reprovingly. God is merely tinkering, when what is needed is a drastic refabrication of the human creature. The recalcitrant mechanism must be returned to the base metal out of which it has been wrought and the components recompacted into some new and more durable organization of spiritual matter if it is to 'rise, and stand' (the sexualized pun is, I suspect, deliberate) at the resurrection. 'O'ethrow mee . . . bend / Your force, to breake, blowe, burn and make me new' he implores. Force lies at the heart of the poem. God, the master technician and designer of the human frame, must be forced to realize that, in dealing with the rare quality, and rare sinfulness, of this particular example of His handiwork, some process more radical than mere refurbishment is called for.

'Batter my heart' is a bravura display of that all consuming 'I' encountered so frequently in Donne's writing, whether of the sacred or profane kind. At a rather more mundane level, it is also a good example of a Renaissance poet's delight in metallic imagery. The forge of Vulcan was not only attractive to visual artists in the period. The forge, with all its connotations of fire, heat, and the violent hammering into shape of new forms from crude metal, proved to be an appealing field of images with which to paint the pangs of despised love among the sonneteers of the generation of poets writing in the 1590s: witness Michael Drayton's sonnet 'My Heart the Anvile where my Thoughts doe Beate' (first published in 1594 in *Ideas Mirrour*) or Spenser's sonnet 'The paynefull smith with force of fervent heat' to be found in *Amoretti* (1595).[4] Each of these poems draws on exactly the same *topos*: that the human being, or at least human passion, can be considered in terms of the metallic creations forged or fashioned by art and artifice. At the same time, 'Batter my heart' is of a piece with other moments in Donne's writing when metallic industry seems to have seized hold of his imagination. What interested Donne was the ductility or malleability of metals, which enabled skilled craft workers to confect objects of enduring worth and beauty by applying the heat of the furnace. Such skill could be encountered at surprising moments. In the *Devotions upon Emergent Occasions* (1624), written out of an illness which came close to killing him, Donne imagines his own frame, wracked by fever, being poured out 'like lead, like yron, like brasse melted in a furnace . . .'.[5]

Donne was attracted by the potential restlessness of the morphology of metals.[6] This potential for change was related to the language and metaphors of alchemy that were so popular in the period, in which the adept was transformed into some better or more refined state.[7] Indeed, the very word 'refined' hints at both a spiritual exultation and the process by which pure metal was extracted from its impure source. Metal could be imagined as the 'soul' or essence of the metallic ore, wrestled from its loamy matrix by miners. New artificial forms were forged out of these natural substances in a process that was akin to parturition – 'the great work' as it was sometimes known among alchemists – while they were also the product of obscure alchemical reactions that might, of course, always prove fruitless or even fraudulent, as Donne (elsewhere) caustically observed:

> . . . such gold as that wherewithal
> Almighty *Chymiques* from each mineral,
> Having by subtle fire a soule out-pulled;
> Are dirtely and desperately gull'd:[8]

Crafted by God, the object that Donne's poetic persona imagines himself becoming in 'Batter my heart' is a metallic or artificial vision of a better existence. It offers the chance to be reborn and restored, and is thus part of that larger vision of machines that promised an optimistic restitution of the fallen human state.

This vision lingered on, in the imagination of the poets, well after the Renaissance. So Donne's Holy Sonnet might be compared to a twentieth-century poetic exploration of the power of the craft worker to produce mechanical life: the final stanza of W. B. Yeats's 'Sailing to Byzantium' (1927):

> Once out of nature I shall never take
> My bodily form from any natural thing,
> But such a form as Grecian goldsmiths make
> Of hammered gold and gold enamelling
> To keep a drowsy Emperor awake;
> Or set upon a golden bough to sing
> To lords and ladies of Byzantium
> Of what is past, or passing, or to come.[9]

Separated as they are by three hundred years, the tone of the two poems is, of course, very different. Where Donne is blusteringly insistent, Yeats's verses are a drowsy, nostalgic, reverie, evoking a distant and magical past. And yet, the similarities, too, are striking. Both poets imagine a transformation into some better version of humanity by surrendering to the prospect of artificiality. For Yeats, the fabulous, mythical, wrought creature he imagines himself becoming ('a form as Grecian goldsmiths make / Of hammered gold and gold enamelling') has no place in nature. Rather, it represents an escape out of nature into a world where temporality no longer holds sway. In his later poem 'Byzantium' (published in 1933), Yeats would return to this theme, writing of exchanging the organic 'complexities of mire and blood' for the 'glory of changeless metal'.[10] Metallic life is, at once, more durable and less complex than the vagaries of fleshly existence. It as if there is something enviable in the perpetual activity of delicate, highly wrought, artificial mechanisms when compared to the transitory nature of human existence. By contrast, although Donne's poem, too, expresses an idea of escape, his vision of God as an artificer or fabricator of humanity is still an entirely orthodox excursion into Christian theology. A few years later, the rather less orthodox Sir Thomas Browne, in his *Religio Medici* (composed in the 1630s, though not published until 1642) would speculate on the possibility that God, in constructing the 'frame of man' had 'played the sensible operator, and seemed not so much to create, as to make him'.[11]

Donne was not alone in his metallic speculations. For the French protestant poet Guillaume de Saluste, Sieur du Bartas (known in England in
the seventeenth century simply as Du Bartas), God was a supremely gifted
mechanician who had fashioned human creatures that were, in turn, capable
of fashioning objects of wonder on their own account. In his encyclopae-
dic account of the creation of the world to be found in his epic poem, La
Semaine (1578–84), Du Bartas celebrated mechanism and mechanical craft,
which he linked directly to the creative power of God. Rapturously, the
poem hymns those purely human skills by which artificial objects, including mechanical objects, are ushered into the world:

> Looke (if thou canst) from East to Occident,
> From *Island* to the *Moores* hot Continent;
> And thou shalt nought perfectly faire behold,
> But Pen, or Pencill, Graving-Toole, or Mould,
> Hath so resembled, that scarce can our eye
> The counterfait from the true thing discrie.
>
> (I. vi. 859–64)[12]

The artist's tools and implements, 'pen, Pencill, Graving-Toole, and Mould',
are deployed to make representations of the world so perfect that the eye
is deceived; the natural and the artificial seem to merge into one another.
Cataloguing those examples of classical art and legend in which human or,
indeed, animal eyes had been misled by artistic skill, Du Bartas exalted in
the rivalry which seemed to exist between art and nature. So, he recalls the
story of the 'brazen Mare' (actually, according to Pliny, a heifer, but horses
were far nobler than cows) said to have been cast by the fifth-century artist
Myron, which was mounted by beguiled stallions, the painted grapes fashioned by Zeuxis that beguiled birds into believing them to be real, and,
finally, the marble statues of Venus carved by Praxiteles and by Appeles,
which were said to have fired Athenian youths with erotic desire (I. vi.
865–77).

Such deceptions proved that human art or cunning could 'Goddess-like
another Nature frame' (I. vi. 875–6). In framing another nature, however,
it was mechanical skill, above all others, which most clearly illustrated the
impress of divine creative force on human ingenuity. So Du Bartas described
a series of artificial mechanical wonders encountered both in antiquity and
among the moderns: the wooden dove of the legendary engineer, Archytas, and the metallic eagle and the fly of Regiomontanus, fashioned by an

art that could 'compack / Features and formes that life and motion lack' (I. vi. 877–8). The human skill involved in the fashioning of these artificial creatures aped the original skill of the creator Himself, who worked by equivalent mechanical principles:

> O devine wit, that in the narrow wombe
> Of a small Flie, could finde sufficient roome
> For all those springs, wheels, counterpoise, and chaines,
> Which stood in steed of life, and spurre, and raines.
>
> (I. vi. 903–6)

It is as if the creative powers of God had been transmitted, in some obscure fashion, into his human imitators. Certainly, when he came to consider the 'Heav'n of Glasse', said to have been assembled for a Persian monarch, the prospect of creating 'New Heav'ns, new stars', models of the heavens akin to those now being assembled by skilled clock and watch makers of the period, suggested 'a curious lust to imitate the best / And fairest Works' of the almighty (I. vi. 963–4). Perhaps such creative energy might even produce something that had never existed before, a purely artificial, machine-driven universe, which would amount to a remoulding of God's original masterwork:

> But who would think, that mortall hands could mold
> New Heav'ns, new stars, whose whirling courses should
> With constant windings, through contrary wayes,
> Marke the true mounds of Yeares, and Months, and Dayes?
>
> (I. vi. 925–8)

The English reader of the poem in Joshua Sylvester's translation was reminded that such fantasies had become reality. A marginal note to the 1605 edition of the poem anchored these mechanical speculations to a well-known example of just such a mechanism: 'Admirable Dialls and Clockes, namely, at this Day, that of Straesbourg'. The great cathedral clock of Strasbourg, refurbished in 1574 and considered one of the mechanical wonders of Europe, suggested the ways in which 'mortall hands could mold / New Heav'ns, new stars'.[13]

Fabricating nature

Du Bartas's admiration for mechanism, along with Donne's meditation on metallic restoration, clearly belong to the optimistic framework that came to surround the wonders of Technē in the Renaissance. Rejecting Ovid's tale of human decline, in which a golden past has been replaced by an iron present, both of these poets admired the human capacity to assemble matter into new forms. Transformed by human energy and skill, matter could be rearranged by the machine makers, forgers, and smiths, working with materials that had been originally created, in turn, either by God, or by God's handmaiden: nature. 'Metals are a creation of nature', wrote Georgius Agricola in De Re Metallica.[14] 'Provident and sagacious Nature', he continued, generates metals 'in the veins, stringers, and seams in the rocks, as though in special vessels and receptacles for such material.'[15] From this natural treasury, a kind of earthy womb, first plundered by the miner, then transformed by the smith in the smelting furnace, the artist and the craft worker created new and wonderful objects, instruments, and devices: 'elegant, embellished, elaborate, useful . . . fashioned in various shapes by the artist from the metals gold, silver, brass, lead, and iron'.[16]

But this process, by which a natural substance was shaped or formed by human craft into something artificial, posed a much larger philosophical problem in the Renaissance, circulating around the status of natural as opposed to artificial objects in the world. In the earlier seventeenth century, around the time that Donne was composing the Holy Sonnets and Shakespeare's Volumnia was fashioning the terrible figure of Coriolanus, 'artificial' objects and devices were considered to belong to a specialized category of created things. So, the rare and wonderful objects contained in the Künstkammer of the Emperor Rudolf were classified (by the German antiquarian Daniel Fröschl) under three principles: naturalia, artificialia, and scientifica.[17] Late-medieval artists, particularly in the field of the applied arts, had struggled to promote what Martin Kemp has termed the 'essential contiguity of the natural and the artificial' in shaping or adapting natural objects to new purposes, but in ways that allowed their original form still to remain apparent.[18] This tradition of linking the natural and the artificial lingered on until well into the sixteenth century. The Künstkammer, or collection of objects assembled by Archduke Ferdinand II, for example, created at the end of the sixteenth century and said to have been inspired by Pliny the Elder's Natural History, sought to make a connection between artefacts and their natural origins.[19] In this sense, nature herself could be understood as an artificer: the hidden metallic veins to be discovered deep within the earth, for example, hinted at nature's mysterious ability to breed forms, far from envious human eyes. Metal, or the ore out of which metal could be wrought, was considered to be a peculiar example of nature's fecundity, as John Milton imagined in his 1634 'Masque' (Comus), where nature:

> . . . in her own loins
> . . . hutched the all-worshipped ore, and precious gems
> To store her children with . . .[20]

But Renaissance artists and writers were also heirs to a long tradition of thought in which artificial and natural objects were held to exist in an uneasy tension with one another.[21]

The view that wrought, inanimate, objects existed in a different sphere from that to be found in nature stretches back at least to Plato. In The Republic, Plato had argued that objects created by human beings were but a poor reflection of the reality of the world of forms created by God, and that the representation of those objects in art or in poetry was placed even further down the chain of existence.[22] So, Aristotle, in the Physics, distinguished between those things which exist by nature, and those things which exist from other causes. In the Aristotelian view, human artefacts and objects discovered in nature existed in a parasitic relationship to one another.[23] It was this tradition that Augustine drew upon, when, in the City of God, he observed that 'living things are ranked above inanimate objects', while things 'which have the power of reproduction, or even the urge towards it, are superior to those who lack that impulse'.[24]

The Augustinian concept of 'reproduction' lay at the core of the theological distinction between art and nature. In this respect, art could be considered a kind of surrogate parent. As the medieval alchemist Arnald of Villanova observed: 'what remains uncompleted by nature may be completed by Art'.[25] Edmund Spenser, too, explored this mysterious process in his depiction of the 'Garden of Adonis' in The Faerie Queene (1596), in which the fecundity of nature is imagined as an endless recycling of 'matter' out of which the 'forme and feature' of natural objects is fashioned (FQ III. vi. 37).[26] It also emphasizes precisely what was at stake in Coriolanus when, as we have seen, the play's hero is said to be artificially 'framed' by his mother, although this term may also be related to the larger, biological, debate among natural philosophers in the period.[27] But reproduction, in the Augustinian sense, was also akin to the more familiar idea of artistic or literary imitation, a process which was understood as the urge to translate objects or stories from one medium to another, or to reproduce or replicate the activities or motions of another. Aristotle had claimed in the *Poetics* that 'the instinct of imitation is planted in man from childhood', and this imitative faculty was both a source of delight and one of the hallmarks by which the human and animal worlds were distinguished from one another.[28]

Constructing the artificial device of a machine or engine, in other words, bore striking affinities to the mysterious process by which the equally artificial device of a poem came into being. For poems and machines were both products of *Technē*. Indeed, the language of machines and Renaissance poetic theory seem to slide seamlessly into one another. Many of the terms applicable to Renaissance machinery, such as 'device', 'contrivance', and 'invention', were also words used to describe the artful effects achieved by the poet or the playwright. In Renaissance poetic theory, moreover, imitation or *mimesis*, defined by Sir Philip Sidney as 'a representing, counterfeiting, or figuring forth', led to the creation of 'a speaking picture', and this was held to be the chief end of poetry.[29] According to Roger Ascham's influential *The Schoolmaster* (1570), 'Imitation', too, could be considered as part of the arsenal of 'tools and instruments' with which eloquent discourse was 'wrought'.[30] In the world of discourse, 'imitation' was closely allied to that other Renaissance rhetorical undertaking 'invention'. Invention, in its modern sense, is suggestive of originality and discovery. In the Renaissance, however, while 'invention' might indeed suggest originality, it also expressed a sense of rediscovering what had been hidden by God from humankind after the Fall.[31] This sense of the term 'invention' was related to the rhetorical idea of 'invention' as a process of bringing to mind the store of texts already lying dormant in the memory.[32]

These ideas help us to understand the intellectual materials out of which Renaissance machines and devices, too, were wrought. Just as the artificer of machines assembled a device that had hitherto never existed in nature, so poets produced in the imagination forms that could not otherwise be found in the world, using the texts, tropes, and metaphors bequeathed to them by their predecessors, particularly their classical predecessors. The imagination, or 'fancy' as it was later termed by Thomas Hobbes, was the operative principle that underpinned all human work. 'All that is beautiful' wrote Hobbes in 1650 'or marvellous in engines and instruments of motion' and which in turn defined the 'civility of Europe' was a function of 'the workmanship of fancy . . . guided by the precepts of true philosophy'.[33] Poets, the Renaissance rhetoricians agreed, were indeed 'makers', and in this respect they could be compared to the fabricators of other kinds of artificial forms in the world. Indeed, one of the most frequently cited classical legends in defence of poetry was that of the construction of Thebes by the power of poetic harmony. As George Puttenham wrote in his *Arte of English Poesie* (1589), the city's walls were 'reared . . . with the stones that came in heaps' to the sound of Amphion's lyre, as though musical harmony was itself a kind of construction device, driven by an instrument, capable of 'the mollifying of hard and stony hearts by . . . sweet and eloquent persuasion'.[34] In similar measure, the task of the architect was to imitate the works of nature, using the laws by which she was held to operate, but deploying an inventive imagination.[35] It was the power of the imagination in such individuals, *euphantasiōtoi* as Puttenham described them, which guaranteed their ability to devise new artificial forms; and this was a trait to be discovered not only in poets, legislators, and politicians, but also (wrote Puttenham) 'cunning artificers and engineers . . . in whose exercises the inventive part is most employed'.[36] By the same token, seventeenth-century readers of Guido Ubaldo's treatise on mechanics learned that the deployment of machinery was an example of the power of art to force nature to work, which could be compared to other human arts, such as medicine or painting. Describing the operation of an Archimedean screw, for example, the seventeenth-century author of a treatise on water mechanisms appropriated the critical language (derived from Ubaldo) used to describe art or poetry to commend the '*actings of this machine*' as 'delightful and ravishing'. For the machine was the 'child of art':

> Art useth either to counterfeit Nature, as in paintings, or else . . . command her, as is seen in divers Ingines. But in this . . . it seems to me to be of power to effect a fourth prank, to wit, that Art can sometimes even cheat and cozen even nature herself.[37]

But the mental world of the Renaissance 'inventor', whether of machines, texts, paintings, or buildings, was still governed by the Aristotelian opposition of art versus nature.[38] If artificiality was celebrated as the means by which art mirrored, replicated, or even improved upon the natural world, then a rhetorical treatise such Puttenham's *Arte of English Poesie* could also list some of the ways in which art and nature were at variance with one another. 'In some cases,' Puttenham wrote, 'we say, art is an aid and coadjutor to nature,' but he also noted how art might, in other circumstances, be considered as an 'alterer' or 'surmounter' of nature, or art might be an 'imitator' or even an 'encounterer' with nature to produce 'effects altogether strange and diverse . . . as she [nature] never would nor could have done herself.'[39]

In some measure, this activity was praiseworthy. Michelangelo, for example, was admired in Giorgio Vasari's *Lives of the Artists*, for his ability to fabricate forms that seemed to blur the dividing line between art and nature: his *Pietà*, sculpted out of marble for St Peter's in Rome, represented '. . . a miracle that a formless block of stone could ever have been reduced to a perfection that nature is scarcely able to create in the flesh'.[40] For Vasari, the peculiar 'aura' of Michelangelo's art lay precisely in its ability to re-create the impression, at least on the surface, of forms which might *almost* convince the onlooker that they were gazing at something 'real', that is to say 'natural'.

But this skill could also be seen as duplicitous or even blasphemous in other contexts. Vasari's juxtaposition of 'a formless block of stone' with 'flesh' is also a manifestation of what has been sometimes termed 'the great art–nature antithesis' of the Renaissance.[41] This antithesis was very rarely a balanced or harmonious meeting of opposites. Instead, these two principles were locked in a seemingly perpetual struggle with one another. So, art might always triumph over nature, replacing the natural object with its confected simulacrum to the confusion of the beholder. All too easily, confusion could give way to duplicity, as the stories and legends surrounding the ambiguous figure of the alchemist in Renaissance culture illustrate. The alchemist, for all that he may have paved the way for a modern understanding of chemical action and reaction, was also dedicated to the science of the artificial in that he strove to 'transmute' natural substances from one form into another. So it is that we find Ben Jonson evoking the energetic thrill of illicit forgery in his play *The Alchemist* (1612). The power of the alchemist lay in his ability to convince his credulous audience that art (by which Jonson means human imitative skill) might, eventually, be able to transplant nature, as Subtle, the alchemist of the play's title, explains:

> . . . He will make
> Nature asham'd of her long sleep when art,
> Who's but a stepdame, shall do more than she,
> In her best love to mankind, ever could:[42]

Weaving alternative realities out of language in order to dazzle and beguile his willing dupes, Subtle's 'art' is, of course, a confection. It is a brilliant manipulation of words, not things. And yet Subtle's programme of fraud echoed the much more serious debates which, among philosophers, artists, engineers, and poets, had come to dominate that 'great antithesis' that so preoccupied Renaissance thinking.

In a more positive context, the replication and reproduction of natural forms was a skill endlessly practised by the makers of art (whether plastic, visual, textual, or technological). For this was a culture which (Anne Goldgar observes) 'took pleasure in blurring the boundaries between art and nature' to produce:

> . . . natural objects in collections turned half into *artificialia* by gilding, etching, carving or artistic arrangement. Coconuts, ostrich eggs, or rhinoceros horns transformed into reliquaries; nautilus shells etched and gilded into luxurious beakers; reindeer antlers fashioned into candelabra: all testified to the desire of artists and collectors to intertwine nature with art.[43]

By the same token, as Pamela Smith writes, 'playing with the divide between nature and art became a favourite conceit of artisans in the sixteenth century, who claimed by their *ars* both to imitate and even rise above the artifice of nature'.[44] Smith goes on to catalogue the technical mastery of the Nuremberg goldsmith, Wenzel Jamnitzer, who 'achieved an exact imitation of nature' by developing the technique of 'casting from life'.[45] The organic bodies of small creatures, even flowers and grasses, formed the basis of a mould into which was poured precious metal. Out of this process were created silvery and golden lizards, frogs, and insects. Such delicate confections, manufactured by burning away organic material to leave an empty but perfect space into which the craftsman could pour the enduring matter of gold or silver, might even suggest that Donne's metallic fantasies of artificial rebirth and transformation may not have been so fantastical after all.

The aesthetic underpinning the fashioning of such objects was interwoven with admiration for the possibility of preserving for eternity natural objects. The seventeenth-century English poet, Robert Herrick, for example, delighted in the *minutiae* of nature transformed into objects of wonder and beauty through human artifice. Just as Du Bartas had wondered at the divine engineering skills of God who, in the 'narrow wombe / Of a small Flie', could find space for all the 'springs, wheels, counterpoise, and chaines' which drove the tiny creature, so Herrick's imagination was stirred by the transformation of insects into objects of art and luxury. In his short poem 'Upon a Flie', Herrick inspects another insect:

A Golden Flie one shew'd to me,
Clos'd in a box of Yvorie:
Where both seem'd proud; the Flie to have

>His burial in any yvory grave:
>The yvorie took State to hold
>A corps as bright as burnisht gold.[46]

Herrick's verses described other such rare objects, a sparrow 'with lilies tomb'd up in a Glasse', for example, as though the ephemeral nature of tiny lives could be memorialized for eternity by human skill.

Yet, the skill with which such objects were fashioned emphasized the distance between art and nature, while also suggesting, paradoxically, that the boundary between the two might be permeable. Within sixteenth- and seventeenth-century protestant intellectual culture, admiration for the human skill in creating artificial forms coexisted with a sense of the disturbing moral ambivalence engendered by gazing on such creations. Hence, the further paradox of the artificial as it came to be understood in the Renaissance. Among the religious reformers of the period, objects crafted by human artisans and artists might be appreciated with a mixture of delighted fascination, and, at almost the same moment, deep moral ambivalence, even distrust. For all that the protestant poet Du Bartas, in late sixteenth-century France, might have celebrated the artistic skill capable of fashioning the 'counterfait', his English co-religionists were often profoundly troubled by just this ability. Such objects, beautiful and beguiling as they might be, were 'vanities'. Worse, they sprang from the same impulse that fashioned other, less innocent, fusions of artifice and organic matter. The transformed rhinoceros horn was emblematic of the problem posed by these curiously compounded things. Here was a marvellously exotic natural object, a wonder of nature, embellished by art and put to an entirely new purpose. But its new role was redolent of vain or even idolatrous superstition, reminding reformers of the creation of marvellously wrought receptacles – reliquaries – for the dead tissue of saints or martyrs.

Such distrust mirrored a more general protestant attitude towards images and representations of the human form that would give rise to the periodic bouts of iconoclasm that swept through the British Isles and the Protestant areas of continental Europe, particularly Germany, the Netherlands, and Switzerland, in the 1560s and later.[47] As John Peacock has observed, England, in common with other Protestant states 'had developed a culture wary of the visual arts'.[48] The puritan, railing against theatrical performance, or the iconoclast tearing down statues of the Virgin and the saints shared, at heart, a deep distrust of the act of representation or (to use a term common to both Du Bartas and Sir Philip Sidney) 'counterfeiting'. In England, the key text which supported the iconoclasts was the Second Commandment: 'Thou shalt not make unto thee any graven image, or any likeness of anything that is in heaven above, or that is in the earth beneath, or that is in the water under the earth' (Exodus 20. 4, *AV* text). The creation of a 'likeness' represented the core of the mimetic arts of poetry, painting or sculpture. But a 'likeness' could encompass a multitude of forms because the biblical text prohibited the reproduction of 'anything' to be found in the created world, and it thus precluded any attempt at representing the world and what it contained by way of the agency of human artefacts.

Moreover, the wonder of art was that it could beguile the senses into confusion, and such confusion was dangerous. It was not the place of art to surpass nature. Rather, as Spenser at his most didactically protestant puts it in *The Faerie Queene*, it was the role of art to play an Aristotelian 'second . . . part' to nature (FQ IV. x. 21). Paradoxically, however, both the literary and the visual culture of the Renaissance valued the endless combat between art and nature. And, ironically, no poet was more adept than was Spenser in exploring this paradox. Thus, in sending the products of human skill, labour, and ingenuity into battle with nature, sixteenth-century intellectual and aesthetic culture delighted in the energy which was thereby released, even while it also regarded the results with a certain moral disdain. So, in Spenser's sinister 'Bowre of Blisse' episode of *The Faerie Queene*, we encounter a world of cunningly contrived fabricated objects, fashioned by an 'art, which all that wrought, appeared in no place' (FQ II. xii. 58). Art, here, is artlessly masquerading as nature, to produce a hybridization of forms, intertwined in a fraught physical union. At first, the union seems secure, even innocent:

> One would have thought, (so cunningly, the rude
>> And scorned parts were mingled with the fine,)
>> That nature had for wantonesse ensued
>> Art, and that Art at nature did repine;
>> So striuing each th'other to vndermine,
>> Each did the others worke more beautifie;
>> So diff'ring both in willes, agreed in fine:
>
> (*FQ* II. xii. 59)

But any appearance of concord between art and nature was, at best, momentary. Cunning and 'wantonness' were loaded words in Spenser's puritan lexicon, balancing positive terms such as beauty and agreement. For all that the union of artifice and nature results in beauty, such beauty was all the more dangerous because it seduced the senses, making it impossible to distinguish between the authentic and the factitious.

Spenser explores this paradox as it is gradually revealed that, despite the beauty of forms that have been manufactured in the Bowre, this is a place of deceit and guile. At the centre of the Bowre is a fountain, which might (at first) remind us of the fountains and grottos of those Italian gardens that Montaigne had observed in his European journey:

> And in the midst of all, a fountaine stood,
>> Of richest substance, that on earth might bee,
>> So pure and shiny, that the siluer flood
>> Through euery channel running one might see;
>> Most goodly it with curious imageree
>> Was ouer-wrought, and shapes of naked boyes,
>> Of which some seemed with liuely iolittee,
>> To fly about, their wanton toyes,
> Whilest others did them selues embay in liquid ioyes.

> And ouuer all, of purest gold was spred,
>> A trayle of yvie in his natiue hew:
>> For the rich metal was so coloured,
>> That wight, who did not well auis'd it vew,
>> Would surely deeme it to be yuie trew:
>> Low his lascivious armes adown did creepe,
>> That themselues dipping in siluer dew,
>> Their fleecy flowers they tenderly did steepe,
> Which drops of Christall seemed for wantones to weepe.

(*FQ* II. xii. 60–1)

Like the creations of the Nuremberg goldsmith, who cast flowers and grass into silver and gold, the ivy turns out not to be natural at all, although it is coloured so that it might be mistaken as 'yuie trew', while even insubstantial dew is transformed into silver.

Long ago, C. S. Lewis breezily remarked of this passage that a description of 'metal vegetation as a garden ornament' might be taken (by a peculiarly obtuse reader of the poem, it is true) as proof of Spenser's 'abominable bad taste'.[49] But bad taste, an inability to discriminate, is exactly the point. Georgius Agricola, in his 1556 treatise, wrote of the alchemists that they 'do not change the substance of base metals, but colour them to represent gold or silver, so that they appear to be that which they are not'.[50] In similar fashion, Spenser's Bowre is a place of falsity, fraud, and deception. It is a place where things (and people) 'appear to be what they are not'. Spenser's Bowre represents the obverse side of the coin described by another manufacturer of finely wrought objects, the sixteenth-century French ceramic artist, Bernard Palissy, who had also deployed the technique of casting from life. Palissy described his art as a fusion of artifice and nature so that his works 'do not appear to involve any appearance or form of the art of sculpture, nor any labour of the hand of man'.[51] But in the context of the sensual world of Spenser's Bowre, when confronted by Puritan sensibilities, such objects represented a fusion of principles that should be kept firmly apart from one another.

At the very heart of the Bowre reclines the enchantress Acrasia, who, in her ability to ensnare and then transform men into beasts, expresses the disarming power of both art and the feminine principal to subvert and then over-master masculine reason. Spenser's Acrasia is herself the product of seductive art. Reclining on a bed of roses, the enchantress is 'arayd' or rather 'disarayd' in a 'veyle of silke and silver thin, / That hid no whit her alabaster skin' (FQ II. xii. 78). Like Michelangelo's statue of the Pietà, which had so ravished Vasari, Acrasia hovers on the edge of the boundary separating the artificial from the natural. Her sensuous appeal lies in this disarming combination of artifice and nature. Associated, too, with the myth of Arachne, the spidery weaver of nets or webs, who deploys craft, cunning, and deceit to ensnare the unwary, there is a poetic justice in Acrasia's own entrapment within a 'cunningly . . . wound' net at the close of the episode (FQ II. xii. 82).[52]

The 'goodly workmanship' which the Bowre represents must be erased with 'rigour pittilesse' (FQ II. xii. 83), because it celebrates both the attraction and the danger of artifice. Hence, the whirlwind of destruction which envelopes Acrasia at the end of Book II of The Faerie Queene. Intemperately, Acrasia's world of artificial or hybridized forms must be destroyed by the exemplars of temperance, the knight Guyon and his companion, the Palmer, or pilgrim, in an act of hooliganism that has long disturbed modern readers of Spenser's poem as a manifestation of 'puritan frenzy'.[53] Iconoclasm must supersede discrimination since, for Protestants of a more extreme temper, any attempt at imitating or representing the world by the devices of art was to be distrusted. Stephen Greenblatt reminds us of this distrust when, in his interpretation of the destruction of the Bowre, he recalls the violent iconoclasm of sixteenth-century England in which 'statues of the virgin were dismembered by unruly crowds, frescos were whitewashed over and carvings in "Lady Chapels" were smashed in order to free men from thraldom to what an Elizabethan lawyer calls, in describing the Pope, "the witch of the world"'.[54] Greenblatt summons up the idea of the threat of 'absorption' to explain the destructive impulse of Guyon and his companion.[55] Such 'absorption' is not merely the dissolution of the (masculine) will in some endless erotic reverie. Rather, it represents the blurring of the boundary between the natural world and the wrought or artificial world. Spenser's own word for this process is 'blend'. To be blended into a world of artifice is the fate of the young man, Verdant, who has been ensnared by Acrasia, and who is released by Guyon and the Palmer: 'His dayes, his goods, his bodie he did spend / O horrible enchantment, that him so did blend' (FQ II. xii. 80). One modern editor glosses 'blend' (variously) as 'blind' and 'defile', but perhaps Spenser's own word is the right one after all.[56] Verdant has become fused – blended – with the artificial world that surrounds him, forgetting what it might be that makes him a reasonable, human creature.

But, as if to add to the confusion, nature, too, could be held to be a master of artifice, as Shakespeare's Polixenes explains to Perdita in The Winter's Tale (1609). Confronted by Perdita's distrust of flowers that have been artificially bred, Polixenes attempts to explain the confused relationship between human and natural artifice. Perdita shuns the 'streaked gillyvors' (variable coloured carnations) since she believes that the flowers betray 'an art which in their piedness shares / With great creating nature'. For the untutored Perdita, art and nature represent categories which must be firmly distinguished from one another. Polixenes responds:

> . . . Say there be,
> Yet nature is made better by no mean
> But nature makes that mean. So over that art
> Which you say adds to nature is an art
> That nature makes. You see, sweet maid, we marry
> And make conceive a bark of baser kind
> By bud of nobler race. This is an art
> Which does mend nature – change it rather; but
> The art itself is nature.
>
> (IV. iv. 88–97)

Whether or not nature is mended or changed, human intervention in the natural world – here the art of grafting – is itself an offshoot of purely natural processes: 'the art is nature'. Or as Leo Marx comments on this scene:

'the artificial is but a special, human category of the natural'.[57] But Perdita is unconvinced. Comparing herself to the flowers, she rejects artifice as tainted, in a simile which draws attention to her own fecundity:

> I'll not put
> The dibble in earth to set one slip of them,
> No more than, were I painted, I would wish
> This youth should say 'twere well, and only therefore
> Desire to breed by me.
>
> (IV. iv. 99–103)

Refusing to allow such artificial things into her own garden, Perdita's rejection of 'painted' flowers is a mirror of that more general protestant distrust of artifice.

Mechanical illusions

Spenser and Shakespeare may have expressed ambivalent attitudes towards the seemingly endless rivalry between art and nature in the late sixteenth century, but in the seventeenth century, this contest began to take on new dimensions. Sir Henry Wotton, in his influential treatise on architecture, design, and taste which was The Elements of Architecture (1624), for example, dismissed the 'Alexandrian delicacies' of pneumatic and hydraulic devices in garden design on grounds of economics as well as aesthetics, castigating 'artificial devices' as being 'of great expence, and little dignity'.[58] Yet, for others, artificiality provided a mark to be aimed at. 'The efficient causes of diverse works are God, Nature, Art', proclaimed Hans Wecker in his popular 'book of secrets' first published in 1559.[59] By art, the work continues, are created 'things artificial . . . by the diligent dexterity of the hand, and cunning Industry of men'.[60] For Ben Jonson, poetry and painting were 'born artificers' while that common Renaissance idea of poetry as a 'speaking picture' inherited from classical theory, might also suggest the idea of a moving, mechanized tableau vivant, or even, as we shall see, an automaton.[61]

In the earlier seventeenth century, the affinity between mechanism and artful illusion underpinned the short-lived cultural phenomenon of the court masque. In the joint ventures of the architect and stage designer Inigo Jones and the poet Ben Jonson, artificiality together with all manner of ingenious mechanical contrivances would become the very essence of this magnificent (and magnificently costly) form of elite entertainment. The court masque was a dream work: a fusion of art and nature designed to ravish the senses through the deployment of all the techniques of artifice, including painting, poetry, music, and movement or dance. Machines and engines of all kinds were integral to the production of the masque, appearing in the form of 'cloud 'or 'wave machines' often derived from Italian models, while complex mechanical artifice was later deployed to achieve dazzling transformational effects.[62] In the opening moments of the masque *Hymenaei* (1606), for example, the audience watched as 'out of a microcosm, or globe, figuring man, with a kind of contentious music, issued forth the first masque, of eight men'.[63] Later, the scene changes:

> Here the upper part of the scene which was all of clouds and made artificially to swell and ride like the rack, began to open, and the air clearing, in the top thereof was discovered Juno sitting in a throne . . . Above her the region of fire with a continual motion was seen to whirl circularly, and Jupiter standing in the top, figuring the heaven, brandishing his thunder . . .[64]

What Jonson and Jones were devising was nothing less than a mechanical representation of the universe itself, mediated by Renaissance Platonism. This 'continual motion' might remind us of the 'perpetual motion' machine which, as we have seen, was to be exhibited to the fascinated King James by the secretive Cornelius Drebbel, and which would, in turn, become emblematic of the king's own perpetually moving mind (so the poets would have it) as he guided his two kingdoms of England and Scotland. In the lengthy descriptive passages that accompanied the text of Jonson's masque, the devices by which these transformative effects were achieved were explained in more detail. Deploying Inigo Jones's inventive architectural genius, the masque used a *machina versatilis* or 'turning machine'. The *machina versatilis*, upon which depended 'the whole machine of the spectacle', was a device dedicated to manufacturing illusion.[65] 'No axle was seen to support it' as the device operated to produce its spectacular effects: a globe filled with countries; 'a mine of several metals'; 'the three regions of the air', and so on. In fact, what Jones and Jonson had devised was a kind of model of the universe, not unlike the perpetually moving armillary sphere confected by Drebbel for King James but on an altogether grander scale. The *machina versatilis* 'imitated with such art and industry as the spectators might discern the motion, all the time the shows lasted, without any mover . . .'[66] Here was artifice at its most refined: a mechanism that moved with no visible mechanical impulse to drive it, allowing airy spirits to descend from the empyrean, or forests to become animated with life and movement.[67] Such contrivances were designed to fascinate the courtly audiences privileged to witness these performances.[68]

Jones's elaborate and ingenious devices overwhelmed the senses in light, colour, sound, and motion. But Ben Jonson's relationship with his inventive designer was famously quarrelsome, although there was no mistake (at least in Jonson's eyes) as to who was the senior member of the partnership. 'Jonson' writes Stephen Orgel 'from the beginning was "the inventor," and Jones's machines were, at least till the final years of the collaboration, realizations of Jonson's poetic symbols.'[69] By the early 1630s, however, the relationship had collapsed into a quarrel that would produce Jonson's invective-laden poem, 'An Expostulation with Inigo Jones'. In his 'expostulation', Jonson turned his back on the whole elaborate edifice that he and Jones had so brilliantly crafted for the Stuart court. Comparing Jones (unfavourably) to 'Archytas / The noblest engineer that ever was' Jonson rounded on those who, watching or performing in his masques, 'cry up the machine' at the expense of the intellectual virtues of the text.[70] 'Painting and carpentry are the soul of masque', he railed, bitterly: 'Pack with your peddling poetry to the stage: / This is the money-get, mechanic age!'[71]

Jonson's *de haut en bas* assault on Jones was particularly barbed. In making his erstwhile partner the epitome of a 'mechanic' age, Jonson was consigning the scholarly Jones to the company of those humble artisans, painters, and carpenters who laboured to create the special effects, which, in his view, were threatening to overwhelm the performance. And that the age was, indeed, becoming 'mechanic' turned out to be true, although not in the sense in which Jonson understood that term. At any rate, prior to the civil wars of the 1640s, the court masque was already collapsing under its own extravagant weight of costly artifice. It has been calculated that the production costs of a single masque were equivalent to the building costs of a country house, an expense that may even have helped precipitate the economic failure of the regime which the court masque sought to celebrate.[72]

'Bodies without souls'

In comparing his partner, unfavourably, to 'Archytas / The noblest engineer that ever was', Ben Jonson was reminding the reader that the skill of the true engineer was related to a larger notion of mechanism as a branch of ancient philosophy. Appealing to classical antiquity in defence of his own art was a characteristic strategy of Jonson, who rarely resisted an opportunity to parade his learning in front of the reader. But Archytas was more than an 'engineer', no matter how noble. He was also a magician.

In the Renaissance, magic had become linked to mechanics through the supposed 'discovery' of the works of Hermes Trismegistus, the 'author' (so it was believed) of 30,000 volumes of esoteric lore.[73] For the occult writer, Henry Cornelius Agrippa, drawing on this well of mystical lore, mechanism and magic were inseparable from one another. In his three books of occult philosophy (published in 1533) Agrippa claimed that the creation of 'Bodies . . . which yet want the animal faculty' was an art known to antiquity. Among these devices were to be found images and automata created by Daedalus, 'statues of Mercury which did speak, and the wooden dove of Arthita [Archytas] which did fly'. Hence, wrote Agrippa:

> . . . a magician, expert in natural philosophy, and mathematics, and knowing the middle sciences consisting of both these, arithmetic, music, geometry, optics, astronomy, and such sciences that are of weights, measures, proportions, articles, and joints, knowing also mechanical arts resulting from these, may without any wonder, if he excel other men in art, and wit, do many wonderful things which the most prudent, and wise men may much admire.[74]

Frances Yates has traced the patterns of thought which gave rise to these mechanical fantasies, speculating that 'some kind of mental association of miraculous Egyptian statues with the works of Hero on mechanics and automata may have stimulated interest in mechanics', and she cites the writings of the Dominican monk and philosopher, Tommaso Campanella (1568–1639) in support of her claim.[75] Certainly, in his Theologia (1613–24), Campanella had classified the mechanician's 'art' as 'real artificial magic':

> Real artificial magic produces real effects, as when Architas made a flying dove of wood, and recently at Nüremberg, according to Boterus, an eagle and a fly have been made in the same way. Daedalus made statues which moved through the action of weights or of mercury . . .[76]

But Campanella also understood such effects to be now firmly rooted in the emerging craft of mechanics, to which there were certain limits:

> This art however cannot produce marvellous effects save by means of local motions and weights and pulleys or by using a vacuum, as in pneumatic

and hydraulic apparatuses, or by applying forces to the materials. But such forces and materials can never be such as to capture a human soul.[77]

Similarly, Campanella's English contemporary, Robert Burton, listed in *The Anatomy of Melancholy* (1628) 'thaumaturgical works' such as we have already encountered – 'Archita's dove, Albertus's brazen head' and so on – but he, too, linked such devices, whether real or imaginary, to more mundane mechanical effects: 'cranes and pulleys . . . mills to move themselves'.[78]

Yet, the black arts of thaumaturgy and the mechanical skills of the engineer might be all too easily confused. Prospero, in Shakespeare's masque-like play, *The Tempest* (composed c. 1610, published in 1623) was able not only to work upon human perception, but also to rearrange the forces of nature, and even blur the boundaries between life and death, while the Aristotelian elements (air, water, fire, and earth) were made to operate at his command (V. i. 40–50). Prospero's own version of the *machina versatilis*, the 'device' or 'instrument' by which these transformations are effected, was the 'potent art' of magic which, at the end of the play, he renounces. In similar fashion, in Christopher Marlowe's *Tragicall Historie of Dr Faustus* (1604, 1616), Faustus is not only the archetype of the Renaissance conjuror, but he is also a mechanician, or at least the master of spirits able to work mechanically: 'Yea stranger engines for the brunt of warre . . . Ile make my servile spirits to inuent' he claims.[79] The fact that the magician-engineer was able to 'invent' or fabricate devices, whether real or imagined, which appeared to be self-motivating, was the clue to the magical or semi-magical power which, it was believed, was possessed by their creators. So, the characters in *The Tempest* believe themselves to be agents of their own fate when, in Prospero's fashioning of reality, they are in fact more like the 'demi-puppets' that he is able to command at his will (V. i. 36). And in this respect, of course, they are the precise equivalent to the very idea of 'characters' formed or fashioned by the inventive genius of the playwright, but who seem to possess, for the brief period of the play's performance, a measure of autonomy which is no more than the product of theatrical illusion.

Illusion, machinery, and magic were intimately linked to one another through the idea of 'motion' in Renaissance aesthetic culture. 'Motion' was a word that described not just movement, but was also applied, in other contexts, to the uncanny art of puppetry. In the final moments of Ben Jonson's *Bartholomew Fair*, first performed in 1614, a 'motion' or puppet is accused of the 'abomination' of transvestism, a charge which it successfully refutes by raising its garments to reveal that 'we have neither male nor female amongst us'.[80] It was considered debateable, moreover, whether certain kinds of 'motion' were the products of machines or magic, so closely allied were the two held to be. Moving images of the human form, akin to puppets, had been fashioned in remote antiquity. And certainly, simple jointed figures designed as religious objects are to be found scattered through many different cultures.[81] In classical Greece and Rome, mechanically operated images and statues were used to deliver oracles. Such devices, known as *neurospasta*, were said to be able to move, bleed, swear, and (even) collapse, though some classical commentators considered them to be 'vulgar'.[82]

Such images were related to the more familiar example of sculptural expressions of human and animal forms. 'Sculpture', Alfred Chapuis and Edmond Droz have observed, 'was for a long period subject to priestly authority, and a statue, like a myth, appeared as the epitome of a divine thought.'[83] In pre-Reformation Europe, this tradition would resurface in the guise of sacred sculpture, endowed with particular devotional significance. In England, late-medieval devotional practice shifted from the cult of relics to the cult of images, as if purely representational devices – paintings and statues – were supplementing or even supplanting the bodily residue of the countless saints and martyrs around which reliquaries, shrines, and chapels had once been constructed.[84] But if such devices were seen to move, then animation was held to be evidence of divine intervention, rather than the result of mechanical craft or skill.[85]

Renaissance inventors, however, investing themselves in the mantle of priestly authority, were intrigued by the possibility of recreating pre-Christian moving devices, which they encountered in both Arabic and Graeco-Roman sources, particularly in the works of Heron of Alexandria, Ctesibius, and Philo of Byzantium.[86] Heron's *Peri automatopoietikes* (*On Automaton-making*, composed in the first century CE), in particular, contained detailed instructions with the help of which it was possible to create moving figures and even entire mechanical theatrical performances.[87] For the Western inheritors of this tradition, two equally alluring prospects lay behind their endeavours to recreate these ancient devices, although their relationship to orthodox Christianity was not always clear. If artificial movement was the product of magic, then might that magic once more be made to operate in the world? Conversely, if magic was dismissed, then might the power of movement nevertheless be harnessed by a more mechanical art?

The arts, whether technological or magical, which could induce movement in seemingly inanimate marble or stone were described in detail by the French cabbalist, Jacques Gaffarel, whose treatise on the 'talismanical

sculptures of the Persians' was continuously reprinted throughout the seventeenth and eighteenth centuries.[88] In England, the influential treatise of the
French hydraulic engineer Isaac de Caus (translated and published in 1659
as *New and rare Inventions of Water-Works*) contained detailed instructions on how
to recreate a speaking statue, powered by sunlight. Such a device, de Caus
wrote, had been described by Tacitus, incorporated into a statue of Memnon
in Egypt.[89] Similar devices had already become a reality, not only in the Italian gardens, but also in the fabulous royal grottoes at St-Germain-en-Laye,
constructed by the father and son team of Thomas and François Francine
for Henri IV between 1589 and 1609.[90] A contemporary viewer, André du
Chesne, described the grottoes at St-Germain, with their hydraulic dragons
(breathing water not fire) fashioned out of bronze, little birds 'which truly
seem not painted or imitated, but alive', and various mythological scenes:
Perseus and Andromeda, Bacchus, and Orpheus playing his lyre.[91]

Underpinning these legendary stories or fictional creations was the Renaissance delight in creating deceptive, moving, artificial figures, as if the
vanished world of classical antiquity, or Eden itself, could be recreated by
a combination of artifice, engineering, and magic – the three being not
always distinguishable. The 1589 translation (into Italian) and publication
of Heron's *Pneumatica* by Giambattista Aleotti acted as a spur to this impulse.[92]
By unlocking the wealth of Greek and Arabic investigations into the actions
of gases and liquids under pressure, Aleotti precipitated the creation of the
gardens which the Francines created in France and which Montaigne had
seen in Italy. The Elizabethan traveller Fynes Moryson described the moving
hydraulic figures to be wondered at in Pratolino in the mid-1590s:

> A head of marble distilleth water; and two little trees by the turning of a
> cocke shed waters abundantly, and a little globe is turned about by Cupid,
> where the images of duckes dabble in the water, and then look around
> them.[93]

Such travellers' descriptions of similar hydraulic marvels reappeared in *The
Unfortunate Traveller* (1594) of Thomas Nashe, producing an imaginary, exotic,
Italian machine-driven garden powered by 'enwrapped art'. Mechanical
creatures – 'bodies without souls' – fashioned by 'mathematical experiments' recreated the first, Ovidian or Edenic garden state, with no poisonous
serpents, roses without blemish, leaves without caterpillars, 'only jays loved
to steal gold and silver to build their nests withal . . . The ant did not hoard
up against winter, for there was no winter, but a perpetual spring, as Ovid

saith.'[94] 'Every man there', concluded Nashe, 'renounced conjectures of art and said it was done by enchantment.'[95]

To populate such theatres of what Nashe termed 'soul-exalting objects', Renaissance designers became skilled in creating bestiaries of moving mechanical animals and figures.[96] A swivel-eyed Bacchus, a self-propelling Diana mounted on a stag, carriages bearing Minerva and Cupid, were culled from exotic nature, the tales of Ovid, and even the scriptures. Clockwork horsemen, eagles, cocks, griffins, parrots, unicorns, camels, lions, and ele-phants pranced, flapped, screeched, or shambled over the tables of the great, coexisting with more sober scriptural scenes: an automated flagellation, Adam and Eve moving through the garden of Eden, even a moving Virgin Mary.[97] Such devices have been described as 'secular analogues to exhibi-tions of relics', although in this mechanical world, there seemed to be little distinction between the sacred and the profane, pagan myth or scriptural story.[98]

Objects of this kind were, of course, constructed to adorn the tables of the wealthy. But these machines were also devised to fulfil multiple, symbolic, roles. A clock, of the type presented by the Jesuit Father Nicholas Trigault, to the Imperial court in China, in 1618, and which depicted, on striking the twelfth hour, 'the history of Christ's birth . . . marvellously enacted by little figures in gilded copper', might be considered as a machine or device whose 'message' amounted to much more than either marking the passage of time, or illustrating elements of the Christian faith.[99] Introduced into a culture that already possessed highly sophisticated devices for measuring time, but which was also fascinated by animated figures, such an instru-ment could be considered as a form of clockwork diplomacy, designed to impress the recipient with the technological prowess of the culture able to produce such an artefact.[100]

On a rather grander scale was the story of the silver statue of Jupiter, created by Benvenuto Cellini for François I of France at Fontainebleau in 1545. By concealing, in the plinth of the statue, a device that enabled a hidden operator to move the statue gently towards the king as he entered the darkened gallery to view the statue for the first time, Cellini endowed his creation with the semblance of movement. The king, much like Leontes in The Winter's Tale confronting the 'statue' of Hermione, was suitably impressed. Cellini recorded François's approbation in his Autobiography: 'we must rate Benvenuto very highly indeed: his work not only rivals, it surpasses the ancients'.[101] As Horst Bredekamp, commenting on this story, observes: 'modern art in the form of a "machina" had outshone the magnificence of antiquity'.[102] Other creatures were more mundane, though no less riveting. In Germany, in 1588, Hans Schlottheim created a pair of automatic lobsters, fashioned out of copper, capable of scuttling across the floor with opening and closing claws.[103] Schlottheim was to become the master of this craft, creating, in the late sixteenth century, a succession of fabulously expensive automata as gift tokens for emperors and royal dukes.

The modern concept of the inventor or engineer was related to a much older belief in the fabricator of machines as a magician or sorcerer of some kind, capable of creating mechanical life. For the Alexandrian mathematician Pappus, writing in his fourth-century CE *Mathematical Collection*, machines might be the work of mechanicians (*mechanikoi*), or machine builders (*mechanopoioi*) or 'gadget designers' (*thaumasiourgoi*). But they might also be the work of 'conjurors' (*manganarioi*) who 'by means of machines (*mechanai*)... lift great weights ... moving them with little force, contrary to nature'.[104] Augustine, in the *City of God* was unsure as to whether the fabrication of such objects was the work of human ingenuity, or demonic craft: 'God's created beings can, by the use of human arts, effect so many marvels ... of a nature so astounding that those unfamiliar with them would suppose them to be the works of God himself.'[105]

Augustine would have been familiar with those Greek myths and legends in which such mechanical wonders abounded. Pindar, in his seventh Olympian Ode, described the people of Rhodes fashioning 'living creatures' (*zooisin*) that were able to move and wander through the streets.[106] Rhodes was also the home of Talus (or Talos), the man of bronze, a survivor (according to Hesiod, in the *Works and Days*) of a whole race of brazen men created by Zeus:

> And Zeus the father made a race of bronze,
> Sprung from the ash tree, worse than the silver race,
> But strange and full of power. And they loved
> The groans and violence of war; they ate
> No bread; their hearts were flinty-hard; they were
> Terrible men; their strength was great, their arms
> And shoulders and their limbs invincible.
> Their weapons were of bronze, their houses bronze;
> Their tools were bronze: black iron was not known.
> They died by their own hands, and nameless went
> To Hades' chilly house.[107]

It is not difficult to see this 'race of bronze' as a reinterpretation of the myth of the three ages of the earth prior to the coming of human beings, in which the gods first fashion a golden race, followed by a race of silver creatures, and then the bronze race of Talos and his kind. The myth may also, however, be understood as an anthropomorphic idealization of tools and weapons, even primitive forms of machines. In some versions of the myth, Talos is imagined as the creation of Hephaestus/Vulcan. Other accounts associate Talos with Daedalus, claiming that Talos, seeking to rival Daedalus, was the inventor of the saw, the potter's wheel, and the compass for measuring circles. In yet another version of the story, that to be found in the *Argonautica* of Appollonius of Rhodes, Talos appears as the artificial defender of Crete against Jason and the crew of the *Argo*. Fashioned with a single vein, stoppered by bronze pin or nail, Talos's mythical task was to process around the island of Crete proclaiming the law, inscribed on bronze tablets.[108]

Talos was to resurface in the Renaissance in the terrible figure of Talus in Book V of Edmund Spenser's *The Faerie Queene*. In Spenser's appropriation of the cycle of tales surrounding Talus/Talos, the artificial creature appears as an implacable figure of retributive justice, bestowed on the knight Artegall by the goddess, Astrea, who has fled the world:

> But when she parted hence, she left her groome
> An yron man, which did on her attend
> Always, to execute her stedfast doome,
> And willed him with *Artegall* to wend,
> And doe what euer thing he did intend.
> His name was *Talus*, made of yron mould,
> Immoueable, resistlesse, without end.
> Who in his hand an yron flale did hould,
> With which he thresht out falsehood, and did truth unfold.
>
> (*FQ* V. i. 12)

Talus, transformed from malleable bronze into more workmanlike iron in keeping with the Ovidian myth of human decline, is the law as Spenser imagined that it should be exercised by the Elizabethan imperium at the expense of rebellious Ireland.[109] Those same qualities that Montaigne found attractive in his contemplation of machines – their singleness of purpose, their dynamic power, their tireless repetition – are here appropriated to produce a vision of machine life anchored to retribution: 'Immoueable, resistlesse, without end'.

But long before Talus was unleashed by Spenser to stalk, in poetry, through the Irish countryside, deceptive mechanical figures had featured prominently in the imaginations of the Renaissance poet's predecessors. Medieval romances abound in automata of all kinds: armoured knights who are revealed to be machines, automata disguised as men or women, or mechanical animals. The brass horse, to be found in Chaucer's *The Squire's Tale* (composed c. 1370–80), is, perhaps, the most famous medieval example of a literary automaton. Such figures began to appear in romance literature around the beginning of the twelfth century, and, for at least three hundred years, reoccur in cycles of romance. In, for example, the *Roman de Troie* (c. 1160) we encounter four automata, two of which are female, and two of which are male. In the twelfth-century *Roman d'Alexandre*, the function of these figures was to act as guardians to a bridge, entrance, or gate of some sort. In *Lancelot* of the early thirteenth century, a series of mechanical knights are encountered, while in *Tristan* (c. 1220) the enchantress Morgan la Fée defends her castle with the aid of copper knights. In the thirteenth-century *Huon de Bordeaux*, two copper men, armed with flails (precursors of Spenser's Talus), guard a castle, and in the cycle of legends surrounding the ambiguous figure of Virgil the Necromancer, brazen spearmen or archers have to be defeated by the questing hero.[110]

Automata, in these narratives, are seldom seen as benign figures. Rather, they are malignant, even daemonic devices, constructed with the aid of magic and sorcery. Appearing first as purely fictional devices, they seem to have migrated, in the later Middle Ages, into the historical narratives of semi-legendary sorcerers, magicians, and natural philosophers. Thus, Albertus Magnus, the thirteenth-century Dominican monk, is said to have laboured for thirty years in the fabrication of an automaton which was endowed with the power of speech. His pupil, Thomas Aquinas, destroyed the creation as the work of the devil, although in some versions of the narrative, it was the creature's garrulousness that is said to have enraged the theologian.[111] Rather later is the tradition of the mechanical fly and artificial eagle, constructed with the aid of magical arts by the mathematician Johan Müller (Regiomontanus) at Nuremberg in the fifteenth century.[112] Other automata, though, were clearly envisaged as sacred devices. Thus, the mid-thirteenth-century engineer, artist, and mason, Villard de Honnecourt (fl. 1220–30) devised a mechanical eagle, incorporated into a lectern, which was designed to turn its head towards the deacon when he began to read the Gospel.[113]

Such a device, activated by the word of God, alerts us to another class of automata, which were seen as oracular messengers of truth. The chief attribute of these machines was that they could speak.[114] Their speech was, however, of a special kind. In the German romance known as 'Valentin und Namelos' (and published as *Valentine and Orson* in English in 1510) two brothers, the eponymous heroes of the tale, who are unaware of their relationship to each other, discover a brass castle in which is installed an artificial brazen head, which reveals to them their true identity.[115] Stories of oracular heads of this kind, related to the familiar story of the Green Knight in *Sir Gawain and the Green Knight*, circulated throughout the Middle Ages. In the poem *Image du Monde* (1245), based on a twelfth-century account to be found in the writings of William of Malmesbury, an artificial speaking head, the creation, once more, of Virgil the Necromancer, was consulted by the Pope. Virgil's device reappears in the *Renart Contrefait* (1319) while, at roughly the same time, in London, the Knights Templar were accused of concealing a two-faced brazen head, which answered any question put to it. John Gower in his *Confessio amantis* (c. 1390) relates how the Oxford scholar (and future Chancellor of the University) Robert Grosseteste laboured, unsuccessfully, to create a brazen head that would foretell the future. Rather more successful was the supposed invention (again at Oxford) of a speaking brazen head by an anonymous magician in the opening years of the sixteenth century. The head, it seems, would only speak on Saturdays. Further afield, in Spain, a brazen head was exhibited in the church of Tavara, whose task (so it was reported) was to speak whenever a Jew attempted to enter the church.[116] These heads are forerunners to the device described in the second part of Cervantes' *Don Quixote* (1614), where Sancho Panza and Don Quixote are shown a speaking brazen head – 'an oracular machine' – able to respond to interlocutors. In contrast to the rather lighter workload imposed by the Oxford speaking head, this device refused to operate on Fridays, perhaps suggesting that it was the product of Islamic ingenuity. The head was made 'by one of the greatest enchanters and sorcerers the world has ever known', though it is later revealed that the instrument is, in fact, a fake: a hidden operator, concealed in another room, controlled it.[117]

The most famous Renaissance oracular artificial creature, however, is that to be found in Robert Greene's play, *Friar Bacon and Friar Bungay* (composed 1589, published 1594). The play tells the story of two monks, one of whom is a fictional version of the Oxford philosopher Roger Bacon, who was supposed to have constructed an oracular brazen head by magic. Greene's primary source for the story was the anonymous prose romance, *The Famous Historie of Fryer Bacon*, composed in the mid sixteenth century, survives in no copy earlier than the seventeenth century. The *Famous Historie* is a curious work, containing not only the story of Bacon's artificial head, but also a prophetic account of mechanical devices of all kinds which, the anonymous author claims, will be created in the future by 'the figuration of Art' (i.e. magic). This 'Vision of Machines' included:

> . . . instruments of navigation [ships] without men to rowe in them, and they shall sayle far more swiftly then if they were full of men. Also chariots shall move with an unspeakable force, without any living creature to stirre them. Likewise an instrument may be made to flye withall, if one sit in the middle of the instrument, and doe turne an Engine by the which the winges being artificially composed may beat ayre after the manner of a flying Bird . . . By art also an Instrument may bee made, wherewith men may walke in the bottome of the sea or rivers without bodily danger.[118]

How are we to account for these ambiguous mechanical figures and these fantasies of an as yet uninvented mechanical life?

In some measure, the heavily armoured European knight of the later Middle Ages bears a more than passing resemblance to a mechanical figure. Encased in a metal carapace, with his face hidden and exhibiting no outward signs of humanity, the medieval mounted warrior could indeed be imagined as a terrible, purposive, mechanical version of the human form. Around 1435, the Swiss artist Konrad Witz (c. 1400–45) painted an altarpiece showing the 'mighty men' of the Old Testament narrative surrounding King David. Perhaps remembering the biblical description of these heroic figures ('the man that shall touch them must be fenced with iron', 2 Samuel 23. 7), Witz's knights have been compared to 'robot-like figures . . . awkward gestures describe their mechanical movements' while the 'geometric casing' renders the figures 'completely anonymous'.[119] Equally, as Jessica Wolfe has observed of Spenser's figuration of Talus, such a creature may be thought of as the 'literalization of a metaphor common to ancient and Renaissance stoicism', that the Stoic should cultivate a stony indifference to the pleasures of the world.[120]

But mechanism in these narratives represents a fantasy of mastery over nature that was part of a technological revival whose roots were to be found in Islamic technology.[121] Islamic engineers and craftsman had become skilled in fabricating fabulously complex devices and machines. Their water-powered clocks and drinking vessels, trick devices, moving figures and automata, were created long before their Western counterparts and imitators were able to reproduce such fine technology.[122] In the West, in the sixteenth century, such devices were to become associated with the devious skills of the conjuror, the magician, the sorcerer, and, of course, the fraud. That they were also the products or oriental rather than occidental skill only added to the aura of luxuriously sinister decadence that came to surround such objects in Western eyes.

The manufacture of such devices was related to the alchemist's illusionary skills. We have already met with Ben Jonson's alchemist, Subtle, claiming that his 'art' is one that can make even nature 'ashamed'. In Jonson's play, Subtle employs the ingenious vocabulary of alchemy, to explain that his task is not merely to translate matter from one form into another, but to create matter entirely anew. He is (he claims) capable, with the help of his 'art', of begetting matter. Alchemy can thus 'produce the species of each metal / More perfect thence, than nature doth in earth'. Jonson's seventeenth-century audience would have appreciated the vaunting ambition that lies behind this absurd assertion, and they would have appreciated, too, the specious and entirely fraudulent reasoning with which Subtle buttresses his claim that he is master of an art capable of producing life:

> Beside, who doth not see in daily practice
> Art can beget bees, hornets, beetles, wasps,
> Out of the carcasses and dung of creatures;
> Yea, scorpions of an herb, being rightly placed
> And these are living creatures, far more perfect
> And excellent than metals.[123]

That 'living creatures' were far more 'perfect . . . than metals' was no more than orthodoxy. And that creatures might be engendered by the process known as *sponte nascentia* or spontaneous generation was a belief that would linger well into the seventeenth century and beyond.[124] But Subtle has confused the issue in claiming that this process is a product of 'art' or human technique. Only nature, working under the impress of God's laws, so it was held, could perform these operations. To think otherwise, as Jonson's audience would also have known, was to set oneself up as a rival to the generational power of God. But was 'art', then, to be considered as a part of nature, or nature's rival?

Jonson's Subtle manages, slyly, to suggest that his arts of fabrication are nearly as great as (if not greater than) those of nature who is able to bring to life bees, hornets, beetles, and wasps out of the discarded detritus of animal existence. Schlottheim's copper lobsters, scuttling across the floor to the delight of his princely audience, belonged to the same world as that evoked by Jonson's duplicitous alchemist. For 'art', so it seemed, had the

power to endow inanimate matter with the semblance of life and movement. In Cesare Ripa's immensely popular book of emblems, Iconologia, first
published in 1593, this problem was given emblematic expression. In the
first English version of Ripa's text, the twenty-seventh image is that of 'Artificio' or 'Artifice'. The image shows a man, with one hand extended towards
a hive of bees, and the other turning a screw mechanism. The English text
explains the image for us:

> A Comely Man whose Garment is richly emroider'd; he lays his Hand upon a
> Screw of perpetual Motion, and by his right shews a hive of bees. He is nobly
> clothed because Art is *noble* of itself. His Hand upon the screw shews that
> *Engines* have been contriv'd by *Industry*; that by them incredible Things like
> the perpetual Motion have been *perform'd*. The Hive declares the *Industry* of
> the *Bees*, which, being very inconsiderable, are nevertheless *great* as to their
> conduct.[125]

Bees, in secular allegory, were attributes of the lost age of pastoral innocence,
while in sacred allegory they expressed the purely human art of eloquence.[126]
But here, they are being re-employed as Virgilian metaphors of industry,
equivalents to the ingenious devices confected by human design and skill.
But bees are also creatures to be found in nature. The 'perpetual motion'
engine, on the other hand, is a representation of pure artifice, though it
might, as we have seen, be understood as a representation of the perpetual
motion engines constructed by God: the macrocosm of the turning universe, and the microcosm of the human being. In Ripa's gradually unfolding
image, however, the intent seems to be to show that art, industry, and the
devices of human ingenuity are in harmonious concord with the products
of nature.

In the earlier seventeenth century, machines that would edify, delight,
amuse, or instil a sense of wonder in the onlooker were at least as important
as machines, which were held to perform a useful task. And even 'useful'
machines might still be held to operate in a philosophical rather than
strictly utilitarian framework. The machine that seemed to imitate or
even improve upon organic life represented the summit of the engineer's
'art'. It confirmed his power over the abstract forces of nature to create a
'second nature' as good as (or even better than) the world in which he
lived. So, more complex devices, automated human forms, began to appear
in the period, particularly in Spain and in Germany: a female automaton
which could dance and play a tambourine, a cittern player, and a 'robot'

that resided in the art gallery, or *Künstkammer*, of the emperor Rudolf II in Prague in 1600.[127] Rudolf's *Künstkammer*, with its collection of automata, has been described as a 'pre-Cartesian' museum which gave the impression (as did the automaton itself) of 'dissolving the boundary between natural and human creations'.[128] The dissolution of such boundaries perhaps appealed to an emperor who was said to have preferred the society of clocks to that of people.[129]

The figures collected by the reclusive emperor were related to the moving figures (*jaquemarts*) to be found on the elaborate public clocks of the period. A moving figure such as that, carved in wood, and painted, to be found at Southwold Church in Suffolk, England (constructed *c.* 1480) 'was a sort of surrogate figure' (Mary Hillier writes) 'replacing the armed guard who formerly kept watch on a tower'.[130] But these devices are also manifestations of a more general fascination with the different ways in which organic life could be emulated by mechanical devices. Thus, in England, in the civic pageantry crafted for Tudor princes, the automaton makes a surprising entrance. Michael Witmore has shown how various different kinds of mechanism, for example, came to feature in the civic pageantry of London in the earlier sixteenth century, listing devices such as a mechanical falcon deployed at the coronation entry of Anne Boleyn in 1533, and a mechanical phoenix which descended at the coronation progress of Edward VI in 1547.[131]

In his *Mathematicall Magick* (1648), John Wilkins saw such devices as a branch of mechanics, which he understood as a means of making inanimate matter '*overcome*, and *advance* nature'. Some of these devices he termed 'moveable and gradient automata representing the motion of living creatures . . . and some of them articulate'.[132] Such 'gradient . . . ambulatory' engines (of the kind attributed to Daedalus, and among which Wilkins included an 'iron spider') were contrasted to 'volant [flying] automata which included '*Archytas* his Dove, and *Regiomontanus* his Eagle'.[133] By the 1640s, it seems, these devices were becoming commonplace, and the magic associated with them had begun to dissipate: 'It is so common an experiment in these times to represent the persons and actions of any story by such self-moving images, that I shall not need to explain the manner how the wheels and springs are contrived within them', wrote Wilkins.[134]

That the 'persons and actions of any story' might be represented by 'self-moving images' alerts us to the ways in which the ambitions of Renaissance fine engineering seemed, in this respect, to mesh with a shifting view of the role of poetry or fiction more generally in Renaissance culture. Heron of Alexandria's automated theatrical performance has been described as producing the effect of a 'moving picture' that, like the 'speaking picture' which was poetry, was driven by the authors' powers of invention and imitation.[135] In this respect, both the automaton-maker and the poet were considered to be capable of ushering forms into the world that were either uncreated by nature, or which had existed (hitherto) only in classical myth and legend. For the poet, in Renaissance poetic theory, was also considered to be a 'maker', a fabricator of forms. So, in his *An Apologie for Poetrie* (1595), Sir Philip Sidney wrote that, for the poet 'lifted up with the vigour of his own invention', the task was to create:

> . . . things either better than nature bringeth forth, or, quite anew, forms such as never were in nature, as the heroes, demi-gods, Cyclops, chime-ras, furies, and such like; so as he goeth hand in hand with nature, not enclosed within the narrow warrant of her gifts, but freely ranging within the zodiac of his own wit.[136]

Machines, particularly machines as they were realized in the fashioning of hydraulic or clockwork-driven automata, drew as extensively as did poetry (or, for that matter, the visual arts) on the lexicon of the mythographers, who plundered the works of Ovid or the scriptures for new subject matter.

Mechanical women

The automaton was a luxurious device designed to provoke admiration and wonder both for the ingenuity and the ostentatious display of wealth that was expressed in its manufacture. At the same time, it seemed to imitate something of the quality of life itself. But other types of Renaissance and early-modern machine were designed to provoke entirely different kinds of pleasure. The very first legendary automata of which we possess a descrip-tion were female. In Book XVIII of Homer's *Iliad*, we read how Hephaestus fashioned female automata as animated prostheses for the lame god who was the legendary originator of the mechanical arts: 'Golden maidservants helped their master. They looked like real girls and could not only speak and use their limbs but were endowed with intelligence and trained in hand-work by the immortal gods.'[137] Other forms of fictional female automata, however, fulfilled a rather more decorative role. In the twelfth-century *Roman de Troie*, by Benoît de Sainte-Maure, for example, we read of a fictional automaton, a young girl crafted out of gold who 'performed and enter-tained and danced and capered and gambolled and leapt all day'.[138] This voyeuristic fantasy was complemented by another group of female automata displaying 'the games that ladies and young girls play'.[139]

Although we cannot say that such imaginative devices were explicitly erotic machines, lower down the mechanical hierarchy there is an intriguing hint (to be found in an aside in Jonson's *The Alchemist*) that the skills of the Renaissance mechanician could be deployed to baser ends, in the production of what may be termed automotive erotica. 'What device should he bring forth now?' asks the gullible Lovewit, contemplating Subtle's ability to manipulate human nature under the guise of manipulating matter:

> . . . Sure he has got
> Some bawdy pictures to call all this ging!
> The Friar and the nun; or the new motion
> Of the knight's courser covering the parson's mare;
> The boy of six year old with the great thing:[140]

Jonson writes, here, as if such bawdy excursions into mechanical life were well known to his audience. Yet, we do not know whether such a crude 'motion' was ever devised in reality. Certainly none has (to my knowledge) survived, though their manufacture would have been entirely within the capacities of sixteenth- or seventeenth-century craft workers.

In poetry, the equivalent to such lascivious mechanisms can be found in Spenser's disturbing image of the two 'naked Damzelles' who, in the Bowre of Blisse section of *The Faerie Queene*, appear to be bathing, but 'ne car'd to hyde, / Their dainty parts from vew of any, which them eyed' (FQ II. xii. 63). Are these erotic visions of female allure even human? Certainly, like the mechanical or hydraulic figures populating the gardens of Tivoli or Pratolino, these forms appear, at first, to be organic. But, given the dissimulating world of the Bowre, can we be absolutely sure that they are not artificial or even mechanical? Acting as though they are a pair of counter-poised weights on a lever or balance, they lift one another up from the waters:

> Sometimes the one would lift the other quight
> Aboue the waters, and then downe againe
> Her plong, as ouer maistered by might,
> Where both awhile would couered remaine,
> And each the other from to rise restraine;

(*FQ* II. xii. 64)

It is as if the strange pool of seductive women to be found in the central panel of Hieronymus Bosch's *Garden of Earthly Delights* (c. 1505–10), or the erotic engravings attached to the works of Aretino, which had begun to circulate in ever-greater quantities in the sixteenth century, had been brought to hydraulic life, in an endless and hedonistic rite of unfulfilled, pneumatic or mechanical pleasure, a courtly rival to the cruder motions of Jonson's 'boy . . . with the great thing'.[141]

In the late seventeenth and early eighteenth centuries, the themes of women, automata, and sex came together in the disturbing story of a female automaton said to have been fashioned by the high-priest of mechanism: René Descartes. In the early 1640s, Descartes was said to have constructed a female mechanical figure modelled on his illegitimate daughter, Francine. The daughter and her mechanical simulacrum were said to be indistinguishable from one another, while Descartes himself was inseparable from his artificial creation.[142] Stephen Gaukroger, the modern biographer of Descartes, believes, convincingly, that the tale of Descartes' automaton 'has all the elements of propaganda including that favourite propaganda weapon, sexual innuendo', and that it came into being as a conscious response to the spread of Cartesian materialism in the eighteenth century.[143] Descartes' 'Francine' might be compared to other later examples of female artifice and artificial which are equally fictional such as Jonathan Swift's prosthetically confected 'Corinna' to be found in his brilliant but disturbing poem 'A Beautiful Young Nymph Going to Bed' (1731), or the female android which features in the novel *L'Eve Future* (1886) by Villiers de L'Isle Adam. De L'Isle Adam's 'bottomly obnoxious science fiction fable' features an entirely synthetic female manufactured for aristocratic male pleasure.[144] These later eighteenth- and nineteenth-century images of artificial women are antecedents to the galaxy of deceptive female androids which have come to inhabit cinema in the modern world: the sinister robotic figure of Maria in Fritz Lang's *Metropolis* (1926), the female android sex-workers in Michael Crichton's *Westworld* (1973), or the beautiful but deadly android Pris ('a basic pleasure model') in Ridley Scott's *Blade Runner* (1982). As Gabby Wood has observed, when men fall in love with androids, believing them to be 'perfect women', then the mistake is usually 'fatal'.[145]

The most famous literary example of the consequences of men falling in love with a mechanism masquerading as organic life is to be found in E. T. A. Hoffmann's story 'The Sandman', published as the first tale in the collection *Nachstücke* (1816). In 'The Sandman' the hero of the story, Nathaniel, is enamoured of Olympia, who is gradually revealed to be a mechanical doll. Hoffmann's story was the starting point of Sigmund Freud's essay 'The Uncanny' in which Freud struggled to submit the irrationalities of Hoffmann's text to a rational explanation. Freud's influential interpretation, was, however, itself struggling against an earlier interpretation: a 1906 paper by the psychoanalyst Ernst Jentsch, which Freud acknowledged (in a rather grudging aside) to be the progenitor of his own thoughts on 'The Sandman'.[146] For Jentsch, 'The Sandman' was a tale in which we find ourselves unsure as to whether 'an apparently animate being is really alive, or conversely, whether a lifeless object might not be in fact animate'.[147] Jentsch's paper referred Freud to examples of this phenomenon:

> . . . the impression made by waxwork figures, ingeniously constructed dolls and automata . . . the uncanny effects of epileptic fits, and of manifestations of insanity, because these excite in the spectator the impression of automatic, mechanical processes at work behind the ordinary appearance of mental activity.[148]

How, in other words, are we to tell if a human being, who seems to exhibit symptoms of mechanism, the uncontrollable twitches and jerks of a fit, say, might not, in reality be a machine? How much worse might it be if machines began to take on a lifelike form? And what if the 'machine' is, at the same time, masquerading as a desirable female?

Published in the same year that Mary Shelley composed her novel of galvanic life, *Frankenstein or the Modern Prometheus*, Hoffmann's 'The Sandman' seems, though, to have transformed both a fashionable pastime and an emerging feature of industry into the matter of neurosis. For the period of composition of 'The Sandman' was also the period in which mechanization was becoming a feature of manufacturing processes. In 1801, for example, the invention (by J. M. Jacquard, in France) of a loom whose operation was controlled by a punched card, and was thus a forerunner of modern, digital, technologies, had demonstrated how a machine was able to function without continuous human intervention.[149] By the time that Hoffmann came to write his fantasy of automation, there were some eleven thousand 'Jacquard looms' in operation in Europe.[150] In this respect, Freud's psychoanalytic precursor Ernst Jentsch was surely right in identifying as 'uncanny' automatism masquerading as humanity. So Hoffmann's story can be thought of as a literary response to that growing distrust of machinery and automatism which, in England, in the period of the composition of 'The Sandman', would result in outbreaks of machine-wrecking or Luddism.[151] Indeed, Olympia's

English entirely non-fictional (male) counterparts were the 'Iron Men', as industrial operatives collectively christened the new factory machines, Hargreaves's spinning jenny, Arkwright's water frame, and Compton's mule, which would revolutionize the European textile industry in the eighteenth century and later.[152]

Mechanical women, however, presented a more sinister threat. In fiction, more often than not, once the mechanical nature of an artificial woman is revealed, 'she' becomes an object of horror and disgust. But perhaps such creatures reflect the lingering suspicion that 'woman' is herself an artful substitution for her masculine prototype: it is no coincidence, obviously, that de L'Isle Adam's mechanical heroine is christened 'Eve'. And lingering behind all these stories of mechanical women is the unspoken threat that the unbiddable or non-compliant organic woman can always be substituted for her compliantly mechanical counterpart.

Marshall McLuhan has shown how, in the twentieth century, women would be surrounded with artifice. Through the deployment of the new technologies of synthetic fibres, rubber, and wire women would appear as 'Nature's Rival'.[153] But Woman as 'Nature's Rival' was already a standard trope among Renaissance writers. In Shakespeare's *Antony and Cleopatra* (1606), for example, the Egyptian queen is described by the overwhelmed Enobarbus as a masterpiece of art, who is capable of creating 'a gap in nature' (II. ii. 224). Enobarbus's language is invested with images and similes of artificiality which produce an image of Cleopatra 'O'er picturing that Venus where we see / The Fancy outwork nature' (II. ii. 207–8). The queen's barge is 'like a burnished throne', with its poop of 'beaten gold', purple sails, and 'silver oars' which keep time to music, her 'pavilion' is fashioned out of 'cloth of gold, of tissue' while she is surrounded by 'pretty dimpled boys, like smiling cupids', together with a 'seeming mermaid' who steers using 'silken tackle' (II. ii. 197–216). The effect is similar to the marvellous effects that the Renaissance automaton makers or masque designers strove to reproduce in their art, where nature is represented and, if possible, surpassed by moving artificiality. Fabulous miniature ships, for example, driven by clockwork mechanisms, with painted sails and moving figures, were a speciality of a sixteenth-century technologist such as Hans Schlottheim, whose richly wrought miniature moving vessels were crafted at fabulous expense for European princes.[154]

As an Egyptian, the Renaissance Cleopatra would have been understood as a master of deceptive art, able to seduce masculine Roman virtue by the power of enchantment. These ideas can also be related to the idea of the

moving statue, or even the statue, which, like the figure of the Commenda-
tore in Mozart's *Don Giovanni* (1787) is brought to life. This is the fantasy with
which Shakespeare closes *The Winter's Tale* (composed *c.* 1609–10, published
1623), where we witness the magical transformation of a marble woman
into flesh, as the 'statue' of Hermione is ushered into life and movement in
a quasi-religious service. Magic, or at least the charge of magic, was always
associated with such enterprises, a charge which Shakespeare carefully side-
steps (though not entirely evades) as he has Paulina protest that her ability to
endow the statue with life is not 'unlawful business' (V. iii. 96). Is Hermione
a living figure or is she, rather, akin to those fabulous marionettes of antiquity, a *neurospaston*? And is Paulina, who has animated the figure, a magician,
a mechanic, or, as Polixines darkly suspects when he asks how Hermione
might have been 'stol'n from the dead' (V. iii. 116), a necromancer?[155]

In these literary images of Renaissance women, artificiality lurks just
beneath the surface, beguiling the men who gaze on these animated figures. Conversely, there was always the possibility of manufacturing an ideal
woman artificially. This, of course, is the theme of the familiar Pygmalion
story, told in Book X of Ovid's *Metamorphoses*. In Ovid's tale, as retold by John
Marston in his erotic poem *The Metamorphosis of Pygmalion's Image* (1598), Pygmalion's fashioning of an artificial female form is born out of his disgust at
women generally. Pygmalion prefers art or artifice to reality, since he:

> Disdain'd to yield servile affection
> Of Amorous suit to any womankind,
> Knowing their wants, and men's perfection:
>> Yet love at length forc'd him to know his fate,
>> And love the shade whose substance he did hate.[156]

Substituting the 'shade' (the statue) for the 'substance' (the woman) which
he hates, the 'high love-hating mind' of Pygmalion prefers a wrought or
fashioned creature to anything encountered within nature, since it offers a
narcissistic view of the maker's own genius:

> He was amaz'd at the wondrous rareness
> Of his own workmanship's perfection.
> He thought that Nature ne'er produced such fairness
> In which all beauties have their mansion;
>> And thus admiring, was enamoured
>> On that fair image himself portrayed.[157]

'On that fair image himself portrayed' suggests that fabrication is a self-reflexive act, a mirror in which the maker can see his own genius reflected. Similarly, in Arthur Golding's version of the tale, published earlier, in 1567, it is the maker's appreciation of his own skill, rather than the product of his skill, which excites the fetishistic adoration of the inanimate female form that he has created: 'In this his worke he tooke / A certaine loue' writes Golding:

> So artificiall was the work. He woondreth at his Art
> And of his counterfetted corse conceyueth loue in hart.
> He often toucht it, feeling if the woork that he had made
> Were verie flesh or Iuorye still.[158]

We might, of course, appeal to ideas of fashion or luxury, particularly in its eighteenth- and nineteenth-century manifestations, to explain why women should appear so often as the products of artifice, or be associated with artificial, inanimate objects. Such a critique of women as artificial creations, luxurious puppets, was well under way in the sixteenth century when the puritan Philip Stubbes, in his *Anatomie of Abuses* (1583), described women who adorned themselves as: 'not naturall women, but artificiall Women, not Women of flesh, & blod, but rather puppits, or mawmets of rags & clowtes compact together'.[159] Yet even here, Stubbes's misogynistic railing seems to hint at some deeper, masculine, fear of woman as a category. As Scott Cutler Shershow has observed of this and similar such passages, terms such as puppet or poppet (related to the French word for doll, *poupée*, a term which was also used to denote an attractive woman) create an idea of 'Woman conceptualised and reified . . . an object (or plaything) of male desire'.[160] In the twentieth century, equally, we could appeal to the literal truth of Simone de Beauvoir's famous proposition in *Le Deuxième Sexe* (1968), that 'On ne naît pas femme: on le devient' ('One is not born a woman, one becomes one') when we consider the ways in which artificial life and femininity have uneasily cohabited together within these male fantasies.[161]

Artificiality as an expression of male anxiety or fear of the feminine, however, seems to take us to deeper, more atavistic, levels of understanding. At their root, these images, fantasies, and fictions depend upon the lingering suspicion that 'woman' may be an inherently unnatural human form, which can only ape the primary creation of the ideal, natural, human form: the Adamic male. This view corresponds to that larger, premodern, understanding of the biological difference between male and female that held that woman was essentially a 'version' of the male: 'man is the measure of all things and woman does not exist as an ontologically distinct category', as Thomas Laqueur writes (his emphasis), quoting that familiar Renaissance dictum, sometimes attributed to Protagoras, *omnium rerum homo mensura est*.[162] The female form was thus held to be belated or secondary – an imperfect realization of the more perfect symmetry and proportion of the male. Just as the machine and the automaton, which were also forms of secondary creation, seem to possess the semblance of life in their various motions, so the female was a manufactured entity, springing from the male body, and created at one remove from that divine *pneuma* which had animated Adam. Scrape back her outward marks of humanity, and what is revealed beneath the surface is a deceptively artificial fabrication: a creature that only superficially resembles its male counterpart. In her exploration of the cycle of stories and traditions surrounding Eve, Helen of Troy, Pandora, and Pygmalion's statue, as well as the widespread stories to be found in folklore of female statues which become animated, Marina Warner writes of the ubiquity of woman as a 'manufactured maiden . . . where woman as original matter and woman as artefact become interchangeable'; hence, Warner argues, 'the definition of woman partakes of the definition of art'.[163] In sharing this definition, the woman as created object shares in the power of art to deceive by its lifelike (but, eventually, false) evocation of the real, or masculine original, which it can only imitate.

Like a machine, then, 'woman' belongs to a category that is not part of nature. Like a machine, too, though, she moves to some purpose, she might be as much a product of art and ingenuity as a purely natural processes. The artificial woman, fashioned as an object of desire, is a manifestation of a more profound narcissism in which the maker turns away from mere flesh and blood, to produce a more perfect realization of his own skill, craft, and artificial cunning. In the later seventeenth century, this impulse would be related to the idea of the 'masculine' birth of science and reason, springing, like Minerva, from the head of Jupiter.[164] But as we shall see in the next chapter, the possibility of fashioning such a race of mechanical beings that might exist in reality was to become a further manifestation of mechanical culture, as it was to emerge in the context of the 'mechanical philosophy' of seventeenth-century England.

6

REASONING ENGINES
The instrumental imagination
in the seventeenth century

The mechanisms, fables, and fantasy devices surveyed in the previous chapter were designed primarily to enthral and entertain. In the case of the 'artificial woman', we can also see how the mechanical impulse was allied to a much wider imaginative debate over the narcissistic inventive genius of the masculine progenitor which, in turn, was a manifestation of that debate between 'art' and 'nature' which so enthralled Renaissance poets, artists, and craft workers. The makers of tools, machines, statues, images or literary texts were all, to a greater or lesser extent, involved in that debate which pitted the Aristotelian world of *Technē* or the process of 'bringing something into being' against nature and natural forms. But as we shall see in this chapter, the appliance of mechanism, in the later seventeenth century, would give rise to a quite different view of nature, and, at the same time, the prospect of the creation of artificial creatures more fantastic than anything that might have been imagined by the poets and mythographers of the sixteenth century.

Buying an instrument

The mechanic philosophers of the later seventeenth century proclaimed their optimistic belief in the eventual conquest of nature with the help of their ingenious machines, devices, and instruments. Yet, the experience of actually confronting nature with the help of a modern apparatus could result in frustration rather than revelation. Certainly, this was Samuel Pepys's experience of first peering at nature through the lens of a microscope. One summer's morning in 1664, Pepys received two tradesmen at his house in London: his tailor 'with a coat I have made to wear indoors' and also 'Mr Reeve, with a microscope and scotoscope'.[1] The microscope was purchased, along with the new coat, while the scotoscope, an image-enhancing apparatus, was given to Pepys *gratis* by the adept salesman, Mr Reeve.[2] Full of pride at his acquisition of these latest technological gadgets, although perhaps concerned, too, to justify the considerable sums involved in the transaction – £5 10s – Pepys breathlessly admired his instruments:

> . . . a great price, but a most curious bauble it is, and he says, as good, nay, the best he knows in England, and he makes the best in the world. The other he gives me, and is of value; and a curious curiosity it is to look at objects in a darke room with. Mighty pleased with this I to the office . . .[3]

The 'curious bauble' entered the Pepys household not so much as a precision scientific instrument, but, rather, as a recreational device. That evening, Pepys scurried back from the office 'to read a little in Dr Power's book of discovery by the microscope to enable me a little how to use and what to expect from my glasse'.[4] Henry Power's recently published *Experimental Philosophy in Three Books* (1664), which described 'new experiments, Microscopical, Mercurial, Magnetical', functioned as a kind of owner's manual for the new instrument.[5] The following evening, having finished Power's book, and accompanied by his wife, Pepys tried to view objects through his microscope 'with great pleasure, but with great difficulty before we could come to find the manner of seeing any thing'.[6] The couple were learning that working with such an instrument demanded a radical readjustment of human perceptions.

This vignette of the enthusiastic couple, struggling to see the wonders of nature with the aid of their new instrument reminds us of how the rise of 'mechanical philosophy' in the seventeenth century was not always an austere communion with nature. The story illustrates for us, too, how the term 'mechanical' had begun to function as a kind of rallying cry or watchword, a hallmark of intellectual fashion in London in the 1660s. For scientific machines and devices had become all the rage. 'The ordinary shops of Mechaniks', Thomas Sprat recorded in 1667, 'are as full of rarities, as the cabinets of the former noblest mathematicians.'[7] To be a 'mechanical philosopher' was to sport modernity as a token or badge of belonging to a circle of adepts, joining the select company of Bacon, Descartes, and Hobbes or (later) Boyle, Willis, or Newton. A French visitor to London in 1663 was impressed by what he understood as this burgeoning democracy of mechanical intellect. Describing his meetings with various *virtuosi* in Restoration London in the course of his journey to England in 1663, the French historian, anglophile, and translator of Thomas Hobbes, Samuel Sorbière, wrote of his encounter with the 'learned *Scotchman*' Sir Robert Moray, the royalist commander and politician, that it was a 'wonderful, or rather very edifying Thing':

> ... to find a person imploy'd in Matters of State, and of such Excellent Merit, and one who had been engaged a great Part of his Life in Warlike Commands, and the affairs of the Cabinet, apply himself in making Machines in *St James's Park*, and adjusting Telescopes . . .[8]

Perhaps naively, Sorbière attributed this fascination with mechanical matters on the part of the nobility as well as the men of business, trade, and commerce, directly to the effect of the civil wars. For 'having no Court to make', Sorbière believed that the nobility had applied themselves to useful labour, and had established 'Elaboratoriaries, made machines, opened mines, and made use of an Hundred Sorts of Artists, to find out some New Invention or other'.[9] We need only recall the notorious John Wilmot, second Earl of Rochester, and his circle to appreciate the extent to which Sorbière was exaggerating the commitment of Restoration aristocrats to mechanical matters, at least in this scientific sense.

Pepys's purchase of a microscope nevertheless foreshadows the ways in which, in the contemporary world, technological 'gadgets' are sold to us as aspirational statements of who or what we consider ourselves to be. 'Early adopters' of technology are often, it has been suggested, 'addicted to technology', acquiring new devices as status objects.[10] Indeed, the beautifully crafted microscopes and telescopes that were now available for purchase in seventeenth-century London and Paris, with their ornate scrollwork, veneered carrying cases, and intricate engraving, were clearly fashioned as ostentatious objects to be seen with, as well as with which to see.[11] Samuel Pepys, with his sometimes over-anxious desire to appear 'modern', was a technological consumerist who was fascinated by new devices of the kind represented by the microscope and the scotoscope. In April 1673, for example, we find him trying out another kind of device, the Otacousticon invented by Sir Samuel Morland. Where the microscope enlarged visual objects, the Otacousticon enlarged sounds. It was a device 'like a great glass bottle' and with its help Pepys was able to hear 'the dashing of the oares of the boats in the Thames to Arundell gallery window, which, without it, I could not in the least do'.[12] Listening to the dash of oars on a distant river was not, of course, the end of the new philosophy of nature. Instead, it was the prospect of conquering nature which underpinned the labours of the natural philosophers, with whom Samuel Pepys wished to be associated. Machines of ever more complex design would be the means by which nature would be wrestled from the imagination of the poets, and made to serve human needs.[13]

Galileo's *Dialogues Concerning Two New Sciences* (1638) was the founding text of this new mechanics, and motion was the key to this new method of enquiry. 'There is in nature perhaps nothing older than motion, concerning which the books written by philosophers are neither few nor small' Galileo dryly observed in the opening to the third 'day' of the *Dialogues*, that concerning *De motu locali* or 'change of position'.[14] But motion had to be divorced from the Aristotelian sense of motion as a change of state, prompted by the will of God or the innate properties of bodies.[15] Rather, motion was to be examined with a mathematical precision: 'only in mathematics' (Galileo wrote) can we be struck by 'the force of rigid demonstrations'.[16] Such 'rigid demonstrations' formed the matter of the *Two New Sciences*, as Galileo explored the relative capacities of differently sized mechanisms, discovering that, for example, a doubling in size of a particular machine by no means resulted in a doubling of its power capacity.[17] Motion now meant something at once local and particular, the 'movement from here to there' as Richard S. Westfall has described Galileo's explorations, which 'denied that anything essential to a body was involved in its motion . . . a body is indifferent to motion or rest'.[18]

Francis Bacon and the reform of mechanism

That natural phenomena were 'indifferent', oblivious to the world around them or of any creational cause, was to become a central tenet of the 'mechanical philosophers' of the seventeenth century. In England in the early seventeenth century Francis Bacon was the great advocate of the power of mechanical art over nature. In Bacon's writings, nature was imagined as being gathered and squeezed in the press of the new philosophy. Nature was to be reduced to a pulpy mass, out of which would be distilled the new liquor of reason and knowledge. No detail in the natural world was too small or insignificant to escape this penetrating process of enquiry. As Bacon wrote in *The Advancement of Learning* (1605): 'For it being the nature of the mind of man, to the extreme prejudice of knowledge, to delight in the spacious liberty of generalities, as in a champain region, and not in the inclosures of particularity.'[19] Particularity may represent an 'inclosure', yet, like Hamlet's nutshell, it could also amount to a place of infinite space for the mind's contemplation. But Bacon was interested, too, in the wider sense of the 'mechanic arts' rather than in the mathematical precision of mechanics that Galileo was to develop later in the seventeenth century.[20]

For Bacon, both mechanics and (by extension) machines inhabited a social as much as an intellectual sphere. When Thomas Sprat wrote approvingly of how the 'ordinary shops of Mechaniks' were now full of 'rarities', he was commenting on the ways in which instruments and devices had penetrated the workplace, rather than being confined to the 'cabinets' of the wealthy collector. But Sprat still thought of 'mechanics' as a socially inferior class. Historically, 'mechanics', irrespective of whether they traded in the world of mechanisms, had long been understood as engaged in crafts that were socially demeaning in some (often unspecified) way, as a glance at the etymology of the word in the *Oxford English Dictionary* will confirm.[21] More than this, in England a 'mechanical' understanding of phenomena, prior to Galileo's mathematical enquiries into materials and motion, actually betokened a *lack* of mathematical or theoretical understanding. Thus, in John Dee's preface to Humphrey Billingsley's 1570 translation of Euclid's *Geometry*, Dee wrote that 'A Mechanicien, or a Mechanicall workman is he, whose skill is without knowledge of Mathematical demonstration.'[22] Dee's 'Mechanicien' is associated with untutored or unskilled work, which could, in turn, signify an a-theoretical approach to a problem. Later, Dee wrote of a particular calculation that it could be done 'naturally . . . and mechanically: yet hath it a good Demonstration Mathematicall'.[23]

It is one of the ironies of the history of science and technology that a subject – mechanics – which was to become so indebted to mathematics, should have been rooted, etymologically, in a term which originally signalled (in England at any rate) an *absence* of mathematical rigour. In this sense 'mechanics' has absolutely nothing whatsoever to do with machines or machinery. Rather, the term suggested 'routine . . . unthinking activity'.[24] Rather than machines and machinery giving birth to the specialized trade or craft of 'mechanics', the reverse was the case. Machines, in their unthinking application of work to a particular task, emerged, as Marx was to argue, as supreme examples of the possibility of transforming repetitive labour into organic attachments to the machine.

Bacon's endeavour was to release the idea of 'mechanics' from the sense of 'routine . . . unthinking activity', while he also linked the term to the contemplation of machines or mechanisms which could (as he understood it) act upon nature in some way. So, the investigation of mechanisms of all kinds formed part of the larger investigation of 'nature altered or wrought'.[25] For Bacon 'the history of nature wrought or mechanical' described the ways in which humanity altered or shaped nature in some fashion. Thus the five simple machines first described by Heron of Alexandria – the lever, the wheel and axle, the wedge, the pulley, and the screw – were enlisted as devices which forced nature out of her course, bending inanimate matter to human will or intellect.[26] Bacon believed that it might be possible to devise operations which forced matter to behave in ways which defied any natural law. 'In things artificial' Bacon imperiously wrote in his *Preparation for a Natural and Experimental History* (published with the *Novum Organum* in 1620): 'nature takes orders from man, and works under his authority'.[27] Nature could be understood as a form of crude metallic ore, which, through the skills of the craftsman could be moulded or even assembled into new and surprising forms. Indeed, mining, metallurgy, and the associated arts of metalwork, were to become dominant metaphors in Bacon's writing as he sought to explain how nature could be bent to the force of machines and mechanisms. For Baconian nature was made up of matter that could be 'reshaped, rearranged, beaten, jostled around by heating, and suchlike'.[28] Like a soft metal, nature was both malleable and ductile; through the application of 'art' she could be put to human 'use': key terms in Bacon's philosophical lexicon.

Thus Bacon envisaged a new 'history' of nature, emended by 'the experiments of the mechanical arts', to become 'confined and harassed . . . forced from its own condition by art and human agency, and pressured and moulded'.[29] Citing three examples of the 'mechanic arts' (printing, gunpowder, and the compass), Bacon wrote that 'no empire or sect or star seems to have exercised a greater power and influence on human affairs than these mechanical things'.[30] Writing as he was prior to Galileo's theoretical and experimental investigations of 'work' and 'force', Bacon nevertheless sensed that the theoretical understanding of machines, even those which had been in use for thousands of years, was still barely understood. More than this, the contemplation of mechanisms was still shrouded in prejudice and obscurantism:

I find some collections made of agriculture, and likewise of manual arts;
but commonly with a rejection of experiments familiar and vulgar. For it is
esteemed a kind of dishonour unto learning to descend to inquiry or meditation upon matters mechanical, except they be such as may be thought
secrets, rarities, and special subtilities.[31]

So, as well as rescuing the term 'mechanics' from its association with unskilled work, this liberation of 'matters mechanical' from the grip of those
who classified mechanisms with 'secrets, rarities, and special subtilities' also
represented Bacon's attempt to sever the mechanical arts from any magical,
occult, alchemical, or cabbalistic approach to nature. No longer would nature
be understood through systems of correspondence, allegory and simili-
tude, or hidden sympathies or antipathies. Nature and natural effects were
to be demystified and industrialized.[32] For all of natural philosophy could
now be divided under two (industrial) headings: 'the mine and the furnace'. The natural philosophers themselves could be divided into two sorts:
'some to be pioneers and some smiths; some to dig, and some to refine and
hammer'. To the first group (the 'speculative') was assigned 'the inquisition of
causes'; to the second (the 'operative') 'the production of effects'.[33] The refiners
and hammerers, among whom were the technologists and fabricators of
engines, were no longer to be dismissed as a rude mechanics. But neither
were they to be invested with the spurious glamour of magic, or praised for
mastery of hidden 'secrets' by which inanimate matter would be given the
semblance of life.

John Donne's image of the human soul, re-forged by the great artificer in
his sonnet 'Batter my heart', corresponds, in a surprising fashion, to this larger
Baconian project. For all Donne's scepticism towards the 'New Philosophy'
expressed most famously in the Anniversary poems of 1611 and 1612, Donne,
writing at the outset of the new age of experiment, had begun to recreate God
as a divine 'operative' of the kind Bacon envisaged as mastering nature. There
was nothing, however, mysterious about this process. Insofar as the end of
the 'operative' natural philosopher was to alter, or bend nature, he could be
considered as a practitioner of 'technical magic', which may be understood
as a transformational power over nature, accomplished with the help of science and technique.[34] Natural magic, for Bacon, was a term that had been
'misapplied and abused', since it was no more than 'natural wisdom, or natural
prudence ... purged from vanity and superstition'.[35] As such, it was a term
worth rescuing from the clutches of the Hermeticists and alchemists.[36]

Bacon was puzzled by the intellectual scorn which was attached to the 'operative' philosopher, or technologist who studied how nature could be put to work. For Bacon, far from this being a rude or demeaning task, it was the most radical and fundamental undertaking of natural philosophy:

> ... the use of history mechanical is of all others the most radical and fundamental towards natural philosophy; such natural philosophy as shall not vanish in the fume of subtile, sublime, or delectable speculation, but such as shall be operative to the endowment and benefit of man's life ... will give a more real and true illumination concerning causes and axioms than is hitherto attained.[37]

Most of the Baconian catchwords are in play here: a 'history mechanical', which is 'operative', giving rise to a 'benefit', which, in turn is the product of 'real and true illumination', based on 'causes and axioms' rather than the 'fume of subtile ... and delectable speculation'. Within this context, it was the task of the machine to 'vex' nature by the application of artifice. The machine or instrument pressurized nature, forcing her to reveal herself in ways that were otherwise hidden from casual observation: 'the passions and vexations of nature cannot appear so fully in the liberty of nature, as in the trials and vexations of art', Bacon wrote.[38]

For Bacon, the study of mechanism was an intellectual as well as a practical art, piercing beneath the superficial appearance of things to attain a 'real and true illumination concerning causes and axioms'. In his sketch of a utopian scientific and intellectual community to be found in the *New Atlantis* (1624), Bacon outlined the institutional means by which he believed the pursuit of 'nature altered or wrought' might be achieved. On the imaginary island of Bensalem, a group of travellers encounter the wonders of Salomons House, 'the noblest foundation' (they are told) 'that ever was upon the earth ... Dedicated to the study of the Works and Creatures of God'.[39] Salomons House is a kind of research institution or college, dedicated to the study of nature through the light of 'experience', rather than mediated by the texts of Aristotle or the ancient philosophers. Sensory experience, indeed, appears to be, at first, the organizing principle of Salomon's House, with each portion of the study of nature particularized into various 'houses', based upon the human senses: 'Perspective-Houses' (for the investigation of light); 'Sound-Houses' (for the exploration of sound and harmony); 'Perfume-Houses' (where Bacon conjoined smell and taste). But there is no 'house' dedicated to 'touch'. Rather, at the heart of Salomons House are the 'Engine-Houses', where 'Engines and instruments for all sorts of motions' are stored:

Ther we imitate and practise to make Swifter Motions than any you have, either out of your Musketts or any Engine that you have; And to Make them and Multiply them more Easily, and with small Force, by Wheeles and other Meanes; and to make them Stronger and more Violent than yours are, Exceeding your greatest Cannons and Basilisks [artillery]. Wee represent also likewise New Mixtures and Compositions of Gun-Powder, Wilde-Fires [bitumen] burning in Water and Unquenchable. Also Fire-workes of all Variety, both for Pleasure and Use. Wee imitate also Flights of Birds; Wee have some Degrees of Flying in the Ayre. Wee have Shipps and Boates for going under Water, and Brooking [enduring] of Seas; Also Swimming-girdles [life-belts] and Supporters. We have divers curious Clocks and other like Motions of Returne [pendulums], And some Perpetuall Motions. Wee imitate also Motions of Living Creatures, by Images of Men, Beasts, Birds, Fishes, and Serpents. Wee have also a great number of other Various Motions, strange for Equality [regularity], Finenesse, and Subtility . . . These are (my Sonne) the riches of Salomons House.[40]

In Bacon's mechanical future, machines will spawn further machines. Bacon's imaginary 'engine-Houses' would emerge, later in the seventeenth century, in the form of William Petty's idea of a 'Gymnasium Mechanicum' dedicated to the study of the 'Advancement of all Mechanicall Arts and Manufactures' as well as in the enthusiastic descriptions of English devotion to mechanism by foreign observers such as Samuel Sorbière.[41]

But the mechanical wonders of Salomons House were not unproblematic tokens of technological optimism. Many of the ingenious inventions that he described were dedicated to violence and destruction. This, the negative side of Bacon's advocacy of technology, was explored more tangentially in the retelling of the myth of Daedalus, the legendary founder (together with Prometheus) of the mechanical arts. In the *De Sapientia veterum* ('Of the Wisdom of the Ancients', first published in 1609) Bacon attributed to Daedalus 'mechanical skill, industry, and curious arts converted to ill uses'.[42] It was Daedalus, Bacon wrote, who 'by his abominal industry and destructive genius' created the labyrinth in which sheltered the monstrous Minotaur. The labyrinth itself was 'a work infamous for its end and design, but admirable and prodigious for art and workmanship'.[43] So, while 'the use of mechanic arts' had benefited human society, Bacon also recognized that the 'same magazine supplies instruments of lust, cruelty, and death'.[44]

The labyrinth of Daedalus, for Bacon, also expressed a larger sense of the mechanic arts. The labyrinth, Bacon wrote:

... contains a beautiful allegory, representing the nature of mechanic arts in general; for all ingenious and accurate mechanical inventions may be conceived as a labyrinth, which, by reason of their subtility, intricacy, crossing, and interfering with one another, and the apparent resemblances they have among themselves, scarce any power of the judgment can unravel and distinguish . . .[45]

Bacon had begun to see technological innovation as cumulative. The task of the natural philosophers was to create an alternative, mechanical, world of artefacts and systems conforming to human designs. In forging this world, a work which might be compared to that idea of the 'Second Creation' by which humankind partially recovers, by its own efforts, from the primal Edenic disaster, the philosophers first had to recreate the natural world around them according to mechanical principles.

Seeing with machines

For all that the audio-voyeuristic possibilities of the Otacousticon had intrigued Samuel Pepys, it was sight rather than sound that was to be the human sense most transformed by the instruments of seventeenth-century technology.[46] Indeed, most if not all of the technical innovations devised or refined by the 'mechanical philosophers' were devoted either to sight, as in the case of the microscope and the telescope, or to measurement as in the instances of the micrometer, barometer, thermometer, wind-gauge, and pendulum clock. And measuring devices such as these may, in any case, be thought of as transforming different sensory impressions into purely visual, and measurable, phenomena. Even a device that we would not, now, associate with sight, such as the universal joint, was first devised in the seventeenth century to make an optical instrument – the telescope – function more accurately.[47]

In the nineteenth century, Charles Darwin would write of how it had become 'scarcely possible to avoid comparing the eye with a telescope . . . perfected by the long-continued efforts of the highest human intellects'.[48] Darwin was used to seeing the world in terms of devices or instruments. But this analogy only underlined the superiority of that process which Darwin was learning to call natural selection, and which, over the course of millennia, was able to produce a 'living optical instrument . . . as superior to one of glass, as the works of the Creator are to those of man'.[49] This process of thinking with the help of instruments was already in train among artists, and poets, as well as natural philosophers, in the seventeenth century as they began to see the world in terms of new devices. And yet, the problem for seventeenth-century natural philosophers, in contrast to Darwin and nineteenth-century biologists and zoologists, was that their new devices and instruments revealed the *imperfection* of the human senses, rather than their superiority over any fabricated works. And such imperfection could not be easily reconciled with the idea of an omniscient creative deity.

For how could one be sure that what one saw with the help of one's instrument was not a delusion? Here, the experience of the artist was to be crucial. The development of perspective, after all, was a technological solution to the problem of representing a three-dimensional world on a flat surface. But it was also an illusionary skill. We tend not to think of perspectival drawing and painting as an instrument or device of any kind, let alone a machine. Yet perspective, just like the machine, was evolving out of a set of precisely calibrated mathematical procedures, deployed in order to create a 'systematic illusion of receding forms behind the flat surface of a panel, canvas, wall or ceiling'.[50] This idea had been in circulation since the fifteenth century. The goal of the artist, according to Alberti's hugely influential treatise *Della Pittura* (*On Painting*) of 1435 was to convince the spectator that what they saw represented on the flat surface, delineated in drawn lines and paint, 'appears to be in relief' in just the same way that forms encountered in nature appeared to posses depth.[51] To Sir Henry Wotton, writing two hundred years after Alberti, the technique by which 'diverse distinct *Eminences*' are made to appear on a flat surface was still reckoned to be nothing less than an '*Artificall Miracle*'.[52] Given the development of what Erwin Panofsky has described as a 'mathematically exact linear perspectival procedure' attributed, long after the event, to Brunelleschi, it was perhaps inevitable that, to the artists of succeeding generations, the view arose that with the help of machines or instruments the illusion might be made even more convincing.[53]

This techno-artistic fantasy, irrespective of whether it was grounded in Italian or Northern European perspectival procedures, was very much a Western phenomenon: 'The ambition to invent a machine or device for the "perfect" imitation of nature appears to have been virtually limited to Renaissance and post-Renaissance Western art – until the universal craze for photography', Martin Kemp has written.[54] More broadly, Kemp sees this process as part of a larger European technological and intellectual movement, manifested in the fashion for perspective machines, *camerae obscurae*, and other devices which ingeniously captured the effects of nature. So, Samuel Sorbière, in the course of his English journey of 1663, recorded seeing 'an instrument, by which a man that has never learnt, may Design and Draw all sorts of Objects'.[55] The device was a tracing instrument of some type, by which the operator moved a 'rule' attached to a pencil, over the object to be drawn, which in turn traced its outline on paper. Svetlana Alpers has recently suggested that the seventeenth-century artist's studio could be thought of as 'an experimental instrument for attending to the world'.[56] Within the studio figured as instrument, the artist could play with the effects of light, colour, mathematical rules, and the texture of paint in an attempt not merely to mimic the exterior world, but to reproduce sometimes better versions of that world, in all its possible variety, within the bounded space of the canvas or wooden panel.

The visual arts would provide a powerful metaphor, in the seventeenth century, for understanding the new mechanical philosophy. In his extravagant ode of celebration 'To the Royal Society' which prefaced Thomas Sprat's *History of the Royal Society* (1667), the poet Abraham Cowley understood the reorganization of knowledge, attendant upon the invention of so many new devices, to be directly comparable to the procedures of the visual artist. For the artist and the natural philosopher now had to learn to see the world anew if they were to represent it accurately:

> Who to the life an exact Piece would make,
> Must not from others Work a copy take;
>> No not from *Rubens* or *Vandike*;
> Much less content himself to make it like
> Th'Idæas and the Images which ly
> In his own Fancy, or his Memory.
>> No, he before his sight must place
>> The Natural and living face;
>> The real Object must command
> Each judgment of his Eye, and Motion of his hand.[57]

The task, whether of science or of art, had become the contemplation of the 'real Object' which was nature, unmediated either by the work of other artists, or the artist's or the philosopher's own preconceptions residing in their 'fancy' or 'memory'. Paradoxically, of course, this unmediated contemplation of the 'real Object' precluded the use of those very instruments or devices to which seventeenth-century natural science was becoming increasingly indebted. Rather, as Cowley describes the process, the eye and the hand each had to become instruments themselves, responding to the 'living face' of nature. Such organic instruments were now understood as enhancing this commitment to the study of the 'real Object'. The dominant image of Cowley's 'Ode' is an imagined machine or device in which nature is squeezed or 'vexed' mechanically. Nature is conceived of as an orchard, into which the natural philosopher strides, purposefully gathering the 'fruit' of knowledge: 'And when on heaps the chosen bunches lay, / He prest them wisely the Mechanic way . . .'[58]

If, once, the Fall of humankind and with it the shameful origins of technology had been expressed in the old story of eating the forbidden fruit, then in Cowley's Ode, we can see philosophy being reorganized as a kind of knowledge machine, operating to reverse the effects of this act of primal disobedience. Or, as the instrument maker, technologist, and one of the founding fellows of the Royal Society, Robert Hooke argued in the preface to his *Micrographia* (1665): 'by the addition of . . . artificial instruments and methods, there may be, in some manner, a reparation made for the mischiefs and imperfections, mankind has drawn upon itself'.[59] Humanity may have fallen from its original state of innocence, but the loss could be made good, not just by religion and faith, but by science and technology.[60]

The 'conquest' of nature by artifice was the goal, and mechanism would be the instrument by which this end would be attained. In 1671, Robert Boyle explained this new undertaking:

> I do not take the term, Mechaniks, in that stricter and more proper sense, wherein it is wont to be taken, when 'tis used onely to signifie the Doctrine about the moving powers (as the Beam, the Leaver, the Screws, and the Wedg) and of framing Engines to multiply force; but I here understand the word *Mechaniks* in a larger sense, for those Disciplines that consist of the Applications of pure Mathematicks to produce or modify motion in inferior bodies.[61]

By way of the 'discipline' of mathematics, nature was to be rendered calculable and (above all) predictable.[62] According to the precepts of 'mechanical philosophy', nature was, in turn, to be conceived of as a gigantic machine. Once nature was so conceived, then the properties of machines began to be mapped onto nature, in much the same way that Darwin in the nineteenth century would come to understand the structure of the eye as a system of lenses of the kind to be found in a microscope or telescope. Nature, far from being unpredictable or capricious (the gendering of 'Nature' as a female goddess by the poets was, of course, particularly resonant in this respect), began to appear as intelligible, even, paradoxically, artificial. This proposition violated the most basic precepts of Aristotelian philosophy, namely, that there was a distinction between the contrived and the natural. More than that, nature began to appear as altogether more mundane, and certainly far less whimsical or fantastic. As Steven Shapin following Max Weber puts the matter, to recreate nature in terms of machinery was, in effect, to fashion a 'vehicle for taking the wonder out of nature'.[63] The long Renaissance conflict between 'art' and 'nature' which had so energized Renaissance poets and artists was, at last, at an end.

The relationship of machines to the generation of knowledge in the seventeenth century would achieve its clearest expression in Robert Boyle's most renowned invention, the air pump. Boyle's contrivance, which Samuel Sorbière termed a 'Pneumatick Engine', was simply a device for producing a vacuum.[64] But it also expressed, in sum, the ambitions of the 'mechanical philosophy', which, as Shapin together with Simon Schaffer, have observed:

> . . .used the machine not merely as an ontological metaphor, but also, crucially, as a means of intellectual production. The matters of fact that constituted the foundations of the new science were brought into being by a purpose-built scientific machine.[65]

The air pump, constructed for Boyle in 1658–9, and described in detail in his New Experiments Physico-Mechanical, Touching the Spring of the Air (1660) was a 'rarity' of the kind which, in Bacon's sense, served to 'vex' nature. It was thus a representative of a new class of mechanisms. It was quite unlike the machines, say, which Leonardo or Ramelli had devised in their imaginations and in their drawings, or which Montaigne had enjoyed viewing in his travels, or which Fontana had deployed in sixteenth-century Rome. It did not rearrange the landscape, or make human life (at least directly) any the more pleasurable. And though it might, in its operation, instil a sense of awe, wonder, or delight in the observer, sensations of the kind which Pepys was pursuing when he purchased his microscope, these could be considered as by-products of the machine's operation, not intrinsic factors in their design.

Indeed, awe, wonder, and delight were responses to the machine that Robert Boyle, in describing the sequence of experiments undertaken with the device, actively avoided. Instead, Boyle's descriptions of the operation of the air pump, as he watched larks, sparrows, and mice dying within its confines, was tersely factual, pretending to 'a faithful embodiment of the proper form of writing up experiments . . . no rhetorical flourishes, no superfluous citation of authorities, no verbal ornament, but a straight forward account of the phenomena to be investigated'.[66] Neither could the air pump be compared to the fabulous synthetic machines which inhabited the gardens and grottoes beloved of Elizabethan travellers to Italy or France, or to the artful designs of Inigo Jones, whose purpose was to generate illusionary diversions for his courtly audience. Rather, the air pump existed to generate new 'facts' about the world; facts which could (at least in theory) be understood as generated through the disinterested operation of the machine.

But these new devices had another unlooked-for effect, which, paradoxically, acted to call in question the whole foundation of the 'new science' of which they were a technological expression. Following the Baconian idea of attending to the minute details of nature, and trusting firmly in the belief that what could be described was *only* what could be seen, the instruments of the scientific imagination promised a sharper, clearer, picture of nature. But, at almost the same moment, they demonstrated that the human senses, unaided, were profoundly untrustworthy. More than this, as the story of Pepys and his wife struggling to see objects beneath his microscope's lenses reminds us, the human senses had to learn how to adapt to these new instruments. Just as Georgius Agricola, one hundred years earlier, had set about the task of educating the reader of *De Re Metallica* so that they might learn how bodies now had to work in conformity to machines, so the human senses now had to be trained to work with the devices that were becoming available.

This refocusing of the human sensorium involved the realization that unaided sensory experience was an untrustworthy medium for understanding the world. Indeed, the fallibility of the fallen human senses was, if anything, underlined by the growing reliance on instruments of all kinds. Adam in paradise, as Joseph Glanvill pointed out in his *Vanity of Dogmatising* (1661) had no need of either spectacles or the instrument that was '*Galileo's* tube' so perfect was his sight.[67] It was only fallen human beings that had need of such artificial enhancements and prostheses. So, the scientific devices that were gaining currency in the period also announced the inherent fallibility of the undisciplined or untutored senses.[68]

Robert Hooke's artificial bodies

Samuel Pepys eventually mastered his microscope, and, armed with his instrument, he thus numbered himself among those philosophers of nature who had begun to unravel a whole new dimension to the natural world.

Sometimes, though, Pepys sensed that the rage for instrumentation and calculation could be taken a little too far. After a chance encounter (August 1666) in the street with Robert Hooke, Pepys learned that it was now possible to 'tell how many strokes a fly makes with her wings . . . by the note that it answers to in musique during their flying'. Pepys reflected in his diary that such speculations might, perhaps, have become 'a little too much refined'.[69] For Hooke, however, the deployment of instruments, machines, and gadgets that rendered nature measurable, had become a part of his intellectual being.[70] His 'refined' speculations were to become the very essence of the mechanical philosophy. For if a phenomenon could be observed, then it could be measured, and only when it had been measured was it truly comprehensible.

The monument to Hooke's instrumental imagination was his investigation into the minutiae of all forms of natural life under the microscope published as *Micrographia* (1665). The work was hugely popular, and was understood as a perfect expression of the ambitions of the recently formed Royal Society.[71] But it was also merely a foretaste of what Hooke believed would be achievable in the future with the aid of (as yet) uninvented mechanisms. Perhaps, indeed, an Adamic sensory perfection might be attainable once more? Drawing on the example of sight, enhanced with the aid of the artificial device of the microscope and the telescope, Hooke began, hesitantly, to peer into a mechanically contrived future. In the lengthy preface to *Micrographia*, he envisaged a human body whose sensory perception of the world surrounding it had been immeasurably enhanced by a galaxy of uninvented mechanisms and devices: '. . . as *Glasses* have highly promoted our seeing,' he wrote, 'so 'tis not improbable, but that there may be found many *Mechanical Inventions* to improve our other Senses, of *hearing, smelling, tasting, touching*'.[72] The sense of smell, for example, improved or even transformed by (unspecified) 'mechanicall wayes found out, of sensibly perceiving the *effluvia* of bodies' would form part of a larger promotion of 'the use of Mechanical helps for the senses, both in the Surveying the already visible world, and for the discovery of many others hitherto unknown'.[73] The instrument had thus begun to appear as analogous to those voyages of discovery and conquest undertaken by European navigators in the course of the previous two centuries. It had become a device for searching out new and distant terrains that were places of enhanced perception as much as they could be thought of as geographic space. So, the microscope was of a piece with other kinds of instrument and tool which had long been in circulation in early-modern Europe and which were applied to the task of measurement: the theodolite, the cross staff, and the plane table, devices with which the observer's position on the earth's surface was calculated, land was measured, and its ownership apportioned.[74]

Machines might also be a medium of communication. Just as Samuel Pepys marvelled at the Otacousticon's ability to magnify sound, so Hooke, remarking on the property of air to convey sound, described how it was now possible 'by the help of a *distended* wire', to transmit sound over considerable distances 'in an *instant*, or with as seemingly quick a motion as that of light . . . and this not only in a straight line, or direct, but in one bended in many angles'.[75] The 'Sound-Houses' of Francis Bacon's *New Atlantis*, in which artificial devices amplified, dissected, and broadcast sound beyond the normal range of human perception, seemed on the brink of being realized.[76]

But what if some mechanical contrivance could penetrate even more deeply into the human faculties than mere sensory enhancement was capable of? Drawing on the example of printing, by which ideas and experiences were stored, circulated, and made available for subsequent generations, Hooke lamented that this printed record of human experience, designed both to distil and expand human memory, although it had immeasurably benefited humankind, was still imperfect since it was selective and 'for the most part . . . set down very lamely and imperfectly'.[77] What, he wondered, might be the benefit to the '*rational* or deductive *Faculty*' of instantaneous retrieval of the multiplicity of printed texts? So, he imagined:

> . . . readily *adapted*, and rang'd for use, that in a moment, as 'twere, thousands of Instances, serving for the *illustration*, *determination*, or *invention*, of almost any inquiry, may be represented even to the sight? How neer the nature of *Axioms* must all those *Propositions* be which are examin'd before so many *witnesses*? And how difficult will it be for any, though never so subtil an error in Philsophy, to 'scape from being discover'd, after it has indur'd the touch, and so many other *tryals*? What kind of mechanical way, and physical invention also is there requir'd, that might not this way be found out?[78]

Hooke was adept at asking the right questions. Finding answers to these riddles would prove rather more difficult. Nevertheless, fired by his enthusiasm for instruments and devices, Hooke had begun to imagine a world in which instantaneous data retrieval and manipulation (those phrases 'in a moment' and 'before so many *witnesses*' are telling) might become possible.

The world of parallel computing, the Internet, Wikipedia, or Google™ lay far in the future. But Hooke had begun to conceive of a world newly organized, manipulated, indexed, stored, and made available through some as yet unspecified mechanical device. The computer had, in imaginative terms at least, begun to glitter, dimly, on the horizon. And in wondering 'how neer the nature of *Axioms* must all those *Propositions* be which are examin'd before so many *witnesses*', Hooke had also begun to perceive of a universal knowledge device that represented a democracy of the intellect, rather than the preserve of a technocratic elite.

For Hooke, the microscope, however, was the instrument of all instruments. The microscope suggested immensity within a narrowly circumscribed orbit. Was not the miraculous power of the divine engineer, as Du Bartas had observed at the end of the sixteenth century, far more wonderful in the cases of tiny creatures rather than in instances of tremendous size? In his *Religio Medici* (1642), Sir Thomas Browne had dismissed those 'ruder heads' who wondered at the 'prodigious pieces of nature' such as whales or elephants. Such creatures were, it was true, the 'Colussus and Majestick pieces of her [nature's] hand'. But far more wonderful was the ingenuity involved in the manufacture of insects. For in the 'narrow Engines' of 'Bees, Aunts [ants], and Spiders', Browne wrote:

> . . . there is more curious Mathematicks, and the civilitie of these little Citizens, more neatly sets forth the wisdome of their Maker; Who admires not *Regio-Montanus* his Fly beyond his Eagle . . .?[79]

'Go to the ant' (Proverbs 6.6) might have been the proverbial admonition of the sluggard, but in Browne's view, what the sluggard might learn was not just industry, but precision engineering as well as civil behaviour.

Hooke was less concerned with moral behaviour than with the structure of natural forms revealed in all their minute particularity beneath the microscope's lenses: crystalline mineral structures, the residue of flint sparks, snowflakes, the 'stinging points and juice of nettles', plant seeds, fish scales, bee stings, the wings of flies, 'the teeth of a snail', and so on. Each of these instances illustrated a world in which every contrivance or feature was part of a larger, mechanical, whole. Such objects no longer existed to be embellished by the jeweller's or the poet's art, as Robert Herrick had once embellished in poetry a golden fly entombed within an ivory casket. Rather, inspecting nature beneath the microscope, what Hooke saw was the various minute cogs of a gigantic machine. Nature was, indeed, an instrument that seemed endlessly to replicate itself, confounding Aristotle's distinction between those things that are born of themselves, and those things counterfeited by human intelligence. So Hooke peered at nature beneath his microscope, in much the same way that a modern mechanic might contemplate different makes or types of a car engine. Each engine, he discovered, was different in its appearance, and might be 'manufactured' in widely scattered geographical locations, yet their composite functions were always the same, and hence they could be considered as *components*, structures tirelessly repeated in different examples, rather than a bewildering array of mere variety. And this mechanical analogy was, in fact, precisely that to which Hooke turned in the pages of *Micrographia* in order to illustrate the variety of natural forms that he observed beneath his microscope.

Three hundred years before that twentieth-century fascination with the fusion of machine and the animal body which Donna Haraway has traced in the ambiguous figure of the cyborg, Hooke, the seventeenth-century fabricator of instruments, had already begun to see in nature a form of hybridization between mechanisms and organic life.[80] So, to take just one example of this fusion, Hooke's description (Observation 44) of the 'tufted or Brush-horn'd Gnat' is representative of his procedure. The text describing the insect is accompanied by an illustration of the gnat, shown in what might be described as an architectural elevation.[81] Each feature of the insect is carefully labelled, using the device of the keying mechanism that had been so successfully deployed in anatomical works as well as in the printed works of the machine book authors of the sixteenth century and which was now becoming *de rigueur* for all scientific illustration. Describing the insect in its natural habitat, Hooke's opening remarks are composed in approved Royal Society style. Carefully recording the circumstances under which the observation was made, Hooke's comments amount to a small masterpiece of pastoral writing, evoking the commonality of the gnat and the balmy warmth of an English summer's day. One specimen is singled out from its peers to become the object of Hooke's rapt attention, and given in some measure a sense of individuality: 'This little creature was one of those multitudes that fill our *English* air all the time that warm weather lasts, and is exactly of the shape of that I observ'd to be generated and hatch'd out of those little insects that wriggle up and down in rain-water', he begins.[82]

Rescued from obscurity, the gnat is to be given a kind of immortality under an instrument, rather than in a delicate, witty, web of metaphysical verses. Such creatures now no longer prompted any larger contemplation of ephemerality, much less of human mortality, in the way that the poets of the earlier seventeenth century had transformed insect lives in their verses. Instead, they posed a purely taxonomic problem which was a product of the mechanical approach to the works of nature. Was this particular gnat truly representative of its kind? How could Hooke know that he had alighted on what scientists would later describe as the 'type specimen'? The problem was important, since Hooke wanted to show how, in proper Baconian style, his description of this particular insect held good for all others of its kind. Thus, in investigating this instance of 'particularity', he was keen to establish procedures for understanding 'generality', to use Baconian terminology. For the insect which he had memorialized, although it appeared to share its morphology with others, was singular in terms of its size, there being other representatives of the species which he had observed 'playing to and fro in little clouds in the sun, each of which were not a tenth part of the bigness of one of these I have here delineated, though very much of the same shape'.[83] This anxiety led the scientist into a classic zoological blunder, concluding that not only may the 'same kind of creature . . . be produc'd from several kinds of ways, but the very same creature may produce several kinds'.[84] How could this be so? The answer to the riddle lay in the mechanical principles that informed (so Hooke believed) the insect's creation:

> For, as divers Watches may be made out of several materials, which may yet have all the same appearance, and move after the same manner, that is, shew the hour equally true, the one as the other, and out of the same kind of matter, like Watches, may be wrought differing ways; and, as one and the same Watch may, by being diversly agitated, or mov'd by this or that agent, or after this or that manner, produce a quite contrary effect: so may it be with these most curious Engines of Insect's bodies; the all-wise God of Nature, may have so ordered and disposed the little *Automatons*, that when nourished, acted, or enlivened by this cause, they produce one kind of effect, or animate shape, when by another they act quite another way, and another animal is produc'd. So may he so order several materials, as to make them, by several kinds of methods, produce similar *Automatons*.[85]

For all that it was erroneous, the watch/insect simile had enormous theological implications. God, in Hooke's succession of mechanical metaphors, was no longer a generational deity, much less a blind watchmaker. Rather, He was a highly skilled engineer, able to produce new and startling forms from pre-existing assemblies and sub-assemblies. If bodies, whether insect, animal, or human, were composed out of similar components, then why could not the 'all-wise God of Nature' assemble his complex machines according to the same principles deployed by his human counterpart, combining the same component parts to fabricate different kinds of creature?

Insects were peculiarly important to the project of the mechanic philosophers, in part because, with the aid of the microscope, they could now be observed in such detail. They came to be understood as tiny, meticulous engines. They were 'the natural counterparts of machines' as Jessica Wolfe has observed:

> Organic prototypes for the meticulous techniques of Renaissance clock-makers, insects nestle alongside automata, optical devices, and portable scientific instruments in the collections of natural philosophers ... Their breath and blood invisible to the naked eye, insects resemble automatic machinery in that both occupy the liminal space between the natural and the artificial, the living and the merely lifelike.[86]

Because they seemed to be so different from vertebrate life, insects were innately mysterious. They could not have souls, of course. But how did they breathe? How did they reproduce? What thoughts, feelings, even emotions might they possess? What purpose animated their motions? And each of these questions might, imaginatively and metaphorically, be addressed to a complex piece of machinery, which, fabricated as it was by human skill, also seemed to move through its own vital force. More than this, if insects were to be considered as tiny examples of automacity, then might it not be possible, working on the same principles, to assemble entirely new creatures?

Not every natural philosopher, however, shared this optimistic vision of the future. In Margaret Cavendish's critique of Hooke's work which was her *Observations on Experimental Philosophy* (1666), for example, we find a quite different vision of the instrumental imagination of the age. Cavendish reminds us of the paradoxical nature of instruments to unsettle rather than enlighten the observer. Cavendish's *Observations* were published with a fictional addendum entitled *The Description of a New World Called the Blazing World*, in which she, too, imagined a Baconian scientific utopian community based on a commitment to reason. Reason, however, was not to be discovered beneath the lenses of microscopes and telescopes since these are 'false informers and instead of discovering the truth, delude your senses'.[87] To the objection that it may be the organic instruments of perception which are at fault, Cavendish's fictional persona, 'the Empress', responds that 'nature has made your sense and reason more regular than art has your glasses, for they are mere deluders and will never lead you to the knowledge of truth'.[88] As though looking back to the great 'art' versus 'nature' antithesis of the sixteenth century, Cavendish preferred to rely on the evidence of nature, rather than the devices of art. The argument, for Cavendish, was Platonic. The instrument makers and users in *The Blazing World* are like the prisoners in Plato's cave, taking 'more delight in artificial delusions than in natural truths'.[89] Denying that such instruments have the power to rectify the senses, Cavendish's argument has come to fascinate the philosophers of postmodernity and visual reality. For mediated by the lenses and mirrors of an instrument, who was to know if what was glimpsed beneath its polished surfaces was a product of nature or of the instrument itself?[90]

The second Adam

Shown a flea and a louse beneath a microscope, Cavendish's 'Empress' finds the images monstrous; she recoils in horror unable to believe her eyes. Nevertheless, prompted by their growing sense of natural mechanism revealed with the aid of their instruments, the mechanic philosophers set about re-creating all of nature as a machine. Even the fantasies of creating artificial bees, wasps, and scorpions, which we have already encountered in Ben Jonson's early seventeenth-century play *The Alchemist*, seemed, at least for a moment, to be on the brink of being realized. Such creatures would be far more lifelike and alluring than the copper lobsters that had once scuttled across the floor to charm a German emperor.

Hooke's otherwise fantastic claim that, in the future, it might be possible to create 'Mechanical helps for the senses', as though what was envisaged was a more perfect, because mechanically contrived, second Adam, seems to anticipate the ways in which nineteenth-century engineers would use natural phenomena as models.[91] In February 1669/70, for example, the Royal Society witnessed a 'contrivance' engineered by Hooke 'to try, whether a mechanical muscle could be made by art, performing without labour the same office which a natural muscle doth in animals'. The experiment was not a success. Powered by a cumbersome arrangement of heated and then cooled vessels of air, and quite possibly drawing upon Boyle's Law of 1662 governing the volume of gases at different pressures, the artificial muscle was unable to produce 'motion immediately, and with that speed, as it is done in animals'.[92] Art could not yet rival the designs of nature, and Hooke was urged, instead, to consider a system of springs.

A system of springs suggested a quite different approach to the creation of the second Adam: clockwork. This was the route pursued, in imaginative terms, by the printer, map maker, mathematician, and hydrographer, Joseph Moxon who, in 1696, envisaged the creation of a robotic household servant. This mechanical creature would be fashioned according to the well-known principles of clockwork; indeed, Moxon described his mechanical servant as being, in essence, a superior form of 'clock':

> It may be made, that the clock every hour or appointed time, shall atchieve divers offices; so cloks may be made which at a prefixt time of night shall strike fire and kindle a light; and in the same manner they may be so fitted, that they may send forth water or draw it from a well, or so as to snuff candles dexterously, at appointed times.[93]

Moxon imagined the regularity of clockwork being superimposed upon the minor chores of everyday life: making the fire, fetching the water, snuffing candles. Where, in others, this fantasy of automatic labour would have been just that, a daydream of attentive, machine-driven luxury, Moxon was of a more practical cast of mind. As a printer, he specialized in producing abridgements for popular consumption of scientific and practical handbooks and manuals, together with mathematical manuals and tables, navigational textbooks, and treatises on drawing. These were the conceptual tools and instruments that had already become so vital to the construction of seventeenth-century science.[94]

But the prospect of a mechanically redesigned second Adam might also suggest that the Almighty had not, perhaps, been working at the utmost limit of His powers on the sixth day of creation. Was there not room for improvement? Just as human beings had improved upon nature in the production of hybridized plants, while animals had been selectively bred for centuries, might not a human being be artificially enhanced in some way? Many years later, Alexander Pope in his *An Essay on Man* (1733) would speculate on why things were as they were: 'Why has not Man a microscopic eye?' he asked, as though recalling Hooke's breathless speculations as to whether, in the future, some radical reorganization of the human form along mechanical lines might be possible. The answer was metrically and theologically obvious: 'For this plain reason, Man is not a Fly.'[95] What would be the point, Pope asked, in enhancing and remoulding the human form along the mechanical principles suggested by a Robert Hooke? Would such a radical reorganization of matter produce a better understanding of nature? Or would it, rather, present merely new and hitherto unforeseen difficulties?

Say what the use, were finer optics giv'n,
T'inspect a mite, not comprehend the heav'n?
Or touch, if tremblingly alive all o'er,
To smart and agonise at ev'ry pore?
Or quick effluvia darting thro' the brain,
Die of a rose in aromatic pain?[96]

To be killed by the scent of a rose, so finely tuned might the second Adam's senses become, is to underline the absurdity of the claim that man, of all created creatures, could be 'improved' in the way that landscapes could be enhanced by the skills of garden designers. Others, however, did not share Pope's sense of the absurdity of such a project. To them, the creation of a second Adam, an artificially enhanced creature, was not merely a question of modifying what already existed in nature. Rather, it meant beginning again, and framing something that had never existed before; to create, in short, a machine whose artificial motions were indistinguishable from those of a human being.

The manufacture of a second Adam, a creature which possessed the outward form of humanity but which operated according to purely mechanical principles, was an ancient fantasy. In some measure, the fantasy was related to the history of the automaton which we have already explored. But Renaissance automata were rarely, if ever, thought of as performing productive work. Rather, they were luxurious devices designed to delight and divert. Like so many other Renaissance mechanisms, they were objects of consumption, rather than a means of production. Above all, they were not 'useful' in the way that Moxon's mundane mechanism for lighting the fire or snuffing a candle could be thought of as useful. The history of the robot is popularly thought to have begun with the publication of Karel Čapek's 'fantastic melodrama' R.U.R. (1921), in which the word itself (a term derived from the Czech word *robota* meaning 'forced labour') was coined.[97] Yet, the robot, considered as a device or instrument capable of shouldering some of the burdens of humanity, and thus freeing (real) humans from the drudgery of daily existence, was a dream as old as Homer's golden maidservants assisting the lame god Hephaistos to go about his metallic business.

In an intriguing memorandum written by the Italian clockmaker and astronomer Lorenzo della Volpaia (1446–1512), robotic fantasy emerges in its purest, almost childlike, state. So Volpaia wrote: 'to remind myself when I go to stay in Rome to make a wooden man who will stand behind a door, and when someone opens the door that wooden man comes to meet him with a stick to hit him on the head'.[98] Volpaia, a skilled clockmaker, in the 1480s had designed and constructed an astronomical clock, described by the Florentine humanist Angelo Poliziano as a 'self-propelled device' ('*machinula automato*'), which was of such complexity that it was as if he had 'learned the heavens in heaven itself'.[99] Yet Volpaia's primitively violent robotic wooden doorman was also, of course, pure fantasy.

The first robot to have been designed, if not constructed, is often claimed to be that attributed to Leonardo da Vinci. Leonardo's 'lost robot' was, more properly, an automaton of some kind, which exists today only as an ambiguous set of drawings to be found in his scattered manuscript notebooks. Inspired by Greek and Arabic designs for moving mechanical figures, some time around 1495 Leonardo seems to have begun work on an armoured robot knight. The creature's warlike disposition was firmly rooted in its design. On the outside dressed in German-Italian armour of the period, its interior would be purely mechanical: 'Designed to sit up, wave its arms, and move its head via a flexible neck while opening and closing its anatomically correct jaw. It may have made sounds to the accompaniment of automated drums.'[100] It is difficult, however, to be sure whether such a mechanical creation was ever more than an interesting idea, rather than a fully formed workable (if not working) device for Leonardo. The 1490s was the period during which Leonardo was beginning to think of human and animal bodies in mechanical terms. His notebooks from this period show him exploring physiology as engineering.[101] His sketches for the design of the 'robot' may have been not so much investigations into the reality of a mechanical device, as they were translations of anatomical structures into their mechanical equivalents. They existed, in fact, in much the same realm as the mechanical iron hands, arms, and legs, designed in the late sixteenth century by the French surgeon Ambroise Paré as a prosthetic replacement for the severed limbs of soldiers, or in the bizarrely anthropomorphized mechanical figures of Giovanni Battista Bracelli (fl. 1616–50) who, in his *Bizzarie di Varie Figure* (1624) experimented with the creation of robotic simulacra of the human figure.

Contemporary scientists involved in robotic research have suggested that the dream of robotic 'life' is as distant now as it ever was at the time that Leonardo was sketching mechanical movement, or Volpaia was speculating about the creation of his thuggish gatekeeper: 'We are at least a couple of miracles short of the full goal of robotics: to recreate a human being in all its glory – in other words to make an android that is indistinguishable from a human.'[102] Possessed by more optimistic senses of their mechanical craft, seventeenth-century philosophers, by contrast, believed themselves to have been on the brink of perfecting an entirely artificial creature. And yet, none of the devices envisaged in the seventeenth century appeared to possess the capacity to interact with the world around them. Rather, like automata, they could only move or function according to a preprogrammed set of motions, which were determined in advance by the will of their maker, who had invested them with mechanical movement in the first place. A device manufactured in seventeenth-century Milan helps us understand this crucial point. The 'chained slave' possibly designed and built by the scientific instrument maker and collector Manfredo Settala, took the form of a grotesque painted wooden devil, whose mechanism was activated by the weight of the unsuspecting visitor to Settala's collections. The creature was capable of emitting terrifying shrieks while its eyes, tongue, and head jerked into mechanical life.[103]

Setalla's 'slave', summoned into mechanical activity by the weight of a visitor's footfall, is a very early example of an automatic device which possesses 'sense organs . . . conditioned by its relation to the external world, and by the things happening in the external world'.[104] Such devices, automatic doors being a familiar example of this technology in the modern world, work on the principle that a 'message' (in the case of an automatic door, the interception of a beam of light, in the case of Setalla's slave, a visitor's footfall) actuates the device. Contraptions of this kind are qualitatively different from mere automata, since they are able to interact, in however primitive a fashion, with the world around them. They are thus different from automata which (Norbert Wiener writes):

> . . . move in accordance with a pattern, but it is a pattern which is set in advance, and in which the past activity of the figures has practically nothing to do with the pattern of their future activity. The probability that they will diverge from this activity is nil . . . They are blind, deaf, and dumb, and cannot vary their activity in the least from the conventionalised pattern.[105]

Such devices – 'blind, deaf, and dumb' – are not only devoid of thought, but also devoid of even the illusion of thought.

Clockwork reason

Robert Hooke's tiny but perfect living insect machines were understood in terms of clockwork. But insects, like machines, seemed devoid of reason which was an attribute possessed, so it was believed, only by divinely fabricated human beings. Nevertheless, insects moved, and thus they appeared to be driven by a sense of purpose residing in the will of their maker and first mover, God. Clocks, too, moved to a purpose, and one that was well understood. But clocks also expressed a larger sense of mechanical order. 'The clock, not the steam engine, is the key machine of the modern industrial age' Lewis Mumford has written: 'It marks a perfection towards which other machines aspire.'[106] The regularity and predictability of the clockwork-driven mechanism, by the early seventeenth century, had evolved to produce devices of much greater accuracy than had been possible in previous centuries. This gain in accuracy is reflected in the first appearance, in the early 1600s, of watches whose 'faces' (though this anthropomorphic term did not enter into common usage until well into the eighteenth century), marked with half-hour and quarter-hour divisions on the dial, 'reflected not only the improvement of the instrument but the tighter requirements of social time'.[107] In the seventeenth century, astronomical clocks were among the most advanced mechanisms that had ever been constructed, able to show not only the passage of time, but also a panoply of information, all of which was related to the idea of predictability. Such a clock, designed at Augsburg in 1600, for example, as well as showing the time of day, also showed the age and phases of the moon, the days of the week, the movement of planets, sectors for length of day and night, saints' days, dominical letters, the golden number, the 'epact' (the age of the moon on 1 January, used to calculate the date of Easter), and the dates for Easter for the years 1600–87. This array of information was presented in a case which measured just 52 cm in height.[108]

The watch or clock was also a reminder of human mortality, a mechanized *memento mori*. Carried about the person, it warned of the transitory nature of existence, as a short Latin epigram by Thomas Campion (*De horologio portabili*, published in 1619) indicates:

> Times-teller wrought into a little round,
> Which count'st the days and nights with watchful sound;
> How (when once fixt) with busie Wheels dost thou
> The twice twelve useful hours drive on and show.
> And where I go, go'st with me without strife,
> The Monitor and ease of fleeting life.[109]

Such devices were to become not just a means of marking the passage of time, or understanding the movement of heavenly bodies, or even reminders of human mortality. They could help to explain human behaviour. Shakespeare in *Richard II* (1597) had played with just this idea, though to tragic effect, as the imprisoned and soon to be deposed king reflects on the possibility that he has become no more than a clockwork mechanism, working at the behest of the clockmaker or designer who is the rebellious usurper Bolingbroke:

> For now hath time made me his numb'ring clock.
> My thoughts are minutes, and with sighs they jar
> Their watches on unto mine eyes, the outward watch
> Whereto my finger, like a dial's point,
> Is pointing still in cleansing them from tears.
> Now, sir, the sounds that tell what hour it is
> Are clamorous groans that strike upon my heart,
> Which is the bell. So sighs, and tears, and groans
> Show minutes, hours, and times. But my time
> Runs posting on in Bolingbroke's proud joy,
> While I stand fooling here, his jack of the clock.
>
> (V. v. 41–59)

Time, which at the moment that Shakespeare was writing these lines was becoming subjected to an ever-more strict mechanical regime, has ensnared the king in its grasp, transforming him from a free-floating, autonomous entity, into an instrument, a 'numbering clock' created (and operated) by another.[110] In Shakespeare's extended simile, the king's human attributes have been appropriated by mechanism which is, in turn, reducing him to the status of 'jack of the clock' or *jacquemart*, the mechanical figure which struck the bell of the clock and marked the passage of time in public spaces, such as on the great Strasbourg cathedral clock. He has become, in other words, a puppet or 'motion': a body, as Thomas Nashe had observed of other kinds of mechanical figures, robbed of soul.

But was not the human being, in any case, a mechanical wonder? Philosophically, the idea of analysing human and animal bodies in terms of mechanisms of different kinds is associated with Cartesian modes of thinking.[111] But Cartesianism, among whose central tenets was the belief that animal motions represented an infinitely superior form of mechanical motion, was in this respect a system of metaphors and similes which were in play long before the publication of Descartes' *Discourse on the Method* in 1637. In Thomas Dekker's *The Seuen Deadly Sinnes of London* (1606), for example, we read of how humans are restless mechanisms, anatomical machines in perpetual motion. The human being:

> . . . carries certaine *Watches* with *Larums* about him, that are euer strik-ing: for all the *Enginous Wheeles* of the *Soule* are continually going: though the body lye neuer so fast bownde in Slumbers, the imagination runnes too and fro, the phantasie flyes round about, the vitall Spirits walke vp and downe, yea the very pulses shew actiuitie, and their hammers are still beat-ing, so that euen in his very dreames it is whispered in his eare that hee must bee dooing something.[112]

Even when fast asleep, the mechanism (the *Enginous Wheeles* of the *Soule*) is still active, the machine is still ticking over. And when the mechanical creature is awake, every feature of its being reminds it of its essentially mechanical nature:

> His armes haue artificiall cordes and stringes, which shorten or flye [o]ut to their length at pleasure: They winde about the bodye like a siluer Girdle, and being held out before, are weapons to defend it: at the end of the armes, are two beautiful *Mathematicall* Instruments, with fiue seuerall motions in each of them, and thirtie other mouing *Engines*, by which they stirre both. His head likewise standes vppon three *Skrewes* . . .[113]

. . . and so on. Dekker's text, published just a few years after Shakespeare's *Hamlet* had first appeared in print, appealed to exactly the same metaphor which Hamlet had employed when he had commended himself to Ophelia as 'evermore . . . whilst this machine is to him, Hamlet' (II. ii. 120–5). Dis-sociating thoughts and identity from corporeal existence, it was as if both Shakespeare and Dekker had anticipated the existential dilemma of the Car-tesian ghost in the machine.

Some 30 years later, in the poem 'Loves Clock', written in the 1630s by the 'cavalier' poet Sir John Suckling, the tragedy of a clockwork king, which Shakespeare had described in *Richard II*, has given way to comedy, as the poet explores exactly the same trope of the human being as a mechanical device. In the poem, Suckling imaginatively deconstructs his own passion as if it were a watch, spreading the parts out in front of him, and ascribing to each feature of the mechanism some aspect of the psychology of that otherwise most irrational of states of mind, love. 'Lovers have in their hearts a clock' the poem begins:

Hope is the mainspring on which moves desire,
And these do the less wheels, fear, joy, inspire;
The balance is thought, evermore
Clicking
And striking,
And ne'er giving o'er;

Occasion's the hand which still's moving round,
Till it by the critical hour may be found;
And when that falls out, it will strike
Kisses
Strange blisses,
And what you best like.[114]

Suckling's poetry abounds in imagery derived from the skills of the clock-maker.[115] We should not, however, take this poem too seriously as a medita-tion on mechanism. Suckling humorously attributes clockwork precision to something as imprecise as emotion, as though underlining the pretensions of the mechanical philosophers and their batteries of instruments as well as their mechanical metaphors and analogies. Indeed, the ironic point of the poem is to demonstrate the absurdity of the notion of a clockwork lover, and how entirely irrational the 'motions' of love may be.[116]

By the middle of the seventeenth century, in England, France, and Ger-many, the clock metaphor had penetrated deeply into imaginative writing.[117] But neither the clock, nor (to recall Robert Hooke's gnat) the insect, pos-sesses reason. The clock metaphor, like the insect metaphor, may work to explain motion, mortality, society, or even a degree of autonomy. But reason, that 'universal instrument', which, according to Descartes, seemed unique to the human being, could never be replicated by artifice. Paradoxically, however, it was poets rather than natural philosophers who, in the late six-teenth and earlier seventeenth centuries, began to think even of reason in mechanical terms. In Dekker's 'Enginous Wheeles of the Soule', with its punning allusion to engines and the root Latin term of ingenia or ingeniousness, the animating force within the human being is imagined as a kind of constantly turning mechanism. It was not, however, human reason which turned like clockwork, but divine reason. In his hymn to the divine concord of the universe Orchestra, or a Poem of Dauncing (1596), Sir John Davies expressed the conundrum of reason, conceived in mechanical terms:

Who sees a clock mooving in every part,
A sayling Pinesse, or a wheeling Cart,
    But thinks that reason ere it came to passe
    The first impulsive cause and mover was.[118]

Three quite different (though familiar by sixteenth-century standards) technological forms lie behind Davies's analogy: the clock, the sailing vessel, and the wheel and axle.[119] Contemplating these devices, Davies is led into a further mechanical analogy, but one which was far in advance of the technology then available: that reason might be understood, in mechanical terms, as 'an impulsive cause and mover'. The difference, though, between Descartes' later speculations on mechanical reason and this late sixteenth-century meditation on reason is that, for Davies, reason is an anterior force, existing beyond the boundaries of the device itself. For others, however, reason was indeed held to be a mechanical phenomenon, but one that could be thought of as the driving force of the entire human 'mechanism' which was innate to the composition of the human being: 'Man is an Engine, mov'd with Reason's weight, / But *Death*, that stops his breath, unwinds him streight'.[120] So wrote the poet and epigrammatist, Thomas Bancroft in the 1630s in his epigram 'Of man', applying mechanical, or, to be more precise, clockwork, metaphors to the age-old theme of human mortality.

The calculating machine

We have seen how, in the later seventeenth century, mechanical devices had become all the rage, even if their purpose was not always understood. Such devices posed a serious philosophical problem: might it, in fact, be possible to construct a machine which not only moves independently, or that even seems to respond to the world around it, but which, in some measure 'thinks'? If so, what did 'thinking' amount to? In his *Discourse on the Method*, Descartes had argued that, to anyone familiar with the creation of the 'many kinds of automatons, or moving machines the skill of man can devise' it was possible to consider the body as a machine but one which 'having been made by the hands of God, is incomparably better ordered than any machine that can be devised by man, and contains in itself movements more wonderful than those in any such machine'.[121] Descartes concluded, however, that it would be impossible to confuse a human being with a machine, since the artificial creature would lack the facility of language. For Descartes, though a talking machine might be possible, it would only function much like a magpie that has been taught to say 'Good morning' (an analogy he developed in a letter to the Marquis of Newcastle).[122] Language seemed to be the gatekeeper, barring the way to the creation of a fully mechanized simulacrum of the human being.

Descartes had denied that reason could ever be produced mechanically, believing that the production of language, the token of the 'universal instrument' of reason, was far too complicated an operation to be replicated mechanically. His contemporaries and immediate successors, however, were much less certain that mechanism might not come to inhabit even this sphere of human existence. We have already seen how talking statues and speaking heads hovered on that dubious borderline which separated magic from mechanics. But at a more practical level, seventeenth-century natural philosophers were spellbound by the possibility of creating artificial languages, of the kind to be found in John Wilkins' *Essay Towards a Real Character, and a Philosophical Language* (1668), in which a 'Real Universal Character' (i.e. an artificial language) was devised 'that should not signifie words, but things and notions'.[123] If words could be anchored to 'things', then might not 'things' be devised capable of producing words? Fired by such enthusiasm, the Jesuit polymath, Athanasius Kircher, was said to have designed (in the 1660s) what he termed an *Arca glototactica* (a 'linguistic chest'), which, Paula Findeln writes, was a 'communicating device'. Operated by a system of levers, the machine was imagined as generating language.[124] How, exactly, it worked was never, of course, explained in any detail.

But what if reason itself could be constructed, or at least imitated, in a mechanical fashion using a very different means of thinking about the nature of thinking? Might not mathematical calculation, for example, offer an alternative method of devising artificial thought? Mathematics, after all, was a form of reasoning which had long drawn upon different kinds of artificial devices, of which the abacus, in use in the Far East from at least the fourth century BCE, is the most familiar.[125] In Europe, in the late sixteenth century, the possibility of creating sophisticated mechanical calculating devices had become a very real possibility. Such devices may be thought of as 'extensions' to the human sensory-motor capability. John Napier, for example, described his invention of logarithms as artificial aids devised to assist the 'weaknesse of memory', as if they could be understood as prosthetic additions to the rational faculty.[126] But though 'Napier's Bones' represented a multiplication and division device, while the linear slide rule had made its appearance in 1621, nobody would have claimed that these instruments had the capacity to reason.[127] Similarly, the 'arithmetical jewell' devised by William Pratt sometime before 1616 was a prototype, at least in theory, of the miniaturized calculator, or, as Adam Max Cohen describes it, it was a foretaste of the 'hand-held wireless personal computing device'.[128] But automaticity, let alone autonomy, was not one of its properties.

However, shortly after Descartes' *Discourse on the Method* appeared, Blaise Pascal, around 1644, created a primitive adding machine, a system of wheels and falling weights capable of performing addition and subtraction. The mechanism was devised to assist his father, a tax-gatherer.[129] Although the first theoretical adding machine had been proposed as early as 1624, by the Tübingen professor, Wilhem Schickard, and was thus pre-Cartesian, Pascal's machine was the first to demonstrate that these machines were practical possibilities, and he went on to construct about fifty more of these devices. Pascal's machine, however, could only perform addition and subtraction. It was no more (indeed, much less) a rational machine than the talking magpie which Descartes had described to the Marquis of Newcastle.

In England, Thomas Hobbes had also become preoccupied by this problem, which he too believed might be solved with the aid of mathematics. Thinking, which Hobbes termed 'ratiocination' was, after all, no more than a form of 'computation', as he wrote in his *De Corpore* (1655):

> . . . to compute is either to collect the sum of many things that are added together, or to know what remains when one thing is taken out of another. *Ratiocination*, therefore, is the same with *addition* and *subtraction*; and if any man add *multiplication* and *division*, I will not be against it, seeing multiplication is nothing but addition of equals one to another, and division nothing but a subtraction of equals one from another, as often as is possible. So that all ratiocination is comprehended in these two operations of the mind, addition and subtraction.[130]

Was the rational faculty of the human being, therefore, no more than a calculating engine, of the type (only rather more sophisticated) that Pascal had constructed to assist his father in gathering taxes? Hobbes thought that this might indeed be the case. 'By the ratiocination of our mind', he wrote, 'we add and subtract in our silent thoughts, without the use of words', concluding that 'We must not therefore think that computation, that is, ratiocination, has place only in numbers.'[131] Even visual perception, for Hobbes, could be imagined as a form of arithmetical calculation, as he proceeded to argue: an observer, on first seeing an object appearing in their field of vision, would conclude that they saw a body; as the shape came closer, a new idea would be added to the former – an animated body; on hearing speech or seeing 'signs of a rational mind' they would add to their former calculation the term rational; finally, compounding (or adding) together all these perceptions, they would perform the complete calculation, to produce, triumphantly, a single result: '*body – animated – rational, or man*'.[132]

Hobbes's reduction of the human being to a calculating device was to begin an argument that George Dyson has observed 'is far from settled after three hundred and forty years; if reasoning can be reduced to arithmetic . . . then is mechanism capable of reasoning?'[133] Certainly, calculating devices of different kinds were to become an intriguing reality in Restoration London. In 1662, the diplomat, inventor, cryptographer, hydrostatic engineer, and famously indigent Sir Samuel Morland (who in 1681, would be dubbed the king's 'Master of Mechanicks') had presented to the king an arithmetical device, closely allied to Pascal's calculator. Morland's instrument, which Robert Hooke thought 'very silly' but which John Evelyn admired immensely, was described in his *The Description and Use of Two Arithmetick Instruments* published in 1673.[134] At almost the same time, in Germany, G. W. Leibniz had been struck by the many hours of labour involved in calculations that might be done by machines, while he, too, had become fascinated by the philosophical implications of automata.[135] In 1671, Leibniz, then a young diplomat and lawyer and working in collaboration with the French watchmaker Olivier, began to construct a machine capable of performing all four arithmetic operations (addition, subtraction, multiplication, and division) as opposed to the mere two operations of which Pascal's machine was capable.

Early in 1673, in the same year that Morland published his work on mechanical calculation, Leibniz travelled to London to demonstrate to the Royal Society the prototype of his machine, which he termed (in an unmistakable gesture towards Hobbes) the *calculus ratiocinator*.[136] The *machina arithmetica*, as Leibniz would later describe his device in 1685, was an instrument designed to relieve human beings from the drudgery of mechanistic, mathematical calculation: 'for it is unworthy of excellent men to lose hours like slaves in the labour of calculation, which could be safely relegated to anyone else if the machine were used', he claimed.[137] Leibniz's machine, in other words, was not a general labour saving device, but, rather, a means of liberating the virtuoso, distributing the tedium of mere calculation to less skilled operatives who, unthinkingly, work a machine that performs the repetitive labour of computation on their behalf. Intellectual work could thus be distributed on principles which would, later, be termed 'the division of labour', principles which, in France in the later eighteenth century, would be applied more generally to mathematical calculation as the Revolutionary government sought to promote the recently adopted decimal system.[138]

Wiener has suggested that Leibniz's computing machines 'were only an offshoot of his interest in a computing language, a reasoning calculus which again was in his mind, merely an extension of his idea of a complete artificial language'.[139] For all that Leibniz had constructed a machine capable, so it seemed, of calculation he never confused human and mechanical life. What distinguished the two, he believed was the absence of 'thought' or 'perception' in any mechanical device, a phenomenon that, he believed, was far more complex than Hobbesian calculation. Although Leibniz would later write (in a letter of 1714) that it might be possible to invent a 'universal symbolistic [sic] in which all truths of reason would be reduced to a kind of calculus' this was to devise an arithmetical system or method, not a sentient machine.[140] So, in his response to Locke's *Essay Concerning Human Understanding* (1690), which was his *New Essays on Human Understanding* (completed 1704, but not published until 1765), Leibniz took great care to delineate the differences between a machine or instrument and a human being. For Locke, ideas were the product of bodies, operating mechanically, as he put it '*by impulse*, the only way which we can conceive bodies [to] operate in'.[141] For Leibniz, though he agreed that 'impulse' seemed to be a driving force in the human creature ('those imperceptible little urges which keep us constantly in suspense') and that 'impulse' seemed to be mechanical in its nature, like 'so many little springs trying to unwind and so driving our machine along', this was an argument by analogy, once again, with the portable, clockwork driven, timepiece or watch, not a statement of reality.[142] Mechanism may have penetrated deeply into Leibniz's habit of thought, but machines could not (and would never) 'think':

> A sentient or thinking being is not a mechanical thing like a watch or a mill: one cannot conceive of sizes and shapes and motions combining mechanically to produce something which thinks, and senses, too . . .[143]

Even were we to conceive of a machine 'whose structure makes it think, sense and have perception' and imagine it as being like some great mill into which we could wander, Leibniz later argued, all that we would be able to see would be 'parts which push one another, and never anything which could explain a perception'.[144] Machines, even gigantic calculating instruments, were far too cumbersome to explain the delicate nuances of thought.

Mechanical theology

By the later seventeenth century, mechanism had reached an impasse. Driven by the conceptual desire to create thinking things, the philosophers of reason sensed that the technology available to them was not capable of reaching such creational heights, any more than it is in the modern world. Yet, though Descartes or (later) Leibniz appeared to be keen to dispel any notion of mechanical life based on reproducing 'thought' through some artificial means, the wider applicability of mechanism as a means of understanding the world was too seductive to be easily jettisoned: 'Thanks to the *Penetration* of an excellent Philosopher of this age', wrote the French anatomist Dominique Beddevole in 1686 (he was thinking, we may assume, of Descartes), 'it has been discovered that the living body is only a Machine. Men have applied their minds to discover its Springs.'[145] Just as ever-more accurate watches and clocks were now being developed that were able to keep time to within ten seconds a day – a precision that would have been considered impossible at the beginning of the seventeenth century – so, it was believed, the marvellous clockwork mechanism concealed either within the human body or the universe at large would, eventually, be traced with an equivalent sense of accuracy.[146]

This cast of mind had been given new impetus by the proliferation of machines which were appearing in the workshops of the clock and instrument makers. But on an altogether grander and more public scale were machines of the kind erected by engineer speculators such as James Ward who, in the early 1670s, under letters patent granted by the king, had installed a device capable of pumping (so he claimed) a 'tunne of water' in St James's Park: an undertaking which was to bring Ward into tumultuous dispute with the hydrostatically jealous Sir Samuel Morland.[147] As Roy Porter has observed, engineers and investigators such as Ward and Morland, as well as better-known figures such as Gassendi, Boyle, Hooke, Huygens, Newton, and others, had begun to see:

> . . . living creatures mechanistically, as ingenious contraptions made up of skilfully articulated components . . . functioning as levers, pulleys, pipes and wheels, in line with the laws of mechanics, kinetics, hydrostatics, and so forth. The body became a *machina carnis*, a machine of the flesh.[148]

But the effect of the introduction of these devices, and with them, the refashioning of the body as a mechanical enterprise, was as much theological as mechanical. If, as Robert Boyle claimed in 1663, 'a humane Body it selfe seems to be but an Engine, wherein almost, if not more then almost, all the Actions common to Men, with other Animals, are perform'd Mechanically' then what, or who, was the designer?[149] Thus, the argument ran, the evidence of the existence of a clockmaker was to be found in the design of the clock, just as the evidence of the existence of the master artificer, God, would be discovered through the careful study and, perhaps, even imitation of His mechanisms. In the late 1590s, Johannes Kepler, inspired by displays of clocks and automata to be found in *Künstkammern* such as that created by Emperor Rudolf II, had produced models of the cosmos powered by clockwork.[150] In France, too, at the end of the sixteenth century, the mathematician Henri de Monantheuil (Monantholius), in his *Aristotelis mechanica* (1599) sought to convince the world that God was a 'mechanikos' and that the universe was no more than 'a machine . . . doubtless the most powerful, practical, and elegant contrivance of all time'.[151]

But in England in the later seventeenth century, it was in poetry that mechanical theology was explored to its fullest extent, in particular in the enraptured, mystical poetry of Thomas Traherne. Traherne's poetry, which was almost entirely unknown to his contemporaries, was probably written in the late 1660s and the 1670s, around the time that Hooke was peering at tiny insect lives beneath his microscope and heating vessels of air to replicate the motions of muscles, or when Pascal and Leibniz were constructing artificial calculating machines. In Traherne's writings, however, we meet with mechanism and artificiality in an entirely different guise. 'Nature is still nearest to natural things', Traherne observed in his *Centuries of Meditation* (composed c. 1668–71), and yet the ability to work with artificiality also had to be reckoned as being among the freshest of 'inventions' bestowed on humankind by God.[152] In his lengthy hymn of praise which was 'Thanksgivings for the Body', Traherne, deploying his customary enraptured cataloguing style, praised God for the creation of:

> . . . all the mysteries, engines, instruments, wherewith the world is filled, which we are able to frame and use to Thy glory. For all the trades, varieties of operations, cities, temples, streets, bridges, mariner's compass, admirable picture, sculpture, writing, printing, songs and music; wherewith the world is beautified and adorned.[153]

Just as Sir Thomas Browne had commended the living engine of an insect as the greatest wonder of creation, so, for Traherne, the devices and instruments created by human reason were more properly understood as a further manifestation of God's creative genius. Human beings might be the agents by which such artificial 'objects' (a favourite word of Traherne's, along with the word 'use') came into the world, but, true to a belief in God as the ultimate fabricator of all that was to be found in the universe, Traherne saw such contrivances as a form of divine mechanics.

Of course, such 'riches of Invention' were not to be unduly esteemed, and neither should 'vain inventions newly made to please' be allowed to displace other kinds of natural objects, bestowed by God on humankind.[154] Traherne was no mechanist. In fact, he was profoundly opposed to the taxonomic impulse that would become the *raison d'être* of the early supporters of the Royal Society. His mystical Neoplatonism, moreover, was hardly in sympathy with a materialist, Hobbesian, approach to the mechanism of the natural world.[155] And yet, mechanism suggested to Traherne, as it had, paradoxically, to Robert Hooke, a richly imaginative language which could be put to the service of the praise of God. So, God could be hymned (in his poem 'Thoughts I') as the creator of 'heavenly springs . . . machines great . . . engines of felicity', while, within the 'curious fabric' of the human body, were to be discovered 'living engines' of 'glorious worth' ('The Author to the Critical Peruser').[156] Within Traherne's curious mixture of mechanically transcendent metaphors, the study of what he termed 'mechanicisms' [sic] together with 'all kinds of arts [and] trades . . . that adorned the world pertained to felicity'.[157] By the time that Traherne had published his *Christian Ethics* (1675), one of his very few securely dateable works, he seems to have understood the motion of clockwork as a detailed metaphor for the operation of the divinely constructed fabric of the world. 'As in a clock' Traherne wrote:

> . . . 'tis hinder'd-force doth bring
> The wheels to order'd motion, by a spring;
> Which order'd motion guides a steady hand
> In useful sort at figures just to stand;
> Which, were it not by counter-balance stay'd,
> The fabric quickly would aside be laid
> As wholly useless: so a might too great,
> But well proportion'd, makes the world complete.
> Power well-bounded is more great in might,
> Than if let loose 'twere wholly infinite.[158]

The essence of Traherne's clock–universe analogy is restraint, the sense that the interior mechanisms of both the world and the timepiece function through the balancing force of springs and counter-balances, set in place by the divine watchmaker.

'Motion is always attended by life', Traherne wrote in the second of his *Centuries of Meditation*, probably composed in the late 1670s; but what then of clocks and watches? Were they, too, alive in some obscure fashion? 'Can . . . these things move so without a life, or spring of motion?' he puzzled.[159] This conundrum led him into a further set of mechanical analogies:

> . . . the wheels in watches move, and so doth the hand that pointeth out the figures. This being a motion of dead things. Therefore hath God created living ones: that by lively motions and sensible desires, we might be sensible of a Deity. They breathe, they see, they feel, they grow, they flourish, they know, they love. O what a world of evidences! We are lost in abysses, we now are absorbed in wonders and swallowed up in demonstrations . . . Let us therefore survey their order, and see by that whether we can discern their Governor.[160]

Fascinatingly, led by meditation and contemplation of the divine, Traherne seems to have guessed at a set of mechanical principles that would not, in reality, become incorporated into machinery until the late eighteenth century. God as the 'governor' (i.e. ruler) of the universe is, of course, a theological commonplace. But God manufacturing the universe in answer to the construction of human-built devices is a conceit entirely of Traherne's own fashioning, as is his application of the term 'Governor', in the sense of a device for self-regulating the motion of a machine.[161]

Political machines

A governor is a ruler, whether in a theological, mechanical, or political sense. Government, of course, was the theme of the greatest sustained exploration of politics in the mid-seventeenth century, the *Leviathan* (1651) of Thomas Hobbes, a work that is indebted at every turn to ideas of mechanical motion, artificial devices, and machinery more generally. For Hobbes, the clockwork metaphor revealed a fundamental truth about both human beings and the world which they inhabited. Indeed, to term Hobbes's idea of mechanism a 'metaphor' is to underestimate the enormous importance which Hobbes attached to machinery in understanding the structure of the world. 'For seeing life is but a motion of Limbs, the beginning whereof is in some principall part within; why may we not say that all *Automata* (Engines that move themselves by springs and wheeles as doth a watch) have an artificial life?', Hobbes demanded in the famous opening sentences to *Leviathan*.[162] For Hobbes, life, whether it was the life of individuals or societies, was essentially 'motion', a mechanical phenomenon, which could be investigated with the clockmaker's precision and skill. And so with God's greatest work, the human being, as Joseph Glanvill wrote in his propagandizing work on behalf of the Royal Society:

> To suppose a *watch*, or any other the most curious *Automaton* by the blind hits of *chance*, to perform diversity of orderly *motions*, to indicate the *hour*, day of the *moneth*, *Tides*, age of the *moon*, and the like with an unparalleled exactness, and all without the regulation of Art, this were the more pardonable absurdity. And that this admirable *Engine* of our Bodies, whose functions are carried on by such a multitude of *parts*, and *motions*, which neither interfere, nor impede one another in their operations; and by an *harmonious sympathy* promote the perfection and good of the whole: that this should be an undesigned effect, is an assertion, that is more than *Melacholies Hyperbole*.[163]

In this passage from the *Vanity of Dogmatising* (1661), Glanvill compared the human body to a 'table' or 'tabernacle' clock, of the type that had begun to appear in Europe in the mid-sixteenth century. For Glanvill, the 'regulation of art' was a more convincing proof of the existence of God than 'the blind hits of chance'. Complex machines such as clocks, the product of careful design, were motive proof of the existence of their maker. In observing, too, that the parts of the marvellous clockwork of the human body 'neither interfere, nor impede one another in their operations', Glanvill was suggesting the superiority of the human mechanism to the artificial mechanism of the clock, since (discounting the effects of age, injury, and illness) the human body appeared to be a frictionless device. In clock design, the conquest of friction could be understood as the holy grail of the clockmaker's art, since every additional moving part increases the friction and with it the irregularity of the mechanism.[164] But friction, the rubbing together of parts to the detriment of the overall mechanism, had a social dimension for Glanvill. Born in 1636, and writing, as he was, after the cataclysm of civil war, Glanvill might well have come to value a system in which 'functions are carried on by such a multitude of *parts*, and *motions*, which neither interfere, nor impede one another in their operations'.

Clockwork had also become an index of rational thought and behaviour as well as a vision of harmony and concord. It was the *orderly* nature of the machine that excited the imaginations of seventeenth-century observers, and led them to think of forms of government and society in terms of the more complex machines evolving around them. We can see this habit of mind in the writings of another founder member of the Royal Society (and friend of Hobbes), Sir Kenelm Digby, author of the vast *Treatise of the Nature of Bodies* (1644). As a young man, in the 1620s, Digby had travelled in Spain where, much like Montaigne in his travels, he had been struck by the new machines that were coming into being around him. Two devices in particular commanded his attention in the course of his Spanish journey: a water-raising engine or pump which had been constructed at Toledo, and the Spanish Royal mint (also water-powered) located at Segovia. The mint was an object of rapt interest to Digby. A system of hydraulically powered machines, each with its particular task, beat the gold into shape, stamped the blank discs, cut and filed the coin, and delivered the finished currency into a reserve. For Digby, the machine expressed a harmony of purpose and design which was political, as much as it was mechanical. So, though he was no political radical, Digby observed that 'though every part and member [of the machine] be, as it were, a complete thing of itself, yet every one, requireth to be putt on its motion by another . . . for the use and service of the whole'.[165]

The machine, in other words, was evolving into an example of a regulated, harmonious, communitarian society. It had become a mechanized rival to the far more ancient metaphor of society as a communitarian body, an analogy that can be traced back at least to St Paul's idea of the Christian community as a 'body' of believers. As Digby's description made clear, one of the obvious, but rarely remarked upon qualities of machines and clockwork is that they possess no innate hierarchy. Rather, the smooth, efficient running of the complete mechanism depends on the harmonious operation of all the parts of the machine. Unlike the machines to be found in the printed machine books of the sixteenth century, economy of design was also becoming a feature of mechanisms. In theory, at least, no one part is any less important than any other, while no part can be considered superfluous to the overall design of the mechanism. This was an aspect of mechanism which, to the philosophers of the seventeenth century, was of enormous importance in their efforts to understand the world. So, John Wilkins, that deviser of tables and language systems, writing in the late 1630s and observing that 'Wee allow every Watch-maker so much wisdome as not to put any motion in his Instrument, which is superfluous, or may bee supplied an easier way' concluded that nature, too, must be organized with an equivalent economy of mechanical design: 'and shall wee not thinke that Nature ha's as much providence as every ordinary Mechanicke?' he demanded.[166]

The more complex clocks and mechanisms now appearing in Europe also introduced complexity itself as a factor in understanding the wider phenomena of nature.[167] When, in the mid-seventeenth century, the human body began to be understood as a kind of mechanism, the apparent 'purposefulness' of each part, together with an appreciation of the overall complexity of the machine, came into direct confrontation with a much older form of analysis, one that stressed hierarchy or the relative 'nobility' of the different parts. In the older, Galenic, physiology, the body was believed to consist of a hierarchy of parts, some of which were considered 'noble' (the heart, the liver) and some considered less 'noble' (the skin, the cartilage). Mechanical systems do not, however function in such a fashion, as the Dutch anatomist Paul Barbette observed in his *Anatomia practica* of 1659:

> All things in our body are joined together, as in a clock, one cannot be without the other, neither is the most despicable wheel less necessary than the Hand of the Clock itself without which it cannot be accounted a clock.[168]

If the human body was considered (in the words of the Royal Physician, Walter Charleton, in 1680) as 'a system of innumerable engines, by infinite wisdom fram'd and compacted into one greater automaton', then it also existed within a newly defined political relationship, one which was more akin to a republican model than an autocratic model of kingly authority, perched on top of a social pyramid of declining nobility.[169]

Sex machines

It is tempting to invoke the success of their watch and clock designers and manufacturers, as much as the philosophical impact of the ideas of Descartes, to explain why the seventeenth-century argument over mechanism raged most fiercely in autocratic, Catholic, France.[170] These arguments would, in the course of time, culminate in the publication of the extreme statement of materialist philosophy, Julien Offray de la Mettrie's *L'Homme Machine* (1748). Rejecting the dualism of Descartes and the hesitations of Leibniz, *L'Homme Machine* boldly set out its thesis, encapsulated in its title: 'The Human Machine'. 'Man is a machine . . . The human body is a machine which winds itself up, a living picture of perpetual motion.'[171]

La Mettrie derived his philosophy of human behaviour from the claim that all activity, thought, emotion, instinct was, essentially, mechanical in nature. The foundation of La Mettrie's argument was to be discovered in that principle which had so fascinated Descartes, the phenomenon of reflexive movement in humans and in animals. To this end, La Mettrie drew up a long list of vivisectionist experiments investigating this apparently mechanical phenomenon in organic beings: palpitating animal flesh after death, the retraction of severed muscles, the reanimation of dissected frogs' hearts when warmed, even the leaping away from fire of a human heart torn from an executed criminal (a story recounted by Francis Bacon).[172] La Mettrie concluded that all these phenomena pointed to the mechanical nature of the animal body. And so, too, of the human mechanism:

> Let us go into more details concerning these springs of the human machine. All the vital, animal, natural and automatic movements are carried out thanks to them. When the body draws back, struck with terror at the sight of an unexpected precipice, when the eyelids blink under the threat of a blow, as we have said, when the pupils contract in bright light to protect the retina and dilate to see objects in the dark, surely all this happens mechanically?[173]

It was the absence of conscious will or volition, in other words, which sustained this vision of mechanism.

But if there was one feature of human beings that, more than any other, pointed to their mechanical nature, it was sex. Desire, particularly the physiology of male desire, underlined the extent to which the human being was no more than a system of springs, regulated by mechanical force. Remarking (perhaps inevitably) on the 'singular spring, as yet little known ... despite all our knowledge of anatomy' that prompted the erection of the penis, La Mettrie offered a view of sexuality which was hydraulic rather than biological let alone emotional:

> Why does the sight, or the mere idea of a beautiful woman cause singular movements and desires in us? Does what happens then in certain organs come from the very nature of those organs? ... All we have here is one spring, excited by the Ancients' 'beneplacitum' or by the sight of beauty, exciting another one, which was very drowsy when the imagination awoke it. And what can cause this except the riot and tumult of the blood and spirits, which gallop with extraordinary rapidity and swell the hollowed out organs?[174]

Here is perhaps the first expression of sexual desire as a hydraulic force.[175] But if human beings were indeed machines, driven by 'impulses' over which they could have no control, then what sense would morality, a knowledge of right and wrong, make? Could a machine be accused of acting or behaving immorally? As Warren Chernaik puts it (here in the context of Hobbesian psychology) 'there [was] no room for the self-regulating mechanism or inner barometer . . . providing "bounds" for "desires" . . .'[176]

The human machine, whether understood as a system of self-activating springs, interlocking wheels, or as a crude hydraulic device, was a mechanism in which morality played no necessary part in its interior constitution. This was the essence of libertine philosophy, where good and evil became 'terms indicating preferences' rather than absolute moral alternatives.[177] It is easy to see how, in late seventeenth-century London, libertinism – a French import every bit as luxurious as Julien Leroy's clocks and watches – chimed with the idea of mechanism. Libertinism, with its combination of Hobbesian materialism and bastardized Epicureanism, in which the sum total of human endeavour was held to be the pursuit of pleasure and the avoidance of pain, had a quixotic affinity with machines.[178] Machines, or humans considered as a species of machine, either work or they fail to work and if their maker has endowed them with 'ungovernable' appetites and passions, then should we not blame the designer, rather than the device?

By the end of the seventeenth century, machines had become contrivances that seemed to lift some of the burden of guilt from human existence. Optimism, in this sense, had begun to prevail once more over pessimism. Human beings were no more than purposeful machines, designed by a master-manufacturer. Thus, the machine promised a degree of theological restitution in at least two senses: on the one hand, there was the Baconian promise that, with the help of ingenious devices, humankind would soften the effects of that primary fall from grace, recounted in the story of Eve's and Adam's expulsion from Eden into a world of labour. And on the other hand, if human beings were to be considered as highly complex devices, created by the divine clockmaker, then that tormenting Calvinist interior search for signs of redemption could, at last, be abandoned: blame, if blame should be apportioned, was laid at the door of the machine maker, and not his mechanical creations.

In England, this argument was to be explored in its most extreme forms in the poetry of the notorious John Wilmot, second Earl of Rochester. Human beings were guilt-ridden, fallen creatures, or so conventional morality would have it. Human machines, by contrast, were merely acting according to the maker's design. Why, then, should the human being, conceived of as a machine, feel guilt or be obsessed with a sense of depravity and sin? Influenced as he was by Hobbes, in whose writings the body politic and the natural body were analysed in terms of a multitude of springs, levers, and pulleys, Rochester would find himself both attracted and repelled by this conception of mechanism. The attraction, of course, lay in the promised freedom that the machine enjoyed, unburdened by any sense of sin. The repulsion, however, lay in the sterility of mechanistic philosophy: its rejection of appetite and passion, both of which seemed, to Rochester, to transcend mere mechanics, and offer a more convincing account of the stimuli which lay behind human behaviour.

So, although in his poetry we find people (and bodies) that seem to operate in an unthinkingly mechanistic fashion, mechanism, in the end, is not to be trusted either: 'Huddled in dirt, the reas'ning *Engine* lyes, / Who was so proud, so witty, and so wise' (*Poems*, p. 92).[179] Thus, in Rochester's *Satyr against Mankind* ('Were I who to my cost already am . . .'), the human 'engine', stumbling towards death, is no more than a malfunctioning calculating device, of the kind which Leibniz had demonstrated to the Royal Society in London just three years before the poem is said to have been composed.[180] Indeed, it is difficult to read these lines, once we know of Leibniz's demonstration of his calculating apparatus, or of the arithmetical engine presented to Charles II in 1662 by Sir Samuel Morland and described in his publication of 1673, without suspecting that Rochester had heard tales of, or perhaps even seen, the imperfect operation of a *calculus ratiocinator*. And certainly, the poem's scornful description of the 'reas'ning *Engine*' as 'huddled in dirt' is entirely in keeping with Rochester's aristocratic disdain for the earnest mechanical philosophers of the Royal Society with their fantastic batteries of heated vessels and pumping systems by which they sought to emulate the action of human muscle.[181]

In heaping dirt on the discarded machine of the human being, Rochester had, metaphorically, returned it to the dust out of which (so orthodox belief would agree) it was first formed. Rochester's disposable, dirt-encumbered engine is an ironic commentary on mechanical devices, on orthodox religion, *and* on Cartesian rationality, for these were precisely the mechanical terms with which Descartes believed it was possible to understand the human machine. As Descartes had observed in *The Passions of the Soul* (1649) we nowhere become more aware of the affinity of the human body with machines than when we contemplate (as Rochester has us contemplate) a corpse:

> ... the difference between the body of a living man and that of a dead man is just like the difference between, on the one hand, a watch or other automaton (that is, a self-moving machine) when it is wound up and contains in itself the corporeal principle of the movements for which it is designed ... and, on the other hand, the same watch or machine when it is broken and the principle of its movement ceases to be active.[182]

Hence, Rochester is not as easily enlisted in the ranks of the mechanists as might at first appear to be the case. His most philosophically coherent poem – the *Satyr Against Mankind* – is a rational diatribe against rationalism, with its absurd (for Rochester) denial of sensual appetite, and 'certain instinct' in favour of the mechanical organization of time and human affairs (*Poems*, p. 92). Confronted by some 'formal Band, and Beard', representing the clerical establishment, who rehearses the conventional defence of the divinity of human reason, Rochester is unequivocal:

> Hunger call's out, my Reason bids me eat;
> Perversely your's your Appetite does mock,
> This asks for Food, that answers what's a Clock?

> (*Poems*, p. 94)

In a brilliant philosophical *coup de main*, Rochester's sceptical narrator turns mechanical thinking on its head, arguing that his opponent, the defender of divine reason, is himself enslaved to mechanism, which he has allowed to regulate his natural appetites. For Rochester, reason is dominated by the body's more pressing demands, demands which seem to him far more 'reasonable' than it is to bind appetite to the artificial motions of a clock.

Rochester's rage against the body which seems so omnipresent in his 'obscene' poems is paradoxically entirely in keeping with a fundamental *opposition* to mechanistic philosophy, even while his verses, at every turn, seem indebted to mechanical metaphors and modes of thought. For the body rarely (if ever) seems to operate according to either its maker's design or its owner's desires. The interior system of springs and levers was always on the brink of catastrophic mechanical or hydraulic collapse. So, 'The Imperfect Enjoyment', a poem recounting in explicit and exquisite detail male sexual dysfunction, hinges precisely on the failure of those 'springs' and 'impulses' to achieve the desired outcome. The poem begins with bodies operating as if they were well-maintained mechanisms, operating, as does the machine, through action and reaction in an entirely predictable sequence of mechanical movements:

The nimble *Tongue* (*Love's* lesser Lightning) plaid
Within my *Mouth*, and to my thoughts conveyd
Swift Orders, that I shou'd prepare to throw,
The *All-dissolving Thunderbolt* below.

(*Poems*, p. 30)

Everything, at first, seems to be in working order. 'Swift Orders' are transmitted fluidly and with precise efficiency around the mechanized organism: from tongue, to mouth, to that magnificently comic, vainglorious, 'thunderbolt' which is ready to be released 'below'. The soul 'sprung' with the 'pointed kiss' hovers in anticipated ecstasy as each part performs according to its design, locking into place, ready to cement the union. Everything is in perfect working order. But then, disaster! 'In liquid *Raptures*, I dissolve all'ore, / Melt into Sperme, and spend at ev'ry pore' (*Poems*, p. 31). Rather than a precisely calibrated instrument of passion, designed, like a mechanical trebuchet or catapult to bring all its pent up weight and force into play at the crucial moment, the machine dissolves into a chaotic organic mess of ejaculate, leaking out of newly discovered orifices. At once, a new and quite different mechanical sequence takes over: 'Eager desires . . . succeeding shame . . . And *Rage*, at last confirms me impotent' (*Poems*, p. 31). If the body was a machine, then it was also a supremely ill-designed machine in Rochester's view: 'Trembling, confus'd, despairing, limber, dry, / A wishing, weak, unmoving lump I ly' (*Poems*, p. 31). Instead of some satisfying post-coital reverie, this is the automotive response of a body thwarted by mechanical malfunction, an engine which now moves to no useful purpose.

Mechanical bodies were mechanical failures. Compared to the machine said to have been erected in St James's Park in the early 1670s, and capable of pumping vast quantities of water, Rochester's own body was an inefficient mechanism at best. Indeed, in Rochester's most memorably obscene poem, which was also set in St James's Park where James Ward had set up his pumping engine to the chagrin of his rival, Sir Samuel Morland, the heroine of the poem, the proud (but undiscriminating) Corinna acts like a human suction engine, draining liquid from her various lovers, '. . . drawn / From Porters backs and Footmen's brawn' (*Poems*, p. 67). As though readjusting social levels hydraulically, the aristocratic female suction device which is Corinna draws fluid from the lower orders with mechanical efficiency, within the borders of the park which, in reality, housed the new pumping engines devised by mechanical philosophy. Rochester's own body, by contrast, is a far less efficient mechanism, able to serve up only a 'dram of sperm . . . for the digestive surfeit water' compared to the reservoirs of fluid which Corinna has extracted from 'halfe the Town' in the course of her nocturnal adventures (*Poems*, p. 67).

Simpler devices might, however, prove rather more reliable as a route to some form of satisfaction. No reader of Rochester's verses can fail to ignore his obsession with the artificial 'substitute' (as some would have it) for the male member, which the dildo seemed to represent. Here was a device that, unlike Rochester's own organ, seemed incapable of malfunction. More than this, we can see how, in an age obsessed with the invention of ingenious artificial instruments, the dildo represented the obscene underside of a world of prosthetic devices and mechanisms: those various 'extensions of the human sensorium' beloved of the Royal Society. With its 'plain leather coat', its 'virtuous abilities', its 'discretion and vigor', together with the fact that, compared to the 'nasty devices' of 'candle, Carret [carrot], or thumb' it was 'sound, safe, ready, and dumb', the dildo represented a more trustworthy route to female enjoyment than mere 'Flesh and blood' (as Rochester's encomium to the dildo concludes) which could only come 'wobbling after' to the sound of scornful female laughter (*Poems*, pp. 75–8).

The problem, too, with machines was that their very regularity, their un-thinking maintenance of cycles of repetition, easily led to a world of bore-dom, listlessness, and *ennui*:

> Let the *Porter*, and the *Groome*,
>   Things designed for dirty *Slaves*,
> Drudge in fair *Aurelia's Womb*,
>   To get supplies for Age, and Graves.

(Poems, p. 25)

As 'things' it is the servile task of the lower orders to 'drudge' at the mechan-ical labour of copulation, leaving Rochester and his kind to pursue the more Grecian pleasures of endless boozy befuddlement (engendering 'Wit') or better still pederasty.[183] Human life, once liberated from the bondage of morality, but reduced to the mechanical regularity of the machine, becomes dull, stifled, perverse, even, as Rochester explained in his poem '*Regime d'Viver*':

> I Rise at Eleven, I Dine about Two,
> I get drunk before Seven, and the next thing I do,

I send for my *Whore*, when for fear of a *Clap*,
I Spend in her hand, and I Spew in her *Lap*:
Then we quarrel, and scold, till I fall fast asleep,
When the *Bitch*, growing bold, to my Pocket does creep;
Then slyly she leaves me, and to revenge th'affront,
At once she bereaves me of *Money*, and *Cunt*.
If by chance then I wake, hot-headed and drunk,
What a coyle do I make for the loss of my *Punck*?
I storm and roar, and I fall in a rage,
And missing my *Whore*, I bugger my *Page*:
Then crop-sick, all *Morning*, I rail at my *Men*,
And in bed I lye Yawning, till Eleven again.

(*Poems*, p. 130)

As Warren Chernaik comments on these lines, 'sex could hardly seem less enjoyable [or] more mechanical'.[184] And that, of course, was the point. Marking the passage of hours over a twenty-four hour period, the poem proceeds like the remorseless ticking of a clock. The jog-trot rhythm of these verses (technically, the metre is an anapaestic tetrameter) with their related effect of machine-like regularity and repetition, underlines the poem's queasy relationship to clockwork and mechanical movement.[185] It is as though Rochester has imagined himself as his own ghastly *jaquemart*, animated by merely 'impulsive' functions and passions, to recall the dispute between Locke and Leibniz. These impulses represent an interminable round of mechanical repetition, living life according to a timetable that could (so the metre implies) continue, cyclically, forever.

In his behaviour, too, Rochester proclaimed the truth that he had discovered in his own malfunctioning frame: that once the body is conceived of as a type of machine, then rather than this being the triumphant expressions of the mind of a rational maker, it is in fact a deeply flawed mechanism. If we are clocks, then we are not very effective clocks, and investing any degree of certainty in our mechanical devices is foolish. This is the context in which we might read the notorious drunken incident in which Rochester and his companions, acting like aristocratic Luddites (though lacking the moral force of true Luddites), were said to have vandalized the king's glass sundials, set up in the Privy Garden in Whitehall. In the summer of 1675, so a contemporary record runs: 'My Lord Rochester in a frolic after a rant did yesterday beat down the dial which stood in the middle of the Privy garden, which was esteemed the rarest in Europe.'[186] Accounts of what was said on the occasion vary. In one version, and addressing the dials, Rochester is said to have remarked: 'Kings and Kingdoms tumble down and so shall thou', which turns the act into a directly political statement, in keeping with the pseudo-republican sentiments expressed in his 'Satire on Charles II': 'I hate all Monarchs, and the thrones they sit on / From the Hector of France to the Culley of Britain' (*Poems*, p. 75).[187] But equally possible, and certainly in a more authentically Rochesterian vein, is the remark, recorded by John Aubrey: 'What, said the Earl of Rochester, doest thou stand heer to marke [fuck] time? Dash they fell to worke.'[188] Of course, it is perfectly possible to understand this drunken anti-horological sally against the king's phallically intrusive chronometers (Aubrey records them as resembling 'something of Candlesticks') as 'a direct challenge to authority and respectability' as well as at a 'more philosophical level, to time and mortality'.[189] But it is not time that Rochester is vandalizing, so much as the instruments that measure time. His scorn was for the king's delight in such devices, which was an echo of the enthusiasm with which the mechanic philosophers had invested their instruments.

Instead of representing the apotheosis of perfect movement, or the lineaments of a more organized human society, or liberation from the drudgery of the daily round of work or labour, machines, for Rochester, had become expressions of boredom and failure. In this respect, rather than seeing Rochester's brilliant and beguiling verses as being in the vanguard of seventeenth-century rationalism, they might equally be taken as hearkening back to an older, pre-Baconian view of the relationship between human beings and their inventions. Here, as we shall see in our next chapter, Rochester shares something of the paradoxical fascination with mechanism, tinged with profound distrust, of his poetic contemporary, though not sympathetic partisan in either political or moral terms: John Milton. And it is to Milton's writings, and specifically, to his fabulous poetic engines that we must now turn, in order to complete our exploration of the mechanical culture of the early-modern world.

7

MILTON AND THE ENGINE

Mechanical language

To the savants of the Royal Society, the reform of language and the promotion of the mechanical philosophy were seen as allied endeavours. If machines had no need of rhetoric in their operation, then why should language, which was a token of the presence of the 'universal instrument' of human reason (to recall Descartes), deploy such strategies? Language, too, had to operate mechanically with mathematical regularity and precision. The tropes, conceits, metaphors, similes, the entire panoply of rhetorical devices beloved by the poets, had to be banished in order to produce a 'strict account' of nature.

So, Thomas Sprat, in his *History of the Royal Society* (1667) proclaimed the advent of a new kind of language: one which would 'separate the knowledge of *Nature*, from the colours of *Rhetorick*, the devices of *Fancy*, or the delightful deceits of *Fables*'.[1] Language had to be purged of its grosser elements, as though the removal of figures, tropes, and allusions would be akin to creating the rarefied atmosphere that it was the business of the air pump to create. Language should operate like an 'admirable instrument', as though language was itself an artificial device or mechanism. Thus, some sixty years before Jonathan Swift's satirical invention of a language machine in *Gulliver's Travels* (1726), in which language and the concept of a machine are held to be interrelated, the Royal Society, prompted by its devotion to instruments and mechanisms, had begun to conceive of a new discourse of reason.[2] Divested of 'ornament', mechanical language would, so it was hoped, result in a recovered purity of speech and understanding. To this end, the mechanical philosophers would have to develop 'a close, naked, natural way of speaking; positive expressions; clear senses, a native easiness: bringing all things as near the mathematical plainness as they can: and preferring the language of Artizans, Countrymen, and Merchants, before that of Wits, or Scholars'.[3] Mathematics, the driving force behind the new mechanics, was the goal to be aimed at, echoing Hobbes's claim in the *De Corpore* that 'all ratiocination' was, essentially, mathematical.[4]

Ironically, then, the mechanical philosophy demanded that its mechanical language should be derived from the language of those who would formerly have been dismissed as 'mere' mechanics. The elegant refinements of the learned were to be jettisoned in emulation of the speech of 'Artizans' and 'Countrymen' as well as that of the bourgeois 'Merchants'. The mechanical world, Sprat implied, would necessitate an intellectual if not social revolution. It would, of course, be a mistake to see the newly formed Royal Society as constituting a democratic institution of the intellect. The bulk of the Society's earlier membership – well over half according to Michael Hunter – were drawn from the landed gentry and professional classes who made up just five per cent of the population as a whole in the years after the Restoration.[5] In 1663, the Society formed eight committees to undertake work in its different areas of interest. Of these eight groups, three – the committees for mechanics, for the 'history of trades', and for agriculture – drew the widest membership, and it was the committee on mechanics that was the largest of all, with sixty-eight members, including seventeen noblemen and twenty-two knights.[6] And yet, there is some substance to Sprat's socio-linguistic manifesto when it is recalled that nearly a quarter of the membership was also drawn from sons of merchants, artisans, and yeomen.[7] But, in advancing its programme of linguistic reform along mechanical principles, the Royal Society and its adherents would prompt the implacable hostility of the failed political revolutionary, John Milton.

For Milton, committed (as he was) to a language impregnated with simile, fable, allusion, and reference, Thomas Sprat's attack on the language of 'wits and scholars', published in the same year that *Paradise Lost* first appeared, was an attack on his very identity as a poet and as an intellectual.[8] More than that, Sprat's appeal to the language of 'artisans', 'countrymen', and 'merchants' was an appeal to the language of the practical men of business who, in their anxiety to secure their economic privileges had (so Milton believed) been foremost in betraying the ideal of an English Republic. For Milton, it was precisely these interests who bore greatest responsibility for the collapse of the 'good Old Cause'. These were the men, he wrote in the second edition of *The Readie and Easie Way to Establish a Free Commonwealth* (1660), who were 'so affected, as to prostitute religion and libertie to the vain and groundless apprehension, that nothing but kingship can restore trade' (*CPW* VII. 461).[9] A mechanical universe, then, of the kind that was now being explored by the philosophers of the Royal Society, and a theologically driven universe of the kind which Milton was creating, at almost the same moment in the pages of *Paradise Lost*, were separated from one another by more than simply an intellectual chasm. Rather, reading Sprat's 1667 manifesto, let alone Robert Hooke's earlier speculations on the possibility of moulding an enhanced second Adam through the agency of mechanics, it becomes easier to understand the political as well as the emotional and imaginative nature of Milton's argument with the emergent mechanical philosophy. For all that there may have been a measure of agreement between puritans who were anxious to deny any possibility of 'self-determination in a world dominated by irresistible external forces', and the operation of a machine, we should not underestimate the hostility, on the part of Milton, towards the arguments of the mechanical philosophers.[10]

Mechanical sight

But this hostility was paradoxical. Milton may have decried the ideology and the political sympathies of those who promoted mechanism as a way of understanding the world, yet, in his poetry he also thrilled to the energy, power, and force which machines and engines seemed to unleash upon the world. Milton's paradoxical engagement with mechanism becomes readily apparent in what he has to say about that sense which was most transformed by instruments in the seventeenth century: sight. Joseph Glanvill, in his *Vanity of Dogmatising* (1661) pondered over whether Adam in paradise would have had any need either for spectacles or the instrument that was 'Galileo's tube', so perfect was his sight.[11] For Milton, an instrument such as the telescope could never provide grounds of certainty of understanding. True, it was an instrument of reason, but created, as it was, by human reason which was itself tainted by the Fall, how could it offer more security of knowledge than that offered by the inner 'celestial Light' of God (PL III. 51)? More than this, it is difficult to resist the suspicion that, to advise the poet that the wonders of the created universe could best be appreciated by way of the optical instruments, air pumps, and assorted engines which now so delighted the mechanical philosophers, was to play a particularly cruel joke at his expense. Of all the human senses, it was sight which was most enhanced by the devices which captivated the mechanical philosophers. But, as Karen Edwards has reminded us, it is unlikely that Milton ever looked into a microscope.[12] And there was a perfectly good reason for his neglect of one of the foremost instruments of seventeenth-century science. By the time that Robert Hooke had demonstrated a microscope to the Royal Society, in 1663, Milton had been blind for many years.

Milton's blindness, perversely, is a neglected factor in the story of mechanism in the later seventeenth century. To jettison the book of scripture, in favour (say) of the solemn contemplation of the deaths of small animals in a vacuum was a task that was unlikely to prove congenial to the austere scholar, poet, and philosopher, even if he had been able to see the experimental results that were obtained by these procedures. For Milton, more than most, knew just how fallible arguments from sensory experience were. This, after all, was a philosopher who, in the ringing phrases of the invocation to heavenly light which opens Book III of *Paradise Lost*, spent his days:

> . . . from the cheerful ways of men
> Cut off, and for the book of knowledge fair
> Presented with a universal blank
> Of nature's works to me expunged and razed,
> And wisdom at one entrance quite shut out.
>
> (PL III. 46–50)

The poignancy of that 'universal blank', as well as the finality of the phrase 'shut out', reminds us of just how isolated from the visual world Milton had become, and how much, therefore, imagination and memory were involved in the production of the startling visual effects on page after page of *Paradise Lost*. An almost casual remark alerts us to the sense of intellectual isolation Milton experienced as a result of his loss of sight. In 1656, four years after the onset of his blindness, in a letter to an acquaintance, Milton described how he had considered buying an atlas. But 'since painted maps can hardly be of use to me because of my blindness, whilst I traverse the circle of the world in vain with blind eyes, I am afraid that the more I paid for that book, the more I shall seem to mourn for my loss'.[13]

Of course, Milton's capacity for dramatic self-presentation should never be underestimated. The cloak of blindness, to one who saw his destiny as acting as a voice of prophesy amid the chaotic collapse of the Republic, was very much the appropriate costume to adopt in order to present himself in the dramatic production which was *Paradise Lost*. But Milton *was* blind, and he *was* thereby cut off from the sight of the visible natural world, and of new attempts to understand that world.[14] So neither should we over-look the force of these lines, when they are juxtaposed with the rhetoric of the mechanical philosophers. Traversing 'the circle of the world in vain with blind eyes' is a telling phrase when applied to the closing moments of *Paradise Lost*, in which sight is exalted to almost mystical proportions. Joseph Glanvill may have speculated on pre-lapsarian Adam's lack of any need for spectacles, but for Adam after the Fall, it was quite a different matter. The immeasurable enhancement of human vision guaranteed by the microscope or the telescope is re-imagined, in *Paradise Lost*, in terms of an angelic opti-cal device, 'a magical enhancement of sight . . . to set forth great things by small'.[15]

Setting forth great things by small was, of course, the whole endeavour of Galileo when, observing the movement of spots over the surface of the sun through the telescope some time before 1611, he deduced (correctly) the rotation of the sun.[16] Famously, Milton claimed to have met Galileo in the course of his Italian journey of 1638–9, around the time, that is, when Galileo was publishing the product of his labours on force and motion which was *The Two New Sciences*. Earlier in his career, Milton had held Galileo up as a hero of intellectual freedom, or, at least, a hero of opposition to Roman Catholic dogma, recording the meeting in the pages of *Areopagitica* (1644).[17] But when, twenty years later, Galileo was ushered into *Paradise Lost* in the guise of the 'Tuscan artist', he would be associated, even if indirectly, with Satan. His telescopic observations would be qualified as 'less assured' in comparison to angelic sight, his lunar studies dismissed as the creation of '*imagined* lands and regions in the moon'(PL V. 262, 263, my empha-sis).[18] Galileo, in his *Letters on Sunspots* (1613) had brusquely dismissed the view that the sunspots he had studied through his telescope were 'mere appearances or illusions of the eye of the lenses of the telescope'. Rather, these tiny objects were, he believed, 'enormous in bulk . . . as large as those clouds that sometimes cover a large province of the earth'.[19] But by the time he came to compose *Paradise Lost*, Milton had begun to find this deductive argument unconvincing. In one of his most tellingly anti-scientific similes, Milton had compared Satan, landing on the surface of the sun, to a 'spot' which no amount of peering through a 'glazed optic tube' would ever reveal (PL III. 590).

To reveal the nebulous horizons of human history, a far subtler instrument was called for. Milton describes the creation of this 'instrument' in great detail. Adam and Michael are perched on the highest hill of Paradise, where the world, at least visually, lies all before them. But a telescopic vision of earth's geography is not enough. So that Adam's 'eye' might see into a distant future, his visual sense has to be 'purged' of its deluded 'film' of knowledge engendered by the Fall:

> . . . to nobler sights
> Michael from Adam's eyes the film removed
> Which that false fruit that promised clearer sight
> Had bred; then purged with euphrasy and rue
> The visual nerve, for he had much to see
>
> (PL XI. 411–15)

Like Samuel Pepys and his wife, peering into their recently purchased microscopes, Milton's Adam has to learn to see anew, but with a far more complex instrument than could ever have been purchased in the shops of the instrument makers. Clearer sight is purchased not by the promise of the 'false fruit' of human knowledge, let alone a clumsy arrangement of lenses and mirrors. Instead, it is as if Milton had imagined Adam's visual cortex being rearranged to produce a radical reorganization of the human creature's sensorium. So, drops from the 'well of life' are 'instilled' into Adam, so that he begins to see with 'the inmost seat of mental sight' (PL XI. 418). Implicitly, this 'inmost seat of mental sight' is contrasted to the mere enhancement of human vision that the devices of Galileo or his followers were developing. And from this point onwards, Milton's text is infused with injunctions to look, to see, and to comprehend: 'ope thine eyes, and first behold . . .'; 'his eyes he opened, and beheld . . .'; '. . . direct thine eyes . . .' (PL XI. 423, 429, 711), while the angel Michael is addressed by Adam as 'True opener of mine eyes' (PL XI. 598), and the verbal formulation 'He looked and saw . . .' becomes a repeated refrain of these passages (PL XI. 556, 638, 712, 840).

It might be objected that this insistence on blindness, sight, and vision betrays a naively autobiographical understanding of *Paradise Lost*. But we perhaps need to remind ourselves that Milton's quarrel with the mechanic philosophers was not just an intellectual difference. It was a clash of ideologies, of temperaments, and of physical capacities. It was also a clash of attitudes. What irked Milton most in the arguments of the mechanical philosophers was the arrogant certainty that Nature could be put to 'useful' ends. In Abraham Cowley's *A Proposition for the Advancement of Experimental Philosophy* (1661), the Royalist poet and (after Thomas Sprat) chief propagandist on behalf of the Royal Society, had argued that it was now the task of philosophers to pursue nature with what he termed a 'virtuous covetousness'.[20] As Cowley's manifesto proceeds, it is almost as if he had targeted Milton in his sights: 'Certainly the solitary and unactive Contemplation of Nature, by the most ingenious Persons living, in their own private Studies' could never achieve this 'virtuous covetousness', he wrote.[21] And then, as if rubbing salt into the wound, Cowley described the core of the mechanical philosophy in the form of a programme to which Milton could never assent:

> Our reasoning Faculty as well as Fancy, does but Dream, when it is not guided by sensible Objects. We shall compound where Nature has divided, and divide where Nature has compounded, and create nothing but either Deformed Monsters, or at best pretty but impossible Mermaids. 'Tis like Painting by Memory and Imagination which can never produce a Picture to the Life . . . Whereas since the Industry of Men has ventured to go abroad, out of Books and out of Themselves, and to work amongst Gods Creatures, instead of Playing amongst their Own, every age has abounded with excellent Inventions . . .[22]

'Memory and Imagination' were, of course, the only tools that Milton had at his disposal when Cowley promulgated this manifesto. But in a broader sense, it was as if Cowley was accusing all of philosophy of fruitless onanism prior to the advent of the Royal Society. As Milton understood the world, it was not the task of God's creation to submit itself to humankind. Rather, it was humanity's task to submit itself to God. Here, though, was a philosophy of enquiry that violated every principle he had learned to live by. Divested of sight, how could he be guided by 'sensible Objects'? How else could Milton 'paint' other than by 'memory and imagination'? Where else was he to look for illumination of God's purpose, other than in the books of the ancients, and in his own sense of conviction?

As if in revenge, Milton projects the self-authorizing, triumphalist tone of voice he encountered in the rhetoric of the *virtuosi* of the Royal Society into the mouth of Satan in *Paradise Lost*, as the arch fiend stands before his fallen hosts, explaining to them that their task, like the philosophers in their pursuit of nature, was now to enquire with the utmost rigour into the newly created world of humanity. The rhetoric of Thomas Sprat or Abraham Cowley has been appropriated to infernal mechanistic ends. 'Thither let us bend all our thoughts', argues Satan confronting the fallen angels, but addressing them as though he was addressing a meeting of the Royal Society, contemplating a new research programme:

> . . . to learn
> What creatures there inhabit, of what mould,
> Or substance, how endued, and what their power,
> And where their weakness, how attempted best,
> By force or subtlety:
>
> (*PL* II. 354–7)

Only that last comment ('by force or subtlety') reminds us that we are in Hell rather than at an earnest gathering of the Society in Restoration London.

Of course, to read *Paradise Lost* as a series of veiled topical allegories is to reduce the poem to little more than a system, undoubtedly complex, of historical codes possessing all the charm and subtlety of a crossword puzzle. The poem is not a *roman à clef*, as Christopher Hill, one of the poem's most insistently topical readers, has nevertheless reminded us.[23] Satan, in this respect, does not 'represent' seventeenth-century science for all that he has been understood by one distinguished critic as initiating Eve into the mysteries of empiricism at the moment of temptation in *Paradise Lost*.[24] Yet, the fact that no contemporary philosopher of nature other than Galileo appears in Milton's poem is, in this respect, significant. When, in Book VIII of *Paradise Lost*, Adam begins to demonstrate vestiges of interest in the mechanical philosophy (he has begun to 'compute' or calculate the 'magnitudes' of the heavenly bodies) his enquiries are forestalled by the angel Raphael, who warns him that, in pursuing this line of reasoning, he may become the butt of a vast, cosmic joke (*PL* VIII. 16, 17). Both Copernican and pre-Copernican philosophy may be no more than an unwitting human invention, designed to amuse the omnipotent creator. The universe is a vast instrument, but one which, fabricated by God, could never be imitated by mechanical reasoning:

> . . . or if they list to try
> Conjecture, he [God] his fabric of the heavens
> Hath left to their disputes, perhaps to move
> His laughter at their quaint opinions wide
> Hereafter, when they come to model heaven
> And calculate the stars, how they will wield
> The mighty frame, how build, unbuild, contrive

To save appearances, how gird the sphere
With centric and eccentric scribbled o'er,
Cycle and epicycle, orb in orb . . .

(PL VIII. 75–84)

Even were human beings, in the future, to devise fantastic models of the universe, deploy ingenious calculation, and frame fabulous designs in imitation of the movement of the stars, such devices would result only in more confusion.

The semi-omnipotent engine

For all Raphael's scorn, however, by the time that Milton was composing his epic poem, London had become a city dedicated to mechanism, and not just in the philosophical or instrumental sense associated with the contrivances that had so delighted Samuel Pepys and his friends. In 1652, for example, rumours of a remarkable new machine had begun to circulate in the city. The Commonwealth government had heard accounts of experiments being conducted by the Dutch engineer Caspar Calthoff to apply the motive power of steam to raise water. Calthoff was invited to London to work with Edward Somerset (later second Marquis of Worcester) with whom he had collaborated on various ingenious devices and inventions in the late 1620s, particularly the perpetual motion machines which had diverted the king and his court. Installing themselves in the former Royal Ordnance works in Vauxhall, Calthoff and Somerset laboured to bring their 'engine' to perfection.[25] Whether they were successful or not we do not know. No working model of the Calthoff–Somerset engine has survived. But when Somerset came to write an account of his labours, published as *A Century of Inventions* (1663), he was unequivocal: his 'Water Commanding Engine' was a device, driven by fire, with the help of which it was possible to draw water 'like a constant Fountaine-streame forty foot high'.[26]

Foreign observers, too, were impressed by the 'hydraulic machine' as it was termed by that enthusiastic cataloguer of English mechanical achievement Samuel Sorbière, who had seen the device in operation in 1663.[27] Six years later, in 1669, another foreign visitor, Cosimo de' Medici III, Grand Duke of Tuscany, visited the works at Vauxhall, enthusiastically recording the fact that the device 'raises water by more than forty geometrical feet by the power of one man only, and in a very short space of time will draw up four vessels of water through a tube or channel not more than a span in width'.[28] What was this device? At the end of his *Centuries of Invention*, the marquis christened his machine the 'semi-omnipotent engine'. The 'semi-omnipotent engine', Somerset wrote, 'worked the *Primum mobile* forward or backward, upward or downward, circularly or corner-wise, to and fro, straight, upright, or downright' and was so remarkable that he determined to have a model of the device buried with him.[29] Whether this oxymoronic machine was, in reality, constructed is impossible to tell. Given the many other kinds of device to be found in the *Centuries*, including limpet mines, perpetual watches, calculators, an 'imprisoning chair', and those old stand-bys of the speculative inventor, the artificial flying bird, and that *machina ex dei*, the flying machine itself, a degree of scepticism is warranted.[30] But the idea that the steam engine, the foundational mechanism of the eighteenth-century industrial revolution, might have been born on the banks of the Thames rather than the Clyde, and in the very city where John Milton was labouring on the first great imaginative account of industrial labour which was *Paradise Lost* is intriguing.

In what sense can we think of Milton's poem as responding to an idea of industrial labour? Economic historians, after all, tell us that the first 'factory' to be constructed in Britain was the silk-throwing mill constructed in the East Midlands in 1718–21 by Thomas Lombe. Lombe's six-floor factory, which employed over three hundred workers (most of them women and children), harnessed water power to drive machines comprised of over twenty-five thousand wheels, generating over ninety thousand movements.[31] Given that this gigantic operation did not commence until fifty years after the publication of *Paradise Lost*, and long after Milton's death, how can we think of Milton as the poet of the factory, or the herald of industry?

In fact, of course, factories and machine houses had been established throughout Britain and on the Continent long before Lombe's Derbyshire mill machines had begun to turn. Seventeenth-century London, in particular, was a hive of mechanized industrial activity. As we have already seen, machines, mills, and pumping engines were appearing along the banks of the Thames or in St James's Park in the 1650s and the 1660s. In the 1620s, the London silk factories were employing between 7,000 and 8,000 'silk throwers' who operated water-powered 'Engine Looms' derived from Dutch machines devised at the end of the sixteenth century.[32] Perhaps unsurprisingly, the first English factory to be so termed was associated with the mechanical operation of the printing press. Thus, in 1618, the Stationers' Company was described as erecting a 'factory for books and a Press' in London.[33] The earliest English factory may, however, have been heard rather than seen: a contemporary account of women workers singing, again in London in 1595, registers the aural presence of what may indeed have been one of the first factories in England.[34]

We do not know whether or not Milton had witnessed the operation of such machines either in London or in the course of his Italian journey of 1638–9. A modern silk-spinning factory, we might guess, would not have ranked very high on the list of Milton's humanist concerns as he journeyed through Italy in the years prior to the outbreak of civil war in England. Similarly, even if he had, as he later claimed, met the aging Galileo who was then at work on the labours that would result in the exploration of force, weight, and movement contained in the *Two New Sciences*, Milton makes no mention of Galileo's interests in mechanics or the power of machines. But Milton did not have to travel to Italy, or even Derbyshire, to appreciate the glare, noise, and din of industrial labour. For it was the old Royal Ordnance Works in Vauxhall, where Somerset and Calthoff laboured on their 'semi-omnipotent engine', and where they had once worked together in the design of perpetual motion machines, which represented the mechanical heart of seventeenth-century London.

Vauxhall in the eighteenth century would become associated with pleasure and vice. In the seventeenth century, however, it was a place of useful labour, containing a rambling assembly of buildings, sheds, and outhouses clustered along the Thames adjacent to Lambeth Palace, just a short walk down river from Milton's residence in Hammersmith in the period 1631–8. The Works were far more than either an armaments depot or even a munitions factory. Rather, since their establishment in 1629, they had evolved into an industrial complex, where all manner of ingenious devices and engines were set to work.[35] In some sense, we can think of the Vauxhall Works as the concrete realization of Francis Bacon's vision of 'engine-Houses' described in the *New Atlantis* of 1624. And certainly, after the defeat of the Royalist cause in 1645, the Works were to become the site for a planned 'College for Inventions and Advancement of All Mechanical Arts and Industries', envisaged as the technological branch of a putative 'University of London'. In 1649, a memorandum 'For setting Faux-hall apart for Publick Use' was drawn up by the Scottish educational reformer and republican, John Dury. Dury's memorandum detailed the ways in which the Ordnance Works might be transformed into a projected College of Mechanism, arguing that it was vital to preserve the 'Ingenuities, rare Models and Engines which may bee useful for the Common-wealth' and which were already installed at Vauxhall.[36]

Vauxhall was a treasure trove of mechanical ingenuity which the 1649 Memorandum recognized as a valuable public asset: 'The convenience of forges, furnaces, mills, and all manner of tooles for making of Models and Experiments being there already will be a great losse to the Common-wealth if they should bee destroyed . . .'[37] We know a great deal about the contents of the Works in the civil war period, since an intriguing inventory of 'all his Ma[jesty's] Goods, Engines and Materialls whatsoever in his Ma[jesty's] said house at Fauxhall and in the Workhouses and Outhouses belonging to the same' was made on behalf of the Parliamentary authorities in September 1645. Presumably, the new masters of London wanted to know exactly what had now fallen into their hands following the defeat of Royalist forces at the battle of Naseby earlier in the summer of that year. So the Inventory lists the forges, bellows, anvils, vices, scales, cranes, mills, iron spindles, tools, and grindstones, to be found in the workshops, together with many different kinds of 'engine' that had been gathered alongside the Thames. These devices spanned the whole range of seventeenth-century mechanical technology, though at times their precise function was obscure even to contemporaries: an 'engine for the mocion [sic] of water' or another 'engine for a waterworke' might have been any kind of pumping or milling device, while an 'endless scrue of iron for a mocion worke of water' would have been an Archimedean screw, and an 'iron engine for drilling' and an 'engine of brasse' were probably used in the manufacture of musket and carbine barrels. 'Wooden frames for some mocion worke' is intriguingly ambiguous, but the 'Seaven great wheeles made for perpetuall mocion' is perhaps all that remained of the perpetual motion machine that Somerset and Calthoff had once demonstrated to the king and court before the outbreak of war. The Works was also a form of experimental laboratory in which collections of models of many different kinds of speculative engine were stored. If 'one modell for a waggon to go without horses' hints at mechanical fantasy, then the 'modell of an engine to cutt Tobacco upon' and a 'modell of a lether engine to cast water out of a Trench' suggest a more practical sense of purpose.

As might be expected, however, it was the vast array of warlike 'engines' that made up the bulk of the contents of the Ordnance Works in 1645. These were the many devices used in manufacturing artillery and firearms in the period. This was the demesne of John Bishop, the King's 'Engineer and Overseer of all the Instruments of Warre made, moulded and contrived in Fauxhall' together with his 'gun founder' William Lambert, and another 'engineer' William Joulden. Bishop and Joulden seemed to have cooperated with the parliamentary inventory makers, helping to bestow 'proper names to the severall Engines which other wise could not have been discovered'. Just as modern technology can baffle the onlooker, so seventeenth-century military technology had its own arcane language. The inventory went on to list the hundreds of musket and carbine barrels (both 'stockt' and 'not stockt') which were piled up, together with pikes, musket barrels 'cut dragoone length' (i.e. shortened), breech-loading muskets 'completed upp', and the numerous brass engines, and machines which were used in the manufacture of 'great guns' or artillery in the period. Finally, as though the inventory makers had exhausted their repertoire of mechanical language, or the engineers Bishop and Joulden, had finally wearied of the incessant questions concerning the uses and names of the vast quantity of machines and devices contained in the Works, the Inventory simply records the 'divers other . . . materialls for severall uses unknowne too tedious to number'.[38]

The presence of the Ordnance Works on the banks of the Thames throughout the 1630s and 1640s, with its agglomeration of furnaces, forges, instruments, devices, and machines, gives some substance to one of the most evocative passages describing a city on the brink of war to have been written in the seventeenth century: Milton's description of London preparing for war in *Areopagitica*, and written when the Ordnance Works must have been operating at full stretch:

> Behold now this vast City, a City of refuge, the mansion house of liberty . . . the shop of warre hath not there more anvils and hammers waking, to fashion out the plates and instruments of armed Justice in defence of beleaguer'd Truth, then there be pens and heads there, sitting by their studious lamps, musing, searching, revolving new notions and idea's wherewith to present, as with their homage and their fealty the approaching Reformation: others as fast reading, trying all things, assenting to the force of reason and convincement.
>
> (*CPW* II. 553–4)

Here, intellectual labour ('pens and heads') perpetually 'revolving new notions and ideas' and 'assenting to the force of reason' is imagined in terms of the hammers and forges of an organization very much like the Ordnance Works. In Milton's imagination 'Armed justice in defence of beleaguer'd Truth' was being manufactured on an industrial scale, as the toil of seventeenth-century armourers becomes a metaphoric vision of London transformed into one gigantic 'shop' of activity and energy dedicated to the preservation of the 'mansion house of liberty' which, in 1644, Milton believed was the destiny of the city.[39] It is difficult to resist the image of Milton, who in the period prior to the outbreak of war had lived almost within hearing of the Ordnance Works, responding to the sound of those 'anvils and hammers', as he, too, laboured on the great work of hastening the 'approaching Reformation'. And certainly, something very like the Works seems to have entered deeply into his imagination, when, many years later, he began work on his poem in defence of the truly omnipotent engine of the universe which is God in *Paradise Lost*.[40]

The idea of the engine

For all that *Paradise Lost* may be read as a poem in which Milton was struggling with the implicit challenge to orthodox belief proposed by seventeenth-century philosophy, the poet was plainly fascinated with mechanisms, engines, and devices of all kinds. Milton, like Montaigne, could be suspicious of novelty or modernity, as his explanatory note on the verse of *Paradise Lost* in the second edition (1674) of the poem testifies, with its crusty condemnation of the 'jingling' sound of rhyme as the modern 'invention of a barbarous age'.[41] Significantly, it was the *sound* of rhyme, with its mechanical insistence on similarity, to which Milton chiefly objected. Yet, just like Montaigne, Milton also seems to have responded to the imaginative force of the 'engine' as an expression of restless energy and motion. So, while the many examples of 'engines' in *Paradise Lost* are usually (though not invariably) associated with daemonic power, his poetry nevertheless manages to invest such devices with a compensatory sense of titanic force and inventiveness that is in many ways admirable. Almost at the outset of *Paradise Lost* we read how the fallen angel Mulciber was unable to escape God's wrath for all his invention of devious and cunning engines (PL I. 750). In their counsels, the fallen angels speculate as to how they will meet God's 'almighty engine', which is a device whose purpose and function is never explained, except that, like so many machines, it generates 'noise' (PL II. 65) much like the noise of Chaos which is compared to the 'battering engines' deployed by Bellona, goddess of war (PL II. 923).[42] In the opening to Book IV of the poem, Satan is compared to a 'devilish engine' which 'back recoils / Upon himself' (PL IV. 17) as if he had been transformed into a kind of artillery piece, or, recalling the Latin root of the word *ingenia*, into an infernal calculating machine which has, at least temporarily, lost its bearings. In the war in heaven the 'devilish enginery' of gunpowder-powered artillery is deployed (PL VI. 553), and these same 'deep throated engines' (PL VI. 586) are held to be the invention of Satan, whose 'cursed engines . . . new and strange' (PL VI. 650) can only be thwarted by the angelic trick of launching geography 'the seated hills with all their load' (PL VI. 644) against the transgressors. Not only in the pages of *Paradise Lost* does Milton reveal his fascination with engines. In *Samson Agonistes* (1671), the blinded Samson becomes a *primum mobile*, harnessed to the treadmill and threatened by his persecutors with yet another unnamed engine to 'assail and hamper' him (CSP, p. 389). Only very rarely do Milton's engines appear as benign devices. In the second of his two early poems commemorating the death of Hobson, the Cambridge University carrier, written in 1631, the dead Hobson is remembered as an apparatus 'Made of sphere-metal', which eventually runs down 'Like an engine moved with wheel and weight', a clock that has, at last, ceased to tick (CSP, p. 125).

The 'semi-omnipotent engine' on which Somerset and Calthoff laboured in the Vauxhall Ordnance Works, as well as Milton's recourse to a language of 'enginery', indicates the ways in which, in the middle years of the seventeenth century, a new vocabulary of engines was emerging. The 'engine' might appear, in seventeenth-century discourse, at surprising times, and in surprising contexts. As might be expected in the civil war period, there was a growing fascination with the idea of inventing some fabulous new 'engine' or war machine that might turn the tide of war. Speculative inventors such as Edmund Felton, brother of John Felton the assassin of the Duke of Buckingham, promised to develop unspecified 'engines' that might replace large bodies of men and bring the war to a successful conclusion.[43] Equally, the very idea of the 'engine' with its connotations of cunning inventiveness seems to have appealed to seventeenth-century writers of very different persuasions. The 'engine' (or 'gin' as it would become known in its shortened form) was not only a mechanical apparatus of some kind, but it was also a way of exercising leverage and force, whether mental or mechanical, by which an obstacle might be shifted. A scriptural or devotional text, for example, might be described as a kind of 'engine' insofar as it strove to persuade its readers of the author's arguments.[44] In a macabre footnote to the history of mechanics, the regicides of 1649 were said to have devised an 'engine to draw his late majesties head down to the block in case of refusal', though the device, even if it had been invented, was not needed. The king was famously compliant in his own execution.[45] But perhaps it was felt that the terrible act of regicide could only be accomplished with the help of an engine to exert sufficient force. Certainly, the idea of an engine designed to apply mental force lies behind George Herbert's dislocatingly poetic 'engine against the almighty' to be found in 'Prayer (I)' first published in 1633.[46] In Herbert's image, the force of prayer is imagined as a mental siege engine ranged against God, as if the deity could be made to succumb to the battery of the multiple prayers of the faithful. Like a torsion catapult of the kind to be found in the books of machines, prayer was an 'instrument' by which fallen humanity pressed its claims on God's attention. Engines, too, could refer both to precision instruments and primitive tools that, today, we would be unlikely to describe as a species of 'engine'. Thomas Fuller, for example, writing in 1662, records a chest being forced open by thieves 'with what engines unknown', while the *savant* Henry Power, in 1664, referred to the microscope as 'our modern engine'.[47] All of these ideas circulating around the notion of an 'engine' help us understand the context in which Milton, too, deployed his poetic engines.

Milton's evident fascination with the idea of the 'engine' was, in part, a function of the inherent ambiguity of the engine in the seventeenth century. Related to the idea of *ingenium* or human ingenuity, a seventeenth-century engine might, at almost the same instant, be understood as an artillery piece, a vast battering instrument, a clumsy crowbar, a precision apparatus, or even an idea or a text. For Milton, engines were products of ingeniousness, and hence, fittingly, they were associated with Satanic energy and inventiveness. In *Paradise Lost* Book VI, having been thrown into disarray by their first encounter with God's angelic armies, the fallen angels cast about them for the means by which to defeat their omnipotent foe. With a theatrical flourish ('Not uninvented that, which thou aright / Believst so main to our success' PL VI. 470–1) of the kind that a speculative 'inventor' such as Edmund Felton would have envied, Satan reveals to his followers his new 'inventions':

> . . . hollow engines long and round
> Thick-rammed, at the other bore with touch of fire
> Dilated and infuriate shall send forth
> From far with thundering noise among our foes
> Such implements of mischief as shall dash
> To pieces, and o'erwhelm whatever stands
> Adverse . . .
>
> (PL VI. 484–90)

The unveiling of his new invention – gunpowder powered artillery – sends a frisson of entrepreneurial envy among the rebel angels. Like visitors to the

Vauxhall Ordnance Works, the fallen angels cluster around these miraculous contraptions:

> The invention all admired, and each, how he
> To be the inventor missed, so easy it seemed
> Once found, which yet unfound most would have thought
> Impossible:
>
> (*PL* VI. 498–501)

As with so many technological innovations, the fallen angels have discovered that once the principles of the new device are grasped, it becomes difficult to imagine how they had ever been missed in the first place.

The 'devilish engine' of artillery is presented in *Paradise Lost* as a daemonic invention. This invention had intrigued Milton since his earliest years. One of his earliest (Latin) poetic compositions 'In inventorum bombardae' ('On the Inventor of Gunpowder'), published for the first time in 1645, appears to offer a paradoxical encomium to Prometheus, the mythical donator of fire to humanity, who is thus credited as the first inventor of the substance which would power those 'hollow engines' operated with 'touch of fire'. But Prometheus is shown to be far less inventive than his human successor, who turns fire into an agent of destruction:

> In their blindness the ancient's praised Japetus's son for bringing down heavenly fire from the sun's axle. But I think this man greater, who, we may believe, has snatched from Jove his ghastly weapons and three-forked thunderbolt.
>
> (*CSP*, p. 36)

Was there not something perversely commendable, Milton seems to be saying, in the cunning theft of heavenly weaponry?

Milton was also the creator of what has become, for modern literary critics, the most puzzling engine of the seventeenth century. Milton's own speculative 'engine' was not, however, to be found in a technical treatise, let alone discovered deep beneath the earth's surfaces in the treatises of the mining engineers of the period. Rather, it was a purely imaginative creation to be found in a poem of loss, mourning, remembrance, and consolation. In 'Lycidas' (1638), we encounter the famously obscure 'two-handed engine', which stands 'at the door . . . ready to smite once, and smite no more' (CSP, p. 249). This engine, which has been described as 'the most celebrated (non-textual) crux in English literature', clearly represents a threat of some kind.[48] Its target is the 'grim wolf with privy paw' which, in the poem's veiled system of allegory, may be taken as the proselytizing power of Catholicism in mid-century England, particularly the power of the Jesuits whose founder, Ignatius Loyola, incorporated the figure of the wolf into his armorial device.[49]

Today, accounts of what, exactly, Milton's 'two-handed engine' might have been are legion, fostering a flourishingly ingenious offshoot of the Milton industry among latter-day commentators and interpreters. Is the device a complex allegory of the Old and the New Testaments? A two-handed broadsword? A printer's device? The two nations of England and Scotland? The keys to heaven?[50] Or rather more literally, perhaps it is simply a black-powder firearm of the type which, by the time the poem had been republished in 1645, had been deployed in the volleys of fire unleashed at Naseby and Marston Moor in the civil wars, or which had been manufactured on Milton's doorstep throughout the 1630s at Vauxhall. In the form of the matchlock pistol, which required two hands to fire, or the flintlock musket, which in the everyday guise of the fowling piece would indeed have stood 'at the door' of many a country house in the seventeenth century, this device would have been instantly recognizable to Milton's contemporary readers.[51]

But the 'two-handed engine' crux is a puzzle since it seems so entirely out of place in the poem's succession of figures, metaphors, and allusions. It occurs at the end of a digressive section of 'Lycidas' where the verses seem to swerve from the more familiar theme of Christian solace to prophesy 'the ruin of our corrupted clergy then at their height', as the headnote to the poem explained when it was republished in 1645 (CSP, p. 239). Whatever its precise nature, the engine forms part of an interruption, a pause in the unfolding of the verses, associated with some violent dislocation in the pastoral calm which the poem otherwise evokes. Into a landscape of 'fountain, shade, and rill', which was once the haunt of Lycidas, the poetic persona of the drowned young man whom the poem remembers, the engine is an intrusion, just as the religious conflicts of the 1630s may equally be understood in the poem as a modern interruption, disturbing the classical calm of the world inhabited by Orpheus and Amaryllis. The engine should have no place in the pastoral or sylvan world, with its Ovidian echoes of the lost golden age. And it is in this context that we might begin to understand Milton as the first poet of industry.

Milton and industry

We do not often think of *Paradise Lost* as being a poem of industry or the factory. But then, we do not often think of the London in which Milton was living and working in the 1640s and the 1650s as a city of industry and the factory. If it is true, however, that the 'semi-omnipotent engine' of Calthoff and Somerset was indeed a precursor of the steam engine, then it would also be true to say that *Paradise Lost* is a poetic precursor of later, Romantic, visions of human industry and technology. Certainly, Milton's vision of Babel in *Paradise Lost*, together with the infernal labours of Satan and his cohorts would come to inform later reinterpretations of Milton's poetry, whether in the prophetic lines of Blake's *Milton* (1808) where Satan is associated with 'Mills & Ovens and Cauldrons' in his work of 'eternal death', or in the apocalyptic illustrations of John Martin incorporated into his *The Paradise Lost of John Milton* (1827), in which new visions of nineteenth-century industry were combined with Milton's biblical narrative, to evoke a titanic industrial presence.[52]

But we do not need to peer so far forward in time to understand the ways in which Milton's poem was engaged with technology. For Milton, technology, or, to give the term its seventeenth-century (non-rhetorical) flavour, 'invention', was invariably expressive of the Fall: the collapse of a divinely ordered, harmonious, universe into something catastrophic, despotic, redolent of tyranny. We have seen how, in Abraham Cowley's propagandist hymn to the nascent Royal Society, published in the same year that *Paradise Lost* appeared, nature was imagined a being 'pressed' mechanically to reveal her secrets to the followers of Bacon. That was not, however, how Milton imagined the matter. Rather, the climactic image of *Paradise Lost* is that of nature sighing, groaning, and trembling, as she and the earth feel the 'wound' which Eve and then Adam create as they gorge themselves on the fruits of the tree of knowledge (PL IX. 780–3, 1001).

For Milton, human invention and inventiveness, in a technological sense, is the direct result of this catastrophic act of transgression. Such inventiveness, equally, carried with it none of the optimistic sense of restitution, no matter how partial, with which patristic and contemporary commentators struggled to accommodate the artificial world of *Technē*. Rather, the human arts, civilizing as they may appear, are understood within Milton's wider theological plan as a confirmation of humanity's fallen state. The busy industry which surrounded Milton in seventeenth-century London, and which we have seen him evoking to such rhetorical effect in *Areopagitica*, was a constant reminder of the Fall. Hence, in Milton's poetry the term 'industry' takes on a surprisingly modern register in his poetic lexicon, as though he was already beginning to glimpse the lineaments of a world driven by ever-more powerful machines and instruments, 'semi-omnipotent' engines, rather than the truly omnipotent creator.

In Milton's poetry, 'industry' was truly daemonic in that it signified an endlessly restless, Godless, pursuit of self-gratification and self-aggrandizement. We may recall Mulciber, that builder of engines in *Paradise Lost* who is sent, by Milton, 'with his industrious crew to build in hell' (PL I. 171); or the fallen angel Belial who is 'to vice industrious, but to nobler deeds / Timorous and slothful' (PL II. 116–17) as though only the alluring prospect of vice can raise him to the pitch of activity. Industry, moreover, was a sign of movement to no purpose, as in the image of the wandering earth 'industrious of her self' (PL VIII. 137) moving through Raphael's scornfully evoked Copernican model of the heavens. Even where the term appears in what, at first, seems a more positive light, its context leaves the reader ambiguously uncertain as to its true import. In *Paradise Regained* (1671), Milton may have described the '. . . sound / Of bees' industrious murmur', which lulls the scholar to the delightful lassitude of 'studious musing' (CSP, p. 501), but the epithet is spoken by Satan, and acts as a memory of the simile of the bees with which the infernal legions are described in their entrance to Pandaemonium in *Paradise Lost* (PL I. 768–77). In *Samson Agonistes* (1671), by contrast, the term 'industry' is unambiguously yoked to tyranny, in the evocation of the:

> . . . brute and boisterous force of violent men
> Hardy and industrious to support
> Tyrannic power . . .
>
> (CSP, p. 385)

Tyranny, brutality, and violence are the by-products of industrious energy.

Certainly, brutality and violence is the context in which we find Milton's poetic description of industry in the sense of mass production, though the setting might seem, at first, unlikely. In his 'Masque Presented at Ludlow Castle' (Comus) first performed in 1634, and published in 1637, the enchanter Comus, who lurks in the wilderness of the forest, attempts to seduce the Lady by juxtaposing what he terms her 'lean and sallow abstinence' with his evocation of the 'full and unwithdrawing hand' of nature (CSP, pp. 211–12). For Comus, nature works like a master craft worker, fashioning delicate and ravishing objects, tastes, and sensations for human use. These artificial things,

Comus argues, are there to be consumed by discriminating connoisseurs such as himself. By refusing his invitation to become either a consumer or something to be consumed, the Lady, according to Comus, denies both nature's fecundity and her organizational skill. For nature is also capable of mass production, filling the seas and air with organic life. And among her greatest gifts are the techniques with which she produces luxurious items of consumption on an unimaginably vast scale, such as her natural silk-spinning factories where insects, or at least their larval progenitors, labour in the service of humanity. Nature, acting like the thousands of silk spinners working their engine looms in seventeenth-century London, works on an industrial scale in order to:

> . . . set to work millions of spinning worms,
> That in their green shops weave the smooth-haired silk
> To deck her sons . . .
>
> (*CSP*, p. 212)

Silk, in the seventeenth century, was indeed a luxurious commodity, which would have been available only to 'deck' the frames of those who could afford it, as opposed to woollen products, which Comus dismisses as the products of domestic labour, manufactured by 'coarse complexions / And cheeks of sorry grain', who serve to 'ply / The sampler and to tease the housewife's wool' (Milton, CSP, p. 214). Though silk, with all its connotations of hedonistic luxury, aroused the ire of Puritan commentators, the industrial manufacture of silk was one of the flourishing industries of seventeenth-century London, producing what can be described as a literature of silk in the period.[53] Later in the seventeenth century, Robert Boyle would combine both industry and nature in a way that is reminiscent of Milton's toiling caterpillars, to describe the silk worm as being itself a productive 'living engine'.[54]

Comus, who evokes nature as an industrial presence in the midst of the wild green wood in his seductive speech in praise of excess, is the first of Milton's daemonic spokesmen for industry, mechanism, instrumentation, and mechanical labour. But it is in *Paradise Lost* that industry, the engine, and labour are brought together in what soon begins to emerge as one of the earliest accounts of industrial labour in English poetry. Almost the very first concrete image that we meet with in *Paradise Lost* is related to industry and industrial process. When Satan turns his eyes around him to view his new demesne, Hell, the sight which greets him is 'A dungeon horrible, on all sides round / As one great furnace flamed' (PL I. 61–2), reminding us that he has indeed been 'cast' out of heaven, to be remoulded as a true 'engine against the Almighty'. Later, the flaming furnace that is hell becomes the setting for the construction of gigantic structures, which are produced with infernal technological ingenuity.

Recovering from the shock of their headlong expulsion, the fallen angels soon set about the task of improving their new home by creating Pandaemonium. The archetype of Pandaemonium is Babel, which we have already met in the context of the optimistic celebration of human art and industry in the work of Northern European artists of the late sixteenth and seventeenth centuries. But this is Babel re-imagined and 'improved' by an energy that far surpasses anything of which humans are capable:

> . . . And here let those
> Who boast in mortal things, and wondering tell
> Of Babel and the works of Memphian kings
> Learn how their greatest monuments of fame,
> And strength and art are easily outdone
> By spirits reprobate . . .

(PL I. 692–7)

Milton's Babel is a monument (albeit vanished) of 'fame, / And strength and art', which (in one of those reversions of chronology which are characteristic of *Paradise Lost*) has become the fictional precursor of Pandaemonium. The belated human fabricators of Babel could never, however, match the purposefulness of their Satanic precursors. For the construction of Pandaemonium is also a vision of industrial process, the daemonic counterpart to that busy industry which, over a hundred years earlier, Georgius Agricola had described in his technical descriptions of miners delving beneath the earth's crust to retrieve precious metals in the pages of his *De Re Metallica* (1556).

For Agricola, mining was a civilizing task, a heroic labour in quest of the metallic ore out of which objects of beauty and worth could be fabricated. For Milton, however, the pioneering work of the rebel angels was transgressive, an echo of that Ovidian fable in which the earth is harrowed by human greed. The mining activities of the fallen angels open in the earth a 'spacious wound' from which 'ribs of gold' are extracted, as though the earth was an organic body, flayed, as Agricola had shown it flayed in his treatise on mining, by the tools and implements of the fallen angels (PL I. 689, 690). This wound in the organic earth is a foretaste of the later 'wound' felt by the earth in Book IX of the poem, at the moment of human disobedience. The architect of Pandaemonium is Mulciber, the biblical prototype of Hephaistos/Vulcan who, even before his fall, was a plunderer of the earth's contents. From him, human beings learn how to delve into the earth in a work of impiety:

> Men also, and by his suggestion taught,
> Ransacked the centre, and with impious hands
> Rifled the bowels of their mother earth
> For treasures better hid.
>
> *(PL* I. 685–7)

An inventive miner, Mammon leads the fallen angels 'armed' with 'spade and pickaxe' to retrieve the 'metallic ore' out of which Pandaemonium is constructed (PL I. 676, 673).

The construction of Pandaemonium out of the spoils of the earth is, too, a triumph of daemonic organization, which is at least comparable to that earlier deployment of human time, energy, and skill which Domenico Fontana had summoned into being in Renaissance Rome when he shifted the pagan monuments of antiquity at the behest of his patron, the Pope. The fallen angels are masters of organization, far outdoing the labours performed in classical antiquity or in scripture in rearing Babel or the pyramids. These 'spirits reprobate' are able to perform:

> . . . in an hour
> What in an age they with incessant toil
> And hands innumerable scarce perform.
>
> *(PL* I. 698–700)

Just as we have seen John Wilkins, in 1648, commending Fontana's skill in marshalling human labour with such economy of purpose when compared to the multitudes and the ages required to rear the monuments of antiquity, so Milton's hell is a technocracy, led by the technocratic Satan and his lieutenants. Together they embark on the industrial project that is the creation of their new abode:

> Nigh on the plain in many cells prepared,
> That underneath had veins of liquid fire
> Sluiced from the lake, a second multitude
> With wondrous art founded the massy ore
> Severing each kind, and scummed the bullion dross:

A third as soon had formed within the ground
A various mould, and from the boiling cells
By strange conveyance filled each hollow nook,
As in an organ from one blast of wind
To many a row of pipes the sound-board breathes.
Anon out of the earth a fabric huge
Rose like an exhalation . . .

(*PL* I. 701–11)

Hell has been transformed into a gigantic workshop in which multitudes of fallen angels work with 'wondrous art', at their 'strange conveyance'. Much like the 'millions' of spinning worms in 'Comus', or the thousands of spinning workers in seventeenth-century London, labour has been conceived here on an industrial scale. Although Pandaemonium is a structure reared with fiery insubstantiality, which rises 'like an exhalation', it is, for all that, suffused with industrial reality.[55] Wreathed in fumes and smoke, Pandaemonium hints at a coming age of industry and vapour from which already, in seventeenth-century London, some were recoiling. The diarist John Evelyn, for example, complained in his *Fumifugium* (1661) of how modern industry was enveloping London in a 'Hellish and dismal cloud . . . an impure and thick Mist accompanied with a fuliginious and filthy vapour'.[56] Amid similar mists and fumes, Milton's fallen angels labour (as Agricola had shown his miners labouring in the pages of *De Re Metallica*) in sociable harmony, dividing the tasks among themselves according to those principles by which labour had been divided in the mines of Bohemia, and which had been so exhaustively analysed in Agricola's text. Long before Adam Smith had remarked upon the ways in which pins might be manufactured more efficiently by dividing up the many tasks involved in their manufacture, Milton's fallen angels had grasped the principles of 'division of labour' required for the fabrication of Pandaemonium.

As though placing the whole poem in parentheses, Babel, to which Pandaemonium had been compared at the outset of the poem, makes its reappearance at the end of *Paradise Lost*, in the lesson in human futurity which is given to the now fallen Adam by the angel Michael. Babel becomes a bleak story of political despotism, interlaced with a prophetic account of industrialization, encapsulated in the story of Nimrod:

. . . till one shall rise
Of proud ambitious heart, who not content

> With fair equality, fraternal state,
> Will arrogate dominion underserved
> Over his brethren, and quite dispossess
> Concord and law of nature from the earth . . .

(PL XII. 24–9)

Like restless emigrant industrial workers, Nimrod and his 'crew' swarm westwards, leaving Eden far behind them:

> He with a crew, whom like ambition joins
> With him or under him to tyrannize,
> Marching from Eden towards the west, shall find
> The plain, wherein a black bituminous gurge
> Boils out from under ground, the mouth of hell;
> Of brick, and of that stuff they cast to build
> A city and tower, whose top may reach to heaven;

(PL XII. 38–44)

Nimrod's followers are described as a 'crew'. In Milton's poetry, 'crews' are invariably 'horrid', 'banished', 'rebellious', 'hapless', 'godless', 'wicked', 'atheist', 'cursed', 'monstrous', 'infernal', 'impious', or 'damned' (PL I. 51, 751; IV. 573; V. 879; VI. 49, 277, 370; VI. 806; XI. 474; CSP, pp. 436, 373, 112). Unless they are a part of God's angelic hosts, vast purposeful groups of labourers, whether they are silk-spinning caterpillars, or labouring fallen angels, are rarely to be admired, even if Milton delighted in the different ways in which multitudes of soldiers, angels, or workers could be described. But it was the lone individual, or small groups of individuals such as the 'fit audience . . . though few' who are imagined as the potential readers (and understanders) of *Paradise Lost* in the invocation to Book VII of the poem (PL VII. 31) who were almost always to be preferred over nameless agglomerations of peoples.

The hallmark of 'industry', in the emerging sense of the factory, was that it involved masses of individuals conforming to a single collective purpose. Milton seems to have distrusted collective purpose of any kind. But Milton was also ideologically, philosophically and temperamentally opposed to the kind of optimism expressed by Robert Boyle who, just five years before *Paradise Lost* appeared, was proclaiming the triumph of mechanism in terms which would have been immediately recognizable to the author of a poem which recounts the history of Adam, Eve, and their human progeny:

> ... if *Adam* were now alive, and should Survey that great Variety of Man's Productions, that is to be found in the shops of Artificers, the Laboratories of Chymists, and other well-furnished Magazines of Art, he would admire to see what a new world, as it were, or set of Things has been added to the Primitive Creatures by the Industry of His Posterity.[57]

The 'industry' of Adam's 'posterity' might have been, for Robert Boyle, a wonder, but this was not how Milton understood the energy and activity of the silk spinners, operatives, mechanists, instrument-makers, and engineers to be found in seventeenth-century London. Rather, their work was to be understood as the culmination of the long history of human folly and cruelty by which humanity had severed itself from the pastoral Eden it had once enjoyed. The industrious world of Techne was, for Milton, quite literally, the mark of Cain, as he explained in the later books of *Paradise Lost*.

This pessimistic view of human technological accomplishment is given full rein in *Paradise Lost* in the course of the lesson in universal history which Adam receives in the closing books of the poem. 'And now prepare thee for another sight' (PL XI. 555) advises the archangel Michael midway through the penultimate book of the poem. Peering into the future, Adam is groping towards an understanding of the world shared by the readers of the poem, the fallen world of Techne.[58] This 'other sight' seems, at first, to be a scene of tranquillity: a spacious plain, 'tents of various hue', grazing cattle, and the sound of 'instruments that made melodious chime' (PL XI. 557, 559). Into this pastoral world, ringing with harmony, however, a disturbing presence intrudes: the presence of human industry, and with it the arrival of artifice which disturbs and then destroys the pastoral idyll:

> In other part stood one who at the forge
> Labouring, two massy clods of iron and brass
> Had melted (whether found where casual fire
> Had wasted woods on mountain or in vale,
> Down to the veins of earth, thence gliding hot
> To some cave's mouth, or whether washed by stream
> From underground) the liquid ore he drained
> Into fit moulds prepared; from which he formed
> First his own tools; then, what might else be wrought
> Fusile or graven in metal.

> (PL XI. 564–73)

This Vulcanic figure is Tubalcain, a descendent of Cain, and the progenitor, as the Bible has it, of metallic technology: 'an instructor of every artificer in brass and iron' (Genesis 4. 22). As the vision progresses, Tubalcain and his kind are joined by another group who are committed not to mechanical but intellectual labour:

> . . . by their guise
> Just men they seemed, and all their study bent
> To worship God aright, and know his works
> Not hid, nor those things last which might preserve
> Freedom and peace to men . . .
>
> (*PL* XI. 577–80)

At first, Adam greets this vision of his future with hope. Despite his 'fault', it seems that his posterity will enjoy a restitution, akin to that optimistic vision of a technologically enlightened age which Francis Bacon and his seventeenth-century followers believed was heralded by the new world of rational instruments, devices, and mechanisms: 'Much better seems this vision, and more hope / Of peaceful days portends . . .' (PL XI. 599–600) exclaims Adam. Michael soon disabuses him:

> Those tents thou saw'st so pleasant, were the tents
> Of Wickedness, wherein shall dwell his race
> Who slew his brother; studious they appear
> Of arts that polish life, inventors rare,
> Unmindful of their maker, though his Spirit
> Taught them, but they his gifts acknowledged none.
>
> (*PL* XI. 607–12)

The true future-history of human *Technē* – the 'arts that polish life' – following the Fall is revealed to be a cataclysmic series of disasters laying waste all human skill and ingenuity: 'towns and rural works . . . / Cities of men with lofty gates and towers' are subjected to 'battery, scale and mine . . . / dart and javelin, stones, and sulphurous fire' (PL XI. 639, 656, 658). The pasturing herds are slain, the 'ensanguined' fields deserted, and 'infinite / Manslaughter, shall be held the highest pitch of human glory' (PL XI. 692–3). It is a vision of despair culled directly from Ovid.

In the story of Nimrod, and in the vision of Tubalcain and his descendants promised to Adam, Milton rehearses the outline of arguments which, in

the modern world, have become almost a commonplace of contemporary technophobia. Milton was not, however, alone and neither was he the first to sense that the human technological impulse might have disastrous consequences. Paradoxically, one of the strongest condemnations of technology in the Renaissance was to be found in a work which was dedicated to the promotion of technology. Five hundred years before our modern preoccupation with the effects of industrialization on the environment, Georgius Agricola, the German mining engineer, evoked the catastrophic effects of the very industry which his great work, *De Re Metallica* also celebrated. 'The strongest argument of the detractors' of such industry, Agricola wrote 'is that the fields are devastated by mining operations.' He continued, summoning up a vision of a landscape poisoned by industrial processes, two hundred years before the coming of industrial revolution:

> . . . woods and groves are cut down, for there is need for an amount of wood for timbers, machines, and the smelting of metals. And when the woods and groves are felled, then are exterminated the beasts and birds . . . Further, when the ores are washed, the water that has been used poisons the brooks and streams, and either destroys the fish or drives them away. Therefore the inhabitants of these regions, on account of the devastation of their fields, woods, groves, brooks, and rivers, find great difficulty in procuring the necessaries of life . . .[59]

The pastoral or sylvan world is shown to be a fragile entity in the face of the rapacious enthusiasm of the miner, or his counterpart, the fallen angel. But it was not just the link between 'daemonic energy', industrial labour, and fallen humanity which Milton's poem sought to unravel. His quarrel with mechanism existed at a far more profound level, a level that takes us to the philosophical and theological core of *Paradise Lost*.

Milton and the machine

Adam, leaping into life and motion in the pages of *Paradise Lost* is not, of course, a machine. Yet, he is in many ways the true predecessor of Rochester's anti-Hobbesian, dirt-encumbered and redundant 'reas'ning Engine' that lies, huddled in despair, in the opening of the 'Satyr Against Mankind'.[60] Philosophically speaking, Milton's engagement with the problem of the 'reasoning engine' should be no great surprise given that he was the author of a poem whose purpose was to proclaim the essential freedom of the human creature to choose between right and wrong within the wider theological context of the Calvinist idea of predestination. When, in *Paradise Lost*, Milton has Adam recall his own moment of entering into a sense of being and animated life, the human creature's recollection is of springing (the word is Milton's) into action in a mechanical, though smooth and free-flowing fashion which Rochester's faulty mechanisms could only have envied. As Adam, a fabricated being, arises into consciousness of his own existence, so he gazes heavenwards until 'raised / By quick instinctive motion up I sprung, / As thitherward endeavouring' (PL VIII. 258–60).

That phrase – 'By quick instinctive motion up I sprung' – might have been culled from the writings of Descartes or Boyle rather than the text of Genesis.[61] For Adam does not understand or know why or even how he moves. Instead, like a machine, he moves passively, driven by some motive force whose origin is uncertain. Adam then subjects his body to an exploratory survey or autopsy, testing its mechanical operation:

> My self I then perused, and limb by limb
> Surveyed, and sometimes went, and sometimes ran
> With supple joints, and lively vigour led:
> But who I was, or where, or from what cause,
> Knew not . . .

(PL VIII. 267–71)*

This famous passage can be compared to a directly Cartesian moment. In his *Traité de l'homme* or *Treatise on Man*, composed during 1639–40, but suppressed by its author and not published until 1662, just five years before the first appearance of *Paradise Lost*, Descartes had posited the existence of a newly created race of human beings, whose principles of motion were entirely mechanical.[62] When the *Treatise* did finally appear, it was clear that the philosopher had sketched the outlines of the Miltonic dilemma by imagining, like Milton, a newly created race of human beings. Descartes' newly fashioned creatures are much like humanity as it exists, save that God consciously forms them as automata, or, as they are described in the text, like 'a statue or machine made of earth'.[63] Described throughout the *Treatise* as machines, the new race is, however, a divinely organized mechanism, and hence far more complex than anything that can be made by human skill:

> We see clocks, artificial fountains, mills, and other such machines which, although only man-made, have the power to move of their own accord

in many different ways. But I am supposing this machine to be made by the hands of God, and so I think you may reasonably think it capable of a greater variety of movements than I could possibly imagine in it, of exhibiting more artistry than I could possibly ascribe to it.[64]

By the time that this passage first appeared, in the *Treatise* of 1662, the body-machine had become the new orthodoxy, even if it sat uneasily with the older certainty of a creature infused with an autonomous will by its Creator. And this, of course, was precisely the certainty that Milton's poem set out to proclaim.

'Cartesian animals', writes Dennis des Chene, 'are self-moving machines.'[65] In such creatures, both the internal and the external functions rely on mechanical forethought or design rather than the presence of a soul. Descartes' human machines would operate according to:

. . . the mere arrangement of the machine's organs every bit as naturally as the movements of a clock or other automaton follow from the arrangement of its counter-weights and wheels. In order to explain these functions . . . it is not necessary to conceive of this machine as having any vegetative or sensitive soul or other principle of movement or life.[66]

For all that Milton's Adam may possess *some* of the quality of an automaton, he is clearly not a Cartesian machine of this kind. Instead, he has self-knowledge by which he understands that he cannot be self-created, and that the 'cause' of his being must, therefore, lie outside himself.

In other words, Milton has exposed the paradox at the centre of the Cartesian model of the human being as an automaton: a machine which 'knows' itself to be a fabricated object, and which therefore knows that it has been fashioned by a maker, cannot, in truth, be thought of as a machine. Only human beings have the capacity to sense that they might *not* be autonomous agents. By contrast, the fallen angels in *Paradise Lost* lack this facility of self-knowledge and hence an understanding either of their divine maker or the divine workmanship which has been deployed in their making. In the denial of their own created state, and hence in the denial of their maker 'who . . . formed the powers of heaven / such as he pleased' (PL V. 824–5), the rebel angels in *Paradise Lost* are revealed to be acting as though they were indeed automata. In Satan's ironic riposte to the seraph Abdiel, who endeavours, without success, to remind his leader that they have no autonomous being, we see Milton wrestling, with what might be termed the reverse of the

Cartesian paradox: that a machine which believes itself *not* to be a machine is acting in a truly machine-like fashion. 'That we were formed then say'st thou?' asks Satan:

> . . . Strange point and new!
> Doctrine which we would know whence learned: who saw
> When this creation was? Remember'st thou
> Thy making, while the maker gave thee being?
> We know no time when we were not as now;
> Know none before us, self-begot, self-raised
> By our own quickening power . . .

(PL VI. 853–61)

Memory, so Satan believes, is the key to autonomy. Parodying the primacy of sight in the accounts of the mechanical philosophy, Satan poses the impossible question: 'who saw / When this creation was?' Evidence from sight, as we have seen, had become a vital part of the credo of the mechanical philosophers. But relying on the negative evidence that 'We know no time when we were not as now', Satan's dream of autonomy is equally false.

Seventeenth-century arguments over artificial existence and human autonomy, and with them the precise corollary to Satan's reasoning, can be found in the writings of the Cambridge Platonist Nathaniel Culverwell. In the opening pages of his *Discourse of the Light of Nature* (1652), Culverwell, with the help of Plato, attacked the view of those who, following Aristotle, had descended into 'a most stupid Atheisme', by proposing that all 'beings' are the product either of 'nature', 'fortune', or 'art'.[67] Of those creatures ('the first and chief corporeal beings') said to have been the product of a God-less 'Nature', Culverwell scornfully protested against the view, which is also Satan's opinion of his own creation, that they have 'sprung from eternity into being by their own *impetus*, and by their own virtue and efficacy . . . like so many natural *automata*, they were the principles of their own being and motion . . .'[68] Milton was certainly aware of this form of argument because, many years earlier in *Areopagitica*, he had appealed to the idea of an automaton as well as to the examples of puppets or 'motions' to promote the idea of the essential freedom of the human being created by God. For the human being was able to exercise that faculty of reason which was to so bedevil the fabricators of artificial, machine-driven life in the seventeenth century:

> Many there be that complain of divin Providence for suffering *Adam* to transgresse, foolish tongues! When God gave him reason, he gave him freedom to choose, for reason is but choosing; he had bin else a meer artificiall *Adam*, such an *Adam* as he is in the motions.
>
> (*CPW* II. 527)

An 'artificiall *Adam*', of the kind which had mechanically jerked its way through Eden in the form of an exquisite automaton fashioned by sixteenth- and seventeenth-century craft workers, let alone of the type which Robert Hooke has imagined confecting out of heated and cooling vessels, could never be illustrative of the human capacity of exercising reason.

Milton's point, though, was a more generally theological one, which forms the intellectual core of his great poem of justification. For the lines in which Satan argues for his own self-generation, deploying those crucial terms 'self-begot' and 'self-raised', are central to any understanding of the poem.[69] As Regina Schwartz writes, 'the entire epic constitutes an extended refutation of Satan's heresy of self-begetting'.[70] Yet, those same self-reflexive terms express much of the quality of machinery as it was appreciated by Milton's contemporaries: the ability of a machine to appear as if it were a self-motivating force, endowed with a 'quickening' (i.e. lifelike) 'power'. And as we have also seen, the very word 'automatism' or self-movement, used in Italy as early as the 1480s in the context of Volpaia's '*machinula automato*' or 'self-propelled device', proclaimed an idea of self-activation that came to be associated with machines of all kinds.

The word 'auto', from whence are derived so many of our words to describe machinery, can be translated as 'self'. In Greek drama, it was suggestive not only of self-movement, but of the 'blood-tie . . . a place of incest, of parricide, and of suicide', all of which are transgressions associated by Milton with Satan.[71] And the word 'self', deployed grammatically as a prefix, seems to have held a peculiarly attractive poetic resonance for Milton. Again and again in his poetry Milton returned to this linguistic structure, to condemn activity that seems to operate at one remove from the paths laid down by God. So, allied to Satan's mistaken claim that he and his companion fallen angels are 'self-begot, self-raised' in *Paradise Lost*, we find evil in the masque *Comus* described (by the Elder Brother) as 'self-fed, and self-consumed' (CSP, p. 205); Eve in *Paradise Regained* described as 'self-deceived' (CSP, p. 489); the human creatures in *Paradise Lost* depicted by God before their Fall as 'self-tempted, self-depraved' (PL III. 130); Satan, in the opening speeches of *Paradise Lost* proclaiming that he and his legions will regain their seat in heaven 'self-raised' (PL I. 634); the fallen angels in *Paradise Lost* described by Raphael as 'self-lost', corruptible humankind termed 'self-knowing', while humanity as a whole is termed 'self-left' by God (PL VII. 154; VII. 510; II. 93).

These reflexive compounds might be no more than a peculiar poetic trick of Milton's – a species of linguistic tic – were it not for the fact that the 'self' prefix had acquired a remarkable potency in the mid-seventeenth century. The OED, in what amounts to a short linguistic essay marking the impossibility of ever cataloguing the infinite number of usages of the word 'self', records the fact that the 'self-' prefix:

> ... was greatly augmented towards the middle of the seventeenth century, when many new words appeared in theological and philosophical writing, some of which had apparently a restricted currency of about fifty years (e.g. 1645–90) ...[72]

In other words, in deploying this particular structure, Milton can be thought of as being linguistically modish. But there is, too, a theologically appropriate means of explaining this reflexive quirk of Milton's. For Satan's project is indeed parricidal. His ambition is to destroy his own maker, while knowledge of (and love for) one's maker was, for Milton, one of the marks of humanity. In Satan's ironic affirmation of his own autonomy (and hence denial of his maker), and in the frequency with which characters and actions in his poetry are invested with this rebellious sense of selfhood, Milton was underlining the wider theological point that God's creatures do not possess the degree of autonomy that they might wish upon themselves. Although they are not machines, acting like automata, neither are they entirely self-moving. Rather, their primary impulse springs from God, their true fabricator.

For Descartes, writing in 1644 in the *Principles of Philosophy*, the relationship between the designer and the machine was vital to the understanding of what it was to be human. Descartes' description of this relationship has a singular force when applied to *Paradise Lost*. What, after all, is Milton's poem about but the exercise of human choice, the evidence of human freedom? For Descartes, too, humans were 'free', while machines, by contrast, were bounded by the will of their designer:

> ... it is a supreme perfection in man that he acts voluntarily, that is, freely; this makes him in a special way the author of his actions and deserving

of praise for what he does. We do not praise automatons for accurately producing all the movements they were designed to perform, because the production of these movements occurs necessarily. It is the designer who is praised for constructing such carefully made devices, for in constructing them he acted not out of necessity but freely.[73]

This, of course, was exactly Rochester's mechanical point about freedom and guilt, in which it is the maker, rather than His fabrications, who should receive blame or praise for their actions. Like Shakespeare's Coriolanus, who protests that he will not act like a gosling by becoming a slave to instinct, but instead will stand 'as if a man were author of himself' (Coriolanus V. iii. 36), so Descartes (like Milton) reserved for humanity the privilege of autonomy, or authorship, a privilege denied to humanity's mechanical creations.

But what if humanity was to be considered as a kind of mechanical device, of the kind that Descartes had already proposed, through simile and analogy, in the Discourse on the Method? Theologically, if not philosophically, this argument exposed the dilemma in mechanistic thinking, as the natural philosophers attempted to reconcile their machines, mechanical contrivances, and mechanistic comparisons with orthodox theology. The arguments of Thomas Willis or Robert Boyle, that the human being was essentially a 'singular artifice' much like the 'motions of a clock or engine' posed a dilemma which could not easily be reconciled with orthodoxy.[74] If God were considered to be the fabricator of the human machine, in what sense was the human different from the automaton, imprisoned within the bounded will of its designer?[75] How could the human machine be considered 'free' if it ran only in the predetermined grooves of its maker's master plan?

So complex had clockwork mechanisms become at the time that Paradise Lost was being written that they did, indeed, suggest a kind of autonomy to seventeenth-century observers. We have already seen the great cathedral clock of Strasbourg firing the imagination of the French poet Du Bartas, in terms of its complex mechanical motions. Such a device, with its galaxy of moving angelic figures and its history of Christ's passion, excited the imagination of sixteenth- and seventeenth-century observers, prompting them to speculate on the degree to which such devices seemed to exhibit a sense of purpose. Such devices suggested that mechanism had become infused with a kind of artificial autonomy. So Robert Boyle in his Considerations Touching the Usefulnesse of Experimental Naturall Philosophy (1663) described the 'curious engine' of the Strasbourg clock as composed out of parts which

... are so fram'd and adapted, and are put into such a motion, that though the numerous Wheels, and other parts of it, move several ways, and that without any thing either of Knowledge or Design; yet each performs its part in order to the various Ends for which it was contriv'd, as regularly and uniformly as if it knew and were concern'd to do its Duty; and the various Motions of the Wheels, and other parts concur to exhibit the *Phaenomena* design'd by the Artificer in the Engine, as exactly as if they were animated by a common Principle, which makes them knowingly conspire to do so . . .[76]

Of course, Boyle knew this analogy to be false. A clock could not 'knowingly conspire' to do its duty any more than could Montaigne's oxen turning the Persian watermill compute their revolutions: 'I do not imagine that any of the Wheels, &c. or the Engine it self is endowed with Reason, but commend that of the Workman who fram'd it so Artificially', Boyle hastily explained.[77]

It was an explanation of which John Milton's God would have approved. For Boyle, like Descartes, knew that the human being, unlike the machine, was the 'author of his actions'. And it was authorship, too, which Milton sought to affirm in claiming that his human creatures were 'free'. So, Milton's Calvinist God justified the immutable laws of predestination that condemned His human creations to expulsion from Paradise, in terms of 'authorship'. Was the human 'free'? God's answer, according to Milton, was unequivocal:

> So without least impulse or shadow of fate,
> Or aught by me immutably foreseen,
> They trespass, authors to themselves in all
> Both what they judge and what they choose; for so
> I formed them free, and free they must remain,
> Till they enthrall themselves: I else must change
> Their nature . . .

> (*PL* III. 120–6)

Milton's use of the term 'impulse' here is revealing. In our own age, to act 'impulsively' is to act without premeditation or thought for any possible outcome, the very opposite of the careful forethought inherent to the design of a mechanism. Machines cannot (yet) contain within themselves a capacity for 'impulsive' behaviour, since that would be to invest them with autonomy. By contrast, in the seventeenth century, 'impulse' was, as we have seen in

292 MILTON AND THE ENGINE

the case of Leibniz's argument with Locke, a term fraught with mechanical implications. Although the word was beginning to carry its modern connotation of recklessness, the term was still anchored to its older, Latinate, root *impellere*, meaning to impel through the application of sudden exterior force, which creates motion. 'Impulse' belonged (as both Leibniz and Locke would later agree) primarily to the realm of artificial devices. But if human beings were considered as a species of machinery, then it became easier to understand how they, too, might be driven by 'impulse'.[78] Hence, Milton's denial of impulse, in both its mechanical sense and its modern sense of acting without forethought, as a factor in God's plan. Surrounded and fiercely opposed to the surge of mechanistic thinking promoted by the adherents of the Royal Society, for Milton human beings could never be understood as automata, acting on pure, mechanistic, 'impulse'.

By contrast, Milton's Adam springs into motion 'by instinct', which is discovered to be a force implanted in him whose origin lies beyond himself. And yet, Milton's creatures are also 'formed' by God, as though they were indeed mechanical puppets, whose natures could (if God chose) be changed. Or rather, it is as if the poet allows his creatures to choose, in a severely circumscribed fashion, whether or not to 'enthrall' themselves to the slavery of 'impulse' or passion. The dilemma of whether or not the creatures of Milton's cosmos are genuinely 'free' has, of course, plagued generations of the poet's readers ever since the first appearance of *Paradise Lost*. And this dilemma can be thought of as inherent to the particular branch of puritan theology – the Calvinist view of predestination – that is the frame for the poem's drama.[79]

Milton was struggling with exactly the dilemma with which extreme mechanists such as Hooke were also struggling. What if the human creature was, indeed, no more than a mechanical contrivance? Mechanism, the child of the machine, thus lay at the very core of Milton's great poetic enterprise. At the heart of *Paradise Lost*, which Humphrey Jennings for one saw as the foundational text of all subsequent writings on industry and the machine, lies the spectre not of a ghost in the machine, but of human beings who, divorced from God, have become machine-like. Responding imaginatively to the world of mechanism that had come into being around him in seventeenth-century London, Milton's poetry also looked forwards to an alternative vision of human existence. At the close of *Paradise Lost*, the world of Pandaemonium has invaded Eden. Glancing over their shoulders, Adam and Eve are witnesses to the collapse of the first garden of the world, overrun by a terrible new force:

They looked back, all the eastern side beheld
Of Paradise, so late their happy seat,
Waved over by that flaming brand, the gate
With dreadful faces thronged and fiery arms:

(*PL* XII. 641–4)

Walking away from the fiery daemonic industry and energy which has overwhelmed them, Adam and Eve set out to find a place of safety and rest
in some other part of the world which lies all before them. Where such a
world was to be found takes us back to the opening pages of this book, and
towards the conclusion of our enquiry into the birth of mechanical culture
in Renaissance Europe.

8

THE MACHINE STOPS

At the end of *Paradise Lost*, the human figures walk out into the world, hand in hand, to find their new home. In reality, of course, the descendants of Adam and Eve were to find no such idyll of repose. Rather, what they were to encounter was a life of endless toil and labour which the world of *Technē* was devised to alleviate. But the idea of an eventual restoration, a return to a more innocent and more secure existence is implicit in Milton's story of exile and loss. Paradoxically, however, it was *Technē* itself, the entire realm of artificial devices, which now acted as the equivalent to that flaming sword brandished over the heads of Adam and Eve as they were forced to abandon Paradise. Modernity or novelty had triumphed over antiquity and tradition. No matter how much the poets and artists might struggle to recreate the Ovidian fantasy of the lost golden age, the presence of the machine would come to symbolize all that humanity had lost in losing Eden.

The interrupted idyll of Andrew Marvell

Leo Marx, in his now classic study of American literature, *The Machine in the Garden* (1964), has described the confrontation between mechanical culture and nature as manifestations of what he has termed the 'interrupted idyll'. The 'interrupted idyll' can be traced back to the much more ancient literary genre of pastoral, familiar to Renaissance writers and readers through the countless poetic imitations of Virgil's *Eclogues*, in which the pastoral landscape offers an escape from the social world inhabited by fallen human beings.[1] But in Marx's view, this Arcadian idyll is, invariably, shown to be a fragile retreat, easily shattered by the intrusion of the machine erupting into the landscape. Mechanical disturbance constituted the essence of the 'interrupted idyll': the sudden intrusion of mechanical power, and particularly noise, into a formerly tranquil countryside. In the nineteenth century, steam-powered locomotives would become the favourite vehicles of such disruption:

> The sensory attributes of the engine – iron, fire, steam, smoke, noise, speed – evoke the essence of industrial power and wealth . . . set against the attributes of a natural terrain – fecundity, beauty, serenity, and ineffable numinosity . . . The recurrence of the 'interrupted idyll' testifies to the salience of the conflict of meaning and value generated by the onset of industrial capitalism. It prefigured the emergence of what has proved to be a major cultural divide, separating those Americans who accept material progress as the primary goal of our society from those who – whatever their ideals of the fulfilled life – do not.[2]

Leo Marx saw this conflict as a peculiarly American phenomenon of the nineteenth and twentieth centuries, and he cites a galaxy of American writers, from Thoreau to Ernest Hemingway, in support of this beguiling thesis. But perhaps the conceit of the 'interrupted idyll' surfaced in earlier periods too?

Certainly, early-modern culture was constantly threatened by the interruption of artifice. One version of that disturbance can be found in the poetry of Andrew Marvell, written in the midst of that larger political interruption of the mid-century wars of religion and ideology affecting the three kingdoms of England, Ireland, and Scotland in the 1640s and the 1650s. Unlike John Milton, Marvell did not thrill to the 'daemonic' force of the machine, but neither did he decry the restless enterprise of industrious labour. Rather, in his sequence of 'Mower poems', Marvell explored the way in which the world of nature and natural forms was invaded by transforming human energy. But this energy was also tainted by human vice. In 'The Mower Against Gardens', it is 'luxurious man' who:

> Did after him the world seduce:
> And from the fields the Flow'rs and Plants allure,
> Where Nature was most plain and pure.[3]

In the artificial world of the garden, as opposed to the more natural world of the meadows, a disturbing perversity has begun to flourish which is a consequence, once more, of the Fall. Appropriating the fashionable horticultural language of hybridization by which new 'improved' stocks of plants were developed, Marvell imagines the plants and flowers primping themselves like young girls exploring cosmetics for the first time or, since the use of powder and paint in the seventeenth century was not solely a female preoccupation, they are like so many old *rouées*, hoping to disguise the ravages of age by the application of art:

> With strange perfumes he did the roses taint.
> And Flow'rs themselves were taught to paint.
> The Tulip, white, did for complexion seek;
> And learned to interline its cheek:[4]

The tulip hunting after 'white' is searching for white lead, a toxic component in the manufacture of cosmetics, which is of a piece with the production of 'forbidden mixtures . . . uncertain and adult'rate fruit'.[5] Perversity, which is also *Technē*, has come to invade the quiet, green world of meadows and woods.

In Marvell's poetry, the natural world is always on the point of being overwhelmed by the artificial, even when it seemed most secure and most divinely ordered. Thus, in his evocation of a pastoral idyll encountered by a band of Puritan voyagers in his poem 'Bermudas' (composed c. 1654), Marvell has his pious travellers hymn the creator of the 'grassy Stage' of the New World in terms that elide the natural and the artificial:

> He lands us on a grassy Stage;
> Safe from the storm and Prelat's rage.
> He gave us this eternal Spring,
> Which here enamells everything;
> And sends the Fowl's to us in care,
> On daily visits through the Air.
> He hangs in shades the Orange bright,
> Like golden lamps in a green Night.
> And does in the Pomegranates close,
> Jewels more rich than *Ormus* show's.[6]

Even at its most natural, the world is contaminated by artifice. For the psalm-chanting refugees from the Old World bring with them not only their faith, but also their language, metaphors, tropes, and similes which will transform this paradise. So, Marvell imagines the newly discovered, tropical world to be the work of a master craftsman, or even a set designer in the mould of Inigo Jones, masque designer to the Stuart court: the grass is a 'stage'; the 'eternal spring' 'enamells' the natural world; the oranges are 'golden lamps'; the pomegranate, when opened, discloses its fruit as 'jewels'. Metaphors and similes, the artificial 'devices' of poetry, have already set about their transformational work of replicating the natural world as a place of luxurious consumption. What particle of nature could remain untainted by vice associated with the artificial?

In his meditation upon the civil wars of the 1640s, which was his poem 'Upon Appleton House, to My Lord Fairfax', Marvell ushers in the mowers with an appropriately mechanical image culled from the artificial world of the staged court masque, with its fabulous mechanisms of transformation:

> No scene that turns with Engines strange
> Does oftner than these Meadows change.
> For when the Sun the grass hath vext,
> The tawny Mowers enter next . . .[7]

Let loose amid the fields, with their 'whistling' scythes, Damon and his kind 'massacre' the grass and the creatures who hide within it, and in doing so they come to 'detest' their strokes; the bloodied edges of their tools put them in mind of their own dissolution, as well as the larger dissolution of civility which has overtaken the Commonwealth. So, there is a kind of poetic justice in the poem 'Damon the Mower' when the mower himself, erstwhile spokesman for the natural as opposed to the artificial, becomes a victim of his own adept (though still primitive) technology. For Damon, too, is engaged in shaping the natural world to an artificial mould:

> While thus he threw his Elbow round,
> Depopulating all the Ground,
> And, with his whistling Sythe, does cut
> Each stroke between the Earth and Root,
> The edged Stele by careless chance
> Did into his own Ankle glance;

> And there among the Grass fell down,
> By his own Sythe, the Mower mown.[8]

'Damon the Mower' is undoubtedly the wittiest exploration in English poetry of what (at the risk of bathos) we might now term an agricultural accident: the mower mows, is mown, and so moans, while the poem as a whole is a 'complaint' or extended moan. But in the poem, Marvell manages to express some larger and more troubling relationship between human beings, organic nature, and the urge to render the world serviceable to human design through the agency of technology. In an epithet more usually associated with the martial valour of swordsmen than mowers, the 'edged Stele' which glances into the mower's own ankle can, without too much difficulty, be taken as a knowing metaphor for the self-laceration which had come to infect the English polity as a whole in the 1640s and the 1650s. Yet, the contrast between nature and artificiality still holds. The pastoral world, which Marvell continuously delighted in invoking in his poetry, has been redrawn as a demarcation line from behind which the poet wages guerrilla warfare against the threat of the artificial.[9]

It was no coincidence that Marvell turned against the artificial at this particular moment in the mid-seventeenth century. Writing, as he was, in the period when the mechanical philosophy was emerging as the dominant intellectual movement in England and in Europe more generally, but when older pastoral forms still exercised enormous influence in art and in literature, Marvell seems to have found the quest to submit nature to the 'use' of humankind profoundly disturbing. Humans, after all, could never emulate the perfection with which nature produced her own designs. In his poem 'Upon the Hill and Grove at Bill-borow To the Lord Fairfax' nature is shown to produce forms more perfect than anything which could be achieved with the help of humanity's instruments of reason and artifice:

> See how the arched Earth does here
> Rise in a perfect hemisphere!
> The stiffest Compass could not strike
> A line more circular and like;
> Nor softest Pensel draw a Brow
> So equal as the Hill does bow.
> It seems as for a Model laid,
> And that the World by it was made.[10]

Paradoxically, it is Nature herself who is able to produce the most perfect designs through her own deployment of an artifice that is shown to be more accomplished than anything that might be fabricated by human instruments and designs.[11]

For the philosophers of reason, of course, nature did indeed operate according to mechanical principles. In 'The Garden', Marvell seems to gesture towards this mechanization of natural processes when he closes the poem with an evocation of time being measured not by mechanical clocks but by an insect mechanism: 'th'industrious bee', which 'computes its time as well as we'.[12] Marvell's 'industrious bee' busily computing or calculating the time spent in its labour of pollination, seems to be working to a precisely calibrated schedule or programme of work. The 'computation' of time, labour, and human society was intrinsic to the triumph of mechanical culture in the seventeenth century. Although, in Milton's *Paradise Lost* Adam's efforts to 'compute' the motions of the heavens would result in an angelic reprimand, and while Marvell's Damon offers no critique of an emerging 'industrial' world, these poems nevertheless hint at the ways in which mechanism and artifice has stealthily transformed the world even as it seems to be still suffused with an older pastoral stillness.

The happy return

But what if the clock was to be wound backwards or even forwards, and humankind offered the chance to begin again by erasing the troubling technology that had come to surround it, and which, to recall Freud's gloomy sadness, has come to trouble prosthetically endowed humanity? The idea of a 'happy return' to a pre-technological world acts as a counterweight to our many fables of technology, whether they be derived from Greek myth or the Bible, transcribed in Renaissance art, or uncovered in the philosophies we have developed to accommodate the presence of the machine in our midst. This, in essence, is the vision of human futurity with which Milton's *Paradise Lost* seems to conjure. What would the world look like were we to be allowed to return to the Edenic state?

Or perhaps the rediscovery of Eden might be forced upon us, as the natural world rebels against encroaching artifice? In his *Man and Technics* (1931), Oswald Spengler, in his customarily apocalyptic style, predicted the catastrophic outcome of humanity's reliance on technology:

All things organic are dying in the grip of organization. An artificial world is permeating and poisoning the natural . . . Civilization itself has become a machine that does, or tries to do, everything in mechanical fashion . . . we cannot look at a waterfall without mentally turning it into electric power; we cannot think of a countryside full of pasturing cattle without thinking of its exploitation as a source of meat supply . . .[13]

Of course, it is difficult to imagine a time in the human past when a herd of pasturing cattle were *not* seen as a potential source of food. Pastoralism, after all, is yet another manifestation of *Technē*. But for Spengler, the machine had come to represent 'Faustian civilization', which was doomed to dissolution and decay: 'machine-technics will end . . . and one day will lie in fragments, forgotten – our railways and steamships as dead as the Roman roads and the Chinese wall', Spengler prophesied.[14]

Understood as a product of a purely technological culture, the machine and all that it has come to symbolize have often been seen as fundamentally opposed to ideas such as 'nature', 'art', or 'culture'. The 'technologico-Benthamite' world of the machine can have little sympathy, so it has often been claimed, with the human world of the imagination as it is to be discovered in art or in poetry.[15] In fact, as Heidegger observed, poetry, art, and the machine are all equally the products of *Technē*. Equally too, among artists and poets, as well as among architects and designers, the machine has had its passionate defenders, who, at times, have reached a pitch of religious intensity.[16] In the early twentieth century, for example, Futurism, with its provocative exultation of speed, dynamism, and mechanism, together with its enraptured adoration of machinery challenged the older, organicist view of things. Futurism's 'motor car, which seems to run on shrapnel', replacing 'the victory of Samothrace' was held to be more beautiful than anything that could have been devised in remote antiquity.[17]

In 1919, the diarist and diplomat Harold Nicolson recorded a conversation with a Bolshevik commissar who had announced the 'triumph of the machine' in Soviet Russia. To the question 'what machine?', the commissar responded, wrote Nicolson, by making 'a vague gesture embracing the whole world of mechanics'.[18] But, as Aldous Huxley's *Brave New World* (1932) with its presiding deity of Our Ford testifies, machines were still ambiguous presences in human life. For all that the former front-line soldier and novelist Ernst Jünger might have hymned the fusion of the human form and the machines encountered on the Western Front, writing of nerves and blood being intertwined with iron and steel, such an unholy cybernetic fusion was not necessarily the rule of modernism.[19] In D. H. Lawrence's poetry, for example, the machine was imagined as triumphing only for 'one sad century' while nature would eventually revolt against 'mechanical man, in triumph seated upon the seat of his machine'.[20] Even if his writing, in common with that of other modernist writers, was steeped in metaphors of technology, yet Lawrence himself still proclaimed the belief that no implement or device could fathom the depth of the human soul: 'no engine can reach into the marshes and depths of a man'.[21]

For Spengler, as much as for Lawrence, 'machine-technics' would one day 'lie in fragments, forgotten'. Presumably, both these German and English prophets of the collapse of mechanical culture knew the outcome of just such an experiment in the earlier twentieth century:

> Cottage industries boomed, largely undetected by statisticians, as the peasants sought to manufacture all those household products they had once bought from the towns but which were now unavailable or too expensive for them to buy. Rural craftsmen fashioned simple ploughs and sickles out of old scrap iron. Flax and hemp were grown for clothes and rope; timber was cut to make wheels and furniture; reeds were gathered to make baskets; clay was dug for pottery; and oil-producing seeds were grown for fuel . . .[22]

This is not a description of an imagined retreat into a Rousseauesque state of nature, and neither is it the screenplay to some futuristic film, in which the survivors of a natural or man-made catastrophe live amid the crumbling detritus of technological civilization. Rather, it is a description of Russia in 1918, when, under the pressure of industrial crisis, the great cities were all but abandoned as millions fled to the countryside in search of food. For a contemporary observer of the cataclysm that overwhelmed Russia, the historical parallels were immediate. 'Russia returned to its rural past', seeking a haven in the middle ages when:

> Rus' had neither railways nor steamboats, nor steam-mills, nor factories, nor any other 'European invention', when handicraftsmen fed, clothed, and heated the whole of Russia and made its footwear, when everything was done by them on a tiny scale and very coarsely – with a hand chisel instead of a lathe, with an axe instead of a saw.[23]

The result of this enforced retreat from modernity would be the deaths of countless numbers of individuals from hunger, disease and the effects of war. Russia's experience of the 'retreat' into pastoralism during 1918–19 was, of course, unplanned. In this respect it was quite unlike a more recent attempt to jettison the trappings of 'machine technics' as experienced by the Cambodian people under the Khmer Rouge regime in the 1970s, when the cities were all but abandoned as virtually the entire population was forced into a new form of ruralism.

François Ponchaud claims that the goal of the Khmer Rouge was the creation of a 'new concept of society, in which there is no place for the idea even of a city', which would be exchanged for the ideal of 'an egalitarian rural society'.[24] The result of this experiment in a late twentieth-century version of Virgilian pastoral was catastrophic. But it is, nevertheless, important to remind ourselves what a modern world, suddenly divested of technology in fact amounts to, since, no matter that a world without the machine is a comfortless place, imaginative literature has long been entranced by just this prospect. Hence, the beguiling fantasy of 'beginning again' – a Year Zero endeavour, in which humankind is imagined as stripped of its technology, and returned to a purer 'primitive' state. In the nineteenth century, these fantasies would emerge in the antiquarian and imaginative contemplation of ruined cities and civilizations, returning to the wilderness of the forest or the desert in an ironic commentary on human ephemerality. Mary Shelley's novel The Last Man (1826), for example, conjures with a world struck by a devastating plague that has all but destroyed humanity. Set in England, at the end of the twenty-first century, the last few survivors in Shelley's novel cling to the remnants of civilization, until only the book's narrator survives. As the grass grows in the streets of the cities, the last rites for humanity's technologically reliant existence are pronounced:

> Farewell to the giant powers of man . . . to the power that could put a barrier to mighty waters, and set in motion wheels, and beams, and vast machinery, that could divide rocks of granite or marble, and make the mountains plain![25]

The fantasy of nature's eventual triumph over the works of humanity, and with it the end of that old 'art' versus 'nature' antithesis which so enthralled Renaissance poets and inventors, seems to have been peculiarly vivid when the impact of new industrial processes was at its height. In poetry and in art, the reconquest of human art and artifice by nature formed the essence of Romantic meditations of the kind to be found in Percy Shelley's poem of ruins 'Ozymandias' (1818), or in the apocalyptic visions of artists such as

John Martin in the 1820s. Leonardo's fantasies of a world overwhelmed by the forces of nature, erasing the works of humanity had returned, at least in the imagination. Later still, the theme of the solitary survivor, brooding over the debris of civilization, would act as a counterpoint to that high Victorian energy unleashed by industrialization. It was to be found in images such as Octave Saunier's *Paris en ruines* (1899) or Gustave Doré's final engraving for his *London: A Pilgrimage* (1872), known as *The New Zealander*, in which an oddly medieval figure surveys a ruined cityscape, which is gradually crumbling into the encroaching swamps.[26]

The forms and gestures of Renaissance pastoral, which Leo Marx has traced in American literature of the nineteenth and twentieth centuries, continue to surface. Perhaps unsurprisingly, following the devastation suffered by European and Asian cities in the Second World War, the theme of technological collapse, and with it a revised form of pastoral, haunts twentieth-century science fiction. In George R. Stewart's futuristic eco-novel *Earth Abides* (1949), a deadly virus strikes down humanity, and, gradually, the technology surrounding the few scattered survivors begins to collapse. Generators and turbines run down. The motorways crumble. Abandoned cars rust in the driveway. As the lights are extinguished, humanity is surrounded by the encroaching darkness of wild nature. At first, like Daniel Defoe's eponymous hero in *The Life and Strange and Surprising Adventures of Robinson Crusoe* (1719) the survivors live, like scavengers, off the shipwrecked technology that surrounds them. Abandoned shops and stores provide a seemingly limitless means of meeting the necessities of life.[27] But, by the end of Stewart's novel, a new form of existence has come into being, one that harmoniously coexists with the nature that has returned to replace vanished civilization. Retreating into a stone-age world of magic, and ancestor worship, where the most advanced technological device available is the longbow, the descendants of the few survivors achieve a kind of felicity, which exactly parallels the Arcadian idyll of the Renaissance poet. Asked, by the last of the survivors of the original catastrophe, whether he is happy in a world which has never known the light bulb or the refrigerator, the young man who represents the future of what has emerged as the 'tribe' responds: 'Yes, I am happy. Things are as they are, and I am part of them.'[28] Quiescently accepting its new role, humanity has, at last, achieved a kind of maturity. The only artefact from the technologically sophisticated past which the descendants employ are the millions of scattered dimes, nickels, and quarters (the novel is set in what was once Northern California) which are put to new and unforeseen uses; they are beaten into arrowheads.[29] The erasure of money, and the reappearance of the 'true', primitive, value of metal,

reminds us that, at heart, Stewart's novel is profoundly conservative, conforming to what I. F. Clarke has described as the survival narrative in which
the 'happy return to the primeval state' represents:

> ... the most extreme statement in the argument against the imputed
> indifference and inhumanity of industrialized society ... the symbol of an
> absolute separation between humanity and technology, of a total disjunc-
> tion between the industrial past and the inchoate future.[30]

In such works, 'the imagined annihilation of the contemporary world' produces, in the end, a feeling of happiness derived from 'the contemplation of
the return to the uncomplicated, primeval state of nature'.[31]

The renaissance equivalent to this 'happy return to the primeval state' was
inherited from the Eclogues of Virgil who first mapped the geography of
Arcadia. The pastoral world of shepherds and shepherdesses, beloved of the
Spenserian generation of poets and their imitators (Sir Philip Sidney, Michael
Drayton, Samuel Daniel, Giles and Phineas Fletcher, George Wither, and, in
certain moments, Shakespeare and Milton), would culminate, in England,
in the poetry of Andrew Marvell. This, however, was a world in retreat from
any idea of modernity.[32] The pastoral mode was the 'literature of stasis', a
retreat into frozen time, devoid of human ambition.[33] The pastoral poet or
writer evoked an imagined antiquity in which 'nature serves man with the
necessities and even the luxuries he requires' in contrast to the modern
world where a 'struggle for survival' is the rule.[34] Pastoral writing thus looks
back to the past while it also prophesies an imagined future which is also a
return to a golden age, based on the vision of futurity to be found in Virgil's
Fourth Eclogue:

> Justice is to return, and the rule of Saturn is to begin anew. The Age of Iron
> will pass gradually from the earth, and a golden race of men will inherit
> it. The earth will produce fruit without man's toil, the ox will no longer be
> frightened by the lion ... In time there will be no more shipping, no more
> wars, and no wounding of the earth with ploughs.[35]

This is not a world where technology has failed, so much as it is a mental
construction in which there is simply no need for technology. What point
would there be for the 'prostheses' of tools, devices, or engines, when
nature is already, willingly, moulding herself to a simpler pattern of human
desire? In this respect, although pastoral writing could operate as a mask

from behind which the Elizabethan or Jacobean poet could grumble, discontentedly, at the corruption of courtly life and contemporary politics, pastoral forms were fundamentally opposed to the modernity preached by those, such as Bacon, who had begun to envisage the conquest of nature by human artifice.[36]

It is not, I think, coincidence that the vogue for pastoral writing should have reached its climax, in England at any rate, in the last years of the sixteenth century and the early years of the seventeenth century when a new vision of modernity, fashioned by mechanical culture, was springing into being. Shakespeare was particularly alert to the possibilities and impossibilities of pastoral: 'Hath not old custom made this life more sweet / Than that of painted pomp?', asks Duke Senior in *As You Like It* (1600) (II. i. 2–3). Banished from civility into the wild woods of the Forest of Arden, the duke and his court discover true civility. 'Are not these woods / More free from peril than the envious court?' (II. i. 3–4) he continues, rehearsing the familiar pastoral trope that only in the civilized world is there to be found true savagery. Pastoral of this kind has been described as conforming to a three-fold pattern: first the expulsion or the retreat, then the 'sojourn in a pastoral setting', and finally a return to the ordinary, everyday, world.[37] But pastoral also parallels, perhaps surprisingly, the modern idea of the 'survivor narrative'. Exiled from the normal world, the refugees in Arcadia learn to start again, and, once their time in Arcadia is played out and they have returned to their rightful position in the world then they can be reckoned as survivors twice over. They have survived the original catastrophe, and, purged of worldly pomp and vanity, they have survived the sometimes-dubious pleasures of the brief return to a purer state of being.

Shakespeare's exploration (and satirization) of pastoral forms in his account of the fortunes of the banished court in *As You Like It* can be thought of as an earlier version of the 'survivor narrative' that he later explored more completely in *The Tempest* (1611). But *The Tempest* also gestures towards a central theme with which we have been concerned throughout this study: the dominion over the brute forces of nature by human cunning and artifice. Indeed, if any play by Shakespeare *should* have been written by Francis Bacon, it is, surely, *The Tempest*, so Baconian are its concerns. *The Tempest* begins with the seventeenth-century equivalent of a technological catastrophe: the shipwreck which casts Alonso, King of Naples and his retinue onto the island inhabited by another set of survivors, Prospero and his daughter Miranda. For all his magical powers, Prospero is a truly Baconian figure, overmastering nature by means of his superior technology, and what the play terms his 'art'. Prospero bends nature to his capricious will just as he binds the elements and the indigenous inhabitants of the island, Caliban and Ariel, to his service. Prospero's 'staff' and 'book' are, in this respect, the equivalent of those technological prostheses by which nature is subdued, channelled, and finally bent to human ends in the more familiar story of technological evolution. For Prospero and Miranda did not stumble upon the magical island entirely divested of the technological prowess necessary to survive. Rather, as Prospero explains, they were cast adrift in a way that is familiar to all such survival narratives. Like Crusoe, or like the central character of Stewart's *Earth Abides*, who labours to protect the contents of the university library as an ark from which, he believes, one day, civilization will be reared once more, Prospero carries with him his 'volumes that / I prize above my dukedom' (I. ii. 167–9). It is through these books and his staff, instruments of his 'rough magic' that, in a fantasy of control over the forces of nature of which Leonardo could only dream and Bacon merely envy, Prospero has tampered with the stupendous forces of nature. For all that this art is abandoned by the close of the play, the story of Prospero and Miranda conforms to those later 'survival narratives' where survivors of the wreck of civilization are allowed to deploy the last vestiges of their superior technology to subdue the wilderness which they encounter around them.

But set against Prospero's mastery of nature by art, the play proposes an alternative vision of survival, one indebted to the modes of pastoral, once more, in which an imagined future is created, in which technology has all but vanished. This is the vision of Gonzalo, courtier to Alonso, who, seeking to consol the king, offers him the beguiling prospect of Year Zero. For the shipwreck, which has cast them on to Prospero's island, is an opportunity to begin again:

> I'th'commonwealth I would by contraries
> Execute all things. For no kind of traffic
> Would I admit, no name of magistrate;
> Letters should not be known; riches, poverty,
> And use of service, none; contract, succession,
> Bourn, bound of land, tilth, vineyard, none;
> No use of metal, corn, or wine, or oil;
> No occupation, all men idle, all;
> And women too – but innocent and pure;
> No sovereignty –
>   . . .

All things in common nature should produce
Without sweat or endeavour. Treason, felony,
Sword, pike, knife, gun, or need of any engine,
Would I not have; but nature should bring forth
Of its own kind all foison, all abundance,
To feed my innocent people.

(II. i. 148–72)

To an idealist such as Gonzalo, the arrival on the island of the sophisticated European court offers a chance to turn the clock back to the supposedly primitive origins of human culture.

And yet, there is a paradox at the heart of Gonzalo's project, a paradox which, in John Carey's words, haunts all such utopian visions of a better world to be created out of the ruins of the old. Such visions, Carey writes 'aim at a new world, but most destroy the old . . . The aim of all utopias, to a greater or lesser extent, is to eliminate real people'.[38] In forbidding the establishment of trade ('traffic'), supremacy ('magistrate'), writing and communication ('letters'), hierarchies founded upon economic power ('riches, poverty . . . use of service'), legal title and ownership ('contract, succession, bourn, bound of land'), agricultural and industrial technology ('tilth, vineyard . . . metal, corn . . . wine . . . oil') and labour ('occupation'), Gonzalo has created a true 'contrary:' a plantation which is dedicated to regression, and which thus denies the very reason for its establishment. Undaunted, Gonzalo pushes his radical experiment forward: common ownership of the means of production, abolition of labour and the capital crime of treason, abandonment of the instruments of war, and, finally, a retreat into the very kernel of 'nature', the collapse not just of civility, but of civilization itself, with the forbidding of 'the need of any engine'. Recreating the Virgilian world, Gonzalo's commonwealth in *The Tempest* is a counter-argument to that restless, Baconian project of technological optimism that came to inform the seventeenth-century urge to master nature with the aid of devices, instruments, and artefacts. Indeed, Bacon's vision of a technologically driven future which he outlined in the pages of *New Atlantis* (1624) might easily be read as a riposte to visionaries such as Gonzalo, who believed that only by returning to a primitive state would humankind regain its forfeited place in Eden.

Gonzalo's fantasy is a familiar one. To abandon technology and to thus return to a supposedly more primitive state, is to set about re-creating what Gonzalo calls the 'perfection' of the 'Golden age', that land of lost content which is discovered sometimes in the re-creation of an imagined past, and sometimes in the anticipation of an imagined future. It has proved seductive to visionaries over the centuries. It is also a flight out of the modern world, with all its confusion and complexity, into something supposedly cleaner, purer, and simpler. We meet a similar vision in Ben Jonson's *Volpone: Or, The Fox* (1607), when the anti-hero of the play, the cunningly inventive Volpone, offers a justification of his peculiar art whereby human greed is transformed into gold:

> . . . I gain
> No common way; I use no trade, no venture;
> I wound no earth with plough-shares, fat no beasts,
> To feed the shambles; have no mills for iron,
> Oil, corn, or men, to grind them into powder:
> I blow no subtle glass, expose no ships
> To threat'nings of the furrowed sea;
> I turn no monies in public bank,
> Nor usure private.[39]

Volpone's defence of his scurrilous activities rests on a revised vision of pastoral, in which the arts of civilization and civility, which include trade, 'venture', commerce, and industry, are foresworn. Volpone's specious self-defence hinges on a vision of fallen technology, in which the human and animal worlds are no longer wounded and ground down in the 'mills of iron' which, as we have seen, were already a reality in early seventeenth-century London.

In *The Tempest*, Shakespeare culled Gonzalo's vision from Montaigne's essay, 'Of Cannibals' which evoked the precise opposite, or as Gonzalo would say 'contrary', to civilized European life. Citing the accounts of an unnamed returnee from what he called 'Antarctic France' (Brazil, in 1557), Montaigne's essay evoked a pre-lapsarian Eden, untainted by civility where nature exists in a purer form: 'We have so overloaded the beauty and richness of [nature's] works by our inventions that we have quite smothered her' Montaigne observed.[40] Shakespeare, too, seems, at least momentarily, to have been seduced by a similar vision. Writing, it would seem, with an opened copy of Montaigne's *Essays*, in the translation of John Florio published in 1603 before him, in Gonzalo's speech Shakespeare transcribed, virtually word for word, an image of a better society, which had returned to the mythical past of the golden age:

> It is a nation, would I answer *Plato*, that hath no kinde of traffike, no knowledge of Letters, no intelligence of numbers, no name of magistrate, nor of

politike superiority; no use of service, of riches or of povertie; no contracts, no successions, no partitions, no occupation but idle; no respect of kindred, but common, no apparell but naturall, no manuring of lands, no use of wine, corne, or mettle.[41]

But the idylls of Gonzalo and Montaigne are defined not by what they are, but by what they are not. They are enterprises founded on absence.

Gonzalo's desire to start over once more and to remould the world according to some better pattern has proved seductive. In England, within thirty years of the first appearance in print of The Tempest, Gerrard Winstanley and his comrades (the 'Diggers' or 'True Levellers') had sought to construct a rather different kind of Eden with the establishment of their own 'plantation' at St George's Hill, near Cobham in Surrey in 1649. Writing after the collapse of his project, and surrounded and opposed by the spiritual and political heirs of Antonio and Sebastian who mock Gonzalo's imagined future in The Tempest, Winstanley explained the kernel of his 'revelations', which was nothing less than the restoration of the earth so that it would become, once more, Edenic. Just like Shakespeare's Gonzalo (though with rather more analytical force) in his Fire in the Bush (1650), Winstanley imagined a future in which commerce and trade had been abolished, since 'buying and selling of the earth, with the fruits of the earth' was no more than 'an imaginary art', a purely artificial manipulation of human wants and desires.[42] Unlike Gonzalo's vision, however, Winstanley's doomed experiment in primitive communism was not rooted in a distrust of technology or 'improvement'.[43] Winstanley's utopia in fact broadly shares a Baconian spirit of optimism. Thus, in The Law of Freedom in a Platform (1652) Winstanley wrote that the 'five fountains whence all arts and sciences have their influences' embrace husbandry, gardening, mining, pastoralism, and the work of those 'carpenters, joiners, thrusters [turners?], plough-makers, instrument-makers' by whose labours we 'may find out the secret[s] of nature'.[44]

For Thomas Hobbes, on the other hand, a return to a more primitive form of existence could only spell disaster. In the famous cadences of the thirteenth chapter of Leviathan (1651) Hobbes spelt out precisely what the Year Zero endeavour of pastoral visionaries would, in his view, amount to. 'In such condition', Hobbes wrote:

... there is no place for Industry; because the fruit thereof is uncertain: and consequently no Culture of the Earth; no Navigation nor use of the commodities that may be imported by Sea; no commodious Building; no

Instruments of moving, and removing such things as require much force; no Knowledge of the face of the Earth; no account of Time; no Arts; no Letters; no Society; and which is worst of all, continuall feare and danger of violent death; And the life of man, solitary, poore, nasty, brutish, and short.[45]

Hobbes's description of the 'Natural Condition of Mankind' in the absence of that 'common Power' which was the sovereign force in the commonwealth produces not the scriptural Eden, nor the Golden Age, nor Montaigne's natural primitivism, but a state of endless terror, punctuated, one may imagine, by the fearful cries of the victims of such a return to simplicity, in a world without machines or instruments.[46]

Conclusion: The machine stops

At the heart of the argument over technology lies that original Aristotelian opposition of art against nature that we have been tracing throughout this book. Today, that argument has resurfaced in the form of argument and counter-argument over environmental degradation and its effects on the planet and the human and animal life which is sustained by a nature which is not, as seventeenth-century mechanists once believed, truculently ungovernable and only to be mastered by overwhelming force. We might therefore conclude that the mental world of our Renaissance forbears who set about the task of submitting nature to human ingenuity was, in this respect, vastly different from our own. Yet, as we have seen, a sixteenth-century mining engineer such as Georgius Agricola could write with great eloquence of the destructive impact that his beloved miners could make on the surrounding landscape, while John Milton's argument with the machine centred on the deluded (so he believed) sense that humanity could somehow operate autonomously.

A quite different approach to the 'art versus nature' antithesis has been canvassed by those who, today, argue that the distinction between art and nature, or between the organic and the manufactured, has all but collapsed: 'the overlap of the mechanical and the lifelike increases year after year . . . The meanings of "mechanical" and "life" are being stretching until all complicated things can be perceived as machines, and all self-sustaining machines can be perceived as alive.'[47] *Contra* Aristotle, not only it is at least possible to imagine machines that are capable of replication, or even reproduction, but machines may even be said to possess the beginnings of that mimetic facility which had once been seen as the preserve only of human beings. So, too, microbiologists have begun to conceive of the 'natural' form of the body as a complex sequence of mechanical activities, operating at the molecular level. 'Molecular machines', composed out of protein, are understood as 'the main engineering material of living cells':

> Just as today's engineers build machinery as complex as piano players and robot arms from ordinary motors, bearings, and moving parts, so tomorrow's biochemists will be able to use protein molecules as motors, bearings, and moving parts to build robot arms which will themselves be able to handle individual molecules.[48]

Whether or not this imagined future comes to pass, here is the reproductive fantasy of the technologist, which we have already encountered in those narcissistic fantasies of male generation that flourished in the sixteenth and seventeenth centuries, in their most acute form. Nature has, at last, been recreated as artificial.

But are these reproductive fantasies of artificial life anything more than metaphors? Writing in the early 1950s, Norbert Wiener pointed out that 'the nervous system and the automatic machine are fundamentally alike in that they are devices which make decisions on the basis of decisions they have made in the past'.[49] For Wiener, however, the fact that the machine and the body might be 'fundamentally alike' did not mean that machines should be understood as being 'alive' in any sense. Such a confusion of the organic and the inorganic was a semantic rather than a scientific issue:

> Now that certain analogies of behaviour are being observed between the machine and the living organism, the problem as to whether the machine is alive or not is, for our purposes, semantic and we are at liberty to answer it one way or the other as best suits our convenience. As Humpty Dumpty says about some of his more remarkable words, 'I pay them extra, and make them do what I want.'[50]

Alive to the seductive power of metaphor, Wiener's mechanical bodies existed as statements of similarity, not reality.

However, under the pressure of new, digital, technologies, the world about us has been re-mapped. A regime of artificiality or (to appropriate a phrase coined by the French 'urbanist' and theorist, Paul Virilio) 'total . . . motorization' has come into being, at least in theory.[51] In the postmodern world inhabited by Jean Baudrillard, the distinctions between the natural and the artificial simply no longer apply. Thus, Baudrillard can describe the 1991 conflict in the Arabian Gulf as 'war stripped bare by its technicians, and then re-clothed by them with all the artifices of electronics, as though with a second skin'.[52] Even the categories of 'real' and 'unreal' have buckled, as Baudrillard urges us to contemplate 'models of a real without origin or reality: a hyperreal'.[53] This new reality is a product of the reproductive or 'replicative' capacities of systems, programmes, machines, mechanisms, or even games, whereby an artificial order has come into being. This order is the product of 'miniaturized cells, matrices, and memory banks, models of control – and it can be reproduced an infinite number of times from these'.[54]

Herbert A. Simon, a computer scientist, psychologist, and (in 1978) Nobel Laureate in Economics, agrees with the philosophers of machine-made reality that 'The world we live in today is much more a man-made, or artificial, world than it is a natural world.'[55] For Simon, the world, which has been understood since the late-seventeenth century by way of the agency of 'natural science' is now in need of what he terms 'artificial science'. Such a science would be devoted to the study of the world of artefacts and artificial systems, rather than natural forms and phenomena. Yet, for all the celebration of artificiality above nature on the part of modern theorists of the real and the simulated, Simon recognizes that the project of 'artificial science' has to overcome a deeply engrained human prejudice, which is betrayed at the level of language. This prejudice is implicit in the Aristotelian and Augustinian views of the world we have touched upon in this account. So, Simon remarks upon the many synonyms which exist for the very word 'artificial:' 'affected, factitious, manufactured, pretended, sham, simulated, spurious, trumped up, unnatural', together with antonyms such as 'actual, genuine, honest, natural, real, truthful, unaffected'. Surveying this vocabulary of artifice, Simon argues that 'our language seems to reflect man's deep distrust of his own products'.[56]

And yet, as Mary Tiles and Hans Oberdiek observe:

> Once we start to think about it, it is not easy to see how to draw the line between natural and artificial ... It may be easy enough to distinguish between imitation pearls and real ones, but how much more difficult to classify domesticated animals (Siamese cats, Jersey cows, Swaledale sheep) or fi-hybrid tomatoes.[57]

Paradoxically or ironically, depending on your point of view, an insistence on the 'real' may only serve to heighten the aura of artifice that has come to surround us. By the same token, for all that modern cultural theorists might hymn that uncomfortable fusion of artifice and nature represented by the cyborg, such quasi-organic creations, as they are imagined in cinema or in science fiction, are rarely benign.[58] The cyborg has, however, come to mark the *terminus ad quem* of any boundary between the organic and the artificial. 'From the seventeenth century till now', writes Donna Haraway, 'machines could be animated – given ghostly souls to make them speak or move or to account for their orderly development and mental capacities.'[59] Haraway, commenting on the ubiquity of cyborgs – 'creatures simultaneously animal and machine, who populate worlds ambiguously natural and crafted' – in contemporary science fiction, in medicine, in industry and in the military complex, proposes a history of mechanism which is, in essence, a history of the 'crafted' as opposed to the 'natural'.[60] Such creatures, like Shakespeare's Coriolanus, are forged rather than born, and may be considered the product of technique rather than biology. Although we might recall that the very word 'forgery' is derived from the Latin *fabricare*, to make or fabricate, the distinction between the fake or inauthentic, and the real or authentic, has been eroded (Haraway argues) to the point where policing that boundary has become all but impossible.[61] Instead, a new machine has come into being, and with it a new order of reality:

> Late twentieth-century machines have made thoroughly ambiguous the difference between natural and artificial, mind and body, and many other distinctions that used to apply to organisms and machines. Our machines are disturbingly lively, and we ourselves frighteningly inert.[62]

Contemplating the conceptual world of early-modern people, we might assume that any such anxiety over the boundaries which separated human beings from their devices or mechanisms was altogether alien to their sensibilities. How could a pre-industrial culture, in other words, harbour a residual fear that their instruments, devices, and machines might undermine the distinction between the biological and the artificial? But as we have seen, the possibility of nature being overwhelmed by 'art' was, in fact, the mainspring of so many Renaissance ideas about the power of human invention. In this respect, modern theorists of artificial reality may be unknowingly tracing a landscape whose features first began to be mapped in the European Renaissance.

Works of fiction, particularly science fiction, have, of course, endlessly exploited the tendency to conceive of technology as possessing vestiges of latent humanity, even savagery. In the late nineteenth century, in Samuel Butler's novel of a dystopic society, *Erewhon* (1872), machines have been either destroyed or consigned to the museum, not because of what they are, but because of what they might become, as a philosopher of Erewhon explains: 'I fear none of the existing machines; what I fear is the extraordinary rapidity with which they are becoming something very different to what they are present.'[63] That Darwinian possibility, that machines might evolve in obedience to a set of laws that lie outside the designs of their creators, is a theme which has become a mainspring of contemporary science fiction. Underpinning such fantasies is the belief that machines might triumph (if they have not done so already) over the ultimate power which humans hold over them: that we can simply switch them off, pull the plug, disconnect them. Struggling to resist being switched off, as it wages psychological warfare against its human opponent, is the endeavour of the softly spoken, eminently reasonable, and murderously destructive computer HAL in Stanley Kubrick's film, *2001: A Space Odyssey* (1968), which is yet another modern manifestation of our propensity to see machines, in fiction if not in real life, as dangerous rivals.[64]

Machines will outlive us. That is the message of fictions such as Brian Aldiss's 1958 short story *But Who Can Replace A Man?* and Ray Bradbury's *There Will Come Soft Rains* (1950).[65] These two stories, published within a few years of the detonations of the atom bombs at Hiroshima and Nagasaki, both powerfully evoke a world in which all that survives of humankind is its technology, still restlessly performing its mechanized rituals, but to no purpose, since human life has disappeared. A similar idea informs Joan Didion's essay 'At the Dam' (1970), in which she recalls her first visit to the Hoover Dam. The essay ends with a vision of a world given over to technology, with no human presence whatsoever:

> Of course that was the image I had seen always, seen it without quite realizing what I saw, a dynamo finally free of man, splendid at last in its absolute isolation, transmitting power and releasing water to a world where no one is.[66]

Alternatively, of course, machines might simply switch themselves off. In E. M. Forster's short story, *The Machine Stops*, first published in the *Oxford and Cambridge Review* of 1909, humankind is imagined as being sustained by an enormously complex machine, responsible for every aspect of existence. As time passes, however, no single person can any longer understand the workings of the machine, which has taken on the attributes of a deity, rather than a technological device. But this technological deity proves to be untrustworthy:

> No one confessed that the Machine was out of hand. Year by year it was served with increased efficiency and decreased intelligence. The better a man knew his own duties upon it, the less he understood the duties of his neighbour, and in all the world there was not one who understood the monster as a whole . . . Humanity, in its desire for comfort had overreached itself.[67]

Gradually, the machine grinds to a halt, and with it perishes mere fleshly existence. For the machine is conceived of as a 'sin against the body . . . centuries of wrong against the muscles and the nerves'.[68]

Writing before Freud had begun to describe technology as a 'graft', Forster conceived of his machine in terms of some form of original sin perpetuated against the organic body. Probably few people, today, would conceive of machines and technology in such directly theological terms. And yet the British environmentalist writer George Monbiot begins a recent work on the causes, effects, and remedies of global warming by rehearsing the familiar story of Faustus, in Christopher Marlowe's version. Monbiot refuses to read the Faust story as an allegory, preferring to interpret the Faustian narrative as a 'metaphor' for the impact of humanity on its environment.[69] Perhaps, however, he need not have been so circumspect, since, as we have seen, early-modern people saw the entire technological impulse as the result of the catastrophic collapse represented by the Fall of humankind.

But even if we have abandoned the overt language of sin, the accompanying idea of a catastrophic collapse is not so easily jettisoned. Indeed, it has been argued that the collapse of technology and our technological systems seems to hover just over the horizon. 'In the present age of terror', writes Steven E. Jones, 'technology is both a threat and a potential target, a means of destruction as well as the "fabric" (network, web, weave) of society that is threatened with destruction.'[70] Or as John Gray writes, the 'fragility' of modern life is increasing: 'as human beings become more closely interlinked, breakdowns in one part of the world spread more readily to the rest'.[71] The human world is envisaged as a gigantic network of interlinked mechanical and digital functions, which, in Gray's view, are on the brink of collapse. We have never, it seems, been as close to a retreat back into the pastoral as we are now.

For all its dynamic optimism, the artistic, intellectual, technological and literary culture of the European Renaissance was constructed around a very similar idea of failure. First, there was the original collapse of humanity, which provided the theological basis of so much art and literature in the period. Second, and particularly for humanist intellectuals, there was the spectre of the collapse of that great source of ideas, rituals, architecture, literature, art, and technology which was ancient Rome. In Edmund Spenser's poem 'The Ruines of Time' (1591), the Roman past is catalogued, and then evoked as 'dust':

> High towers, faire temples, goodly theatres,
> Strong walls, rich porches, princelie palaces,
> Large Streetes, brave houses, sacred sepulchres,
> Sure gates, sweete gardens, stately galleries,
> Wrought with faire pillours, and fine imageries,
> All those (ô pitie) now are turned to dust,
> And overgrowen with blacke oblivions rust.[72]

Like an abandoned and discarded tool, the 'wrought' world of Rome has rusted over. Based on a sixteenth-century French original, Spenser's poem might nevertheless function perfectly well as a futuristic vision of London or New York after the apocalypse.[73]

The spectre of the Roman collapse was mournfully alluring to a poet such as Spenser, as much as it was to the historian, Edward Gibbon when, in the opening page of his *History of the Decline and Fall of the Roman Empire* (1776–88), he described the Roman collapse as 'a revolution which will ever be remembered, and is still felt by the nations of the earth'.[74] The decay of the Roman Empire is a phenomenon that still has the power to fascinate, engendering multiple and contradictory explanations among historians of culture, technology, and human society.[75] Rome is, for us as much as our early-modern ancestors, quite literally the *locus classicus* of all our narratives, myths, images, and legends of ruin. Gazing at the ruins of Rome, and speculating on how such an enterprise could have so completely vanished from human life, Montaigne was driven to uncover a technological parallel. In 1581 Montaigne surveyed the ruins of Rome and struggled to make sense of the fragments that lay scattered around him:

He said that one saw nothing of Rome but the sky under which it had stood and the plan of its site; that this knowledge that he had of it was an abstract and contemplative knowledge of which there was nothing perceptible to the senses; that those who said that one at least saw the ruins of Rome said too much, for the ruins of so awesome a machine would bring more honour and reverence to its memory: this was nothing but its sepulchre.[76]

Overwhelmed by melancholy, Montaigne compared the ruins of this 'awesome . . . machine' to a 'wonderful body' whose 'disfigured limbs' were 'broken and shattered' by the terrified survivors of the catastrophe.[77] Contemplating the ruined mechanism, Montaigne perceived only fragments, 'paltry rubble . . . pieces of tile and broken pots'.[78] Nothing else remained of the mighty engine, save what could be harvested by the imagination.

NOTES

Preface

1 Humphrey Jennings, *Pandaemonium 1660–1886: The Coming of the Machine as Seen by Contemporary Observers* ed. Mary-Lou Jennings and Charles Madge (London: André Deutsch, 1985), p. xxxv.

2 Jennings, *Pandaemonium 1660–1886*, p. xxxvi.

3 Jennings, *Pandaemonium 1660–1886*, p. 5.

4 See, in particular, Carlo M. Cipolla, *Clocks and Culture 1300–1700* (1978, reprint, New York and London: W. W. Norton, 2003); Otto Mayr, *Authority, Liberty, and Automatic Machinery in Early Modern Europe* (Baltimore and London: Johns Hopkins University Press, 1986); Horst Brederkamp, *The Lure of Antiquity and the Cult of the Machine* trans. Allison Brown (Princeton: Markus Wiener, 1995); Henry Heller, *Labour, Science and Technology in France 1500–1620* (Cambridge: Cambridge University Press, 1996); Dennis Des Chene, *Spirits and Clocks: Machine and Organism in Descartes* (Ithaca and London: Cornell University Press, 2001); Jessica Wolfe, *Humanism, Machinery, and Renaissance Literature* (Cambridge: Cambridge University Press, 2004); Adam Max Cohen, *Shakespeare and Technology: Dramatizing Early Modern Technological Revolutions* (New York and London: Palgrave Macmillan, 2007).

5 See Lewis Mumford, *Technics and Human Civilization* (1934, reprint, New York and London: Harcourt Brace, 1963), p. 151–5.

6 J. A. Mazzeo, *Renaissance and Revolution: The Re-making of European Thought* (London: Secker and Warburg, 1967), p. 306. For a more recent work in this vein see Victor Davis Hanson, *Why the West Has Won: Carnage and Culture from Salamis to Vietnam* (London: Faber and Faber, 2001).

7 John Hooper and Kate Connolly, 'Berlusconi Breaks Ranks over Islam' *The Guardian* (27 September 2001), p. 3.

8 See Arnold Pacey, *Technology in World Civilization* (Cambridge, MA: MIT Press, 1990), pp. 73–107; James E. McClellan III and Harold Dorn, *Science and Technology in World History* (Baltimore and London: Johns Hopkins University Press, 1999), pp. 99–174; John M. Hobson, *The Eastern Origins of Western Civilization* (Cambridge: Cambridge University Press, 2004), pp. 29–96.

9 Douglass C. North and Robert Paul Thomas, *The Rise of the Western World: A New Economic History* (Cambridge: Cambridge University Press, 1973), p. 1.

10 John Gray, *Al Qaeda and What It Means to Be Modern* (London: Faber and Faber, 2003), p. 101. For further reflections on this theme, see Philip Brey, 'Theorizing Modernity and Technology' in Thomas J. Misa, Philip Brey, and Andrew Feenberg (eds), *Modernity and Technology* (Cambridge, MA, and London: MIT Press, 2003), pp. 33–71; Robert Friedel, *A Culture of Improvement: Technology and the Western Millenium* (Cambridge, MA, and London: MIT Press, 2007), pp. 1–11.

11 Abbot Payson Usher, *A History of Mechanical Inventions* (Cambridge, MA: Harvard University Press, 1954), p. 116.

12 Michael Fores, '*Technik*: Or Mumford Reconsidered' in A. Rupert Hall and Norman Smith (eds), *History of Technology* vol. 6 (London: Mansell, 1981), p. 129.

13 See Michael Fores, 'Uneven Mirrors: Towards a History of Engines' in Graham Hollister-Short (ed.), *History of Technology* vol. 19 (London and Washington: Mansell, 1997), p. 93.

14 These definitions are offered, respectively, by Garet Garrett (1926), Donald Michael (1962), Norbert Weiner (1954), Henry Ford (1926), and Ludvic Aškenazy (1958). See Arthur O. Lewis Jr (ed.), *Of Men and Machines* (New York: E. P. Dutton, 1963), p. xiv.

1 The Renaissance machine and its discontents

1 Aristotle, *Ethics* trans. J. A. K. Thomson (Harmondsworth: Penguin Books, 1953), p. 208.

2 Aristotle, *Ethics*, p. 208.

3 Martin Heidegger, 'The Question Concerning Technology' in David Farrell Krell (ed.), *Martin Heidegger Basic Writings 1927–1964* (London: Routledge, 1978), p. 318. For a helpful commentary on Heidegger's essay, see Don Ihde, 'Heidegger's Philosophy of Technology' in Robert C. Scharff and Val Dusek (eds), *Philosophy of Technology: The Technological Condition* (Oxford: Blackwell Publishing, 2003), pp. 277–92.

4 The OED claims 1628 as the first appearance of the English word 'technologie', though this term was not (according to the OED) applied to the 'mechanical or industrial arts' until the eighteenth century. Jessica Wolfe has traced the sixteenth-century uses of the Latin term *technologia* (derived from the Greek τεχνολογια), relating them 'not to mechanical practices but rather to rhetorical or philological methods' associated with humanism. See Jessica Wolfe, *Humanism, Machinery, and Renaissance Literature* (Cambridge: Cambridge University Press, 2004), pp. 3–4.

5 Sigmund Freud, *Civilization and Its Discontents* in *The Standard Edition of the Complete Psychological Works* vol. 21, trans. and ed. James Strachey (1961, reprint, London: Vintage, Hogarth Press, Institute for Psychoanalysis, 2001), p. 90.

6   Freud, *Civilization and Its Discontents*, pp. 90–1.

7   Freud, *Civilization and Its Discontents*, p. 89.

8   Freud, *Civilization and Its Discontents*, pp. 91–2. For a wide-ranging analysis of Freud's ideas on prosthesis in relation to modernism, see Tim Armstrong, *Modernism, Technology and the Body* (Cambridge: Cambridge University Press, 1998), pp. 77–105.

9   On the 'dialectic' between utopian and dystopian views of technology, see R. L. Rutsky, *High Technē: Art and Technology from the Machine Aesthetic to the Posthuman* (Minneapolis and London: University of Minnesota Press, 1999), pp. 73–4.

10 The concept of the 'Second Creation' may be traced back, via Johannes Scotus Erigena (Duns Scotus) and Hugo of St Victor, to Cicero's ideas in the *De natura deorum*, whereby humans create a 'second nature' by 'channelling the rivers . . . sowing and fertilizing the soil . . . planting trees . . . transforming the land into a new Garden of Eden'. See Thomas P. Hughes, *Human-Built World: How to Think About Technology and Culture* (Chicago and London: University of Chicago Press, 2004), p. 17.

11 Francis Bacon, *The Advancement of Learning* (1605) ed. G. W. Kitchin (London: J. M. Dent, 1973), p. 138.

12 See John Plamenatz, *Hegel, Marx and Engels, and the Idea of Progress* rev. M. E. Plamenatz and Robert Wokler (2nd edition, London and New York: Longman, 1992), p. 301.

13 See R. Murray Schaffer, *The Tuning of the World* (Toronto: McClelland and Stewart, 1977), pp. 43–67; Bruce R. Smith, *The Acoustic World of Early Modern England: Attending to the O-Factor* (Chicago and London: University of Chicago Press, 1999), p. 49. One of the earliest attempts to recreate the sound texture of pre-industrial life is to be found in the masterful opening of Johan Huizinga's *The Waning of the Middle Ages* (1925). As Francis Haskell has observed of Huizinga's work: 'No serious historical masterpiece has ever responded so spontaneously to the sights and sounds of earlier human societies.' See Francis Haskell, *History and Its Images: Art and the Interpretation of the Past* (New Haven and London: Yale University Press, 1993), p. 470.

14 Kenneth Sisam (ed.), *Fourteenth Century Verse and Prose* (Oxford: Clarendon Press, 1925), p. 169. The poem is found in the British Library MS. Arundel 292 (f. 71b), which dates from the first half of the fifteenth century.

15 Sisam (ed.), *Fourteenth Century Verse and Prose*, p. 170.

16 David Landes, *The Wealth and Poverty of Nations: Why Some are So Rich and Some So Poor* (1998, reprint, London: Little, Brown, 2001), p. 46.

17 Thomas Dekker, *The Seven Deadly Sinnes of London* (London, 1606), pp. 25–6.

18 John Ruskin, *The Two Paths* (1859) in Alasdair Clayre (ed.), *Nature and Industrialization* (Oxford: Oxford University Press, 1977), pp. 137, 138.

19 Tomas Deloney, *The Pleasant Historie of Iohn Winchcomb in his yonguer yeares called Iack of Newbery* (London, 1626), sig. D2. On the popularity of Deloney's work in the seventeenth century, see Paul Salzman, 'Deloney, Thomas (*d*. in or before 1600)', *Oxford Dictionary of National Biography* (Oxford University Press, 2004), Internet: www.oxforddnb.com/view/article/7463. Accessed 3 February 2007. I am grateful to Gary Taylor for alerting me to this reference.

20 See Steven E. Jones, *Against Technology: From the Luddites to Neo-Luddism* (New York and London: Routledge, 2006), p. 202.

21 Francis D. Klingender, *Art and the Industrial Revolution* ed. and rev. Arthur Elton (St Albans: Granada Publishing, 1975), p. 51.

22 James Snyder, *Northern Renaissance Art: Painting, Sculpture, The Graphic Arts from 1350 to 1575* rev. by Larry Silver and Henry Luttikhuizen (2nd edition, Upper Saddle River, NJ: Prentice Hall, 2005), p. 475.

23 R. H. Tawney, *Religion and the Rise of Capitalism* (1922, reprint, Harmondsworth: Penguin Books, 1966), p. 229.

24 Walter Endrei, 'Jean Errard (1554–1610) and his *Book of Machines: Le Premier Livre des instruments mathématiques méchaniques* of 1584' in Graham Hollister-Short and Frank A. J. L. James (eds), *History of Technology* vol. 17 (London: Mansell, 1995), p. 180.

25 Klingender, *Art and the Industrial Revolution*, pp. 51–2. Klingender (p. 52) sees this interest in representing the labour of ordinary craftsman as a 'strange intrusion' of an alien (that is protestant) tradition into Florentine artistic culture.

26 These works can be associated with the many representations of the forge of Vulcan or Hephaistos, blacksmith to the gods, to be found in pictures by (for example) Jan Brueghel (1568–1625), Diego Velásquez (1599–1660), and Mathieu le Nain (1607–77), in which a mythological subject was treated with a degree of technological realism. On the realistic qualities of the Velásquez *Forge of Vulcan* (painted before 1634), see Jonathan Brown, *Velázquez: Painter and Courtier* (New Haven and London: Yale University Press, 1986), p. 74.

27 Ovid, *Metamorphoses* trans. Mary M. Innes (Harmondsworth: Penguin Books, 1984), pp. 31–2.

28 Ovid, *Metamorphoses*, p. 33.

29 Jeffey Chipps Smith, *The Northern Renaissance* (London: Phaidon Press, 2004), p. 334.

30 See Neil MacLaren, *National Gallery Catalogues: The Dutch School 1600–1990* rev. Christopher Brown, 2 vols (London: National Gallery Publications, 1991), I, pp. 383–4, 387. Ruisdael has been described as the first European artist to make machines the 'principal theme' of his work. This claim is only sustainable if we ignore the vast body of technical illustration circulating in Europe from the late fifteenth century onwards. See Seymour Slive, *Jacob van Ruisdael Master of Landscape* (London: Royal Academy of Arts, 2005), p. 5.

31 Slive, *Jacob van Ruisdael*, pp. 11–12.

32 MacLaren, *National Gallery Catalogues: The Dutch School 1600–1990*, I, pp. 96, 112, 145–6.

33 Svetlana Alpers, *The Art of Describing: Dutch Art in the Seventeenth Century* (London: John Murray, 1983), p. 142.

34 For an account of the polder in Dutch culture, see Jared Diamond, *Collapse: How Societies Choose to Fail or Survive* (London: Penguin Books, 2006), pp. 219–20.

35 Simon Schama, *The Embarrassment of Riches: An Interpretation of Dutch Culture in the Golden Age* (London: Fontana Press, 1987) pp. 42, 44.

36 Anon., *The Pilgrimage of the Lyfe of the Manhode* ed. Avril Henry (London: Early English Text Society/Oxford University Press, 1985), p. 37.

37 The emblem, entitled '*spiritus vivificat*' is to be found in Zacharias Heyns, *Emblem-*

ata, Emblems Christienes, et Morales (Rotterdam, 1625). See Slive, *Jacob van Ruisdael*, p. 124.

38 On different kinds of watermill (overshot, undershot, and horizontal) and their relative efficiency, see Vacalav Smil, *Energy in World History* (Oxford: Westview Press, 1994), pp. 103–9.

39 Martha Teach Gnudi and Eugene S. Ferguson (eds), *The Various and Ingenious Machines of Agostino Ramelli* (New York and Aldershot: Dover Publications/Scolar Press, 1976), p. 50.

40 See Gnudi and Ferguson (eds), *The Various and Ingenious Machines of Agostino Ramelli*, p. 570. Treadmills, described in the *De Architectura* of Vitruvius, as well as in the *Codice Atlantico* of Leonardo da Vinci, were held to be suitable devices for slaves to operate. See Rhys Jenkins, 'An Elizabethan Human-Power Engine: John Payne and the History of the Treadmill' in Rhys Jenkins, *Links in the History of Engineering and Technology from Tudor Times: The Collected Papers of Rhys Jenkins* (1936, reprint, Freeport, NY: Books for Libraries Press, 1971), pp. 1–8.

41 Snyder, *Northern Renaissance Art*, p. 521.

42 On the device of the opened window in Northern Renaissance art, see Craig Harbison, *The Mirror of the Artist: Northern Renaissance Art in its Historical Context* (Upper Saddle River, NJ: Prentice Hall, 1995), p. 134.

43 On the role of shame in the 'civilizing process', see Norbert Elias, *Power and Civility* trans. Edmund Jephcott (New York: Pantheon Books, 1982), pp. 292–300.

44 The 'technology as gift' narrative was related to the Promethean story, to be found in the *Prometheus Unbound* of Aeschylus, which opens with the 'rebel' Prometheus punished for stealing the 'flowery splendour / Of all fashioning fire' from Zeus. See Aeschylus, *Prometheus Unbound* trans. Philip Vellacott (Harmondsworth: Penguin Books, 1961), p. 20.

45 St Augustine, *Concerning the City of God against the Pagans* trans. Henry Bettenson (Harmondsworth: Penguin Books, 1984), p. 1072.

46 Augustine, *City of God*, p. 1075.

47 David Noble, *The Religion of Technology: The Divinity of Man and the Spirit of Invention* (London: Penguin Books, 1999), p. 12.

48 Clive Gamble, *Timewalkers: The Prehistory of Global Colonization* (Harmondsworth: Penguin Books, 1993), p. 3.

49 See Colin Chant and David Goodman (eds), *Pre-Industrial Cities and Technology* (London and New York: Routledge in association with the Open University Press, 1999), p. 1.

50 Peter Harrison, *The Bible, Protestantism and Natural Science* (Cambridge: Cambridge University Press, 1998), p. 211.

51 Bacon, *The Advancement of Learning*, p. 38.

52 On Renaissance interpretations of Babel in terms of linguistic confusion, see Stuart Clark, 'The Rational Witchfinder: Conscience, Demonological Naturalism and Popular Superstitions' in Stephen Pumfrey, Paolo L. Rossi, and Maurice Slawinski (eds), *Science, Culture and Popular Belief in Renaissance Europe* (Manchester and New York: Manchester University Press, 1991), pp. 242–3; Timothy J. Reiss, *Knowledge, Discovery and Imagination in early Modern Europe* (Cambridge: Cambridge University Press, 1997), pp. 31, 46.

53 On Kircher's *Turris Babel*, see Paula Findeln, 'Introduction: The Last Man Who Knew Everything . . . or Did He?' in Paula Findeln (ed.), *Athanasius Kircher, The Last Man Who Knew Everything* (New York and London: Routledge, 2004), p. 4.

54 Antony Grafton, 'Kircher's Chronology' in Findeln (ed.), *Athanasius Kircher*, p. 173.

55 For an account of the Babel story in terms of the origins of technology, see Jonathan Sawday, 'The Fortunes of Babel: Technology, History, and Genesis 11:1–9' in Kevin Killeen and Peter Forshaw (eds) *The Word and the World: Biblical Exegesis and Early Modern Science* (Basingstoke: Palgrave Macmillan, 2007), pp. 191–214.

56 Dante Alighieri, *The Divine Comedy 3: Paradisio* trans. John D. Sinclair (London and New York: Oxford University Press, 1971), p. 379; Augustine, *City of God*, p. 657.

57 Polydore Vergil, *On Discovery (De inventoribus)* ed. and trans. Brian P. Copenhaver (Cambridge, MA, and London: Harvard University Press, 2002), p. 459.

58 Ovid, *Metamorphoses*, p. 184.

59 Ovid, *Metamorphoses*, p. 185.

60 Ovid, *Metamorphoses*, p. 185.

61 Ovid, *Metamorphoses*, p. 185.

62 On the fate of similar overreachers in Renaissance art, see Malcolm Bull, *The Mirror of the Gods: Classical Mythology in Renaissance Art* (London: Allen Lane, 2005), p. 145.

63 Christopher Marlowe, *The Works* ed. C. F. Tucker Brooke (Oxford: Clarendon Press, 1941), p. 146.

64 On Leicester's political ambitions, see Simon Adams, 'Dudley, Robert, Earl of Leicester (1532/3–1588)', *Oxford Dictionary of National Biography* (Oxford University Press, September 2004), Internet: www.oxforddnb.com/view/article/8160. Accessed 10 August 2006.

65 Ovid, *The xv. bookes of P. Ovidius Naso, entytuled Metamorphosis, translated oute of Latin into English meeter, by Arthur Golding Gentleman* (London, 1567), sig. A3ᵛ.

66 Robert Jones, *The First and the Second Book of Songs and Ayres Set Out to the Lute* (London, 1601), sig. Bᵛ.

67 See Christopher Allen, 'Ovid and Art' in Phillip Hardie (ed.), *The Cambridge Companion to Ovid* (Cambridge: Cambridge University Press, 2002), pp. 336–67. The subject of Icarus had a wide pictorial appeal. Illustrations based on the woodcuts of Virgil Solis, which first appeared in the edition of the *Metamorphoses* (Basel, 1543) by Jakob Micyllus, were recycled throughout the sixteenth century and later, as were those by Bernard Salomon, which first appeared in the *Metamorphose figurée* (Lyons, 1557). Among the artists (in addition to those mentioned above) who turned to the theme of Icarus and Daedalus in the period, were Tomaso Manzuoli (Maso da San Friano) (1531–71), Elias Greither (*c.* 1565–1646), Carlo Saraceni (1579–1620), and Rubens (1577–1640).

68 W. H. Auden, *Collected Shorter Poems 1930–1944* (London: Faber and Faber, 1962), p. 19.

69 On *Landscape with the Fall of Icarus*, see Michael Levey, *High Renaissance* (London: Penguin Books, 1975), p. 185; E. H. Gombrich, *The Story of Art* (London: Companion Book Club, 1956), p. 281.

70 Ovid, *The xv. bookes of P. Ovidius Naso*, pp. 98–9.

71 Ovid, *P. Ovidii Nasonis Metamorphosis* (Antwerp, 1591), p. 195.

72 For a reading of the 'heroic' figure of the ploughman, see Robert Baldwin, 'Peasant Imagery and Brueghel's "Fall of Icarus"' *Konsthistorisk Tidskrift/Journal of Art History* 55 (1986), pp. 101–14.

73 Marsilio Ficino, *Platonic Theology (Theologia platonica de immortalitate animorum)*, 6 vols, ed. and trans. Michael J. B. Allen and James Hankins (Cambridge, MA, and London: Harvard University Press, 2001–), IV, p. 173.

74 Snyder, *Northern Renaissance Art*, p. 523. For accounts of alternative, alchemical, readings of the image, see Pamela H. Smith, *The Body of the Artisan: Art and Experience in the Scientific Revolution* (Chicago and London: University of Chicago Press, 2004), p. 136.

2 Philosophy, power, and politics in Renaissance technology

1   See Paolo Galluzzi (ed.), *The Art of Invention: Leonardo and the Renaissance Engineers* (Florence: Giunti/Instituto e Museo di Storia della Scienza, 1996), p. 84.

2   Irma A. Richter (ed.), *The Notebooks of Leonardo da Vinci* (Oxford: Oxford University Press, 1980), p. 18.

3   Richter (ed.), *Notebooks of Leonardo*, p. 23. On the mechanical basis of Leonardo's anatomical studies, see Galluzzi (ed.), *The Art of Invention*, p. 78.

4   See E. H. Gombrich, Martin Kemp, and Jane Roberts, *Leonardo da Vinci* (London: Yale University Press/South Bank Centre, 1989), pp. 130–6.

5   Richter (ed.), *Notebooks of Leonardo*, p. 19.

6   Richter (ed.), *Notebooks of Leonardo*, p. 26.

7   Kenneth Clark, 'Introduction' to Carlo Pedretti, *Leonardo da Vinci Nature Studies from the Royal Library at Windsor Castle* (Catalogue to the exhibition at the J. Paul Getty Museum, Malibu, 15 November 1980–15 February 1981, The Metropolitan Museum of Art, New York, 4 March–7 June 1981) (n.p.; Johnson Reprint Corporation, 1980), p. 11.

8   Kenneth Clark, *Leonardo da Vinci: An Account of His Development as an Artist* (1939, revised edition, Harmondsworth: Penguin Books, 1967), p. 148.

9   Michael White, *Leonardo: The First Scientist* (London: Abacus Books, 2001), pp. 25, 292.

10 Michel Jeanneret, *Perpetual Motion: Transforming Shapes in the Renaissance from Da Vinci to Montaigne* trans. Nidra Poller (Baltimore and London: Johns Hopkins University Press, 2001), pp. 57, 61.

11 Giorgio Vasari, *Lives of the Artists* (2nd edition, 1568) trans. George Bull (Harmondsworth: Penguin Books, 1965), p. 256.

12 Galluzzi, *Art of Invention*, p. 55.

13 Galluzzi, *Art of Invention*, p. 61.

14 Hunter Rouse and Simon Ince, *History of Hydraulics* (Iowa Institute for Hydraulic Research: State University of Iowa, 1957), p. 44. Note that Galluzzi claims that 'it is not clear' what part Leonardo played in the Arno project; see Galluzzi, *Art of Invention*, p. 70.

15 Martin Kemp, 'The Vortex' in Gombrich, Kemp, and Roberts, *Leonardo da Vinci*, p. 119.

16 Galluzzi, *Art of Invention*, pp. 188–91.

17 Bruce R. Smith, *The Acoustic World of Early Modern England: Attending to the O-Factor* (Chicago and London: University of Chicago Press, 1999), pp. 49–51, 57.

18 Abbott Payson Usher, *A History of Mechanical Inventions* (Cambridge, MA: Harvard University Press, 1954), p. 337.

19 Technically, water power is a form of solar energy. Water-driven devices harness the force of falling water, which has been transported from lower levels (the oceans) to higher levels (rivers and streams) by evaporation caused by the sun's heat, and then fallen as rain or snow. See Terry S. Reynolds, *Stronger than a Hundred Men: A History of the Vertical Water Mill* (Baltimore and London: Johns Hopkins University Press, 1983), p. 9.

20 The mills produced 4.5 tonnes of flour each day. See Robert H. J. Sellin, 'The Large Roman Water Mill at Barbegal (France)' in Norman Smith (ed.), *History of Technology* vol. 8 (London and New York: Mansell, 1983), p. 101.

21 Paul Roberts, *The End of Oil: The Decline of the Petroleum Economy and the New Energy Order* (London: Bloomsbury, 2004), p. 26.

22 See Wolfgang von Stromer, 'Nuremberg as Epicentre of Invention and Innovation toward the End of the Middle Ages' in Graham Hollister-Short (ed.), *History of Technology* vol. 19 (London and Washington: Mansell, 1997), pp. 29–31. See also Norman F. Cantor, *In the Wake of the Plague: The Black Death and the World it Made* (New York: Harper Perennial, 2002), p. 24. For a sceptical view of the idea that the depletion of the human population led to technological innovation, see William H. McNeil, *Plagues and Peoples* (London: Scientific Book Club, 1979), pp. 183–4.

23 As Henry Heller observes, quoting a sixteenth-century French observer who decried the way in which forests were being cut down: 'Virtually all manufacturing was dependent on wood as a raw material . . . Deforestation threatened to destroy the basis of French industrial activity.' See Henry Heller, *Labour, Science and Technology in France 1500–1620* (Cambridge: Cambridge University Press, 1996), p. 86.

24 Roberts, *The End of Oil*, p. 26. See also William H. Te Brake, 'Air Pollution and Fuel Crises in Pre-Industrial London, 1250–1650' in Terry S. Reynolds and Stephen H. Cutcliffe (eds), *Technology and the West: A Historical Anthology from Technology and Culture* (Chicago: University of Chicago Press, 1997), pp. 91–2.

25 Terry S. Reynolds and Stephen H. Cutcliffe, 'Technology in the Preindustrial West' in Reynolds and Cutcliffe (eds), *Technology and the West*, pp. 37–8. See also Thomas T. Read, 'The Earliest Industrial Use of Coal' *Transactions of the Newcomen Society* 20 (1939), pp. 119–33.

26 On the proliferation of patents for pumping devices in England in the sixteenth and seventeenth centuries, see Rhys Jenkins (ed.), *R. Dacres's The Art of Water Drawing* (Cambridge: Newcomen Society, 1930), p. ix.

27 On early-medieval transformation in animal and wind power (as well as water power), see Richard Shelton Kirby, Sidney Withington, Arthur Burr Darlington, and Frederick Gridley Kilgour, *Engineering in History* (1956, reprint, New York: Dover Publications, 1990), pp. 96–100.

28 The Netherlands was an exception to the development of water-powered machinery, preferring to draw on wind power because in flatlands it is, of course, impossible to develop a sufficient 'head' of water to power water-driven devices. On the development of wind power in the Netherlands, see Vaclav Smil, *Energy*

in World History (Oxford: Westview Press, 1994), pp. 108–12. See also E. M. Gardner, 'Some Notes on Dutch Water-Mills' *Transactions of the Newcomen Society* 27 (1949), pp. 199–202. In the Dutch context, Simon Schama has identified what he terms a 'humanist philosophy of hydraulics'; see Simon Schama, *The Embarrassment of Riches: The Interpretation of Dutch Culture in the Golden Age* (London: Fontana Press, 1987), pp. 42–3.

29 A. Goubert, *The Age of Water: The Urban Environment in the North of France AD 300–1800* (College Station: Texas A & M University Press, 1988), p. 52, cited in Colin Chant and David Goodman (eds), *Pre-Industrial Cities and Technology* (London: The Open University in association with Routledge, 1999), p. 150. On the provision of water to medieval communities, see the authoritative account to be found in Roberta J. Magnusson, *Water Technology in the Middle Ages: Cities, Monasteries, and Waterworks after the Roman Empire* (Baltimore and London: Johns Hopkins University Press, 2001), especially pp. 52–115. On water provision in early-modern cities in general, see Christopher R. Friedrichs, *The Early Modern City 1450–1750* (London and New York: Longman, 1995), pp. 262–4. For later developments, see Cesare S. Maffioli, *Out of Galileo: The Science of Waters 1628–1718* (Rotterdam: Erasmus, 1994).

30 See David Landes, *The Wealth and Poverty of Nations: Why Some are So Rich and Some So Poor* (1998, reprint, London: Little, Brown & Co., 2001), p. 46. Landes's account of pre-industrial technology acts as a valuable corrective to the view of earlier generations of historians who saw Renaissance Europe as a fundamentally pre-technological society. Thus, J. R. Hale has claimed that 'love of ingenuity for its own sake . . . acted as a check upon the implementation of mechanical ideas on a large and economically useful scale'. See J. R. Hale, *Renaissance Europe 1480–1520* (London: Collins, 1971), p. 154.

31 On the survival, and (in some regional instances) repair of Roman water-delivery systems, see Magnusson, *Water Technology*, pp. 3–7.

32 By 1650, annual coal output in England had reached 2 million tonnes, while 'almost all of the country's coal fields were opened up between 1540 and 1640'. See Smil, *Energy in World History* p. 159. On the spread of coalmining in the West in the sixteenth and seventeenth centuries, see R. A. Buchanan, *The Power of the Machine: The Impact of Technology 1700 to the Present* (London: Penguin Books, 1992), pp. 87–90.

33 Jean Gimpel, *The Medieval Machine: The Industrial Revolution of the Middle Ages* (London and New York: Penguin Books, 1976), pp. 10–12.

34 On the sound of mills, see Thomas Hardy's nineteenth-century description (in *The Trumpet Major*) of the 'patter' of the great wheel, combining with the sound of other mechanical components to produce 'a remote resemblance to the stopped diapason in an organ'; quoted in Murray Schaffer, *The Tuning of the World* (Toronto: McClelland and Stewart, 1977), p. 57. On the sound of various pre-industrial technological devices, see also Smith, *Acoustic World of Early Modern England*, p. 50.

35 Reynolds, *Stronger than a Hundred Men*, p. 62.

36 These figures are derived from Heller, *Labour, Science and Technology in France 1500–1620*, pp. 12–15.

37 Magnusson, *Water Technology in the Middle Ages*, p. 169; Rhys Jenkins, 'Notes on

the London Bridge Water Works' in Rhys Jenkins, *Links in the History of Engineering and Technology from Tudor Times: The Collected Papers of Rhys Jenkins* (1936, reprint, Freeport, NY: Books for Libraries Press, 1971), pp. 131–40. For an evocation of the 'endless grinding and reverberation' of the water mills of London Bridge at the end of the sixteenth century, see Peter Ackroyd, *London: The Biography* (London: Chatto and Windus, 2000), p. 74.

38   London's water supply was guaranteed not only by Morris's system of water wheels, but also by the horse-driven chain pumps installed by the speculative mining engineer, Bevis Bulmer, in 1594. This machine was located at Broken Wharf, off Upper Thames Street. These devices, in turn, would be replaced by the horse-driven suction pumps installed by Sir Edward Ford, under letters patent granted by Oliver Cromwell in 1655. See Rhys Jenkins, 'Bevis Bulmer' in Rhys Jenkins, *Links in the History of Engineering and Technology*, pp. 24–7; Rhys Jenkins, 'A Chapter in the History of the Water Supply of London: A Thames-side Pumping Installation and Sir Edward Ford's Patent from Cromwell' *Transactions of the Newcomen Society* 9 (1928), pp. 43–51.

39   On the *Stangenkunst* system, see G. Hollister-Short, 'The Vocabulary of Technology' in A. Rupert Hall and Norman F. Smith (eds), *History of Technology* vol. 2 (London: Mansell, 1977), pp. 132–47; Alex Keller, 'Technological Aspirations and the Motivation of Natural Philosophy in Seventeenth-Century England' in Graham Hollister-Short and Frank A. J. L. James (eds), *History of Technology* vol. 15 (London: Mansell, 1993), p. 81; Reynolds, *Stronger than a Hundred Men*, pp. 141–2. On the development of water power, see Arthur Stowers, 'Observations on the History of Water Power' *Transactions of the Newcomen Society* 30 (1955), pp. 239–56; N. A. F. Smith, 'The Origins of Water Power: A Problem of Evidence and Expectations' *Transactions of the Newcomen Society* 55 (1983), pp. 67–84.

40   Among the 'scores of previously manual tasks', Smil lists the following processes driven by water mills: sawing, milling, wood turning, oil pressing, paper making, cloth fulling, tanning, ore crushing, iron making, wire pulling, stamping, cutting, metal grinding, blacksmithing, wood and metal burning, majolica glazing, polishing. See Smil, *Energy in World History*, p. 107. Around 1500, Leonardo had drawn up a list of industrial processes (to be found in the *Codex Atlanticus*) that might be encouraged were the river Arno to be 'improved' allowing for the development of further mills. These activities included 'sawmills, fulling mills, paper mills, hydraulic trip hammers, flour mills, mills for burnishing arms, grinding and sharpening knives, manufacturing gunpowder and saltpetre, spinning silk, weaving ribbons, and shaping jasper and porphyry vases with water-activated lathes'. See Reynolds, *Stronger than a Hundred Men*, p. 136.

41   Reynolds, *Stronger than a Hundred Men*, p. 122. Reynolds also observes (p. 156) that '. . . mechanized factories of the nineteenth century were simply the culmination of a process whose roots went unbroken back to medieval Europe'.

42   I. F. Clarke, *The Pattern of Expectation 1644–2001* (London: Jonathan Cape, 1979), p. 34. On the Marly machine, see Joel Mokyr, *The Lever of Riches: Technological Creativity and Economic Progress* (New York and Oxford: Oxford University Press, 1990), pp. 66–76; J. J. Ermenc, 'The Machine of Marly' *French Review* 29 (1956), pp. 242–4.

43 Michel de Montaigne, *The Complete Works* trans. Donald M. Frame (London: Everyman's Library, 2003). All references to Montaigne's writings are to this edition.

44 Jean Starobinski, *Montaigne in Motion* trans. Arthur Goldhammer (Chicago and London: University of Chicago Press, 1985), p. 226.

45 Starobinski, *Montaigne in Motion*, p. 226.

46 On Montaigne's travel journal, see Donald M. Frame, *Montaigne: A Biography* (London: Hamish Hamilton, 1965), pp. 201–22.

47 The chief river systems Montaigne followed were those of the Marne, Moselle, Rhine, Adige, and Po.

48 The public water supply at Augsburg, though possibly the most advanced in Europe by the end of the sixteenth century, was not the first of its kind. On medieval civic water systems supplies, see Usher, *History of Mechanical Inventions*, pp. 337–8; Chant and Goodman, *Pre-Industrial Cities and Technology*, pp. 149–50; Magnusson, *Water Technology in the Middle Ages*, pp. 8–11, 134.

49 R. D'acres, *The Art of Water-drawing, or A Compendious Abstract of All Sorts of Water-Machins, or Gins, Practised in the World* (London, 1660), p. 26.

50 On the possibility that Montaigne's attitude towards machinery was influenced by his physiological difficulties, see Margaret Healy, 'Journeying with the "Stone": Montaigne's Healing *Travel Journal*' *Literature and Medicine* 24 (2005), pp. 231–49 (p. 242); Jonathan Sawday, 'In Search of the Philosopher's Stone: Montaigne, Interiority and Machines' *Dalhousie Review* 85 (2005), pp. 195–220.

51 A. R. Hall, 'Epilogue: the Rise of the West' in Charles Singer, E. J. Holmyard, A. R. Hall, and Trevor I. Williams (eds), *A History of Technology* 7 vols (Oxford: Clarendon Press, 1954–78), vol. 3, *From the Renaissance to the Industrial Revolution*, p. 714.

52 Edward Chaney, *The Evolution of the Grand Tour: Anglo-Italian Cultural Relations since the Renaissance* (London and Portland, OR: Frank Cass, 2000), p. xii.

53 See Roy Strong, *The Renaissance Garden in England* (London: Thames and Hudson, 1979), pp. 73–137.

54 Francis Bacon, *The Essays* ed. Michael J. Hawkins (London: J. M. Dent 1972), p. 141. See also John Dixon Hunt and Peter Willis (eds), *The Genius of the Place: The English Landscape Garden 1620–1820* (Cambridge, MA, and London: MIT Press, 1988), pp. 6–7 (editors' introduction).

55 Montaigne's engagement with 'useful' technology has been attributed to his work as a magistrate, 'the bourgeois roots of his family', the influence of his 'Calvinist relatives', and, above all, 'the management of his own estates'. See Heller, *Labour, Science and Technology in France 1500–1620*, pp. 133–5.

56 The word *Noria* is of Arabic origin. The device probably originated in the ancient Middle East. See Eugene S. Ferguson 'Technical Annotations and a Pictorial Glossary' in Martha Teach Gnudi and Eugene S. Ferguson (eds), *The Various and Ingenious Machines of Agostino Ramelli: A Classic Sixteenth-Century Illustrated Treatise on Technology* (New York and Aldershot: Dover Publications/Scolar Press, 1976), p. 574. On ancient irrigation devices more generally, see Rouse and Ince, *History of Hydraulics*, pp. 4–8; Trevor I. Williams, *A History of Invention from Stone Axes to Silicon Chips* rev. William A. Schaaf Jr (London and New York: Little, Brown, 1999), pp. 29–31.

57 Frame, *Montaigne: A Biography*, p. 212.

58 Frame, *Montaigne: A Biography*, p. 211.

59 A. G. Keller writes that the smoke jack, a 'primitive "rottisomat" . . . was the first practical heat engine – the first machine to be driven by an artificially produced power, rather than one provided by nature or human muscle'. See A. G. Keller, *A Theatre of Machines* (London: Chapman and Hall, 1964), p. 45.

60 Quoted in Keller, *Theatre of Machines*, p. 37. The German traveller, Arnold von Harff, also reported the existence of the '*filatoio da aqua*' in Florence before 1497 (Keller, *Theatre of Machines*, p. 37).

61 Otto Mayr (ed.), *Philosophers and Machines* (New York: Science History Publications, 1976), p. 4.

62 Montaigne's fascination with mechanical movement might be compared to the 'glorification of mechanical motion' beloved of the Futurists at the beginning of the twentieth century or to the 'fantasy machines' or *Métamatics* created by the modern Swiss kinetic artist, Jean Tinguely (1921–91), which are dedicated to illustrating the very Montaignian proposition that 'Everything moves continuously. Immobility does not exist.' See Sylvia Martin, *Futurism* (Cologne and London: Taschen, 2005), p. 19; Heidi E. Violand-Hobi, *Jean Tinguely: Life and Work* (Munich and New York: Prestel Verlag, 1995), p. 33.

63 See Donald Cardwell, *The Fontana History of Technology* (London: Fontana Press, 1994), p. 88. On the distinction between a 'mechanism' that modifies motion, as opposed to a machine which modifies energy, see Brian S. Baigrie, 'Descartes's Scientific Illustrations and La Grande Méchanique de la Nature' in Brian S. Baigrie (ed.), *Picturing Knowledge: Historical and Philosophical Problems Concerning the Use of Art in Science* (Toronto and London: Toronto University Press, 1996), pp. 86–134.

64 Lewis Mumford, *Technics and Civilization* (1934, reprint, New York and London: Harcourt Brace, 1963), p. 9. Mumford is here relying on a modern definition of a machine, such as 'a device for overcoming a resistance at one point by the application of force at some other point'. See T. C. Collocott and A. B. Dobson (eds), *Chambers Dictionary of Science and Technology* 2 vols (Edinburgh: Chambers, 1975), II, p. 712.

65 Franz Reuleaux, *Kinematics of Machinery, Outlines of a Theory of Machines* trans. A. B. W. Kennedy (1876) quoted in Usher, *A History of Mechanical Inventions*, p. 117.

66 Mumford, *Technics and Civilization*, p. 52.

67 Mark E. Rosheim, *Robot Evolution: The Development of Anthrobotics* (New York and Chichester: John Wiley and Sons, 1994), p. 321.

68 Montaigne might, however, have known the passage in *The Golden Ass* of Apuleius, in which the narrator is transformed into an ass, and finds himself put to work powering a mill. The passage is a famously empathetic account of imagining what it might be like to be something other than a human being. See Apuleius, *The Golden Ass* trans. Robert Graves (Harmondsworth: Penguin Books, 1950), pp. 179–81.

69 Cited in Frame, *Montaigne: A Biography*, p. 207.

70 Erich Auerbach, *Mimesis: The Representation of Reality in Western Literature* trans. Willard Trask (New York: Doubleday, 1957), p. 257.

71 Mokyr, *The Lever of Riches*, p. 73.

72 Releaux, *Kinematics of Machinery*, quoted in Usher, *A History of Mechanical Inventions*, p. 117.

73 Cardwell, *History of Technology*, p. 85.

74 Stillman Drake and I. E. Drabkin (eds), *Mechanics in Sixteenth-century Italy. Selections from Tartaglia, Benedetti, Guido Ubaldo, and Galileo* (Madison: University of Wisconsin Press/Publications in Medieval Science, 1969), p. 241.

75 'After Galileo . . . all machines have the common function of applying "force" as efficiently as possible . . . Once this has been accepted a rational science of machines becomes possible.' Cardwell, *History of Technology*, p. 89. On the concept of mechanisms being devised which 'cheat' nature (of which the perpetual motion machine is a prime example), see Alan Gabbey, 'Between *ars* and *philosophia naturalis*: Reflections on the Historiography of Early Modern Mechanics' in J. V. Field and Frank A. J. L. James (eds), *Renaissance and Revolution Humanists, Scholars, Craftsmen and Natural Philosophers in Early Modern Europe* (Cambridge: Cambridge University Press, 1993), pp. 133–45 (particularly pp. 142–4). On the power output of different kinds of pre-industrial machine, see Smil, *Energy in World History*, pp. 268–9.

76 Karl Marx, *The Poverty of Philosophy* (1847) in Karl Marx, *Selected Writings* ed. David McLellan (1997, reprint, Oxford: Oxford University Press, 2002), pp. 219–20.

77 Mokyr, *Lever of Riches*, p. 57.

78 See James E. McClellan III and Harold Dorn, *Science and Technology in World History: An Introduction* (Baltimore and London; Johns Hopkins University Press, 1999), pp. 94, 180–1; Jared Diamond, *Guns, Germs and Steel: A Short History of Everybody for the Last 13,000 Years* (London: Vintage, 1988), pp. 249–50. It has, however, been argued that 'though the pharaohs in Egypt may have had vast resources of manpower, Greek and Roman building contractors rarely had more than a small labour force'. See J. G. Landels, *Engineering in the Ancient World* (1978, revised edition, London: Constable, 1998), p. 10. Moreover, in the anonymous *De rebus bellicis* (*c.* 375 CE) it is proposed that machines should supplement a growing shortage of human labour in the Empire: see Walter Endrei, 'Count Theodore Batthyány's Paddle-wheel Ship' in Graham Hollister-Short and Frank A. J. L. James (eds), *History of Technology* vol. 15 (London: Mansell, 1993), p. 93. On Roman mechanical 'blindness', see Norman A. F. Smith, 'Attitudes to Roman Engineering and the Question of the Inverted Siphon' in A. Rupert Hall and Norman Smith (eds), *History of Technology* vol. 1 (London: Mansell, 1976), p. 48. For a vigorous defence of the innovative nature of Roman and Greek technology, see D. L. Simms, 'Archimedes the Engineer' in Graham Hollister-Short and Frank A. J. L. James (eds), *History of Technology* vol. 17 (London: Mansell, 1995), particularly pp. 86–93.

79 A. Rahman, 'A Perspective on Technology in India' in A. Rahman (ed.), *History of Indian Science, Technology, and Culture AD 1000–1800* (New Delhi: Oxford University Press/Project of History of Indian Science, Philosophy, and Culture, 1998), p. 247.

80 See Karl Wittfogel, *Oriental Despotism: A Comparative Study of Total Power* (New Haven: Yale University Press, 1957). The so-called 'Wittfogel Thesis' has been much challenged for its technological determinism. For a critique, see Arnold Pacey, *Tech-*

nology in World Civilization (Cambridge, MA: MIT Press, 1990), pp. 18–19. In the 1970s, the Khmer Rouge regime in Kampuchea (Cambodia), dedicated itself to gigantic irrigation projects to solve the 'problem of water' that involved the forced mobilization and ruralization of virtually the entire Cambodian population. See François Ponchaud, *Cambodia Year Zero* trans. Nancy Amphoux (Harmondsworth: Penguin Books, 1978), pp. 93–9.

81 Peter F. Drucker, 'The First Technological Revolution and Its Lessons' in Terry S. Reynolds and Stephen H. Cutcliffe (eds), *Technology and the West: A Historical Anthology from Technology and Culture* (Chicago: University of Chicago Press, 1997), pp. 40–1.

82 Lynn White Jr, *Medieval Technology and Social Change* (London and Oxford: Oxford University Press, 1962), p. 134.

83 Michael Adas, *Machines as the Measure of Men: Science, Technology, and Ideologies of Western Dominance* (Ithaca and London: Cornell University Press, 1989), p. 21.

84 Richard Shelton Kirby, Sidney Witherington, Arthur Burr Darlington, Frederick Gridley Kilgour, *Engineering in History* (New York: Dover Publications, 1990) p. 96. Yet, the *Mendelschen Zwölf-Brüder-Stiftung*, a treatise showing illustrations of workmen using different instruments, issued in Nuremberg around 1390–1400, shows medieval machines such as the pole driven lathe, or the bow-string drill, that had been in use for a thousand years or more before the advent of Christianity. See Derek Birdsall and Carlo M. Cipolla, *The Technology of Man: A Visual History* (London: Wildwood House, 1980), p. 107.

85 William Barclay Parsons, *Engineers and Engineering in the Renaissance* (1939, reprint, Cambridge, MA: MIT Press, 1976), p. 105.

86 On the construction of the Suez Canal using forced labour, see Kirby *et al.*, *Engineering in History*, p. 451.

87 See Jaques Le Goff, *Time, Work, and Culture in the Middle Ages* trans. Arthur Goldhammer (Chicago and London: University of Chicago Press, 1990), p. 90. Le Goff comments, too, (p. 80) on the way in which the ability of early-medieval monks to construct mechanical devices was understood as proof of their thaumaturgical knowledge rather than their technical prowess.

88 See Marc Bloch, 'The Watermill and Feudal Authority' in Donald MacKenzie and Judy Wajcman (eds), *The Social Shaping of Technology* (Buckingham and Philadelphia: Open University Press, 1999), pp. 152–5.

89 See E. P. Thompson, *The Making of the English Working Class* (1963, reprint, Harmondsworth: Penguin Books, 1980), pp. 604–5.

90 Joan Thirsk and J. P. Copper (eds), *Seventeenth-Century Economic Documents* (Oxford: Clarendon Press, 1972), p. 294. For a historical and sociological analysis of Luddism, see Keith Grint and Steve Woolgar, *The Machine at Work: Technology, Work and Organization* (Cambridge: Polity Press, 1997), pp. 39–64. For a cultural analysis of Luddism, see Steven E. Jones, *Against Technology: From the Luddites to Neo-Luddism* (New York and London: Routledge, 2006), particularly pp. 45–75.

91 Geoffrey Chaucer, *The Complete Works* ed. W. W. Skeat (1912, reprint, London: Oxford University Press, 1973), p. 426. Chaucer does not say whether his fictional miller runs a watermill or a windmill. However, in the retaliatory tale offered by the Reeve, there is no ambiguity: the Reeve's miller, Simkin, operates a watermill, on

a brook not far from Trumpington near Cambridge. See Chaucer, *Complete Works*, p. 468.

92   Bloch, 'The Watermill and Feudal Authority', p. 152. On Chaucer's miller and the 'crucial if still somewhat obscure role' that millers played in medieval society, see Lee Patterson, '"No Man His Reson Herede" Peasant Consciousness, Chaucer's Miller and the Structure of the *Canterbury Tales*' in Valerie Allen and Ares Axiotis (eds), *Chaucer: New Casebooks* (London: Macmillan, 1997), pp. 169–92.

93   See Langdon Winner, 'Do Artefacts Have Politics?' in Mackenzie and Wajcman (eds), *The Social Shaping of Technology*, pp. 28, 30–1; Lewis Mumford, 'Authoritarian and Democratic Technics' *Technology and Culture* 5 (1964), pp. 1–8.

94   Lewis Mumford, 'The Myth of the Machine' in Robert C. Scharff and Val Dusek (eds), *Philosophy of Technology: The Technological Condition* (Oxford: Blackwell, 2003), p. 348.

95   Lewis Mumford, 'The First Megamachine' in Donald L. Miller (ed.), *The Lewis Mumford Reader* (Athens, GA, and London: University of Georgia Press, 1995), pp. 315–16.

96   On the rebuilding of Rome under Sixtus V, see Peter Murray, *The Architecture of the Italian Renaissance* (London: Thames and Hudson, 1969), p. 206; Loren Partridge, *The Renaissance in Rome 1400–1600* (London: Weidenfeld and Nicolson, 1966), pp. 32–40. On schemes for transforming Berlin, Rome, and Moscow in the 1930s, see William J. R. Curtis, *Modern Architecture since 1900* (London: Phaidon Press, 1982), pp. 211–22; Ruth Eaton, *Ideal Cities: Utopianism and the (Un)Built Environment* (London: Thames and Hudson, 2002), pp. 154–213.

97   On the transporting of obelisks in antiquity, see M. J. T. Lewis, 'Roman Methods of Transporting and Erecting Obelisks' *Transactions of the Newcomen Society* 56 (1984), pp. 87–110; Brian Curran, *The Egyptian Renaissance: The Afterlife of Ancient Egypt in Early Modern Italy* (Chicago and London: The University of Chicago Press, 2007), pp. 77–81.

98   Colin Chant and David Goodman (eds), *The Pre-industrial Cities and Technology* (London and New York: Routledge/Open University Press, 1999), p. 136. Chant and Goodman give the translated text of the edict in full.

99   Chant and Goodman (eds), *Pre-industrial Cities*, p. 136.

100   Parsons, *Engineers and Engineering in the Renaissance*, p. 162.

101   'Christianizing' the obelisk was an important element in the project. In the earlier sixteenth century it was believed that the top of the obelisk contained the ashes of the Emperor Gaius Caesar. See Sebastiano Serlio, *The Five Books of Architecture* trans. anon. (London, 1611), III, ch. 4, fol. 29. Serlio's *Archittetura* was first published at Venice in 1537–47.

102   Dick Parry, *Engineering the Pyramids* (Stroud: Sutton Publishing, 2004), pp. 106–8.

103   Parry, *Engineering the Pyramids*, p. 110.

104   For an account of cathedral construction in the Middle Ages, see Frances and Joseph Gies, *Cathedral, Forge, and Waterwheel: Technology and Invention in the Middle Ages* (New York: HarperCollins, 1994), particularly pp. 192–200.

105   Elizabeth Eisenstein, *The Printing Press as an Agent of Change: Communications and Cultural Transformations in Early Modern Europe* (Cambridge: Cambridge University Press, 1979), p. 261.

106 David Nye, *American Technological Sublime* (Cambridge, MA, and London: MIT Press, 1994), p. 34.

107 Nye, *American Technological Sublime*, pp. 35–6.

108 Partridge, *The Renaissance in Rome*, p. 36.

109 Eaton, *Ideal Cities*, pp. 48–9.

110 Partridge, *The Renaissance in Rome*, p. 36.

111 Chant and Goodman (eds), *Pre-industrial Cities and Technology*, p. 183.

112 On the resistance to utopian plans by sixteenth-century property owners, see Friedrichs, *The Early Modern City 1450–1750*, pp. 26–7.

113 See John Peacock, *The Stage Designs of Inigo Jones: The European Context* (Cambridge: Cambridge University Press, 1995), p. 73. As Peacock points out (pp. 30–1), Fontana had also designed the catafalque for his papal master, adorning it with examples of his architectural work. These included the obelisks that he had so successfully transported through the city.

114 John Wilkins, *Mathematicall Magick or the Wonders that May be Performed by Mechanicall Geometry* (London, 1648), p. 67.

115 Wilkins, *Mathematicall Magick*, pp. 73, 74. For modern estimates of the total manpower required in pyramid construction, see Parry, *Engineering the Pyramids*, pp. 152–62.

116 Wilkins, *Mathematicall Magick*, p. 75. For more recent calculations, see Smil, *Energy in World History*, p. 155.

117 Wilkins, *Mathematicall Magick*, p. 75.

118 William Bray (ed.), *The Diary of John Evelyn* 2 vols (London: J. M. Dent, 1911), I, p. 119.

119 Michel Foucault, *Discipline and Punish: The Birth of the Prison* trans. Alan Sheridan (Harmondsworth: Penguin Books, 1977), p. 153.

120 Foucault, *Discipline and Punish*, p. 149.

121 On the Benedictine origin of the timetable, see Arno Borst, *The Ordering of Time: From the Ancient Computus to the Modern Computer* trans. Andrew Winnard (Cambridge: Polity Press, 1993), p. 26.

3 The turn of the screw: machines, books, and bodies

1 Carlo M. Cipolla, *Clocks and Culture 1300–1700* (New York and London: W. W. Norton, 2000), p. 119.

2 See J. Z. Young, *An Introduction to the Study of Man* (Oxford: Clarendon Press, 1971), pp. 477–8.

3 The principle of the screw was well known to the ancient world. But it was not until the fifteenth century in Europe, particularly among armourers, that screws appeared as fastening devices. Arguably, the screw is the foundational device of mechanical culture, since it allows a device not only to be assembled, but to be disassembled for repair, maintenance, or redesign. On the history of screws, see Witold Rybczynski, *One Good Turn: A Natural History of the Screwdriver and the Screw* (New York and London: Simon and Schuster, 2000), particularly pp. 87–93.

4 On the potter's wheel, see T. K. Derry and Trevor I. Williams, *A Short History of Technology from the Earliest Times to AD 1900* (New York: Dover Publications, 1960), p. 76.

5   Jaques Le Goff, *Time, Work, and Culture in the Middle Ages* trans. Arthur Goldham-mer (Chicago and London: University of Chicago Press, 1980), p. 90.

6   For a theoretical analysis of work in the Renaissance, see Agnes Heller, *Renaissance Man* trans. Richard E. Allen (New York: Schocken Books, 1978), pp. 394–412.

7   Ken Alder, *The Measure of All Things* (London: Abacus, 2004), p. 3.

8   See Joel Mokyr, *The Gifts of Athena: Historical Origins of the Knowledge Economy* (Princeton and Oxford: Princeton University Press, 2002), p. 60. See too the 'complex of kinships, resemblances, and affinities' described in Michel Foucault, *The Order of Things: An Archaeology of the Human Sciences* (London: Tavistock, 1974), pp. 54, 55.

9   On standardized measurement in the case of artillery, see Charles Messenger, 'Weapons and Armour' in Ian McNeil (ed.), *An Encyclopaedia of the History of Technology* (London and New York: Routledge, 1990), pp. 977, 981.

10 On Bodin and wage labour, see Henry Heller, *Labour, Science and Technology in France 1500–1620* (Cambridge: Cambridge University Press, 1996), pp. 135–7.

11 Karl Marx, *Grundrisse* in Karl Marx, *Selected Writings* ed. David McLellan (1977, 2nd edition, Oxford: Oxford University Press, 2000), p. 408.

12 Marx, *Selected Writings*, p. 408.

13 Marx, *Selected Writings*, pp. 408–9.

14 Marx, *Selected Writings*, p. 409.

15 On the distinction between 'tool' and 'machine' see Marx's letter to Friedrich Engels (28 January 1863) in Marx, *Selected Writings*, pp. 565–7.

16 Marx, 'Wage-Labour and Capital' (from articles published in the *Neue Rheinische Zeitung*, April 1849), in Marx, *Selected Writings*, p. 291.

17 Marx, *Selected Writings*, p. 291.

18 Adam Smith, *The Wealth of Nations* (1776) with an introduction by D. D. Raphael (New York, London, and Toronto: Everyman's Library, 1991), p. 6.

19 Smith, *Wealth of Nations*, p. 9. On Smith's analysis of the division of labour, see J. H. Plumb, *England in the Eighteenth Century* (1950, reprint, Harmondsworth: Penguin Books, 1972), pp. 22–3; Roy Porter, *Enlightenment: Britain and the Creation of the Modern World* (London: Allen Lane/Penguin Books, 2000), pp. 392–3. The view that Smith's advocacy of the division of labour principle 'reduced the worker to a "hand", a mentally stunted, slave-like machine' is vigorously contested in Alexander Brodie, *The Scottish Enlightenment: The Historical Age of the Historical Nation* (Edinburgh: Birlinn, 2001), p. 105.

20 Porter, *Enlightenment*, p. 392.

21 On the interrelationship between Smith and the entrepreneurial and technological culture of late eighteenth-century Glasgow, see Peter Hall, *Cities in Civilization: Culture, Innovation, and Urban Order* (London: Weidenfeld and Nicolson, 1998), pp. 348–76.

22 Smith, *Wealth of Nations*, p. 227.

23 Charles Babbage, *Selected Works* ed. Anthony Hyman (Cambridge: Cambridge University Press, 1989), p. 130. On Babbage and the Difference Engine, see, in particular, Doron Swade, '"It will not slice a Pineapple": Babbage, Miracles, and Machines' in Francis Spufford and Jenny Uglow (eds), *Cultural Babbage: Technology, Time, and Invention* (London and Boston: Faber and Faber, 1996), pp. 34–51.

24 Babbage, *Selected Works*, p. 130.

25 Babbage, *Selected Works*, p. 130.

26 See William J. Barber, *A History of Economic Thought* (Harmondsworth: Penguin Books, 1967), p. 68.

27 Marx, too, saw the development of the clock as vital to the expansion of manufacturing industry. See Marx, *Selected Writings*, p. 566.

28 Peter Heinlein (1480–1542) of Nuremberg is credited with being the first fabricator of portable clocks or watches, following his invention of the mainspring. Nuremberg watches were oval in shape and hence their comparison to eggs. See Ilan Rachum, *The Renaissance: An Illustrated Encyclopaedia* (London: Octopus, 1979), pp. 234, 338.

29 David Landes, *Revolution in Time: Clocks and the Making of the Modern World* (London and New York: Viking, 2000), p. 92.

30 Cipolla, *Clocks and Culture*, p. 116. But note Arno Borst's comment that the 'revolutionary influence' of clocks and watches has been 'overrated by modern scholars'. See Arno Borst, *The Ordering of Time: From the Ancient Computus to the Modern Computer* (Cambridge: Polity Press, 1993), p. 92.

31 Schmidt's *Shakespeare Lexicon* lists no fewer than eighty instances of characters referring specifically to *clock* time in Shakespeare's plays. See Alexander Schmidt, *Shakespeare Lexicon and Quotation Dictionary* 2 vols (1902, 3rd edition, New York: Dover Publications, 1971), I, pp. 207–8. See also John Kerrigan's comments on Shakespeare's use of clock time in William Shakespeare, *The Sonnets and A Lover's Complaint* ed. John Kerrigan (Harmondsworth: Penguin Books, 1999), pp. 33–46 (editor's introduction).

32 Christopher Hill, *Society and Puritanism in Pre-Revolutionary England* (1964, reprint, Harmondsworth: Penguin Books, 1986), p. 127.

33 Elizabeth L. Eisenstein, *The Printing Press as an Agent of Change: Communications and Cultural Transformations in Early Modern Europe* (Cambridge: Cambridge University Press, 1979), p. 81.

34 Terry S. Reynolds, *Stronger than a Hundred Men: A History of the Vertical Water Mill* (Baltimore and London: Johns Hopkins University Press, 1983), p. 156.

35 Eisenstein, *Printing Press as an Agent of Change*, p. 264; on technical illustration, see also David Landau and Peter Parshall, *The Renaissance Print 1470–1550* (New Haven and London: Yale University Press, 1994), p. 259.

36 It is, of course, true that illustrations could be degraded over time as they were reproduced in successive printed editions of a work. But, note Eisenstein's comments in the case of the *Cosmography* of Sebastian Munster, first published in 1544, and which went through thirty-five editions prior to 1628: 'As each edition became bigger, more crammed with data, and more profusely illustrated, each was also provided with more tables, charts, indexes which made it possible for readers to retrieve the growing body of information that was being stored in the work' (Eisenstein, *Printing Press as an Agent of Change*, p. 109).

37 See Eugene S. Ferguson, *Engineering and the Mind's Eye* (Cambridge, MA: MIT Press, 1992), pp. 107–13; Thomas J. Misa, *Leonardo to the Internet: Technology and Culture from the Renaissance to the Present* (Baltimore and London: Johns Hopkins University Press, 2004), pp. 26–8.

38 As well as the work of Eisenstein and Bennett (see below), see Mark U. Edwards Jr, *Printing, Propaganda, and Martin Luther* (Berkeley and Los Angeles: University of California Press, 1994); Alberto Manguel, *A History of Reading* (London: HarperCollins, 1997); Peter Murray Jones, 'Medicine and Science' in Lotte Hellinga and J. B. Trapp (eds), *The Cambridge History of the Book in Britain* (Cambridge: Cambridge University Press, 1999), III, pp. 433–48; Peter Burke, *A Social History of Knowledge: From Gutenberg to Diderot* (Cambridge: Polity, 2000), pp. 149–96; Ian Green, *Print and Protestantism in Early Modern England* (Oxford: Oxford University Press, 2000).

39 Lotte Hellinga, 'Printing' in Hellinga and Trapp (eds), *The Cambridge History of the Book in Britain*, p. 69.

40 On the spread of the printing presses and the diffusion of books, see Neil Rhodes and Jonathan Sawday, 'Paperwolds: Imagining the Renaissance Computer' in Neil Rhodes and Jonathan Sawday, *The Renaissance Computer: Knowledge Technology in the First Age of Print* (London and New York: Routledge, 2000), p. 1.

41 See Walter Ong, *Orality and Literacy: The Technologizing of the Word* (London and New York: Routledge, 1982), pp. 115–29.

42 On author's attending (or failing to attend) the presses, see H. S. Bennett, *English Books and Readers 1475–1640* 3 vols (Cambridge: Cambridge University Press, 1970), III, pp. 211–12.

43 Eisenstein, *Printing Press as an Agent of Change*, p. 56.

44 Eisenstein, *Printing Press as an Agent of Change*, p. 55.

45 The European heavy plough, the *carucca*, was to transform agriculture in the Middle Ages. See Joel Mokyr, *The Lever of Riches: Technological Creativity and Economic Progress* (New York and Oxford: Oxford University Press, 1990), p. 32.

46 On spinning and weaving in early-modern Europe, see Ann Rosalind Jones and Peter Stallybrass, *Renaissance Clothing and the Materials of Memory* (Cambridge: Cambridge University Press, 2000), pp. 104–33.

47 Lucien Febvre and Henri-Jean Martin, *The Coming of the Book* trans. David Gerard (London and New York: Verso, 1997), p. 62.

48 Michel Foucault, *Discipline and Punish: The Birth of the Prison* trans. Alan Sheridan (Harmondsworth: Penguin Books, 1977), pp. 135, 165.

49 Bennett, *English Books and Readers*, I, p. 218.

50 Bennett, *English Books and Readers*, III, p. 204.

51 On printing rates, see Bennett, *English Books and Readers*, II. p. 290. But note the forms of book production introduced in Paris in the thirteenth century, which amounted to an industrialization of the tasks of copying manuscripts. See Christopher de Hamel, *A History of Illuminated Manuscripts* (London: Phaidon Press, 1994), pp. 130–2.

52 Anon, *Plaidorie pour la reformation de l'imprimerie* (Paris, 1572), fol. 3^{r-v}, quoted in Heller, *Labour, Science and Technology in France 1500–1620*, p. 25.

53 See D. F. McKenzie, *Making Meaning: 'Printers of the Mind' and other Essays* ed. Peter D. McDonald and Michael F. Suarez (Amherst and Boston: University of Massachusetts Press, 2002), pp. 18–56.

54 Samuel Hieron, *All the sermons of Samuel Hieron minister of Gods Word, at Modbury in Deuon heretofore sunderly published, now diligently reuised, and collected together into one volume* (London, 1614), sig. ¶2.

55 Marshall McLuhan, 'The Playboy Interview' *Playboy Magazine* (March 1969), Internet:

www.newcastle.edu.au/school/design-comm-info/intranet/ems/play_mcl/. Accessed 12 August 2005.

56 For a comprehensive critique of McLuhan's ideas, see Eisenstein, *Printing Press as an Agent of Change*, pp. 16–17.

57 Marshall McLuhan, *The Guttenberg Galaxy: The Making of Typographic Man* (Toronto: University of Toronto Press, 1962), p. 141.

58 On the continuing authority of Galen in the realm of anatomy in the sixteenth century, see Andrew Cunningham, *The Anatomical Renaissance: The Resurrection of the Anatomical Projects of the Ancients* (Aldershot: Scolar Press, 1997).

59 Vitruvius, *The Ten Books of Architecture* trans. Morris Hicky Morgan (New York: Dover Publications, 1960), p. 283.

60 Vitruvius, *The Ten Books of Architecture*, p. 283. The *ballista* and the *scorpio* were siege weapons, the *anisocycli* was a system of gears.

61 On Greek and Roman technology, and particularly the machines to be found described in works by, (*inter alia*), Aristotle, Heron, and Vitruvius, see John W. Humphrey, John P. Oleson, and Andrew N. Sherwood (eds), *Greek and Roman Technology: A Sourcebook* (London and New York: Routledge, 1998), pp. 23–74; J. G. Landels, *Engineering in the Ancient World* (1978, 2nd revised edition, London: Constable, 2000), pp. 58–98, 199–218. On Arabic machines and devices more generally, see Donald R. Hill, *Islamic Science and Engineering* (Edinburgh: Edinburgh University Press, 1993), pp. 92–121.

62 See Alexander G. Keller, 'A Manuscript Version of Jaques Besson's Book of Machines with his Unpublished Principles of Mechanics' in Bert S. Hall and Delna C. West (eds), *On Pre-Modern Technology and Science: A Volume of Studies in Honour of Lynn White Jr* (Malibu: Undena Publications, 1976), pp. 75–103. On the work of medieval engineers, particularly Villard de Honnecourt and Guido da Vigevano, see Bertrand Gille, *The Renaissance Engineers* trans. anon. (London: Lund Humphries, 1966), pp. 24–34.

63 On Kyeser and the 'German school' of engineers, see Gille, *Renaissance Engineers*, pp. 55–77.

64 See L. D. Reynolds and N. G. Wilson, *Scribes and Scholars: A Guide to the Transmission of Greek and Latin Literature* (2nd edition, Oxford: Clarendon Press, 1974), pp. 108–46.

65 Donald R. Hill, *A History of Engineering in Classical and Medieval Times* (London: Croom Helm, 1984), p. 128.

66 On the manuscripts of the Sienese engineers, and their many different machine designs, see Paolo Galluzzi, *The Art of Invention: Leonardo and Renaissance Engineers* (Florence: Instituto e Museo di Storia della Scienza/Giunti, 1999), pp. 118–86. On the transmission of Heron's writings, see, in particular, Marie Boas, 'Hero's *Pneumatica*: A Study of Its Transmission and Influence' *Isis* 10 (1949), pp. 90–100. On the transmission of the works of Philo and Archimedes, see Reynolds and Wilson, *Scribes and Scholars*, pp. 48–51. For further information on Heron and Philo, see A. G. Drachmann, *Ktesibios Philon and Heron: A Study in Ancient Pneumatics* (Copenhagen: Ejnar Munksgaard, 1948), pp. 41–161.

67 Galluzzi, *Art of Invention*, pp. 118–19, lists ten manuscript volumes associated with the Sienese School.

68 For an analysis of the relatively slow replacement of earlier technologies of warfare by gunpowder technology, see Bert S. Hall, *Weapons and Warfare in Renaissance Europe* (Baltimore: Johns Hopkins University Press, 1997).

69 The phrase was heard in a dispute between an architect and masons engaged in the construction of Milan cathedral around 1400. See Burke, *Social History of Knowledge*, p. 83. On the 'architecture of humanism', see Rudolph Wittkower, *Architectural Principles in the Age of Humanism* (4th edition, London: Academy Editions, 1973), *passim*.

70 Galluzzi, *Art of Invention*, pp. 20–1.

71 On the ox hoist, see Galluzzi, *Art of Invention*, pp. 23–4, 99–116; Ross King, *Brunelleschi's Dome: The Story of the Great Cathedral in Florence* (London: Pimlico, 2001), pp. 58–71.

72 On the circulation and influence of Taccola's manuscripts, in which many of Brunelleschi's devices were recorded and hence preserved, see Frank D. Prager and Gustina Scaglia, *Brunelleschi: Studies of his Technology and Inventions* (Mineola, NY: Dover Publicatiions, 2004), pp. xi–xiii.

73 The first of the (datable) *Probierbüchlein* seems to have been published at Magdeburg in 1524, and they were continuously reissued throughout the sixteenth and seventeenth centuries, with the last appearing as late as 1782. See Georgius Agricola, *De Re Metallica* trans. Herbert Clark Hoover and Lou Henry Hoover (New York: Dover Publications, 1950), 'Appendix B' (pp. 612–13).

74 For the publication history of the *Pirotechnia* and *De Re Metallica*, see Vannoccio Biringuccio, *The Pirotechnia* trans. and ed. Cyril Stanley Smith and Martha Teach Gnudi (New York: Dover Publications, 1990), pp. xix–xxiii; Agricola, *De Re Metallica* pp. xvi–xviii (translators' introduction).

75 See Jonathan Sawday, *The Body Emblazoned: Dissection and the Human Body in Renaissance Culture* (London and New York: Routledge, 1995), pp. 134–5. On Agricola's illustrations, see O. Hannaway, 'Reading the pictures: The Context of Georgius Agricola's Woodcuts' *Nuncius: Annali di Storia della Scienza* 12 (1997), pp. 49–66.

76 Agricola, *De Re Metallica*, p. xxv. The illustrations were based upon drawings made by Basilus Wefring. Publication of *De Re Metallica* was considerably delayed while the woodcuts were in preparation. See Agricola, *De Re Metallica*, p. xvi (translators' note).

77 Francis D. Klingender, *Art and the Industrial Revolution* ed. and rev. Arthur Elton (St Albans: Granada Publishing, 1975), p. 50.

78 Gary Taylor has suggested to me that these images perhaps served as the prototype of seventeenth-century 'industrial' images showing black slaves tending machinery on New World plantations. See also Gary Taylor, *Buying Whiteness: Race, Culture, and Identity from Columbus to Hip-Hop* (New York and Basingstoke: Palgrave Macmillan, 2005), pp. 278–9.

79 Originating in the late medieval church as small books that contained the forms to be observed by the priest in administering the sacraments, the 'manual' evolved into the idea of a concise treatise or abridgment of a subject. Erasmus's *Enchiridion militis christiani*, in its English version was sub-titled (on the title page) the 'manuel of the christien knight' when published in 1533.

80 Eisenstein, *Printing Press as an Agent of Change*, p. 65.

81 Technically, the machine is an overshot watermill, driving an angular camshaft, into which are set tappets, which raise metal-headed stamps.

82 Agricola, *De Re Metallica*, pp. 279–86.

83 Agricola, *De Re Metallica*, pp. 288–9.

84 Foucault, *Discipline and Punish*, pp. 152–3.

85 The work is first reported as being 'in hand' in 1529, in a letter to Erasmus. In 1533, Agricola reported that he hoped to publish the work 'if he lives'. In 1546, the book was reported to be close to completion. Although it was apparently finished in 1550, it was not sent to the printer until 1553. It finally appeared in 1556, twenty-seven years after it was first heard of. See Agricola, *De Re Metallica*, p. xvi (editors' introduction). Clearly, not every author responded to the quickening pace of the mechanical press.

86 See Wolfgang von Stromer, 'Nuremberg as Epicentre of Invention and Innovation toward the End of the Middle Ages' in Graham Hollister-Short (ed.), *History of Technology* vol. 19 (London and Washington: Mansell, 1997), pp. 22–4. The *Verlag* system however, seems to have been more like a rationalization of labour among individual firms, than a means of dividing a particular process into specific tasks.

87 Eisenstein, *Printing Press as an Agent of Change*, p. 65.

88 Pamela H. Smith, *The Body of the Artisan: Art and Experience in the Scientific Revolution* (Chicago and London: University of Chicago Press, 2004), p. 150.

89 Agricola practised for much of his life as a physician in the Bohemian mining district of Joachimstahl (now known as Jáchymov) in the Erzgebirge (ore-bearing mountains), in the northwestern region of what is now the Czech Republic. The region was famous for its silver mines. See Derry and Williams, *Short History of Technology*, p. 129. On Agricola's intellectual background, see O. Hannaway, 'Georgius Agricola as Humanist' *Journal of the History of Ideas* 53 (1992), pp. 553–60.

90 See Donne's sermon of April 1620/1 on the text 'Hast thou found honey?' in George R. Potter and Evelyn M. Simpson (eds), *The Sermons of John Donne* 10 vols (Berkeley and Los Angeles: California University Press, 1953–62), III, p. 235.

91 Agricola, *De Re Metallica*, p. vii (translators' introduction). In the period 1520–4, Agricola had been engaged on a revision of Galen's works.

92 Michael Camille, *Mirror in Parchment: The Luttrell Psalter and the Making of Medieval England* (London and Chicago: University of Chicago Press/Reaktion Books), p. 213.

93 Camille, *Mirror in Parchment*, p. 180.

94 Camille, *Mirror in Parchment*, p. 220. Camille also remarks (p. 220) upon the principal artist of the Luttrell Psalter, that he had 'a special interest in rotary machinery'.

95 Agricola, *De Re Metallica*, p. 23.

96 Agricola, *De Re Metallica*, p. 20. On Agricola, see Lewis Mumford, *Technics and Civilization* (1934, reprint, New York and London: Harcourt Brace, 1963), pp. 65–74.

97 Galuzzi, *Art of Invention*, p. 59. But see, also, the more recent analysis of the possible methodology behind Leonardo's various machine designs in Pamela O. Long, 'Objects of Art/Objects of Nature: Visual Representation and the Investigation of Nature' in Pamela H. Smith and Paula Findlen (eds), *Merchants and Marvels: Commerce, Science, and Art in Early Modern Europe* (London and New York: Routledge, 2002), pp. 67–82.

98   Quoted in King, *Brunelleschi's Dome*, p. 58.

99   Long, 'Objects of Art/Objects of Nature', p. 63.

100   Kenneth J. Knoespel, 'Gazing on Technology: *Theatrum Mechanorum* and the Assimilation of Renaissance Machinery' in Mark L. Greenberg and Lance Schachterle (eds), *Literature and Technology* Research in Technology Studies 5 (London and Toronto: Associated University Presses, 1992), p. 99. See, also, Jonathan Sawday, 'Forms such as Never Were in Nature: The Renaissance Cyborg' in Erica Fudge, Ruth Gilbert, and Susan Wiseman (eds), *At the Borders of the Human: Beasts, Bodies and Natural Philosophy in the Early Modern Period* (1999, reprint, Basingstoke: Palgrave Macmillan, 2002), pp. 179–80.

101   Martha Teach Gnudi and Eugene S. Ferguson (eds), *The Various and Ingenious Machines of Agostino Ramelli: A Classic Sixteenth-Century Illustrated Treatise on Technology* (New York and Aldershot: Dover Publications/Scolar Press, 1976), p. 26 (editors' introduction).

102   Jessica Wolfe, *Humanism, Machinery, and Renaissance Literature* (Cambridge: Cambridge University Press, 2004), p. 237.

103   See Marcus Popplow, 'Protection and Promotion: Privileges for Inventions and Books of Machines in the Early Modern Period' in Graham Hollister-Short (ed.), *History of Technology* vol. 20 (London and New York: Mansell, 1998), p. 113.

104   Many different kinds of books published in the early modern period contained illustrations or descriptions of machines and devices, but often these were part of some larger project, particularly (as in the case of Biringuccio's *Pirotechnia* of 1540 or Georgius Agricola's *De Re Metallica* of 1556) on mining and metallurgy. Similarly, works such as John Bate's *Mysteries of Nature and Art* (London, 1629) and John Wecker's *Eighteen Books of the Secrets of Art and Nature* translated by Richard Read (London, 1660) contain illustrations and descriptions of mechanical devices. The first printed work containing illustrations of machines seems to have been the *De Re Militari* (Verona, 1472) of Roberto Valturio (Valturio of Rimini), while Giovanni Rusconi's edition of Vitruvius, published in 1590, represented an attempt at 'reconstructing' ancient machines described in the text. The chief (though not the only) machine books of the period are Jaques Besson, *Livre Premiere Des Instruments Mathematiques et Mechaniques* (n.p., n.d.) [Orleans, 1569]; Jean Errard, *Le Premier Livre des instruments mathématiques méchaniques* (Nancy, 1584); Agostino Ramelli, *Le diverse et Artificiose Machine* (Paris, 1588); Vittorio Zonca, *Novo Teatro di machine et edificii* (Padua, 1607); Heinrich Zeising, *Theatri machinarum* 2 vols (Leipzig, 1607–12); Fausto Veranzio (Fausto Vrančić), *Machinae Novae* (Venice, 1616); Jacobus [Octavius?] de Strada, *Kunstliche Abrisz allerhand Wasser- Wind- Rosz- und Handt Mühlen* (Frankfurt, 1617); Giovanni Branca, *Le Machine* (Rome, 1629); Isaac de Caus, *New and Rare Inventions of water Works* (London, 1659); Georg Boeckler, *Theatrum machinarium novum* (Nuremberg, 1661). Conversely, a work such as Giacomo Torelli's *Scene e Machine* (Paris, 1654) though it contains many mechanical designs, is not truly a machine book, in that it is concerned more with effects (in this instance stage effects) than mechanism *per se*. The same might be said of Achille Tarducci's *Delle Machine Ordinanze et Quartieri* (Venice, 1601) which is, primarily, a book on military design. On the bibliography of the machine book and its precursors, see T. Beck, *Beiträge zur Geschichte des Maschinenbaues* (Berlin,

1899); Gille, *Renaissance Engineers*, pp. 247–53; Eugene S. Ferguson, *Bibliography of the History of Technology* (Cambridge, MA, and London: Society for the History of Technology/MIT Press, 1968), pp. 10–11, 39–52.

105 The Earl of Arundel, for example, owned a copy of the *Machinae Novae* of Veranzio, along with more familiar artistic and architectural works by Vitruvius, Lomazzo, and Palladio. See Linda Levy Peck, *Consuming Splendor: Society and Culture in Seventeenth-century England* (Cambridge: Cambridge University Press, 2005), p. 127.

106 Eisenstein, *Printing Press as an Agent of Change*, pp. 261–2.

107 A. G. Keller, *A Theatre of Machines* (London: Chapman and Hall, 1964), p. 4.

108 Otto Mayr (ed.), *Philosophers and Machines* (New York: Science History Publications, 1976), p. 3.

109 Wolfe, *Humanism, Machinery, and Renaissance Literature*, p. 8.

110 The seven 'mechanical arts' were held to encompass the crafts or trades of cloth making, shipbuilding, navigation, agriculture, hunting, healing, and acting. See Burke, *Social History of Knowledge*, p. 84. As the OED reminds us, social distinctions were to become embedded in the terms used to describe different kinds of mechanical artefacts. Thus a carpenter works with 'tools', but a surgeon operates with 'instruments', although, as in the case of the saw, both might find themselves manipulating exactly the same device.

111 See Minta's comment (*Leonardo to the Internet*, p 13) on Renaissance technologists' fascination with courtly pursuits: 'warfare, city building, courtly entertainments . . . dynastic displays' as opposed to industry or commerce.

112 Ramelli, *Machines*, p. 13 (editors' introduction); Heller, *Labour, Science and Technology in France 1500–1620*, pp. 126–31.

113 Besson was identified as Leonardo's successor in A. K. Corry, 'Engineering, Methods of Manufacture and Production' in McNeil (ed.), *An Encyclopaedia of the History of Technology*, p. 393.

114 Keller, *A Theatre of Machines*, p. 8.

115 On Errard's career, see Walter Endrei, 'Jean Errard (1554–1610) and his Book of Machines: *Le Premier Livre des instruments mathématiques méchaniques* of 1584' in Graham Hollister-Short and Frank A. J. L. James (eds), *History of Technology* vol. 17 (London: Mansell, 1995), pp. 181–2.

116 Keller, *A Theatre of Machines*, p. 8.

117 Vittorio Zonca, *Novo teatro di machine* (Padua, 1621), title page; Keller, *A Theatre of Machines*, p. 8.

118 Burke, *A Social History of Knowledge*, p. 153. For the text of the patent granted to Brunelleschi, see Prager and Scaglia, *Brunelleschi*, pp. 111–12; on the granting of privileges, particularly at Venice and Florence, for machine designs more generally, see Popplow, 'Protection and Promotion', pp. 106–12.

119 On English patents, see Charles Webster, *The Great Instauration: Science, Medicine, and Reform 1626–1660* (London: Duckworth, 1975), p. 344; Harold W. Brace, *History of Seed Crushing in Great Britain* (London: Land Books, 1960), pp. 160–1.

120 Ramelli, *Machines*, p. 55. The extent to which the different authors were copying or adapting one another's devices is still a disputed topic. Ramelli's work, for example, which drew upon the Sienese tradition was certainly used by Zeising, Veranzio,

and Boeckler: see Eugene S. Ferguson 'The Influence of Ramelli's Book' in Ramelli, *Machines*, pp. 37–9.

121   Popplow, 'Protection and Promotion', p. 113.

122   Leonhard Christoph Sturm, *Vollständige Mühlen Baukunst* (Augsburg, 1718), preface, quoted in Popplow, 'Protection and Promotion', p. 118.

123   Ramelli, *Machines*, p. 43.

124   This typology is set out in Ken Baynes and Francis Pugh, *The Art of the Engineer* (Guilford: Lutterworth Press, 1981), pp. 14–15.

125   Mokyr, *Gifts of Athena*, p. 62. For a discussion of Ramelli's designs as 'articulations' of the possibility of mechanism, see Bert S. Hall, 'The Didactic and the Elegant: Some Thoughts on Scientific and Technological Illustrations in the Middle Ages and the Renaissance', in Brian S. Baigrie (ed.), *Picturing Knowledge: Historical and Philosophical Problems Concerning the Use of Art in Science* (Toronto and London: Toronto University Press, 1996), pp. 3–39 (particularly pp. 21–6, 34–7).

126   So, Lawrence Manley comments that convention 'acted as the guide to Renaissance activity *in all its forms*' (my emphasis). See Lawrence Manley, *Convention 1500–1700* (Cambridge, MA, and London: Harvard University Press, 1980), p. 138.

127   See Pamela O. Long, 'Power, Patronage, and the Authorship of Ars: From Mechanical Know-How to Mechanical Knowledge in the Last Scribal Age' *Isis* 88 (1997), pp. 1–41.

128   Sir Philip Sidney, *The Countess of Pembroke's Arcadia* ed. Maurice Evans (Harmondsworth: Penguin Books, 1977), p. 41 (editor's introduction).

129   Ramelli, *Machines*, pp. 70, 72, 74.

130   Ramelli, *Machines*, pp. 110, 150.

131   Ramelli, *Machines*, p. 170.

132   Ramelli, *Machines*, p. 44.

133   Ramelli, *Machines*, p. 54.

134   Eugene S. Ferguson, 'Pictorial Glossary' (note) in Ramelli, *Machines*, p. 596. Some machine morphologists include a sixth device – the inclined plane.

135   Thus, Jaques Besson's *Livre premiere Des Instruments Mathematiques, et Mechaniques* became *Theatre des Instruments mathematiques et mechaniques . . .* when it was reissued at Lyons in 1579. The theatrical element was preserved when a Latin edition was issued: *Theatrum intrumentorum et machinorum* (1582). Similarly, the works of Zonca, Zeising, and Boeckler deployed the 'theatre' convention in their titles.

136   On the dramatic role of the body in the Renaissance anatomy theatre, see Sawday, *Body Emblazoned*, pp. 39–53.

137   On the importance of perspective and the 'solidity that came from the use of realistically observed shading' to the origins of engineering drawing, see Baynes and Pugh, *The Art of the Engineer*, pp. 29–30.

138   Eisenstein, *Printing Press as an Agent of Change*, p. 262.

139   Ramelli, *Machines*, p. 53.

140   Ramelli, *Machines*, pp. 49, 53.

141   Leon Battista Alberti, *The Ten Books of Architecture: The 1755 Leoni Edition* trans. James (Giacomo) Leoni (New York: Dover Publications, 1986), p. 124.

142   Alberti, *The Ten Books of Architecture*, p. 125.

143 Klingender, *Art and the Industrial Revolution*, p. 63.

144 Ramelli, *Machines*, pp. 234, 178.

145 Cyprian Lucar, *A Treatise Named Lucarsolace devided into Fower Bookes* (London, 1590), p. 107.

146 See George Basalla, *Evolution of Technology* (Cambridge: Cambridge University Press, 1988), p. 209.

147 Thus, plates from Ramelli's work were copied by the German instrument maker Jacob Leupold for his multi-volume *Theatrum machinarum* (Leipzig, 1724–39). The Glasgow instrument maker James Watt was said to have learned German in order to study these designs. See Eugene S. Ferguson, 'Leupold's *Theatrum Machinarum*' *Technology and Culture* 12 (1971), pp. 64–6.

148 See B. S. Hall, 'A Revolving Bookcase by Agostino Ramelli', *Technology and Culture* 11 (1970), pp. 389–400; Anthony Grafton, *Commerce with the Classics: Ancient Books and Renaissance Readers* (Ann Arbor: University of Michigan Press, 1977), p. 59; Leah S. Marcus, 'The Silence of the Archive and the Noise of Cyberspace' in Rhodes and Sawday (eds), *The Renaissance Computer*, p. 19.

149 Ramelli, *Machines*, p. 508.

150 See Graham Hollister-Short, 'Cranks and Scholars' in Graham Hollister-Short and Frank A. J. L. James (eds), *History of Technology* vol. 17 (London: Mansell, 1995), p. 217.

151 There is still some dispute as to whether or not Ramelli's 'book wheel' is, in fact, a workable device at all. Keller (*Theatre of Machines*, p. 95) claims that the detailed circular inset, which shows the working of the mechanism, has arranged the gears in such a way that 'as the rollers . . . revolve in the same direction of the drum . . . the books will fall onto the floor'.

152 John Wilkins, *Mercury or the Secret and Swift Messenger* (London, 1641), pp. 2–3. On language conceived of as a machine, see Roy Harris, *The Language Machine* (London: Duckworth, 1987), pp. 9–36.

153 Ben Jonson, *Timber* (1640–1) in Ian Donaldson (ed.), *Ben Jonson: The Oxford Authors* (Oxford and New York: Oxford University Press, 1985), pp. 570–1. For Bacon, speech was a 'remembrance or suggestion' of what was already known, rather than an invention or discovery of 'that we know not'. See Francis Bacon, *The Advancement of Learning* (1605) ed. G. W. Kitchin (London: J. M. Dent, 1973), p. 127.

154 Thomas Hobbes, *Leviathan* ed. Richard Tuck (Cambridge: Cambridge University Press, 1991), p. 24.

155 Hobbes, *Leviathan*, p. 24.

156 Derry and Williams, *A Short History of Technology*, p. 214; Young, *Introduction to the Study of Man*, p. 516.

157 Young, *Introduction to the Study of Man*, p. 516. On the evolution of writing in different human societies, see Jared Diamond, *Guns, Germs and Steel: A Short History of Everybody for the Last 13,000 Years* (London: Vintage, 1998), pp. 215–38.

158 Margaret Mann Phillips, *Erasmus on His Times: A Shortened Version of the Adages of Erasmus* (Cambridge: Cambridge University Press, 1980), pp. 22, 23.

159 Phillips, *Erasmus on His Times*, p. 23.

160 Michel de Montaigne, *The Complete Works* ed. and trans. Donald Frame (London: Everyman, 2003), p. 226.

161 Sir William Petty, *The Advice of W. P. to Mr Samuel Hartlib for the Advancement of Some Particular Parts of Learning* (London, 1647), sig. A2. On Petty's copying machine, see Peck, *Consuming Splendor*, p. 258.

162 Petty, *The Advice of W. P.*, sig. A2.

163 It has been claimed that, in the seventeenth century, scriveners manipulated this power for economic gain, producing documents that were illegible to any except themselves. See Joe Nickell, *Detecting Forgery: Forensic Investigation of Documents* (Lexington: University of Kentucky Press, 1996), p. 15.

164 Anon., *A Summer's Divertisement of Mathematical and Mechanical Curiosities* (Edinburgh, 1695), p. 8.

165 Donald Cardwell, *The Fontana History of Technology* (London: HarperCollins, 1994), p. 423.

166 The *Epiostola de Magnete* (*c.* 1269) of Petrus Peregrinus (or Peregrinus de Maricourt), speculates on the possibility of creating a perpetual motion device employing magnets. See *The Hutchinson Dictionary of Scientists* (Oxford: Helicon, 1996), pp. 380–1.

167 Oswald Spengler, *Man and Technics: A Contribution to a Philosophy of Life* trans. anon. (1931, reprint, Honolulu: University Press of the Pacific, 2002), pp. 84–5. On Spengler, see Jeffrey Herf, *Reactionary Modernism: Technology, Culture, and Politics in Weimar and the Third Reich* (Cambridge, Cambridge University Press, 1984), pp. 38–9.

168 Martin Kemp, 'The Vortex' in E. H. Gombrich, Martin Kemp, and Jane Roberts, *Leonardo da Vinci* (London: Yale University Press/South Bank Centre, 1989), pp. 127. Leonardo's comments precede his own investigations (in Codex Forster II) of designs for a 'perpetual wheel'.

169 Robert Park, *Voodoo Science: The Road from Foolishness to Fraud* (Oxford: Oxford University Press, 2000), pp. 6–7.

170 The chief English works on perpetual motion (or which contain accounts of perpetual motion devices) in the period are: Johannes Taisnierus, *A Treatise on Continuall Motions* (London, 1579); Thomas Tymme, *A Dialogue Concerning Perpetual Motion* (London, 1612); R. D'acres, *The Art of Water-drawing, or A Compendious Abstract of All Sorts of Water-Machins, or Gins, Practised in the World* (London, 1660); Thomas Powell, *Humane Industry or A History of Most Manual Arts* (London, 1661). To these can be added continental works such as James Zabarella, *De Inventione Æterni Motoris* (Frankfurt, 1618). Robert Fludd's perpetual motion device can be found in his *Tractatus secundus de naturae simia seu technica macrocosmi historia in partes undecim divisia* (Oppenheim, 1618), pp. 456, 462. John Dee's device is described in John Dee, *Preface to Euclid, The Elements of Geometrie* trans. Henry Billingsley (London, 1570), p. 34.

171 Henry Dircks, *Perpetuum Mobile or a History of the Search for Self-Motive Power from the 13th to the 19th century* (London, 1870), p. 23. Schott's machine was taken from his *Magiae universalis naturae et artis* (Herbipoli [Würzburg], 1658).

172 Park, *Voodoo Science*, p. 110.

173 Popplow, 'Protection and Promotion', p. 106.

174 Edward Somerset, second Marquis of Worcester, *A century of the names and scantlings of such inventions as at present I can call to mind* (London, 1663), pp. 37–8. On

Somerset's inventions, see Henry Dircks, *The Life, Times, and Scientific Labours of the Second Marquis of Worcester* (London, 1865).

175 William Bray (ed.), *The Diary of John Evelyn* (London: J. M. Dent, 1937), II, p. 37.

176 Isaak de Caus, *A New and Rare Invention of Water-Works shewing the Easiest Waies to raise Water Higher than the Spring. By which invention the Perpetaul Motion is Proposed* trans. John Leak (London, 1659), p. 21.

177 Anon. [attrib. Cressy Dimmock], *An Invention of Engines of Motion lately Brought to Perfection* (London, 1651), sig. A2^v. This 'invention' claimed to be able to perform 'any work now done in England or elsewhere . . . either by wind, water, cattel, or men' (title-page).

178 Francis Bacon, *New Atlantis* in Brian Vickers (ed.), *English Science, Bacon to Newton* (Cambridge: Cambridge University Press, 1987), p. 35.

179 Thomas Powell, *Humane Industry or A History of Most Manual Arts* (London, 1661), p. 25.

180 John Wilkins, *Mathematicall Magick. Or the Wonders That May be Performed by Mechanicall Geometry* (London, 1648), p. 2.

181 Wilkins, *Mathematicall Magick*, p. 3.

182 Wilkins, *Mathematicall Magick*, sig. A5^r.

183 Wilkins, *Mathematicall Magick*, p. 224.

184 Wilkins, *Mathematicall Magick*, p. 224. This observation would later be explained in terms of the First Law of Thermodynamics, which governs the 'conservation of energy'. See T. C. Collocott and A. B. Dobson (eds), *Chambers Dictionary of Science and Technology* 2 vols (Edinburgh: Chambers, 1975), II, p. 1178.

185 See Arthur W. G. H. Ord-Hume, *Perpetual Motion: History of an Obsession* (New York: St Martin's Press, 1977).

186 D'acres, *Art of water-drawing*, p. 24.

187 Although, as D'acres observed, human and animal life was not so much an example of perpetual motion ('*motus perennis*') as 'a motion holding throughout some numbers of years' ('*motus perannis*'). See D'acres, *Art of Water-drawing*, p. 20.

188 Svetlana Alpers, *The Art of Describing: Dutch Art in the Seventeenth Century* (London: John Murray, 1983), p. 5. According to Alpers, Rubens had dismissed the perpetual motion machine of Drebbel as 'nonsense'. On Drebbel, see L. E. Harris, 'Cornelius Drebbel: A Neglected Genius of Seventeenth Century Technology' *Transactions of the Newcomen Society* 31 (1957), pp. 195–204. Smith (*Body of the Artisan*, p. 163) notes that Drebbel claimed that his perpetual motion machine derived its motion 'from the eternal movement of all things', and was thus a machine powered by theology, rather than in conformity with any mechanical law.

189 Thomas Tymme, *A Dialogue Philosophicall. Wherein Natures Secret Closet is Opened, and the Cause of Motion in Nature Shewed out of Matter and Form* (London, 1612), p. 61.

190 Tymme, *A Dialogue Philosophicall*, p. 62.

191 Tymme, *A Dialogue Philosophicall*, p. 62. On the importance of secrecy, as an ideal of kingship within the Jacobean court, of which Drebbel's perpetual motion machine may be taken as emblematic, see the persuasive reading of the episode of James and the perpetual motion engine offered in Wolfe, *Humanism, Machinery, and Renaissance Literature*, pp. 65–7.

192 Shakespeare, *The Sonnets* ed. Kerrigan, p. 35.

193 Hugo Grotius (attrib.), '*In organum motus perpetui quod est pennes / Maximum Britanniacum Regem* Jacobum' trans. Henry Vaughan in Henry Vaughan, *The Works* ed. L. C. Martin (Oxford: Clarendon Press, 1957), p. 682.

194 Vaughan, *Works*, p. 466.

195 King James VI and I, *Political Writings* ed. Johann P. Sommerville (Cambridge: Cambridge University Press, 1994), p. 46.

4 Women and wheels: gender and the machine in the Renaissance

1 In Germany, this redistribution was perhaps surprising given National Socialist devotion to the cult of *kinde, küche,* and *kircher*. Nevertheless, Niall Ferguson claims that 'more women entered the German and Japanese workforce during the [second] war than in Britain and America'. See Niall Ferguson, *The Cash Nexus: Money and Power in the Modern World 1700–2000* (London: Allen Lane/Penguin Books, 2001), p. 401. On women's labour in Europe in the prewar and wartime periods, see Richard Vinen, *A History in Fragments: Europe in the Twentieth Century* (London: Abacus, 2002), pp. 131–6. On the motherhood 'cult' in Nazi Germany, see Michael Burleigh, *The Third Reich: A New History* (London: Macmillan, 2000), pp. 229–32.

2 The connection between Rosie and Isaiah was first noted in the *Kansas City Star*, 6 June 1943, which published Rockwell's image besides that of Michelangelo.

3 On 13 May 1943, just over a fortnight before Rockwell's image appeared in the *Saturday Evening Post*, the 94th and 95th US Bombardment groups, based in East Anglia, flew their first combat missions over Germany. See David Reynolds, *Rich Relations: The American Occupation of Britain 1942–1945* (London: HarperCollins, 1996), pp. 284, 286.

4 On women's wartime labour, see Pamela E. Mack, 'What Difference Has Feminism Made to Engineering in the Twentieth Century?' in Angela N. H. Creager, Elizabeth Lunbeck, and Londa Schiebinger (eds), *Feminism in Twentieth-Century Science, Technology, and Medicine* (Chicago and London: University of Chicago Press, 2001), p. 155.

5 See Merry E. Wiesner, *Working Women in Renaissance Germany* (New Brunswick, NJ: Rutgers University Press, 1986); Susan Cahn, *The Industry of Devotion: The Transformation of Women's Work in England, 1500–1660* (New York: Columbia University Press, 1987); Deborah Simonton, *A History of European Women's Work, 1700 to the Present* (London and New York: Routledge, 1998).

6 Marina Warner, *From the Beast to the Blonde: On Fairy Tales and Their Tellers* (New York: Farrar, Strauss and Giroux, 1994), pp. 136–7.

7 Wayne Franits, *Paragons of Virtue: Women and Domesticity in Seventeenth-century Dutch Art* (Cambridge: Cambridge University Press, 1993), p. 36.

8 See Patricia Baines, *Flax and Linen* (Princes Risborough: Shire Publications, 2003), p. 12.

9 It has been suggested that the production of large-scale tapestries was a response to theories that the plague was airborne, and that they were designed to cover the windows of the affluent. See Norman F. Cantor, *In the Wake of the Plague: The Black Death and the World It Made* (New York: Harper Perennial, 2002), pp. 22–3.

10 Svetlana Alpers, *The Vexations of Art: Velázquez and Others* (New Haven and London: Yale University Press, 2005), p. 149.

11 Mary Sidney, Countess of Pembroke, 'Even Now That Care' in Danielle Clarke (ed.), *Isabella Whitney, Mary Sidney, and Aemilia Lanyer: Renaissance Women Poets* (London: Penguin, 2000), p. 47.

12 On the 'rediscovery' of the narrative content of the painting see Jonathan Brown, *Velázquez: Painter and Courtier* (New Haven and London: Yale University Press, 1986), p. 302.

13 Ovid, *Metamorphoses* trans. Mary M. Innes (Harmondsworth: Penguin Books, 1984), p. 138. For a reading of the Ovidian story in terms of webs or networks of intertextuality, see Sarah Annes Brown, 'Arachne's Web: Intertextual Mythography and the Renaissance Acteon' in Neil Rhodes and Jonathan Sawday (eds), *The Renaissance Computer: Knowledge Technology in the First Age of Print* (London and New York: Routledge, 2000), pp. 120–34.

14 Is the classically draped Arachne standing in front of her tapestry? Or is she, rather, a part of it? For a survey of these conflicting views, see Brown, *Velázquez*, p. 303 (notes 36–7).

15 See, in particular, Ann Rosalind Jones and Peter Stallybrass, *Renaissance Clothing and the Materials of Memory* (Cambridge: Cambridge University Press 2001), pp. 89–103; Alpers, *The Vexations of Art*, pp. 133–80.

16 Brown, *Velázquez*, pp. 252–3.

17 Brown, *Velázquez*, p. 253. See also Alpers, *Vexations of Art*, p. 177.

18 As Carr points out, in capturing the 'transient optical effects of motion in the static medium of paint' Velásquez was following classical precedent: Pliny's *Natural History* (a copy of which the artist owned) commended painterly skill in capturing the movement of wheels. See Dawson W. Carr, 'Painting and Reality: The Art and Life of Velásquez', in Dawson W. Carr, Xavier Bray, John H. Elliott, Larry Keith, and Javier Portús, *Velásquez* (catalogue to the exhibition held at the National Gallery, London, 18 October 2006–21 January 2007) (London: National Gallery/Yale University Press, 2006), p. 50.

19 This woman's posture, her isolation, her dress, her lowly seated position, the unskilled task in which she is engaged, and, above all, her dark complexion, suggest that Velásquez wishes us to identify her either as a *Morisca* – a Spanish Moor – or as a *Zincala*: a gypsy. On anti-gypsy prejudice in seventeenth-century Spain, see Amy Motomura, 'Gypsy Legislation in Spain 1499–1783' *Concord Review* 14 (2003), pp. 141–62. The Moors were finally exiled from Spain to North Africa in 1610. Significantly, in 1627, Velásquez had taken part in an artistic competition (of which he was the winner) based on representing the expulsion of the *Moriscos* from Spain under Philip III. The painting is now lost. See Brown, *Velázquez*, pp. 60–1. *Moriscos* were well known for their participation in the Spanish silk industry. See Thomas F. Glick, 'Moriscos and Marranos as Agents of Technological Diffusion' in Graham Hollister-Short and Frank A. J. L. James (eds), *History of Technology* vol. 17 (London: Mansell, 1996), p. 117.

20 Jones and Stallybrass, *Renaissance Clothing*, p. 89.

21 Edmund Spenser, *The Faerie Queene* ed. A. C. Hamilton (London and New York: Longman, 1977), p. 296; William A. Oram *et al.* (eds), *The Shorter Poems of Edmund Spenser* (New Haven and London: Yale University Press, 1989), p. 428.

22 The centrality of the three central female figures in the image would once have been more emphatic in the picture's original state. See Brown, *Velázquez*, p. 252. The attributes of the fates are usually the distaff or, more rarely, a spinning wheel (Clotho), the spindle (Lachesis) and the shears (Atropos). See James Hall, *Dictionary of Subjects and Symbols in Art* (1974, revised edition, London: John Murray, 1987), p. 302.

23 Jones and Stallybrass, *Renaissance Clothing*, p. 93.

24 Sigmund Freud, *New Introductory Lectures of Psycho-Analysis* (1933) in *The Standard Edition of the Complete Psychological Works of Sigmund Freud* 24 vols ed. and trans. James Strachey in collaboration with Anna Freud (London: Vintage, 2001), XXII, p. 132.

25 Freud's reading is perhaps given more substance it if is recalled that, in the sixteenth-century, a slang term for the penis was 'loom'. I am grateful to Dr Suzanne Trill for alerting me to this etymology.

26 This famous question, attributed to John Ball at the time of the Peasants' Revolt (1381), was probably derived from an earlier source: a text by Richard Rolle of Hampole (*c.* 1300–49). See *Brewer's Dictionary of Phrase and Fable* (London: Cassell, 1999), p. 1260.

27 Freud, *New Introductory Lectures of Psycho-Analysis*, p. 132.

28 Sadie Plant, *Zeros + Ones: Digital Women + The New Technoculture* (London: Fourth Estate, 1998), p. 25.

29 Alpers, *Vexations of Art*, p. 189.

30 T. K. Derry and Trevor I. Williams, *A Short History of Technology from the Earliest Times to A. D. 1900* (1960, reprint, New York: Dover Publications 1993), p. 192.

31 George Basalla, *The Evolution of Technology* (Cambridge: Cambridge University Press, 1988), p. 11.

32 On non-wheeled transport methods, see S. M. Cole, 'Land Transport without Wheels' in Charles Singer, E. J. Holmyard, and A. R. Hall (eds), *A History of Technology* 7 vols (London and New York: Oxford University Press, 1954–78), I, pp. 704–15.

33 Wheels are said to have made their first appearance around 4000 BCE, possibly in Mesopotamia, but abandoned in favour of the camel as a more efficient means of transporting goods and people in the region. See Basalla, *Evolution of Technology*, pp. 8–9; V. Gordon Childe, 'Wheeled Vehicles' in Singer *et al.* (eds), *History of Technology*, I, pp. 716–29. On the disappearance of wheeled transport from the medieval Arab world, see Richard W. Bulliet, *The Camel and the Wheel* (New York: Columbia University Press, 1990), pp. 1–27, 216–36.

34 Basalla, *Evolution of Technology*, p. 8.

35 See M. T. Wright, 'Rational and Irrational Reconstruction: The London Sundial-Calendar and the Early History of Geared Mechanisms' and J. V. Field, 'Some Roman and Byzantine Portable Sundials and the London Sundial Calendar' in Graham Hollister-Short and Frank A. J. L. James (eds), *History of Technology* vol. 12 (London and New York: Mansell, 1990), pp. 65–102, 103–35. The Antikythera Mechanism (1st century BC) is the oldest known example of toothed gearing. On the discovery and operation of the Antikythera Mechanism, see Jo Marchant, 'In Search of Lost Time' *Nature* 444 (30 November 2006), pp. 534–8.

36 Lorne Ladner, *Wheel of Great Compassion: The Practice of the Prayer Wheel in Tibetan Buddhism* (Boston, MA: Wisdom Publications, 2000), pp. 15, 27–8.

37 Lynn White Jr, *Medieval Technology and Social Change* (London and Oxford: Oxford University Press, 1962), p. 86. It has been suggested that various aspects of European wheel technology (the ball and chain governor, the vertical axis windmill, and even the hot-air turbine) may have been the result of Western encounters with various forms of Tibetan 'prayer technology'; see Ladner, *Wheel of Great Compassion*, p. 30.

38 See Bulliet, *Camel and the Wheel*, p. 226.

39 See Katherine A. Winstead, *Chaste Passions: Medieval English Virgin Martyr Legends* (Ithaca and London: Cornell University Press, 2000), pp. 115–16.

40 The association of Catherine with a broken wheel has led some commentators to assume (erroneously) that she herself was 'broken' on the wheel. See Marina Warner, *Monuments and Maidens: The Allegory of the Female Form* (London: Picador, 1985), p. 159.

41 Edward Gibbon, *The History of the Decline and Fall of the Roman Empire* ed. Dean Milman, M. Guizot, and Sir William Smith 8 vols (London: John Murray, 1908), II, p. 130.

42 Jacobus de Voraigne, *The Golden Legend: Readings on the Saints* ed. and trans. William Granger Ryan 2 vols (Princeton, NJ: Princeton University Press, 1993), I, p. 338.

43 Winstead, *Chaste Passions*, p. 155.

44 To be 'broken on the wheel' would become a form of punishment deployed in the early modern period, particularly in France and Germany. Depictions of early-modern execution sites often included wheels, hoisted high into the air, upon which the broken bodies of felons would be exhibited: Brueghel's *Carrying of the Cross* (1564) shows such a detail. Michel Foucault cites an eighteenth-century catalogue of punishments, among which 'to be broken alive and to die on the wheel' was reserved for 'more serious crimes'. In the twentieth century, the wheel as an instrument of punishment was to reappear in the form of the infamous 'Field Punishment No. 1', which involved tying the malefactor to the wheel of a cart or gun limber: a penalty which was still in use in the British Army during the First World War. See Michel Foucault, *Discipline and Punish: The Birth of the Prison* trans. Alan Sheridan (Harmondsworth: Penguin Books, 1977), p. 32; Dennis Winter, *Death's Men: Soldiers of the Great War* (London: Penguin Books, 1978), pp. 42–3.

45 Franz Kafka, *Metamorphosis and Other Stories* (Harmondsworth: Penguin Books, 1974), pp. 167–99.

46 Foucault, *Discipline and Punish*, p. 40.

47 Winstead, *Chaste Passions*, p. 155.

48 Simon Schama, *The Embarrassment of Riches: An Interpretation of Dutch Culture in the Golden Age* (London: Fontana Press, 1987), p. 16.

49 Schama, *Embarrassment of Riches*, p. 402.

50 Merry E. Wiesner, 'Spinsters and Seamstresses: Women in Cloth and Clothing Production' in Margaret W. Ferguson, Maureen Quilligan, and Nancy J. Vickers (eds), *Rewriting the Renaissance: The Discourses of Sexual Difference in Early Modern Europe* (Chicago and London: University of Chicago Press, 1986), p. 202.

51 Alpers, *Vexations of Art*, p. 209.

52 On the use of spindles and distaffs, see Derry and Williams, *Short History of Technology*, pp. 79–80. Distaff, through its association with female labour, came to be a means of describing matrilineal lines of descent.

53 Donald Cardwell, *The Fontana History of Technology* (London: Fontana Press, 1994), pp. 34–5; Baines, *Flax and Linen*, pp. 10–11.

54 The term 'spinster' as a legal definition of a single woman seems to have arisen, in England, in the late sixteenth century. See Susan S. Lanser, 'Singular Politics: The Rise of the British Nation and the Production of the Old Maid' in Judith M. Bennett and Amy M. Froide (eds), *Singlewomen in the European Past 1250–1800* (Philadelphia: University of Pennsylvania Press, 1999), p. 298.

55 Alfred P. Wadsworth and Julia de Lacy Mann, *The Cotton Trade and Industrial Lancashire 1600–1780* (Manchester: Manchester University Press, 1931), p. 11.

56 Wadsworth and de Lacy Mann, *The Cotton Trade and Industrial Lancashire*, p. 11.

57 By contrast, some early-modern communities perceived the solitary spinning woman as an economic threat. See Merry E. Wiesner, 'Having Her Own Smoke: Employment and Independence for Singlewomen in Germany 1400–1750' in Bennett and Froide (eds), *Singlewomen in the European Past 1250–1800*, pp. 197–8. In England, too, the *fem sole* was understood as a threat to the guild system. See Mary Prior, 'Women and the Urban Economy: Oxford 1500–1800' in Mary Prior (ed.), *Women in English Society 1500–1800* (London and New York: Methuen, 1985), p. 110.

58 Jones and Stallybrass, *Renaissance Clothing*, pp. 127–8.

59 Adam Smith, *The Wealth of Nations* (1776) with an introduction by D. D. Raphael (New York, London, and Toronto: Everyman's Library, 1991), p. 227; Derry and Williams, *Short History of Technology*, p. 97.

60 Derry and Williams, *Short History of Technology*, p. 97.

61 On the mechanization of spinning in the fourteenth century, see Joel Mokyr, *The Lever of Riches: Technological Creativity and Economic Progress* (New York and Oxford: Oxford University Press, 1990), p. 54.

62 Jane Whittle, 'Housewives and Servants in Rural England, 1440–1650: Evidence of Women's Work from Probate Documents' *Transactions of the Royal Historical Society* 15 (2005), pp. 51–74 (p. 53).

63 John May, *A Declaration of the Estate of Clothing Now Used within this Realme of England* (London, 1613), p. 2.

64 Whittle, 'Housewives and Servants', pp. 68, 73.

65 Elizabeth Wayland Barber, *Women's Work: The First 20,000 Years Women, Cloth, and Society in Early Times* (New York and London: W. W. Norton, 1994), p. 29.

66 See Alice Clark, *Working Life of Women in the Seventeenth Century* (1919, reprint, London and New York: Routledge, 1982), p. 95.

67 Prior, 'Women and the Urban Economy: Oxford 1500–1800', p. 95.

68 Barber, *Women's Work*, p. 33. On women and technology in later periods, see, in particular, Martha Moore Trescott (ed.), *Dynamos and Virgins Revisited: Women and Technological Change in History* (Metuchen, NJ: Scarecrow Press, 1979); Judith A. McGaw, 'Women and the History of American Technology' *Signs: Journal of Women in Culture and Society* 7 (1982), pp. 798–828; Judy Wajcman, *Feminism*

Confronts Technology (University Park: Pennsylvania State University Press, 1991); Ellen Lupton, *Mechanical Brides: Women and Machines from Home to Office* (New York: Cooper-Hewitt National Museum of Design/Smithsonian Institution/ Princeton Architectural Press, 1993); Ruth Oldenziel, *Making Technology Masculine: Men, Women, and Modern Machines in America, 1870–1945* (Amsterdam: Amsterdam University Press, 1999). A useful overview of work in this area may be found in Carroll Pursell, 'Feminism and the Rethinking of the History of Technology' in Creager *et al.*(eds), *Feminism in Twentieth-Century Science, Technology, and Medicine*, pp. 113–27.

69 Martha Moore Trescott, 'Introduction' in Trescott (ed.), *Dynamos and Virgins*, p. 3.

70 Whittle, 'Housewives and Servants', p. 52.

71 Cynthia Cockburn, 'Caught in the Wheels: The High Cost of Being a Female Cog in the Male Machinery of Engineering' in Donald MacKenzie and Judy Wajcman (eds), *The Social Shaping of Technology* (Buckingham and Philadelphia: Open University Press, 2003), p. 128.

72 See Mokyr, *The Lever of Riches*, p. 51.

73 Judy Wajcman, *TechnoFeminism* (Cambridge: Polity Press, 2004), p. 16.

74 Wajcman, *TechnoFeminism*, p. 16.

75 It should be noted, however, that a male operative is shown working a multiple spinning device based on a crank in Jean Errard's book of machine illustrations, *Premier Livre des instruments mathématiques méchaniques* (1584). See Walter Endrei, 'Jean Errard (1554–1610) and his Book of Machines: *Le Premier Livre des instruments mathématiques méchaniques* of 1584' in Hollister-Short and James (eds), *History of Technology*, vol. 17, p. 186.

76 In contrast to the spinning wheel, the horizontal frame loom (which tended to be operated by men) and which was the other innovation that revolutionized the medieval woollen industry, has been described as, technically, not so much a 'fundamental advance' as it was, rather, a 'matter of convenience to the weaver'. See Derry and Williams, *Short History of Technology*, p. 97. Spinning was a far more laborious task than weaving: 'six spinners were needed to supply each weaver in the late sixteenth century if they all worked full time' (Whittle, 'Housewives and Servants', p. 72).

77 Cockburn, 'Caught in the Wheels', p. 127.

78 Cynthia Cockburn, 'The Material of Male Power' in MacKenzie and Wajcman (eds), *The Social Shaping of Technology*, pp. 190–1.

79 Jones and Stallybrass, *Renaissance Clothing*, p. 125.

80 Lena Cowen Orlin, 'Three Ways to be Invisible in the Renaissance: Sex, Reputation, and Stitchery' in Patricia Fumerton and Simon Hunt (eds), *Renaissance Culture and the Everyday* (Philadelphia: University of Pennsylvania Press, 1999), pp. 183–203 (p. 189).

81 Thomas Blundeville, *His Exercises . . . in Cosmographie, Astronomie, Geographie* (London, 1594), fol. 135. See, also, S. K. Heninger Jr, *The Cosmographical Glass: Renaissance Diagrams of the Universe* (San Marino, CA: Huntington Library, 1977), p. 34.

82 Geoffrey Chaucer, *The Complete Works* ed. W. W. Skeat (London: Oxford University Press, 1973), p. 142. On the iconography of *Fortuna*, see Rudolph Wittkower,

'Chance, Time, and Fortune' *Journal of the Warburg Institute* 1 (1937–8), pp. 313–21; Samuel C. Chew, 'Time and Fortune' *English Literary History* 6 (1939), pp. 83–113; Jerold C. Frakes, *The Fate of Fortune in the Early Middle Ages: The Boethian Tradition* (New York: E. J. Brill, 1988).

83   On sixteenth-century and early-seventeenth-century translations of Boethius, see Michael Witmore, *Culture of Accidents: Unexpected Knowledges in Early Modern England* (Stanford, CA: Stanford University Press, 2001), pp. 45, 173.

84   See St Augustine, *Concerning the City of God against the Pagans* trans. Henry Bettenson (Harmondsworth: Penguin Books, 1984), p. 182 (I. V. III).

85   Robert Graves interprets this myth in terms of the 'burning wheels rolled downhill at European midsummer festivities, as a sign that the sun has reached its zenith and must now decline again until the winter solstice'. See Robert Graves, *The Greek Myths* 2 vols (Harmondsworth: Penguin Books, 1955), I, p. 209.

86   The history plays are concerned not only with shifts in estate, but also with cycles of repetition akin to the Greek idea of *dike*: a restoration comparable to our idea of atonement. See Brian Vickers, *Towards Greek Tragedy* (London and New York: Longman, 1973), p. 24.

87   See Henninger, *Cosmographical Glass*, pp. 4–6. Recorde's title page is given architectural expression in the timber-framed manor house of Little Moreton Hall, near Congleton in Cheshire, where the allegorical figures of Destiny and Fortune (together with their inscriptions derived from Recorde) are represented in the gallery of the house.

88   Witmore, *Culture of Accidents*, p. 23.

89   Christopher Marlowe, *The Works* ed. C. F. Tucker Brooke (Oxford: Clarendon Press, 1941), p. 384.

90   Sir Walter Raleigh, 'The 21st (and last) Book of the Ocean to Cynthia' in Gerald Hammond (ed.), *Sir Walter Raleigh: Selected Writings* (Harmondsworth: Penguin Books, 1984), pp. 38–9 (ll. 81–5).

91   On the relationship between Raleigh and the Queen, see William A. Oram, 'Raleigh, The Queen, and Elizabethan Court Poetry' in Patrick Cheney, Andrew Hadfield, and Garrett A. Sullivan Jr (eds), *Early Modern English Poetry: A Critical Companion* (New York and Oxford: Oxford University Press, 2007), pp. 113–24.

92   Stephen Greenblatt, *Renaissance Self-Fashioning: From More to Shakespeare* (Chicago and London: University of Chicago Press, 1980), pp. 136–7.

93   Sir Thomas Wyatt, *Collected Poems* ed. Joost Daalder (Oxford and London: Oxford University Press, 1975), p. 21.

94   Wyatt, *Collected Poems*, p. 147.

95   Isabella Whitney, 'The Auctor to the Reader' in Clark (ed.), *Renaissance Women Poets*, p. 5.

96   Thomas Carew, 'Elegy upon the Death of the Dean of St Paul's, Dr John Donne' (1633) in Thomas Clayton (ed.), *Cavalier Poets: Selected Poems* (Oxford and London: Oxford University Press, 1978), p. 196.

97   Cynthia Marshall, 'Wound-Man: *Coriolanus*, Gender, and the Theatrical Construction of Interiority', in Valerie Traub, M. Lindsay Kaplan, and Dympna Callaghan (eds), *Feminist Readings of Early Modern Culture: Emerging Subjects* (Cambridge: Cambridge University Press, 1996), pp. 93–118 (p. 109).

98   Jones and Stallybrass, *Renaissance Clothing*, p. 110.

99   Janet Adelman, *Suffocating Mothers: Fantasies of Maternal Origin in Shakespeare's Plays, Hamlet to The Tempest* (New York and London: Routledge, 1992), p. 148.

100 See Brian Cotterell and Johan Kamminga, *Mechanics of Pre-Industrial Technology* (Cambridge and New York: Cambridge University Press, 1990), pp. 188–9. See, also E. W. Marsden, *Greek and Roman Artillery – Historical Development* (Oxford: Clarendon Press, 1969). For an earlier reading of Coriolanus in the context of machinery, see Jonathan Sawday, '"Forms such as Never Were in Nature": The Renaissance Cyborg' in Erica Fudge, Ruth Gilbert, and Susan Wiseman (eds), *At the Borders of the Human: Beasts, Bodies and Natural Philosophy in the Early Modern Period* (Basingstoke and New York: Macmillan/St Martin's Press, 1999), pp. 171–95. Richard Wilson has described Coriolanus as 'the motor of the future', suggesting that he is comparable to an 'instrument of England's industrial revolution, the threshing machine'. See Richard Wilson, *Will Power: Essays on Shakespearean Authority* (New York and London: Harvester Wheatsheaf, 1993), pp. 87–8. This is beguiling, but unlikely. Though Coriolanus is indeed associated with agricultural labour in Volumnia's description of him as being 'like to harvest-man that's tasked to mow', in the sixteenth century threshing was undertaken with the help of animal hooves, boards studded with flints, and jointed flails. The threshing machine did not make its first appearance until 1784, the invention of the Scottish millwright, Andrew Meikle. See Derry and Williams, *Short History of Technology*, pp. 58, 672–3.

101 See Norbert Weiner, *Cybernetics or Control and Communication in the Animal and the Machine* (1948, reprint, Cambridge, MA: MIT Press, 1996), pp. 40–1.

5 'Nature wrought': artifice, illusion, and magical mechanics

1   Norbert Weiner, *Cybernetics or Control and Communication in the Animal and the Machine* (1948, reprint, Cambridge, MA: MIT Press, 1996), p. 39.

2   John Donne, *Poetical Works* ed. Sir Herbert Grierson (1937, reprint, London: Oxford University Press, 1973), p. 299.

3   Thus Augustine: '. . . God is the great artificer in the great things; but that does not mean he is an inferior artist in the small.' Augustine, *City of God* trans. Henry Bettenson (Harmondsworth: Penguin Books, 1984), II. XI. 22 (p. 454), and II. XI. 26 (p. 459).

4   Maurice Evans (ed.), *Elizabethan Sonnets* (London, Melbourne, and Toronto: Everyman's Library, 1977), pp. 104, 127.

5   John Donne, *Selected Prose* ed. Neil Rhodes (Harmondsworth: Penguin Books, 1987), p. 102.

6   See, too, Donne's fascination with the expansive properties of gold traced in John Carey, *John Donne: Life, Mind and Art* (London: Faber and Faber, 1981), pp. 184–6.

7   Marcos Martinón-Torres and Thilo Rehren, 'Alchemy, Chemistry and Metallurgy in Renaissance Europe: A Wider Context for Fire-Assay Remains' *Historical Metallurgy* 39 (2005), pp. 14–28 (p. 18).

8   Donne, *Poetical Works*, p. 87.

9   W. B. Yeats, 'Sailing to Byzantium' in Norman Jeffares (ed.), *W. B. Yeats: Selected Poetry* (London: Macmillan, 1969), p. 105.

10 Yeats, 'Byzantium' in Jeffares (ed.), *Yeats: Selected Poetry*, p. 154. The Byzantine Empire was famous for its marvellous automata. See Gerard Brett, 'The Automata of the Byzantine "Throne of Solomon"' *Speculum* 29 (1954), pp. 477–87.

11 Sir Thomas Browne, *The Major Works* ed. C. A. Patrides (Harmondsworth: Penguin Books, 1984), p. 105.

12 Guillaume de Saluste, Sieur du Bartas, *The Divine Weeks and Works* trans. Joshua Sylvester, ed. Susan Snyder, 2 vols (Oxford: Clarendon Press, 1979). All references to the poem are to this edition.

13 Du Bartas, *Divine Weeks*, II, p. 803 (editor's note). Compare this praise of the Strasbourg clock to Nicodemus Frischlin's *Carmen de astronomico horologio Argentortatensi* (1575): 'O divine inventions of the human hand! What work does either God or nature do anywhere which we do not imitate . . .' Quoted in Francis C. Haber, 'The Clock as Intellectual Artefact' in Klaus Maurice and Otto Mayr (eds), *The Clockwork Universe: German Clocks and Automata 1550–1650* (Washington, DC, and New York: Smithsonian Institution and Neale Watson Academic Publications, 1980), p. 18.

14 Georgius Agricola, *De Re Metallica* trans. Herbert Clark Hoover and Lou Henry Hoover (New York: Dover Publications, 1950), p. 18.

15 Agricola, *De Re Metallica*, p. 12.

16 Agricola, *De Re Metallica*, p. 19. On metal work in the Renaissance, see B. G. Awty, 'The Blast Furnace in the Renaissance Period: *Haut Fourneau* or *Fondene?*' *Transactions of the Newcomen Society* 61 (1989), pp. 65–78.

17 Paula Findlen, 'Rudolf II and the Prague Court' in Malcolm Oster (ed.), *Science in Europe 1500–1800: A Secondary Sources Reader* (Basingstoke: Palgrave Macmillan/The Open University, 2002), p. 115. On the classificatory principles informing early-modern cabinets of curiosity, see Claire Preston, 'In the Wilderness of Forms: Ideas and Things in Thomas Browne's Cabinets of Curiosity' in Neil Rhodes and Jonathan Sawday (eds), *The Renaissance Computer: Knowledge Technology in the First Age of Print* (London and New York: Routledge, 2000), pp. 170–83. For a taxonomy of objects to be found in the *wunderkammern* culture of the period, see Martin Kemp, '"Wrought by No Artist's Hand": The Natural, the Artificial, the Exotic, and the Scientific in Some Artifacts of the Renaissance' in Claire Farago, *Reframing the Renaissance: Visual Culture in Europe and Latin America 1450–1650* (New Haven and London: Yale University Press, 1995), pp. 177–96 (pp. 177–8). On the display of objects in *wunderkammern* crafted with the help of new optical instruments, see Linda Levy Peck, *Consuming Splendor: Society and Culture in Seventeenth-century England* (Cambridge: Cambridge University Press, 2005), pp 154–6. Claire Preston has traced the rise of 'spoof' collections, such as Sir Thomas Browne's *Musæum Clausum* (1684), with its collection of imaginary books, images, and objects parodying the *wunderkammern* of the period. See Claire Preston, *Thomas Browne and the Writing of Early Modern Science* (Cambridge: Cambridge University Press, 2005), pp. 155–74.

18 Kemp, 'Wrought by No Artist's Hand', p. 181.

19 See Marina Belozerskaya, *Luxury Arts of the Renaissance* (London: Thames and Hudson, 2005), p. 25.

20 John Milton, *Complete Shorter Poems* ed. John Carey (London: Longman, 1968), p. 212.

21 Steven Shapin, *The Scientific Revolution* (Chicago and London: University of Chicago Press, 1996), p. 31.

22 Plato, *The Republic* trans. Desmond Lee (London: Harmondsworth, 1955), pp. 421-6 (X. 595-8b). On the complex question of the distinction between art and nature in antiquity, see, in particular, Lawrence Manley, *Convention 1500-1700* (Cambridge, MA, and London: Harvard University Press 1980), pp. 25-36.

23 As Lorraine Daston and Katharine Park write of this Aristotelian distinction: 'Artefacts lack ontological identity, or "natures"... They are necessarily posterior to and parasitic upon natural objects.' See Lorraine Daston and Katharine Park, *Wonders and the Order of Nature* (New York: Zone Books, 2001), p. 264.

24 Augustine, *City of God*, II. XI. 16 (p. 447).

25 Quoted in Charles Nicholl, *The Chemical Theatre* (London: Routledge and Kegan Paul, 1980), p. 27.

26 See Edmund Spenser, *The Faerie Queene* ed. A. C. Hamilton (London and New York: Longman, 1977), p. 362.

27 Thus, in 'framing' Coriolanus, Volumnia may be said to have usurped the (Aristotelian) role of the male principle in the act of generation: that of investing the material body with its sensitive soul – a process which Volumnia has, moreover, corrupted. See Thomas Laqueur, *Making Sex: Body and Gender from the Greeks to Freud* (Cambridge, MA, and London: Harvard University Press, 1990), p. 30.

28 Aristotle, *The Poetics* ed. and trans. S. H. Butcher (New York: Dover Publications, 1951), p. 15 (IV. 2-5).

29 Sir Philip Sidney, *An Apology for Poetry* (1595) ed. Geoffrey Shepherd (Manchester: Manchester University Press, 1973), p. 101.

30 Roger Ascham, *The Schoolmaster* (1570) in Brian Vickers (ed.), *English Renaissance Literary Criticism* (Oxford: Clarendon Press, 1999), p. 145.

31 Marcus Popplow, 'Privileges and Promotion: Privileges for Invention and Books of Machines in the Early Modern Period' in Graham Hollister-Short (ed.), *History of Technology* vol. 20 (London and New York: Mansell, 1998), p. 107.

32 Terence Cave, *The Cornucopian Text: Problems of Writing in the French Renaissance* (Oxford: Clarendon Press, 1979), p. 76. For a more general discussion of the role of imitation and invention in Renaissance poetic theory and practice, see Thomas M. Greene, *The Light in Troy: Imitation and Discovery in Renaissance Poetry* (New Haven and London: Yale University Press, 1982), particularly pp. 28-53.

33 Thomas Hobbes, 'The Answer of Mr Hobbes to Sir Will. Davenant's Preface Before Gondibert' (1650) in David F. Gladish (ed.), *Sir William Davenant's Gondibert* (Oxford: Clarendon Press, 1971), p. 49.

34 George Puttenham, *The Arte of English Poesie* (1589) in Vickers (ed.), *English Renaissance Literary Criticism*, p. 194.

35 See John Peacock, *The Stage Designs of Inigo Jones: The European Context* (Cambridge: Cambridge University Press, 1995), p. 20.

36 Puttenham, *The Arte of English Poesie* in Vickers (ed.), *English Renaissance Literary Criticism*, pp. 201-2.

37 R. D'acres, *Art of Water-drawing* (London, 1660), p. 37. This passage is a translation of a section of the Preface to Ubaldo's *Mechanicorum Liber* (1577).

38 Daston and Park, *Wonders and the Order of Nature*, p. 265.

39 Puttenham, *The Arte of English Poesie* in Vickers (ed.), *English Renaissance Literary Criticism*, pp. 292–3.

40 Giorgio Vasari, *Lives of the Artists* trans. George Bull (Harmondsworth: Penguin Books, 1976), p. 336.

41 Frank Kermode, *English Pastoral Poetry, from the Beginnings to Marvell* (London: Harrap, 1952), p. 37.

42 Ben Jonson, *The Complete Plays* ed. Felix E. Schelling, 2 vols (London: Everyman's Library, 1967), II, p. 17.

43 Anne Goldgar, 'Nature as Art: The Case of the Tulip' in Pamela H. Smith and Paula Findlen (eds), *Merchants and Marvels: Commerce, Science, and Art in Early Modern Europe* (New York and London: Routledge, 2002), pp. 325–6. See also Patrick Mauries, *Cabinets of Curiosities* (London: Thames and Hudson, 2002), pp. 69–93.

44 Pamela H. Smith, *The Body of the Artisan: Art and Experience in the Scientific Revolution* (Chicago and London: University of Chicago Press, 2004), p. 76.

45 Smith, *Body of the Artisan*, pp. 74–5.

46 Robert Herrick, *The Complete Poetry* ed. J. Max Patrick (New York: Anchor Books, 1963), p. 248.

47 See Craig Harbison, *The Mirror of the Artist: Northern Renaissance Art in its Historical Context* (Upper Saddle River, NJ: Prentice Hall, 1995), p. 110.

48 Peacock, *Stage Designs of Inigo Jones*, p. 36.

49 C. S. Lewis, *The Allegory of Love: A Study in Medieval Tradition* (1936, reprint, London: Oxford University Press, 1972), p. 325.

50 Agricola, *De Re Metallica*, p. xxix.

51 Quoted in Kemp, 'Wrought by No Artist's Hand', p. 191.

52 On the mythology surrounding Arachne, and on the more general fascination with nets in the Renaissance, see Sawday, 'Towards the Renaissance Computer' in Rhodes and Sawday (eds), *The Renaissance Computer*, pp. 35–40; Sarah Annes Brown, 'Arachne's Web: Intertextual Mythography and the Renaissance Acteon' in Rhodes and Sawday (eds), *The Renaissance Computer*, pp. 120–34.

53 Harry Berger Jr, *The Allegorical Temper: Vision and Reality in The Faerie Queene Book II* (New Haven: Yale University Press, 1957), p. 218.

54 Stephen Greenblatt, *Renaissance Self-Fashioning: From More to Shakespeare* (Chicago and London: University of Chicago Press, 1980), p. 189.

55 Greenblatt, *Renaissance Self-Fashioning*, p. 172.

56 Spenser, *The Faerie Queene*, p. 296 (editor's note).

57 Leo Marx, *The Machine in the Garden: Technology and the Pastoral Idea in America* (1964, revised edition, Oxford and New York: Oxford University Press, 2000), p. 67.

58 Sir Henry Wotton, *The Elements of Architecture* (London, 1624), pp. 112–13. See also John Dixon Hunt and Peter Wills (eds), *The Genius of the Place: The English Landscape Garden 1625–1820* (Cambridge, MA: MIT Press, 1998), p. 50.

59 John Wecker, *Eighteen Books of the Secrets of Art and Nature, being the Summe and Substance of Naturall Philosophy* trans. R. Read (London, 1660), p. 249.

60 Wecker, *Eighteen Books of the Secrets of Art and Nature*, p. 249.

61 Ben Jonson, '*Discoveries (1640–1)*' in Ian Donaldson (ed.), *Ben Jonson* (The Oxford Authors) (Oxford and New York: Oxford University Press, 1985), p. 561.

62 Allardyce Nicoll notes that the 'homely' term 'engine' was used to describe these devices in earlier masques such as *The Masque of Blacknesse* (1605), *Hymenai* (1606), and *Lord Hay's Masque* (1607), but that this term gave way to the word 'machine' derived from the Italian *macchina* in the *Masque of Oberon* (1611) and later. See Allardyce Nicoll, *Stuart Masques and the Renaissance Stage* (London: Harrap, 1937), p. 60.

63 Ben Jonson, *Selected Masques* ed. Stephen Orgel (New Haven and London: Yale University Press, 1970), p. 51. On the staging of theatrical effects, in addition to Orgel's helpful introduction to the *Selected Masques*, and Peacock's work, see Lily B. Campbell. *Scenes and Machines on the English Stage During the Renaissance* (1923, reprint, New York: Barnes and Noble, 1960); Richard Southern, *Changeable Scenery: Its Origin and Development in the British Theatre* (London: Faber and Faber, 1952); Philip Butterworth, *Theatre of Fire: Special Effects in Early English and Scottish Theatre* (London: Society for Theatre Research, 1998).

64 Jonson, *Selected Masques*, pp. 54–5.

65 On the operation of the *machina versatilis* which gave way to the *scena ductilis* or succession of tractable scenes see John Harris, Stephen Orgel, and Roy Strong, *The King's Arcadia: Inigo Jones and the Stuart Court* (London: Arts Council of Great Britain, 1973), p. 45.

66 Jonson, *Selected Masques*, p. 69.

67 See Michael Leapman, *Inigo. The Life of Inigo Jones: Architect of the English Renaissance* (London: Headline, 2003), p. 82.

68 Peacock speculates (*Stage Designs of Inigo Jones*, p. 165) that it may have been Queen Anne who 'was the real devotee of floating islands, revolving thrones, and all that other retardataire paraphernalia'.

69 Jonson, *Selected Masques*, pp. 17–18 (editor's note).

70 Donaldson (ed.), *Ben Jonson*, p. 462. On the quarrel between Jonson and Jones, see Donaldson's note to the poem (Donaldson (ed.), *Ben Jonson*, p. 721) together with D. J. Gordon, 'Poet and Architect: The Intellectual Setting of the Quarrel between Ben Jonson and Inigo Jones', in Stephen Orgel (ed.), *The Renaissance Imagination. Essays and Lectures by D. J. Gordon* (Berkeley: University of California Press, 1976), pp. 77–101.

71 Donaldson (ed.), *Ben Jonson*, p. 463.

72 John Summerson, *Inigo Jones* (1966, reprint, New Haven and London: Paul Mellon Centre for Studies in British Art/Yale University Press, 2000), p. 12; Leapman, *Inigo. The Life of Inigo Jones*, p. 6.

73 On the Hermetic tradition in the Renaissance, see M. J. B. Allen, 'Marsilio Ficino, Hermes Trismegistus and the Corpus Hermeticum' in John Henry and Sarah Hutton (eds), *New Perspectives on Renaissance Thought* (London: Duckworth, 1990), pp. 38–47. On the broader Renaissance fascination with Egyptian antiquities, see Brian A. Curran, 'The Renaissance Afterlife of Ancient Egypt' in Peter Ucko and Timothy Champion (eds), *The Wisdom of Egypt: Changing Visions Through the Ages* (London: UCL Press/Institute of Archaeology, 2003), pp. 101–31.

74 Henry Cornelius Agrippa, *Three Books of Occult Philosophy* trans. James Freake, ed. Donald Tyson (St Paul, MN: Llewellyn Publications, 2004), p. 233.

75 Frances Yates, *Giordano Bruno and the Hermetic Tradition* (1964, reprint, London

and Chicago: Routledge and Kegan Paul/University of Chicago Press, 1982), p. 149 (note).

76 Quoted in Yates, *Giordano Bruno*, p. 147.

77 Quoted in Yates, *Giordano Bruno*, p. 148.

78 Robert Burton, *The Anatomy of Melancholy* (1628) (London: Chatto and Windus, 1908) (Part 2, Section 2 Member 4 'Exercise Rectified'), p. 354.

79 C. F. Tucker Brooke (ed.), *The Works of Christopher Marlowe* (Oxford: Oxford University Press, 1941), p. 149.

80 Jonson, *Complete Plays*, II, p. 260.

81 Alfred Chapuis and Edmond Droz, *Automata: A Historical and Technical Study* trans. Alan Reid (1928, reprint, Neuchatel/London: Editions du Griffon/Batsford, 1958), p. 24. On jointed figures, see Mary Hillier, *Automata and Mechanical Toys: An Illustrated History* (1976, reprint, London: Bloomsbury, 1988), p. 11.

82 See Susan Murphy, 'Heron of Alexandria's *Automaton-Making*' in Graham Hollister-Short and Frank A. J. L. James (eds), *History of Technology* vol. 17 (London: Mansell, 1996), p. 5. Chapuis and Droz (*Automata*, p. 17) claim that such devices were still being manufactured in the medieval period.

83 Chapuis and Droz, *Automata*, p. 13.

84 Eamon Duffy, *The Stripping of the Altars: Traditional Religion in England 1400–1580* (New Haven and London: Yale University Press, 1992), p. 167.

85 See Hillier, *Automata*, p. 18.

86 See Chapuis and Droz, *Automata*, p. 40. On the Arabic transmission of Hellenistic texts on mechanisms and engineering, see Donald R. Hill, *Islamic Science and Engineering* (Edinburgh: Edinburgh University Press, 1993), particularly pp. 122–3.

87 Murphy, 'Heron of Alexandria's *Automaton-Making*', p. 1.

88 Edmund Chilmead (trans.), *Unheard of Curiosities concerning the Talismanical Scultures of the Persians* (London, 1650), title page.

89 Isaak de Caus, *New and rare Invention of Water-works* trans. John Leak (London, 1659), p. 33. John Bate's *The Mysteries of Arts and Nature* (London, 1635) also contained descriptions (pp. 24, 25) of moving statues and 'sounding' statues, as well as more conventional machinery such as water-raising devices.

90 Chapuis and Droz, *Automata*, p. 43.

91 Chapuis and Droz, *Automata*, pp. 43–6.

92 Chapuis and Droz, *Automata*, p. 40.

93 Quoted in Roy Strong, *The Renaissance Garden in England* (London: Thames and Hudson, 1979), p. 79.

94 Thomas Nashe, *The Unfortunate Traveller* ed. J. B. Steane (Harmondsworth: Penguin Books, 1972), pp. 327, 329.

95 Nashe, *Unfortunate Traveller*, p. 328.

96 Nashe, *Unfortunate Traveller*, p. 330.

97 Illustrations of these Renaissance automata may be found in Klaus Maurice and Otto Mayer (eds), *The Clockwork Universe: German Clocks and Automata 1550–1650* (Washington, DC, and New York: Smithsonian Institution and Neale Watson Academic Publications, 1980), pp. 234–88.

98 Belozerskaya, *Luxury Arts*, p. 71.

99 Chapuis and Droz, *Automata*, p. 80. Chapuis and Droz suggest (p. 77) that clocks

and watches, used as gifts, enabled the Jesuits to establish themselves in Beijing in 1601.

100 See Arnold Pacey, *Technology in World Civilization* (1991, reprint, Cambridge, MA: MIT Press, 2000), pp. 35–6, 96.

101 Benvenuto Cellini, *Autobiography* trans. George Bull (Harmondsworth: Penguin Books, 1956), p. 298.

102 Horst Bredekamp, *The Lure of Antiquity and the Cult of the Machine* trans. Allison Brown (Princeton: Markus Wiener, 1995), p. 2.

103 One of Schlottheim's copper lobsters has survived (though damaged in 1945), and is now housed in the Dresden Staatliche Kunstammlungen.

104 Pappus of Alexandria, *Mathematical Collections* (8. 1–2) in John W. Humphrey, John P. Oleson, and Andrew N. Sherwood (eds), *Greek and Roman Technology: A Sourcebook* (London and New York: Routledge, 1998), p. 47. On Pappus and mechanics, see also, John Fauvel and Jeremy Gray (eds), *The History of Mathematics: A Reader* (London: Macmillan in association with the Open University Press, 1987), pp. 199–200.

105 St Augustine, *City of God* trans. Henry Bettenson (Harmondsworth: Penguin Books, 1972) pp. 974–5 (V. xxi. 6).

106 See Marina Warner, *Monuments and Maidens: The Allegory of the Female Form* (London: Picador, 1987), p. 226.

107 Dorothea Wender (trans), *Hesiod and Theogonis* (Harmondsworth: Penguin Books, 1973), p. 63.

108 On the confusing mythic ancestry of Talus/Talos see Robert Graves, *The Greek Myths* 2 vols (Harmondsworth: Penguin Books, 1962), I, p. 312, II, p. 247. On the Renaissance interpretation of the legend of Talus, see Jessica Wolfe, *Humanism, Machinery, and Renaissance Literature* (Cambridge: Cambridge University Press, 2004), p. 211.

109 Michael O'Connell, 'The Faerie Queene, Book V' in A. C. Hamilton, Donald Cheney, W. F. Blissett, David A. Richardson, and William W. Barker (eds), *The Spenser Encyclopaedia* (1990, reprint, London: Routledge, 1996), p. 280.

110 These examples of medieval automata are all culled from J. Douglas Bruce, 'Human Automata in Classical Tradition and Medieval Romance' *Modern Philology* 10 (1913), pp. 511–26.

111 The story seems to have first been told by Matteo Corsini in his *Rosnio della Vita* (1373). See Gaby Wood, *Living Dolls: A Magical History of the Quest for Mechanical Life* (London: Faber and Faber, 2002), p. xv; Steven Connor, *Dumbstruck: A Cultural History of Ventriloquism* (Oxford: Oxford University Press, 2000), p. 339.

112 See Eli Maor, *Trigonometric Delights* (Princeton, NJ: Princeton University Press, 1998), p. 49 (note 5). The story was propagated by Ramus in the later sixteenth century.

113 See Bertrand Gille, *The Renaissance Engineers* trans. anon. (London: Lund Humphries, 1966), p. 27.

114 See J. Voskuil, 'The Speaking Machine through the Ages' *Transactions of the Newcomen Society* 26 (1947), pp. 259–67.

115 See Arthur Dickson, *Valentine and Orson: A Study in Late Medieval Romance* (New York: Columbia University Press, 1929).

116 See John Webster Spargo, *Virgil the Necromancer: Studies in Virgilian Legends* (Cambridge, MA: Harvard University Press, 1934); Dickson, *Valentine and Orson*, pp. 203, 208, 211, 214.

117 Miguel de Cervantes, *The Adventures of Don Quixote* trans. J. M. Cohen (Harmondsworth: Penguin Books, 1950), p. 875.

118 Anon., 'The Vision of Machines' in *The Famous Historie of Fryer Bacon, Containing the Wonderfull Thinges That He Did in His Life* (London, 1627), sig. C4. 'The Vision of machines' forms the substance of a later work by 'T. M.', which is attributed to John Dee: See T. M., *Friar Bacon His Discovery of the Miracles of Art, Nature, and Magic Faithfully Translated Out of Dr Dees Own Copy* (London, 1659), pp. 18–19.

119 James Snyder, *Northern Renaissance Art Painting, Sculpture, The Graphic Arts from 1350–1675* rev. Larry Silver and Henry Luttikhuizen (2nd edition, Upper Saddle River, NJ: Prentice Hall, 2005), p. 78.

120 Wolfe *Humanism, Machinery, and Renaissance Literature*, p. 211.

121 Lorraine Daston and Katherine Park, *Wonders and the Order of Nature 1150–1750* (New York: Zone Books, 2001), p. 95.

122 The chief sources for such designs were the *Book of Ingenious Devices* (*Kitāb al-Hiyal*) of the Banū Mūsà brothers (Baghdad, ninth century), the *Mafātih al-'Ulūm* (a tenth-century scientific encyclopaedia), an eleventh-century treatise on water clocks written in Muslim Spain, and the machine book of Ibn al-Razzāz al-Jazarī written at the beginning of the thirteenth century. Many Islamic designs and devices were collected in a compilation, the *Libros del Saber de Astronomia* (1277) written in Castilian. For a comprehensive account of these works, see Hill, *Islamic Science and Technology*, pp. 122–48. On the Book of Ingenious Devices, see Donald R. Hill, 'The Banū Mūsà and their *Book of Ingenious Devices*' in A. Rupert Hall and Norman Smith (eds), *History of Technology* vol. 2 (London: Mansell, 1977), pp. 39–76.

123 Ben Jonson, *Complete Plays*, II, p. 27.

124 On the trope of *sponte nascentia*, see Jonathan Sawday, '"The Chief Mystery of the Seminall business": Andrew Marvell, William Harvey, Abraham Cowley and the Politics of Fertility in the Seventeenth Century' *English: The Journal of the English Association*, 56 (2007), pp. 107–125.

125 Pierce Tempest, *Iconologia: or Moral Emblems by Caesar Ripa* (London, 1709), p. 7. On Tempest's English version of Ripa, see Michael Bath, *Speaking Pictures; English Emblem Books and Renaissance Culture* (London and New York: Longman, 1994), pp. 259–61.

126 See James Hall, *Dictionary of Subjects and Symbols in Art* (1974, revised edition, London: John Murray, 1987), p. 43.

127 Mark E. Rosheim, *Robot Evolution: The Development of Anthrobotics* (New York and Chichester: John Wiley and Sons, 1994), p. 21.

128 Bredekamp, *The Lure of Antiquity*, pp. 31–2, 34. The contents of Rudolf's *Kunstkammer* ('long considered the product of a deranged mind') are known from an inventory dated 1607–11.

129 Neils Van Holst, *Creators, Collectors and Connoisseurs: The Anatomy of Artistic Taste from Antiquity to the Present Day* trans. Brian Battershaw (Cologne and London: Dumont Presse/Thames and Hudson, 1976), p. 107; Paula Findeln, 'Rudolf II

and the Prague Court' in Malcolm Oster (ed.), *Science in Europe, 1500–1800: A Secondary Sources Reader* (Basingstoke: Palgrave Macmillan/The Open University, 2002), p. 116.

130 Hillier, *Automata*, p. 18.

131 Michael Witmore, 'The Mechanics of Tudor Civic Pageantry' (unpublished paper). I am extremely grateful to Professor Witmore for allowing me to see an early draft of his work.

132 John Wilkins, *Mathematicall Magick or The Wonders that may be Performed by Mechanicall Geometry* (London, 1648), p. 172.

133 Wilkins, *Mathematicall Magick*, pp. 176, 191.

134 Wilkins, *Mathematicall Magick*, p. 174.

135 Murphy, 'Heron of Alexandria's *On Automaton Making*', p. 6.

136 Sir Philip Sidney, *An Apology for Poetry* ed. Geoffrey Shepherd (Manchester: Manchester University Press, 1973), pp. 100–1.

137 Homer, *The Iliad* trans. E. V. Rieu (Harmondsworth: Penguin Books, 1976), p. 348.

138 Quoted in Belozerskaya, *Luxury Arts*, p. 70.

139 Belozerskaya, *Luxury Arts*, p. 70.

140 Jonson, *The Complete Plays*, II. p. 75.

141 See David O. Frantz, *Festum Voluptatis: A Study of Renaissance Erotica* (Columbus: Ohio University Press, 1989), pp. 43–6; Paula Findlen, 'Humanism, Politics, and Pornography in Renaissance Italy' in Lynn Hunt (ed.), *The Invention of Pornography: Obscenity and the Origins of Modernity, 1500–1800* (New York: Zone Books, 1993), pp. 49–108.

142 Stephen Gaukroger, *Descartes: An Intellectual Biography* (Oxford: Clarendon Press, 1995), p. 1.

143 Gaukroger, *Descartes*, pp. 1, 418 (note).

144 Jonathan Swift, *Poetical Works* ed. Herbert Davis (London and New York: Oxford University Press, 1967), pp. 517–18; Connor, *Dumbstruck*, p. 358. On *L'Eve Future*, see also R. L. Rutsky, *High Technē: Art and Technology from the Machine Aesthetic to the Posthuman* (Minneapolis and London: University of Minnesota Press, 1999), p. 42.

145 Wood, *Living Dolls*, p. xvii.

146 Sigmund Freud, 'The Uncanny' in Albert Dickson (ed.), *Sigmund Freud: Art and Literature* (The Pelican Freud Library vol. 14) trans. James Strachey (Harmondsworth: Penguin Books, 1985), p. 354.

147 Freud, 'The Uncanny', p. 347; Ernst Jentsch, 'On the Psychology of the Uncanny' ('Zur Psychologie des Unheimlichen') *Angelaki: Journal of the Theoretical Humanities* 2 (1995), pp. 7–16.

148 Freud, 'The Uncanny', p. 347. See also Tom Standage, *The Mechanical Turk: The True Story of the Chess Playing Machine that Fooled the World* (London: Penguin Books, 2002), pp. 6–13. For an insight into the extent to which automata had captured the popular imagination in the nineteenth century, see the collection of cuttings assembled by G. S. Peckham (*c.* 1840) entitled *Exhibitions of Mechanical and Other Works of Ingenuity*, now in the British Library (call mark 1269.h.38).

149 On the operation of the 'Jacquard Loom', see Donald Cardwell, *The Fontana History*

of Technology (London: HarperCollins, 1994), pp. 186–8. In 1741, silk workers of Lyons rioted because they were fearful (as Tom Standage writes) of being transformed into 'human parts in what would be, in effect, a huge automaton'. See Standage, *The Mechanical Turk*, p. 12.

150 T. K. Derry and Trevor I. Williams, *A Short History of Technology from the Earliest Times to AD 1900* (1960, reprint, New York: Dover Publications, 1993), p. 570.

151 See Adrian J. Randall, 'The Philosophy of Luddism: The Case of the West of England Woollen Workers, ca. 1790–1809' in Terry S. Reynolds and Stephen H. Cutcliffe (eds), *Technology and the West: A Historical Anthology from Technology and Culture* (Chicago and London: University of Chicago Press, 1997), p. 182.

152 See Keith Grint and Steve Woolgar, *The Machine at Work: Technology, Work and Organization* (Cambridge: Polity Press, 1997), p. 63; Phyllis Deane, *The First Industrial Revolution* (1965, 2nd edition, Cambridge: Cambridge University Press, 1995), pp. 89–91.

153 Marshall McLuhan, *The Mechanical Bride: Folklore of Industrial Man* (1951, reprint, Corte Madera, CA: Gingko Press, 2002), p. 94.

154 On Schlottheim's ship automata see Julia Fritsch (ed.), *Ces Curieux navires: Trois automates de la Renaissance* (Paris: Editions de la Réunion des Musées Nationaux, 1999).

155 Compare Shakespeare's story of the revivification of Hermione in *The Winter's Tale* with Henry Cornelius Agrippa's accounts of 'men [that] have slept for many years together, and in the time of sleep, until they awaked, there was no alteration in them, as to make them seem older' in Henry Cornelius Agrippa, *Three Books of Occult Philosophy* trans. James Freake, ed. Donald Tyson (St Paul, MN: Llewellyn Publications, 2004), p. 183. Hermione, of course, is unaltered even after she has 'awaked'.

156 John Marston, 'The Metamorphosis of Pygmalion's Image' in Sandra Clark (ed.), *Amorous Rites: Elizabethan Erotic Verse* (London: Everyman, 1994), p. 117.

157 Marston, 'The Metamorphosis of Pygmalion's Image' in Clark (ed.), *Amorous Rites*, p. 118.

158 Arthur Golding (trans.), *The xv. bookes of P. Ouidius Naso, entytuled Metamorphosis* (London, 1567), p. 127.

159 Philip Stubbes, *The Anatomie of Abuses Contayning a Discouerie, or Briefe Summarie of such Notable Vices and Imperfections, as Now Raigne in Many Christian Countreyes of the Worlde* (London, 1583), sig. F6ᵛ. See also Scott Cutler Shershow, *Puppets and 'Popular' Culture* (Ithaca and London: Cornell University Press, 1995), p. 72.

160 Shershow, *Puppets and 'Popular' Culture*, p. 71.

161 Simone de Beauvoir, *Le Deuxième Sexe* 2 vols (Paris: Gallimard, 1977), I, p. 285.

162 Laqueur, *Making Sex*, p. 62.

163 Marina Warner, *Monuments and Maidens*, pp. 224, 225.

164 See Jan Golinski, 'The Care of the Self and the Masculine Birth of Science', *History of Science* 40 (2002), pp. 125–45.

6 Reasoning engines: the instrumental imagination in the seventeenth century

1 Samuel Pepys, *The Diary of Samuel Pepys* ed. Henry B. Wheatley, 8 vols (London: G. Bell and Sons, 1938), IV, pp. 201–2.

2 On the operation of the scotoscope, see Lisa Jardine, *Ingenious Pursuits: Building the Scientific Revolution* (London: Little, Brown, 1999), p. 44.

3 Pepys, *Diary*, IV, p. 202. The sum Pepys paid for his microscope was equivalent to over £500 in modern money.

4 Pepys, *Diary*, IV, p. 202.

5 Henry Power, *Experimental Philosophy in Three Books* (London, 1664), title page.

6 Pepys, *Diary*, IV, p. 203.

7 Thomas Sprat, *The History of the Royal Society* (1667), ed. Jackson I. Cope (London: Routledge and Kegan Paul, 1966), p. 80. 'Shop' here means workshop rather than our modern idea of a retail outlet. On the London trade in scientific instruments, see James A. Bennett, 'Shopping for Instruments in Paris and London' in Pamela H. Smith and Paula Findlen (eds), *Merchants and Marvels: Commerce, Science, and Art in Early Modern Europe* (London and New York: Routledge, 2002), pp. 370–95. On scientific instruments more generally, see Deborah Jean Warner, 'What is a Scientific Instrument, When Did it Become One, and Why?' *British Journal for the History of Science* 23 (1990), pp. 83–93.

8 Samuel Sorbière, *A Voyage to England, Containing Many Things Relating to the State of Learning, Religion, and Other Curiosities of that Kingdom* trans. anon (London, 1709), p. 30. On Moray's political and intellectual life, see David Allan, 'Moray, Sir Robert (1608/9?–1673)', *Oxford Dictionary of National Biography* (Oxford University Press, September 2004), Internet: www.oxforddnb.com/view/article/19645. Accessed 27 September 2006.

9 Sorbière, *A Voyage to England*, pp. 32, 33.

10 See Jennifer Tann, 'Space, Time and Innovation Characteristics: The Contribution of Diffusion Process Theory to the History of Technology', in Graham Hollister-Short and Frank A. J. L. James (eds), *History of Technology* vol. 17 (London: Mansell, 1995), p. 149.

11 On the scientific instrument as an item of luxurious consumption in the seventeenth century, see Linda Levy Peck, *Consuming Splendor: Society and Culture in Seventeenth Century England* (Cambridge: Cambridge University Press, 2005), pp. 306–7, 324–5, 339.

12 Pepys, *Diary*, VII, p. 362.

13 On the rise of the mechanical philosophy in the seventeenth century, see the two classic accounts: Marie Boas, 'The Establishment of the Mechanical Philosophy' *Osiris* 10 (1952), pp. 412–541; E. J. Dijksterhuis, *The Mechanization of the World Picture* trans. C. Dikshoorn (Oxford: Clarendon Press, 1961).

14 Galileo Galilei, *Dialogues Concerning Two New Sciences* (1638) trans. Henry Crew and Alfonso de Salvio (1914, reprint, New York: Dover Publications, 1954), p. 152.

15 On medieval conceptions of motion, see John E. Murdoch and Edith D. Sylla, 'The Science of Motion' in David C. Lindberg (ed.), *Science in the Middle Ages* (Chicago and London: University of Chicago Press, 1978), pp. 206–64.

16 Galileo, *Dialogues Concerning Two New Sciences*, p. 276. On the 'turn to mathem-

atics' (as opposed to rhetoric and logic) among sixteenth-century humanists, see Timothy J. Reiss, *Knowledge, Discovery and Imagination in Early Modern Europe* (Cambridge: Cambridge University Press, 1997), pp. 110–31 (p. 110).

17 These are just some of the phenomena explored by Galileo. See Galileo, *Dialogues Concerning Two New Sciences*, pp. 2–5, 110–52, 160–70, 244–94.

18 Richard S. Westfall, 'Mechanics' in Wilbur Applebaum (ed.), *Encyclopaedia of the Scientific Revolution from Copernicus to Newton* (New York and London: Garland, 2000), p. 415.

19 Francis Bacon, *The Advancement of Learning* ed. G. W. Kitchin (London: J. M. Dent, 1973), p. 99.

20 On Bacon's attitude towards mechanics in the Galilean sense, see Stephen Gaukroger, *Francis Bacon and the Transformation of Early-Modern Philosophy* (Cambridge: Cambridge University Press, 2001), p. 93.

21 Thus, the OED: 'Mechanic: 'each mechanick slave, Each dunghill peasant . . .' (Marston, 1599); 'painting in Oyle . . . is more mechanique and will robbe you of overmuch time from your more excellent studies' (Peacham, 1622); 'though noble by descent, Mechanik by profession and indigent' (Stanley, 1655). Mechanical: 'A seruant meanly trained in some mechanical sciences' (Day, 1586); 'mechanicall and men of base condition' (anon., 1589); 'a crew of patches, rude mechanicals' (Shakespeare, 1590), 'beggarly mechanicals' (Holland, 1603).

22 H. Billingsley (trans.), *Elements of the Geometrie of Euclid . . . With a Preface by John Dee* (London, 1570), sig. A3^v.

23 Billingsley (trans.), *Elements of the Geometrie of Euclid*, sig. C3.

24 On the shifting meanings of 'mechanics', see Raymond Williams, *Keywords: A Vocabulary of Culture and Society* (London: Fontana Press, 1976), p. 201.

25 Bacon, *The Advancement of Learning*, p. 70.

26 On the five basic machines, see Ian McNeil, 'Basic Tools, Devices and Mechanisms' in Ian McNeil (ed.), *An Encyclopaedia of the History of Technology* (London and New York: Routledge, 1996), pp. 17–18.

27 Francis Bacon, *The New Organon* ed. Lisa Jardine and Michael Silverthorne (Cambridge: Cambridge University Press, 2000), p. 224.

28 Peter Dear, *Revolutionizing the Sciences: European Knowledge and its Ambitions, 1500–1700* (London: Palgrave, 2001), p. 64.

29 Bacon, *The New Organon*, pp. 20–1.

30 Bacon, *The New Organon*, p. 100. Of these three technologies, however, Brian Stock observes: 'all were Chinese and two were known to medieval man'. See Brian Stock, 'Science, Technology and Economic Progress in the Early Middle Ages' in Lindberg (ed.), *Science in the Middle Ages*, p. 29.

31 Bacon, *The Advancement of Learning*, p. 71.

32 Agnes Heller, *Renaissance Man* trans. Richard E. Allen (New York: Schocken Books, 1981), p. 407.

33 Bacon, *The Advancement of Learning*, p. 90.

34 James Barry Jr, *Measures of Science: Theological and Technological Impulses in Early Modern Thought* (Evanston, IL: Northwestern University Press, 1996), p. 103.

35 Bacon, *The Advancement of Learning*, p. 90.

36 On Bacon's quixotic relationship to the alchemists, see John C. Briggs, *Francis*

Bacon and the Rhetoric of Nature (Cambridge, MA, and London: Harvard University Press, 1989), pp. 148–9.

37 Bacon, *The Advancement of Learning*, pp. 72–3.

38 Bacon, *The Advancement of Learning*, p. 73.

39 Francis Bacon, *New Atlantis* in Brian Vickers (ed.), *English Science, Bacon to Newton* (Cambridge: Cambridge University Press, 1987), p. 35.

40 Bacon, *New Atlantis*, pp. 41–2.

41 Sir William Petty, *The advice of W. P. to Mr Samuel Hartlib for the Advancement of Some Particular Parts of Learning* (London, 1647), p. 7.

42 Francis Bacon, 'Of the Wisdom of the Ancients' in Joseph Devey (ed.), *The Moral and Historical Works of Lord Bacon* (London: George Bell and Sons, 1888), p. 236.

43 Bacon, 'Of the Wisdom of the Ancients', p. 236.

44 Bacon, 'Of the Wisdom of the Ancients', p. 237.

45 Bacon, 'Of the Wisdom of the Ancients', p. 237.

46 For an exploration of this theme in its relationship to poetry, see Jane Partner, 'Poetry and Vision in England 1650–1670' unpublished PhD dissertation, Cambridge University, 2005.

47 See Alex Keller, 'Technological Aspirations and the Motivation of Natural Philosophy in Seventeenth-Century England' in Graham Hollister-Short and Frank A. J. L. James (eds), *History of Technology* vol. 15 (London: Mansell, 1993), p. 80.

48 Charles Darwin, *The Origin of Species by Means of Natural Selection* (1859) (London: John Murray, 1910), p. 136.

49 Darwin, *The Origin of Species*, p. 137.

50 Martin Kemp, *The Science of Art: Optical Themes in Western Art from Brunelleschi to Seurat* (New Haven and London: Yale University Press, 1990), p. 7. See, also, Martin Kemp, 'Wrought by No Artist's Hand: The Natural, the Artificial, the Exotic, and the Scientific in Some Artefacts from the Renaissance' in Claire Farago (ed.), *Reframing the Renaissance: Visual Culture in Europe and Latin America 1450–1650* (New Haven: Yale University Press, 1995), pp. 177–96.

51 Leon Battista Alberti, *On Painting* ed. Martin Kemp, trans. Cecil Grayson (London: Penguin Books, 2004), p. 87.

52 Sir Henry Wotton, *The Elements of Architecture* (London, 1624), p. 83.

53 Erwin Panofsky, *Perspective as Symbolic Form* trans. Christopher S. Wood (1991, reprint, New York: Zone Books, 1997), p. 62.

54 Kemp, *The Science of Art*, p. 167. But see also Michelangelo's disdain for those sculptors and architects who rely on artificial devices – compasses, ruler, T squares – rather than the trained eye of the artist as described by Robert J. Clements, *Michelangelo's Theory of Art* (London: Routledge and Kegan Paul, 1963), pp. 29–31.

55 Sorbière, *A Voyage to England*, p. 28.

56 Svetlana Alpers, *The Vexations of Art: Velázquez and Others* (New Haven and London: Yale University Press, 2005), p. 4.

57 Abraham Cowley, 'To the Royal Society' in Sprat, *History of the Royal Society*, sig. B2^{v}.

58 Cowley, 'To the Royal Society', sig. B2^{v}.

59 Robert Hooke, *Micrographia* (1665) (Mineola, NY: Dover Publications, 2003), sig. a^{r}.

60 On the idea of reversing the effects of the Fall through the application of science

and technology, see Charles Webster, *The Great Instauration: Science, Medicine and Reform 1626–1660* (London: Duckworth, 1975), pp. 324–35.

61 Robert Boyle, *Some Considerations Touching the Usefulness of Experimental Natural Philosophy . . . The Second Tome* (London, 1671), p. 1.

62 On the concept and history of the academic 'discipline', see Peter Burke, *A Social History of Knowledge from Gutenberg to Diderot* (Cambridge: Polity Press, 2000), pp. 90–1.

63 Shapin, *The Scientific Revolution*, p. 36.

64 Sorbière, *A Voyage to England*, p. 34.

65 Steven Shapin and Simon Schaffer, *Leviathan and the Air Pump: Hobbes, Boyle, and the Experimental Life* (Princeton, NJ: Princeton University Press, 1985), p. 26.

66 Brian Vickers (ed.), *English Science, Bacon to Newton* (Cambridge: Cambridge University Press, 1987), p. 45.

67 Joseph Glanvill, *The Vanity of Dogmatising* (London, 1661), p. 5.

68 Shapin and Schaffer, *Leviathan and the Air Pump*, p. 37.

69 Pepys, *Diary*, V. 369.

70 Jim Bennett, 'Hooke's Instruments' in Jim Bennett, Michael Cooper, Michael Hunter, and Lisa Jardine, *London's Leonardo: The Life and Work of Robert Hooke* (Oxford: Oxford University Press, 2003), p. 64. See also Lisa Jardine, *The Curious Life of Robert Hooke – The Man Who Measured London* (London: Harper Perennial, 2003), p. 42.

71 On the popularity and evolution of *Micrographia*, see Elizabeth Spiller, *Science, Reading and Renaissance Literature: The Art of Making Knowledge 1580–1670* (Cambridge: Cambridge University Press, 2004), p. 137; Michael Hunter, 'Hooke the Natural Philosopher' in Bennett *et al.* (eds), *London's Leonardo*, pp. 105–62 (especially pp. 124–31).

72 Robert Hooke, *Micrographia or some Physiological Descriptions of Minute Bodies made by magnifying Glasses* (1665) (New York: Dover Publications, 2003), sig. B2^r. A few years later, Robert Boyle would take these speculations a stage further when he published his two pamphlets *Experiments and Observations about the Mechanical Production of Odours* (London, 1675) and *Experiments and Observations about the Mechanical Production of Tasts* (London, 1675).

73 Hooke, *Micrographia*, sigs c, d2$^{r–v}$.

74 The operation of these instruments was discussed in works such as Leonard Digges, *Techtonicon* (London, 1592), and Aaron Rathborne's *The Surveyor* (London, 1616). See Bernhard Klein, *Maps and the Writing of Space in Early Modern England and Ireland* (Basingstoke: Palgrave Macmillan, 2001), pp. 42–60; Andrew Gordon and Bernhard Klein (eds), *Literature, Mapping and the Politics of Space in Early Modern Britain* (Cambridge: Cambridge University Press, 2001).

75 Hooke, *Micrographia*, sigs b2$^{v–r}$.

76 Since the late sixteenth century, Tom Standage writes, 'there had been persistent rumour across Europe of a miraculous device that allowed people many miles apart to spell out messages to each other letter by letter'. It was not until the late eighteenth century, however, that the 'telegraph' (conceived of as a means of sending visible rather than audible signals) came into being. See Tom Standage, *The Victorian Internet* (London: Phoenix, 1999), p. 6.

77 Hooke, *Micrographia*, sig. d.

78 Hooke, *Micrographia*, sig. d^{r-v}.

79 Sir Thomas Browne, *Selected Writings* ed. Sir Geoffrey Keynes (London: Faber and Faber, 1968), p. 20. As Karen Edwards notes, this passage from Browne was copied verbatim into the preface of Henry Power's *Experimental Philosophy* (1664). See Karen L. Edwards, *Milton and the Natural World: Science and Poetry in Paradise Lost* (Cambridge: Cambridge University Press, 1999), p. 48.

80 See Donna J. Haraway, *Simians, Cyborgs, and Women* (London: Free Association Books, 1991), pp. 149–81.

81 Lisa Jardine has speculated that Sir Christopher Wren may have been responsible for some of the larger-scale illustrations in *Micrographia*. See Jardine, *The Curious Life of Robert Hooke*, p. 362 (n. 17).

82 Hooke, *Micrographia*, p. 193.

83 Hooke, *Micrographia*, p. 193.

84 Hooke, *Micrographia*, p. 193.

85 Hooke, *Micrographia*, pp. 193–4.

86 Jessica Wolfe, *Humanism, Machinery, and Renaissance Literature* (Cambridge: Cambridge University Press, 2004), p. 189.

87 Margaret Cavendish, Duchess of Newcastle, 'The Blazing World' in Paul Salzman (ed.), *An Anthology of Seventeenth-century Fiction* (Oxford and New York: Oxford University Press, 1991), p. 268.

88 Cavendish, 'The Blazing World', p. 269.

89 Cavendish, 'The Blazing World', p. 269.

90 On Cavendish's writing, see Lisa T. Sarahsohn, 'A Science Turned Upside Down: Feminism and the Natural Philosophy of Margaret Cavendish' *Huntington Library Quarterly* 47 (1984), pp. 289–307.

91 Studying *Teredo navalis* or the ship worm, Marc Isambard Brunel, for example, discovered that its foot operated as a 'fulcrum' and that its muscles worked by 'rotary motion'. It was the mechanical action of the shipworm's jaws that formed the basis of Brunel's design of the first mechanical tunnelling equipment in the early years of the nineteenth century. See Richard Beamish, *Memoir of the Life of Sir Marc Isambard Brunel* (1862) quoted in Humphrey Jennings, *Pandæmonium 1660–1886: The Coming of the Machine as seen by Contemporary Observers* ed. Mary-Lou Jennings and Charles Madge (London: André Deutsch, 1985), p. 140; Ian McNeil, 'Roads, Bridges and Vehicles' in McNeil (ed.), *Encyclopaedia of the History of Technology*, p. 468.

92 'Minutes of the Royal Society' in Thomas Birch, *The History of the Royal Society* (London, 1756) quoted in Jennings, *Pandæmonium 1660–1886*, p. 15. On Hooke's mechanical muscle, see Bennett, 'Hooke's Instruments', p. 81. Shapin (*Scientific Revolution*, p. 111) reminds us that Boyle's explorations of the volume of gases under pressure resulted in 'a law that Boyle never called a law and to which he never gave symbolic mathematical expression'.

93 Joseph Moxon, *Mechanick Powers: or, The Mistery of Nature and Art Unvail'd* (London, 1696), p. 247.

94 For information on Moxon's life and publications, see the editors' 'Introduction' to Joseph Moxon, *Mechanick Exercises on the Whole Art of Printing* ed. Herbert

Davis and Harry Carter (1958, 2nd edition, New York: Dover Publications, 1962), pp. xix–lv.

95 John Butt (ed.), *The Poems of Alexander Pope* (London: Methuen, 1968), p. 511.

96 *Poems of Alexander Pope*, p. 511.

97 Karel Čapek, 'R. U. R. (*Rossum's Universal Robots*)', in Arthur O. Lewis Jr (ed.), *Of Men and Machines* (New York: E. P. Dutton, 1963), p. 3.

98 Quoted in Mark E. Rosheim, *Robot Evolution: The Development of Anthrobotics* (New York and Chichester: John Wiley and Sons, 1994), p. 19.

99 See Angelo Poliziano, *Letters* ed. Shane Butler (Cambridge, MA, and London: Harvard University Press, 2006), p. 271.

100 Mark E. Rosheim, 'Leonardo's Lost Robot' in Paolo Galluzzi (ed.), *The Art of Invention: Leonardo and Renaissance Engineers* (Florence: Instituto e Museo di Storia della Scienza, 1999), p. 234.

101 Michael White, *Leonardo the First Scientist* (London: Abacus, 2000), pp. 188–9.

102 David Akin (Maryland University) quoted in Robin McKie and David Smith, 'Face of the Future?' *The Observer* (18 July 2004), p. 17. For rather more optimistic accounts of developments in robotics, see Kevin Warwick, *March of the Machines* (London: Century, 1997); Hans Moravec, *Robot: Mere Machine to Transcendent Mind* (Oxford: Oxford University Press, 1999); Rodney A. Brooks, *Robot; The Future of Flesh and Machines* (London: Allen Lane/Penguin Books, 2002).

103 For a description of the 'slave' see Patrick Mauries, *Cabinets of Curiosities* (London: Thames and Hudson, 2002), p. 116.

104 Norbert Wiener, *The Human Use of Human Beings: Cybernetics and Society* (1954, reprint, Cambridge, MA: Da Capo Press, 1988), p. 23.

105 Wiener, *The Human Use of Human Beings*, p. 21.

106 Lews Mumford, *Technics and Civilization* (1934, reprint, New York and London: Harcourt Brace, 1963), pp. 14–15.

107 David S. Landes, *Revolution in Time: Clocks and the Making of the Modern World* (1983, revised edition, London and New York: Viking, 2000), p. 118. The OED ascribes the first use of the term 'face' to describe a clock's dial to 1751.

108 See Landes, *Revolution in Time*, p. 64.

109 The Latin text ('*Temporis interpres . . .*') was first published in Campion's *Epigrammatum Libri II. Embra. Eligiarum liber unus* (London, 1619). See Walter R. Davies (ed.), *The Works of Thomas Campion* (New York: W. W. Norton, 1967), p. 416. It was translated (possibly by Henry Vaughan), and published in Thomas Powell, *Humane Industry: Or, A History of Most Manual Arts* (London, 1661), p. 11. See Henry Vaughan, *The Works* ed. L. C. Martin (2nd edition, Oxford: Clarendon Press, 1957), p. 681.

110 A 'numbering clock' was a mechanical device, as distinct from alternative forms of time measurement such as an hourglass.

111 See Dennis Des Chene, *Spirits and Clocks: Machine and Organism in Descartes* (Ithaca, NY, and London: Cornell University Press, 2001), particularly pp. 71–115.

112 Thomas Dekker, *The Seuen Deadly Sinnes of London* (London, 1606), pp. 24–5.

113 Dekker, *Seuen Deadly Sinnes of London*, p. 25.

114 Sir John Suckling, 'Loves Clock' in Thomas Clayton (ed.), *Cavalier Poets* (Oxford and New York: Oxford University Press, 1978), p. 235.

115 As Suckling's modern editor observes, the 'clock and its works are a favourite conceit of Suckling' (*Cavalier Poets*, p. 235).

116 Suckling's fictional human clock employs a 'balance', an innovation in clock making which did not appear until the late sixteenth century. See Landes, *Revolution in Time*, p. 127.

117 Otto Mayr, *Liberty, Authority and Automatic Machinery in Early Modern Europe* (Baltimore and London: Johns Hopkins University Press, 1986), p. 53. Among English writers who deployed the metaphor of the clock in the seventeenth century, Mayr notes (as well as those already mentioned in this account) John Donne, John Davies of Hereford, Michael Drayton, Thomas Middleton, John Webster, Ben Jonson, William Cartwright, John Norden, George Herbert, William Davenant, and Thomas Tynne. See Mayr, *Liberty, Authority and Automatic Machinery*, pp. 207–13.

118 Sir John Davies, *Poems* ed. Robert Kreuger (Oxford: Clarendon Press, 1975), p. 121.

119 Note that Wolfe (*Humanism, Machinery, and Renaissance Literature*, p. 76) glosses the word 'pinesse' in Davies's poem as 'the rotating plates at the end of an astrolabe'. A pinnace, however, was also 'a small light vessel, generally two-masted and schooner-rigged' (OED).

120 Thomas Bancroft, 'Of Man' (Epigram No. 199) in *Two Bookes of Epigrammes, and Epitaphs* (London, 1639), sig. E4.

121 René Descartes, *Discourse on the Method* (1637) in *The Philosophical Writings of Descartes* ed. and trans. John Cottingham, Robert Stoothoff, and Dugald Murdoch, 3 vols (Cambridge: Cambridge University Press, 1985), I, p. 139.

122 Descartes, 'Letter to the Marquis of Newcastle, 23 November 1646' in *Philosophical Writings of Descartes*, III. p. 303. On the role of language in the construction of artificial intelligence, see Steven Pinker, *The Language Instinct: The New Science of Language and Mind* (London: Penguin Books, 1994), pp. 192–6.

123 John Wilkins, *An Essay Towards a Real Character, And a Philosophical Language* (London, 1668), p. 13. On the seventeenth-century quest for 'artificial' (or 'Universal') language systems, see Murray Cohen, *Sensible Words: Linguistic Practice in England 1640–1785* (Baltimore and London: Johns Hopkins University Press, 1977), pp. 1–42.

124 Paula Findlen, *Possessing Nature: Museums, Collecting, and Scientific Culture in Early Modern Italy* (Berkeley and Los Angeles: University of California Press, 1994), p. 86. Kircher's machine was related to other quasi-magical communicative devices such as his *Machina Cryptologica*, which (writes Haun Saussy) formed part of Kircher's 'exhibition of language machines' designed 'to automate the operations of translation, coding, and composition'. See Haun Saussy, 'Magnetic Language: Athanasius Kircher and Communication' in Paula Findlen (ed.), *Athanasius Kircher: The Last Man Who Knew Everything* (New York and London: Routledge, 2004), p. 275. Such devices were to become the object of Jonathan Swift's scorn when he satirized the composition instrument shown to Gulliver by the philosophers of Laputa in *Gulliver's Travels* (1726).

125 See Hebert Ohlman, 'Information: Timekeeping, Computing, Telecommunications and Audiovisual Technologies' in Ian McNeil (ed.), *An Encyclopaedia of the History of Technology* (London and New York: Routledge, 1996), p. 698.

126 John Napier, *A Description of the Admirable Table of Logarithms* trans. Edward Wright (London, 1616), sig. A4. Napier's invention of logarithms was first announced in

his *Mirifici logarthimorum canonis descriptio* (1614). See H. S. Bennett, *English Books and Readers 1603–1640* 3 vols (Cambridge, Cambridge University Press, 1970), III, p. 161.

127 On the invention of 'Napier's Bones', see Trevor I. Williams, *A History of Invention from Stone Axes to Silicon Chips* (1987, revised edition, London and New York: Little, Brown, 1999), pp. 306–7.

128 See Adam Max Cohen, *Shakespeare and Technology: Dramatizing Early Modern Technological Revolutions* (New York and London: Palgrave Macmillan, 2006), ch. 1.

129 Joel Shunkin, *Engines of the Mind: The Evolution of the Computer from Mainframes to Microprocessors* (1984, revised edition, London and New York: W. W. Norton, 1996), p. 33.

130 Thomas Hobbes, *Human Nature and De Corpore Politico* (1655) ed. J. C. A. Gaskin (Oxford: Oxford University Press, 1994), p. 186.

131 Hobbes, *De Corpore*, pp. 187, 188.

132 Hobbes, *De Corpore*, p. 187.

133 George Dyson, *Darwin amongst the Machines* (London: Penguin Books, 1997), p. 7. On analogies between the brain's operation and other kinds of 'instrument' (in particular computers and radar), see J. Z. Young, *An Introduction to the Study of Man* (Oxford: Clarendon Press, 1971), pp. 608–9.

134 On Morland's calculating engine, see *The Description and Use of Two Arithmetick Instruments* (London, 1673), and Pepys, *Diary* VII, pp. 338–9. On Hooke's response to Morland's device, and on the various inventions attributed to Morland, see Alan Marshall, 'Morland, Sir Samuel, first baronet (1625–1695)' *Oxford Dictionary of National Biography* (Oxford University Press, 2004), Internet: www.oxforddnb.com/view/article /19282. Accessed 7 April 2006. Evelyn records seeing Morland's 'inventions and machines, arithmetical wheels, quench-fires, and new harp' in July 1667. See William Bray (ed.), *The Diary of John Evelyn* 2 vols (London: J. M. Dent, 1937), II, p. 28.

135 See Shunkin, *Engines of the Mind*, p. 34. On the philosophical implications of automata for Leibniz, see Guido Giglioni, 'Automata Compared: Boyle, Leibniz and the Debate on the Notion of Life and Mind' *British Journal for the History of Philosophy* 3 (1995), pp. 249–78.

136 On Leibniz's calculating engine, see Dyson, *Darwin Amongst the Machines*, pp. 36–7; Shunkin, *Engines of the Mind*, p. 35; Peggy Aldrich Kidwell, 'Calculating Machine' in Applebaum (ed.), *Encyclopaedia of the Scientific Revolution*, pp. 113–14.

137 G. W. Leibniz, *Machina arithmetica in qua non additio tantum subtractio* tr. Mark Kormes, in Fauvel and Gray (eds), *The History of Mathematics*, p. 584.

138 See Fauvel and Gray (eds), *History of Mathematics*, pp. 584–6.

139 Wiener, *The Human Use of Human Beings*, p. 19.

140 Leibniz, letter to Nicholas Remond, 10 January 1714, quoted in Dyson, *Darwin Amongst the Machines*, p. 36.

141 John Locke, *An Essay Concerning Human Understanding* ed. Peter H. Nidditch (Oxford: Clarendon Press, 1975), pp. 135–6.

142 G. W. Leibniz, *New Essays on Human Understanding* ed. Peter Remnant and Jonathan Bennett (Cambridge: Cambridge University Press, 1996), p. 166.

143 Leibniz, *New Essays*, p. 66.

144   Leibniz, *New Essays*, p. lxxvii (editors' note).

145   Domique Beddevole, *Essays of Anatomy wherein the Formation of the Organs and their Mechanical Operations are Clearly Explained, according to the New Hypothesis* trans. J. Scougall (2nd edition, London, 1696), sig. A5ᵛ.

146   On the evolution of clock design in the seventeenth century, see Landes, *Revolution in Time*, pp. 132–3.

147   See the invective laden exchange to be found in Samuel Morland, *Sir Samuel Morland's Answer to Several Papers of Reasons against his Bill for his New Water Engines* (London, 1676/7), and James Ward, *An Answer to Sir Sam. Moreland's Bill and Printed Paper* (London, 1677).

148   Roy Porter, *Flesh in the Age of Reason* (New York and London: W. W. Norton, 2003), p. 51.

149   Robert Boyle, *Some Considerations Touching the Usefulnesse of Experimental Naturall Philosophy* (London, 1663), pp. 27–8.

150   Bredekamp, *The Lure of Antiquity*, p. 37.

151   Quoted (and translated) in Bredekamp, *The Lure of Antiquity*, p. 39.

152   Thomas Traherne, *Selected Poems and Prose* ed. Alan Bradford (London: Penguin Books, 1991), p. 231.

153   Traherne, *Selected Poems and Prose*, p. 172.

154   Traherne, *Selected Poems and Prose*, p. 86.

155   See Carol Marks, 'Thomas Traherne and Cambridge Neoplatonism' *Publications of the Modern Language Association of America* 81 (1966), pp. 521–34. For a more extended survey of Traherne's response to the new science of the seventeenth century, see Sawday, *The Body Emblazoned*, pp. 256–66.

156   Traherne, *Selected Poems and Prose*, pp. 60, 80.

157   Traherne, *Selected Poems and Prose*, p. 245.

158   Traherne, *Selected Poems and Prose*, p. 157.

159   Traherne, *Selected Poems and Prose*, p. 204.

160   Traherne, *Selected Poems and Prose*, p. 204.

161   Self-regulating devices, attached to engines to control their power output (sometimes known as 'governors') did not emerge until the late eighteenth century. James Watt's 'centrifugal governor' ('a deliberately contrived feedback device') first appeared on his rotative engines in 1788. See Ian McNeil, 'Basic Tools, Devices and Mechanisms' in McNeil (ed.), *Encyclopaedia of the History of Technology*, p. 31.

162   Thomas Hobbes, *Leviathan* (1651) ed. Richard Tuck (Cambridge: Cambridge University Press, 1991), p. 9.

163   Glanvill, *Vanity of Dogmatising*, p. 43. Glanvill's reference to 'Melacholies Hyperbole' is an allusion to the rhetorical skills of the German rhetorician, Melancthon. I am indebted to Neil Rhodes and Jane Pettegree for this explanation.

164   Landes, *Revolution in Time*, p. 131.

165   Sir Kenelm Digby, *Treatise of the Nature of Bodies* (Paris, 1644), p. 208. For a more extended discussion of these devices, see Jonathan Sawday, 'The Mint at Segovia: Digby, Hobbes, Charleton, and the Body as a Machine in the Seventeenth Century' *Prose Studies* 6 (1983), pp. 21–35.

166   John Wilkins, *A Discourse concerning A NEW world and Another Planet In 2 Bookes* (London, 1640), p. 204.

167 So, in modern technological systems James R. Chiles has observed that 'machine disasters nearly always require multiple failures and mistakes to reach fruition'. See James R. Chiles, *Inviting Disaster: Lesson from the Edge of Technology* (New York: HarperBusiness, 2002), p. 6.

168 Paul Barbette, *The Chirurgicall and Anatomical Works* trans. anon. (London, 1672), p. 206.

169 Walter Charleton, *Enquiries into Human Nature in VI Anatomic Praelections* (London, 1680), sig. B^r.

170 On French arguments over mechanism, particularly as they were to be applied to animals, see A[ntoine] D[illy], *De L'Ame des Bêtes* (Lyon, 1676); Jean Darmanson, *La Beste transformée en machine* (Amsterdam, 1684).

171 Julien Offray de la Mettrie, *Machine Man and Other Writings* ed. Ann Thomson (Cambridge: Cambridge University Press, 1996), pp. 5, 7.

172 La Mettrie, *Machine Man*, pp. 26–7.

173 La Mettrie, *Machine Man*, p. 28.

174 La Mettrie, *Machine Man*, p. 29.

175 Joseph Bristow, *Sexuality* (London and New York: Routledge, 1997), p. 171.

176 Warren Chernaik, *Sexual Freedom in Restoration Literature* (Cambridge: Cambridge University Press, 1995), p. 31.

177 Chernaik, *Sexual Freedom*, p. 31.

178 See Brian P. Copenhaver and Charles B. Schmitt, *Renaissance Philosophy* (Oxford and New York: Oxford University Press, 1992), pp. 198–9.

179 All references to Rochester's poetry are to John Wilmot, Earl of Rochester, *Poems* ed. Keith Walker (Oxford: Blackwell, 1984).

180 The date of composition of Rochester's *Satyr* is usually held to be 1674, though it was not published until 1679. See Rochester, *Poems*, p. 282 (editor's note).

181 On the distrust of the culture represented by Rochester among the rather more sober members of the Royal Society, see Michael Hunter, *Science and Society in Restoration England* (Cambridge: Cambridge University Press, 1981), p. 166.

182 *Philosophical Writings of Descartes*, I. pp. 329–30.

183 I am indebted to Neil Rhodes for this point.

184 Chernaik, *Sexual Freedom*, p. 71.

185 I am grateful to Nigel Fabb for his advice on the technical aspects of Rochester's verse. There is some doubt as to whether the poem entitled 'Regime d'Viver' is actually by Rochester, or about Rochester. See Rochester, *Poems*, p. 311 (editor's note). Chernaik (*Sexual Freedom*, pp. 233–4) is, however, convinced (as am I) of Rochester's authorship of this poem.

186 Graham Greene, *Lord Rochester's Monkey: Being the Life of John Wilmot, Second Earl of Rochester* (London: Futura, 1976), p. 105.

187 Greene, *Lord Rochester's Monkey*, p. 105.

188 Oliver Lawson Dick (ed.), *Aubrey's Brief Lives* (London: Secker and Warburg, 1960), p. xcv. I follow Chernaik (*Sexual Freedom*, p. 79) in preferring 'fuck' to the Bowdlerized 'mark'. 'Mark', however, may yet prove to be the correct term since in the mid-seventeenth-century sundials were still used to correct clocks. See Landes, *Revolution in Time*, pp. 132–3.

189 Dick (ed.), *Aubrey's Brief Lives*, p. xcv; Chernaik, *Sexual Freedom*, p. 79.

7 Milton and the engine

1   Thomas Sprat, *The History of the Royal Society* (1667), ed. Jackson I. Cope (London: Routledge and Kegan Paul, 1966), p. 62.
2   Roy Harris, *The Language Machine* (London: Duckworth, 1987), p. 12. For a discussion of the link between language, instruments, and mechanical devices see Thomas L. Hankins and Robert J. Silverman, *Instruments and the Imagination* (Princeton, NJ: Princeton University Press, 1995), pp. 113–47.
3   Sprat, *History of the Royal Society*, pp. 112, 113.
4   Thomas Hobbes, *Human Nature and De Corpore Politico* ed. J. C. A. Gaskin (Oxford: Oxford University Press, 1994), p. 186. On the role of mathematics as a model for language reform, see Charles Webster, *The Great Instauration: Science, Medicine and Reform 1626–1660* (London: Duckworth, 1975), p. 200.
5   See Michael Hunter, *Science and Society in Restoration England* (Cambridge: Cambridge University Press, 1981), pp. 60–1.
6   See Linda Levy Peck, *Consuming Splendor: Society and Culture in Seventeenth-Century England* (Cambridge: Cambridge University Press, 2005), p. 318. See, also, Michael Hunter, *Establishing the New Science: The Experience of the Early Royal Society* (Woodbridge: Boydell Press, 1989), pp. 73–122.
7   See Hunter, *Science and Society in Restoration England*, pp. 60–1. Hunter's calculations must throw some doubt on Christopher Hill's claim that 'the Royal Society was the Establishment *par excellence* in restoration England'. See Christopher Hill, *The Experience of Defeat: Milton and Some Contemporaries* (London: Faber and Faber, 1984), p. 264.
8   For a general discussion of the effect of the new philosophy on literary style, see John M. Steadman, *The Hill and the Labyrinth: Discourse and Certitude in Milton and his Near Contemporaries* (Berekeley, Los Angeles, and London: University of California Press, 1984), particularly pp. 101–12.
9   References to Milton's prose and poetry are as follows: John Milton, *Paradise Lost* ed. Alistair Fowler (London: Longman, 1968), hereinafter *PL*; John Milton, *Complete Shorter Poems* ed. John Carey (London: Longman, 1968), hereinafter *CSP*; John Milton, *Complete Prose Works* 8 vols, ed. Douglas Bush *et al.* (New Haven and London: Yale University Press, 1953–1982), hereinafter *CPW*.
10 John Rogers, *The Matter of Revolution: Science, Poetry, and Politics in the Age of Milton* (Ithaca, NY, and London: Cornell University Press, 1996), p. 5.
11 Joseph Glanvill, *The Vanity of Dogmatising* (London, 1661), p. 5.
12 Karen L. Edwards, *Milton and the Natural World: Science and Poetry in Paradise Lost* (1999, reprint, Cambridge: Cambridge University Press, 2005), p. 138. For a discussion of 'visual rationality' in seventeenth-century culture, see Stuart Clark, *Vanities of the Eye: Vision in Early Modern European Culture* (Oxford: Oxford University Press, 2007), pp. 329–56.
13 Milton French, *The Life Records of John Milton* 5 vols (New Brunswick, NJ: Rutgers University Press, 1949–58) IV, p. 125.
14 In a letter dated 28 September 1654, Milton had described the loss of his sight some two years earlier (he was virtually blind by March 1652) in mechanical terms: '. . . there used to shine out a copious glittering light from my shut eyes; than that, as my sight grew less from day to day, colours proportionately duller would burst

from them, as with a kind of force and audible shot from within'. See French, *Life Records of John Milton*, II. p. 339.

15 David Norbrook, *Writing the English Republic: Poetry, Rhetoric and Politics 1627–1660* (Cambridge: Cambridge University Press, 1999), p. 466.

16 See Stllman Drake (ed.), *Discoveries and Opinions of Galileo* (New York: Doubleday Anchor, 1957), p. 82.

17 Milton, *CPW* II, p. 538. On the veracity of Milton's account of meeting Galileo, see George F. Butler, 'Milton's Meeting with Galileo: A Reconsideration' *Milton Quarterly* 39 (2005), pp. 132–9.

18 On Galileo and the image of the telescope in Milton, see Marjorie Nicholson, 'Milton and the Telescope' *English Literary History* 2 (1935), pp. 1–32.

19 Drake (ed.), *Discoveries and Opinions of Galileo*, pp. 98–99.

20 Abraham Cowley, *A Proposition for the Advancement of Experimental Philosophy* (London, 1661), sig. A5.

21 Cowley, *A Proposition* sigs A5^{r-v}.

22 Cowley, *A Proposition* sig. A5^v.

23 Christopher Hill, *Milton and the English Revolution* (London: Faber and Faber, 1977), p. 398.

24 Stanley Fish, *Surprised by Sin: The Reader in Paradise Lost* (1967, reprint, Berkeley, Los Angeles, and London: University of California Press, 1971), p. 250.

25 My account of the collaboration of Calthoff and Worcester in devising their 'water-commanding engine' is derived from W. H. Thorpe, 'The Marquis of Worcester and Vauxhall' *Transactions of the Newcomen Society* 13 (1932), pp. 75–88. See, also, Stephen K. Roberts, 'Somerset, Edward, second Marquis of Worcester (*d.* 1667)', *Oxford Dictionary of National Biography* (Oxford University Press, 2004), Internet: www.oxforddnb.com/ view/article/26006. Accessed 14 April 2006.

26 Edward Somerset, Marquis of Worcester, *A Century of the Names and Scantlings of such Inventions as at Present I can call to Mind to Have Tried and Perfected* (London, 1663), p. 48.

27 See Samuel Sorbière, *A Voyage to England, Containing Many Things Relating to the State of Learning, Religion, and Other Curiosities of that Kingdom* trans. anon (London, 1709), p. 29.

28 Thorpe, 'The Marquis of Worcester and Vauxhall', p. 77.

29 Somerset, *Century of Inventions*, pp. 66–7. On Somerset's engine, see also Edward Somerset, *An Exact and True Definition of the most Stupendious Water-Commanding Engin . . . Presented to his Most Excellent Majesty Charles the Second* (London, 1663). The British Library copy of this text contains the patent, granted by Charles II, enabling Somerset to benefit from the operation of his machine.

30 For a defence of Somerset as the originator of the steam engine, see Henry Dircks, *The Life, Times, and Scientific Labours of the Second Marquis of Worcester* (London, 1865), pp. 476–99. Somerset's device may have been related to the heat engine described in R. D'acres, *The Art of water-drawing* (London, 1660). In this context, Rhys Jenkins notes that a patent to 'raise water from lowe pitts by fire' had been granted as early as 1630. See Rhys Jenkins (ed.), *R. D'acres's The Art of Water Drawing* (Cambridge: Newcomen Society, 1930), p. vii (introduction).

31 Peter Mathias, *The First Industrial Revolution: An Economic History of Britain*

1700–1914 (2nd edition, London and New York: Routledge, 1995), p. 116, Peck, *Consuming Splendor*, p. 110.

32 Alfred P. Wadsworth and Julia de Lacy Mann, *The Cotton Trade and Industrial Lancashire 1600–1780* (1931, reprint, Manchester: Manchester University Press, 1965), pp. 106, 98–9. In 1675, a petition of the ribbon weavers, defending their 'engine looms' against attack from the London Company of Weavers opens by announcing that 'engine looms or looms called broad looms have been in England above seventy years . . . working silk or cotton . .'. See Joan Thirsk and J. P. Cooper (eds), *Seventeenth-century Economic Documents* (Oxford: Clarendon Press, 1972), p. 294.

33 James Usher, letter to William Camden (1618) in Richard Parr, *The life of the Most Reverend Father in God, James Usher, late Lord Arch-Bishop of Armagh . . . with a Collection of three hundred letters* (London, 1686), p. 64.

34 Bruce R. Smith, *The Acoustic World of Early Modern England: Attending to the O-Factor* (Chicago and London: University of Chicago Press, 1999), p. 26.

35 Thorpe, 'The Marquis of Worcester and Vauxhall', p. 75; Rhys Jenkins, 'The Vauxhall Ordnance Factory of Charles I' in Rhys Jenkins, *Links in the History of Engineering and Technology from Tudor Times: The Collected Papers of Rhys Jenkins* (1936, reprint, Freeport, NY: Books for Libraries Press, 1971), pp. 28–33.

36 Webster, *The Great Instauration*, p. 364.

37 Webster, *The Great Instauration*, p. 365.

38 The Inventory (dated 26 September 1645) may be found in Thorpe, 'The Marquis of Worcester and Vauxhall', pp 80–6 (Appendix I). The Inventory makers, working on behalf of the Revenue Committee of Parliament, were Phillip Darrell (Auditor) and John Freeman (messenger).

39 For a commentary on this passage, see Francis Barker, 'In the Wars of Truth: Violence, True Knowledge and Power in Milton and Hobbes' in Thomas Healy and Jonathan Sawday (eds), *Literature and the English Civil War* (Cambridge: Cambridge University Press, 1990), p. 95.

40 According to Aubrey, *Paradise Lost* was composed during 1658–63. See Oliver Lawson Dick (ed.), *Aubrey's Brief Lives* (London: Secker and Warburg, 1960), p. 202.

41 Milton, *Paradise Lost* ed. Fowler, p. 39.

42 Fowler explains the 'almighty engine' as a 'machine of war' but also as a reference to the chariot of the Messiah (*PL* VI. 750–9) based both on Ezekiel's vision 'God in a machine' and the triumphal chariots to be found in Renaissance pageants. See Milton, *Paradise Lost* ed. Fowler, pp. 345–6.

43 Felton claimed that he had invented 'engines' capable of replacing 'five-thousand pikemen' in his *Engines Invented to save much Blood and Moneys* (London, 1644), p. 7. On Felton and his engines, see Timothy Raylor, 'Providence and Technology in the English Civil War: Edmond Felton and his Engine', *Renaissance Studies* 7 (1993), pp. 398–413.

44 See Ralph Harford, *A Gospel-engine, or Streams of Love and Pity to Prevent New Flames in England* (London, 1649) and John Maudit, *The Christian Souldiers Great Engine, or The mysterious and Mighty Workings of Faith* (Oxford, 1649).

45 Anon, *Englands Deliverance or, The Great and Bloody Plot Discovered* London, 1660), title-page. As Andrew Marvell noted in his 'An *Horatian* Ode upon *Cromwel's*

Return from *Ireland*', the king 'bow'd his comely Head, / Down as upon a Bed' at the moment of execution. See H. M. Margoliouth (ed.), *The Poems and Letters of Andrew Marvell* 2 vols (Oxford: Clarendon Press, 1971), I, p. 93.

46 George Herbert, *The English Poems* ed. C. A. Patrides (London: J. M. Dent, 1974), p. 70.

47 Thomas Fuller, *The History of the Worthies of England* ed. P. Austin Nuttall 3 vols (London, 1840), III, p. 58; Henry Power, *Experimental Philosophy in Three Books* (London, 1664), Preface, p. 7.

48 Edward S. Le Comte, *A Milton Dictionary* (New York: Philosophical Library, 1961), p. 114.

49 Milton, *CSP*, p. 249 (editor's note).

50 On the possible interpretations to the two-handed engine puzzle, see Carey's comprehensive note to these lines in Milton, *CSP*, pp. 238–9, together with Esmond L. Marilla, 'That 'Two-handed Engine' Finally?' *Publications of the Modern Language Association* 67 (1952), pp. 1183–4; Leon Howard, '"That Two-Handed Engine"Once More' *Huntington Library Quarterly* 15 (1952), pp. 173–84; J. Milton French, 'Milton's Two-Handed Engine' *Modern Language Notes* 48 (1953), pp. 229–31; Alan R. Smith, 'Milton's "Two-Handed Engine" and the Last Judgment' *American Notes and Queries* 20 (1981), pp. 43–5; James F. Forrest, 'Milton and the Divine Art of Weaponry: "That Two-Handed Engine" and Bunyan's "Nameless Terrible Instrument" at Mouthgate' *Milton Studies* 16 (1982), pp. 131–40; Joyce Stith, 'The Two-Handed Engine: A Personal Interpretation' *Milton Quarterly* 18 (1984), pp. 61–2; Robert Leigh Davis, 'That Two-Handed Engine and the Consolation of "Lycidas"' *Milton Quarterly* 20 (1986), pp. 44–8; James S. Baumlin, 'William Perkins's *Art of Prophesying* and Milton's "Two-Handed Engine": The Protestant Allegory of "Lycidas"' *Milton Quarterly* 33 (1999), pp. 66–71; Hill, *Milton and the English Revolution*, p. 51.

51 See Charles Messenger, 'Weapons and Armour' in Ian McNeil, *An Encyclopaedia of the History of Technology* (London and New York: Routledge, 1990), pp. 977, 979. If the 'two-handed engine' is indeed a firearm, then published as the poem first was in 1638, these lines amount to an insurrectionary and violent call to arms against the encroaching forces of Episcopalianism. Milton would indeed have preferred an elusively deniable metaphor to cloak such militancy. Conversely, by calling attention to this passage in the headnote to the 1645 edition of the poem ('by occasion foretells the ruin . . .'), Milton was able to appear as presciently aware of the coming violence.

52 William Blake, *Milton* ed. Kay Parkhurst Easson and Roger R. Easson (London: Thames and Hudson, 1978), p. 66; Francis D. Klingender, *Art and the Industrial Revolution* ed. and rev. Arthur Elton (St Albans: Granada Publishing, 1975), pp. 106–7. On Martin's illustrations to *Paradise Lost*, see Marcia R. Pointon, *Milton and English Art* (Manchester: Manchester University Press, 1970), pp. 183–5.

53 See, e.g., Thomas Moffett, *The Silkwormes and Their Flies* (London, 1599); Olivier de Serres, *The Perfect Use of Silke-Wormes and Their Benefit* trans. Nicholas Geffe (London, 1607); William Stallenge, *Instructions for the Increasing of Mulberie Trees* (London, 1609). The illustrations contained in the *Vermis Sericus* of Jan van der Straet (Giovanni Stradano) published in Amsterdam around 1600, showed how silk production could be organized on an industrial scale. In the 1650s, Samuel

Hartlib would become one of a number of enthusiastic advocates for establishing an American silk production industry. On the London silk industry, see Peck, *Consuming Splendor*, pp. 1, 74, 85–9, 90–1, 103, 274–5.

54 Robert Boyle, *Some Considerations Touching the Usefulness of Experimental Natural Philosophy . . . The Second Tome* (London, 1671), p. 38.

55 Alistair Fowler notes the scholarly tradition of glossing the simile 'rose like an exhalation' in terms of 'the machinery of a masque – artificial, temporary, illusory' (*PL*, I. 711, editor's note).

56 John Evelyn, *Fumifugium, or The Inconvenience of the Aer and Smoak of London Dissipated* (London, 1661), p. 5. For a more extended reading of Milton's image of Babel in terms of Evelyn's text, see Edwards, *Milton and the Natural World*, pp. 194–5.

57 Boyle, *Usefulnesse of Experimental Naturall Philosophy*, p. 20.

58 Or as one commentator puts it: 'Adam is given what Milton's readers already have, a view of history whole.' See Marshall Grossman, *'Authors to Themselves' Milton and the Revelation of History* (Cambridge: Cambridge University Press, 1987), p. 180.

59 Georgius Agricola, *De Re Metallica* trans. Herbert Clark Hoover and Lou Henry Hoover (1912, reprint, New York: Dover Publications, 1950), p. 8.

60 Certainly Rochester knew Milton's poetry. In a letter to his friend George Savile, Viscount Halifax (July 1678), Rochester quotes lines from Book I of *Paradise Lost*. His short poem 'Sab[rina]: Lost' has been read as a 'reversal' of Milton's *Comus*, while his poem 'The Fall' ('How blest was that created state / Of Man and Woman, e're they fell') is an erotic reverie based on pre-Lapsarian life in Eden, which amplifies those passages of 'conjugal attraction' to be found in *Paradise Lost*. See John Wilmot, Earl of Rochester, *Poems* ed. Keith Walker (Oxford: Blackwell, 1984), pp. 26, 239 (editor's note); John Wilmot, Earl of Rochester, *Letters* ed. Jeremy Treglown (Oxford: Blackwell, 1980), p. 202.

61 Though note William Kerrigan's portrait of a determinedly unphilosophical Milton: 'I doubt whether he read Descartes.' See William Kerrigan, 'Milton's Place in Intellectual History' in Dennis Danielson (ed.), *The Cambridge Companion to Milton* (Cambridge: Cambridge University Press, 1989), p. 267.

62 For an explication of this text, see Dennis Des Chene, *Spirits and Clocks: Machine and Organism in Descartes* (Ithaca, NY, and London: Cornell University Press, 2001), pp. 7–31. Descartes suppressed the *Treatise*, fearing a similar fate to that which Galileo had met at the hands of the Roman Inquisition in 1629.

63 René Descartes, *Philosophical Writings* ed. and trans. John Cottingham, Robert Stoothoff, and Dugald Murdoch 3 vols (Cambridge: Cambridge University Press, 1985), I, p. 99. A Latin edition of the work first appeared in 1662 at Leiden, and a French edition in 1664 at Paris. See Descartes, *Philosophical Writings*, I, p. 79 (editors' note).

64 Descartes, *Philosophical Writings*, I, p. 99.

65 Des Chene, *Spirits and Clocks*, p. 13.

66 Descartes, *Philosophical Writings*, I, p. 108.

67 Nathaniel Culverwell, *An Elegant and Learned Discourse of the Light of Nature* (1652) ed. Robert A. Greene and Hugh MacCullam (Toronto: University of Toronto Press, 1971), p. 24.

68 Culverwell, *Discourse of the Light of Nature*, p. 24.

69 Rogers, *The Matter of Revolution*, p. 122.

70 Regina M. Schwartz, *Remembering and Repeating: On Milton's Theology and Poetics* (Chicago: University of Chicago Press, 1988), p. 22.

71 See Sophocles, *Antigone* ed. Mark Griffith (Cambridge: Cambridge University Press, 1999), p. 120 (editor's gloss).

72 OED (compact edition), II, p. 2715.

73 René Descartes, *Principles of Philosophy* (1644) in Descartes, *Philosophical Writings*, I, p. 205.

74 Thomas Willis, *Practice of Physick* 2 vols (London, 1684), II, p. 32.

75 For a discussion of the 'argument from design' in the seventeenth century, see Peter Harrison, *The Bible, Protestantism, and the Rise of Natural Science* (Cambridge: Cambridge University Press, 1998), pp. 169–76.

76 Robert Boyle, *Considerations Touching the Usefulnesse of Experimental Naturall Philosophy* (London, 1663), p. 71.

77 Boyle, *Usefulnesse of Experimental Naturall Philosophy*, p. 74.

78 See Milton's use of the term 'impulse' to describe God's refusal to intervene in man's fate in *Paradise Lost*, where the word describes the disturbance of the equilibrium of a balance: '. . . no decree of mine / Concurring to necessitate his fall, / Or touch with lightest moment of impulse / His free will to her inclining left / In even scale' (*PL* X. 43–7).

79 On Milton's theology, see C. A. Patrides, W. B. Hunter, and J. H. Adamson, *Bright Essence: Studies in Milton's Theology* (Salt Lake City: University of Utah Press, 1971).

8 The machine stops

1 See Richard Mallette, *Spenser, Milton, and Renaissance Pastoral* (London and Toronto: Associated University Presses, 1981), p. 34.

2 Leo Marx, *The Machine in the Garden: Technology and the Pastoral Ideal in America* (1964, reprint, Oxford and New York: Oxford University Press, 2000), p. 374.

3 Andrew Marvell, *Poems and Letters* ed. H. M. Margoliouth 2 vols (3rd edition, Oxford: Clarendon Press, 1971), I, p. 43.

4 Marvell, *Poems and Letters*, I, pp. 43–4.

5 Marvell, *Poems and Letters*, I, p. 44. On the manufacture and consumption of perfumes and cosmetics in the seventeenth century, see Linda Levy Peck, *Consuming Splendor: Society and Culture in Seventeenth-century England* (Cambridge: Cambridge University Press, 2005), p. 146.

6 Marvell, *Poems and Letters*, I, p. 18

7 Marvell, *Poems and Letters*, I, p. 74.

8 Marvell, *Poems and Letters*, I, p. 47.

9 For an exploration of the role of pastoral in Marvell's 'Mower Poems', see David Kalstone, 'Marvell and the Fictions of Pastoral' in Harold Bloom (ed.), *Andrew Marvell: Modern Critical Views* (New York and Philadephia: Chelsea House Publishers, 1989), pp. 123–35.

10 Marvell, *Poems and Letters*, I, p. 60.

11 On 'nature' compounded out of 'artifice', see Thomas Healy, 'Marvell and Pastoral',

in Patrick Cheney, Andrew Hadfield, and Garrett A. Sullivan Jr (eds), *Early Modern English Poetry: A Critical Companion* (New York and Oxford: Oxford University Press, 2007), p. 306.

12 Marvell, *Poems and Letters*, I, p. 53.

13 Oswald Spengler, *Man and Technics: A Contribution to a Philosophy of Life* (1931, reprint, Honolulu: University Press of the Pacific, 2002), p. 94.

14 Spengler, *Man and Technics*, p. 103.

15 See, in particular, F. R. Leavis, 'Why Four Quartets Matters in a Technologico-Benthamite Age' first given as the Clark Lectures in 1967 and published in F. R. Leavis, *English Literature in Our Time and the University* (London: Chatto and Windus, 1969), pp. 109–32; F. R. Leavis, '*Hard Times*: The World of Bentham' in F. R. Leavis and Q. D. Leavis, *Dickens the Novelist* (Harmondsworth: Penguin Books, 1972), pp. 251–81.

16 Thus, it has been suggested that German architects in the early twentieth century used 'machine metaphors' to articulate 'a modern machine-based culture analogous to the religion-based culture' of the Middle Ages. See Thomas P. Hughes, *Human-Built World: How to Think about Technology and Culture* (Chicago and London: University of Chicago Press, 2004), p. 112.

17 Harold Osborne (ed.), *The Oxford Companion to Twentieth Century Art* (Oxford: Oxford University Press, 1988), p. 210; Sylvia Martin, *Futurism* (Cologne and London: Taschen, 2005), p. 7.

18 Richard Vinen, *A History in Fragments: Europe in the Twentieth Century* (London: Abacus, 2002), p. 183.

19 Ernst Jünger, *Feuer und Blut* (1929) trans. and quoted in Jeffrey Herf, *Reactionary Modernism: Technology, Culture, and Politics in Weimar and the Third Reich* (Cambridge: Cambridge University Press, 1984), p. 79. For an account of the opposition to 'machine culture' among modernists, see Tim Armstrong, *Modernism, Technology and the Body: A Cultural Study* (Cambridge: Cambridge University Press, 1998), particularly pp. 114–20.

20 D. H. Lawrence, 'The Triumph of the Machine' in D. H. Lawrence, *Collected Poems* ed. Vivian de Sola Pinto and Warren Roberts (London: Penguin Books, 1977), p. 624. Lawrence's poem was first published in 1930. As Richard Aldington noted in 1932 (Lawrence, *Collected Poems*, p. 597) meditations on evil, 'especially the evil machine' became a favourite theme of Lawrence's final years.

21 Lawrence, *Collected Poems*, p. 624.

22 Orlando Figes, *A People's Tragedy: The Russian Revolution 1891–1924* (London: Pimlico, 1996), p. 608.

23 Figes, *A People's Tragedy*, p. 608.

24 François Ponchaud, *Cambodia: Year Zero* trans. Nancy Amphoux (Harmondsworth: Penguin Books, 1978), p. 37.

25 Mary Shelley, *The Last Man* (1826) ed. Pamela Bickley (Ware: Wordsworth Editions, 2004), p. 256.

26 For an illuminating survey of the literature and art of nineteenth-century apocalyptic literature, see I. F. Clarke's introduction to Jean-Baptiste François Xavier Cousin de Grainville, *The Last Man* (1805) ed. and trans. I. F. and M. Clarke (Middleton, CT: Wesleyan University Press, n.d.), pp. xi–xli.

27　See the famous analysis of *Robinson Crusoe* in terms of 'economic individualism' in Ian Watt, *The Rise of the Novel: Studies in Defoe, Richardson and Fielding* (1957, reprint, Harmondsworth: Penguin Books, 1970), pp. 62–95.

28　George R. Stewart, *Earth Abides* (1949, reprint, London: Millenium, 2003), p. 292. For a more recent meditation on this theme, see Alan Weisman, *The World without Us* (London: Virgin Books, 2007).

29　By contrast, in more recent Hollywood-style post-apocalypse films such as the *Mad Max* trilogy (1979–85) (dir. George Miller), or *Waterworld* (1995) (dir. Kevin Reynolds) the survivors do not so much regress, technologically, as struggle to preserve the vestiges of their technology which has become fetishized to the point of comic absurdity.

30　I. F. Clarke, *The Pattern of Expectation 1644–2001* (London: Jonathan Cape, 1979), pp. 294, 295. Clarke identifies other examples of the 'survival narrative' where technology collapses, particularly John Wyndham's, *The Day of the Triffids* (1951), J. G. Ballard's *The Drowned World* (1962), and Doris Lessing's *Memoirs of a Survivor* (1975).

31　Clarke, *The Pattern of Expectation*, p. 294.

32　Renato Poggioli, 'Pastorals of Innocence and Happiness' in Bryan Loughrey (ed.), *The Pastoral Mode* (London: Macmillan, 1984), p. 98.

33　Thomas H. Cain, 'The Shepheardes Calender' (introduction) in William A. Oram, Einar Bjorvand, Ronald Bond, Thomas H. Cain, Alexander Dunlop, and Richard Schell (eds), *The Yale Edition of the Shorter Poems of Edmund Spenser* (New Haven and London: Yale University Press, 1989), p. 3.

34　William Alexander McClung, *The Country House in English Renaissance Poetry* (Berkeley, Los Angeles, and London: University of California Press, 1977), p. 12. On pastoral writing more generally, see, in particular, Paul Alpers, 'Pastoral and the Domain of the Lyric in Spenser's *Shepheardes Calender*' in Stephen Greenblatt (ed.), *Representing the English Renaissance* (Berkeley, Los Angeles and London: University of California Press, 1988), pp. 163–80.

35　Peter Lindenbaum, *Changing Landscapes: Anti-Pastoral Sentiment in the English Renaissance* (Atlanta and London: University of Georgia Press, 1986), p. 12.

36　On the political dimension of English pastoral writing in the late sixteenth and earlier seventeenth centuries, see David Norbrook, *Poetry and Politics in the English Renaissance* (London: Routledge and Kegan Paul, 1984), particularly pp. 91–108.

37　Lindenbaum, *Changing Landscapes*, p. 127.

38　John Carey (ed.), *The Faber Book of Utopias* (London: Faber and Faber, 1999), pp. xi–xii.

39　Ben Jonson, *The Complete Plays* ed. Felix E. Schelling 2 vols (London: J. M. Dent, 1967), I, p. 405.

40　Michel de Montaigne, *The Complete Works* trans. Donald M. Frame (London: Everyman, 2003), p. 185.

41　John Florio, *The Essays on Morall, Politike, and Militarie Discourses of Lo. Michaell de Montaigne* (1603) ed. A. R. Waller 3 vols (London: J. M. Dent, 1910), I, p. 220.

42　Gerrard Winstanley, *The Law of Freedom and Other Writings* ed. Christopher Hill (Cambridge: Cambridge University Press, 1983), p. 234.

43　On Leveller commitment to agrarian improvement, see Christopher Hill, *The World*

Turned Upside Down: Radical Ideas During the English Revolution (Harmondsworth: Penguin Books, 1978), pp. 130–1.

44 Winstanley, *The Law of Freedom and Other Writings*, p. 363–4.

45 Thomas Hobbes, *Leviathan* ed. Richard Tuck (Cambridge: Cambridge University Press, 1991), p. 89.

46 Among anthropologists, the despondent history of the Ik people of Northern Uganda, who have all but abandoned any form of social organization, including even childcare after the age of three, is sometimes cited as the mirror of Hobbes's 'state of nature'. See Joseph A. Tainter, *The Collapse of Complex Societies* (Cambridge: Cambridge University Press, 1988), pp. 17–19. Tainter's account of the Ik seems to parallel the more familiar fictional narrative of a regression to 'primitivism' to be found, for example, in William Golding's *Lord of the Flies* (1954).

47 Kevin Kelly, *Out of Control: The New Biology of Machines* (London: Fourth Estate, 1994), p. 3. As David Edgerton has observed, 'one of the more enduring ideas about technology in the twentieth century suggests that the essentially human has been taken over by the artificial. Such "nightmares" also involve the "breakdown" of the "complex world of artifice that makes modern life possible"', David Edgerton, *The Shock of the Old: Technology and Global History since 1900* (London: Profile Books, 2006), p. 75.

48 K. Eric Drexler, *Engines of Creation: The Coming Era of Nanotechnology* (New York: Anchor Books, 1990), pp. 5, 9. For a similarly breathless account of our nano-futures, see Damien Broderick, *The Spike: How Our Lives Are Being Transformed by Rapidly Advancing Technologies* (New York: Forge, 2001), particularly pp. 202–35.

49 Norbert Wiener, *The Human Use of Human Beings: Cybernetics and Society* (1954, reprint, Cambridge, MA: Da Capo Press, 1988), p. 33.

50 Wiener, *Human Use of Human Beings*, p. 32.

51 Paul Virilio, *The Art of the Motor* trans. Julie Rose (Minneapolis and London: University of Minnesota Press, 1995), p. 133.

52 Jean Baudrillard, *The Gulf War Did Not Take Place* trans. Paul Patton (Sydney: Power Publications, 2004), p. 64.

53 Jean Baudrillard, *Simulacra and Simulation* trans. Sheila Faria Glaser (Ann Arbor: University of Michigan Press, 1994), p. 1.

54 Baudrillard, *Simulacra and Simulation*, p. 2. For further reflections in this vein, see Benjamin Woolley, *Virtual Worlds: A Journey in Hype and Hyperreality* (London: Penguin Books, 1993).

55 Herbert A. Simon, *The Sciences of the Artificial* (1996, reprint, Cambridge, MA: MIT Press, 1999), p. 2.

56 Simon, *The Sciences of the Artificial*, p. 4.

57 Mary Tiles and Hans Oberdiek, *Living in a Technological Culture: Human Tools and Human Values* (London and New York: Routledge, 1995), p. 23.

58 For an exploration of the cyborg in art, literature, and in the reality of engineering, see the essays gathered in Chris Hables Gray (ed.), *The Cyborg Handbook* (New York and London: Routledge, 1995).

59 Donna Haraway, 'A Manifesto for Cyborgs: Science, Technology, and Socialist Feminism in the 1980s' in Linda J. Nicholson (ed.), *Feminism/Postmodernism* (New York and London: Routledge, 1990), p. 220.

60 Haraway, 'A Manifesto for Cyborgs', p. 191.

61 See Nick Groom, *The Forger's Shadow: How Forgery Changed the Course of Literature* (London: Picador, 2002), pp. 16–17.

62 Haraway, 'A Manifesto for Cyborgs', pp. 193–4.

63 Samuel Butler, *Erewhon* ed. Peter Mudford (London: Penguin Books, 1985), p. 203. In some respects Butler's fantasy is extraordinarily prescient. See his comments on how machines of the future 'will probably greatly diminish in size' (Butler, *Erewhon*, p. 202).

64 The computer HAL reveals its latent 'humanity' by regressing into an impossible nostalgic reverie, singing an Edwardian music-hall song (Harry Dacre's 1892 'Daisy Bell' or 'A Bicycle Made for Two') as, slowly, its 'memory' is disconnected, and it 'feels' its 'mind' beginning to slip away.

65 Both stories may be read in Arthur O. Lewis Jr (ed.), *Of Men and Machines* (New York: E. P. Dutton, 1963), pp. 335–49.

66 Joan Didion, 'At the Dam' in Richard Rhodes (ed.), *Visions of Technology: A Century of Vital Debate about Machines, Systems, and the Human World* (New York and London: Simon and Schuster, 1999), p. 301.

67 E. M. Forster, *The Machine Stops* (1909) in Lewis (ed.), *Of Men and Machines*, p. 284.

68 Forster, *The Machine Stops*, p. 290.

69 George Monbiot, *Heat: How to Stop the Planet Burning* (London: Allen Lane, 2006), p. 3. Monbiot's idea of the human development of fossil-fuel technology as a 'Faustian pact' contains uncomfortable echoes of Oswald Spengler.

70 Steven E. Jones, *Against Technology from the Luddites to Neo-Luddism* (New York and London, Routledge, 2006), p. 212.

71 John Gray, *Heresies against Progress and Other Illusions* (London: Granta Books, 2004), p. 61. Gray's essay charting the fragility of modern life is entitled, significantly 'When the Machine Stops'.

72 Oram *et al.* (eds), *The Yale Edition of the Shorter Poems of Edmund Spenser*, p. 237.

73 Spenser's 'Ruines of Time' was based, very loosely, on the French poet Joachim Du Bellay's *Les Antiquitez de Rome* (1558), a work which Spenser translated and published as 'Ruines of Rome' (1591).

74 Edward Gibbon, *The History of the Decline and Fall of the Roman Empire* ed. Dean Milman, M. Guizot, and Sir William Smith 8 vols (London: John Murray, 1908), I, p. 137.

75 For an overview of some of the many conflicting accounts of the cause of the collapse of the Roman Empire, see Tainter, *The Collapse of Complex Societies*, pp. 11, 49–50, 53, 63, 128–51.

76 Michel de Montaigne, *The Complete Works* trans. Donald M. Frame (London: Everyman's Library, 2003), p. 1150.

77 Montaigne, *The Complete Works*, pp. 1150–1.

78 Montaigne, *The Complete Works*, p. 1151.

INDEX

Note: page numbers in *italic* indicate illustrations.

Adagorum Collectanea (Erasmus) 114
Adams, Simon 324 n. 64
Adamson, J. H. 379 n. 79
Adas, Michael 56
Adelman, Janet 162
Adoration of the Magi (Bosch) 11
Advancement of Learning, The (F. Bacon)
    20, 113, 211
Aeschylus 323 n. 44
Agricola, Georgius (Georg Bauer) 180–1;
    see also De Re Metallica
Agrippa, Henry Cornelius 186, 363 n. 155
air pumps 220–1
Akin, David 369 n. 102
Alberti, Leon Battista 96, 109, 217
Albertus Magnus 193
Alchemist, The (Jonson) 176, 196, 200
alchemy 168, 176, 196
Alciati (Andreas Alciatus) 97
Alder, Ken 335 n. 7
Aldington, Richard 380 n. 20
Aldiss, Brian 314
Aleotti, Giambattista 189
Allan, David 364 n. 8
Allen, Christopher 324 n. 67
Allen, M. J. B. 358 n. 73

Alpers, Paul 381 n. 34
Alpers, Svetlana 137, 142, 218, 322 n. 33,
    348 n. 10
Anatomic practica (Barbette) 248
Anatomie of Abuses (Stubbes) 205
Anatomy of Melancholy, The (Burton)
    187
Annanberg altarpiece 7
Antikythera Mechanism 349 n. 35
Antony and Cleopatra (Shakespeare) 203
Apollonius of Rhodes 192
Apologie for Poetrie, An (P. Sidney) 199
'Apology of Raymond Sebond, An'
    (Montaigne) 51
Apuleius, Lucius 330 n. 68
Aquinas, St Thomas 193
Archytas of Tarentum 185, 186
Areopagitica (Milton) 261, 269–70, 287–8
Aretino, Pietro 201
Argonautica (Apollonius of Rhodes) 192
Aristotelis mechanica (Monantheuil) 243
Aristotle 1, 173, 174
Armstrong, Tim 380 n. 19
Arnald of Villanova 173
Arte of English Poesie (Puttenham) 175
artillery designs 85–6

As You Like It (Shakespeare) 76–7, 151, 305
Ascham, Roger 174
Aškenazy, Ludvik 320 n. 14
'At the Dam' (Didion) 314
Aubrey, John 256, 376 n. 40
Auden, W. H. 26–8
Auerbach, Erich 53
Augsburg: astronomical clock 233; entry system 47; public water supply 41, 42–3
Augustine of Hippo, St 19–20, 167, 173, 191
'Author to the Critical Peruser, The' (Traherne) 244
Autobiography (Cellini) 190
automata 117, 120, 191–9, 228–32, 245–6, 290, 355 n. 10; animals 170, 193; birds 45, 170–1, 186, 187, 193, 198; brazen heads 187, 194; Daedalus's 186; figures 189–93, 195, 197, 199–206, 229, 232; hydraulic figures 189–90; insects 170–1, 186, 193; Islamic 195; knights 193, 195; lobsters 191, 196; mechanical women 193, 197, 199–206; men 193; robots 195, 197–8, 230–1; ships 203; Talos/Talus 191–2; *see also* puppets
autonomy 286, 287–8, 289–91
Awty, B. G. 355 n. 16

Babbage, Charles 75
Babel, tower of 20–4
Bacon, Francis 3, 45, 118–20, 267, 305, 307; and mechanism 210–16; *see also Advancement of Learning, The*
Bacon, Roger 194
Baigrie, Brian S. 330 n. 63
Baines, Patricia 347 n. 8
Baldwin, Robert 325 n. 72
Ball, John 136
Bancroft, Thomas 237
Barber, Elizabeth Wayland 351 n. 65
Barber, William J. 336 n. 26
Barbette, Paul 248
Barker, Francis 376 n. 39
Barry, James Jr 365 n. 34
Bartholomew Fair (Jonson) 187–8

Bartolommeo, Fra 15
Basalla, George 344 n. 146
Basilicon Doron (James VI and I) 123
Bate, John 341 n. 104
'Batter my heart' (Donne) 166–7, 168–9, 213
Baudrillard, Jean 312
Bauer, Georg, *see* Agricola, Georgius
Baumlin, James S. 377 n. 50
Baynes, Ken 343 n. 124
Beamish, Richard 368 n. 91
'Beautiful Young Nymph Going to Bed, A' (Swift) 201
Beauvoir, Simone de 205
Beck, T. 341 n. 104
Beddevole, Dominique 242
Belozerskaya, Marina 355 n. 19
Bennett, H. S. 370 n. 126
Bennett, James A. 364 n. 7, 367 n. 70
Benoît de Sainte-Maure 193, 199–200
Berger, Harry, Jr 357 n. 53
Berlusconi, Silvio xvii
'Bermudas' (Marvell) 296–7
Besson, Jacques 101, 341 n. 104, 343 n. 135
Biblical references 15, 195, 224; Babel 20; Ezekiel's visions 123; the Fall 3–4, 19, 95; Second Commandment 179; Uzziah 18–19
Billingsley, Humphrey 211
Birch, Thomas 368 n. 92
Biringuccio, Vannoccio 87, 339 n. 74, 341 n. 104
Bishop, John 268–9
Bizzarie di Varie Figure (Bracelli) 231
blacksmiths 4–5
Blade Runner (film) 163, 201
Blake, William 275
Bles, Herri met de 7, 8
Bloch, Marc 57, 332 n. 88
Blundeville, Thomas 151
Boas, Marie 338 n. 66, 364 n. 13
Bodin, Jean 72
Boeckler, Georg Andreas 98, 119, 341 n. 104, 342 n. 120, 343 n. 135; *Cochlergon* apparatus 118

Boethius, Anicius Manlius Severinus 152

Bol, Hans 28

Book of Knowledge of Ingenious Mechanical Devices (al-Jazari) 85

Borst, Arno 336 n. 30

Bosch, Hieronymus 10–11, *12*, 201

Boyle, Robert 277, 281–2, 367 n. 72; and air pump 220–1; human body as machine 242–3; mechanics, definition of 219, on Strasbourg clock 290–1

Brace, Harold W. 342 n. 119

Bracelli, Giovanni Battista 231

Bradbury, Ray 314

Branca, Giovanni 111, 144, *145*, 341 n. 104

Brave New World (Huxley) 300

Bray, William 371 n. 134

Bredekamp, Horst 190–1, 361 n. 128

Brekelenkam, Quirijn Gerritsz. van 129, *130*

Brett, Gerard 355 n. 10

Brey, Philip 320 n. 10

Briggs, John C. 365 n. 36

Bristow, Joseph 373 n. 175

Broderick, Damien 382 n. 48

Brodie, Alexander 335 n. 19

Brooke, C. F. Tucker 359 n. 79

Brooks, Rodney A. 369 n. 102

Brown, Jonathan 134, 348 n. 12

Brown, Sarah Annes 348 n. 13

Browne, Sir Thomas 169, 224

Bruce, J. Douglas 360 n. 110

Brueghel, Jan the Elder 11

Brueghel, Jan the Younger 11

Brueghel, Pieter the Elder 21, *23*, 141; *see also Carrying the Cross*; *Hunters in the Snow*; *Landscape with the Fall of Icarus*

Brunel, Marc Isambard 368 n. 91

Brunelleschi, Filippo 86, 102

Buchanan, R. A. 327 n. 32

Building of a Double Palace, The (Piero di Cosimo) 9

Bull, Malcolm 324 n. 62

Bulliet, Richard W. 349 n. 33

Bulmer, Bevis 328 n. 38

Buontalenti, Bernardo 44

Burke, Peter 367 n. 62

Burleigh, Michael 347 n. 1

Burton, Robert 187

But Who Can Replace A Man? (Aldiss) 314

Butler, George F. 375 n. 17

Butler, Samuel 314

Butt, John 369 n. 95

Butterworth, Philip 358 n. 63

'Byzantium' (Yeats) 169

Cahn, Susan 347 n. 5

Cain, Thomas H. 381 n. 33

calculating devices 238–41; man as 239–40

Caligula, Caius, emperor 59

Calthoff, Caspar 265

Cambodia 302, 331 n. 80

Camille, Michael 95

Campanella, Tommaso 186–7

Campbell, Lily B. 358 n. 63

Campion, Thomas 233

Canterbury Tales, The (Chaucer) 57, 193

Cantor, Norman F. 326 n. 22

Čapek, Karel 230

Cardwell, Donald 330 n. 63

Carew, Thomas 159–60

Carey, John 307, 354 n. 6, 377 n. 50

Carlyle, Thomas 75

Carr, Dawson W. 348 n. 18

Carrying the Cross (Pieter Brueghel the Elder) 15, 18, 350 n. 44

Carter, Harry 368 n. 94

Cartesianism 234; *see also* Descartes, René

Castle of Knowledge, The (Recorde) 155, *156*

Catherine of Alexandria, St 139–42, *140*

Cave, Terence 356 n. 32

Cavendish, Margaret 227–8

Cellini, Benvenuto 190

Centuries of Inventions (Somerset) 265, 266

Centuries of Meditation (Traherne) 243, 245

Cervantes, Miguel de 194

Chaney, Edward 44

Chant, Colin 67, 333 n. 98

Chapuis, Alfred 188, 359 nn. 81 & 99
Charleton, Walter 248
Chaucer, Geoffrey 57, 193
Chernaik, Warren 250, 255, 373 n. 185, 373 n. 188
Chew, Samuel C. 352 n. 82
Childe, V. Gordon 349 n. 33
Chiles, James R. 373 n. 167
Chilmead, Edmund 359 n. 88
Christian Ethics (Traherne) 244
Christianity: technology and 55–7, 58–63, 64–8
Cicero, Marcus Tullius 321 n. 10
Cipolla, Carlo 76, 334 n. 1
Ciro di Pers 122
City of God (Augustine) 19–20, 173, 191
Civetta, see Bles, Herri met de
Clark, Alice 146
Clark, Kenneth 32–3
Clark, Stuart 323 n. 52, 374 n. 12
Clarke, I. F. 304, 328 n. 42, 380 n. 26
Claude Lorraine 18
Clements, Robert J. 366 n. 54
clocks 76–8, 122, 138, 190, 198, 242, 244–5; astronomical 231, 233; as metaphor 232–7; Strasbourg cathedral 171, 290–1
clockwork 228–9; as metaphor 245–8; and reason 232–7; Traherne on 244–5
Cockburn, Cynthia 146–7, 149
Codde, Pieter 11
Codice Atlantico (Leonardo) 323 n. 40, 328 n. 40
Coecke van Aelst, Pieter 15
Cohen, Adam Max 239, 371 n. 128
Cohen, Murray 370 n. 123
Cole, S. M. 349 n. 32
Collocott, T. C. 330 n. 64
Comus (Milton) 173, 276–7, 288
Confessio amantis (Gower) 194
Connor, Steven 360 n. 111
'Consideration upon Cicero, A' (Montaigne) 114–15
Considerations Touching the Usefulness of Experimental Naturall Philosophy (Boyle) 290–1
Copenhaver, Brian P. 373 n. 178

Copper Mine, The (Bles) 7, 8
copying device 115–16
Coriolanus (Shakespeare) 160–5, 173, 290
Corry, A. K. 342 n. 113
Corsini, Matteo 360 n. 111
Cosmography (Munster) 336 n. 36
Cotterell, Brian 354 n. 100
Countess of Pembrokes Arcadia, The (Sir Philip Sidney) 105
Cowley, Abraham 218–19, 263
Crichton, Michael 201
Culverwell, Nathaniel 287
Curran, Brian 333 n. 97, 358 n. 73
Curtis, William J. R. 333 n. 96
Cutcliffe, Stephen H. 326 n. 25
Cuyp, Aelbert 11
cyborgs 313

D'acres, R. 346 n. 187, 375 n. 30
'Damon the Mower' (Marvell) 297–8
Dante Alighieri 21
Darmanson, Jean 373 n. 170
Darwin, Charles 216
Daston, Lorraine 356 n. 23
data retrieval 223–4
Davies, Sir John 236–7
Davis, Herbert 368 n. 94
Davis, Robert Leigh 377 n. 50
De Architectura (Vitruvius) 83–4, 323 n. 40
de Caus, Isaak 118, 189
De Consolatione philosophiae (Boethius) 152
De Corpore (Hobbes) 239, 258
de Federico Barocci, Ambrogio 10
de Hamel, Christopher 337 n. 51
De inventoribus rerum (Vergil) 24
De re aedificatoria (Alberti) 109
De Re Metallica (Agricola) 7, 172, 278, 284, 341 n. 104; analysis of tasks 90–1; illustrations 87–9, 89, 91, 92–6, 94; readership 88–9; women in 148
De Re Militarii (Valturio) 341 n. 104
De rebus bellicis (Anon.) 331 n. 78
De Sapientia veterum (F. Bacon) 215
Deane, Phyllis 363 n. 152

Dear, Peter 365 n. 28

Dee, John 117, 211

Defoe, Daniel 303

Dekker, Thomas 5, 6, 139, 234–5, 236

Della Pittura (Alberti) 217

Della tranquilitià dell'animo (Alberti) 96

Della Transportione dell'obelisco vaticano (D. Fontana) 60, 63

Delle Machine Ordinanze et Quartieri (Tarducci) 341 n. 104

Deloney, Thomas 6

Derry, T. K. 137

Des Chene, Dennis 286, 369 n. 111

Descartes, René 201, 234, 236, 285–6; freedom 289–90; on human body and machine 251–2; human machines 286; talking machines 237–8

Description and Use of Two Arithmetick Instruments, The (Morland) 240

Description of a New World Called the Blazing World, The (Cavendish) 227–8

designer–machine relationship 289–90

Deuxième Sexe, Le (Beauvoir) 205

Devotions upon Emergent Occasions (Donne) 168

Dialogues Concerning Two New Sciences (Galileo) 210

Diamond, Jared 322 n. 34, 331 n. 78

Dick, Oliver Lawson 373 n. 188

Dickson, Arthur 361 n. 115

Didion, Joan 314

Digby, Sir Kenelm 247

Digges, Leonard 367 n. 74

Dijksterhuis, E. J. 364 n. 13

Dilly, Antoine 373 n. 170

Dircks, Henry 345 n. 170, 375 n. 30

Discourse of the Light of Nature (Culverwell) 287

Discourse on the Method (Descartes) 237

Discovery of Honey, The (Piero di Cosimo) 9

Distant View of Dordrecht, A (The Large Dort) (Cuyp) 11

Diverse et Artificiose Machine, Le (Ramelli) 15–18, 102–3, 106, 107, 112, 148

division of labour 92, 240–1; gender divisions in 148–50; in Hell (*Paradise Lost*) 280; K. Marx on 74; pin making and 74; printing and 80–1

Djehutihotpe, Egyptian provincial governor 64

Domesday Book 36–7

Don Giovanni (Mozart) 204

Don Quixote (Cervantes) 194

Donne, John 93–5, 159–60, 166–7, 168–9, 172, 213

Doré, Gustave 303

Drachmann, A. G. 338 n. 66

Drake, Stillman 331 n. 74, 375 n. 16

Drayton, Michael 168

Drebbel, Cornelius 121–2, 184

Drexler, K. Eric 382 n. 48

Droz, Edmond 188, 359 n. 99

Drucker, Peter F. 332 n. 81

Du Bartas (Guillaume de Saluste, Sieur du Bartas) 170–1, 172, 177, 178

du Chesne, André 189

Duffy, Eamon 359 n. 84

Dürer, Albrecht 139, 140

Dury, John 267

Dyson, George 240

Earth Abides (Stewart) 303–4, 306

Eaton, Ruth 66, 333 n. 96

Eclogues (Virgil) 294–5, 304

Edgerton, David 382 n. 47

Edward II (Marlowe) 157

Edwards, Karen 260, 368 n. 79

Edwards, Mark U., Jr 337 n. 38

Eighteen Books of the Secrets of Art and Nature (Wecker) 341 n. 104

Eisenstein, Elizabeth 66, 78, 80, 99, 109, 336 n. 33

Elements of Architecture, The (Wotton) 183

Elias, Norbert 323 n. 43

emblem books 13, 14, 97

Emblemata (Alciati) 97

Emblemata, Emblems Christienes, et Morales (Heyns) 13, 14

Endrei, Walter 322 n. 24, 331 n. 78

energy sources 34–47; animals 35, 51–2, 328 n. 38; coal 35, 36, 327 n. 32; human

treadmills 41; water 34, 35–47; wind 35, 326 n. 28; wood 34–5
engine looms 266
Enginous Wheeles of the Soule (Dekker) 236
England: water power in 36–7
entertainment 183–5
Erasmus, Desiderius 114, 339 n. 79
Erewhon (S. Butler) 314
Errard, Jean 101, 341 n. 104, 352 n. 75
Essay Concerning Human Understanding, An (Locke) 241
Essay on Man, An (Pope) 229
Essay Towards a Real Character, and a Philosophical Language (Wilkins) 238
Essays (Montaigne) 40, 308
Eve Future, L' (Villiers de Lisle Adam) 201
Evelyn, John 68, 118, 240, 280
Experimental Philosophy in Three Books (Power) 208
'Expostulation with Inigo Jones, An' (Jonson) 185

Fable of Arachne, The (Velásquez) 132–7, *133*, 155–7
factories 266–7
Faerie Queene, The (Spenser) 105, 152, 157, 173, 179; Acrasia 181; 'Bowre of Blisse' episode 135, 179–82, 200; Talus 192
Fall: in *Paradise Lost* 275; technology and 3–4, 9–10, 19
Famous Historie of Fryer Bacon, The (Anon.) 194–5
Fauvel, John 360 n. 104
Febvre, Lucien 81
Felton, Edmund 271
Ferguson, Eugene S. 329 n. 56, 336 n. 37, 341 n. 104, 343 n. 134, 344 n. 147
Ferguson, Niall 347 n. 1
Ficino, Marsilio 29
Field, J. V. 349 n. 35
Figes, Orlando 380 n. 22
Findlen, Paula 238, 324 n. 53, 355 n. 17, 362 n. 141
Fire in the Bush (Winstanley) 309

Fish, Stanley 375 n. 24
Florio, John 308
Fludd, Robert 117
Fontana, Carlo 62, 65
Fontana, Domenico 59–63, *60*, 64–6, 68
Ford, Sir Edward 328 n. 38
Ford, Henry 320 n. 14
Fores, Michael 320 nn. 12 & 13
Forrest, James F. 377 n. 50
Forster, E. M. 314–15
Foucault, Michel 68, 81, 91, 110, 141, 350 n. 44
Fowler, Alistair 376 n. 42, 378 n. 55
Frakes, Jerold C. 352 n. 82
Frame, Donald 46, 329 n. 46
France: water power in 34, 36, 37, 38
Francine, Thomas and François 189
François I, king of France 190
Franits, Wayne 347 n. 7
Frantz, David O. 362 n. 141
French, Milton 374 n. 13, 377 n. 50
Freud, Sigmund 2–3, 30, 136, 160; prosthesis 2, 24; uncanny 202
Friar Bacon and Friar Bungay (R. Greene) 194
Friedel, Robert 320 n. 10
Friedrichs, Christopher R. 327 n. 29
Frischlin, Nicodemus 355 n. 13
Fritsch, Julia 363 n. 154
Fröschl, Daniel 172
Fuller, Thomas 272
Fumifugium (Evelyn) 280
Futurism 300, 330 n. 62

Gabbey, Alan 331 n. 75
Gaffarel, Jacques 188–9
Galileo Galilei 54, 59, 210, 261, 267
Gallego, Fernando 139
Galluzzi, Paolo 325 nn. 1 & 14
Gamble, Clive 323 n. 48
'Garden, The' (Marvell) 299
Garden of Earthly Delights, The (Bosch) 10–11, 201
Gardner, E. M. 326 n. 28
Garrett, Garet 320 n. 14
Gassel, Lucas van 7

Gaukroger, Stephen 201, 362 n. 142, 365 n. 20

Geffe, Nicholas 377 n. 53

gender issues: division of labour 148–50; Rosie the Riveter 125–8, *126*; sexual difference 205–6; spinning 129–36

Ghiberti, Lorenzo 86

Gibbon, Edward 141, 316

Gies, Frances and Joseph 333 n. 104

Giglioni, Guido 371 n. 135

Gille, Bertrand 338 n. 62

Gimpel, Jean 36–7

Giorgio Martini, Francesco di 84–5, 86

Giuliano da Sangallo 86

Glanvill, Joseph 221, 246, 259, 261

Glick, Thomas F. 348 n. 19

Gnudi, Martha Teach 323 n. 39

Golden Ass (Apuleius) 330 n. 68

Golden Legend (Jacobus de Voragine) 139–41

Goldgar, Anne 177

Golding, Arthur 25, 28, 205

Golinski, Jan 363 n. 164

Gombrich, E. H. 324 n. 69, 325 n. 4

Goodman, David 67

Gordon, Andrew 367 n. 74

Gordon, D. J. 358 n. 70

Goubert, A. 327 n. 29

Gower, John 194

Goyen, Jan van 11

Grafton, Anthony 20–1, 344 n. 148

Graves, Robert 353 n. 85

Gray, Chris Hables 382 n. 58

Gray, John xvii, 315–16

Great Machine of Marly 38, *39*

Green, Ian 337 n. 38

Greenblatt, Stephen 159, 181–2

Greene, Graham 373 n. 186

Greene, Robert 194

Greene, Thomas M. 356 n. 32

Greither, Elias 324 n. 67

Grint, Keith 332 n. 90

Groom, Nick 383 n. 61

Grosseteste, Robert 194

Grossman, Marshall 378 n. 58

Grotius, Hugo (Huig de Groot) 122

Grundrisse (K. Marx) 72–3

Guillaume de Deguileville 13

Gulliver's Travels (Swift) 257

Haber, Francis C. 355 n. 13

Hale, J. R. 327 n. 30

Hall, A. R. 329 n. 51

Hall, Bert S. 339 n. 68, 343 n. 125, 344 n. 148

Hall, Peter 335 n. 21

Hall, James 349 n. 22

Hamlet (Shakespeare) 72, 99–100, 153–4, 235

Hankins, Thomas L. 374 n. 2

Hannaway, O. 339 n. 75, 340 n. 89

Hanson, Victor Davis 319 n. 6

Haraway, Donna 225, 313

Harbison, Craig 323 n. 42

Hardy, Thomas 327 n. 34

Hare, Maurice E. ix

Harff, Arnold von 330 n. 60

Harford, Ralph 376 n. 44

Harris, John 358 n. 65

Harris, L. E. 346 n. 188

Harris, Roy 374 n. 2

Harrison, Peter 379 n. 75

Hartlib, Samuel 377 n. 53

Haskell, Francis 321 n. 13

Healy, Margaret 329 n. 50

Healy, Thomas 379 n. 11

Heidegger, Martin 1, 300

Heinlein, Peter 336 n. 28

Hell: division of labour in 280; representations of 11, *12*

Heller, Agnes 365 n. 32

Heller, Henry 326 n. 23

Hellinga, Lotte 337 n. 39

Heninger, S. K. Jr 352 n. 81

Henry, Avril 322 n. 36

Henry V (Shakespeare) 101, 104, 154, 155

Henry VI (Shakespeare) 154–5; *Part 1*: 24–5; *Part 3*: 25, 157

Herbert, George 271–2

Herf, Jeffrey 345 n. 167

Hermes Trismegistus 186

Heroides (Ovid) 161

Heron of Alexandria 108, 188, 189, 198–9
Herrick, Robert 177–8
Hesiod 191
Hesse, Hans 7
Heyns, Zacharias 13, 14
Hieron, Samuel 82
Hilanderas, Las (Velásquez) 132–7, 133, 155–7
Hill, Christopher 77–8, 264, 374 n. 7, 381 n. 43
Hill, Donald R. 338 nn. 81 & 65, 361 n. 122
Hillier, Mary 198, 359 n. 81
History of the Decline and Fall of the Roman Empire (Gibbon) 316
History of the Royal Society (Sprat) 257–8
Hobbes, Thomas 113, 174, 239–40, 258, 309–10; clockwork metaphor 245–6
Hobson, John M. 320 n. 8
Hoffmann, E. T. A. 201–2
Holbein, Hans the Younger 7
Hollister-Short, Graham 328 n. 39
Holst, Neils Van 361 n. 129
Holy Sonnet (Donne) 166–7, 168–9
Homer: Iliad 199; Odyssey 161
Homme Machine, L' (La Mettrie) 248
Hooke, Robert 219, 240; Brush-horn'd Gnat 225–6; instruments 222–8
Hooper, John 319 n. 7
Horenbout, Gerard 21–4
Howard, Leon 377 n. 50
Hughes, Thomas P. 380 n. 16
Huizinga, Johan 321 n. 13
human autonomy 287–8, 289–91
human body: clockwork metaphor 245–8; hierarchy of parts 248
Humane Industry or a History of Most Manual Arts (Powell) 120, 122
Hume, David ix
Humphrey, John W. 338 n. 61
Hunt, John Dixon 329 n. 54
Hunter, Michael 258, 367 n. 71, 373 n. 181, 374 n. 6, 374 n. 7
Hunter, W. B. 379 n. 79
Hunters in the Snow (Pieter Brueghel the Elder) 13–15, 16
Huon de Bordeaux 193

Huxley, Aldous 300
Huygens III, Constantijn 11–13
hydraulic figures 189–90
hydraulic machines (Calthoff–Somerset engine) 265–6
hydraulic societies 55
Hymenaei (masque) 184

iconoclasm 178–9, 181–2
Iconologia (Ripa) 197
Ihde, Don 320 n. 3
Iliad (Homer) 199
illusions 183–4
Image du Monde 194
imagery: forge of Vulcan 167–8
'Imperfect Enjoyment, The' (Rochester) 252–3
In Der Strafkolonie ('In the Penal Settlement', Kafka) 141
In inventorum bombardae (Milton) 273
industry: Milton as poet of 274–6; in Paradise Lost 277–84
Inquiry into the Nature and Causes of the Wealth of Nations (Adam Smith) 74–5
insects: automata 186, 193; as metaphor 226–7, 236
instruments 207–56; air pumps 220–1; calculating devices 238–41; drawing devices 217–18; Hooke and 222–8; measuring devices 216; telescopes 216, 227, 259, 261; for the transmission of sound 223, 367 n. 76; see also clocks; microscopes
intellectual theft 102–3
'interrupted idyll' 294–5
irrigation civilizations 55
Italy: gardens 44–5; water technology 43–7

Jacobus de Voragine 139, 141
Jacquard, J. M. 202
James VI and I, king of Scotland and England 123, 184
Jamnitzer, Wenzel 177
Jardine, Lisa 364 n. 2, 367 n. 70, 368 n. 81
al-Jazari 85

Jeanneret, Michel 33
Jenkins, Rhys 328 n. 38, 375 n. 30, 376
    n. 35
Jennings, Humphrey xv–xvi, 292
Jennings, Mary-Lou 368 n. 91
Jentsch, Ernst 202
Jones, Anne Rosalind 135, 348 n. 15
Jones, Inigo 67, 183–5
Jones, Peter Murray 337 n. 38
Jones, Robert 25
Jones, Steven E. 315
Jonson, Ben 113, 183–6, 187–8, 308; The
    Alchemist 176, 196, 200
Joulden, William 268–9
Jünger, Ernst 300–1

Kafka, Franz 141
Kalstone, David 379 n. 9
Keller, Alexander 330 n. 59, 338 n. 62, 344
    n. 151, 366 n. 47
Kelly, Kevin 382 n. 47
Kemp, Martin 33, 172, 217, 345 n. 168, 355
    n. 17, 366 n. 50
Kepler, Johannes 243
Kermode, Frank 357 n. 41
Kerrigan, John 122
Kerrigan, William 378 n. 61
Khmer Rouge 302
Kidwell, Peggy Aldrich 371 n. 136
King, Ross 339 n. 71
King Lear (Shakespeare) 153, 158, 159
Kirby, Richard Shelton 326 n. 27
Kircher, Athanasius 20–1, 238
Klein, Bernhard 367 n. 74
Klingender, Francis D. 7, 322 n. 25, 377
    n. 52
Knoespel, Kenneth 97
Kubrick, Stanley 414
Künstkammer, Prague 172, 197–8
Kyeser, Konrad 84

La Mettrie, Julien Offray de 248–9
labour: alienation of 72–4, 96, 110;
    division of 74, 80–1, 92, 148–50, 240–1,
    280; gender divisions in 148–50
Ladner, Lorne 350 n. 36

Lambert, William 268
Lancelot 193
Landau, David 336 n. 35
Landels, J. G. 331 n. 78
Landes, David 5, 35–6, 76, 369 n. 107
Landscape with the Fall of Icarus (Bol) 28
Landscape with the Fall of Icarus (Pieter
    Brueghel the Elder) 26–8, 27, 29–30
Landscape with the Marriage of Isaac and
    Rebekah (Claude Lorraine) 18
Lang, Fritz 201
language 113, 244; artificial 237–8, 241;
    mechanical 257–9
Lanser, Susan S. 351 n. 54
Laqueur, Thomas 206, 356 n. 27
Last Man, The (M. Shelley) 302
Last Supper (Coecke van Aelst) 15
Law of Freedom in a Platform, The
    (Winstanley) 309
Lawrence, D. H. 301
Le Comte, Edward S. 377 n. 48
Le Goff, Jacques 332 n. 87
Leapman, Michael 358 n. 67
Leavis, F. R. 380 n. 15
Leibniz, G. W. 240–1
Leonardo da Vinci 67, 68, 86, 96, 303, 323
    n. 40; deluge drawings 32–3; machine
    designs 31, 33, 35; on perpetual motion
    117; physiology as engineering 231;
    robots 231; and water 32–4; water-
    powered industrial processes 328 n. 40
Lesseps, Ferdinand de 56
Letters on Sunspots (Galileo) 261
Leupold, Jacob 344 n. 147
Levey, Michael 324 n. 69
Leviathan (Hobbes) 113, 245–6, 309–10
Lewis, Arthur O. 383 n. 65
Lewis, C. S. 180
Lewis, M. J. T. 333 n. 97
libertinism 250
Life and Strange and Surprising Adventures
    of Robinson Crusoe, The (Defoe) 303
Ligorio, Pirro 44
Lindenbaum, Peter 381 n. 35
Lives of the Artists (Vasari) 33, 176
Locke, John 241

logarithms 238
Lombe, Thomas 266
London: A Pilgrimage (Doré) 303
Long, Pamela O. 340 n. 97, 343 n. 127
'Love wing'd my hopes and taught me how to fly' (Anon.) 25–6
'Loves Clock' (Suckling) 235–6
Lucar, Cyprian 111
Lucretius 53
Luddism 57
Lupton, Ellen 351 n. 68
Luttrell Psalter, The 95, 129, *131*, 340 n. 94
'Lycidas' (Milton) 273–4

McClellan, James E., III: 320 n. 8
McClung, William Alexander 381 n. 34
McGaw, Judith A. 351 n. 68
Machine, Le (Branca) 144, *145*
machine books 83–96, 97–104; artillery in 85–6; and intellectual theft 102–3; main texts 341 n. 104; and Mannerism 103–4; mining and metallurgy 87–96 (*see also De Re Metallica*); in Siena 84–6; as 'theatres' of machinery 109
machine breaking 57
Machine Stops, The (Forster) 314–15
machines 68; and alienation of labour 72–4; and anatomy 108–11; definitions of xix–xx, 330 n. 64; designer–machine relationship 289–90; in fantasy 96–7; and human senses 216–21, 222; Luddism 57; Milton and 284–93; self-replicating 310–11; and social power 54–7; *Technē* 1–4
Mack, Pamela E. 347 n. 4
McKenzie, D. F. 82
MacLaren, Neil 322 n. 30
McLuhan, Marshall 82–3, 203
McNeil, Ian 365 n. 26, 368 n. 91, 372 n. 161
McNeil, William H. 326 n. 22
Mad Max (film trilogy) 381 n. 29
Madge, Charles 368 n. 91
Madonna and Child with the Young John the Baptist (Fra Bartolommeo) 15
Maffioli, Cesare S. 327 n. 29

magic 187–8, 204, 213
Magnusson, Robert J. 327 n. 29
Mallette, Richard 379 n. 1
Manguel, Alberto 337 n. 38
Manley, Lawrence 343 n. 126
Mannerism 103–4, 128, 134
manuals 339 n. 79; estate management 111; naturalism in 92–3; *see also De Re Metallica* (Agricola)
Manzuoli, Tomaso (Maso di San Friano) 324 n. 67
Maor, Eli 360 n. 112
Marchant, Jo 349 n. 35
Marcus, Leah S. 344 n. 148
Marilla, Esmond L. 377 n. 50
Marks, Carol 372 n. 155
Marlowe, Christopher 25, 157, 187
Marsden, E. W. 354 n. 100
Marshall, Alan 371 n. 134
Marshall, Cynthia 353 n. 97
Marston, John 204–5
Martin, Henri-Jean 81
Martin, John 275
Martin, Sylvia 380 n. 17
Martinón-Torres, Marcos 354 n. 7
Marvell, Andrew 295–9, 376 n. 45
Marx, Karl xx, 54–5, 72–4, 75, 336 n. 27; alienation of labour 96, 110; and division of labour 92
Marx, Leo 182–3, 294–5, 303
Maso da San Friano (Tomaso Manzuoli) 324 n. 67
masques 183–5; *Comus* (Milton) 173, 276–7, 288; *machina versatilis* in 184–5, 187
Mathematical Collection (Pappus of Alexandria) 191
Mathematicall Magick (Wilkins) 120, 198
mathematics 44, 100, 109, 210, 238–9, 258; calculating devices 238–41; logarithms 238; *see also Mathematicall Magick* (Wilkins)
Mathias, Peter 375 n. 31
Maudit, John 376 n. 44
Maurice, Klaus 359 n. 97
Mauries, Patrick 369 n. 103
Maxentius, Roman emperor 141

May, John 351 n. 63
Mayr, Otto 49, 100, 330 n. 61, 370 n. 117
measurement 222–3; measuring devices
216; of time, see clocks
'mechanic': OED definition of 365 n. 21
mechanical arts 342 n. 110
mechanical creatures, see automata
mechanical philosophy 207–9
mechanical theology 242–5
Mechanicorum liber (Ubaldo) 54
mechanism: theology and 242–5
Medici, Cosimo III de' 265
Medici, Francesci I de' 9
megamachines 58–69; Deir el-Bersheh/
Hermapolis, Egypt 63–4; Rome, Sixtine
renovation of 58–63, 64–8
Mendelschen Zwöfl-Brüder-Stiftung 332
n. 84
Merian, Mattheus the Elder 22
Messenger, Charles 377 n. 51
metallurgy 168; see also De Re Metallica
(Agricola); mining industry
Metamorphoses (Ovid) 9, 24, 25, 28–9;
Arachne 132–4; Pygmalion 204
Metamorphosis of Pygmalion's Image, The
(Marston) 204–5
metaphors: clocks 232–7; clockwork 245–
8; insects 226–7, 236; of technology
300–1
Metropolis (Lang) 201
Michael, Donald 320 n. 14
Michelangelo Buonarroti 176; Sistine
Chapel ceiling 125, 127, 139
microbiology 311
Micrographia (Hooke) 219, 222
microscopes 208, 222, 224–5, 227, 272;
Milton and 260, 261
Micyllus, Jakob 324 n. 67
Milton (Blake) 275
Milton, John 173, 258–93, 299; blindness
of 260–1, 263; engines, idea of
270–4; and industry 266, 274–84; and
machines 284–93; and mechanical
language 258–9; and optical
instruments 259–65; Prometheus 273;
reasoning engine 284–5; 'self' prefix

288–9; semi-omnipotent engines 265–
70; and technology 275; travels 40–7,
267; two-handed engine 274; use of
'impulse' 291–2; see also Paradise Lost
mimesis 174, 178–9, 310–11
mining industry 7, 148, 278, 341 n. 104;
technical/machine books 87–96; see
also De Re Metallica
mint, Spanish Royal 247
Misa, Thomas 336 n. 37
Moffett, Thomas 377 n. 53
Mokyr, Joel 103, 328 n. 42, 335 n. 8
molecular machines 311
Monantheuil, Henri de (Monantholius)
243
Monbiot, George 315
Montaigne, Michel de 38–53, 67, 68,
308–9, 316–17; on human intelligence
51; on machines 96–7; on movement 53;
on poetry 52–3; on writing 114–15
Montefeltro, Duke Federico da 7–9
morality 250
Moravec, Hans 369 n. 102
Moray, Sir Robert 209
Morland, Sir Samuel 209–10, 240, 242
Morris, Peter 37
Moryson, Fynes 189
Moses Defending the Daughters of Jethro
(Saraceni) 15, 17
motion/movement 53, 187–8, 210; see also
puppets
Motomura, Amy 348 n. 19
moving statues 188–90
'Mower Against Gardens, The' (Marvell)
295–6
Moxon, Joseph 229
Mozart, Wolfgang Amadeus 204
Müller, Johan (Regiomontanus) 170–1,
193
Mumford, Lewis 50, 58, 233, 330 n. 64,
333 nn. 94 & 95
Munster, Sebastian 336 n. 36
Murdoch, John E. 364 n. 15
Murphy, Susan 359 n. 82
Murray, Peter 333 n. 96
'Musée des Beaux Arts' (Auden) 26–8

'My Heart the Anvile where my Thoughts doe Beate' (Drayton) 168
Mysteries of Nature and Art (Bate) 341 n. 104
Myth of Prometheus, The (Piero di Cosimo) 9
mythology: Acrasia 181; Arachne 132–7, 181; Daedalus, labyrinth of 24, 215–16; Fates 135, 150, 151, 161; Fortune/Fortuna 151, 152, 153, 154, 155, 157, 158; Icarus 24–9; Ixion 153; Prometheus 9, 273, 323 n. 44; Talos/Talus 191–2, 195; Vulcan/Hephaistos 9

Nachstücke (Hoffman) 201–2
Napier, John 238
Napier's Bones 238
Nashe, Thomas 189–90, 234
naturalism: in manuals 92–3
needlework/embroidery 150; see also tapestries
neurospasta 187, 204
New and Rare Inventions of Water-Works (de Caus) 118, 189
New Atlantis (F. Bacon) 120, 214, 267, 307
New Essays on Human Understanding (Leibniz) 241
New Experiments Physico-Mechanical, Touching the Spring of the Air (Boyle) 220
New Zealander, The (Doré) 303
Nicholl, Charles 356 n. 25
Nicholson, Marjorie 375 n. 18
Nickell, Joe 345 n. 163
Nicoll, Allardyce 358 n. 62
Nicolson, Harold 300
Noble, David 20
noise: early-modern world 4–6, 34, 37; poetry about 4–5; see also sounds
Norbrook, David 375 n. 15, 381 n. 36
Noria 46
North, Douglas C. 320 n. 9
Novo Teatro di machine (Zonca) 47–9, 48
Novum Organum, The (F. Bacon) 118, 212
Nuremburg Egg 76
Nye, David 66

Obelisk project, Rome 58–63, 64–7
Oberdiek, Hans 312
Observations on Experimental Philosophy (Cavendish) 227
O'Connell, Michael 360 n. 109
Odyssey (Homer) 161
'Of Cannibals' (Montaigne) 308
'Of Gardens' (F. Bacon) 45
'Of Man' (Bancroft) 237
Ohlman, Herbert 370 n. 125
Oldenziel, Ruth 351 n. 68
On the Economy of Machinery and Manufactures (Babbage) 75
'On the Education of Children' (Montaigne) 52–3
Ong, Walter 79–80
optical instruments 259–60; telescopes 216, 227, 259, 261; see also microscopes
optimism/pessimism 3, 14, 19, 21, 26, 250; and machines 68
Oram, William A. 353 n. 91
Orchestra, or a Poem of Dauncing (Davies) 236–7
Ord-Hume, Arthur W. G. H. 346 n. 185
Orgel, Stephen 185
Orlin, Lena Cowen 150
Osborne, Harold 380 n. 17
Otacousticon 209–10
Othello (Shakespeare) 100
Ovid (Publius Ovidius Naso) 161; Metamorphoses 9, 24, 25, 28–9, 132–4, 204
'Ozymandias' (P. Shelley) 302

Pacey, Arnold 320 n. 8
Palissy, Bernard 181
Panofsky, Erwin 217
Pappus of Alexandria 191
Paradise Lost (Milton) 259, 260–2, 270, 299; Adam 262, 264, 282–3, 284, 285, 286, 292–3; Babel 275, 278–80; engines in 270–1, 272, 276, 277–8; the Fall 275; fallen angels 270, 272–3, 276, 278–80, 286, 289; Galileo in 261; industry in 277–84; Mammon 279; Michael 262, 282, 283; Mulciber 270, 276, 278–9;

Nimrod 280–1; Pandaemonium xvi, 278–80; pessimism in 282; Raphael 264–5; Royal Society in 263–4; Satan 261, 263–4, 270–1, 272, 277–8, 286–7, 288–9; sight/blindness 260–2; Tubalcain 282–3
Paradise Lost of John Milton, The (Martin) 275
Paradise Regained (Milton) 276, 288
Paré, Ambroise 231
Park, Katharine 356 n. 23
Park, Robert 345 n. 169
Parry, Dick 333 n. 102
Parsons, William Barclay 56
Partner, Jane 366 n. 46
Partridge, Lauren 333 n. 96
Pascal, Blaise ix, 239
Passions of the Soul, The (Descartes) 251–2
pastoral writing 225, 296–9, 302–3, 304–5
Patenier, Joachim 6
patents 102, 117
Patrides, C. A. 379 n. 79
Patterson, Lee 333 n. 92
'paynefull smith with force of fervent heat, The' (Spenser) 168
Peacock, John 178, 334 n. 113, 358 n. 68
Peck, Linda Levy 364 n. 11
Peckham, G. S. 362 n. 148
Pedretti, Carlo 325 n. 7
Pélerinage de la vie humaine, Le (Guillaume de Deguileville) 13
Pepys, Samuel 208, 209–10, 221–2, 371 n. 134
Peri automatopoietikes (Heron of Alexandria) 188
perpetual motion 116–24; change and 153; main works on 345 n. 170
perpetual motion machines 116, 117–20, 121–3, 197, 331 n. 75
perspective, development of 217
Petrus Peregrinus 116
Petty, Sir William 115–16, 215
Phillips, Margaret Mann 344 n. 158
Physics (Aristotle) 173
Piero di Cosimo 9

Pietà (Michelangelo) 176
Pindar 191
Pinker, Steven 370 n. 122
Pirotechnia (Biringuccio) 87, 341 n. 104
plague 34
Plaidorie pour la reformation de l'imprimerie (Anon.) 337 n. 52
Plamenatz, John 321 n. 12
Plant, Sadie 136
Plato 173
Platonic Theology (Ficino) 29
Pleasant Historie of Iohn Winchcomb, The (Deloney) 6
ploughs/ploughmen 28–30, 81, 95
Plumb, J. H. 335 n. 19
Pneumatica (Heron of Alexandria) 189
Poems (Rochester) 251–6
Poetics (Aristotle) 174
poetry: imitation/mimesis 174; invention 174; Montaigne on 52–3; about noise 4–5
Poggioli, Renato 381 n. 32
Pointon, Marcia R. 377 n. 52
Polhem, Christopher 108
Poliziano, Angelo 231
Ponchaud, François 302
Pope, Alexander 229–30
Popplow, Marcus 341 n. 103
Porter, Roy 74, 242, 335 n. 19
Powell, Thomas 120, 122, 345 n. 170
Power, Henry 208, 272
Prager, Frank D. 339 n. 72
Pratt, William 238–9
prayer as siege engine 272
Premier Livre des instruments mathématiques et méchaniques, Le (Errard) 352 n. 75
Preparation for a Natural and Experimental History (F. Bacon) 212
Preston, Claire 355 n. 17
Principles of Philosophy (Descartes) 289
printing 78–80; deadlines 81–2; development of 81–2; and division of labour 80–1; presses 266; and technical illustrations 78; and Western mechanical culture 82–3

Prior, Mary 146, 351 n. 57
Probierbüchlein 87
Proposition for the Advancement of Experimental Philosophy, A (Cowley) 263
prosthesis 4, 231; dildos 254; Freud and 2, 24; myth of Icarus 24–9; *see also* instruments
puppets 187–8, 234; *see also* automata
Pursell, Carroll 351 n. 68
Puttenham, George 175

R.U.R. (Čapek) 230
Rahman, A. 331 n. 79
railways 7
Raleigh, Sir Walter 158
Ramelli, Agostino 101, 105–8, 109, 110–11, 341 n. 104; book wheel 111–13, *112*, 114, 116; gender divisions in labour 148–9; *see also Diverse et Artificiose Machine, Le*
Randall, Adrian J. 363 n. 151
Rape of Europa, The (Titian) 134
Rape of Lucrece, The (Shakespeare) 154
Rathborne, Aaron 367 n. 74
Raylor, Timothy 376 n. 43
Read, Thomas T. 326 n. 25
Readie and Easie Way to Establish a Free Commonwealth, The (Milton) 259
reason 238; and clockwork 232–7; and optical instruments 259
Recorde, Robert 155, *156*
'Regime d'Viver' (Rochester) 254–5
Regiomontanus (Johann Müller) 170–1, 193
Reid, George Agnew 128
Reiss, Timothy L. 364 n. 16
Religio Medici (Browne) 169, 224
Renart Contrefait 194
reproduction 173–4
Republic, The (Plato) 173
Rest of the Holy Family on the Flight into Egypt 15
Reuleaux, Franz 50
Reynolds, David 347 n. 3
Reynolds, L. D. 338 n. 64
Reynolds, Terry S. 326 n. 25, 328 n. 41
Rhodes, Neil 337 n. 40

Richard II (Shakespeare) 234
Richter, Irma A. 325 n. 2
Ripa, Cesare 197
Roberts, Paul 326 n. 21
Roberts, Stephen K. 375 n. 25
robots 230–1
Rochester, second Earl of (John Wilmot) 250–6, 284
Rockwell, Norman 125, *126*
Rogers, John 374 n. 10
Roman d'Alexandre 193
Roman de Troie (Benoît de Sainte-Maure) 199–200
Rome: collapse of 316–17; Sistine renovation of 58–63, 64–8
Rosheim, Mark E. 330 n. 67, 369 n. 100
'Rosie the Riveter' 125–8, *126*
Rouse, Hunter 325 n. 14
Royal Ordnance Works, Vauxhall 265, 267–70
Royal Society 222, 228, 257–8; in *Paradise Lost* 263–4
Rubens, Peter Paul 324 n. 67, 346 n. 188
Rudolf II, Holy Roman Emperor: *Künstkammer* 172, 197–8
'Ruines of Time, The' (Spenser) 316
Ruisdael, Jacob van 11
ruralism: in Cambodia 302, 332 n. 80
Rusconi, Giovanni 341 n. 104
Ruskin, John 5–6
Russia 300, 301–2
Rutsky, R. L. 321 n. 9
Rybczynski, Witold 334 n. 3

'Sailing to Byzantium' (Yeats) 169
Sainte-Beuve, Charles-Augustin 52
Salomon, Bernard 324 n. 67
Salomons House 214–15
Salzman, Paul 321 n. 19
Samson Agonistes (Milton) 271, 276
'Sandman, The' (Hoffmann) 201–2
Saraceni, Carlo (Carlo Veneziano) 15, *17*, *18*, 324 n. 67
Sarahsohn, Lisa T. 368 n. 90
'Satire on Charles II' (Rochester) 256
Saturday Evening Post 125, *126*

Satyr against Mankind (Rochester) 251, 252, 284
Saussy, Haun 370 n. 124
Sawday, Jonathan 324 n. 55, 329 n. 50, 339 n. 75, 341 n. 100, 357 n. 52, 361 n. 124, 372 n. 165
Scene e Machine (Torelli) 341 n. 104
Schaffer, R. Murray 321 n. 13
Schaffer, Simon 220, 367 n. 68
Schama, Simon 13, 142
Schickard, Wilhelm 239
Schlottheim, Hans 191, 203
Schmidt, Alexander 336 n. 31
Schmitt, Charles B. 373 n. 178
Schoolmaster, The (Ascham) 174
Schott, Gaspar 117
Schwartz, Regina 288
scotoscopes 208
Scott, Ridley 163, 201
screws: as fastening devices 71
scriveners: power of 115
sculpture 188
Second Creation 3, 216
Sellin, Robert H. J. 326 n. 20
Semaine, La (Du Bartas) 170–1
Serlio, Sebastiano 333 n. 101
Serres, Olivier de 377 n. 53
Settala, Manfredo 232
Seuen Deadly Sinnes of London, The (Dekker) 5, 234–5
sexuality 248–56
Shakespeare, William 160–5, 173, 290; sonnets 122; *see also individual plays*
Shapin, Steven 220, 356 n. 21, 367 n. 68, 368 n. 92
Shelley, Mary 302
Shelley, Percy 302
Shershow, Scott Cutler 205, 363 n. 159
Shunkin, Joel 371 n. 129
Sidney, Mary, Countess of Pembroke 132
Sidney, Sir Philip 105, 132, 174, 199
Siena: machine books in 84–6
sight 282–3; blindness 260–2; mechanical 259–65; *see also* optical instruments

silk industry 47, 266, 277, 348 n. 19, 362 n. 149
Silverman, Robert J. 374 n. 2
Simms, D. L. 331 n. 78
Simon, Herbert A. 312
Simonton, Deborah 347 n. 5
Sir Gawain and the Green Knight 194
Sisam, Kenneth 321 n. 14
Six Books on the Commonwealth (Bodin) 72
Sixtus V, pope 59–61, 66, 67
Slive, Seymour 322 n. 30
Smil, Vaclav 328 n. 40
Smith, Adam 74–5, 144; and division of labour 92; pin manufacture 74
Smith, Alan R. 377 n. 50
Smith, Bruce R. 376 n. 34
Smith, Jeffrey Chipps 322 n. 29
Smith, Norman A. F. 328 n. 39, 331 n. 78
Smith, Pamela H. 92, 177, 346 n. 188
Snyder, James 322 n. 22
Somerset, Edward, second Marquis of Worcester 118, 265–6
Sorbière, Samuel 209, 217–18, 220, 265
sounds: instruments for transmission of 223; Otacousticon 209–10; *see also* noise
Southern, Richard 358 n. 63
Space Odyssey, A (film) 314
Spargo, John Webster 361 n. 116
speech 113
Spengler, Oswald 116–17, 299–300, 301
Spenser, Edmund 316; *see also Faerie Queene, The*
Spiller, Elizabeth 367 n. 71
Spinner, The (Brekelenkam) 129, *130*
spinning 6, 81, 129–36, 142–6; distaffs 129, 142–3; Penelope and 161; as punishment 142; spindles 142, 143; *Spinhuis* 142, 147; *Spinnstuben* 143, 147; *see also* spinning wheels
spinning wheels 129–32, 134–6, 137, 143–4, 148–9, *150*; great wheels 129, 142–3; as instrument of punishment 143–4; Saxon wheels 144; water-powered 47–9, *48*

spinsters 143, 151
Sprat, Thomas 208, 211, 257–8
Stallenge, William 377 n. 53
Stallybrass, Peter 135
Standage, Tom 362 nn. 148 & 149, 367 n. 76
Stangenkunst system 37
Starobinski, Jean 38–40
Stationers' Company 266
Steadman, John M. 374 n. 8
steam engines (Calthoff–Somerset engine) 265–6
Stewart, George R. 303–4, 306
Stith, Joyce 377 n. 50
Stock, Brian 365 n. 30
Stowers, Arthur 328 n. 39
Strada, Jacobus (Octavius?) de 111, 341 n. 104
Strasbourg: cathedral clock 171, 290–1
Stromer, Wolfgang von 326 n. 22
Strong, Roy 44
Stubbes, Philip 205
Suckling, Sir John 235–6
Suez Canal 56
Summerson, John 358 n. 72
survivor narratives 305–6, 314
Swade, Doron 335 n. 23
Sweet Nosegay, A (Whitney) 159
Swift, Jonathan 201, 257, 370 n. 124
Sylla, Edith D. 364 n. 15
symbolism: bees 197; open windows 15, 18; of wheel 139, 151–4, 160

Taccola (Mariano di Iacopo) 84–5, 86
Tainter, Joseph A. 382 n. 46
Taisnerius, Johannes 345 n. 170
Tann, Jennifer 364 n. 10
tapestries 132–4
Tarducci, Achille 341 n. 104
Tawney, R. H. 7
Taylor, Gary 339 n. 78
Te Brake, William H. 326 n. 24
technology 275; Christianity and 58–63, 64–7; etymology of 320 n. 4; and politics 58–67; as spectacle and ceremony 61–4

'technology as gift' narrative 19
telegraphs 367 n. 76
telescopes 216, 227; Galileo and 261; Milton and 259, 261
Tempest, Pierce 361 n. 125
Tempest, The (Shakespeare) 187, 305–8, 309
Templum Vaticanum (C. Fontana) 62, 65
textile industry: factory machines 202–3; silk industry 47, 266, 277, 348 n. 19, 362 n. 149
'Thanksgivings for the Body' (Traherne) 243
'That to Philosophise is to Learn How to Die' (Montaigne) 53
Theatrum Machinarum Novum (Boeckler) 98, 118, *119*
Theologia (Campanella) 186
theology 3; and mechanism 242–5; *see also* Christianity
There Will Come Soft Rains (Bradbury) 314
Thirsk, Joan 376 n. 32
Thompson, E. P. 332 n. 89
Thorpe, W. H. 375 n. 25
thought: Montaigne on 52–3
Tiles, Mary 312
Tinguely, Jean 330 n. 62
Titian (Tiziano Vecellio) 134
'To the Royal Society' (Cowley) 218–19
tool use 71, 72–3
Torelli, Giacomo 341 n. 104
torture 141
Torture of St Catherine of Alexandria, The (Dürer) 139, *140*
Tower of Babel, The (Pieter Brueghel the Elder), *23*
Tragicall Historie of Dr Faustus (Marlowe) 25, 187
Traherne, Thomas 243–5
treadmills 323 n. 40
Treatise of the Nature of Bodies (Digby) 247
Treatise on Man (Descartes) 285–6
'Treatise on Water' (Leonardo) 33
Très Riches Heures, Les (Duc de Berry) 95

Trescott, Martha Moore 146, 351 n. 68
Trigault, Nicholas 190
Triptych of the Haywain (Bosch) 11, *12*
Tristan 193
Triumph of Death (Pieter Brueghel the
    Elder) 141
Turing, Alan 51
Turris Babel (Kircher) 20–1
Twelfth Night (Shakespeare) 100
'21st and Last Book of the Ocean to
    Cynthia, The' (Raleigh) 158
Two New Sciences (Galileo) 59
Tymme, Thomas 121, 345 n. 170

Ubaldo, Guido 54, 175
'Uncanny, The' (Freud) 202
Unfortunate Traveller (Nashe) 189–90
unskilled female labour 148
'Upon a Flie' (Herrick) 177–8
'Upon Appleton House, to My Lord
    Fairfax' (Marvell) 297
Upon the Hill and Grove at Bill-borow *To
    the Lord Fairfax* (Marvell) 298–9
Usher, Abbott Payson 320 n. 11
Usher, James 376 n. 33

Valckenborch, Lucas and Martin van 7
'Valentin und Namelos' (*Valentine and
    Orson*) 193–4
Valturio, Roberto (Valturio of Rimini) 341
    n. 104
Van Der Borcht, Pieter 28–9
van der Straet, Jan (Giovanni Stradano)
    377 n. 53
Vanity of Dogmatising (Glanvill) 221, 246,
    259
Vasari, Giorgio 9, 33, 176
Vaughan, Henry 122–3, 369 n. 109
Vauxhall, *see* Royal Ordnance Works,
    Vauxhall
Velásquez, Diego 132–7, *133*, 142, 155–7
Veranzio, Fausto (Verantius, Vrančić) 101,
    341 n. 104, 342 n. 120
Vergil, Polydore 24
Verlag system 92
Vickers, Brian 353 n. 86, 367 n. 66

*View of the Waal from the Town Gate at
    Zaltbommel* (Huygens III) 11–13
Villard de Honnecourt 193
Ville, Arnold de 38
Villiers de Lisle Adam, Philippe-Auguste,
    comte de 201, 203
Vinen, Richard 380 n. 18
Violand-Hobi, Heidi E. 330 n. 62
Virgil (Publius Vergilius Maro) 294–5, 304
Virgil Solis 324 n. 67
Virgil the Necromancer 193, 194
Virilio, Paul 311
Vitruvius (Marcus Vitruvius Pollio) 83–4,
    111, 323 n. 40
Volpaia, Lorenzo della 230–1
Volpone: Or, The Fox (Jonson) 308
Voskuil, J. 360 n. 114
Vulcan and Aeolus (Piero di Cosimo) 9

Wadsworth, Alfred P. 376 n. 32
Wajcman, Judy 147–8, 351 n. 68
Ward, James 242
Warner, Deborah Jean 364 n. 7
Warner, Marina 129, 206, 350 n. 40
Warwick, Kevin 369 n. 102
watches 233
water 32–4; destructive power of 32–3; as
    power/energy source 34, 35–8
water-driven devices 42–3; fountains
    42–3, 44, 180; *Noria* 46; siphons 43;
    spinning wheels 47–9, *48*; *see also*
    watermills
water power: in England 36–7; in France
    34, 36, 37, 38
water technology: in Italy 43–7
watermills 11, 13–15, *16*, *18*, 34, 35–8
Waterworld (film) 381 n. 29
Watt, Ian 381 n. 27
Watt, James 344 n. 147, 372 n. 161
weaving 6, 81, 132, 136; horizontal frame
    looms 352 n. 76
Webster, Charles 366 n. 60
Wecker, Hans 183
Wecker, John 341 n. 104
weights and measures 71–2
Weisman, Alan 381 n. 28

Wender, Dorothea 360 n. 107
Westfall, Richard S. 210
Westworld (Crichton) 201
'Wheel of Fortune' game show 160
wheels 137–9; of fortune 123, 150–60;
    potter's wheels 71, 137, 192; prayer
    wheels 138; and punishment/torture
    139–42; symbolism of 138, 139, 151–4,
    160; *see also* spinning wheels
White, Lynne Jr 138, 332 n. 82
White, Michael 33, 369 n. 101
Whitney, Isabella 159
Whittle, Jane 351 n. 62
Wiener, Norbert 166, 232, 241, 311, 320
    n. 14, 354 n. 101, 369 n. 104
Wiesner, Merry E. 347 n. 5, 350 n. 50, 351
    n. 57
Wilkins, John 67–8, 113, 120, 198, 238;
    on economy of mechanical design
    247–8
William of Malmesbury 194
Williams, Raymond 365 n. 24
Williams, Trevor 137, 329 n. 56
Willis, Thomas 290
Wilmot, John, *see* Rochester, second Earl
    of
Wilson, Richard 354 n. 100
Windmill by a River, A (Goyen) 11
windmills 11–13, 15, 18
Winner, Langdon 333 n. 93
Winstanley, Gerrard 309
Winstead, Katherine A. 350 n. 39

Winter, Dennis 350 n. 44
Winter's Tale, The (Shakespeare) 182–3,
    204
Witmore, Michael 157, 198, 353 n. 83
Wittfogel, Karl 55
Wittkower, Rudolph 339 n. 69, 352, n. 82
Witz, Konrad 195
Wolfe, Jessica 97, 195, 227, 320 n. 4, 370
    n. 119
women: artificiality of 205; division of
    labour 148–50; mechanical 193, 197,
    199–206; 'Rosie the Riveter' 125–8, *126*
Women Operators (Reid) 128
Wood, Gabby 201, 360 n. 112
Wooley, Benjamin 382 n. 54
Works and Days (Hesiod) 191
Wotton, Sir Henry 183, 217
Wright, M. T. 349 n. 35
writing 113–15
writing devices: copying device 115–16;
    'writing engine' 116
Wyatt, Sir Thomas 159

Yates, Frances 186
Yeats, W. B. 169
Young, J. Z. 371 n. 133

Zabarella, James 345 n. 170
Zeising, Heinrich 341 n. 104, 342 n. 120,
    343 n. 135
Zonca, Vittorio 47–9, *48*, 101–2, 111, 117,
    341 n. 104, 343 n. 135